W0008657

LIZARDS

OF THE AMERICAN SOUTHWEST

A Photographic Field Guide

LAWRENCE L. C. JONES and **ROBERT E. LOVICH**, editors

With text and photography contributions from 77 experts
and a foreword by

LAURIE VITT

Maps by **ESTHER I. NELSON** and **LAWRENCE L. C. JONES**
Line drawings by **RANDALL D. BABB**

RIO NUEVO PUBLISHERS
TUCSON, ARIZONA

Rio Nuevo Publishers®
P.O. Box 5250, Tucson, Arizona 85703-0250
(520) 623-9558, www.rionuevo.com

Text, illustration, and photography copyright © 2009 as follows: the contributions by Edward W. Acuña, Brad Alexander, Ralph W. Axtell, Randall D. Babb, Aaron M. Bauer, Cameron W. Barrows, Kent R. Beaman, Daniel D. Beck, Robert L. Bezy, Russell Blaine, Thomas C. Brennan, Tracey K. Brown, Doug Burkett, Paulette M. Conrad, James R. Dixon, Eric A. Dugan, Taylor Edwards, Erik F. Enderson, Robert E. Espinoza, Mark Fisher, Lee A. Fitzgerald, Stanley F. Fox, David J. Germano, Harry W. Greene, L. Lee Grismer, Robert Haase, Marla Hibbitts, Terry Hibbitts, Toby Hibbitts, Troy Hibbitts, Wendy L. Hodges, Bradford D. Hollingsworth, Craig S. Ivanyi, Randy D. Jennings, Lawrence L. C. Jones, Thomas R. Jones, Matthew A. Kwiatkowski, Megan E. Lahti, Adam D. Leaché, Allison F. Leavitt, Daniel J. Leavitt, Jeffrey M. Lemm, Julio A. Lemos-Espinal, William Leonard, Lauren J. Livo, Kim Lovich, Robert E. Lovich, Clark R. Mahrdt, Brad Moon, Daniel G. Mulcahy, Gary Nafis, Larry Neel, Charles W. Painter, Trevor B. Persons, Philip M. Ralidis, Charles S. Rau, Jonathan Q. Richmond, James C. Rorabaugh, Philip C. Rosen, Erica Bree Rosenblum, Mason J. Ryan, Cecil R. Schwalbe, Michael J. Sredl, Brian K. Sullivan, Dale S. Turner, Robert G. Webb, William Wells, Steve Wilcox, John W. Wright, and Kevin V. Young are the property of the respective contributors.

See pages 545–548 for photography and illustration credits. On the front cover: Male Greater Earless Lizard in breeding colors. On the back cover: San Lucan Rock Lizard. On the spine: (top) Sonoran Collared Lizard, (bottom) Greater Short-horned Lizard. On page 2: Eastern Collared Lizard, Cochise Co., AZ; Cochise Co., AZ; page 9, Mountain Skink; page 10: Desert Iguana, Pima Co., AZ.

All rights reserved. No part of this book may be reproduced, stored, introduced into a retrieval system, or otherwise copied in any form without the prior written permission of the publisher, except for brief quotations in reviews or citations.

Design: Karen Schober, Seattle, Washington

Printed in Korea

10 9 8 7 6 5 4 3

Library of Congress Cataloging-in-Publication Data

Lizards of the American Southwest : a photographic field guide / Lawrence L. C. Jones and Robert E. Lovich, editors ; with text and photography contributions from 76 species experts and a foreword by Laurie Vitt.
p. cm.
Includes index.
ISBN-13: 978-1-933855-35-6 (pbk. : alk. paper)
ISBN-10: 1-933855-35-5 (pbk. : alk. paper)
1. Lizards—Southwest, New. 2. Lizards—Southwest, New—Pictorial works.
I. Jones, Lawrence L. C., 1954- II. Lovich, Robert E., 1970-
QL666.L2L596 2009
597.950979—dc22

2008051676

DEDICATION

We dedicate this book to all of the herpetologists who have fostered our appreciation and understanding of lizards as researchers, land managers, ecotourists, hobbyists, and photographers.

While many people have excelled in the study of lizards, we wish to particularly acknowledge certain individuals who are not authors in this book. Hobart Smith, the author of the groundbreaking *Handbook of Lizards,* led the way for giving us a greater understanding and appreciation of lizards. Robert C. Stebbins, Roger and Isabel Conant, and Joe Collins, all authors of the Peterson Field Guides to amphibians and reptiles, were instrumental in our development as budding young herpetologists. Eric Pianka and Laurie Vitt, who have both used lizards as a medium to examine the concepts of ecology, have made a profound impact on the biological sciences.

Of course, we also dedicate the book to our families, who endured our relentless fascination with scaly critters. Janet Jones missed several years of vacations to put up with her husband's need to "go look for lizards." Kim Lovich tolerated her husband's working on some lizard book while supposedly "on vacation" with the family. Domino the Wonder Dog tried to help, but he kept scaring the lizards away. Without our families, we might be living with the lizards.

—Larry Jones and Rob Lovich

AUTHORS

Edward W. Acuña
Raph W. Axtell
Randall D. Babb
Aaron M. Bauer
Cameron W. Barrows
Kent R. Beaman
Daniel D. Beck
Robert L. Bezy
Russell Blaine
Thomas C. Brennan
Tracey K. Brown
Doug Burkett
Matthew D. Caron
Paulette M. Conrad
James R. Dixon
Charles A. Drost
Eric A. Dugan
Taylor Edwards
Erik F. Enderson
Robert E. Espinoza
Gary M. Fellers
Mark Fisher
Lee A. Fitzgerald
Stanley F. Fox
David J. Germano
Harry W. Greene
L. Lee Grismer
Robert Haase
Wendy L. Hodges
Bradford D. Hollingsworth
Jeffrey M. Howland
Craig S. Ivanyi
Randy D. Jennings
Lawrence L. C. Jones
Matthew A. Kwiatkowski
Megan E. Lahti
Adam D. Leaché
Allison F. Leavitt
Daniel J. Leavitt
Jeffrey M. Lemm
Julio A. Lemos-Espinal
Lauren J. Livo
Kim Lovich
Robert E. Lovich
Clark R. Mahrdt
Daniel G. Mulcahy
Charles W. Painter
Trevor B. Persons
Philip M. Ralidis
Charles S. Rau
Jonathan Q. Richmond
James C. Rorabaugh
Philip C. Rosen
Erica Bree Rosenblum
Mason J. Ryan
Cecil R. Schwalbe
Michael J. Sredl
Brian K. Sullivan
Don E. Swann
Dale S. Turner
Robert G. Webb
John W. Wright
Kevin V. Young

A complete listing of all contributors and their affiliations, including photographers and their photo credits, is shown on pages 545–548.

SPONSORS

WE GRATEFULLY ACKNOWLEDGE THE FINANCIAL SUPPORT OF THESE SPONSORS FOR THEIR HELP IN MAKING THIS BOOK POSSIBLE, THEREBY MAKING THIS INFORMATION AVAILABLE TO VIRTUALLY ANYONE WANTING TO LEARN MORE ABOUT LIZARDS OF THE AMERICAN SOUTHWEST:

Arizona Game and Fish Department
Arizona-Sonora Desert Museum
California State Parks Foundation
Colorado Division of Wildlife
Conservation Biology Institute
Endangered Habitats League
Friends of PARC, Inc.
The Herpetologists' League
Nevada Department of Wildlife
San Bernardino / Leslie Canyon National Wildlife Refuge
Society for the Study of Amphibians and Reptiles
Southwestern Association of Naturalists
Tucson Herpetological Society

None of the contributors received any compensation, and 100% of the royalties will be donated to a grant program of The Herpetologists' League to fund research on amphibians and reptiles of the American Southwest and adjacent Mexico.

Contents

LIST OF MAPS AND ILLUSTRATIONS

FOREWORD

For any aspiring naturalist, the American Southwest offers a remarkable opportunity to explore the miraculous world of biology firsthand. Most habitats are relatively open, so it is easy to observe animals and plants in their natural habitats; the climate is generally warm and dry; and of the thousands of species of insects flittering around, few stop to take a blood meal. Most striking, even to the casual observer, is the abundance and diversity of lizards inhabiting these open lands.

Whiptail lizards march around continually sampling the substrate with their tongues, in search of food and mates, while keeping an alert eye on virtually everything that moves around them, while horned lizards sit perfectly motionless, blending into their backgrounds, as they sit and wait for prey. From the canopy of mesquites and Creosote Bushes, Long-tailed Brush Lizards scan the leaves and limbs for ants and other small insects, as Desert Spiny Lizards crash into packrat nests at the bases of Ironwoods. In some sandy areas, from a single vantage point literally dozens of Desert Iguanas can be seen feeding on yellow flowers, and leopard lizards can be seen hiding in the shadows in wait of an unwary whiptail or Common Side-blotched Lizard that ventures too close. Meanwhile, fringe-toed lizards skate across the sands, silently disappearing into a dune, leaving a well-defined trail that can be easily followed by the single primate to colonize North America.

This is a land of lizards that carry on their own complex soap operas day after day in their struggle to both survive to the next day and produce offspring that will carry their genes into the next generation. These fascinating animals, which ran around in the shadows of dinosaurs that themselves didn't make it into the Cenozoic, have diversified into the second-largest group of terrestrial vertebrates, the Squamata (which includes snakes), exceeded in diversity only by birds.

Aside from their spectacular diversity, lizards have proven to be one of the best model systems available for asking questions in conceptual biology. They are often abundant and easy to capture and manipulate, their evolutionary relationships are relatively well known, and they have adapted to nearly every imaginable ecological niche within the temperate and tropical environments. Studies on lizards have expanded our knowledge of basic behavioral, ecological, and physiological processes, and much of what we have learned can be directly applied to other organisms, including man. Questions asked by lizard biologists span the entire field of biology: Why do some lizards move around continually in search of prey, whereas others sit and wait for prey to pass before attacking? How do lizards maintain body temperatures high enough to sustain high activity levels, and how do some remain cool enough to keep from frying under the desert sun? How are some lizards able to produce offspring without males, and what are the possible consequences of producing daughters that are genetically identical to their mothers and grandmothers? Why do some lizards lose their tails and then regenerate them, only to lose them again? Why do male lizards often have brilliant coloration during the breeding season, and in some cases have increased head size? Why do some lizards produce many small offspring and others produce a few large offspring? Why in the world would one of the smallest lizards, the Desert Night Lizard, produce live offspring rather than deposit eggs, and in addition live to be ten or more years old? Why does one species of lizard, the Gila Monster, produce venom, and how can this be used in modern medicine? These are only a few of the thousands of questions that can be asked about our scaly friends.

As a budding naturalist during the early 1970s, I was drawn into the field that would define my career, lizard ecology, by lizards in the American Southwest. During my graduate studies at Arizona State University, along with two dear colleagues, Justin Congdon and Dick van Loben Sels, I zigzagged across southern Arizona, learning everything I could from the four-legged, scaly, ectothermic vertebrates that peeked at me from every nook and cranny. At the time, few biologists had conducted ecological studies on these fascinating animals, and like most of us, I had my list of heroes, including Ken Norris, Wilbur Mayhew, John Wright, and the notorious Chuck Lowe, all of whom I would get to know later in my career. Little did I know at the time that another budding lizard ecologist, Eric Pianka, was also amassing a huge amount of data on desert lizards. To that point in time, the only available books containing good information on lizards of the American Southwest were Robert C. Stebbins' *Field Guide to Reptiles and Amphibians of the Western United States* and Hobart Smith's *Handbook of Lizards.*

Lizards of the American Southwest: A Photographic Field Guide is a beautifully done book that combines accurate biological information and photographs in a format accessible to everyone from the weekend naturalist to professional biologists. Two things strike me right off about this nice book. First, in addition to the standard information that we expect in such a book, we find detailed descriptions about how to actually observe each species of Southwest lizard. It is clear from these accounts that each author has had firsthand experience with the animals in their natural habitats, and they have provided information making it possible for the user to repeat those valuable experiences. Second, it is indeed a pleasure to see the large number of people involved in writing the various species accounts, ranging from herpetologists in academia to those in public agencies.

Lizard biology is alive and well in the great American Southwest, and this book goes a long way toward making the lives of these animals accessible to the public.

—Laurie J. Vitt

George Lynn Cross Research Professor and Curator of Reptiles

Sam Noble Oklahoma Museum of Natural History and

Zoology Department

University of Oklahoma

Norman, Oklahoma

PREFACE

The Marijilda Experience

Although I hail from southern California (I was a beach bum/desert rat hybrid), most of my adult career as a professional biologist was spent doing research in the Pacific Northwest on amphibians (especially salamanders) and a host of other creatures, including American Martens, small mammals, and birds. While I enjoyed working with "wet herps" (amphibians) as much as the next guy, especially in pristine mountain stream settings, I was lured back to the Southwest by abundant sunshine, the incredible biodiversity, and the chance to enjoy "dry herps" (reptiles) once again (thanks to Greg Green for these alluring vernacular terms in quotes!). While living in the Northwest I never forgot my roots, so I spent multitudes of vacations in the land of dry herps, especially Arizona, California, New Mexico, Texas (Big Bend area), and Mexico. Then I was finally able to move to my "Graceland" in southern Arizona in 2002. I traded in my Cope's Giant Salamanders for Gila Monsters. And I went from researcher to public servant with a public land management agency. When I first arrived in Safford, Arizona, I immediately began poking around to see what the resident reptiles were. So on weekends, I did systematic snake and lizard surveys. My lizard surveys were focused on Marijilda Canyon, in the south end of the Pinaleño

Lower Marijilda Canyon, Graham Co., AZ.

Mountains, near Safford. There I discovered a treasure trove of lizards. Not only were they common as dirt, but also I recorded nineteen species in a small area, which is the highest diversity of lizards I could find reference to in the U.S. (and I know there is at least one more species that is evading my detection). Of course I knew, along with all other herpetologists, that there was a general dearth of books on herps of Arizona and the American Southwest, so this "Marijilda Experience" was my beckoning to produce a book devoted to lizards of the region. For the next five years, nearly all of my annual leave was spent on lizarding vacations across the borderlands from southern California to Big Bend, Texas, and in adjacent Mexico. But in order to pull off editing a lizard book, I needed help, especially from a comrade in southern California, which has a very diverse but different lizard fauna from the inland areas. I was ecstatic when Rob stepped forward and offered himself up, despite a rather busy schedule with his family, graduate school, and Central American adventures. While I look forward to doing other things after this book is published (like traveling to look for snakes, and snorkeling and fishing in the Sea of Cortez), I know that I have become irreversibly obsessed, and wherever I go I will be looking for that tell-tale silhouette of a basking lizard.

—Larry Jones

A Love of Lizards Is Born

My beginnings in herpetology were probably set long before I realized. My brother and I grew up hunting and fishing in the Appalachian/Allegheny Mountains of Virginia and Pennsylvania. A love for the outdoors was the result of these experiences in our youth. However, by the time I understood the difference between amphibians and reptiles, my older brother was already an undergraduate student headed for graduate school and a lifetime of contributions to herpetology. My first focused research on lizards was in graduate school with Lee Grismer, Ron Carter, and Bill Hayes as advisors at Loma Linda University. Lee's lab was a place where I experienced a true passion for herpetology and lizard research in particular, both from Lee and from all of his students. This passion was contagious. Ron and Bill were exceptional influences in herpetology as well, with equally infectious and dynamic labs. The rules were simple: work hard and have fun. Much was expected in the form of academic excellence, but we worked hard because we enjoyed our lizard research. Sure, some folks were looking at other organisms, but I have never been surrounded by so much lizard research since that time. I completed my master's thesis on the phylogeography of the Granite Night Lizard, and discovered that earthquake fault zones were responsible for the tremendous degree of genetic diversity seen in the species. Collecting the samples needed for that study throughout southern California allowed me the opportunity to carefully flip what felt like way too many thousands of rocks in search of the target species. In undertaking this project, I became captivated by the lizards and their rocky refugia. Following my master's degree, I worked for Robert Fisher and sampled herpetofauna throughout southern California. This work allowed me personal contact with every lizard known from the region, not to mention other critters of all shapes and sizes. Lizards gave me my graduate degree, and in return a lifetime of admiration for their natural history, evolution, and all the unknown aspects of their biology.

Larry and I certainly hope that this book will help increase the fan base and human support for lizards of the American Southwest and neighboring Mexico. We've had a lot of fun working together on it, and hope that our enthusiasm for lizards translates well. This region has an incredibly diverse lizard fauna, and it is fascinating to observe the interactions of lizards on the dramatic stage set by Mother Nature in this region. We look forward to seeing you in the field with us, enjoying the lizards and their incredible habitats!

—***Rob Lovich***

Portrait of a Granite Night Lizard.

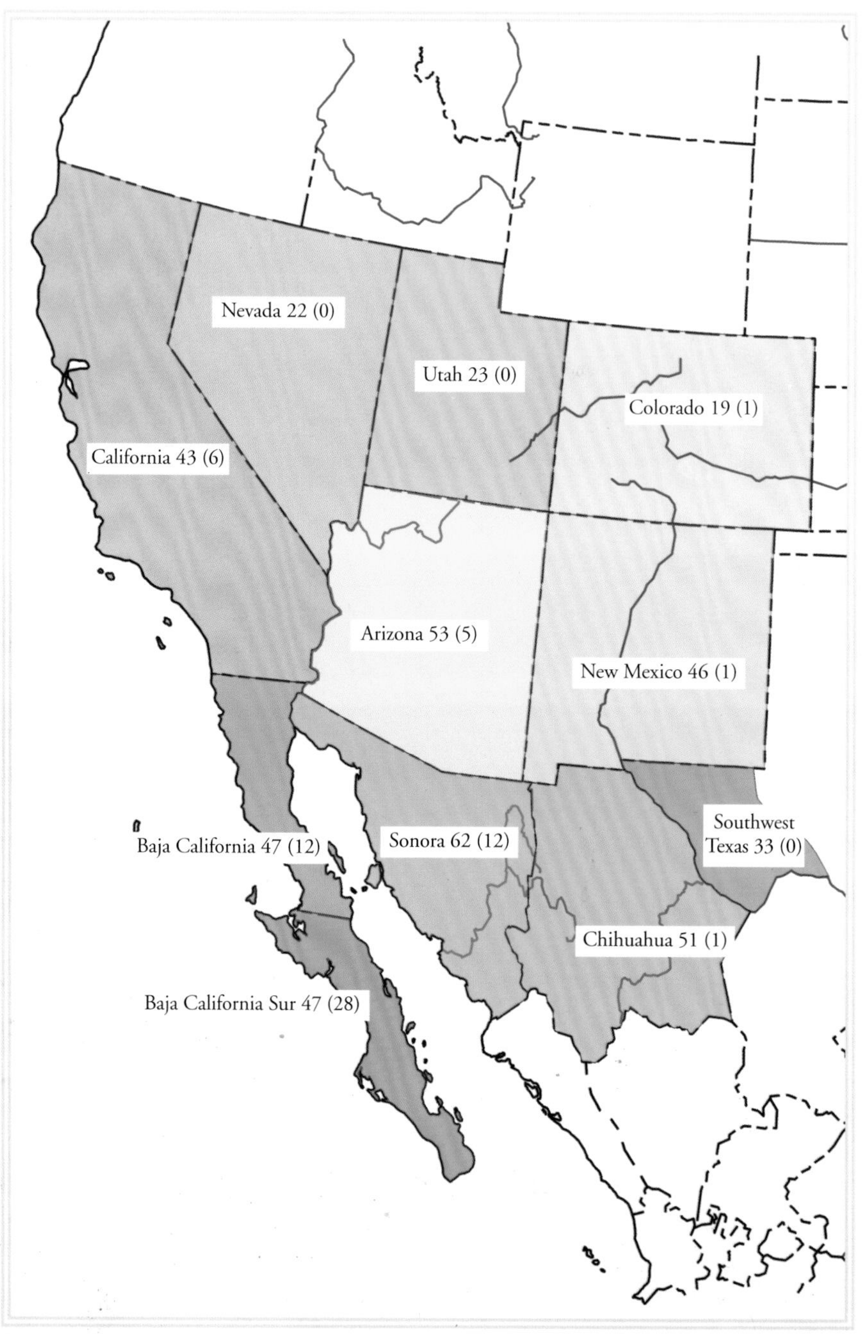

Map 1. Geographic scope of coverage, with species counts and endemics. The number of native species for each state is shown, with numbers of endemic species in parentheses.

FACING PAGE: Mohave Fringe-toed Lizard.

INTRODUCTION TO LIZARDS OF THE AMERICAN SOUTHWEST

GETTING STARTED

ABOUT THIS BOOK

Welcome to the world of lizards! The American Southwest has the highest diversity of lizards anywhere in the country; in fact, as one travels north, no additional species are picked up, so this book also covers the species throughout the West. *Lizards of the American Southwest: A Photographic Field Guide* was written to provide a current synthesis of what is known about all 96 native species of lizards of Arizona, California, Colorado, Nevada, New Mexico, Texas (west of the Pecos River), and Utah, and to provide multiple photographs of all species. Also, because Mexico is so close to our southern border, and the lizard fauna beckons us, we included sections on the Mexican states of Baja California, Baja California Sur, Chihuahua, and Sonora. We also included a master checklist near the end of the book that includes both the American and Mexican states. (You might want to check with the U.S. State Department for the latest travel advisories for Mexico.)

Lizards are among the most familiar and interesting creatures in the American Southwest, yet few books are devoted to them—in fact, the last book to address the full repertoire of species of the area was written over sixty years ago by the esteemed herpetologist Hobart Smith. A lot has changed since that time. We have discovered new species, genetics has become an everyday word, and travel and urbanization have altered the face of the landscape. So, after sixty years, we thought it was time to write another book devoted to the complete lizard fauna of our region. It is not intended to be a complete scientific treatise, as was Hobart Smith's work, but a more generalized and photo-rich synthesis of species and lizard biology. This book is intended for a wider target audience, ranging from ecotourists to herpetologists.

You will notice this book has an unusual format for a field guide. We have chosen to edit it, with taxa experts as our authors, to ensure that each account is based on the best available science from someone intimately familiar with the subject matter. Each author of a species account was asked to synthesize what is known in 1,000 words or less. The accounts were also peer-reviewed.

Because there are so few books devoted to lizards, we did not stop at just having species accounts and photographs. We included sections on anatomy and identification, habitats, life and natural history and behavior, taxonomy and nomenclature, non-native species, environmental ethics, management, conservation, laws, and lizards in captivity—plus information for people who want to go lizard-watching.

We collected hundreds of color photographs in the book to aid in identifying lizards and their habitats. Whenever possible, we tried to obtain photographs of males, females, and juveniles, as well as some of the normal variation encountered in nature. Photographs of some species are shown for the first time in any publication (or at least tied to their current common and scientific names).

And finally, we wanted to help the reader know how, where, and when to look for lizards—and of course, how to identify them, especially through binoculars. Lizards are largely an "untapped market" among ecotourists, but they are truly fascinating creatures and eminently watchable; this is obvious when one notices the number of people on nature hikes taking note of lizards, or at lizard displays. As a group, lizards tend to be common, widespread, diurnal, predictable, and readily observable with close-focus binoculars, and they have fascinating behavioral traits that are easily observed. We hope all readers will benefit from the text and photographs and gain a better understanding and appreciation of the lizards of the American Southwest. Not only are they fun to look at, but they play important roles in the ecology of the region and have become portals to the world of science and nature!

ABOUT LIZARDS

Authors: Robert E. Lovich and Lawrence L. C. Jones

Most people living in the American Southwest are familiar with their scaly neighbors, the lizards. For the most part, these vertebrates are small, four-legged, long-tailed, scaly reptiles that are active during the daytime, but there are notable exceptions. Some are large like the Common Chuckwalla, Gila Monster, and Desert Iguana. Some even have only two legs and live underground, like the Five-toed Worm Lizard found south of the Mexico border in Baja California. Indeed, some lizards lack legs altogether (including one of our native species), which renders them similar in appearance to their relatives, the snakes.

Taxonomically, lizards belong to the order Squamata—the same order as snakes—attesting to the close relationship of these two groups. Lizards belong to the suborder Lacertilia (= Sauria), while snakes belong to the suborder Serpentes (or Ophidia), and both are believed to have come from common ancestors. Although lizards may be smaller than some of their reptilian cousins (save the mighty Komodo Dragon of Indonesia, a lizard reaching a whopping 3 m in length!), they are no less impressive. Our southwestern species range in size from several centimeters in length (some of the night lizards) to half a meter (Gila Monster), and are found in a variety of habitats from below sea level to over 3,000 m in elevation.

Ancient Native American petroglyph.

Lizards have proven resilient throughout their long history, surviving many changes in the earth's history. Fossils of modern lizard relatives first appeared 250 million years ago in the Upper Permian or Lower Triassic, with lizards as we know them basically appearing around the late Jurassic, about 140 million years ago. Continental shifts, ice ages, and changes in sea level have occurred during their history. Lizards are an important part of many ecosystems on a global scale in today's world. Early in their evolution, two groups arose, the Iguania and the Scleroglossa. Iguanians have a fleshy tongue used in feeding, whereas Scleroglossans have a hard tongue and use their jaws rather than tongues when feeding. Lizards of today are incredibly diverse, with over 4,200 species recognized, and they are by far the dominant group among reptiles—over half of all reptile species are lizards.

The highest diversity of native lizards in the U.S. is in the American Southwest. There are about 96 species known from the region, belonging to about 10 families (depending on how experts divvy up the species and families). Iguanians include lizards in the families Iguanidae, Crotaphytidae, and Phrynosomatidae. All other families covered in this book are Scleroglossan lizards. Lizards are common in the Southwest largely because of the climate. As they lack the internal thermoregulatory control of mammals and birds, they require enough heat from their surrounding environments to regulate their metabolism and activities, such as digestion, breeding, and development. This is why lizards do not inhabit polar regions, where temperatures are too low for appropriate metabolic regulation—they simply would perish there. They are found on all continents except for Antarctica.

Almost all lizards are carnivorous or omnivorous, with herbivory being relatively uncommon. Some species are rather specialized, such as most horned lizards, which feed primarily on ants. Collared lizards and leopard lizards are well known to eat other smaller lizards extensively, as well as other prey items. Lizards in the Southwest reproduce by both egg laying and by bearing live young. Some groups of closely related lizards, such as horned lizards, produce offspring by both mechanisms. Horned lizards in northern, cooler regions are live bearing, while the more southern species that inhabit warmer regions are egg layers.

Lizards have long been popular in our cultures and mythology. Petroglyphs of lizards in the Southwest date back thousands of years, and Native Americans ate and traded them and their parts. Native Americans also influenced the distribution of some species that were used for traditional purposes, such as a food source. A familiar way of confirming the importance of lizards to ancestral Americans is by visiting public lands with petroglyphs to see how frequently lizards and snakes appear—obviously, these animals were important to native cultures. In modern times, there is still a fascination with these animals, and most cities in the Southwest have some form of lizard public artwork. Highway and municipal structures are adorned with their images, establishments are named after them (for example, "Horny Toad Saloon"), and school mascots are frequently named after them. Also, street signs in Gila Bend, Arizona, picture Gila Monsters, and one of us (LLCJ) lives on the corner of Spiny Lizard Way in Tucson, Arizona. Chuckwalla Street is a couple of blocks down.

For millennia, lizards have been an integral part of the American Southwest, both ecologically and culturally. They are for the most part innocuous (except for venomous Gila Monsters—but virtually all bites are from people "messing with them"), and none are known to prey specifically on humans or to pose a real threat. They can be colorful and enjoyable to watch, as they are easily approached for the most part and are diverse in species and habits. The authors truly hope that each reader of this book, casual or otherwise, will find a new appreciation for these creatures instilled in them. Take a minute, and go enjoy your local lizards when the opportunity presents itself!

LIZARD HABITAT

Authors: Lawrence L. C. Jones and Robert E. Lovich

The word "habitat" is often used generically to describe the features of an area where plants and animals are found. There is a dizzying array of terms to categorize habitats, as the topic is complex. We will keep the information rather general, since this is only a field guide. Habitat descriptions can best be considered hierarchically, from a large scale to a smaller scale; more precisely, from ecoregion to plant community to habitat feature to microhabitat. If you think of habitat in this way, you can quickly determine how and where to find different assemblages of lizard species and why they are distributed the way they are. In the photographs and captions accompanying this section, we will point out different habitat levels, from ecoregion down to microhabitat in scale (as applicable).

Ecoregions. These are large, two-dimensional areas that are geographically constrained, having similar climatic, geologic, topographic, and biotic conditions. There are many different maps showing various interpretations of ecoregions, but for our lizard-centric purposes, our accompanying ecoregions map should suffice. In the U.S., our ecoregions include the Sonoran, Mojave (or Mohave), Chihuahuan, and Great

Sonoran Desert Ecoregion, Arizona Upland subdivision, desert scrub, Tucson, AZ.

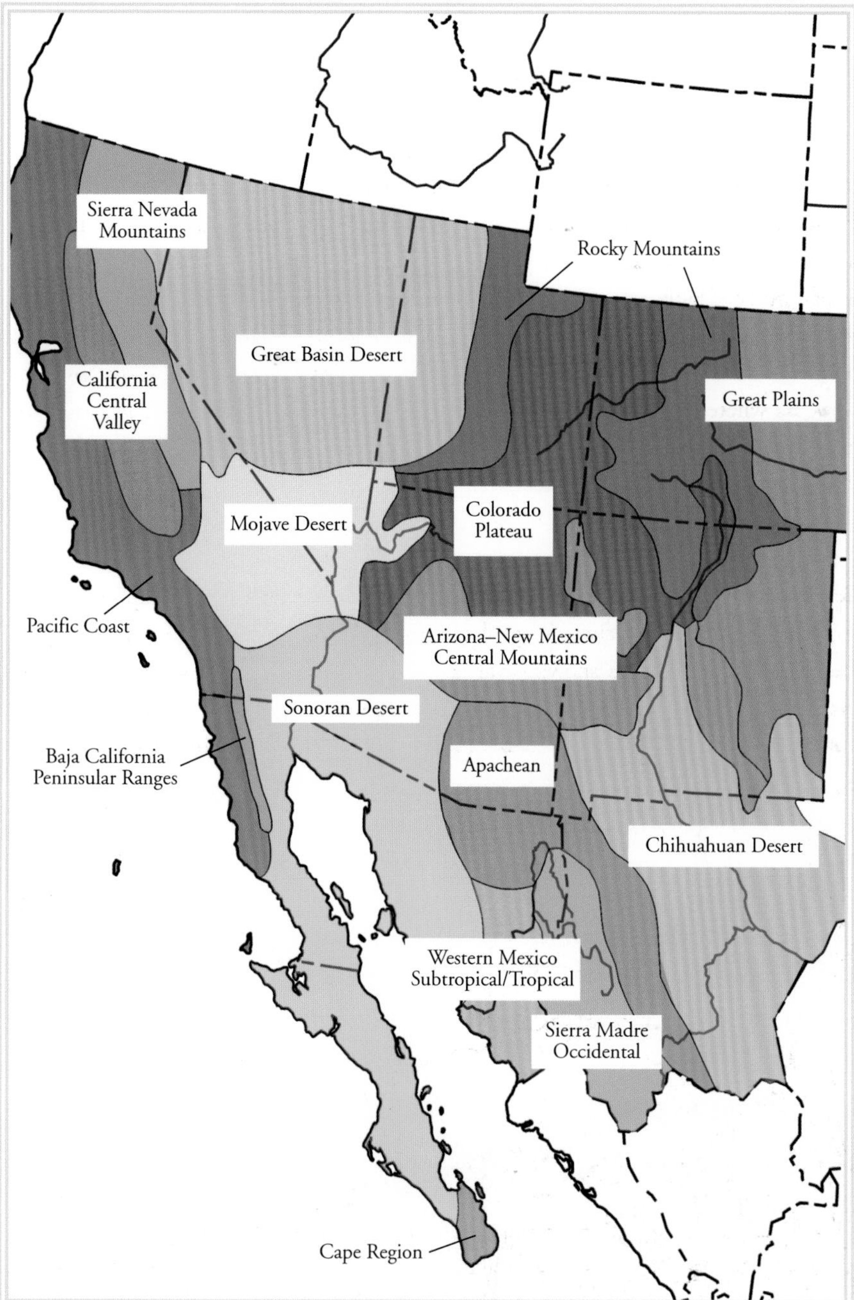

Map 2. Ecoregions map. This simplified map's delineations help explain lizard distribution (including lack of species). Yellows are desert-dominated ecoregions, greens are mountain-dominated, blue-greens are maritime, browns are grassland-dominated, purples are tropical and subtropical, and reds are valleys and plateau ecoregions.

Colorado Plateau Ecoregion: rocky escarpments and shrubs, Vermilion Cliffs, AZ.

Basin deserts; Apachean; Pacific Coast; California Central Valley; Colorado Plateau; Great Plains; Sierra Nevada Mountains; Baja California Peninsular Ranges; Rocky Mountains; and Arizona and New Mexico Central (Mogollon) Mountains. Within these ecoregions, there are many distinctive and unique plant and animal communities. Although ecoregions correspond to large map areas, they blend into one another, so boundaries are not as clearly defined as they appear on the map. Because ecoregions are two-dimensional, at this scale a valley bottom and adjacent mountaintop may be in the same ecoregion, but they will have very different plant and animal communities, including different lizard faunas. However, the lizard fauna of montane habitats within one ecoregion can be similar to, yet distinct from, the lizard fauna of montane habitats in another ecoregion. The greatest lizard diversity lies in the southern ecoregions, especially in the Sonoran and Chihuahuan deserts and in the Apachean and Baja California Peninsular Range ecoregions. More northerly ecoregions, including the Rocky Mountains Ecoregion, have fewer species and a less-distinctive lizard fauna. Also, the Mojave and Great Basin desert ecoregions have but a subset of species found in the Sonoran Desert Ecoregion to the south. At the species level, there is only one endemic lizard in the Mojave Desert, and none in the Great Basin Desert. However, at the subspecies level, there are greater distinctions between these and other ecoregions.

Plant (and Biotic) Communities. Biotic communities are plant and animal assemblages that are usually nested within (but sometimes across) ecoregions. In the literature, we tend to see much more reference to plant communities. However, animal assemblages usually align with one or more plant communities fairly well. There are many ways to categorize plant communities, as there are many definitions and tiers. As with ecoregions, for our lizard-centric perspective, we can do well to think of generalized plant communities (which vary in species composition) across elevation, longitude, and latitude. These plant communities include desert scrub, shrubland, grassland, chaparral, oak woodland, piñon/juniper woodland, pine forest, montane meadow, and montane coniferous forest. As expected, the highest lizard diversity tends to be in plant communities found in southern ecoregions and low elevations, as most lizard species require warm temperatures for survival.

Desert scrub communities are characterized by plants that can tolerate seasonally hot, dry conditions, such as low-growing, drought-resistant shrubs and cacti. Each of the four deserts has its own characteristic plant communities, although there may be overlap. For example, the Mojave, Sonoran, and Chihuahuan deserts have extensive Creosote Bush shrublands, while Creosote Bush is replaced by the more cold-tolerant sagebrush species in the Great Basin Desert. The characteristic plant of the upper elevations of the Mojave Desert is the Joshua Tree, an impressive tree-like species of yucca. There are some other diagnostic plant species, while others are commonly found in the adjacent, contiguous Sonoran and Great Basin deserts as well. The Sonoran Desert is famous for the hallmark Saguaro Cactus, but this species is not found throughout this desert, and in some areas of the Mexican Sonoran Desert, it is replaced by (or co-occurs with) the larger Cardon Cactus, and other species like the strange-looking Cirio or Boojum Tree. Other conspicuous plants include Velvet Mesquite, Ironwood, and various chollas and prickly pear cacti. The Chihuahuan Desert's most diagnostic plant is the Lechuguilla, a species of agave. The Great Basin Desert lacks the high diversity of cacti of the other deserts, so its most distinctive plants are sagebrushes and other shrubs, such as saltbushes and Greasewood. All deserts are prime lizard habitat and account for a large portion of the diversity in the American Southwest.

Chihuahuan Desert Ecoregion, Big Bend NP, TX.

Non-desert valleys and coastlines are also usually characterized by low-growing plants (the California Redwoods are a notable exception!), especially grasses, shrubs, and small trees. Grasslands are quite varied and well distributed across the Southwest. The best-known grasslands are those of the vast Great Plains Ecoregion, which includes both short-grass and tall-grass prairies, but in our area it is generally composed of short-grass prairies. Although the Great Plains lie on the fringe of the area we consider the American Southwest, they are an important element; Great Plains lizard species are best observed in eastern Colorado and adjacent New Mexico. On the southern end, the Great Plains transition into the semi-desert grasslands of the Apachean Ecoregion. Grasslands are also found in the other ecoregions, where ecological conditions are conducive to growth (e.g., association with oak woodland or as mountain meadows). Many of our native grasslands have been lost to—or are at risk from—invasion by non-native grasses, many of which are able to outcompete native species, especially in disturbed areas.

Along coastal southern California and northwestern Baja California, there is a Mediterranean climate that is typified by mild weather and coastal marine fog resulting from the interface of warm terrestrial temperatures with the cold waters of the Pacific Ocean. These coastal shrublands can harbor very dense plant communities. Coastal shrublands are another disappearing ecosystem—one that is being lost primarily to urbanization. Grasslands and shrublands have a surprisingly diverse lizard fauna.

Apachean Ecoregion: Madrean oak woodland with rock features, Chiricahua Mountains, AZ.

Sandia Mountains, NM, an isolated mountain range.

In foothills and lower mountain slopes, we find various woodland plant communities, typically characterized by open evergreen and/or deciduous trees, dominated by oaks and/or junipers. The characteristic species change as one travels to different ecoregions, but the life form structure is similar: grasslands with dominant canopy trees, to dense copses with a high canopy closure largely lacking an understory. Lizards are typically found in the more open areas where they can bask and thermoregulate. Relatively few lizard species are actually found in these habitat types, because montane environments are relatively cold.

Chaparral, which is composed of dense, low-growing shrubs, such as manzanitas and small oaks, is typically found at elevations where you might find oaks and juniper/woodlands, or where growth conditions otherwise favor its development. Coastal chaparral is found from California's coastal foothills inland to the Sierra Nevada Mountains. Interior chaparral is prevalent in the Arizona and New Mexico Central Mountain Ecoregion. Fortunately for lizard aficionados, chaparral (which grows so densely that it is difficult for a person to navigate through) has only a moderate lizard diversity, and there are few endemics.

Pine, pine/oak, and conifer forests are found at high elevations and northern latitudes. These forests are composed of a variety of species, especially in California, but Ponderosa Pine is well distributed across much of the western United States. The largest Ponderosa Pine forest in the world stretches almost continuously across northern Arizona and New Mexico. At the lower elevations, pine forests mix with oaks and may be interspersed with grasslands and chaparral. At higher elevations, they give way to Douglas-firs, true firs, Giant Sequoias, and other conifers (plus some hardy deciduous trees, such as Quaking Aspen), depending on location. As you might expect, these conifer and mixed conifer/deciduous forests are rather low in lizard diversity, but there are some notable exceptions that have mastered life in these harsh environments through special adaptations. At elevations above treeline, lizards are virtually absent.

Habitat Features. These are physical and biotic attributes nested within the above habitat types. For our purposes, we consider the *biotic attributes* to be relatively simple and homogeneous plant assemblages. For example, Creosote Bush flats are dominated by a single dominant species, the Creosote Bush. In fact, Creosote Bush is the dominant shrub in the state of California, even though deserts are only a portion of the entire state! In these habitats, Creosote Bushes are fairly evenly distributed across the landscape and may extend for many miles in all directions. This seemingly simple ecosystem harbors quite a variety of lizard species, because the environment is not as simple as it appears (see the next section on microhabitats). Similarly, the sagebrush flats of the Great Basin Desert harbor many of the same species as Creosote Bush flats, because these two different shrubland types are physically similar.

Riparian areas occur from the lowest elevations to the highest elevations in any type of upland plant community. Usually, a given lizard species is associated with particular upland plant communities (i.e., a particular elevational range). However, riparian areas may act as linear corridors for mesic, or moist, habitats that allow some species to persist despite being surrounded by drier climes. Most skinks and alligator lizards are good examples of lizards that may often be found in riparian corridors and other cool, moist habitats.

Physical attributes include rocky hillsides, rock outcrops, boulder fields, talus fields, open areas, badlands, dunes, roads, urban areas, suburban areas, washes, log jams, debris piles, aquatic habitats, and so on. For lizards, there is a lot of reference to

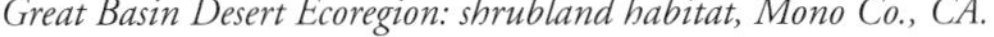

Great Basin Desert Ecoregion: shrubland habitat, Mono Co., CA.

rocky terrain because most species of lizards are found in rocky places where they may naturally thermoregulate, look for prey, seek refuge, and establish territorial promontories. A single rock does not offer all of these features, but when the rocky features are complex, they can meet a multitude of needs. Some species prefer open areas where they can run swiftly, but there must be some sort of cover. Hence, badlands, open dunes, parking lots, or other open areas without structure tend to have a low to absent lizard fauna. However, if you add some structure (vegetation, rocks, etc.), dunes and other open areas can be great lizarding grounds. Dunes stabilized by vegetation, especially Creosote Bush or mesquites, are a particularly great place to look for lizards, as the sand can be littered with tracks of lizards and countless other animals—at least until the next windstorm. There are many stories to be deciphered from patterns in the sand—including where a lizard may have sought refuge from a predator and buried itself under the surface. Washes also attract a multitude of species and may act as an interface with associated microhabitats.

Great Basin Desert Ecoregion: shrubland and riparian vegetation.

Microhabitats. The smallest scale of habitat is the aptly termed "microhabitat." In common usage, this refers to the immediate surroundings and other physical factors of an individual plant or animal within its larger habitat, or a particular component of the habitat for a particular life history need. A single surface or cover object (such as a log) is often referred to as a microhabitat. However, a log on the ground actually consists of numerous microhabitats. Underneath, it provides shelter and a more mesic environment, and it may harbor specific prey species. The upper surface provides a place to bask and search for prey. The edge serves as a runway for both predators and prey, and will provide shade during certain times of the day. Continuing with the example above about the Creosote Bush flats as a lizard-rich biotic habitat feature, a single, large Creosote Bush provides a number of microhabitats: burrows for escaping predators and thermoregulating; open surfaces for gathering radiant heat; dappled light for concealment; leaves, flowers, and leaf litter to attract insect prey; and

Mojave Desert Ecoregion with signature Joshua Trees.

branches to climb for a variety of reasons. A premier example of a lizard that capitalizes on all the benefits of a Creosote Bush is the Long-tailed Brush Lizard. In fact, within its range it has evolved along with the Creosote Bush and similar shrubs. It is very cryptic (difficult to detect) when lying along the axis of one of the Creosote Bush's stems and will move up and down the stem in response to temperature and moisture changes and to seek out prey. This species is rarely found away from the safety of its shrub. Similarly, the aptly named Slevin's Bunchgrass Lizard is closely tied to certain bunchgrasses. Surface objects such as refuse or discarded waste in the form of plywood, metal sheets, tires, etc., are also well known as microhabitat structures, and herpetologists will often look under them (note the ethical and legal ramifications of disturbing microhabitats discussed elsewhere in this book), because some species of lizards (and snakes and arthropods) are seldom found out in the open. Rocks provide a variety of microhabitats for lizards. There are many species associated with cracks and boulders, and interstices between boulders, including Common Chuckwallas, most night lizards, and geckos, among others. Chuckwallas are so closely associated with crevices in boulders that they have evolved the ability to inflate their bodies to become wedged in cracks to avoid extraction by predators. Night lizards and geckos are dorsoventrally flattened and have splayed limbs (as well as other adaptations) so that they can maneuver into and exploit very small areas that are difficult for predators to access, but provide shade and prey abundance.

Rock fissures, Anza-Borrego Desert State Park, CA.

LIFE HISTORY AND BEHAVIOR

Author: Stanley F. Fox

Lizards of the American Southwest are a fascinating and amazing lot. They come in all sizes, shapes, and colors. They live in every kind of terrestrial habitat and are impressive in their specializations to survive and propagate. Lizards are ectotherms and use their environment to maintain warm body temperatures so that they can carry out their daily activities. As such, the greatest density and diversity of lizards in the U.S. occur in the warm, sunny deserts and mountains of the Southwest. Here we see lizards that are diurnal and nocturnal; oviparous (egg-producing) and viviparous (live-bearing); large and long-lived; small and short-lived; some that guard their eggs and some that do not; and even some species that lay unfertilized eggs that are genetic copies of themselves! These Southwestern lizards show all kinds of interesting behavior, as well. Some are territorial, and large, colorful males defend their females from other males with striking visual displays of push-ups, head bobs, lateral displays, and circling behavior. Sometimes they attack each other, biting and fighting viciously. In some species, territorial males can be cuckolded by less colorful and furtive "sneaker" males. Instead of being territorial, some males follow their mated females around, defending their paternity. Most species eat insects, spiders, scorpions, etc., but others are herbivores. Some species find their food by constant movement and searching, while others sit still and ambush prey as it comes near. All sorts of anti-predator behaviors are seen, with the most bizarre being blood squirting from the eye and tail autotomy. Lizards are a showcase for evolution and diversity.

Life History

Life history deals with growth, survival, and reproduction. A characteristic related to these is body size. Lizards of the American Southwest such as tree and brush lizards, horned lizards, skinks, whiptails, and geckos are mostly small (less than 50 g), but some, like Gila Monsters, reach impressive sizes (more than 1 kg). Island forms often reach larger sizes than their mainland counterparts. Generally,

Flat-tailed Horned Lizards, mating.

Texas Alligator Lizard, Nuevo Leon, Mexico, with her clutch.

males are larger than females, although this is sometimes reversed, as in the horned lizards.

How long most lizard species live in the wild is not known; most probably live only two to five years. The larger lizards, like the Common Chuckwalla and the Gila Monster, can live up to twenty to thirty years. Surprisingly, horned lizards (which are not big) have been known to live eight to ten years in captivity. The Madrean Alligator Lizard has lived fifteen years and night lizards up to nine years in captivity. On the other hand, Common Side-blotched Lizards in western Texas mostly live less than a year, dying after spring breeding; those in more northern populations live longer.

Some animals can breed in only one season and then die; others can breed in multiple years. All the species included in this book belong to the latter group, although the western Texas population of the Common Side-blotched Lizard mentioned above comes close to the former, because the majority of the population breeds only in its first full summer. Nevertheless, a small fraction of the population lives another year and breeds again.

Most lizards of the American Southwest can breed the year after they begin life, but some species, especially the larger-bodied ones, have deferred maturity in order to have time to grow large. For example, the Common Chuckwalla does not breed until it is two to five years old and the Gila Monster after it is at least three years old. Night lizards also do not breed until they reach three years of age. Yearling Eastern Collared Lizard males usually do not breed (at least in Oklahoma and probably in the rest of the species' range), even though they are physiologically capable of inseminating females. They are kept away from females by the aggressive behavior of older males, who guard their females inside their territories. This same phenomenon may occur in other long-lived species in which territorial males guard females. Common Chuckwallas, Gila Monsters, and Great Plains Skinks don't necessarily breed each year once they begin reproduction, whereas other species of southwestern lizards breed annually.

Lizards can be oviparous or viviparous. Both modes are seen in lizards of the American Southwest, although oviparity is the most common. Some examples of viviparous lizards are the night lizards, some species of alligator lizards, the California Legless

Lizard, the high-elevation (or northern latitude) Pygmy Short-horned and Greater Short-horned Lizards, and Yarrow's and Crevice Spiny Lizards. The Mountain Skink is oviparous, but there is one published account of viviparity for a female in captivity.

Clutch or litter size varies from just a couple (banded geckos, night lizards, legless lizards) up to thirty to fifty (horned lizards). Whiptails sometimes lay only one or two eggs, probably so as not to be overly burdened by a large, heavy clutch as they actively forage. Most other southwestern species of lizards lay four to eight eggs per clutch, but this can vary a lot depending on weather and food.

Hatchlings or neonates usually resemble adults, except that they are often more strongly patterned (e.g., hatchlings and juveniles of most skinks have much brighter longitudinal lines and bluer tails than adults, especially adult males). For reasons yet unknown to science, hatchling Great Plains Skinks are coal black with white labial scales (see Figure 3) and a bright blue tail, whereas the adults vary between gray and tan, with each scale edged with black or dark brown. The difference is so great that juveniles and adults were for a time regarded as two separate species! As males of many southwestern lizard species mature, they often develop striking breeding coloration, like the brilliant blue or blue-green dorsum of the Eastern Collared Lizard, the orange to red lips of the Many-lined, Western, and Four-lined Skinks (whole head and throat of Gilbert's Skink), or the bright blue undersides and throats of spiny lizards.

Most lizard species of the American Southwest choose a nest site, lay their eggs, and then leave; the eggs and subsequent hatchlings get by on their own. Even viviparous species do not rear their offspring. However, some (maybe all) of the oviparous species of alligator lizards and perhaps all the skinks brood their eggs (it is unknown if Little Brown Skink, which barely enters the geographical area of this book, has the same brooding behavior). Some skinks, such as the Great Plains Skink, even care for the hatchlings a little. Parental care by skinks consists of nest construction and maintenance, hydroregulation and thermoregulation of the nest, coiling around and brooding eggs, brood defense, ingestion of spoiled or unfertilized eggs, manipulation or retrieval of eggs, parental assistance of neonates during hatching, and help with neonatal feeding.

When lizards shed their skin, it is usually sloughed in pieces, as seen in this juvenile Ctenosaura macrolopha, *Sonora, Mexico.*

Yarrow's Spiny Lizards emerging from hibernation in the Chiricahua Mountains, AZ. They are dark with melanin pigments until they warm up.

A final, very bizarre twist in life history among lizards is seen in the large group of all-female whiptails of the American Southwest. *Aspidoscelis tesselata, A. exsanguis, A. neomexicana, A. velox, A. flagellicauda, A. sonorae, A. uniparens, A. dixoni,* and *A. neotesselata* reproduce parthenogenetically, without the need to have their eggs fertilized. However, not all species of *Aspidoscelis* are parthenogenetic; the other 12 species that occur in the American Southwest are typical bisexual species having both males and females. Each of the parthenogenetic species is the product of hybridization between two bisexual *Aspidoscelis* species (sometimes with a subsequent hybridization with one of the same parental species or even a third species). The parthenogenetic species consist of multiple clones of individuals. Each clone is a lineage of genetically identical female lizards—except for subsequent mutations.

Behavior

Social behavior is how conspecifics (individuals of the same species) interact with one another. The most common and archetypical social organization in lizards is territoriality. Chiefly, a male defends an area against rival males. Inside this territory reside one to several adult females with which he mates. The male spends a lot of time during the breeding season guarding his territory and expelling male intruders who might try to sneak in. He uses visual displays (and sometimes chemical scent marks) to defend his territory. His defense is so vigorous that sometimes he fails to eat enough during the breeding season and loses weight. In species like the Eastern Collared Lizard or Yarrow's Spiny Lizard, whose habitat is patchy rock outcrops, lizard densities reach high levels, and it is common for a large male to stake out territories that contain several females. Those females are his harem, and for the most part, he alone copulates with them. A second kind of social organization that is seen when lizards are grouped together quite densely is a dominance hierarchy. Males are grouped in dominance rank so that the most dominant has priority of access to space, food, or females, and all others give way to him. The second-most-dominant has second-place priority, and so forth down the line. The top lizard on the totem pole is the largest, brightest male who displays the most. A variation on this social system is one in which the most dominant male is a tyrant, equally respected by all other males, but the subordinate males are not organized in a hierarchical fashion. In some places and under crowded conditions, the Common Chuckwalla has just such a despotic social organization and only the tyrant mates. In other populations even when they are crowded, the males are territorial.

Conversely, some species of lizards don't defend a territory and wander widely in search of food and mates. Good examples of this behavior are seen in whiptails and the alligator lizards. Sometimes males will guard females after copulation to keep away other males and ensure their paternity. Mate-guarding is known in the Striped Plateau Lizard and the Common Side-blotched Lizard (and likely in the Great Plains Skink).

The Common Side-blotched Lizard, probably the most widely distributed lizard of the American Southwest, can display a complex mixture of mating behavior. In the Central Valley of California, adult males come in three (fixed) forms according to the color of their throat: blue, yellow, or orange. The orange-throated males are the most aggressive and maintain large territories with females inside them; but yellow-throated males, who do not defend territories, sneak into the territories of the orange-throated males at opportune times and copulate with the resident's females. Blue-throated males also do not defend territories, but instead mate-guard their females after copulation. This mate guarding is effective against yellow-throated males, but not against the super-aggressive

Male Common Side-blotched Lizard doing a "push-up" display.

Adult male Eastern Collared Lizard attacking a subadult male of the same species.

orange-throated males. Thus, each morph dominates one of the other morphs, but in turn is dominated by the third—like the child's game of rock-paper-scissors. This circularity means that no one strategy can take over the system; there will be an alternate strategy that can do better against it. Consequently, the relative frequencies of the three color morphs cycle over years due to natural selection. A rare strategy increases when the morph it can outperform is in high frequency; but then when this second morph reaches high frequency, the third morph, which does better against the second, starts to increase, and so on. Orange à Yellow à Blue à Orange—round and round they go over the years.

To accompany all this social life, lizards sport an impressive array of visual displays to communicate with one another. (Lizards for the most part do not vocalize, except that geckos chirp and squeak, and the Long-nosed Leopard-lizard sometimes squeaks or hisses upon capture; Great Plains Skinks will also sometimes hiss when captured.) The quintessential lizard display is the push-up, in which a male raises and lowers the front part of its body, usually with the colored dewlap exposed. Each species has a distinctive sequence of taller and shorter up-and-down movements to form the complete display. Interestingly, the Spanish word for lizard is *lagartija,* and the same word also means "push-up," as in calisthenics. Push-ups are fairly generic signals that are used to warn distant males to keep out of a male's territory, to try to bluff and repel a close-by male, and to court females. A less intensive version of the push-up is the movement up and down in the same species-specific pattern of just the head, called a headbob. If two males are very close to one another, or a male is courting a female, you are apt to see a display called a "full show." The male orients sideways to the receiver, compresses his body laterally, extends his dewlap, arches his back, stands as tall as possible, and delivers several energetic push-ups one after the other. After several "full shows," usually one of the males gives up and flees, or the female accepts or rejects her suitor. Accompanying the "full shows" is circling movement in which the opponents move in an arc to size up one another, like boxers in a ring. If all these ritualized displays don't do the trick, the two males will often escalate their aggression, with one or both combatants charging in and biting the other. Big lizards with strong jaws, e.g., Eastern Collared Lizards, can do considerable damage to one another if the interaction turns fierce. In fact, recent studies have shown that bite force, and not body size or head size, will determine the winner of such interactions among similar-sized combatants. Once males bite one another, they don't need to repeat it much; the ritualized displays will be enough to reinforce who is dominant.

Another important behavior of lizards is foraging. Most species of the American Southwest are carnivores, eating mostly insects, spiders, scorpions, and sometimes even other lizards, although Desert Iguanas and the Common Chuckwalla are herbivores (both species also eat some insects). Collared lizards, California rock lizards, night lizards, fringe-toed lizards, and in particular whiptails supplement their animal diet with seeds, flowers, and tender shoots and leaves of plants.

Most species are diurnal, although geckos and some night lizards are nocturnal. The Gila Monster can be diurnal or nocturnal, depending on the time of year, location, and weather. Not all night lizards are strictly nocturnal; they may also be active during the day in darkened crevices or under plant debris or rock slabs.

Lizards are either sit-and-wait foragers (also called "ambush foragers") or active foragers. Sit-and-wait foragers position themselves immobile at the edge of a bush or on an elevated rock and wait for moving prey, usually insects or spiders, to come within reach. Once they have a suitable prey close, they make a quick dash to capture it, then return to their place or find a nearby, similar hunting post. Opposite to this rather sedentary hunting strategy is that of active foragers, who move around searching out suitable prey, spending most of their time on the move. The families Gekkonidae, Eublepharidae, Phrynosomatidae, and Crotaphytidae employ the sit-and-wait strategy, whereas Teiidae, Scincidae, Anguidae, and Helodermatidae employ active foraging. The Xantusiidae are probably active foragers, given their phylogenetic affinities with other active foragers, but this is not certain.

Escaping predation is another important behavior of lizards. Most lizards rely on either flight or crypsis. Lizards know the suitable refuges inside their territories or home ranges (e.g., old mammal burrows, holes, under logs or rocks, clumps of plants, rocky cracks, and crevices) and seek their protection when danger threatens. Whiptails, collared lizards, leopard lizards, fringe-toed lizards, Desert Iguanas, Greater Earless-lizards, and Zebra-tailed Lizards run fast and often cover considerable distances

Greater Roadrunner, an efficient predator of lizards.

This Round-tailed Horned Lizard employs the defensive strategy of making itself look larger and more threatening to the photographer.

when threatened by a potential predator. The Zebra-tailed Lizard and the Greater Earless-lizard often run (sometimes bipedally like collared lizards, leopard lizards, and Desert Iguanas) with the tail curled over their back, showing off their prominent black-and-white banded caudal underside in an attempt to fool the predator when they suddenly stop running and lower their tail. This hides the black-and-white tail coloration and probably disorients the predator. Fringe-toed lizards and earless lizards run and suddenly dive into the sand to hide from would-be predators. Crevice-dwelling lizards, like Common Chuckwallas and Crevice Spiny Lizards, retreat into tight spaces and inflate their bodies to resist extraction.

Other species rely on crypsis to escape the notice of predators. Long-tailed Brush Lizards, with their cryptic, elongate bodies and delicate limbs, often align themselves along a branch or tree trunk, and are quite difficult to make out. Probably the most cryptic lizards of the American Southwest are the horned lizards. The master of these is the diminutive Round-tailed Horned Lizard, which is plain-bodied and has no marginal, pointed, fringe scales (see Figure 4) like other species of the genus. It lives in arid areas with gravel or cobblestone substrates and escapes notice by hunching up its body and mimicking a stone!

Unique among the lizards of the American Southwest is the Gila Monster in that it is both venomous and brightly colored with orange and black—the exact opposite of crypsis. Its bold coloration is a warning to would-be predators of its dangerous venom.

This autonomized tail saved a lizard from this House Cat.

Easily the most bizarre adaptation to deter a would-be predator is the ability of some species of horned lizards to release a spurt of blood from a sinus at the corner of the eye, usually in response to rough handling by a coyote or dog. It has been shown that the squirted blood carries a chemical that irritates the eyes and mucous membranes of the canid. A dog or coyote at the receiving end of such a defense gives up its potential prey and retreats, wiping its eyes and mouth.

Finally, a quintessential lizard defense is tail autotomy, the ability of some species to allow the tail to break free of the body when grasped by a predator. The detached tail, often brightly colored, wriggles violently and may distract the predator, enabling the "lizard part" of the lizard to escape. Most lizards of the American Southwest have this ability, but not collared, leopard, and horned lizards, Gila Monsters, or adult Common Chuckwallas. Tail autotomy is not simply tearing the tail away from the body. There exists a whole suite of adaptations to allow the release of the tail from the body along a series of "fracture planes" down the tail. In most species the break occurs through a preweakened vertebra, not between them. At these fracture planes, the muscles separate along septa, and blood loss is reduced by contraction of sphincter valves in the blood

Madrean Alligator Lizard with regenerated tail. The new portion of a tail looks different than the original.

vessels. Then, these species have the ability to regenerate the tail—so that it can be lost again if need be! However, the regenerated part of the tail is just cartilage (covered with scales) and lacks bone and new fracture planes, so if tail autotomy occurs again (and this is not uncommon), the break occurs only in the original base of the tail, not in the new part. Tail autotomy may save the life of the lizard, but it obviously comes with costs. After autotomy, lizards have to deal with a major wound, are left with less caudal fat reserves, don't run and maneuver as well, don't have a tail to lose if a predator strikes before regeneration is complete, and (at least in subadult Common Side-blotched Lizards) fall in social status among conspecifics. This loss of social status can adversely affect a lizard's chance of survival and decrease a male's ability to defend a territory and mate. Thus, tail autotomy as a defense against predation is a last-ditch effort.

EXTERNAL ANATOMY AND IDENTIFICATION

Authors: Lawrence L. C. Jones and Randall D. Babb

Most lizards have an overall shape that is relatively elongate and prostrate, with a distinct head, neck, torso, front limbs, and hind limbs. This is similar to most salamanders (with which they are sometimes confused), but there is one very important difference—salamanders are amphibians and have smooth, usually slimy skins, while lizards are reptiles and have dry, scaly skin. From this generalized shape, there are many variations and exceptions. The variations in the shapes of lizards are often diagnostic at the family and genus level. For example, some lack legs, some are dorsoventrally flattened, some have very long tails, and so on.

Most species of the American Southwest can be differentiated in the field with the aid of close-focusing binoculars, based on their overall shape and color pattern. However, there may be considerable variation in color patterns, even within a species. This variation is often diagnostic for differentiating age classes, sexes, subspecies, pattern classes, and reproductive mode, but there is also normal variation to be expected within a single taxon. For example, there may be color-matching, where a lizard generally matches the background, as with horned lizards. The Greater Short-

Adult male Cophosaurus texanus, *Maricopa Co., AZ.*

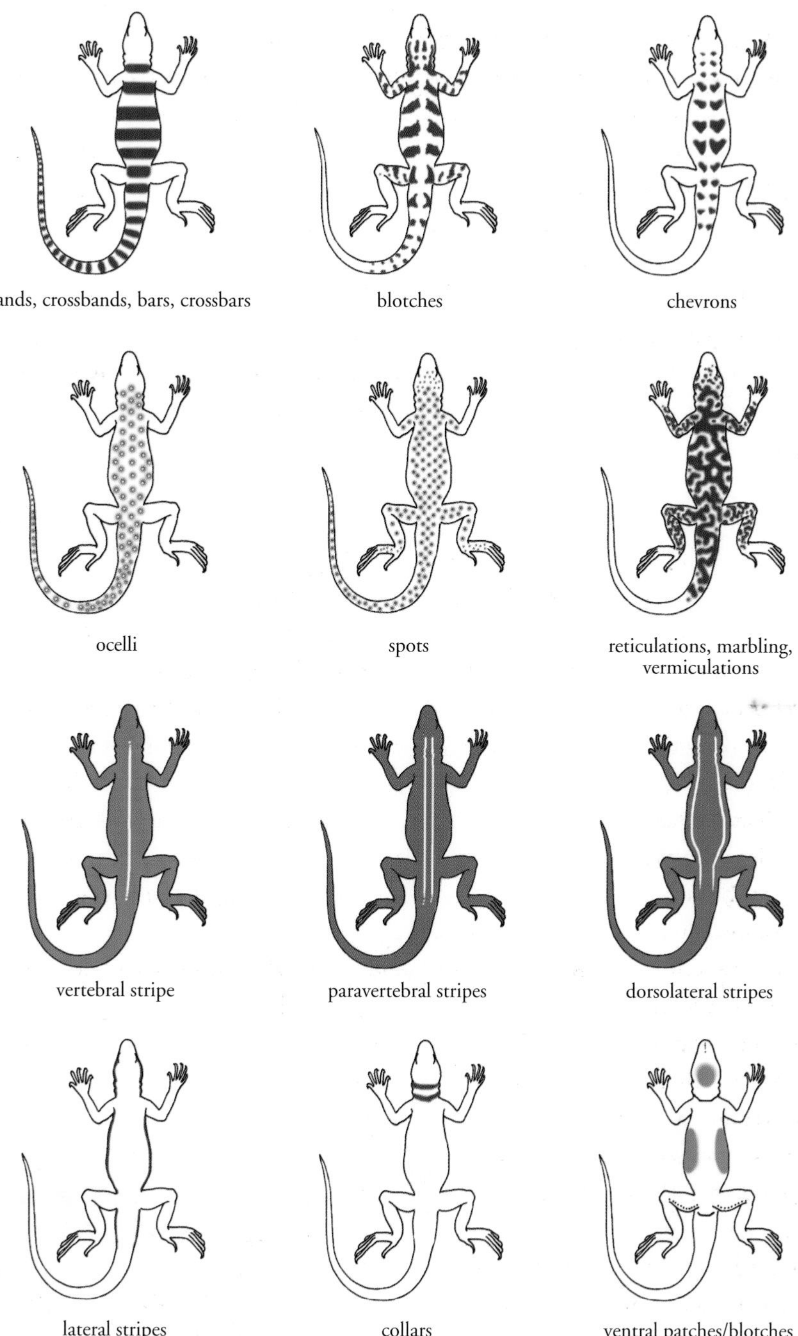

Figure 1. Color patterns and markings of lizards.

horned Lizard may be black in areas of lava beds, red in redrock country, and pale in areas with light-colored soils. Also, when lizards are cold, many tend to be dark, while when they are warm, they tend to be lighter. This is an aid to thermoregulation to maintain their body temperatures at optimal levels. When in breeding condition, the females (and occasionally males) often have reddish orange colors concomitant with a particular stage in the reproductive mode, and adult males (especially) tend to have showy ventral colors (especially blue) for territorial and reproductive displays. Because there may be so much variation in color patterns, it is best to always read the description and subspecies and variations sections in the text entirely, to get an understanding of the full range of possibilities. It is also important to read about the scalation, as that is usually diagnostic, even when color pattern is not.

Scalation is a very important feature long used by herpetologists to differentiate taxa, as it tends to be a more reliable indicator of taxonomy than color and pattern. The gross types and arrangements of scales also tend to vary on the family and genus level. More subtle differences in scalation can be used to differentiate many species, subspecies, and even sexes. For example, many whiptails can be differentiated by the presence/absence or shape of certain scale types (e.g., number of scales across the mid-body, mesoptychial scales, and postantebrachial scales (see Figure 4). When scalation must be used to differentiate species, the animal must usually be captured and viewed in the hand, often with a hand-lens.

Enlarged dorsal scales of a Long-tailed Brush Lizard.

Some other anatomical features may be important diagnostic characteristics at various taxonomic levels, such as the presence or absence of external ear openings, eyelids, vertical pupils; the shape of the toes; and so on.

The brief general description of shape, scalation, and color patterns of families and genera below will help a novice quickly become familiar with lizards at these taxonomic levels; this will help narrow down the choices when trying to identify species. Use these descriptions in concert with the Thumbnail Guide to Families and Genera given on page 560.

Crotaphytidae (Collared and Leopard Lizards). Crotaphytids have a large head, long limbs, and long tail. They are mostly covered in granular scales (see Figure 4). Collared Lizards (*Crotaphytus*) have black collars and males are often brightly colored, while leopard lizards (*Gambelia*) lack collars and are often cryptically colored.

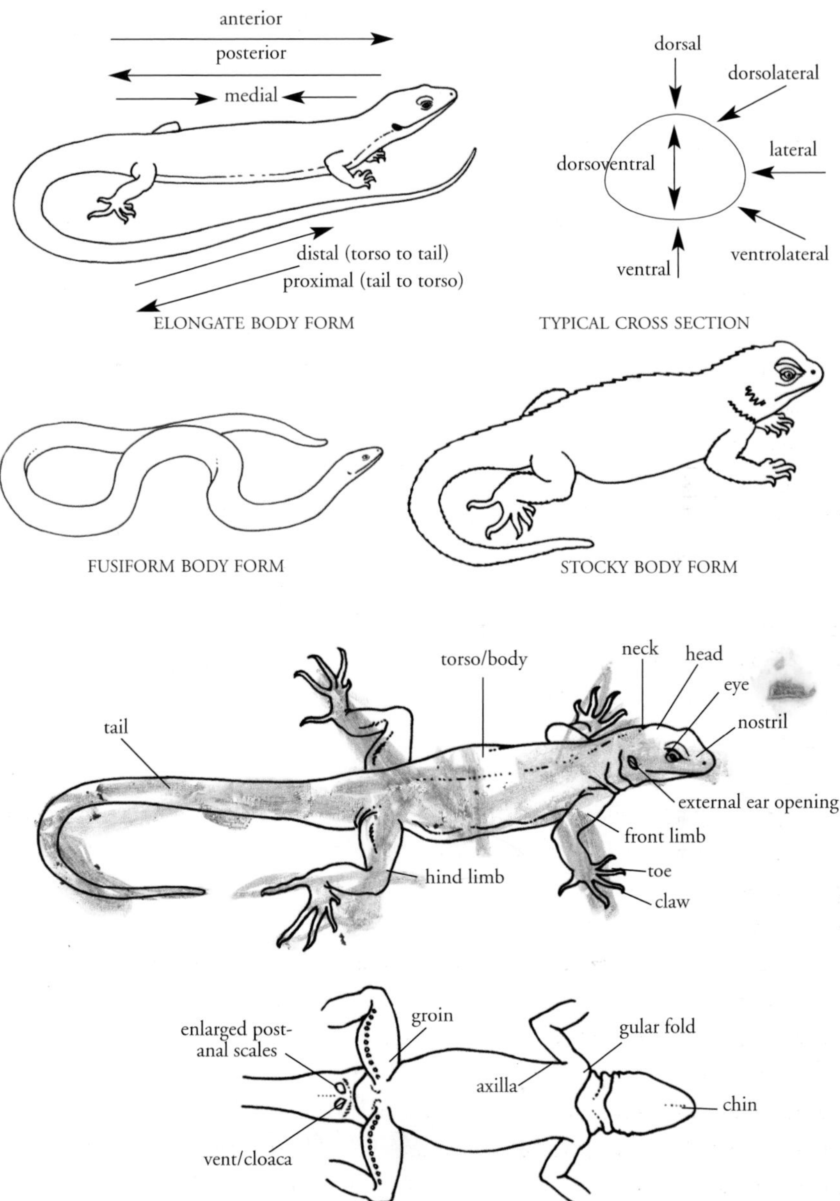

Figure 2. General lizard anatomy. TOP HALF OF PAGE, CLOCKWISE FROM TOP LEFT: Body forms with directional terms: elongate (*Elgaria*), general cross section (typical lizard), stocky (*Sceloporous*), fusiform/tubular/cylindrical (*Anniella*). BOTTOM HALF OF PAGE, TOP TO BOTTOM: External features: dorsolateral view, ventral view.

Iguanidae (Iguanas and Chuckwallas). Members of this family are typically large. Chuckwallas (*Sauromalus*) are heavy bodied and Desert Iguanas (*Dipsosaurus*) are more elongate. They are mostly covered in granular scales. Desert Iguanas and female (and juvenile) Common Chuckwallas are cryptically colored, while male Common Chuckwallas are quite variable in color.

Fringes on the toes of the aptly named fringed-toed lizards are adaptations for running on sand dunes.

Phrynosomatidae (Phrynosomatid Lizards). It is hard to generalize for this diverse family of several genera and many species. Typically, these are small to medium-sized lizards with various scalation. Sand lizards (*Callisaurus, Cophosaurus, Holbrookia,* and *Uma*) are generally adapted for loose soils. *Cophosaurus* and *Holbrookia* lack external ear openings and *Uma* has the diagnostic fringed toes. *Cophosaurus* and *Callisaurus* have a diagnostic black and white banding under the tail. Horned lizards (*Phrynosoma*) are dorsoventrally flattened and usually have large pointed head scales. Spiny lizards (*Sceloporus*) have large keeled scales (some more so than others; see Figure 4) and males often have blue ventral patches. The remaining genera (*Petrosaurus, Urosaurus,* and *Uta*) are difficult to characterize briefly, so refer to the Family and Species Accounts.

Eublepharidae (Eyelidded Geckos). *Coleonyx* (banded geckos) is the only genus in this family that is found in the Southwest; this genus is characterized by lizards that walk relatively upright on the ground; have vertical pupils; possess eyelids; have small, granular scales; and generally have a banded color pattern, which may become spotted.

Gekkonidae (Geckos). This group of geckos belonging to one southwestern genus (*Phyllodactylus*) is dorsoventrally flattened and able to walk on vertical surfaces because of their flattened, modified toes. Scales are granular and tuberculate. The coloration is cryptic, matching the background.

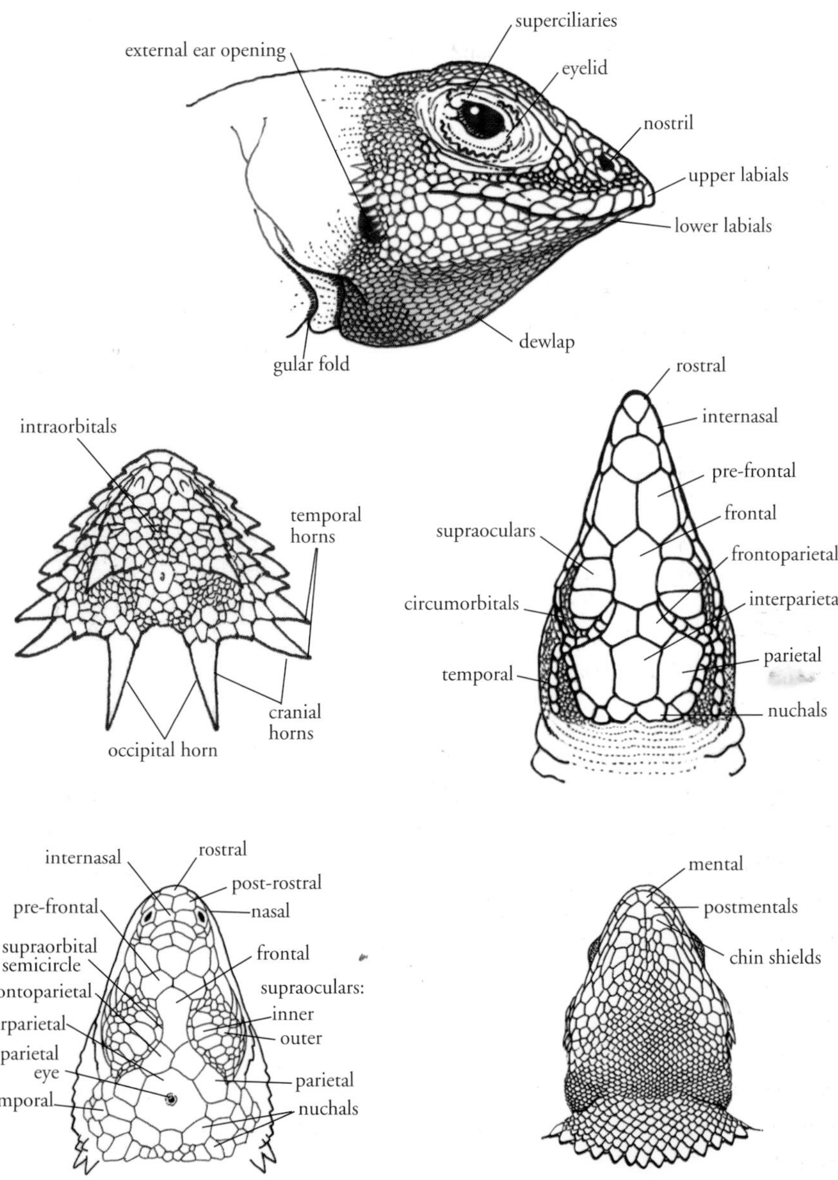

Figure 3. Head scales of lizards. CLOCKWISE FROM TOP: Lateral scales (*Uma*), dorsal scales (*Aspidoscelis*), gular/mesoptychial scales (composite drawing), dorsal scales (*Urosaurus*), dorsal scales (*Phrynosoma*).

Teiidae (Whiptails). One large genus (*Aspidoscelis*), whose members are very similar in form. They are elongate, relatively cylindrical in cross-section, and have a pointed snout and long tail. They are mostly covered in small scales dorsally and large scales ventrally, but there are other diagnostic and variously sized and shaped scale groups, particularly the mesoptychials and postantebrachials. They tend to have one or more of the following patterns: marbled/reticulated, striped, and spotted. The striped-and-spotted whiptails are the most difficult to identify at the species level, so scalation and other subtle differences are key to proper identification. To make matters worse, there are often marked differences between age classes. For example, *A. burti stictogramma* starts out as striped, then becomes striped and spotted, and may end up completely spotted...and some of the intermediate patterns could be considered marbled/reticulated!

Xantusiidae (Night Lizards). The single southwestern genus (*Xantusia*) is composed of small, dorsoventrally flattened lizards (one exception). Most scales, except dorsal head and ventral, are small and granular. Generally, they are cryptically colored, or have a subtle, but variable, pattern of spots and sometimes lines.

Scincidae (Skinks). Both southwestern genera (*Plestiodon* and *Scincella*) are characterized by small to medium, short-limbed lizards, with smooth, shiny scales. Juveniles often have brightly colored tails that tend to fade with age; adults are variously colored and patterned, but tend to be striped or monocolored. Breeding males often have bright reddish upper lips.

Anguidae (Legless and Alligator Lizards). The legless lizards (our sole genus is *Anniella*) are diagnostic on that feature alone. Alligator lizards (*Elgaria* and *Gerrhonotus*) are medium to large elongate animals, with short limbs, a long tail, and pointy snout, which renders them superficially similar to whiptails and skinks, but the dorsolateral fold of scales is always diagnostic.

Helodermatids are called beaded lizards because of their osteoderms.

Helodermatidae (Beaded Lizards). These are large, robust lizards, with large heads and short, fat tails. The single genus (*Heloderma*) has characteristic beaded scales that are actually underlaid with bone. They have a bold coloration pattern of yellow to orange or pink and black, which serves as a warning of their venom.

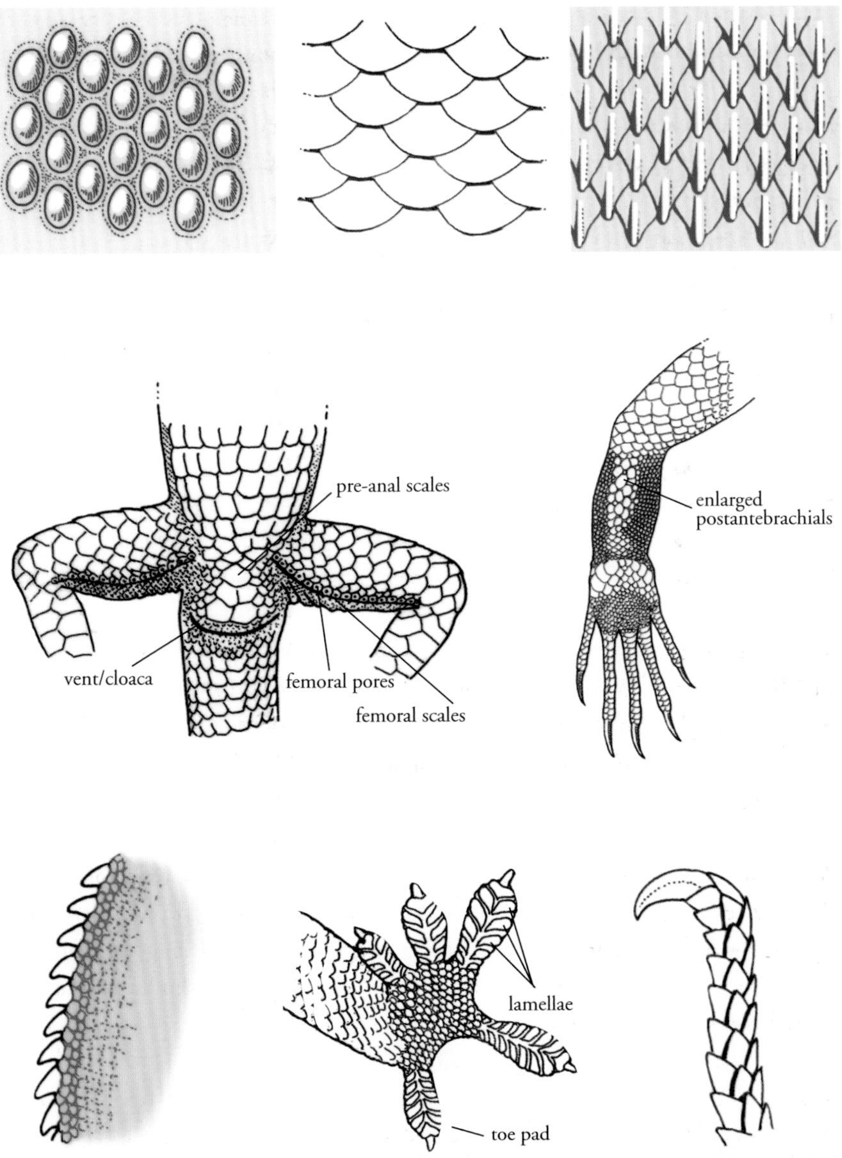

Figure 4. Scalation of lizards. UPPER ROW, LEFT TO RIGHT: Beaded or granular (*Heloderma*); smooth, cycloid (*Plestiodon*); keeled, mucronate (*Sceloporus*). CENTER ROW, LEFT TO RIGHT: Ventral scales in the hind limb/cloacal area (*Aspidoscelis*); postantebrachials of forearm (enlarged, *Aspidoscelis*). BOTTOM ROW, LEFT TO RIGHT: Fringe (*Phrynosoma*), underside of foot (Gekkonidae), and laminate.

NON-NATIVE SPECIES

Authors: Lawrence L. C. Jones and Robert E. Lovich

In the American Southwest, there are relatively few non-native species of lizards that have established breeding populations in the wild (unlike Florida and Hawaii). None are considered invasive, so they pose no known significant threat to other native species at this time. Only one non-native species is well distributed in the Southwest, the Mediterranean House Gecko (*Hemidactylum turcicus*). In our area, it has been recorded in southern California; Las Vegas, Nevada; southern Arizona; southern New Mexico; and southern Texas. It was originally introduced from Europe and Asia, probably through accidental transport (e.g., egg masses in potted plants), but has spread rapidly and is still spreading. Its niche is primarily in the urban environment (i.e., homes and other residential areas), where none of our neighboring species might be potential predators, prey, or competitors. So far, it has not been shown to have a significant detrimental effect on any other native species. However, one of us (LLCJ) has seen this species in a wild setting, on roadcuts in southwestern Texas.

The other non-invasive, non-native species have either been intentionally or unintentionally introduced to various areas, but have more limited distributions in their non-native habitats. Spiny-tailed iguanas (genetically shown to be hybrids) were introduced to the grounds of the Arizona-Sonora Desert Museum in the 1970s, where they are often observed. However, they do not seem to be expanding their range, and few individuals have been noted outside the museum grounds. This species has also become established in the vicinity of Fullerton, California, but it, too, does not seem to be expanding its range. The Moorish Wall Gecko (*Tarentola mauritanica*) has become established in the San Diego area, as has the Green Anole (*Anolis carolinensis*), which is common on the grounds of the San Diego Zoo. Green Iguanas (*Iguana iguana*), Texas Horned Lizards (*Phyrynosoma coronutum*), house geckos (*Hemidactylus* spp.), Bearded Dragons (*Pogona vitticeps*), Savannah Monitors (*Varanus exanthematicus*), Nile Monitors (*V. niloticus*), and Water Monitors (*V. salvator*) have been seen in that region as well. Jackson's Chameleon (*Chamaeleo jacksonii*) has become established in coastal California.

Some other species have "expanded" their range from human introduction. The Green Anole (*Anolis carolinensis*) has become established in Big Bend National Park, Texas, at the Rio Grande Village. This species is native to eastern Texas but is uncommon in the park, and is not likely to spread into the arid environments farther west. A small population of the New Mexico Whiptail (*Aspidoscelis neomexicana*) has been established in Petrified Forest National Park, Arizona. In southern California, two

Spiny-tailed iguanas are found on the grounds of the Arizona-Sonora Desert Museum in Tucson, but they have not become established in the surrounding Tucson Mountains.

species of lizard, the Common Side-blotched Lizard (*Uta stansburiana*) and Southern Alligator Lizard (*Elgaria multicarinata*) have become established on some of the Channel Islands. The Southern Alligator Lizard is also established in Las Vegas. In the Santa Catalina Mountains of the Coronado National Forest, there is an interesting situation. The Catalinas are one of the more northerly "sky islands" and are the only range (including the adjoined Rincon Mountains) among the higher sky islands that is naturally lacking Yarrow's Spiny-lizard (*S. jarrovii*). Instead, a fence lizard (*S. cowlesi or S. tristichus*; identification not genetically confirmed, but previously referred to as *S. undulatus tristichus*) is apparently the native montane spiny lizard in that range. Recently, *S. jarrovii* has been introduced to the range in the vicinity of the Palisades Visitors Center; it is too soon to know if it will spread farther or if there will be an ecological impact from its introduction. The Plateau Striped Whiptail (*A. velox*), a Southwest native, has become established at Cove Palisades State Park, Oregon. There are probably other human-caused range extensions that we are not aware of, and there will no doubt be more in the future.

Northwestern Mexico also has its share of non-native lizards and human-caused range extensions, but still not as many species as one would predict, given the tropical

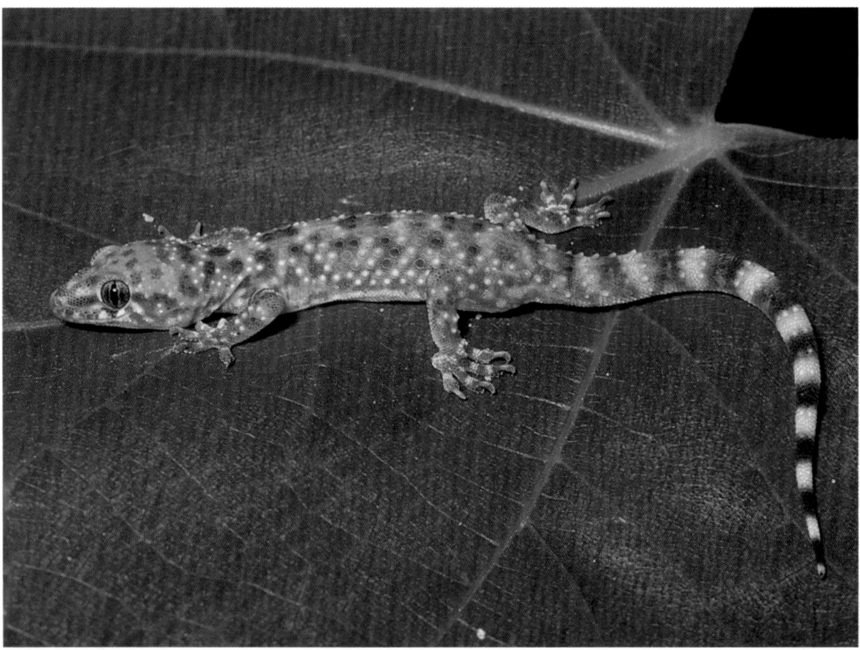

The Mediterranean House Gecko is well established and widespread in the American Southwest, but it is mostly an urban dweller, where there is no competition with native species.

and subtropical climates of the southern parts of Sonora, Baja California, and Chihuahua. The Mediterranean House Gecko, Stump-toed Gecko (*Gehyra mutilata*), and Common House-gecko (*Hemidactylus frenatus*) have become established. Isla Alcatraz is a tiny island in Kino Bay on the Sonora side of the Sea of Cortez (also called Gulf of California) that has three species of chuckwallas (*Sauromalus ater*, *S. hispidus*, and *S. varius*). All three freely hybridize and have produced a hybrid swarm. Of these, only *S. ater* is believed to be native to the island, as it is abundant on the nearby mainland; the other larger species are believed to have been introduced from other islands in the Sea of Cortez by the native Seri peoples as a food source. *Sceloporus varius* was also introduced to Isla Roca Lobos near Bahía de Los Angeles.

Although no non-native lizards are known to be invasive in the American Southwest, we should be cognizant of non-native species as a potential threat to native species and ecosystems. The American Southwest is similar ecologically to numerous other areas, and has good environmental potential for many species of lizards. In this age of rapid global transport and a burgeoning reptile pet trade, we must all be aware that the possibility for the introduction of invasive species exists.

OBSERVING LIZARDS

Authors: Lawrence L. C. Jones and Robert E. Lovich

LIZARD-WATCHING BASICS

If you are a bona fide wannabe lizard-watcher, you are in luck: lizards are fairly predictable. The key to knowing where and how to look for them requires only a little baseline knowledge. A variety of lizards occur in most of the American Southwest and adjacent Mexico.

Ecotourist multi-tasking: lizards and butterflies.

Where to Locate Lizards

As a rule, there are more species as you go south, and more species in valleys and foothills than in montane environments. Hence, the greatest diversity of lizards in the U.S. is near the Mexican border, in the valleys and foothills. As you might expect, mountains in our northern states have a relatively depauparate to nonexistent lizard fauna. If you want to look for a particular species, read the Viewing Tips section for that particular lizard in the Species Accounts. If you want to look for many different species of lizards in a short time, a logical progression is to think of lizard assemblages (groups of lizards associated with characteristic habitat types) in terms of ecoregions, plant (biotic) communities, and habitat features, and where these habitats types converge. For example, Palm Springs, California, is a good base camp at an ecological convergence zone: within a short day's drive, you can see species allied with the Sonoran Desert, Mojave Desert, Peninsular Ranges, and Coast Ranges (and you might be back in time for an afternoon tee-off). When you are at the right location, look in a variety of habitats such as foothills, boulders, Creosote Bush flats, shrub-stabilized sand dunes, washes, and riparian areas. Once you have an idea of how this approach to identifying lizard habitat works, armed with the individual species accounts, the serious lizarder can find most species of lizards fairly easily (there are some notable exceptions). Places that are generally poor for lizards include cities (but suburbs can be good), badlands, and open dunes, but there are some exceptions.

Merging ecoregions near Palm Springs, CA.

When to Observe Lizards

Lizards tend to be surface-active mostly in the spring and summer, but activity patterns vary according to climatic and environmental conditions. For example, it is generally best to view lizards in the Lower Colorado subdivision of the Sonoran Desert during the spring, because activity coincides with the spring bloom and the abundance of wildflowers and insects following winter rains. Because there is no monsoon, it gets extremely hot and dry during summer months and there is no summer bloom, so most lizard species reduce surface activity or aestivate (a state of dormancy during hot, dry summer conditions). Conversely, in an area with a monsoon, it is possible to see lizards well into the summer. Late summer and early fall are usually the best times to see juvenile lizards, but they also emerge from brumation (hibernation) in spring. Keeping an eye on temperatures (and moisture) is the key to knowing when lizards will be surface-active. In the spring, when temperatures are mild, lizards tend to be late risers. As a general rule, small-bodied lizards are the first to appear, while large-bodied lizards appear later in the day. In the spring, lizards are active for much of the day, when daytime temperatures are in the 24–32°C range. In the summer, diurnal lizards typically have a bimodal daily activity pattern. They are most active during the morning hours, after the air and soil temperatures have warmed up sufficiently to allow them to bask. They then seek shade and shelter during the heat of the day. By late afternoon, it has cooled off somewhat and there are long shadows, and some species may be seen surface-active again. The real trick is simply to avoid extreme temperatures if you want to see lizards.

Winter rains off the Pacific Coast are critical to a spring wildflower bloom, which allows for a good lizarding season.

Wildflower blooms following winter rains mark the onset of good insect production and hence a good lizarding season.

The summer monsoon in some areas of the American Southwest brings thunderstorms, and some lizard species have adapted to this second, more substantial rainy season.

Some families of lizards are decidedly observable during the day, including most of the species of the Phrynosmatidae, Teiidae, Crotaphytidae, and Iguanidae. The teiids bask on the surface and are generally observed while on the prowl searching for prey—an activity that is rather fun to watch, as they are very adept predators. The others normally bask on structures, such as rocks and logs. The Eublepharidae, Gekkonidae, and Xantusiidae are either nocturnal or hide in shelters during the day. Most nocturnal species can be observed at night near their haunts, or sometimes on roads. Other species, including those of the Scincidae and Anguidae, rarely venture far from cover, so are difficult to find on the surface. Helodermatids are mostly diurnal during the spring and nocturnal during the summer—but the key to finding a Gila Monster is to spend just enough time in the right place at the right time. Eventually, you will see one.

Moisture is another environmental factor that is a key to lizard activity. If there has been a winter drought, it will translate into a poor spring bloom, which means a poor prey base (invertebrates), so lizard activity is reduced. Some species cope with drought by becoming less surface-active. They may switch diets to more abundant but less preferred food sources, abstain from breeding, and reduce basking. So, wet winters (especially with early winter moisture, which produces a good wildflower season) are a green light for lizard-watching. Also, rainfall can have an immediate effect by stimulating surface activity. As a rule, lizards are active when it is sunny, not windy, and temperatures are right.

How to Look for Lizards

If you are at the right place at the right time, how do you look for lizards? First, arm yourself with a good set of close-focusing binoculars. When shopping for binoculars, if you can focus on your toenails while standing, you will be able to see details of lizards that are relatively close. Many lizards are fairly approachable, so this is important. Of course, some are not, but close-focus binoculars are also designed to see into the distance. The other important feature is resolution. You may need to see diagnostic features clearly in order to identify lizards by species or subspecies. Some species are very similar from a distance, but become very distinct when viewed with binoculars. Another option is to photograph lizards and identify them later. There are a host of cameras and lenses, but that is beyond the scope of this book; suffice it to say, a point-and-shoot camera normally doesn't cut it—you need macro (long-distance macro), telephoto, or zoom capability. Always remember to get clear photographs of the entire lizard in a variety of poses. Make sure the photograph isn't back-lit, or you won't be able to see the diagnostic characters. Shadows and highlights also wreak havoc with photographs (and many lizards seek out areas of dappled sunlight).

Most species of diurnal lizards are best viewed while they are basking on rocks or other objects. The key is in recognizing that telltale shape of a lizard on a rock from a distance, then slowly closing in on it. Many lizards can be seen while you drive *slowly* on little-traveled roads. In fact, many lizards will allow a closer approach while you are in a car, but the minute you get out, they bolt. If you are getting out of a car to look at a lizard, do it a long way from the lizard. The more aesthetically pleasing way to look for lizards is to walk slowly along a trail or wash or foothills while scanning the environment. You can see the habitat in much better detail than when driving and are more likely to see certain species. You will see not only basking lizards, but also active foragers such as whiptails, plus lizards that are somewhat hidden. For example, in Creosote Bush flats, look into the shade of the shrub, as well as the limbs. Allow your eyes time to adjust. In dunes and washes, be sure to look for lizard tracks (and wear sunglasses!), and you may even discover where a lizard is hiding by following its tracks. Lizards in cracks in boulders are often quite visible if you have a mirror or

Kevin Baker employs the ethically sound method to look for crevice-dwelling species during the day.

The telltale silhouette of a lizard basking on a rock is the search image needed for lizard spotting. Pictured is a Common Chuckwalla at Valley of Fire State Park, NV.

flashlight to illuminate the crevice. Nocturnal lizards may be seen crossing roads or by viewing them while you're on foot. For example, Granite Night Lizards and Baja California Leaf-toed Geckos can be seen on the surface or base of giant boulders in appropriate habitats. For viewing nocturnal lizards, lamps, lanterns, and flashlights all do the trick, although some are better than others. Choose a lamp that is right for you when weighing cost, weight, and battery life, but ultimately make sure it provides enough illumination for walking at night and looking for lizards.

Some lizards are not readily watchable by these conventional, non-intrusive methods, and you must actively search for them by looking under surface objects. NEVER EMPLOY ETHICALLY UNSOUND METHODS TO LOOK FOR THESE CRYPTIC SPECIES (see the Environmental Ethics section for more guidelines on this subject). Only cover-objects on the ground that can be returned to their exact original position are fair game, if you have the necessary permit and are in a place where this is legal. For example, plywood on the ground will make any herpetologist drool and is fair game on most public lands (or private, with permission). There are often herpetological delights under those boards, seeking out the moist, cool environment. Looking under a board may reveal some cryptic species, such as alligator lizards and skinks—as well as rattlesnakes, Copperheads, Bark Scorpions, and coral snakes—so caution is always warranted! Wearing gloves and using a tool such as a snake hook are recommended to lift and lay down surface objects.

Catching Lizards

You can differentiate the vast majority of species by viewing through binoculars, or knowing the ranges of some very similar species, but some are best identified in the hand. The most useful characteristics for differentiating lizard species are the numbers and arrangements of scales, which are illustrated in the External Anatomy and Identification section of this book.

Some species are fairly easy to approach, while others are far more wary. For example, fence lizards are among the easiest to catch, while the Granite Spiny Lizard, which belongs to the same genus, is one of the most difficult. The former may sometimes be caught by hand, whereas the latter may bolt when you get out of a car a quarter of a mile away! Most lizards lie in between these extremes.

By far the most useful tool for catching lizards is the lizard noose. It consists of a small sliding loop placed at the end of a pole. The noose can be made of a variety of materials, including dental floss, thin copper wire, or monofilament. Each person has his or her own preference. To make a noose, tie a small loop (say, around a toothpick) with a square knot, cut off the excess, and run the end through the small loop. Tie the other end to the end of your pole and there you have it—the most commonly used tool of lizard researchers! The size of the noose depends on the size of the head of the species being caught, but if the noose dangles too far off the end of the pole, it will get blown around in wind, which can be really aggravating, or caught on twigs, which can be really, really aggravating. If the loop is too small, it cannot open large enough to get over the head of larger lizards. A 2-meter-long collapsible fishing pole makes for a nice pole, as it can be stored out of the way when not in use.

Using your hands alone is sometimes the most logical approach, especially for cryptic species, or species that do not bask on rocks. For example, if you turn over a piece of plywood and find an alligator lizard beneath, the best method to catch it is to grab its body (not its tail, which is easily lost—or the rattlesnake coiled nearby!) before it has time to escape. Hands are also useful when lizards are in a position that renders them difficult to noose. For example, whiptails are inherently difficult to noose, and it is sometimes useful to have several people to surround

A lizard noose caught this Elegant Earless Lizard.

Anne Casey and Lyndsay Hellekson noosed this Eastern Collared Lizard, which inspired them to be lizard aficionados.

the animal and catch it as it tries to hide or escape. This multi-person approach works well when lizards are hiding in the bases of shrubs.

Whether catching a lizard by hand or using a noose or other technique, the key is a stealthy approach. Also, it is far easier to catch a cold lizard that has just emerged to bask than one that has reached its preferred body temperature. Lizards are very wary creatures, and flight is initiated when they feel threatened. Approach a lizard slowly—the closer you get, the stealthier you need to be. Don't let your shadow fall on the lizard. If you can, approach it from behind. Avoid quick movements, and stop if the lizard is looking at you and you feel you may trigger a flight response. Have the noose ready to go long before you get close enough to noose it. The noose should be a little larger than the head. Simply lower the noose over the head, and pull back on the pole fast enough to catch the lizard, but not with such vigor that you will injure the beast. Quickly grab the lizard before it wriggles free, and remove the noose. Voila! If you do it correctly, it is completely harmless to the lizard. Note that most lizards will bite, and bites from species with large heads and strong jaws can be fairly painful. A good way to look at, or photograph, the venter (underside) of a lizard is to rub its belly until it is very calm, then carefully lay it on its back. This is generally how photographs were taken of the ventral view of lizards in this book.

There are other methods to catch lizards, including rubber bands, rubber band guns, pitfall traps, firearms, beanbags, sticky traps, and full-body lunges (beware of cacti!), but we can't recommend such methods to the casual lizarder. Note that these methods are regulated and require permits.

Remember, you must have a hunting license or scientific collecting permit, at a minimum, to catch lizards on public land. Federally threatened and endangered lizards also require a federal permit to handle, as do all lizards in national parks and most national monuments. Other landowners may require their own stand-alone permits, so please do your homework and have the right permits if you plan on doing anything more than observing lizards in a non-invasive fashion. Make sure you know the landowner or manager and abide by their rules and regulations. Never allow a lizard to overheat. Even though they dwell in some of the hottest regions, they are small animals, and their body temperatures can escalate quickly because of small size and large surface area. Never attempt to catch a Gila Monster. Not only is it illegal to do so, but also nearly every bite ever recorded was on some twenty-something macho yahoo enjoying a six-pack, who decided he was more skillful than the Gila Monster. Bites from Gila Monsters are incredibly, exceedingly, excruciatingly painful, and a trip to the hospital is always warranted.

Lizards and Safety

Watching and catching lizards can be an extremely enjoyable pastime, but as with any other activity, you always need to be cognizant of personal safety (e.g., don't ever follow the examples of those foolhardy "television herpetologists"; real herpetologists know their limits and have common sense). In the case of lizards, safety concerns are usually centered on the fact that most species inhabit remote settings and are active during warm temperatures. In fact some species occur only in remote areas, and many like it downright hot! The take-home message is to always be prepared for the worst-case scenario.

- Tell someone where you are going and when you will be back.
- Travel with others.
- Make sure your vehicle is up to the challenge and you have the plethora of spare parts needed for this sort of travel.
- Be extremely careful to avoid heat exhaustion and heat stroke. You may not see these sneaky nemeses coming, and heat stroke can be fatal.
- Never enter a situation that will compromise your ability to cope with the environment. You need to know your abilities from previous experience and stay short of your limits.
- Carry huge quantities of water and electrolytes if you are visiting desert and other hot areas. 
- Slather on high SPF sunscreen liberally.
- Wear light clothing (both color and weight) and a light hat that shades the face and neck.
- Do not forget the awesome power of flash floods! These can appear seemingly out of

nowhere, especially when the rains are many miles away in the mountains. Like heat, a wall of water can be deadly.

- Remember that a number of venomous animals share the same habitats as lizards, including rattlesnakes and scorpions.

The intent is not to frighten you away from lizard-watching, but rather to remind you to assess your preparedness. Even those who are not in tip-top physical condition can enjoy lizards in areas frequently visited by people. Short nature trails around visitors centers are usually very productive lizarding grounds; the lizards tend to be more approachable than they are in more remote areas. They may also be more numerous than they are in the outlying areas. In these places, you tend to be surrounded by other people and you aren't overdoing it (but still take the above precautions). In fact, once you have become familiar with the lizards in this book, you can become an ad hoc naturalist and impress fellow recreationists you run into on the nature trails! And whatever you do, take it easy. Recreational lizarding need not be risky business.

PUBLIC LANDS FOR OBSERVING LIZARDS

Author: Lawrence L. C. Jones

For lizard-watchers, a great feature of the American Southwest is the large amount of public land. On the federal level, public lands are managed by the National Park Service, Bureau of Land Management (BLM), Fish and Wildlife Service, and Forest Service, among others. Federal lands are often large expanses of remote, pristine, and stunningly beautiful places to visit. Many state, county, and city parks are also excellent places to view lizards. In addition, some lands managed by non-government organizations, such as The Nature Conservancy, allow public access for ecotourism.

The following state-by-state accounts offer a tantalizing sampler of places to go and lizards to see. Only some of the many public lands are mentioned, while all of the lizard species are mentioned below (only once). In some cases, a particular lizard can be viewed only in one area (e.g., Sandstone Night Lizard), while most other species may be found in a multitude of localities (e.g., the Common Side-blotched Lizard is found in nearly all desert locations). For more information on where to find lizards, please refer to the Species Accounts.

California

California is a large state characterized by a diversity of habitats. Concomitantly, a large number of species occur there. There is also no shortage of public lands: there are 30 national parks and about 100 state parks. The southern half of California is by far the most biologically diverse, because two deserts, several mountain ranges, and coastal habitats converge there.

Boulder-strewn Anza-Borrego Desert State Park (SP) is a huge chunk of public land and one of the very best lizarding spots in the American Southwest. It has a distinct lizard fauna due to the convergence of the Baja California Peninsular Ranges and the Lower Colorado subdivision of the Sonoran Desert. The park (and its surrounding environs) is the only area in the United States where one can find Baja specialties such as the Banded Rock Lizard, Granite Spiny Lizard, Baja California Collared Lizard, Granite Night Lizard, Baja California Brush Lizard, Peninsular Leaf-toed Gecko, Wiggins' Night Lizard, and the rare and elusive Switak's Banded Gecko. One species—the Sandstone Night Lizard—is endemic to Anza-Borrego Desert SP. The sandy desert portions of the park may yield the Flat-tailed Horned Lizard and Colorado Desert Fringe-toed Lizard.

Two national parks devoted to the Mojave Desert landscape are Joshua Tree National Park (NP) and Mojave National Preserve. At both of these parks, you can find a California Mojave endemic species, the Mohave Fringe-toed Lizard, which is found among the dunes. The Desert Night Lizard tends to remain hidden under fallen Joshua Trees. However, DO NOT search for this lizard inside the park, as it is illegal to disturb the vegetation. Another Mojave Desert park is Death Valley NP; the higher elevations nearby are where to look for the spectacular Panamint Alligator Lizard.

To view the Coast Range lizard fauna, visit Pinnacles National Monument (or NM) or Santa Monica Mountains National Recreation Area (NRA), with characteristic species such as Gilbert's Skink, the Blainville's Horned Lizard, California Legless Lizard, and the Southern Alligator Lizard.

Farther north at Lava Beds NM, it is possible to find the Pygmy Short-horned Lizard and Northern Alligator Lizard.

There are a number of California "endemics" (but

Joshua Tree National Monument, CA.

some are found in adjacent Mexico) not mentioned above that can be viewed in only a few places. The only place to find the Island Night Lizard is at Channel Islands NP. The endangered Blunt-nosed Leopard Lizard can be seen at Carrizo Plain NM, and the Coachella Fringe-toed Lizard may be viewed at the Coachella Valley Preserve, which was established to protect that species and its habitat. Similarly, the Irvine Ranch Land Reserve was established to protect the vanishing coastal sage scrub habitats of extreme southwestern California, home to the Orange-throated Whiptail. North of Baja California, where it is common, Cope's Leopard Lizard is only found in the vicinity of Cameron Corners, Campo, and Portero in extreme southern California on BLM lands. The Sierra Night Lizard can only be seen on private lands, so requires the owner's permission, and as they are difficult to find in century-old crevices, it is best to not even look for this lizard.

Nevada

Valley of Fire State Park, NV, in the Mojave Desert.

Except for the Sierra Nevada Mountains on its west edge, Nevada is almost entirely composed of two ecoregions: the Great Basin Desert and the Mojave Desert. As might be expected from its latitudes and elevations, the Mojave Desert has a higher species richness, but because the two deserts are fairly contiguous, they share many of the same species, including the Common Side-blotched Lizard, Long-nosed Leopard Lizard, Great Basin Collared Lizard, Yellow-backed Spiny Lizard, Desert Horned Lizard, Tiger Whiptail, and Zebra-tailed Lizard. Characteristic species of the Great Basin Desert include the Common Sagebrush Lizard, Western Fence Lizard, and Western Skink.

Suggested public lands to visit include Great Basin NP, Berlin Ichthyosaur SP, and Cathedral Rocks SP. For the best lizarding, stick to the lower elevations in and near these parks. In the Mojave Desert portion of Nevada, any of the public lands near the Colorado River offer excellent lizarding, including Valley of Fire SP, Bend of the Colorado SP, and Lake Mead NRA. Typical lowland desert species occur here, including the Desert Iguana, Western Banded Gecko, Common Chuckwalla, and Long-tailed Brush Lizard.

Arizona

Arizona has the highest diversity of lizards in the Southwest. Three of the four American deserts occur in Arizona, and there is a strong influence from Mexico's Sierra Madre Occidental (in the Apachean ecoregion), the Mogollon Rim, and the Colorado Plateau. Species found in the Lower Colorado subdivision of the Sonoran Desert are the same as in nearby California and Nevada, but the Yuman Fringe-toed Lizard is found only on the Arizona side of the Colorado River.

Heading east from the Colorado River, the elevations rise and you enter the Arizona Upland of the Sonoran Desert. Organ Pipe Cactus NM is very similar to adjacent Sonora. Two lizards to seek out here are the Red-backed Whiptail and Sonoran Collared Lizard; if you are lucky you may find a Goode's Horned Lizard. Saguaro NP, Ironwood Forest NM, and Sonoran Desert NM have a large variety of lizards, including the Desert Spiny Lizard, but be sure to target the Regal Horned Lizard and Gila Monster.

Southeastern Arizona has the greatest diversity of lizards, due to the influence of the Sonoran Desert, Chihuahuan Desert, Sierra Madre Occidental, Mogollon Rim, and Mexican grasslands. The area is composed of "sky islands"—small, discrete mountains ranges separated by desert and grassland valleys. Places to visit include the Coronado National Forest (NF), Saguaro NP (Rincon section), and Coronado NM. Several species found only in southeast Arizona (and adjacent Mexico) include the Arizona Striped Whiptail, Sonoran Spotted Whiptail, Canyon Spotted Whiptail, Madrean Alligator Lizard, Mountain Skink, Elegant Earless Lizard, Clark's Spiny Lizard, Yarrow's Spiny Lizard, Striped Plateau Lizard, and Slevin's Bunchgrass Lizard.

Hiking down the Grand Canyon can take you from the Colorado Plateau to the Mojave Desert. However, it takes a 1,500-m descent to view the canyon's diverse lizard communities!

The Mogollon Rim is mountainous country lying north of the deserts and sky islands. Apache-Sitgreaves NF, Tonto NF, and Prescott NF are the primary public lands here. Look there for the Gila Spotted Whiptail and Bezy's Night Lizard.

North of the Mogollon Rim is the vast Colorado Plateau. Many of the most spectacular backdrops for lizards may be found here, including the Petrified Forest NP, Canyon de Chelly NM, Vermilion Cliffs NM, and upper Grand Canyon NP (the lower portion is in the Mojave Desert).

Look for the Pai Striped Whiptail near Wupatki NM.

The Arizona Night Lizard is found mostly on private lands.

New Mexico

Because it is sandwiched in between Texas and Arizona, New Mexico shares many lizard species with these two states. The Madrean sky islands, Mogollon Rim, and Colorado Plateau are also found in New Mexico, but the state also has the northern extension of the Chihuahuan Desert, the southern extension of the Rocky Mountains, and part of the Great Plains. For a lizard buff, New Mexico is a great place, because many of the recreation areas are at the lower elevations where most of the species occur. Numerous state parks are in the Chihuahuan Desert. Along the Rio Grande Valley, these parks include Caballo Lake, Percha Dam, Leasburg Dam, Mesilla Valley, and Elephant Butte Lake.

Along the Pecos River are five state parks: Brantley Lake, Bottomless Lakes, Villanueva, Santa Rosa, and Sumner Lake SPs, as well as Carlsbad Caverns NP. A good reason to head to these areas (besides swimming, boating, and fishing) is to see the plethora of whiptails and other lizards.

Along the Rio Grande and Pecos valleys you may find the Chihuahuan Spotted Whiptail, Marbled Whiptail, New Mexico Whiptail, Desert Grassland Whiptail, Little Striped Whiptail, Southwestern Fence Lizard, Twin-spotted Spiny Lizard, and Round-tailed Horned Lizard. A must-see for the lizard enthusiast is another public land in the Rio Grande Valley—White Sands NM. Here you can find the bleached phase of the Common Lesser Earless Lizard and the Little White Whiptail.

Caballo Lake State Park, NM.

Another series of dunes straddling the border with the Panhandle and Big Bend area of Texas is the Mescalero Sands. The Mescalero Sands NRA is geared to off-road vehicle use, which has degraded the habitat, but the protected areas nearby are a mecca for lizards, including some species typical of the Great Plains. The endemic Dunes Sagebrush Lizard can be found here.

Texas (Big Bend Area, West of the Pecos River)

With a state as big as Texas, you might expect a big species list. Indeed this is the case, and the area outside the geographic scope of coverage of this book is definitely worth exploring. For example, just east of the Big Bend, you have the Tamaulipan ecoregion, and to the northeast you run into the Edwards Plateau and the Great Plains. But we will stick to the Big Bend area. Big Bend is named for the bend in the Rio Grande between the United States and Mexico. It not only contains some of the best terrestrial and riparian Chihuahuan Desert habitats, but it also has the highest mountains in Texas (yes, there are mountains in Texas!). The premier public land in the Big Bend area is, of course, Big Bend NP. Just west of the national park is Big Bend Ranch SP. Both are situated along the Rio Grande. Many of the Chihuahuan Desert species mentioned in the New Mexico account are also found in the Big Bend, but some Big Bend specialities include the Reticulate Banded Gecko, Plateau Spotted Whiptail, Four-lined Skink, Texas Alligator Lizard, Canyon Lizard, and Gray Checkered Whiptail.

Three other parks in the Big Bend are worth mentioning—Guadalupe Mountains NP, Davis Mountains SP, and Hueco Tanks SP. These parks share some of the same lizard species as parks to the north and south, including the Texas Banded Gecko, Common Checkered Whiptail, Texas Horned Lizard, Crevice Spiny Lizard, and Greater Earless Lizard. Two species that barely enter the Big Bend west of the Pecos are best observed deep in the heart of Texas—the Little Brown Skink and Texas Spiny Lizard.

Utah

The valleys in the southern part of the state should be the destination of the lizard-watcher in Utah, as the higher elevations are less speciose. A tiny piece of the Mojave Desert enters Utah in the extreme southwestern portion near the town of St. George, and several species of true desert dwellers can be seen at Snow Canyon SP. Along the Colorado River, one can also find some Mojave Desert species at Glen Canyon NRA.

Heading east from St. George, you quickly enter the landscape that southeastern Utah and adjacent Arizona are best known for—the red rock country of the Colorado Plateau. This part of Utah is littered with state and federal public lands, including

Lizard-viewing Hot Spots

There are many great places to view lizards, but these are some of our recommended must-sees for a lizard aficionado, having high diversity and large numbers of lizards to view. These areas include trail hikes and/or driving tours.

- **Sabino Canyon, Santa Catalina Mountains, Coronado National Forest, Arizona (near Tucson).** There are fifteen or more species observable here along several trails (the paved trail is great). This area represents a convergence of the Madrean Archipelago and Sonoran Desert. Highlights here include Gila Monsters and Canyon Spotted Whiptails. Lizards here are used to the 1.25 million visitors per year, so are tolerant of human visitation.

- **Borrego Palm Canyon Trail, Anza-Borrego Desert State Park, California (near Borrego Springs).** At least fourteen species are found here or nearby, with several more as you go upstream into the mountains. You should come here to see many of the species found elsewhere only in Baja California, Mexico. Look for the lizards on the desert flats, on boulders, and near the stream and palms. Highlights include the Banded Rock Lizard, Granite Spiny Lizard, Baja California Brush Lizard, and Baja California Collared Lizard. This is a popular ecotourist destination, so lizards are used to human visitors.

- **Marijilda Canyon, Pinaleño Mountains, Arizona (near Safford).** You can drive a high-clearance vehicle or walk the four-mile dirt road, but look along the paved road (Swift Trail), too. At least nineteen species are found here, at a convergence of Sonoran and Chihuahuan deserts, as well as grasslands and montane species. Highlights include four species of horned lizards (usually two are seen), some Madrean species, and green-to-bluish Eastern Collared Lizards.

- **White Dome Road and associated trails, Valley of Fire State Park, Nevada (north of Las Vegas).** This is probably the best that the Mojave Desert has to offer, with at least thirteen species. There is a driving tour with trails, such as Mouse's Canyon Trail. Highlights include Common Chuckwallas, Gila Monsters (the banded subspecies) and several Mojave Desert dwellers. It's a heck of a backdrop for lizard viewing!

- **Alamo Canyon Trail, Organ Pipe Cactus National Monument, Arizona (south of Why and Ajo).** Fourteen or more species can be viewed here and on the road. Highlights include the Sonoran Collared Lizard and Red-backed Whiptail, as well as many other species of the Arizona Upland subdivision of the Sonoran Desert. The Organ Pipe Cactus is a real bonus. This is hot, dry, rugged country, so be prepared!

- **Grapevine Hills Trail, Big Bend National Park, Texas.** At least fourteen species of the Chihuahuan Desert and Great Plains can be viewed here. Highlights include the Plateau Spotted Whiptail, colorful Greater Earless-lizard, Eastern Collared Lizard, Canyon Lizard, and some other Chihuahuan specialties and desert generalists.

There are many honorable mentions, including: Wupatki National Monument, AZ; Mojave National Preserve, CA; San Diego County, CA (the few remaining public areas in native coastal scrub); Cimarron and Comanche National Grasslands, CO; Antelope Pass, NM (at least eighteen species); Mescalero Sands, NM (in Shinnery Oak area, not in the open dunes); state parks near Truth or Consequences, NM (several sympatric whiptails, even on nature tails); Great Basin National Park, NV; Lake Mead National Wildlife Refuge, NV; Red Rock Canyon State Park, NV; Big Bend Ranch State Park, TX; and state parks near St. George, UT.

Coral Pink Sand Dunes SP, Canyonlands NP, Arches NP, Natural Bridges NP, and Monument Valley NP. In these semi-desert parks, look for the Eastern Collared Lizard, Plateau Striped Whiptail, and Ornate Tree Lizard. Western Utah is in the Great Basin Desert, so it has a lizard fauna similar to that described for that ecoregion in Nevada.

Colorado

Great Plains grasslands, Pueblo Co., CO.

The most familiar geological feature of Colorado is the Rocky Mountain Range. The Rockies are better suited to skiers than lizards (e.g., Rocky Mountain NP's reptile checklist shows no lizard species). However, elevations drop on either side of the mountains, and two lizard-friendly ecoregions appear: the Colorado Plateau to the west, and the Great Plains to the east. In the western valleys of the Colorado Plateau, a premier public land to visit for lizards includes Colorado NM. Here you can find some of the usual denizens of the Colorado Plateau, including the Plateau Fence Lizard and Greater Short-horned Lizard.

In the southeastern corner of the state, a good place to observe lizards of the Great Plains is the Cimarron and Comanche National Grasslands. Here you can find Colorado's only endemic lizard, the Colorado Checkered Whiptail, along with the Many-lined Skink, Six-lined Racerunner, Prairie Lizard, and Great Plains Skink.

LIZARDS IN CAPTIVITY

Author: Kim Lovich

Perhaps the easiest way to observe native lizards, without having to keep them at home or hike through scrubland, is to visit your local zoo or nature center. Some facilities will have native reptiles and amphibians on display or have them specially housed to be able to use them in education and outreach programs. Many of the regional nature centers adjoin larger wildlife preserves and host guided field hikes where native species of lizards can be observed and photographed easily. Still others have their own exhibits of native lizards where the public can get up close and personal with the animals.

An outdoor lizard pen with native species is an option for maintaining lizards in captivity, but it requires some thoughtful engineering and lots of food for the lizards.

One regional southwestern zoo that has large-scale naturalistic enclosures for lizard-viewing opportunities is the Arizona-Sonora Desert Museum, just outside of Tucson. It has a very popular lizard pen outside its front entrance, as well as some other enclosures, but remember to visit when the lizards are active (April through early October). Several other regional zoos also have native species on display, but exhibits are subject to change, so it is recommended to call to check current species on display as well as times of programs or presentations and rates. Also, visitors centers often have nature trails, where lizards may be acclimated to human presence, and some even host "lizard walks" to view native species.

Maintaining Lizards in the Home Environment

For many, it is tempting to want to keep a wild lizard as a pet, but many aspects of their care must be considered first; it is generally more prudent to observe lizards in the wild or in zoological parks and visitors centers. Before making a firm decision to keep a native lizard, you should consider your husbandry expertise level, funds availability, and the nutritional and environmental needs of the particular species. The species' specific temperament, hardiness, and tractability should also be addressed before obtaining any reptile as a pet. Housing requirements for various species can be very different, and many need very specific environments in order to survive and thrive. Further, the states require different permits for collecting and housing native lizards, so these should be obtained before collecting any reptile. Many protected species are illegal to keep in captivity unless you have specific permits for bona fide research or education purposes.

The information provided here is by no means meant to suffice as requirements for home husbandry; rather, it is a synthesis of some of the factors to consider when thinking about keeping a native lizard as a pet.

The specific enclosure depends on the husbandry plan to be implemented. In most cases, select as large an enclosure as is feasible. Containers of cement-based products are one alternative; however, unsealed concrete surfaces can be problematic to disinfect between groups of animals. Metal containers, such as galvanized cattle troughs, glass aquaria, and plastic aquaculture tubs, all work well. Containers to be used as water and food bowls should be constructed of easily disinfected materials such as plastic, glass, or fiberglass. Substrate depth and type will depend on the species of lizard being kept. For example, use finer grade sand and gravel for burrowing species and larger gravel and rock for crevice-dwelling species. All containers should have screened lids to prevent lizards from jumping or climbing out. An exception to this can be the larger-scale enclosure where the height of the walls themselves inhibits escaping.

Hiding places, basking spots, and perches are essential for lizards to feel comfortable in their enclosures. Visual barriers are important to reduce stress between adult lizards, particularly males, within the same enclosure, and to reduce stress caused by

Do not house venomous reptiles such as this Gila Monster in a home environment; it is illegal in all states and may encourage a black market trade for these beautiful animals.

activity outside their enclosure. Examples include clay plant pots that have been cut in half lengthwise or have a hole cut in the side large enough for the lizards to enter and exit. Natural or artificial plants can provide additional cover and hiding places. Branches of varying sizes can be stratified so that an animal can seek refuge at a comfortable height. Some of the perches can be placed beneath overhead basking lights, thus increasing thermoregulation opportunities for the lizards.

Where practical, access to natural sunlight is beneficial. Artificial lighting can be provided using compact fluorescent lights, operated by a timer that is set to natural sunlight hours, to simulate daylight in an indoor setup. Ambient lighting should consist of fluorescent, full-spectrum bulbs, and ultraviolet-B (UV) lighting should be provided by using a UV-transmitting flood or spot light. These are available at most larger pet stores or those catering to reptiles. UV light is essential to the lizards for metabolizing vitamins and minerals. Put the basking lights on a timer set to replicate the natural seasons or, for example, to come on for six hours a day in spring and summer, reducing to three hours a day in fall and winter. Offer multiple basking sites for the lizards to warm themselves, and areas where they can take refuge out of the light so they can thermoregulate.

Ambient air temperatures should be maintained near those that the lizard would experience in its native habitat (see species accounts)—usually between 18 and 29°C, with seasonal variation. For example, fall 23°C, winter 18°C, spring 23°C, and summer 29°C might be typical settings for some species. Lizard growth rates and overall health are correlated with environmental temperatures, so it is important to monitor temperatures routinely with a reliable thermometer and adjust it as needed.

Many of the problems associated with metabolic bone disease in adult lizards arise from poor nutrition as juveniles. Mistakes made during a young lizard's developmental phase may result in disease or death. Each species of lizard has specific food sources in the wild and specific ways in which they eat. Meeting these needs in captivity should be attempted wherever possible. Food should be placed in bowls that are easily accessed by lizards or offered free range throughout the enclosure. Uneaten decomposing food should be removed daily. Most native lizards will feed well on domestic crickets, mealworm larvae, mealworm adult beetles, flightless houseflies, wax worm larvae, earthworms, and small roaches. Feeder crickets should be "gut loaded" with a good quality cricket feed, then dusted with a multivitamin/mineral powder just prior to feeding to the lizards. Frequency of feeding will depend upon the season and the size and age of the lizards being kept, but on average lizards should be fed every other day. Remove dead prey items and feces promptly and, if possible, with minimal disturbance. Routine changing of the feeding containers, water bowls, and substrate is important to reduce buildup of organic waste products that can carry or transmit disease to other lizards.

CONSERVATION AND LEGAL ISSUES

Authors: Robert E. Lovich and Lawrence L. C. Jones

ENVIRONMENTAL ETHICS

This book would be incomplete if we did not address something this important: the ethical responsibility of people dealing with lizards in the wild. This ranges from weekend lizard-watchers to illegal poachers and habitat destroyers. The bottom line is that each and every one of us has a responsibility to treat the animals and their environments with respect.

What options are there to avoid unethical uses of lizards and other species? Curiosity about wild animals can be satisfied in a wide variety of formats including books and magazines, zoos, natural history museums, universities, and the Internet. Such resources are tremendous means of learning more about lizards and getting close encounters with them while having no—or minimal—impact on them in the wild. Of course, we still recommend you do enjoy these animals in their natural habitats…and that you take this field guide out with you to some really beautiful spots and enjoy the wonder of the native lizard fauna through binoculars.

Many people in their youth have had experiences with catching animals in the wild and keeping them as "pets." Curiosity about nature is an important and healthy part of growing up (and some curious children even grow up to be biologists!). Unfortunately, the maintenance of wild-caught species in captivity by nature enthusiasts is not always done with the degree of insight of trained personnel in a major zoological institution. The result is frequently a sentence of slow death, granted to the captive species in the fervor of childish wonderment. Lizards are uniquely adapted species, and when placed in aquariums, terrariums, and jars they are not in an ideal habitat. Returning a captive animal back into the wild can be even worse. First, a lizard will likely perish because of its unfamiliarity with an area, or by being chased out into unfamiliar territory by the new resident. Second, if it does survive, it may transmit devastating diseases to native populations. Consider the case of declining amphibians: We have lost hundreds of species across the globe because of a pathogen that likely originated from the release of captive African Clawed Frogs. The resulting epidemic is

Breaking off rock slabs is a heinous, unethical assault on the environment!

now causing the largest extinction event since the Permian Period at the end of the Paleozoic Era. And third, if the lizard is not released to exactly the same spot, there can be genetic mixing and the loss of unique genotypes that have evolved for tens of thousands of years or more. A seemingly thoughtful action of giving an animal its freedom can in turn be devastating to natural populations. People should understand that lizards do the most good for the environment when they are left in the place where they are an integral part of their ecosystem dynamics.

At the time of this writing, commercial collecting of reptiles is legal in some (but not all) states. But commercial collecting is big business, with many thousands of animals being taken out of the wild, and many areas are collected year after year. While it is difficult to take a stance against a legal activity, it is easy to take a stance against the illegal aspect of collecting—poaching. The illegal take of reptiles is much more commonplace than the average reader might imagine. Not all poachers are criminal in looks and demeanor—some are people who just don't bother to get the proper permits to collect, and many of them are fully aware that there are specific regulations. State and federal game agencies have the authority to pursue and arrest game-law violators, and these agencies often have personnel trained specifically for snake and lizard poachers. Unfortunately, under some judges, punishment for offenders may be just a light sentence, despite the potential allowable by law for much harsher penalties. We hope that our society will develop a sense of worth for these wondrous animals and punish the crimes against them.

In addition to the effects of the legal removal of lizards from wild populations on their population dynamics, there are serious concerns about the effects on the environment. One of the more extreme examples of destructive collecting practices is the breaking off of cap rocks to look for crevice-dwelling species. A microhabitat that took thousands of years to develop is gone forever within seconds. The result is not only a loss of valuable lizard microhabitat, but an eyesore for all people wanting to enjoy the splendor of Mother Nature. Pitfall traps are effective devices, but if not checked regularly, they are death traps for as long as they remain intact.

A single pass by an off-road vehicle can scar a desert landscape for hundreds of years.

There are alternative ways to find and view these species without causing irreversible damage, such as visiting the sites at night, viewing inside cracks with the light of a mirror during the day, or using sprigs of grass or twigs to gently manipulate an individual into a better location to view (as has been done to photograph some of our more cryptic lizard species).

Search for crevice-dwelling night lizards during the day by using a mirror to illuminate them in the cracks.

Another potentially damaging practice is the habit of flipping over cover objects. Lizards often seek shelter under logs, rocks, Joshua Tree stems, and other natural and artificial debris, so looking under these cover objects is a well-known method to search for animals. If cover objects must be looked under (always consider alternative methods of viewing first), each object always needs to be replaced in its original position. When you do this, be sure the lizard is off to the side so it isn't squished! Failure to put the object back into the exact spot may result in altering the microhabitat for several years.

We encourage non-invasive enjoyment of lizards and their habitats in the American Southwest and neighboring states of Mexico. We encourage and try our best to uphold environmental standards and integrity that promote the best management and conservation of these species. At a time when habitats and species are under greater pressure than they have ever seen, humans need to have a soft footprint in order to maintain the environment in its healthiest form. While encouraging direct contact and viewing of lizards and their habitats, we also ask you to consider your actions and impacts with responsible ethics. After all, our children and future generations deserve to see these lizards and lizard habitats as well.

CONSERVATION, MANAGEMENT, AND THREATS

The American Southwest contains a tremendous biodiversity and biologically rich habitats. The area has seen huge population growth in the last several decades, with many cities in the region vying for the title of fastest-growing city in the nation. Large, burgeoning metropolitan areas like Los Angeles, Las Vegas, Phoenix, Tucson, Albuquerque, San Francisco, and others have created a less wild and more urban landscape over much of the region. The relatively large and intact parcels of land that remain are diminishing (e.g., Tucson and Phoenix are expanding and growing toward each other). With this growth in the human population, habitats for lizards and other species are being lost at a rapid pace. The combination of population growth with a high biodiversity region poses questions about the value we place on open spaces, the need for maintaining biodiversity, and whether we can strike a balance between urban sprawl and the maintenance of resident lizard faunas in perpetuity. At the present time, some species have already been reduced to numbers that require more than a hands-off approach, and need to be actively conserved and protected, lest they be lost. In other situations, habitats and the species therein need to be managed to avoid the need for costly and species-specific conservation, and threats to habitats and populations need to be mitigated.

Not all lizards appear to be on the downward trend as a result of changing land use. Some species cope better with these changes than others as a result of their biology. For example, Ornate Tree Lizards, some alligator lizards, fence lizards, and skinks occur in urban and suburban settings. Most other species are not quite so resilient. In California, the Orange-throated Whiptail is found only in highly endangered habitats (e.g., coastal sage scrub). While they may be locally abundant in pockets of remaining habitat, their range has been greatly diminished from urbanization and habitat conversion. Challenges exist for the future of lizard populations in striking a balance for the maintenance of all resident species, in both the American Southwest and abroad.

Threats

In order to understand how to conserve and manage lizards, we must first understand the factors that threaten their populations and habitats. A wide range of land conditions exists in the American Southwest, from relatively pristine to completely developed or altered landscapes. While some of the threats facing lizards are natural or innate, such as disease or extremely small ranges, most are due, to or exacerbated by, human-caused factors. Habitat loss and degradation, introduced invasive species, pollution, off-road vehicles, and global climate change are some of the major threats affecting lizards. Collection and unsustainable use are also threats, as discussed in the Environmental Ethics section.

Any activity that changes the landscape is a threat to lizards, as most cannot adapt.

Habitat loss has the single greatest impact on lizards. The human population has never been so large, numbering around six billion, and more and more people continue to move to the largely mild climates of the arid Southwest each year. The growing popu-

This Zebra-tailed Lizard met its fate via the wheels of an all-terrain vehicle.

lation requires more urban areas for homes, infrastructure in the form of roads and shopping centers, and agricultural production and/or shipping to meet supply demands. Electricity is also needed, and we see solar production and wind farms taking up more and more acreage of once-open landscapes in order to meet the energy needs of the population. Water sources, beyond existing rivers and underground aquifers, are also needed, and reservoir numbers and size continue to increase. Habitat loss includes aridification through water loss due to diversion and pumping. A classic example is the loss of Lake Tulare in California. Formerly the largest lake in the western part of the country, it is now completely gone. While Lake Tulare was not itself habitat to any lizards per se, it supported lizard communities in the adjacent upland habitats; its demise created more agricultural land that is no longer lizard habitat. All of these factors limit the available natural lands needed for lizards, as most altered landscapes are either devoid of lizards or are populated only by the few adaptable forms.

Introduced, invasive species represent a considerable threat to lizards. Several examples exist. Invasive ant species have been implicated in the widespread decline of horned lizards from California to Texas, by displacing native ant populations that make up a significant portion of the natural prey for these lizards. In fact, non-native, invasive Argentine Ants form the largest ant colony in the world, stretching from northern Baja California, Mexico, to southern Oregon! Since they are all closely related, they do not compete among colonies and have formed a mega-colony along the Pacific Coast. Fire Ants are a nemesis for the Texas Horned Lizard (and humans!). Introduced Buffelgrass, Russian Thistle, Sahara Mustard, Cheatgrass, and Lehmann Lovegrass are members of a league of insidious non-natives that can completely change a landscape. For example, Buffelgrass is creating a new fire regime in habitats where fire was rare. The Arizona Upland subdivision of the Sonoran Desert may be transformed from a breathtaking land of mighty Saguaros, Ironwoods, and palo verdes to a homogenous landscape of Buffelgrass. Such changes across a landscape can have dramatic impacts on animal populations, either directly or indirectly. Even some aquatic species are known to directly impact lizards. Bullfrogs, for example, are a widespread non-native amphibian known to prey upon lizards.

Global climate change is altering the very weather patterns that habitats have depended upon and evolved in concert with. Continued changes, at a rate well beyond those seen naturally before the human population explosion we are now seeing on Earth, will change distributional patterns and have a negative impact on some lizard populations. It is difficult to predict the future, but climate change is a real phenomenon, and we can expect that species adapted to cooler or wetter climates in the Southwest may be pushed toward extirpation (local elimination of a species) or even extinction.

This Gila Monster on a paved road is at risk of being run over or being collected by poachers.

Off-road vehicle use, as well as vehicle use on paved roads, is deleterious to reptiles. These ectotherms are attracted to the heat retention of road surfaces, luring them to their doom. Lizard mortality as a result of crushing by vehicles is a widespread phenomenon. As we push farther into the suburbs to construct our homes and roads, lizards are increasingly affected. We can expect this trend to continue without the incorporation of wildlife-friendly (including lizard-friendly) culverts, crossings, and barriers. Recreational vehicle use takes traffic from the paved roads into wild areas and can cause severe erosion, substrate compaction, loss of structure, and a host of other problems. Dunes stabilized by vegetation can become open dunes under the onslaught of off-road vehicles, converting the dunes from lizard-rich ecosystems to lizard-free zones. These vehicles can also run over lizards shallowly buried in the substrate, such as fringe-toed lizards and horned lizards, and at the same time compact their loose-soil habitats.

Environmental pollution has known impacts on a wide range of organisms, but is poorly studied relative to lizards. One very real threat is the attractive nuisance of landfills; refuse associated with urban areas attracts large numbers of predators such as crows, ravens, and Coyotes. These species are known to prey upon lizards naturally, and their abundance in disturbed areas with large amounts of refuse and litter is deleterious to lizards.

Disease and parasitism are yet another poorly quantified factor affecting lizards. Much is known about how disease causes deaths in marine and freshwater turtles, crocodilians, desert tortoises, and amphibians, but lizards and snakes have not yet been well studied.

Conservation

"Conservation," for many people, is a word that brings to mind cost and activism. It implies that things that might ordinarily be used need instead to be left alone, or conserved. This is unfortunate, as the word and actions it defines might better be called "maintenance" or "stewardship," because all natural resources, including lizards, are finite. More appropriately, conservation, as applied to natural resources, simply means not using up all the resources that exist. Unfortunately, the opportunity for conservation of many lizard species in the American Southwest is long overdue, and humanity is relegated to trying to grow back some habitat and lizard populations.

Many lizards, along with other reptile species, are declining or have declined historically for myriad reasons. In general, most population declines are due to habitat loss and habitat conversions resulting from the invasion of non-native species. Fortunately, no species of lizard has become extinct in the American Southwest, or neighboring states within Mexico...yet. However, some species are threatened with extinction (per the federal Endangered Species Act), such as the Coachella Fringe-toed Lizard, Blunt-nosed Leopard Lizard, and Island Night Lizard. The first two species have seen their habitats greatly reduced as a result of widespread agricultural and urban development, leaving only fragments of a once larger range. The Island Night Lizard is inherently at risk due to its small range on only a few islands off the coast of southern California. Once thought to be extremely rare, Island Night Lizards have been found to be incredibly abundant in small areas of the islands they inhabit, but their protected status remains until a better assessment can be determined.

There are direct benefits of lizard conservation. Western Fence Lizards harbor a protein in their blood that kills the bacterium known to cause Lyme disease, and the lizards serve as a "sink" to buffer humans from exposure to the disease—meaning the disease cannot reproduce in the host, so the disease does not perpetuate. Several peptides in Gila Monster venom are now being used in the medical profession to treat diabetes, breast cancer, and other maladies. Lizards are an incredibly important part of natural ecosystems (e.g., consider the tremendous number of insects

Texas Horned Lizards are actively conserved, having fallen victim to insecticides and non-native ants.

Radio-tagging Dunes Sagebrush Lizards helps conserve the species through research.

they consume every year) in the American Southwest. Losing our lizard species would mean the unfortunate loss of an integral part of the world's biodiversity. Conservation may sometimes be costly, but other options may be even more costly. How will a healthy humanity persist if the habitats we rely on become unsustainable?

While conservation is really everybody's responsibility, the bulk of major conservation efforts fall on the many public land management agencies. However, an increasing number of private and non-government organizations are taking an active and important part in managing our lizard fauna.

Management

Part of the Coachella Valley was set aside as a refugium for its namesake fringe-toed lizard.

The American Southwest as a region comprises a large amount of open space with many public lands. The history of the western U.S. is synonymous with open space, cowboys, and seemingly endless rangelands for cattle and scenic vistas. Times have changed over the last hundred or more years, but fortunately much of this land area is composed of federal lands that cannot be developed, including national parks and monuments, national forests, national wildlife refuges, national conservation areas, military installations, offshore and coastal reserves, and Bureau of Land Management parcels. States and municipalities have a high number of protected areas as well. All of these areas, as well as many private lands, require management to protect them from threats associated with human encroachment.

Management of lands in the Southwest is a challenge, given the rapid pace of change. Managing lands for lizards specifically is a challenge unto itself. Consider that lands in the Southwest are home to many protected and endangered habitats and species, lizards and otherwise. These areas have to be managed for more than just a single species, or group of species. For instance, managing a habitat to be open with scattered vegetation for some lizards may not provide the best cover or forage for certain birds and mammals. Managing an area to enhance wetlands may counter the habitat requirements for upland lizard species. Within these challenges is a matrix of laws and regulations requiring landowners to protect species, sometimes to the detriment of other species. Federal Endangered Species Act requirements trump many of the other laws and require that habitats be managed to protect listed species. The bias toward legally designated species may undermine addressing the needs of other species that may be equally endangered but do not enjoy the protections afforded the federally listed species. This all may sound a bit confusing—and to that we would say, "Welcome to the life of a Southwest land manager!"

We don't want to end with a completely "doom and gloom" outlook. We should mention that lizards, in general, are faring better than many other species in dealing with impacts to lands in the American Southwest. None of our native species has gone extinct, and relatively few are federally listed as threatened or endangered. Indeed, many species are resilient under changing conditions. But this is not to say we should give up or be irresponsible stewards of the land. We must learn to be respectful of Planet Earth and all of her denizens (especially lizards...because they are fascinating critters!).

Intense wildfires can be a threat to lizards, while lower-intensity wildland fire use and prescribed burns benefit lizards that evolved in landscapes that regularly burn.

LIZARDS AND THE LAW

Lizards are an important part of the ecosystems they inhabit and are a vital part of our natural heritage locally and globally. In keeping with this, legal standards must be maintained to ensure that these species and their habitats persist into the future. Almost all of the species covered in this book require some form of legal permission in order to handle, collect, keep, or, in some cases, disturb them or their habitat. Ultimately, people should do their homework by thoroughly researching the laws and regulations that cover anything beyond simply watching lizards from a distance. For example, to even *photograph* lizards in the Black Gap Wildlife Management Area in the Big Bend of Texas, you need a permit. Here is a summary of some of the common laws and considerations at different levels of government and in different countries.

It is illegal to search under cover objects, such as these Joshua Tree limbs, in protected landscapes such as Joshua Tree National Park.

International Laws

The environment has become a prominent news feature, and it is evident that global environmental needs are dire. Nations are working together to develop strategies and accords that protect the environment while at the same time balancing the needs of the human population toward a sustainable use of resources. One of the global standards, the Convention on International Trade in Endangered Species of Wild Fauna and Flora (CITES), regulates the international trade in a number of species, including some lizards. Simply taking a species from Mexico to the U.S., or vice versa, will result in a violation of CITES and other laws. All imports or exports of wildlife to and from Mexico and the U.S. must be lawfully declared to the appropriate federal authorities, and these activities require permits and other licenses. In fact, if you do not have all of the proper permits from both governments, you could find yourself facing harsh penalties in either country, potentially resulting in imprisonment! The U.S. Fish and Wildlife Service has jurisdiction over international wildlife laws that pertain to lizards, and should be consulted before transporting wildlife across international boundaries.

Federal Laws

Several federal laws pertain to lizards within the U.S. The Endangered Species Act (ESA) protects those species that have been listed as federally threatened or endangered, along with those that have been proposed for listing under ESA. In addition to the three federally protected lizard species in the American Southwest—the Coachella Fringe-toed Lizard, the Blunt-nosed Leopard Lizard, and the Island Night Lizard—a fourth species, the Dunes Sagebrush Lizard, is a candidate for ESA listing and is currently "warranted, but precluded" (meaning there is too much of a processing backlog to proceed with further work on this species at this time). Under the ESA, no person can "take" these lizards. "Take" is defined as any activity or attempt to hunt, harm, harass, pursue, shoot, wound, capture, kill, trap, or collect a species, or its habitat. So even if you don't kill or collect a lizard that is protected, just disturbing it could be considered "take." The penalty for take of a species can be a heavy fine and/or jail time. Take of a federally listed species must be authorized by the U.S. Fish and Wildlife Service.

Other federal laws regulate the commerce or trade in lizards and other wildlife that have been taken from the wild. The Lacey Act prohibits citizens of the U.S. from trading in any wildlife taken illegally, including from outside the country, and can result in substantial fines and penalties. The Sikes Act requires the review of any federal action that has the potential to cause environmental damage. This act is important in that it includes all species that may be affected by an action, with an emphasis on those that are federally protected.

Each federal land management agency (e.g., Forest Service, Bureau of Land Management, or National Park Service) has its own rules, and the extent of laws and regulations is incredibly variable. For example, on most Forest Service and BLM lands, if you want to catch a non-protected species for "personal use," it may be as simple as having a hunting or fishing license (the appropriate state permit). At the other extreme, don't even think of touching a lizard in a national park without a Special Use Permit and a good justification to get that permit, in addition to holding a valid State Scientific Collecting Permit and possibly a Fish and Wildlife Service Scientific Collecting Permit. This may be somewhat surprising, but it is actually legal to collect non-protected species in *some* of our national monuments with a hunting license (but don't you dare cite our book as a reference when they throw you in the slammer because you poached an animal in one of those national monuments or anywhere else where it is absolutely forbidden!). The point is, there may be generalities about permissions among the various land management agencies, but you must always find out about the specifics ahead—and get the rules and permissions in writing! Respective state reptile regulations can be found online.

State Laws

Within the American Southwest, lizards usually fall under the jurisdiction of the state wildlife agencies (Arizona Game and Fish Department, California Department of Fish and Game, Nevada Department of Wildlife, New Mexico Department of Game and Fish, Texas Parks and Wildlife Department, Utah Division of Wildlife Resources, and Colorado Division of Wildlife), and collection of lizards is strictly regulated by state law. In some cases, owning a fishing or hunting license permits the holder to collect, handle, or otherwise capture certain species on certain public lands, while others remain protected by regulations. Lizard species that are protected by state law can in some cases be collected for scientific or other legitimate purposes through an application process for a scientific collecting permit. This process requires a formal proposal to be submitted, reviewed, and approved by the state wildlife agency. The best way to find out specifics is to go online and do a query of respective state reptile regulations.

Like federal land-management agencies, state land-management agencies such as the various state parks also have a variety of regulations about handling lizards. In general, it is rarely a problem to observe lizards through binoculars or photograph them, but more often than not, all species are protected from handling without a Special Use Permit. Again, check with each state land management agency for the latest and greatest regulations for a specific location.

Municipal and Local Laws

An often-overlooked component of lizard and other wildlife regulations is the fact that municipalities frequently have laws that limit or prohibit keeping or trading in wild or captive species, including lizards. It is not unheard of for homeowners' associations also to regulate the wildlife that residents can maintain in captivity. In short, as incidents with captive wild animals gain more media attention, laws and regulations are enacted to keep wild animals away from average citizens. By now, we think you know the drill on finding out more about municipal and local regulations!

Exceptions

We are not advocating in any fashion the exploitation of gaps or loopholes in wildlife laws as they apply to lizards. It is, however, duly noted that existing wildlife laws are not perfect, and some loopholes do exist. Exotic species in many instances are covered poorly, if at all, in regulations, and can sometimes be looked at, captured, handled, released, or even collected with greater ease than native lizards. The take-home message is that ignorance of the law is no excuse, and individuals should know the law as it applies to their conduct, and stay within the law with their actions. No doubt, some of the introduced lizards in our region, such as Mediterranean Geckos, are interesting creatures, worthy of observation and enjoyment. Getting a close-up encounter with such non-native lizards, not covered by specfic laws, may allow the observer freedom to enjoy them more closely. In the end, be knowledgeable, and respect all species you seek to enjoy, safely and from a distance.

TAXONOMY AND NOMENCLATURE

Authors: Robert E. Lovich and Lawrence L. C. Jones

Placement of species in the genus Holbrookia *is a topic that divides many taxonomists.*

The Swedish botanist Carolus Linnaeus (1707–1778) developed the current system of binomial species names that we use today. Taxonomy was until recently an attempt by humans to hierarchically arrange, organize, and group plants and animals based upon their similarities and differences. For lizards, this was usually done by comparing gross morphology and scalation (scale numbers and patterns). This view was pervasive through the 1960s and 1970s, although now much of taxonomy is based on current and historical relationships and includes the use of molecular genetics—an important tool that was not available at that time.

Much emphasis is placed on the species level. A "species" has long been considered a basal taxonomic unit that includes a group of organisms that freely interbreeds and produces viable offspring. The same group does *not* freely interbreed or produce viable offspring with members of other species. However, as any biologist can tell you, this is a vast oversimplification of the modern species concept. Genetic and phylogenetic research is changing our view of the world, by providing information at the molecular level to more precisely resolve the demarcation between individual species and all other living units we recognize.

In taxonomy, there are three general trends of change: lumping, splitting, and reshuffling. With advances in molecular genetics, biodiversity is being revealed at levels never before seen. Molecular techniques have created a landslide of characteristics not previously available, which now can be used to evaluate prior taxonomies that

If one is really interested in why the names of Aspidoscelis gularis *(shown) and* A. scalaris *group have fluctuated over the years, it is best to consult specific research papers.*

were determined largely by using only morphological data. These advances have seen the elimination, or lumping, of many formerly recognized subspecies, and elevated some former subspecies to full species. Changes have been made above the species level as well. Indeed, history has shown that the number of species recognized has been on the increase ever since Linnaeus started picking flowers and science got to work trying to understand the biodiversity that inhabits the earth. Some of the more recent lizard splits include whiptails, night lizards, horned lizards, fence lizards, and collared lizards. However, it is interesting that these newly appearing species had often been named during earlier times! For example, *Phrynosoma goodei,* first described in 1893, was subsequently lumped into *Phrynosoma platyrhinos.* However, as theories and methods have evolved (and data have accumulated), we have come full circle, and as of 2006 we once again recognize this lizard as a distinct species (albeit with new evidence that has shed new light on its distribution and relationship with other horned lizards).

"Nomenclature" refers to the names assigned to the different taxonomic units and is regulated by the International Commission on Zoological Nomenclature (ICZN). This organization is dedicated to "achieving stability and sense in the scientific naming of animals." Such stability is essential to researchers and practitioners of biological sciences around the world to allow for consistent name use when referring to organisms. Latin, Greek, and other languages are used to derive scientific names, and the resulting names chosen are Latinized. All animals are arranged in order by kingdom, phylum, class, order, family, genus, and species, in descending order. Using this system, all lizards would fall under Animalia, Vertebrata, Chordata, Reptilia, and Squamata, followed by respective family, genus, and species. Lizards and other species are named according to their relationships within the hierarchy of scientific nomenclature. For example, the Banded Rock Lizard's scientific name is *Petrosaurus mearnsi* (genus + species).

Taxonomy and nomenclature...gotta love 'em! Although this fluidity of names and relationships may seem maddening to some people, we are actually just proceeding to learn more about the forms of life on our planet. Taxonomy has gone through a history that included lumping of species according to polytypic-species concepts of the mid-twentieth century that were largely based on interbreeding potential. Science now recognizes concepts of species independent of interbreeding potential, and more in keeping with phenetic (observable similarities and differences) distinguishability, diagnosibility, and monophyly (or clade, related species from a common ancestor). These changes in species "concepts" have resulted in resurrecting many of the species formerly "lumped" under the polytypic species concepts. Time and scientific progress will probably continue to refine and better define what a species is.

In this book, we have chosen to use the taxonomy and nomenclature of de Queiroz and Reeder (2008) as the standard for U.S. species and subspecies, and Liner and Casas-Andreu (2008) for Mexican species (in the three Mexico chapters and the Checklist by State in the back of this book). De Queiroz and Reeder is the standard recognized by an inter-society committee representing the Society for the Study of Amphibians and Reptiles, the Herpetologists' League, and the American Society of Ichthyologists and Herpetologists—the primary herpetological societies of the U.S. In some cases, we have adjusted the standard English, Spanish, and scientific names of Liner and Casas-Andreu to be consistent with the names recognized by de Queiroz and Reeder, or to comply with the rules of the inter-society committee, or to correct errors. These changes are noted in the Checklist by State section of this book.

Although we adhere to the prevailing guidelines of these standards, this does not imply that all taxonomic and nomenclatural issues have been resolved, or that we or our authors even agree with them. The guidelines provide a common point of reference at the time of publication. We include designations of subspecies for the same reason—to have a commonly used interpretation of taxonomy and nomenclature. While the concept of "subspecies" is often contested by biologists, we have chosen to retain taxonomy and nomenclature for subspecies. We feel the reference to subspecies often can help interpret

One species or two? We call the top lizard A. gypsi *and the bottom one* A. inornata.

past taxonomies and nomenclatures, explain the variation we see in species, and pave the way for futue taxonomic revisions. Also, subspecies are a target for validation as a taxonomic unit in systematic studies, so their inclusion is useful for researchers, whether or not they agree with the concept or the designations.

Standard English and Spanish names also have utility for designating species, especially among laypersons, but scientific names are usually less variable and more precise (though not without exception). The exceptions seem to be relatively common these days, with widespread taxonomic and nomenclatural changes occurring, resulting in common names becoming more stable than scientific names in some cases.

To summarize, no static and unwavering standards exist in a fluid discipline such as herpetology, and it is absolutely impossible to satisfy all herpetologists, including our authors, about taxonomy and nomenclature. By following a recognized system, we have simply established a baseline for this book. Regardless of how we designate species and subspecies according to the standards adopted by this book, our primary objective is to showcase the incredible diversity of lizards of the American Southwest.

RECENT TAXONOMY AND NOMENCLATURE HIGHLIGHTS

In recent years, there have been many significant changes in the taxonomy and nomenclature of lizards of the American Southwest. For example, two genera have changed to new names within this region: *Aspidoscelis* replaced *Cnemidophorus,* and *Plestiodon* replaced *Eumeces*. Most of the existing literature refers to the taxa by their former genus names, so it is important to know these changes when reviewing older literature. Similarly, there have been some changes among species names, such as the highly contested *Sauromalus ater,* which replaced the long-standing name of *S. obesus*; there is a wealth of entertaining exchanges of opinions among taxonomists on this proposal in the Bulletin of the ICZN!

Several lizard groups in this book, especially certain genera, require morphological and/or molecular studies to determine a more appropriate taxonomy. We review these groups here and present highlights of recent taxonomic and nomenclatural changes. Some of these lizards are inherently difficult to pigeonhole into the current Linnean hierarchy.

Whiptails, genus *Aspidoscelis.* This group of lizards is extremely fascinating from an evolutionary perspective, given the penchant of some species for parthenogenesis (production of clones by all-female forms). These unisexual forms arose from hybridization involving bisexual parent species. Read the section on Family Teiidae for additional information. As if that weren't complicated enough to sort out, whiptails are often very similar to one another, often having few distinct character differences, and they undergo striking ontogenetic changes (changes through development from hatchling to sexually mature adults) that render various life stages similar to other life stages of other whiptails. Add to that the fact that they are relatively mobile and capable of moving into areas occupied by other species, and you have the perfect concoction for a taxonomic and nomenclatural goulash! Fortunately, these intriguing animals have received a lot of attention from many capable herpetologists, and we are continuing to hone in on a better understanding of the taxonomic relationships. Right now, there are twenty-one species recognized by de Queiroz and Reeder for the American Southwest (the most speciose genus in the region), but this will undoubtedly change. There are volumes of literature on this topic, and it even frightens some of the best herpetologists—so if you want to know more, you could spend the rest of your life in a library researching this genus. Here are some recent taxonomic and nomenclatural highlights:

- The genus *Aspidoscelis* replaced *Cnemidophorus* for all North American species in 2002.
- *Aspidoscelis scalaris* is the name used here for the Plateau Spotted Whiptail in Big Bend, Texas, but there is still uncertainty on how this species relates to others of the species complex (e.g., the names *gularis, septemvittata,* and others), especially in Mexico.
- *Aspidoscelis arizonae, A. gypsi,* and *A. pai* are recognized as distinct from *A. inornata.*
- *Aspidoscelis velox* is shown here as including *A. innotata.*
- *Aspidoscelis marmorata* is shown as being distinct from *A. tigris,* but the literature often refers to it as a subspecies of *tigris.*
- *Aspidoscelis xanthonota* is shown here as being distinct from *A. burti,* but the literature often refers to it as a subspecies of *burti.*
- *Aspidoscelis neotesselata* was shown in 1997 to be a distinct triploid, unisexual species, formerly considered *A. tesselata.*

Lesser earless lizard group, genus *Holbrookia*. Currently, there is much disagreement among experts on the taxonomy and nomenclature of this group. Everyone seems to agree that there are at least two species. One is the Common Earless Lizard (*H. maculata*) and the other is the Elegant Earless Lizard (*H. elegans*). Our U.S. standard lists both of these species, while the Mexico standard lists these as well as a third species, *H. approximans,* which could also occur in the U.S. There are many other taxonomic and nomenclatural interpretations about *Holbrookia* with regards to species, subspecies, nomenclature, and color morphs, but without further research that is beyond the scope of this book, there is no way to resolve it at this point. For example, if you have in your hand a *Holbrookia* from the Huachuca Mountains of southern Arizona and you ask various herpetologists what the animal is, the response may be *H. approximans*, *H. elegans*, *H. maculata*, or *H. pulchra* (or more if you include subspecies). But no matter what you call it, it is still the same *Holbrookia* that is found in the Huachuca Mountains (we refer to it as *H. elegans* in our text). We suggest interested readers do a search of the pertinent primary literature and draw their own conclusions. Because of these inconsistencies, we have simplified the range maps by not including any subspecies delineations for *H. elegans* or *H. maculata.* However, because the taxonomy and nomenclature are not universally accepted, the range maps will not be universally accepted either; we see no way to settle the issue until there is more consensus in the scientific community.

Desert Spiny Lizard group, *Sceloporus magister* complex. Our U.S. standard recognizes a recent taxonomic split based on molecular genetics that separated *S. magister* into *S. magister, S. uniformis,* and *S. bimaculosus. Uniformis* and *bimaculosus* were formerly treated as subspecies. This revision elevated them to species level, except that lizards in the Sonoran Desert portion of the range in California, which were *S. m. uniformis,* are now relegated to *S. m. magister.* Similarly, recent literature also shows that *S. m. magister* occurs throughout southern Arizona and east into Hidalgo County, New Mexico; formerly, the magister-complex of southeastern Arizona and Hidalgo County was relegated to *S. bimaculosus* (but there is likely hybridization at this interface). Our maps show these new distributional features. De Queiroz and Reeder recognize two subspecies of *Sceloporus magister: S. m. magister* and *S. m. cephaloflavus.* Recent literature suggests subsumation of *cephaloflavus* into *uniformis,* which would render all of the three magister-complex species without subspecies. Because these two subspecies are recognized, in this area of the interface of *uniformis* and *cephaloflavus* (Colorado Plateau) they are shown in the range maps using their traditional interpretation. It should be noted that the split of *magister* into separate species is not universally accepted among herpetologists (e.g., Liner and Casas-Andreu)—but we as editors are more concerned about the biology of the species in this book. Whether they are species or subspecies, we still discuss them.

Eastern Fence Lizard group, *Sceloporus undulatus* complex. Recently the species formerly recognized as the Eastern Fence Lizard, *Sceloporus undulatus,* was split into four species that were geographically separated. Unfortunately, these four species did not align well with named subspecies, nor did the color patterns. The stalwart research efforts put forth on this species have thus far not been conclusive. This group of little brown lizards is taxonomically in need of further analysis. Try as we might, it often proves difficult to categorize organisms into species for certain groups.

Night Lizards, genus *Xantusia*. These curious little lizards are somewhat of an enigma. The genus is well represented in the American Southwest, and the subtle differences between various species groups do not readily reveal their evolutionary relationships. However, research in molecular genetics is opening the door to understanding these fascinating animals. Not too long ago we recognized three species of xantusiids (*X. vigilis, X. riversiana,* and *X. henshawi*) in the American Southwest. Now we have one additional species in the *henshawi* group (*X. gracilis*), and the *vigilis* group has been split into *arizonae, bezyi, sierrae,* and *wigginsi.* An additional *vigilis* species has been added in Mexico as well. Fortunately, they have distinctive ranges, so we need not rely on external characters to identify them. The subspecies of *X. riversiana* have highly variable patterns, and are not well differentiated, according to our species account expert. They also occur on different islands and require detailed molecular analysis.

Toothy Skinks, genus *Plestiodon*. The long-standing genus *Eumeces* was recently replaced with *Plestiodon. Plestiodon "gilberti"* has the unique distinction of being the only species in our standard with a specific epithet in quotes. This is because it is recognized that this highly variable taxon is only considered a species until someone sorts the group out taxonomically. Likewise, Gilbert's and Western Skinks are closely allied and likely represent a complex yet to be completely deciphered.

Horned Lizards, genus *Phrynosoma*. There have been a number of recent changes to horned lizard taxonomy and nomenclature. Goode's (aka Sonoran) Horned Lizard, *P. goodei,* was split out from the long-established Desert Horned Lizard, *P. platyrhinos,* in 2006. Also, the lizard formerly known as the Coast Horned Lizard, *P. coronatum,* has been split into several species, and *P. coronatum* is now strictly a Baja California form, while the species occurring in California state is now known as Blainville's Horned Lizard (*P. blainvillii*). Herpetologists are still getting used to the changes resulting from the separation of *P. hernandesi* and *P. douglasii* (but these species really are different from one another). De Queiroz and Reeder show clades of horned lizards in parentheses, but we did not follow suit.

OVERLEAF: Phrynosoma blainvillii, *Los Padres National Forest, CA.*

FAMILY AND SPECIES ACCOUNTS

A GUIDE TO THE SPECIES ACCOUNTS

Style and Formatting: For a variety of reasons, we have opted not to include literature citations in the text, nor a complete reference section. Among some of our authors, this was not a popular decision, but the book was already quite large for a field guide, and we decided that if readers (especially herpetologists) really wanted more information, they would go to the usual outlets of the scientific literature to find out more on the subject. Copious literature citations might dissuade the casual reader from fully enjoying the content of the book as well. Hence, we do not mean to suggest that all of the findings are based on the direct research of the respective authors (although often they are), but we do suggest the authors did their homework, and information presented is some of the most up-to-date available on all species.

While we as editors have had to keep writing in check, with standards and guidelines, we have also embraced a large degree of "writer's prerogative." In other words, we tried to retain as much of the authors' content and style as was practicable.

As with our taxonomic and nomenclatural standards of de Queiroz and Reeder and Liner and Casas-Andreu, we capitalize species and subspecies common names, regarding them as proper nouns, regardless of taxon (i.e., it includes lizards, snakes, mammals, insects, and plants). This is not universally accepted, but this approach is gaining in popularity. The primary reason is that without initial uppercase, common names can be misleading. For example, is *Aspidoscelis inornata* a "little striped whiptail"? (Well, yes it is, but so are *A. arizonae, A. gypsi, A. pai, A. velox,* and others.) If you refer to that species as "Little Striped Whiptail," there is no question you are referring to *A. inornata* rather than any of the others. Nicknames are not capitalized, nor are groups of species. For example, "chuckwalla" refers to several species, not just the one we happen to have in the U.S. (Common Chuckwalla). Similarly, when we refer to other animals or plant associations, a distinct species will have initial capital letters and generally be singular (Velvet Mesquite), while groups of related species will be pluralized and without initial capitals (mesquites). For example, some species of lizards are found where there are several species of mesquites or yuccas, while others may be associated with only one species, such as Creosote Bush. Note that plants don't really have standardized common names, so we used common names that are widely recognizable, as shown in popular plant books.

We allowed certain uses of alternative terms—such as parthenogenetic (or all-female, unisexual, asexual); Mohave vs. Mojave (great debates on that one—also, it is usually spelled with the "J" in California and the "H" in Arizona); brumation vs. hibernation (some authors make distinctions, while others do not), and so on—when there is reason. Plant communities are usually joined by a slash, rather than a hyphen, for clarity. For example, spruce-fir reads like Douglas-fir; the former is a group of two genera, and the latter is a single species, so spruce/fir leaves no doubt.

This book targets readers from knowledgable ecotourists (such as bird-watchers and wanna-be lizard-watchers) to professional herpetologists. The use of technical jargon is an unavoidable part of the biological sciences, so instead of trying to find synonyms (which don't always align, anyway), we decided to leave enough technical jargon to make the text accurate, yet readable by our target audience. We have included illustrations and a glossary to help explain the terms. When terms pertaining to scales, scale patterns, and scale clusters are encountered in the text, the reader should refer to Figures 3 and 4. For other biological terms, the reader should refer to the Glossary.

Title Block: This includes the standard English and scientific name of the species, as mentioned above, as well as the person who originally described the species and the year it was described, as it appears in the nomenclatural standard. In keeping with the standard nomenclatural style, the surname of the person(s) who originally described a species (or subspecies) and year of publication of the description follow the scientific name—for example, *Crotaphytus bicinctores* Smith and Tanner, 1972. If the genus is later changed (e.g., from a taxonomic split) the surname of the original describer remains, but is now shown in parentheses, such as *Crotaphytus collaris* (Say, 1823)—hence, Say described this species in 1823, but it was as *Agama collaris*. If the scientific publication comes out in a different year than it was supposed to or there is otherwise ambiguity, you see two dates, such as *Crotaphytus reticulatus* Baird, 1859 "1858," so if searching for the original publication, be on the lookout for either date. Occasionally, a herpetologist will describe a species in someone else's publication, such as *Sceloporus tristichus* Cope *in* Yarrow, 1875. In some cases, you will see the word "unisexual" in parentheses. This denotes an all-female, parthenogenetic whiptail species, as shown in our standard. However, we chose to not show clades of horned lizards in parentheses in the title block, even though our standard does, as clades are not shown for other taxa, and the use of parentheses after a genus is also used to denote subgenera in other literature.

Description: This section describes how to recognize the adults of species, based on size, overall appearance, scale counts and arrangement, coloration, sexual and breeding variations, juvenile differences, and so on. This is the section that usually has the most technical jargon, so the reader may want to mark the glossary and illustration sections for help with the terms commonly used to describe lizards. Herpetologists always express measurements in metric units, and the standard measurements for length are snout-to-vent length (SVL) and total length (TL). Mass (weight) is expressed in grams.

Habitats: Please refer to the Lizard Habitats section, as this includes discussions of ecoregions, plant or biotic communities, habitat features, and microhabitats. Basically, this section within each species account describes where respective species are most commonly found.

Natural History: Some of these life and natural history traits include seasons of surface activity, times of surface activity, preferred temperatures (while surface-active), times of inactivity, home range and territory sizes, spacing patterns (among and between sexes and juveniles), display patterns, breeding and ovipostion (as applicable) sites and times, number of clutches, prey, predators, microhabitat selection, and many other aspects. Authors populated these sections as well as they could, considering that some species are very well understood and others have limited information related to natural history.

Range: This section is a brief synopsis of the distribution of the species, corresponding to a simple range map given for each species.

Taxonomy: This section includes a brief narrative about the current status and understanding of the taxonomy and nomenclature of the species and subspecies, sometimes highlighting information contradictory to the standards we used for taxonomy and nomenclature. It can be very difficult to determine where to draw the line with respect to suggested deviations or changes in taxonomy for different species, and also what particular aspects of the taxonomy are important.

Subspecies and Variation: In this section, the authors show all of the subspecies recognized by our U.S. standard, plus some other discussion of subspecies, as needed. Variation refers to the natural differences that may or may not be captured by the recognition of subspecies. Because aberrant color patterns may crop up in any taxon (e.g., albinism, melanism, piebaldism), these are not discussed here.

Range Maps: The range maps are of a general, shaded type, showing the basic distribution of species and subspecies. The basic method used to produce each range map was to start with large-area, published field guides, then use field guides or reputable websites for specific states, which often have more precise dot maps. In some cases, specific scientific papers were also used. Senior authors reviewed the range maps, but ultimately the editors are responsible for the accuracy of the maps. More precise range maps than those appearing in this book would require a more detailed analysis and verification of museum records, a task beyond the scope of this book. Ranges are not always precisely known, and intergradation and hybridization of some species can lead to very confusing range speculation! Clear delineations for subspecies were the most challenging; we hope the inclusion of named subspecies, wherever possible, will help herpetologists to understand the distribution of various taxa in the future. Whenever possible, we have tried to show ranges of species into Mexico, and Mexican subspecies. As a direct byproduct of relatively poor understanding of ranges of species in Mexico, our maps were in some cases incomplete. Because each species has a map devoted to it, we do not show hybrid zones; rather, we show the range of a given species through its hybrid zones. For example, note the overlap of the Desert Spiny Lizard and Twin-spotted Spiny Lizard in the maps. They overlap in southeastern Arizona (at least) and most likely they hybridize there, but the level of precision between full species and hybrids has never been adequately addressed. In the end, these are general maps, sometimes with imprecise boundaries, and should be treated as such. Please refer to the Guide to Standard Abbreviations, Metric Conversions, and Map Codes page near the back of this book for information on the color-coding of the maps.

As editors of what we hope will be future revisions of this book, we will gratefully accept comments on the ranges of species in this book.

Photographs: We photographed only live animals. We have attempted to portray adult males and females, where they differ, for each species, including normally encountered variation, and some ventral color pattern and habitat shots as needed. Photographs usually show the entire head, body, and tail of each species, rather than zooming in on the torso and head. Close-ups of the head, while interesting to look at, were generally avoided in species accounts to accommodate more photographs showing variation in species and subspecies. Many of the color patterns show the breeding adults, rather than non-breeding adults, because breeding individuals have the same color patterns as non-breeding adults—except that they have additional colors. Ventral photographs were taken when the animals were immobilized by rubbing the venters. We also attempted to show as many juvenile animals (hatchlings to small subadults) as possible, as they usually differ from adults, at least in relative proportions. In addition, we asked that photographic contributors adhere to ethically sound methods of photography and capture (if needed) and to submit photographs of animals *in situ,* or in natural settings. However, in some circumstances, "hand shots" were allowed, especially for young juveniles. Wherever we could, we tried to render the subjects with true-to-life colors (and yes, some really are that vibrant!), as well as help the viewer to separate the lizard from the background visually. The more patient of our photographers sometimes went through great contortions to pay close attention to the background and light settings.

FAMILY CROTAPHYTIDAE: Collared and Leopard Lizards

Author: Lawrence L. C. Jones

This family of large-bodied lizards is restricted to North America and contains relatively few species. Members of this family range from central Oregon east to Missouri and south to northern Mexico. The Crotaphytidae consists of 2 genera: *Crotaphytus*, the collared lizards; and *Gambelia*, the leopard lizards. There are 9 species of *Crotaphytus*, 4 of which are covered in this book. One other species, *C. reticulatus*, is found in Texas, just southeast of our eastern limit of Big Bend, while 4 others (*C. antiquus*, *C. dickersonae*, *C. grismeri*, and *C. insularis*) are known from northern Mexico. There are 3 species of *Gambelia*, all of which are found in the American Southwest. These are *G. sila*, *G. wislizenii*, and *G. copeii*.

Crotaphytids are the epitome of lizards as watchable wildlife—they are large and conspicuous diurnal lizards often observed throughout the arid portions of the American Southwest. The males of many *Crotaphytus* exhibit beautiful coloration, with a conspicuous pattern of spots and/or bars, plus the namesake black collars, as well as well-developed inguinal and throat patches. Females of both genera have vivid reddish-orange coloration in breeding condition; *C. reticulatus* and *G. sila* males also have reddish-orange breeding coloration. Crotaphytids are oviparous and sexually dimorphic. Males are generally larger than females, although the opposite is true in some species. Also, males generally have larger heads than females. Juvenile collared lizards usually have a more reticulated pattern than adults and orange banding on the anterior part of the body. Subadult males may redevelop this orange banding, possibly as a ploy to inhibit territorial disputes with larger adult males. Juvenile leopard lizards have distinctive crossbars and may exhibit vivid red dorsal spots.

The crotaphytids are monophyletic and distinct from other families. Crotaphytids have large heads, long tails, and long limbs. They are covered with many fine, granular scales and possess relatively few large scales. They have gular folds, and many species possess well-developed mite pockets, where parasitic trombiculid mites can commonly be found. Some species have a dark peritoneum, which is apparent in the dark lining of the mouth, a feature that helps these animals cope with intense sunshine by protecting the organs from ultraviolet radiation. Some species have been documented vocalizing. As a group, they are adapted to valley and foothills habitats, and are often seen basking when temperatures are high, when many other species are inactive. Their gait may be bipedal when running to escape predation or attempting to capture prey, which, in addition to large arthropods, may include other lizards or other small vertebrates. Leopard lizards in particular are well known as lizard eaters, and all crotaphytids can be cannibalistic (eating members of their own species). The presence of crotaphytids may be an indicator of a healthy population of smaller lizard species. Crotaphytids are powerful predators that can deliver a substantial bite to anyone trying to handle them. Crotaphytids are preyed upon by a variety of ground and aerial predators.

The crotaphytids have received various taxonomic treatments over the years. In the past, both genera had sometimes been lumped into the single genus *Crotaphytus*, but these 2 genera are pretty well accepted these days. The genera are readily distinguished: collared lizards have broader heads than leopard lizards, plus they have one or 2 black collars bordered with white. Leopard lizards are tan with large brown spots and lack collars.

Collared lizards are typically associated with rocks (except *C. reticulatus*), as in the rocky foothills of mountains, outcrops, or other situations where boulders are present. *Crotaphytus* often bask and watch for predators and prey from their rocky promontories. These rocky areas are usually interspersed with open areas, so they may run after prey or escape predation. Conversely, *Gambelia* are generally associated with open flat lands, such as Creosote Bush, sagebrush, and alkali flats; mesquite dunes; and among bunchgrasses or other low-lying shrubs.

Male Crotaphytus dickersonae, *Sonora, Mexico. Compare to the female on p. 511.*

For the avid lizard-watcher and photographer, crotaphytids are among the most rewarding targets. Seeing a vivid cobalt-blue lizard against the backdrop of the Sea of Cortez (*C. dickersonae* male, though gravid females are also spectacular) or a turquoise lizard with a bright yellow head and yellow feet (*C. collaris* male) in red rock country is breathtaking. Seeing a leopard lizard with another, equal-sized lizard hanging from its maw is also a memorable experience. Pity the poor other lizards (except the mighty Gila Monster, of course) that must compete for the lizard-watcher's attention. After starting this book, I decided to devote one wall of my house to crotaphytid photographs and paintings. Obsess much?

Great Basin Collared Lizard

Crotaphytus bicinctores Smith and Tanner, 1972

Author: Mason J. Ryan

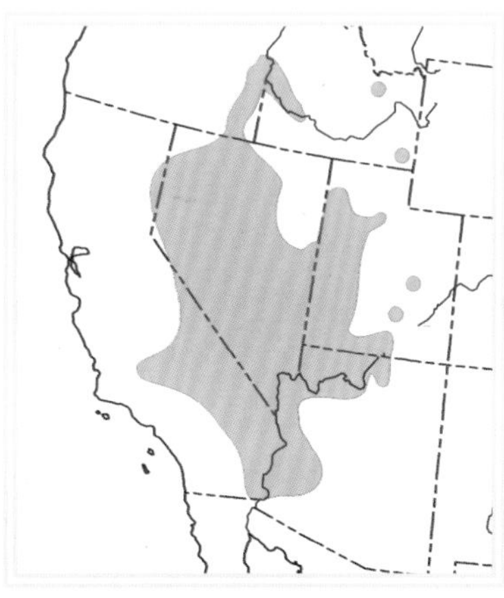

See page 559 for map color codes.

Description: This medium-sized lizard reaches approximately 116 mm SVL, with a large head and 2 black neck collars separated by no more than 12 pale grayish scales. The black collars are complete or near complete middorsally, bordering a gray to yellow central collar. The dorsal ground color is green olive-brown to gray with numerous small, scattered spots, and the spotting pattern becomes more profuse toward the tail and grades into a reticulated pattern on the tail. There are numerous, alternating transverse pale orange to peach bands across the back that end at the base of the tail. The sides of the head have dark spots on a light background. **Sexual Variation:** Adult males are larger and tend to be more colorful than females, with more distinct crossbands. Males possess slate gray to blue dark patches on the throat and groin. The male's tail is laterally compressed and has a pale dorsal stripe; the female's tail is more rounded and lacks the tail stripe. During the breeding season, female Great Basin Collared Lizards develop orange to reddish lateral bars. **Juveniles:** Hatchlings are

Venter of male Crotaphytus bicinctores, *showing the throat and inguinal patches typical of the genus.*

Male C. bicinctores, *Maricopa Co., AZ. Note the male's large, muscular head.*

tan to brown with the reticulations and may have orange banding. The orange banding usually shows up on newly hatched lizards and fades after a few weeks, but the bands reappear in males.

Similar Species: The Great Basin Collared Lizard is similar to the Sonoran Collared Lizard and Eastern Collared Lizard but differs from these 2 by the pale line on top of the tail and the lack of black oral pigment. The Great Basin Collared Lizard can be distinguished from the Baja California Collared Lizard by the Great Basin's 2 black collars encircling a central collar of gray to yellow (as opposed to the Baja California's white central collar). The Baja California Collared Lizard also has narrow, white dorsal bands.

Habitats: The Great Basin Collared Lizard inhabits some of the most inhospitable portions of the Great Basin, Mojave, and Sonoran deserts. It is generally associated with sparsely vegetated, rocky habitats, including alluvial fans, lava flows, hillsides, canyons, and rocky plains. They occur at low elevation from approximately sea level to 2,290 m in desert mountains.

Male C. bicinctores, *Bouse Dunes, La Paz Co., AZ.*

Natural History: This species is chiefly diurnal but may be crepuscular during early spring to late summer, depending on range. Populations in southwest Arizona are known to be active in mid-March, while populations in northwest Nevada are active by mid-April.

Adults can be found basking on top of large rocks and boulders at temperatures over 37°C and may be active between 30 and 43°C. From the vantage point of a boulder, these lizards actively search for potential prey and predators. When startled, they quickly run for cover under the nearest boulder, rock pile, or crevice. These lizards use their speed to capture prey, and once prey is captured they use their powerful jaws to subdue and eat the prey item. They are known to feed on a wide variety of animals including various arthropods such as beetles, wasps, bees, butterflies, and spiders, as well as other lizards. Common Side-blotched Lizards are a frequent prey item, and they may even eat smaller collared lizards. Occasionally, individuals may eat small amounts of vegetation, such as flower and leaf material.

Males are territorial and aggressive toward other males but may share territory with 2 or 3 females. Occasionally, subordinate males may be tolerated within the territory of a dominant male. Courtship and breeding begin in spring (May to June). Egg clutch size can range from 3 to 7 eggs, and females are known to occasionally produce 2 clutches per year. Females deposit eggs in loose sand to a depth of 10–12 cm or in crevices underneath rocks or in rodent burrows. Hatchlings first appear in August.

Range: The Great Basin Collared Lizard occurs in southeastern Oregon, southern Idaho, eastern and southern Utah, much of Nevada, northern and western Arizona, and southeastern California.

Viewing Tips: This lizard is diurnal and best observed in spring and summer (March through August) when they are most active. They frequently can be found basking on boulders or rocky outcrops. It is also possible to find these lizards by walking around the perimeters of boulder and rock outcrops and flushing them out of hiding places. This species can be very quick and skittish, and the best way to observe them is through binoculars. However, sometimes they can be approachable if a person slowly creeps up on them. Good public places to observe this species include Kofa National Wildlife Refuge (AZ), Joshua Tree National Park (CA), Grand Canyon National Park (north of or in the canyon), and Humboldt-Toiyabe Forest and Clan Alpine Mountains Wilderness Study Area (NV).

Taxonomy: The Great Basin Collared Lizard was elevated to the species level in 1996 after decades of taxonomic confusion. It was long confused with the Baja California Collared Lizard from the Peninsular Ranges of southern California and the Eastern Collared Lizard to the east. Recent work has shown that in southwest Arizona the Great Basin Collared Lizard carry haplotypes of the Eastern Collared Lizard, but a hybrid zone has not yet been identified. This suggests that the 2 species hybridized at some time in the past.

Subspecies and Variation: Since a major taxonomic revision of the family Crotaphytidae in 1996, there have been no subspecies of the Great Basin Collared Lizard recognized. There is variation in color and pattern that generally corresponds to their environment. This ability of certain populations to blend in with local substrates serves these animals well in protection from predators and while hunting prey.

Juvenile female C. bicinctores, *Maricopa Co., AZ.*

Remarks: There have been few quantitative treatments of the ecology of this species, but there are many anecdotal notes and descriptions of certain aspects of the natural history.

Eastern Collared Lizard

Crotaphytus collaris (Say, 1823)

Author: Craig S. Ivanyi

Description: Without a doubt, this is one of the most beautiful lizards in our region. The Eastern Collared Lizard is fairly large, reaching 115 mm SVL and up to 356 mm TL. The head is disproportionately large, the tail is long, and the hindlimbs are much longer than the forelimbs. Two black collars around the neck give the lizard its common name. Ground color varies among populations throughout its range, with the small, granular dorsal scales exhibiting tan, bright green, olive, brown, bluish, or yellowish with many light spots and dark crossbands. The belly is whitish. **Sexual Variation:** Males are larger than females, their heads are more heavily muscled, and they are usually more colorful. Color varies from light to bright green, turquoise, or cobalt blue (especially the tail) and, during the breeding season, individuals may develop a yellow head and yellow "socks" on the forelimbs. Also during the breeding season, mature males develop enlarged femoral pores, which exude grayish secretions. When sexually mature, the female is generally smaller and color is less dramatic, tending toward lighter shades of green to tan, with lighter spots and bars on the dorsum. During the breeding season spots and bars of bright red or orange appear on the sides of the female's body and neck, which may indicate that she is gravid; these fade after egg deposition. Immature males may develop a similar orange coloration, which some researchers hypothesize may be

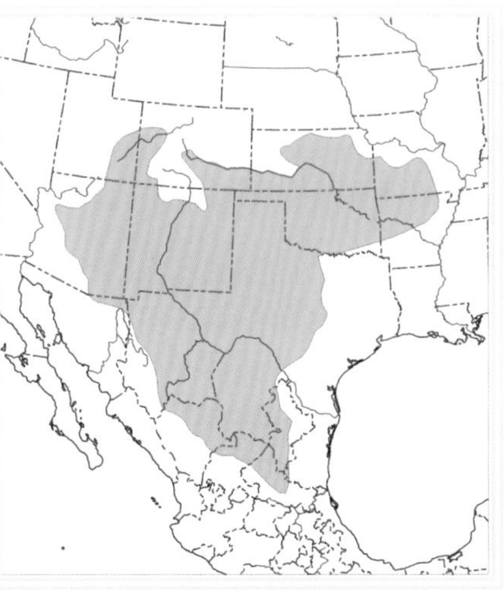

See page 559 for map color codes.

Adult C. collaris, *Wupatki National Monument, Coconino Co., AZ. The toes are elevated to reduce heat intake.*

Male C. collaris, *Wupatki National Monument, Coconino Co., AZ.*

female mimicry, possibly to reduce agonistic behavior of adult males toward the immature lizard. Eastern Collared Lizards have "mite pockets" at the base of the tail and in folds of skin around the legs of both sexes. **Juveniles:** Juveniles have narrower heads and lack the heavy jaw muscles. In addition, they have distinct banding that slowly fades as the animal matures, and the neck collars are broader; otherwise they have subtle pattern and color (especially on the head).

Similar Species: The Long-nosed Leopard Lizard is also smooth-scaled and similar in size and body form, but lacks the black bands around the neck. Spiny lizards (*Sceloporus* spp.) may have one black collar, but never 2. In addition, spiny lizards have sharply pointed, keeled scales.

Habitats: This species occurs in a variety of arid to semiarid habitats, including piñon/juniper, sagebrush, desert scrub, semi-desert and riparian grassland, desert riparian, and riparian gallery forest. Eastern Collared Lizards prefer to view the world from medium-to-large boulders found in areas of sparsely vegetated, open terrain. This lizard can be found from near sea level to 2,440 m in elevation.

Natural History: Eastern Collared Lizards are diurnal and eat a variety of prey including spiders, centipedes, beetles, grasshoppers, and other insects, and other lizards–

Juvenile C. collaris, *Otero Co., CO. Young and gravid females have orange bands.*

including smaller individuals of their own species–along with an occasional small bird or mammal. This species has also been found to consume a variety of plant material. At times, an Eastern Collared Lizard may "bite off more than it can chew." On one occasion (in captivity), an adult Eastern Collared Lizard attempted to eat a hatchling Common Chuckwalla. Both were found dead one morning, because the chuckwalla was too large to swallow; hind legs and tail were protruding out of the mouth of the collared lizard. They are preyed upon by snakes, birds of prey, and smaller carnivorous mammals.

In early summer females may lay 1 to 13 eggs (clutches of up to 22 have been recorded) in shallow depressions in the soil or under rocks. The eggs are generally 11 × 19 mm, and older females are capable of producing 2 clutches of eggs each year. Length of incubation depends upon temperature, but generally lasts 42–94 days. Hatchlings emerge in late summer and early fall. If adequately nourished, they can grow quickly and may reproduce in their first year of life.

When confronted by a predator, an Eastern Collared Lizard quickly dives into rock crevices or under rocks to avoid being eaten. Males are highly territorial and have stereotypical head bobbing and push-up displays. Though much of this behavior appears designed to avoid actual physical contact with other males, males are not averse to physical confrontation, which may consist of chasing and vigorous attacks on smaller individuals, if they fail to give ground to the larger individuals.

Range: With the largest range of any of the collared lizards, this lizard is found in both the U.S. and Mexico. U.S. distribution: occurs from Missouri, Arkansas, and eastern Colorado, through the western two-thirds of Texas, much of New Mexico, and Arizona. Mexican distribution: Eastern Sonora, Chihuahua, Coahuila, Nuevo León, northern Zacatecas, San Luis Potosí, Durango, and Tamaulipas.

Viewing Tips: Due to its size, bright colors, and bold habits, this is a *great* lizard to look for. When you're in rocky areas and hills, look for these lizards, especially males, on small or medium-sized boulders, basking in the sun or on the lookout for potential prey or predators—especially on southeast- to south-facing slopes. Good places to look for this lizard include Wupatki National Monument and on rocky hillsides on the south face of the Santa Catalina Mountains (AZ), Big Bend National Park (TX), Comanche National Grassland in the Southeast and in the West (CO), Colorado National Monument (CO), and Arches and Canyonlands National Parks (UT). They are most active in warm, sunny weather, between 20.5 and 32°C, from late spring to early autumn.

Female C. collaris, *with fading orange bands, Marijilda Canyon, AZ.*

Taxonomy: Up to 6 subspecies have been recognized; most authors no longer recognize these, and some have been elevated to full species.

Subspecies and Variation: No subspecies are currently recognized.

Remarks: The Eastern Collared Lizard is also known as the "mountain boomer" in parts of the Midwest. This name originated with early Oklahoma settlers, who mistakenly believed that this mountain-dwelling lizard was making vocalizations (the sounds were probably coming from unseen frogs and toads). Several melanistic specimens have been reported from lava flows in New Mexico, though some researchers noted that apparent melanistic specimens would lighten in color upon capture.

Large adult male C. collaris, *San Andres Mountains, Doña Ana Co., NM.*

Sonoran Collared Lizard

Crotophytus nebrius Axtell and Montanucci, 1977

Author: Randall D. Babb

Description: This is a medium to large lizard, up to 112 mm SVL, with a stout body, a long slender tail that is round in cross section, and long, muscular back legs with long toes. The head is large and powerfully built with a short snout and wide, heavy temporal region. The scales are granular dorsally but become larger on the front limbs, feet, head, belly, and leading edges of the hind limbs. Seventeen to 22 femoral pores that do not extend beyond the angle of the knee are present on the undersides of thighs. The inside of the throat is black. Two distinct black collars traverse the neck, of which the anterior most completely encircles the throat on males. The rear collar is often broken dorsally at mid-body and terminates on the shoulders laterally. The coloration is variable but is typically drab in nature: yellowish, gray, or tan in ground color with diffused dark or light bars dorsally. The dorsum is typically overlaid with light spots that are about 3 times larger on the top of the back than they are on the sides. These spots give the animal a mottled appearance. Dark blotches are often present on the sides of the body between the front and rear legs. The sides of the head are spotted or mottled, though the top of the head is usually void of markings. There are often light markings on the mandibles. Ventral surfaces of the body are white or cream without markings except for inguinal patches in males (see below). The throat of males and

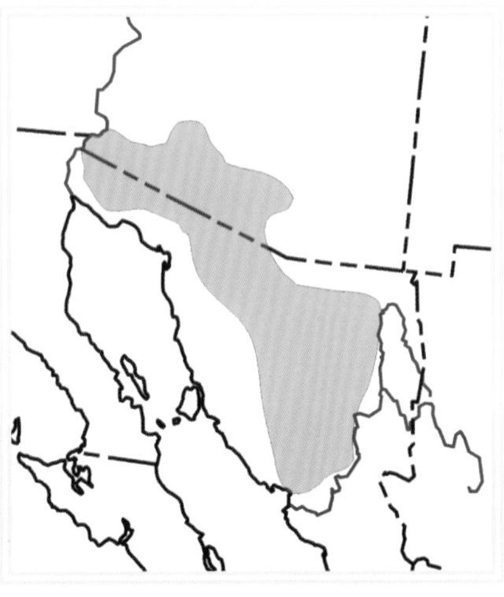

See page 559 for map color codes.

Juvenile C. nebrius, *Maricopa Co., AZ.*

Large male C. nebrius, *Maricopa Co., AZ.*

occasionally females has darker reticulations. **Sexual Variation:** Males have larger, broader heads than females. They also have enlarged post-anal scales and dark inguinal patches. Male Sonoran Collared Lizards are typically more vividly patterned and often have diffuse yellow or orange coloration on the throat. Washes of yellow, orange, or salmon are present on the neck or body of breeding animals. Males are also typically larger than females. Females are smaller with more diffuse or obscure markings. General overall coloration is often browner. **Juveniles:** Young and gravid females have splashes of salmon color on their necks, fore-bodies and sides, which may form bands.

Similar Species: The closely related Long-nosed Leopard Lizard has a longer, narrower head and a longer body, and is typically covered dorsally with dark round spots. Eastern Collared Lizards' anterior collar does not encircle the neck, and they are typically much more vividly colored. Great Basin Collared Lizards have a laterally compressed tail and lack the dark pigment inside the throat. Baja California Collared Lizards have a laterally compressed tail.

Habitats: This species inhabits scrub habitats in Arizona's Sonoran Desert. In Sonora, Mexico, it also frequents tropical deciduous forest habitats in the foothills of the Sierra Madre Occidental, especially open canyons. Sonoran Collared Lizards in the U.S.

Gravid female C. nebrius, *Maricopa Co, AZ.*

favor low, rocky, desert mountains and hillsides. Boulder-strewn canyons, washes, and ridge tops are also frequented by these lizards. Jojoba, Triangle Leaf Bursage, Creosote Bush, Little Leaf Palo Verde, Little Leaf Elephant Tree, Limber Bush, Giant Saguaro, Organ Pipe Cactus, and hedgehog cacti are all common vegetative associates in the United States. Vegetation associated with this lizard is much broader in Sonora, Mexico, and includes Cardon, Senita Cactus, Hecho Cactus, Boat-thorn and other acacias, mimosa, mesquite, etc.

Natural History: Relatively little is known regarding the natural history of the Sonoran Collared Lizard. This diurnal lizard prefers habitats with large rocks, which they use for basking and keeping watch for prey and potential predators. Rocks are also used as retreats during inactive periods such as brumation and for escape from predators. Sonoran Collared Lizards are likely prey for a host of desert animals including whipsnakes and other snakes, hawks, shrikes, foxes, and other small carnivorous mammals. The diet is likely similar to that of other members of the genus, with arthropods and small lizards making up most of their diet. The powerful jaws are designed for seizing prey, which is generally subdued by having its head crushed. Prey is swallowed whole, and collared lizards are well known for their ability to swallow large food items.

Observed activity runs from March through September and likely extends into November in warmer habitats. This species brumates during cooler months. Mating takes place in May–June, after which the female develops a salmon-orange post-breeding coloration known as the "post nuptial blush." Possibly up to 12 eggs are laid in June–July, and the young hatch in July–September. The tails of collared lizards are vital for maintaining balance during bipedal locomotion and are not shed for defense as seen with many other lizard species. If the tail is lost, it does not regenerate.

Range: These lizards are found throughout much of southwestern Arizona from just south of Phoenix southeastward to the vicinity of Tucson and westward to the California border south of the Gila River. The species extends southward into Sonora, Mexico, where it is found over much of the western half of the state to the vicinity of Guaymas.

Viewing Tips: Watch for this lizard atop large rocks and boulders along desert back roads through mountainous and hilly regions, especially on warm spring and early summer days and mornings. When hiking low-desert mountain ranges, keep an eye out for Sonoran Collared Lizards in rocky and canyon habitats. Sonoran Collared Lizards sometimes allow for very close approach and make excellent photographic subjects due to their interesting appearance. Saguaro National Park West, Organ Pipe Cactus National Monument, and the Barry M. Goldwater Range are good places to observe this species.

Male C. nebrius, *Little Ajo Mountains, Pima Co., AZ.*

Taxonomy: The taxonomy of collared lizards was rather confusing until the late 1990s. Work at that time separated the group into several distinct species. The Sonoran Collared Lizard was described in 1977 based on a specimen collected in Sonora, Mexico.

Subspecies and Variation: There are no recognized subspecies.

Remarks: Relatively little is known about this inhabitant of some of the harshest portions of the Sonoran Desert.

Baja California Collared Lizard

Crotaphytus vestigium Smith and Tanner, 1972

Author: Craig S. Ivanyi

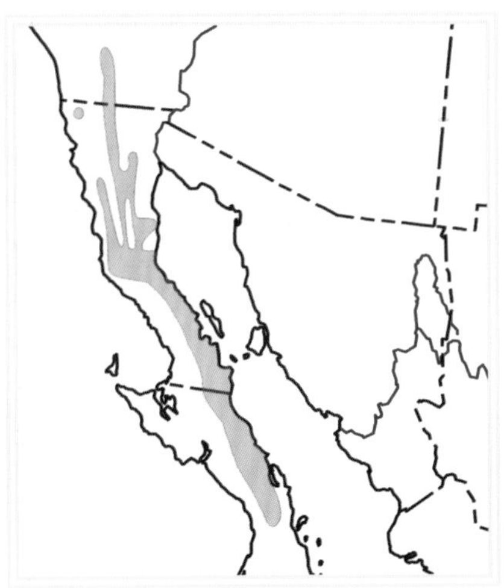

See page 559 for map color codes.

Description: This is a terrestrial, rock-dwelling lizard of moderate size (maximum size ranges from 108 to 125 mm SVL), with a disproportionately large head and granular scales. It has a white collar bordered by 2 black collars immediately behind the head, and transverse dotted and solid lines of white on the dorsal and lateral surfaces of the body. The collars have wide dorsal gaps and the posterior one may be absent. The ground color of this lizard can be black, brown, or tan. Dorsal and lateral aspects of head, limbs, and tail are often vividly blotched, spotted, or marbled. **Sexual Variation:** Males attain a larger size than females. The anterior portion of the throat is olive in color with a black patch posteriorly. Males also have black inguinal patches. Females generally have dark spots on the sides of the body. Reproductive females (and immature males) develop bright orange to red bars on the sides of the body, neck, and posterior portion of the head. **Juveniles:** Young lizards have narrower heads (especially at the angle of the jaw), with less musculature and reduced scale size in ear-flap scales. There is a distinct white banding pattern on larger juveniles, while smaller juveniles and hatchlings have more subtle banding. In addition, color and pattern on the head and throat are very subtle.

Juvenile C. vestigium, *San Diego Co., CA.*

Similar Species: No other *Crotaphytus* occur within the range of *C. vestigium,* though *C. insularis* and *C. grismeri* occur just east of its range (Isla Angel de la Guarda, Sea of Cortez, and northeastern Baja California Norte, Mexico, respec-

Male C. vestigium, *San Diego Co., CA.*

tively) and *C. bicinctores* just north of its range at the San Gorgonio Pass, California. Leopard lizards (*Gambelia* spp.), which are similar in size and appearance, are sympatric with the Baja California Collared Lizard. However, leopard lizards lack the distinct black collars that give collared lizards their name. Some spiny lizards (*Sceloporus* spp.) also overlap the range of this species and may have a single dark collar, but do not have 2 black collars and are much more spiny than the collared lizards.

Habitats: This species frequents a variety of arid rocky habitats, including hillsides, canyons, alluvial fans, and lava flows. The presence of rock outcroppings is critical to its existence. In the U.S., this lizard is found from sea level up to 900 m, whereas in Mexico it has been recorded as high as 2,300 m in elevation.

Natural History: This aggressive, voracious predator feeds upon insects, spiders, and small vertebrates, primarily other lizard species, along with some vegetation such as flowers and leaves. The Baja California Collared Lizard is preyed upon by snakes, birds of prey, and small carnivorous mammals.

This species is capable of leaping considerable distances and running bipedally, with the body held off the ground at a 45-degree angle with tail and forelimbs raised. The stride can be up to 3 times the length of the body. This lizard does not autotomize its tail, as it is useful in maintaining balance as the lizard sprints on hind legs; instead, it's able to lose the skin along the posterior part of its tail. Speed facilitates the capture of prey by this visually oriented predator. Its large head and strong jaw muscles allow it to get a powerful grip on large prey such as other lizards. This species is active from spring through autumn and is often active in extremely hot conditions (up to 38°C). Breeding may occur from spring into late summer, with the female laying 3–8 eggs in underground chambers. Hatchlings emerge in July or August.

Range: This is almost exclusively a lizard of the Baja California peninsula; it enters the U.S. from the border with Mexico to the San Gorgonio Pass, near Palm Springs, California, where it follows the northern extension of the Peninsular Ranges. Additionally, an isolated population on Tecate Peak, along the international border between the U.S. and Mexico, has been reported. In Mexico, they are found along central gulf coast, Vizcaíno, and Magdalena regions.

Viewing Tips: Baja California Collared Lizards are found only in rocky terrain. Look for this lizard atop small or medium-sized boulders, which it uses to survey the surrounding area for potential prey and as a sanctuary if threatened by a predator. Though wary of predators, it may allow close approach before diving for cover. Use binoculars to scan isolated boulders and approach by vehicle if possible, which will often afford closer approach than being on foot (this may allow you to get those close-up photos you want!). In its limited distribution in the United States, look for this

Male C. vestigium, *Imperial Co., CA.*

Gravid female C. vestigium, *Jacumba Mountains, CA.*

species in Anza-Borrego Desert State Park or the southern edge of the San Gorgonio Pass near the town of Cabezon, near Palm Springs.

Taxonomy: This species was originally described as *C. fasciatus* and eventually as *C. fasciolatus. Crotaphytus insularis* and *C. insularis vestigium* have also been used as names for this species, and these 2 species *(C. insularis* and *C. vestigium)* are considered very close relatives. Because of the long-term use of *C. vestigium,* taxonomists have retained this name.

Subspecies and Variation: There are no recognized subspecies, nor are there any described pattern classes. Color varies in relation to background matching, and pattern shifts are noted within its distribution from north to south (spots between light bands are more regular and linearly arranged in the southern part of its range).

Remarks: Researchers have noted that this species is believed by some people in Mexico to have toxic saliva. Though they have powerful jaws and will readily bite when handled, they are not believed to be venomous in any fashion. The word *Crotaphytus* means "head of the hammer" and refers to the large head with strong muscles in the temple region, while *vestigium* translates to "a trace," referring to the reduced collars.

Cope's Leopard Lizard

Gambelia copeii (Yarrow, 1882)

Authors: Clark R. Mahrdt and Kent R. Beaman

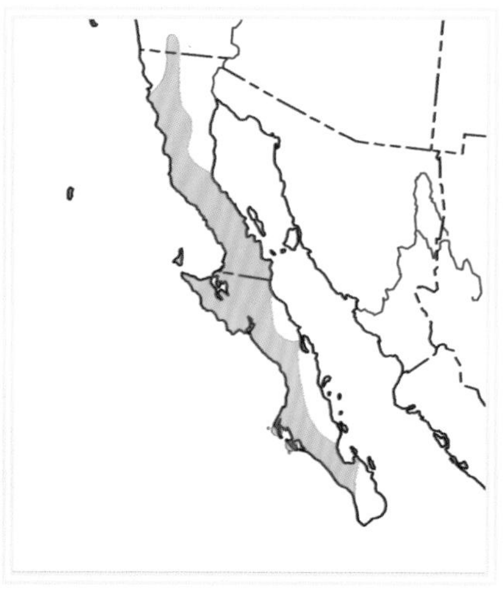

See page 559 for map color codes.

Description: Cope's Leopard Lizard reaches a maximum SVL of 127 mm. The tail is nearly twice as long as the head and body; the snout is elongate. Dorsal color pattern consists of brown, gray, or black paravertebral spots separated by cream-colored transverse bars and a dark brown or tan dorsal ground color. The dorsolateral surface of the body is speckled. The dorsal surface of the head lacks spots and the gular region has longitudinally black or dark brown streaks. The venter is white to pale gray in color. **Sexual Variation:** Males are usually smaller than females, with more pronounced femoral pores; males lack breeding coloration. Gravid females possess orange or red spots on the head or neck. Spots may be present on the flanks and ventral surface of the tail; red or orange pigment may be present on the thighs. Females attain a larger adult size than males. **Juveniles:** Dorsal coloration is dark gray or dark brown and may possess red dorsal spotting and conspicuous cream- or buff-colored banding.

Similar Species: This species is a sister taxon of the Long-nosed Leopard Lizard occurring to the east in the Sonoran and Chihuahuan deserts. The Long-nosed Leopard Lizard is lighter in dorsal ground color and has spots on the head. Gravid coloration is similar to that of the female Cope's Leopard Lizard. Although smaller and more slender in body form, the brown- or gray-colored Tiger Whiptail may be confused with Cope's Leopard Lizard, especially when running. Both species occupy the same habitat and range.

Habitats: This lizard prefers open Chamise chaparral, inland sage scrub, and occasionally oak woodland with fine to coarse granitic soil. Dominant plants include Chamise, California Buckwheat, Great Basin Sage, White Sage, Sugarbush, Laurel Sumac, scrub oak, and prickly pear and cholla cacti. It also occurs on rocky hillsides and within areas containing scattered boulders. The elevational range of this species is 500–900 m.

Adult G. copeii.

Natural History: Very little has been published on the ecology and natural history of Cope's Leopard Lizard, although it is presumed to be ecologically similar to the Long-nosed Leopard Lizard. The species is a sit-and-wait predator utilizing cryptic coloration to prey on other lizards. Its diet consists primarily of insects, although the large head and powerful jaws allow this species to consume lizards, snakes, and small rodents. This lizard also employs speed to subdue its prey. It basks on rocks, on roadside berms, or under sparse vegetation in early morning or late afternoon. Individuals have been observed foraging in sandy open spaces, in washes, and around patches of relatively dense chaparral. The only known predator of Cope's Leopard Lizard is the Loggerhead Shrike. Potential reptilian predators are the Coachwhip, Striped Racer, Western Patched-nosed Snake, and Common Kingsnake. Surface activity has been observed as early as mid-February and extending into mid-August. It is likely that mating occurs in late March to early May. Gravid females have been observed from early May through early July. This lizard is extremely wary and will often run bipedally when approached by a potential predator, usually seeking cover under dense vegetation, under rocks, or in mammal burrows. When threatened, it may remain motionless, relying on its cryptic coloration to avoid detection. When handled, this species may inflict a painful bite.

Juvenile G. copeii, *Cameron Corners, San Diego Co., CA.*

Range: Cope's Leopard Lizard is largely endemic to Baja California, although it occurs in the foothills and valleys of cismontane southern San Diego County. There are records from Cottonwood Canyon (near Barrett Junction) east to Jacumba and from the border of Baja California to approximately 3 km north of Cameron Corners; a record from Dulzura is questionable.

Viewing Tips: Adults may be observed basking on boulders, along roadsides, and crossing dirt trails and roads in early morning or late afternoon in late spring and early summer. During the hot summer months, lizards are very wary and difficult to approach. It is best to use binoculars to observe individuals at a distance. Several confirmed sightings have been reported from the vicinity of the Campo Indian Reservation and approximately 2.5 km northeast of Cameron Corners. Nearly all records are from private property.

Taxonomy: Although the genus *Gambelia* was recently reviewed, the taxonomy of Cope's Leopard Lizard remains problematic. The extensive geographic variation in dorsal color pattern has led some herpetologists to recognize *G. copeii* as a subspecies of the Long-nosed Leopard Lizard, *G. wislizenii*. Both species have a widely separated distribution, *G. copeii* occurring in cismontane Baja California and *G. wislizenii* in the deserts to the east. However, in the vicinity of Paseo de San Matías, where the lower Colorado Desert connects with the more mesic foothill and coastal regions of northwestern Baja California, both species occur syntopically. Molecular analysis and behavioral observations of the Paseo de San Matías population may detect the presence or absence of gene flow and resolve the taxonomic status of *G. copeii.*

Subspecies and Variation: There are no recognized subspecies of Cope's Leopard Lizard. In populations occurring in southern San Diego County and on the Pacific slopes of the Sierra de Juarez and Sierra San Pedro Martir of northwestern Baja California, the dorsal ground color is usually dark brown with large paravertebral spots; spotting is absent from the head and sides of the body. In southern populations, the dorsal ground coloration is a light brown to pale golden tan, peppered with fine pale speckling. The dorsal spots are fragmented and may be indistinguishable; spots on the sides may be present.

Remarks: San Diego County represents the northern extent of the species range. The distributional limits within that county have yet to be determined, although suitable habitat exists north in the vicinity of Buckman Springs. Only 6 specimens from San Diego County have been catalogued in museum collections; in addition, 16 sight records and photo vouchers have been reported. Cope's Leopard Lizard has been included in a habitat conservation plan for southern San Diego County.

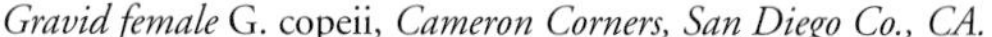

Gravid female G. copeii, *Cameron Corners, San Diego Co., CA.*

Blunt-nosed Leopard Lizard

Gambelia sila (Stejneger, 1890)

Author: David J. Germano

Description: This is a medium-sized lizard that can reach 120 mm SVL. Males average a larger size than females and have correspondingly larger, broader heads. The tail is long and tapering, and is about twice as long as the head and body. The base color of the body is brown to tan with cream-colored thin bars across the back. The tail has brown blotches, and the underside of the tail and body is white or cream-colored, except for juveniles or breeding males. **Sexual Variation:** Most adult males develop a light salmon to orange-salmon coloring over the entire body and onto the tail during much of the active season. Adult females have light to bright rusty-red patches along the sides of their bodies, extending from their ears to hind limbs during most of the active season. This coloration can extend to the underside of the tail. **Juveniles:** Hatchlings have prominent dark red spots on their backs, extending onto their tails. These spots turn brown as the juvenile increases in size, with the cream-colored crossbars becoming prominent. Juveniles also have lemon-yellow to bright-yellow coloring under their hind limbs and tail.

See page 559 for map color codes.

Juvenile G. sila, *Central Valley, CA.*

Similar Species: No other lizard in its range looks like the Blunt-nosed Leopard Lizard, but you could confuse it with the Western Whiptail if you see a large lizard running. The Western Whiptail, though, is gray, much more slender, and has a much smaller, pointed head.

Male G. sila, *Central Valley, CA. Males typically show orange-salmon coloration on body and tail during the active season.*

Habitats: This lizard occurs in a variety of habitats in the desert environment of the San Joaquin and adjacent southwest valleys up into surrounding foothill habitat. They occur from about 40 m elevation in alkali sink habitat with playas, saltbush scrub habitat, non-native grasslands, and *Ephedra* shrub habitat up to 750 m in elevation (their elevational limit), but they do not occur on slopes more than 30°. Much of their range has been converted to agricultural fields or human habitations in which they do not occur. However, Blunt-nosed Leopard Lizards can still be found in all but the most densely developed soil. The past invasion of non-native grasses often renders otherwise good habitat unsuitable in dense grass years.

Natural History: The Blunt-nosed Leopard Lizard is the largest lizard where it occurs and tends to dominate the lizard fauna because it can be abundant and it eats smaller lizards in its habitat, including young of its own species. Much of its diet, however, consists of invertebrates: mostly grasshoppers, crickets, beetles, bees, wasps, and flies. Adult and yearling lizards begin activity in April, and most adult activity ends in July. Males and females obtain breeding colors by May and mate a number of times to the end of June. Males are territorial and often are conspicuous on rises in the terrain, such as kangaroo rat mounds or berms of dirt roads, as they survey surrounding territory. Females usually produce 3–4 eggs (6 maximum) and can produce as many as four clutches by

Female G. sila, *Central Valley, CA.*

mid-July. Young appear above ground from July to September at 45–50 mm SVL and grow rather rapidly until reaching about 90 mm SVL before going underground for the winter in October or early November. Adults can live up to 6 years.

Population abundance fluctuates from year to year based on environmental conditions, but Blunt-nosed Leopard Lizards can reach densities as high as 16 adults/ha and 36 hatchlings/ha. They wander widely over their habitats, and home ranges can vary from one to 18 ha with males having larger home ranges than females. A variety of predators eat leopard lizards, including rattlesnakes, Coachwhips, falcons, hawks, owls, Greater Roadrunners, and shrikes. Good habitat consists of open ground because Blunt-nosed Leopard Lizards flee predators and chase down prey by running. Sometimes they run fast enough to become bipedal for short durations. If cornered, they will bite, and they have extremely powerful jaws.

Range: Blunt-nosed Leopard Lizards only occur in California in the San Joaquin Valley and several smaller, adjacent valleys to the southwest. They can be found in remaining habitat on the west side of the valley to the Panoche Hills, in the remaining grassland habitat in Merced and Madera counties, and southward to the south end of the San Joaquin Valley. They also occur in the Carrizo and Elkhorn plains in San Luis Obispo County and where there is habitat in the Cuyama Valley of San Luis Obispo and Santa Barbara County.

Viewing Tips: Look for Blunt-nosed Leopard Lizards along dirt roads and washes, or on the mounds of kangaroo rat burrows in appropriate habitat. Adults are most active from May to July, and young leopard lizards can be seen from July to October in most years. If you are walking, leopard lizards are most often found when they run as you get near, but they often stop some distance off and can be viewed if you move slowly toward them. They can be viewed on the Elkhorn and Carrizo plains in San Luis Obispo County, which is part of the Carrizo Plain National Monument.

Taxonomy: The species was once considered a subspecies of the wide-ranging Long-nosed Leopard Lizard, and was listed as *Crotaphytus wislizenii silus*. Subsequently the Leopard Lizards were placed in their own genus, *Gambelia*, and the Blunt-nosed Leopard Lizard was determined to be a separate species, *G. sila*, with only minimal genetic exchange with *G. wislizenii* at one contact zone.

Subspecies and Variations: There are no subspecies or significant variations of this species.

Remarks: Much of the habitat for Blunt-nosed Leopard Lizards has been destroyed for agriculture, energy production, and cities. It was one of the original species listed as endangered by the U.S. Fish and Wildlife Service in 1967. It is also listed as endangered by the State of California, but development continues to chip away at its remaining habitat. A series of reserves have been established or are being considered for this and other protected species in the San Joaquin Valley to prevent their extinction.

Male G. sila, *Central Valley, CA.*

Long-nosed Leopard Lizard

Gambelia wislizenii (Baird and Girard, 1852)

Author: Bradford D. Hollingsworth

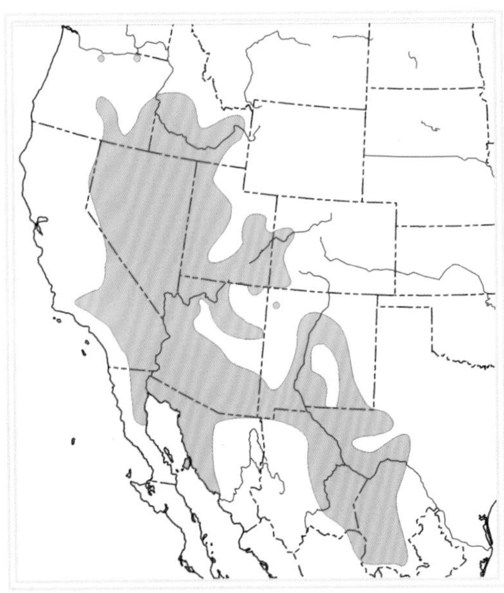

See page 559 for map color codes.

Description: This moderate-sized lizard has a muscular frame, with females reaching larger adult sizes than males. Females measure 144 mm SVL compared to 119 mm SVL of males. The tail is long, more than twice the length of the head and body. This species has a relatively large head, long snout, and distinct neck. Small scales cover the body and head. Femoral pores are present. The dorsal base color varies between white, cream, gray, and sometimes brown, overlaid with prominent darker spots and paler transverse lines. Spots extend onto head and flanks. Dorsal spotting extends onto the tail. Ventral color is uniform and paler, often white or pale gray, with dark gray to black streaks on the chin and throat. Males and females have similar color patterns with the exception of the seasonal gravid coloration of females. **Sexual Variation:** Adult males lack orange or red pigmentation, while a seasonal breeding coloration develops in adult females: orange to red pigment emerges on the sides of the head, flanks, thighs, and the ventral surface of the tail. **Juveniles:** Juveniles are more vivid than adults and have transversely arranged rows of dark red dorsal spots separated by cream-colored crossbars.

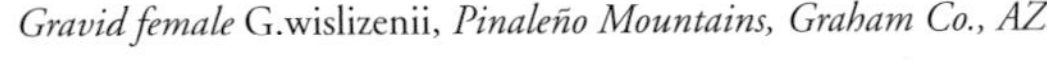

Gravid female G.wislizenii, *Pinaleño Mountains, Graham Co., AZ.*

Adult male G. wislizenii, *Deep Springs Valley, Inyo Co., CA.*

Similar Species: This species is similar to both the Cope's Leopard Lizard and the Blunt-nosed Leopard Lizard; however, these species do not overlap in distribution over the majority of their ranges. The Long-nosed Leopard Lizard differs from the Cope's Leopard Lizard by being paler in coloration and having spots that extend onto the top of the head. It differs from the Blunt-nosed Leopard Lizard by having a more elongate snout and a streaked throat rather than spotted, and males do not develop pink or rust hues during breeding season. More superficially, this species is often mistaken for the Desert Iguana when seen at a distance, but body proportions and color pattern readily distinguish them.

Habitats: This species is largely confined to the flat areas of arid to semiarid lands of western North America. It is associated with Creosote Bush, sagebrushes, bunchgrasses, and other arid-adapted plants. While some populations extend into higher elevation piñon/juniper woodlands, most prefer lower elevation flatlands with sparse vegetation and numerous rodent burrows. They occur from sea level to near 1,800 m.

Natural History: The Long-nosed Leopard Lizard is an agile diurnal predator active from March to October. It prefers flat, open terrain, with intermittent plants to hide beneath. It basks in open areas, on small rocks, or in the open. These lizards often lie motionless in a crouched position beneath a shrub and are superbly camouflaged in the dappled sunlight. When they see prey, they rapidly accelerate to make a capture, sometimes leaping into the air. While omnivorous, this species is most noted for its ability to eat lizards of its own size, including members of its own species. Other vertebrate prey includes snakes and small rodents. It also preys on grasshoppers, beetles, butterflies, and other arthropods. Strangely, it eats wolfberries, usually in mid-summer, possibly as a dietary supplement when prey items become less abundant.

Long-nosed Leopard Lizards are not territorial and have overlapping home ranges. Reproductive timing varies with latitude, with southern populations starting in late April to early May and more northern populations beginning in June. The orange to red breeding coloration of females is hormonally controlled and develops shortly before ovulation and persists to egg-laying. Most populations produce a single clutch, ranging from one to 11 eggs, but averaging between 5 and 7 eggs, usually laid from May to July. Young hatch in approximately 2 months. The Long-nosed Leopard Lizard can emit a wail or squeal. Predators include birds of prey, shrikes, and various species of snakes. They have extensive black pigmentation in the oral cavity, possibly associated with the threat display of mouth gaping. When cornered, this lizard will turn and stand its ground and can deliver a painful bite if not handled cautiously.

Range: This species occurs in western Texas, New Mexico, Arizona, Nevada, Utah, extreme western Colorado, southern Idaho, Oregon, extreme northeastern California, and southern California in the U.S. In Mexico, they occur in northeastern Baja California, northern Sonora, Chihuahua, western Coahuila, eastern Durango, and extreme northern Zacatecas.

Gravid female G. wislizenii *in agonistic encounter (with an adult male), Bouse Dunes, AZ.*

Juvenile G. wislizenii, *Doña Ana Co., NM.*

Viewing Tips: This species is easiest to see while it is basking along the sides of roads that run through open, flat terrain. Individuals can be observed on small rocks or berms on the side of the road, or even on the roadway. Walking slowly among shrubs and carefully looking at the bases can also be productive. When approached, threatened individuals will usually run to the base of a nearby bush, crouch, and remain motionless. This "freeze" behavior can be used to your advantage provided you observe the lizard as it runs off. Pay special attention to which shrub the lizard runs to, as close inspection will usually find it hunkered down in the shade. This species can be seen in most low-lying desert areas. Good places to view this species include Mojave National Preserve (CA), Valley of Fire State Park (NV), and many public lands in the Great Basin Desert.

Taxonomy: There has been little taxonomic confusion in recent years. Originally described as a member of the collared lizard genus (*Crotaphytus*), the Long-nosed Leopard Lizard has been recognized as a member of the Leopard Lizard genus (*Gambelia*) since 1946. The 2 other Leopard Lizard species were formerly recognized as subspecies of the Long-nosed Leopard Lizard, but were elevated back to full species. Future taxonomic questions will center on the contact zone with the Cope's Leopard Lizard in Baja California and the validity of previously described subspecies.

Subspecies and Variations: Currently, no subspecies of the Long-nosed Leopard Lizard are recognized. Differences in size and position of the spots account for most of the variation. Smaller adult sizes are obtained in northern populations than in southern populations.

Remarks: Although widespread, local populations are becoming more threatened as their preferred habitat is easily converted to agricultural fields or engulfed by expanding cities.

FAMILY IGUANIDAE:
Iguanas and Chuckwallas

Author: Matthew A. Kwiatkowski

For our purposes, this family comprises the true iguanas and chuckwallas, although many authorities include the phrynosomatids as a subset (i.e., subfamily Phrynosomatinae), and this is often seen in the literature. Although a relatively small group of around 40 species, the Iguanidae family includes some of the most recognized lizards, such as the Green Iguana and the famous Marine Iguana of the Galápagos Islands. Arguably, the family has contributed disproportionately to the scientific study of lizards; despite being such a small group, Iguanidae have attracted the interest of biologists like a magnet. Although they are unique in a variety of ways, perhaps what distinguishes iguanas and chuckwallas from other lizards the most is their diet. Unlike most lizards, iguanids are almost strictly herbivorous, eating leaves, flowers, fruits, and even algae, in the case of Marine Iguanas. Except for Marine Iguanas, their colons have unique partitions that presumably aid in the digestion of cellulose. Studies of some West Indies iguanas show that passage through the digestive tract will even cause certain seeds to germinate faster.

Iguanids are remarkably diverse ecologically. They range in size from the moderate Desert Iguana at 140 mm SVL to large species in the genus *Cyclura* of the West Indies at over 760 mm SVL. All are found in the western hemisphere except for the 2 species of banded iguanas found on the islands of Fiji and Tonga in the Pacific. Some are found in tropical and subtropical regions, such as the Green Iguanas of Central and South America, the ground iguanas of the West Indies, and the banded iguanas on Fiji and Tonga. Others, such as the Desert Iguana (*Dipsosaurus dorsalis*), chuckwallas (genus *Sauromalus*), and some spiny-tailed iguanas (genus *Ctenosaura*) are found in more arid environments of Mexico, and the southwestern U.S. Iguanas and chuckwallas occupy a wide range of habitats. Some, such as the Desert Iguana, are almost exclusively terrestrial, without venturing much onto plants, trees, or rocks. Others rely on rocky habitat. The Common Chuckwalla takes this to the extreme; it is found almost exclusively with rocky outcrops and will retreat into rocky crevices to escape predators. Accordingly, its body is dorsoventrally flattened, and it can inflate its body to wedge itself into a crevice. Some species will readily use both rocky and terrestrial habitats, such as the Galapagos land iguanas (genus *Conolophus*), some ground iguanas, and some spiny-tailed iguanas. Many, including the Green Iguana (*Iguana iguana*), some spiny-tailed iguanas, and the banded iguanas, are arboreal. The Marine Iguanas of the Galapagos Islands are semi-marine, basking on shore but readily entering the ocean to feed. While all iguanas lay eggs, some species face problems with nesting because of their usual habitat. For species in especially rocky areas, such as some ground iguanas and Galapagos land iguanas, females may have to migrate long distances to find suitable soil for nesting.

Marine Iguana, Galapagos Islands, Ecuador. These curious iguanids are the only species of lizard adapted to the marine environment.

Social structure is similarly diverse, ranging from limited social interactions to territoriality to dominance hierarchies. Desert Iguanas are considered to have weak social structure with little defense of home ranges (i.e., territoriality). Other species, such as the chuckwallas endemic to islands found in the Sea of Cortez (such as *Sauromalus hispidus* and *S. varius*), probably have a similarly weak social system, although more study of these species is needed. By contrast, other species can be intensely territorial. Common Chuckwallas will defend areas rich in food resources. This likely translates to fitness, as more food resources within male chuckwalla territories correlates with overlap in more female home ranges. In other species, males do not seem to defend any resources that might be important to females or their offspring. Instead, males set up small territories for displaying. In Green Iguanas, displays are typically made in treetops, whereas Marine Iguanas aggregate above the high-tide zone along rocky coastlines.

Along with complex social structure, many species exhibit complex social signals. Like other lizards, iguanas and chuckwallas will exhibit visual displays in which the head and upper body are rapidly moved up and down. These "head bobbing" displays are typically used as aggressive signals to other males. Males of many iguanas and chuckwallas species will develop (or intensify) breeding colors during the mating season or as they mature. These colors may be orange (e.g., Green Iguanas and Common Chuckwallas), yellow (e.g., Galapagos Land Iguanas), red (e.g., Marine Iguanas), or even blue (Blue Iguanas). In some populations of the Common Chuckwalla, these colors can tell females how much food is available within a male's territory, because males with higher food resources also have brighter colors. This correlation between food and color exists because the male colors are based, in part, on carotenoid pigments,

Green Iguana, a well-known iguanid often kept as a household pet. Well-cared-for adults can reach about 6 feet in length, but most are not cared for well and die in captivity.

which are produced only by plants or algae and must be acquired through ingestion. While the role of colors as social signals is well established in Common Chuckwallas, their role is less clear in other iguanas and merits further study. Finally, some studies suggest that the spines found along the dorsal part of the body and back of the neck in many species could act as a social signal.

Iguana populations face a variety of threats, including over-collection, habitat loss, and impact by exotic species. West Indian iguanas in the genus *Cyclura* have been especially threatened, with many listed as Endangered or Critically Endangered by the World Conservation Union. Other species should be closely monitored as well. Banded Iguanas of Fiji and Tonga face habitat loss and threats by domesticated animals. In some parts of Central and South America, iguanas can be an important protein source for humans and may, therefore, be susceptible to overharvest. Green Iguanas are especially popular in the pet trade and may also face overharvesting. Certain Common Chuckwalla populations are highly desirable among collectors because of the impressive color patterns found in males. In addition to overharvest, chuckwallas face habitat destruction as collectors often destroy irreplaceable rock crevices. It is clear that this relatively small group of lizards, which has contributed so much to scientific knowledge, deserves careful attention to its conservation.

Desert Iguana

Dipsosaurus dorsalis (Baird and Girard, 1852)

Author: Jeffrey M. Lemm

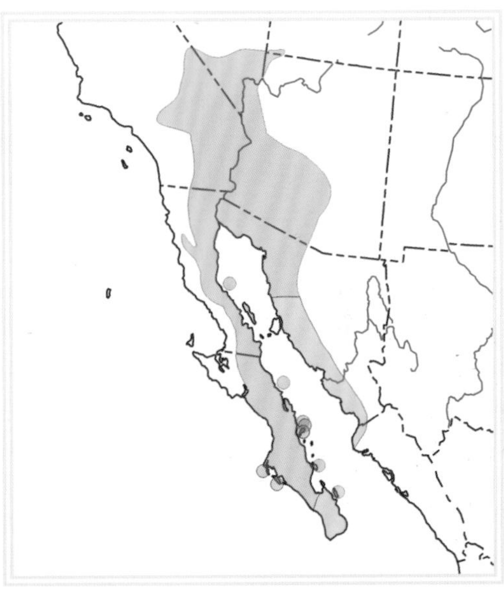

See page 559 for map color codes.

Description: The Desert Iguana is a large, cylindrical lizard with a long tail and small, blunt head. Adult males measure up to 144 mm SVL. The tail may be up to 1.75 times longer than the body. Scales are small and granular, and a row of enlarged, keeled scales down the center of the back forms a well-defined crest that diminishes near the end of the tail. The species is pale gray to whitish above with reddish brown bands or a netlike pattern. The tail is often banded or spotted, and the venter is whitish in color. **Sexual Variation:** Desert Iguanas are sexually dimorphic: adult males are larger than females and have a larger head and femoral pores. Both sexes develop a pinkish hue on the sides of the belly during the breeding season. **Juveniles:** Juveniles are similar to adults but have a bolder pattern.

Adult Dipsosaurus dorsalis, *Anza-Borrego Desert State Park, San Diego Co., CA.*

Similar Species: Desert Iguanas are very distinctive, but are sometimes confused with Tiger Whiptails. Tiger Whiptails are usually much thinner than Desert Iguanas, do not grow as large, lack the dorsal crest, and have a pointed snout. The head of a whiptail lizard also has large scales and a large frontoparietal scale (see Figure 3). From a distance, Desert Iguanas are superficially similar to Long-nosed Leopard Lizards and fringe-toed lizards (genus *Uma*), as these are both fairly large tan lizards, but upon closer inspection, they are quite distinct in body form and color pattern.

Habitats: The Desert Iguana is found in the Mojave and Sonoran deserts and prefers the expansive sandy flats and hummocks dominated by Creosote Bush. They are also found in rocky areas with sparse vegetation; however, Creosote Bush is usually present where iguanas are found. They occur at elevations ranging from below sea level to 1,500 m. Desert Iguanas are often seen around desert towns, provided native vegetation still exists.

Natural History: The Desert Iguana is a large, primarily herbivorous lizard evolved for a desert lifestyle. It remains dormant through the winter in underground burrows and emerges in the spring. It feeds on plants and is closely associated with Creosote Bush; however it also feeds on a variety of other plants and may consume insects, feces, and carrion. Desert Iguanas are most active in hot temperatures (above 35°C) and are considered the most heat-tolerant reptile in North America. Body temperatures have been recorded as high as 45°C, well past the lethal limit for other indigenous reptiles.

Desert Iguanas are territorial during the breeding season, but territories may overlap without aggressive encounters outside of the breeding season. They use a series of dis-

Juvenile Dipsosaurus dorsalis, *Dateland, Yuma Co., AZ.*

plays such as head-bobbing for communication with conspecifics, and also use scent-marking to define territories. Male home ranges of 0.15 ha and female ranges of 0.16 ha have been recorded.

Female Dipsosaurus dorsalis, *Avra Valley, Pima Co., AZ.*

Courtship and copulation occur shortly after emergence in the spring. Egg-laying usually takes place in late May, and the young appear from July to late August. There is considerable variation in these events from year to year and north to south within the range of the species. A single clutch of eggs is laid each year, ranging from 3 to 8 eggs. Adults reduce surface activity after the appearance of the young, which may reduce competition for food. Hatchlings grow quickly and probably reproduce by their second year. Desert Iguanas have a lifespan of 10 years or more. They are host to external parasites such as mites, and are preyed upon by other lizards, snakes, birds, and mammals.

Range: The Desert Iguana ranges from the Mojave Desert regions of east-central California, southern Nevada, and extreme southwestern Utah to western Arizona. The Mexican distribution includes eastern and southern Baja California, northwestern Mexico (Sonora and Sinaloa), and some of the Sea of Cortez islands.

Viewing Tips: Because Desert Iguanas are large and are accustomed to hot temperatures, they are fairly easy to spot in the wild. The easiest areas to find them in are sandy areas containing Creosote Bush and large rocks. In the spring and summer months Desert Iguanas may be observed basking on large rocks or feeding in Creosote Bushes for much of the day. Toward late summer, during the extreme heat of the day, they are more difficult to find. They are best observed from a car, as they are rarely startled by vehicles approaching slowly; however, if a person exits the car or makes sudden movements from an open window, an iguana will usually flee. On foot, they are easily found in the shade of Creosote Bushes and other plants during midday.

Adult Dipsosaurus dorsalis, *Yuma, AZ.*

Taxonomy: The taxonomy of the genus *Dipsosaurus* has been confusing. The taxonomy we are currently using for this book recognizes 4 taxa: *D. catalinensis* (endemic to Santa Catalina Island in the Sea of Cortez, Mexico), *D. dorsalis dorsalis, D. dorsalis lucasensis* (San Ignacio south to the end of the Baja California Peninsula, Mexico, as well as some islands in the Sea of Cortez and the Pacific Ocean), and *D. sonoriensis* (western Sonora and extreme northwestern Sinaloa, Mexico).

Subspecies and Variation: Only one subspecies occurs in the United States, the Northern Desert Iguana, *D. d. dorsalis*. There is some variation in the color among populations.

Remarks: The femoral pores of Northern Desert Iguanas absorb long-wave ultraviolet light. It is believed that the iguanas have visual sensitivity to the secretions from the femoral pores and that they can actually see where an iguana has marked its territory.

Common Chuckwalla

Sauromalus ater Duméril, 1856

Authors: Matthew A. Kwiatkowski, Lawrence L. C. Jones, and Brian K. Sullivan

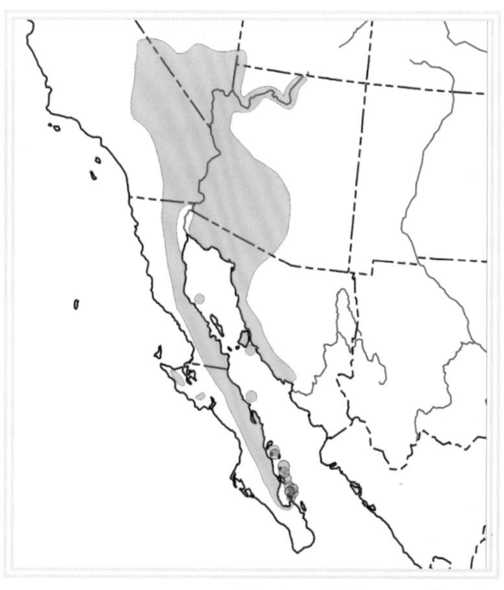

See page 559 for map color codes.

Description: This is a large, bulky lizard, with males reaching about 230 mm SVL, although most adults typically range from 125 to 180 mm SVL. The tail is thick and blunt-tipped, and is approximately the same length as the head and body. This species is somewhat flattened dorsoventrally, with wrinkles on the torso and neck. The legs are short and stout. There is no rostral scale (see Figure 3). **Sexual Variation:** Males are larger and their heads are proportionally longer and wider than in the females. Adult male color can vary considerably among populations, but the head, neck, and legs are typically black, and the tail is uniformly light (cream, yellow, or orange). In all populations, adult females are brown to grayish brown, with dark crossbands on the torso and tail that fade with age. Females may have a light-colored tail, but contrast between the body and tail is usually greater in males. **Juveniles:** Juveniles are similar to females, but banded more intensely, especially on the tail.

Large adult male S. ater *with white torso, San Diego Co., CA.*

Similar Species: Common Chuckwallas are very distinctive; they are not easily confused with any other native lizard species in the American Southwest, except perhaps the Gila Monster, which has a very thick, short tail; a large head;

Large adult male S. ater, *three-color phase, having a red torso, Maricopa Co., AZ.*

beaded skin; and is banded or reticulated with pink or orange coloration. Spiny-tailed Iguanas (*Ctenosaura*) of Mexico (and introduced populations in the U.S.) are superficially similar but have spiny tails.

Habitats: This species is largely confined to the Mojave and Sonoran deserts. Common Chuckwallas are invariably associated with rocks—particularly large boulder piles, lava flows, and outcrops. In some areas (e.g., Phoenix Mountains, Arizona), Common Chuckwallas use burrows as refuges rather than rock crevices, but this is atypical. They occur at low elevations, from sea level to about 1,370 m.

Natural History: Common Chuckwallas are egg-laying herbivores. They generally emerge from brumation in their rocky haunts during the spring to bask and feed on the spring bloom following winter rains. In the Mojave Desert they consume annuals and perennial plants, but in the Sonoran Desert, perennial food plants, including palo verdes, mallows, Ocotillo, Wolfberry, and a variety of composites, are preferred. They do not drink; apparently they obtain sufficient moisture through plants they consume. Salt is excreted through nasal openings. Common Chuckwallas bask for extended periods and prefer to maintain their body temperature between 35 and 40°C.

Common Chuckwallas have a variety of behavioral displays, including head bobbing, chasing, tilting, and biting. Males are territorial, regardless of population size, which ranges from about 3 to 65 animals/ha. Territory size varies inversely with population density (i.e., in dense populations, territories are smaller). Female home ranges are smaller than those of males, and overlap the territories of males as well as home

Juvenile S. ater, *Anza-Borrego Desert State Park, CA.*

ranges of other females. In this polygynous social structure, males defending territories with abundant food plants have access to more females. In the South Mountain population near Phoenix, Arizona, males with the brightest tails (orange) defend high-quality territories and are preferred by females as mates.

Mating occurs in the spring, and eggs are laid in mid- to late-summer. They lay 5–16 (usually 6–8) eggs. Rarely, hatchlings are observed during the fall and winter. Hatchlings are about 45–60 mm SVL. Juveniles may double in size their first year, but growth slows after that. Common Chuckwallas reach sexual maturity at around 140 mm SVL (females) and 125–150 mm SVL (males). They do not breed until at least 2–3 years of age, and females may not breed every year. Common Chuckwallas may live more than 2 decades. They are often a host to pterygosomatid mites and other parasites.

Predators include mammals, raptors, and snakes. To avoid predation, Common Chuckwallas wedge themselves into rocks by gulping air and inflating their lungs. This defense mechanism renders them very difficult to remove from their rocky crevices.

Female S. ater, *Anza-Borrego Desert State Park, CA.*

Range: Common Chuckwallas occur in California, Nevada, Arizona, and extreme southwestern Utah, as well as most of Baja California and western Sonora, Mexico. In the U.S., they are found from the eastern slope of the Peninsular Ranges and western Mojave Desert east to Phoenix, Arizona. Their distribution follows the Colorado and Virgin river drainages into Utah.

Large adult male S. ater, *Maricopa Co., AZ—an orange-tailed form endemic to South Mountain Park near Phoenix.*

Viewing Tips: Because of their size and habitat specificity, these lizards are fairly easy to find. In some areas, nearly every rocky outcrop has a population of Common Chuckwallas. They are wary, so it is best to scan suitable rock outcrops through binoculars from a distance, and then creep up on them, making note of the crevice where they take refuge. The best time of year to view Common Chuckwallas is during the spring (March through early June), when males are actively defending their territories and the animals are surface-active for extended periods. When startled, they will flee into rocky crevices and may be observed in their inflated state; they are sometimes easily observed at close range when in crevices. Good places to observe Common Chuckwallas include Anza-Borrego Desert State Park (CA), Valley of Fire State Park (NV), and South Mountain Park/Preserve (AZ).

Taxonomy: In the U.S. portion of the range, this species has long been referred to as *S. obesus*, but recent analysis suggests that *S. obesus* is conspecific with *S. ater*, as there is poor differentiation between *S. ater*, *S. obesus*, and *S. australis.*

Subspecies and Variation: Until recently, 3 subspecies were recognized. However, research suggests these designations are inconsistent with morphological characters. There are various color patterns (based on adult males), showing geographical consistency. The most common patterns involve 2 or 3 colors: a light tail, black head and limbs, and black, gray, brown, or red (or combination) torso. Populations consisting of gray or yellowish speckled individuals are also known. Virgin River populations are gray banded, and those from the South Mountains are black-bodied with an orange tail. There are other pattern classes in Mexico.

Remarks: Because of its large size, conspicuous nature, and interesting behavioral characteristics, this species has been well studied by researchers.

FAMILY PHRYNOSOMATIDAE:
Phrynosomatid Lizards (Zebra-tailed, Earless, Fringe-toed, Spiny, Tree, Brush, Side-blotched, California Rock, and Horned Lizards)

Author: Adam D. Leaché

The lizard family Phrynosomatidae is a large and diverse group containing 9 genera and more than 130 species. This family has its evolutionary origins in the New World and has a broad distribution across North and Central America from southern Canada to Panama. Most of the species diversity is centered in arid valleys of the American Southwest and Mexico, and as a result, the family is well represented in the lizard communities covered by this field guide. In fact, 39 of the 96 species discussed in this guide are members of the family Phrynosomatidae. Most of the species are among the most commonly encountered reptiles, owing in part to their diurnal nature and tendency to bask in the open sun. Species in this family occupy virtually every type of habitat, including arid deserts, montane ecosystems, and tropical forests. Most species are relatively small to medium-sized, with the largest species reaching about 150 mm SVL. Many species have highly specialized morphological adaptations, which makes them particularly well suited to their ecological niche. As discussed below, some groups are composed of specialized sand dwellers, rock climbers, or arboreal forms,

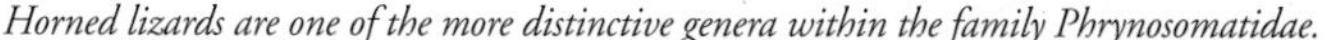

Horned lizards are one of the more distinctive genera within the family Phrynosomatidae.

while others are habitat generalists that are found in a variety of ecological settings. Males (and sometimes females) often have conspicuous color patches (usually blue) on the sides of the belly and/or throat, which are used in aggressive and courtship displays. Most are diurnal insectivores that use ambush foraging to obtain food, and some also eat other lizards or even plant material. Although most species are egg-layers, the ability to give birth to live young has evolved multiple times.

Many species assume the typical lizard-basking pose on rocks and other surfaces as they gather warmth, and are quite easy to view in nature. However, viewing some species is challenging, because their cryptic coloration and sedentary behavior make them extremely difficult to detect against their natural surroundings. This challenge can be overcome with a little skill and perseverance, and detection of these species can be quite rewarding.

Unlike other families in this book, the Phrynosomatidae is very diverse, having several distinctive genera, or groups of genera, so these are briefly described below.

Gravid female Sceloporus slevini, *Chiricahua Mountains, AZ.*

Spiny Lizards (*Sceloporus*) are the most species-rich member of the family, with over 90 species, 15 occurring in the American Southwest. They are small to medium in size (about 40–150 mm SVL) with keeled, pointed, non-overlapping dorsal scales and an incomplete gular fold. Although their general morphology appears somewhat typical between species, their dorsal and ventral color patterns are highly variable. When approached, many species will perform territorial "push-up" displays that are naturally performed in aggressive displays between rival males. Viviparity and sexual dichromorphism have evolved multiple times in the group. Many species of *Sceloporus* are habitat generalists, while others are restricted to rocks, boulders, sand dunes, trees, or shrubs.

Horned Lizards (*Phrynosoma*: about 15 species, 9 of which occur in the American Southwest) are extremely spiny lizards with flat, short bodies and tails. Most species are easy to identify based on the arrangement and orientation of occipital and temporal horns protruding from the head. They mostly inhabit arid deserts, and many species have a specialized diet consisting of native ants. Some species exhibit a bizarre defensive behavior in which blood is squirted from the orbital sinuses. This trait, assumed to be a predatory defense mechanism, is lost in several species. Two groups of Phrynosoma have evolved viviparity, and this may be associated with montane habitats.

Side-blotched Lizards (*Uta*: about 7 species; 1 species occurs in the American Southwest) are small (under 70 mm SVL) terrestrial lizards with a fully developed gular fold. One species (*U. stansburiana*) is widely distributed throughout the western U.S., northern Mexico, and Baja California, while the remaining species are endemic to islands in the Sea of Cortez. It remains unclear how many island populations represent distinct species. Males lack colored belly patches, but some populations have complex mating systems associated with throat color variation.

California Rock Lizards (*Petrosaurus*: 4 species; 1 species occurs in the American Southwest) are small to medium in size (60–180 mm SVL) with flattened heads and bodies, and are distributed throughout Baja California and extreme southern California. One species (*P. mearnsi*) is the only species found in the United States. They are adept rock climbers that are found on large boulders and rocks.

Tree and Brush Lizards (*Urosaurus*: 9 species, 3 of which occur in the American Southwest) are small (under 70 mm SVL) with enlarged and weakly keeled dorsal scales and a fully developed gular fold. Some species are rock dwellers, while others are arboreal and can be found perched on the tips of branches. Males have colored belly patches. *Urosaurus* are distributed throughout the American Southwest and Mexico, and on various islands off the coast of the Sea of Cortez in Mexico.

Sand Lizards (*Callisaurus*, 1 species; *Cophosaurus*, 1 species; *Holbrookia*, 4 species; and *Uma*, 6 species) are small to medium in size (40–124 mm SVL) with granular or minute dorsal scales, smooth and flat ventral scales, long hind-limbs, and a flattened body and tail. All species are adapted to living on sand to some degree, but the fringe-toed lizards (*Uma*) have the most extreme morphological and behavioral adaptations. Scales projecting from the toes form fringes that aid in locomotion on sand. To prevent sand from entering the head when burrowing, the lower jaw is countersunk and the nostrils, ears, and eyes are modified. Some of these features are shared by other sand lizards. Most sand lizards (except *Holbrookia*) have bold black-and-white markings under the tail, and some species curl their tails over their heads to display this unique feature. They are distributed in sand dune areas across the western U.S. and Mexico.

Zebra-tailed Lizard

Callisaurus draconoides Blainville, 1835

Author: Thomas C. Brennan

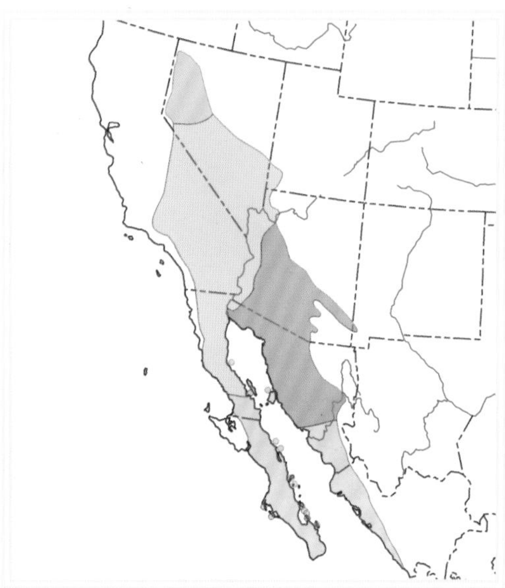

See page 559 for map color codes.

Description: This is a medium-sized lizard with a slender body, long thin limbs, and a slightly flattened tail. Males reach 67–101 mm SVL and females reach 63–87 mm. The snout is wedge-shaped, the lower jaw is countersunk, and a gular fold is present. The dorsal scales are granular, ventrals are larger and smooth, and the eyelids are fringed with small pointed scales. Coloration is grayish tan, usually with a yellow tint on the lower sides. Two longitudinal rows of gray-brown dorsal blotches extend from the shoulders to the base of the tail, where they merge into the dorsal component of the dark tail rings. In adults, dorsal blotches are often faded or obscured by numerous pale dots. Muted gray crossbars usually mark the dorsal surfaces of the hind limbs, and a distinct dark gray horizontal bar runs along the posterior surface of each thigh. Dark tail rings become jet-black ventrally, where they sharply contrast with the white background. Several thin dark lines extend from the labials to a dusky area on the throat; the center of the throat is often rosy. A soft-edged

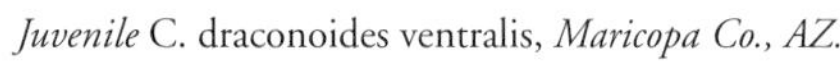

Juvenile C. draconoides ventralis, *Maricopa Co., AZ.*

Male C. draconoides ventralis *waving the underside of its tail, Rainbow Valley, Maricopa Co., AZ.*

orange patch is often present on each side of the venter, just behind the forelimb. Two dark vertical bars mark each side of the body anterior to the midline. These bars extend down onto the sides of the venter. **Sexual Variation:** Males have enlarged postanal scales, black body bars, and a large blue patch surrounding the body bars on each side of the venter. Females lack blue patches on the venter and their body bars are faint or lacking. **Juveniles:** Young usually have distinct brownish dorsal blotches.

Similar Species: The Greater Earless Lizard lacks external ears, and its side-bars emerge from the venter posterior to the midline of the body. Elegant and Common Lesser Earless Lizards lack external ears and tail bands. Fringe-toed lizards have fringed toes and lack distinct bands on the dorsal surface of the tail.

Habitats: The Great Basin, Mojave, and Sonoran deserts are home to this lizard. It inhabits flat, sandy, and open terrain such as dunes, desert pavement, floodplains, arroyos, and drainages within foothills and bajadas at elevations ranging from sea level to 1,450 m. Vegetation in suitable habitat can include Creosote Bush, Broom Snakeweed, Spiny Hopsage, mesquites, and acacias.

Natural History: This diurnal ground-dweller is active from February through October. It is sedentary, spending less than 2% of its waking hours in motion. Upon morning emergence it basks with its ventral surfaces resting on the warm sunlit ground. It is

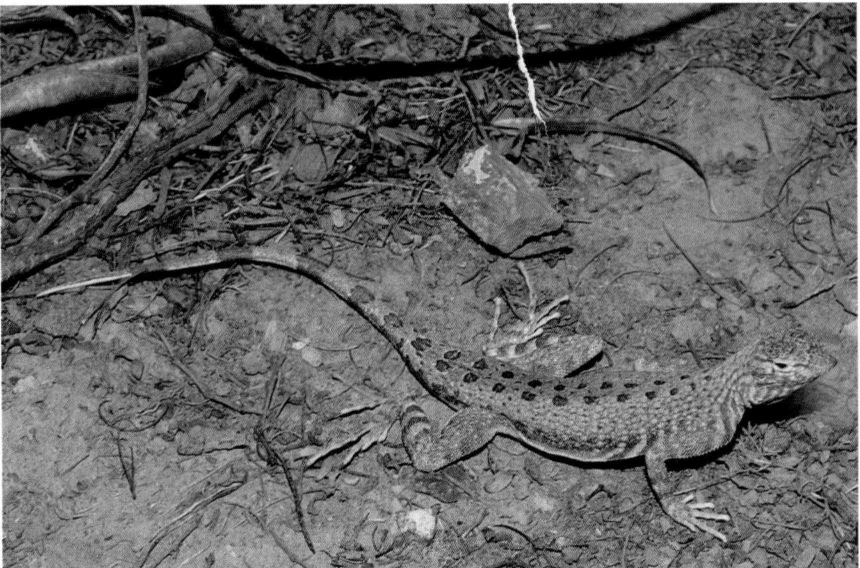

Female C. draconoides rhodostictus, *Yuma Co., AZ.*

exceptionally heat-tolerant and often remains active during the hottest part of the day, when other lizards seek shelter. In high temperatures it basks in an elevated posture with the body, tail, and toes raised, presumably to minimize contact with the hot sand. Its color changes during the course of the day from dark in the morning to chalky white at midday. Light coloration may help it absorb less solar radiation. The light phase is also observed in lizards sleeping on the surface at night.

Crypsis is the first line of defense, followed by flight. With a top sprint speed estimated at over 28 km per hour, this is one of our fastest lizards. When approached it often sprints for a short distance and then curls and wags its tail, displaying the conspicuous black and white banded underside. This may communicate to the predator that it has been spotted by the speedy lizard and that pursuit is not likely to be fruitful. Intermittently displaying the underside of the tail might optically confuse a predator as well. When the conspicuous tail is lowered pre-flight, the cryptic lizard seems to disappear into the environment. If pursued, it flees with an explosive burst of speed, often running 30 meters or more on the hind limbs with the tail curled upward. Fleeing in this posture might divert the predator's attention to the tail, which can be lost and regenerated. Regenerated portions of the tail lack bands. Predators include the Long-nosed Leopard Lizard, Orange-throated Whiptail, Tiger Whiptail, Coachwhip, Nightsnake, patch-nosed snakes, Western Diamond-backed Rattlesnake, Speckled Rattlesnake, and a variety of birds and mammals. This opportunistic carnivore sits and waits for prey to wander within close proximity. It eats beetles, grasshoppers, insect larvae, bees, wasps, roaches, ants, termites, true bugs, flies, spiders, lizards, shed lizard skin, and bits of leaves and flowers.

Males and females of all ages perform territorial displays that include head bobbing, push-ups, expanding the dewlap, and lateral compression of the thorax. Mating begins in April and continues into summer. Male courtship displays are similar to territorial displays. One, possibly 2, clutches of 1–8 eggs are laid from June through August. The incubation period is approximately 30 days, and hatchlings emerge from July to November. Adult size is reached within a year, and maximum lifespan is reported to be 5.9 years.

Range: The distribution of this species involves much of the southwestern United States and northwest Mexico, including southern Nevada, southeastern California, extreme southwest Utah, western and southern Arizona, and extreme southwestern New Mexico.

Viewing Tips: To find this lizard, walk through sandy or gravelly areas in spring or summer, watching for movement between shrubs and along washes. Good places to search include Kofa National Wildlife Refuge (AZ), Saguaro National Park West (AZ), Joshua Tree National Park (CA), and Valley of Fire State Park (NV).

Taxonomy: Three subspecies are found in our area: The Northern Zebra-tailed Lizard (*C. d. myurus*) occurs in northwestern Nevada. It is darker in average coloration than our other subspecies and averages fewer than 16 femoral pores per thigh. The Western Zebra-tailed Lizard (*C. d. rhodostictus*) occurs in southwestern Utah, southern Nevada, western Arizona, and southeastern California. Its tail and hind limbs are longer than those of our other subspecies. The Eastern Zebra-tailed Lizard (*C. d. ventralis*) occurs in southern Arizona and extreme southwestern New Mexico. It averages more than 16 femoral pores per thigh.

Ventral view of male C. d. ventralis, *Four Peaks, Maricopa Co., AZ. Note the anterior placement of markings, and compare to that of* Cophosaurus texanus *on p. 42 and 147.*

Greater Earless Lizard

Cophosaurus texanus Troschel, 1852

Author: Jeffrey M. Howland

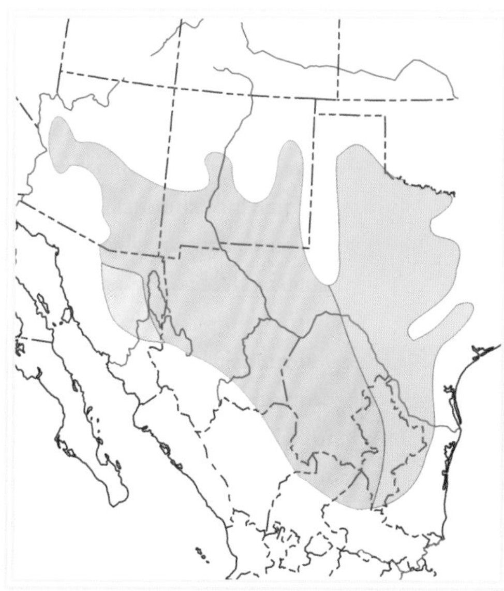

See page 559 for map color codes.

Description: This is a moderate-sized sand lizard, with males occasionally reaching over 80 mm SVL (rarely over 85 mm) and females over 70 mm. The tail is dorsoventrally flattened, longer than the head and body, and its ventral surface is white with bold black bands or spots. The legs are long and thin. There are no external ear openings. The lower jaw is recessed into the upper jaw, and the upper labial scales are flared and separated by grooves. **Sexual Variation:** Males are larger than females, have larger femoral pores, and coloration differs. Males are more brightly colored than females, with 2 pronounced dark bands extending from flank to belly. The ventral surface is white, with a sky-blue to greenish patch surrounding the black bands on each side, and an orange or pinkish wash on chest and throat. Adult females are shades of brown, gray, or greenish, sometimes with a dorsolateral row of darker, irregularly or crescent-shaped transverse blotches on each side. When gravid, females may have patches of orange or pink on the throat, armpits, and sides of belly and chest. The belly is otherwise white, often with a hint of the black bands of males.

Juvenile C. texanus scitulus, *Santa Catalina Mountains, Pima Co., AZ.*

Male C. texanus scitulus *displaying its markings, Big Bend National Park, TX.*

Juveniles: Juveniles have proportionately larger heads than adults, with overall coloration similar to that of females.

Similar Species: Zebra-tailed Lizards have external ear openings and the 2 black bands are farther forward on the sides and belly. Elegant and Common Lesser Earless Lizards have smaller black bands that are farther forward, and lack black markings on the ventral tail surface.

Habitats: Greater Earless Lizards primarily inhabit the Chihuahuan Desert, extending north into shortgrass prairie, east to the Edwards Plateau, and west through the northern Sonoran Desert to the southeastern edge of the Mojave Desert. They usually live in sandy washes or flats, but may venture up onto rocky hillsides. They occur at medium elevations, from about 50 to 1,600 m.

Natural History: Greater Earless Lizards begin activity on sunny spring days after temperatures exceed 25–30°C. Normal active body temperature ranges from 37 to 41°C. Activity is bimodal, peaking in mid- to late-morning, with a secondary peak in late afternoon. They often remain above ground until dusk, at which time they dive head-

Male C. texanus scitulus, *Four Peaks, Maricopa Co., AZ.*

first into sand or other loose substrate, using nose and hind legs to wiggle and push completely under the surface. On an early morning walk up a sun-warmed sandy wash, it is not unusual to see a Greater Earless Lizard pop up from the sand a step or two in front of you and run to a nearby bush or rock. They are ground-dwelling insectivores, ambushing prey from small rocks or other perches in relatively open habitat, sometimes running substantial distances to make a capture. They occasionally leap into the air to catch insects in flight or to snatch them from low flowers. Common prey includes beetles, bees, flies, and spiders.

Mating occurs throughout the breeding season, from April through August. Females lay up to 3 or more clutches of 2–9 (usually 3–6) eggs. Maturity is reached at age 10–12 months, at a size of 48–55 mm SVL for females and somewhat larger for males. Hatchlings are about 26–31 mm SVL and appear in June, with later clutches hatching into October. Growth is rapid for the first year, but in females drops dramatically thereafter as surplus energy is devoted to egg production. Male growth slows more gradually, but nearly stops after age 2. Individuals 3 or more years of age are uncommon, but include some of the largest and most readily observable animals, especially older males. Important predators include Loggerhead Shrikes, Greater Roadrunners, and a variety of snakes and predatory lizards.

Range: Greater Earless Lizards occur in central and west Texas, New Mexico, and Arizona, and in Mexico, from northeastern Sonora to western Tamaulipas. In the U.S., they occur in the western plains of south Texas, north to the Texas panhandle, across southern New Mexico, up the Rio Grande and Pecos River drainages, and from southeast Arizona northwest through the Sonoran uplands, below the White Mountains and Mogollon Rim, to the Big Sandy River drainage and the Hualapai and Cerbat mountains.

Viewing Tips: Although their distribution is patchy, Greater Earless Lizards can be very common, with reported densities as high as 100 animals per ha. Binoculars are helpful for viewing these wary lizards, though they can often be approached to within 2–3 m with careful stalking. They typically use the highest perch at hand, sometimes going out of their way to reach rocks only 1–2 cm high if nothing else is available. When hot, the body is held high on outstretched legs with toes lifted, reducing heat absorption from substrates. When alarmed, they run bipedally. Before and after running, they often raise and wave the boldly patterned tail from side to side, diverting the attention of predators from the body toward the more dispensable tail. Good places to observe Greater Earless Lizards include arroyos and surrounding flats north of Lake Pleasant Regional Park (AZ), or large sandy washes and canyon bottoms in Big Bend National Park (TX).

Taxonomy: *Cophosaurus texanus* is one of the sand lizards, closely allied to species in the genera *Callisaurus*, *Holbrookia*, and *Uma*. There is only one species in the genus *Cophosaurus*.

Subspecies and Variation: There are 2 subspecies in the U.S.: the Chihuahuan Greater Earless Lizard (*C. t. scitulus*) and the more eastern Texas Greater Earless Lizard, with an uncertain range boundary roughly following the Pecos River valley, east of the area covered by this book. A third subspecies occurs in northeastern Sonora, Mexico. Adult males are highly variable in color depending on subspecies, geographic location, and breeding condition. Male Chihuahuan Greater Earless Lizards are brightly colored: head normally gray, upper back and sides salmon to pinkish with gray to lavender spots, and lower back and flanks mottled shades of bright yellow to greenish yellow, with 2 black bands extending from each flank to the ventral surface.

Gravid female C. texanus scitulus, *Santa Catalina Mountains, Pima Co., AZ.*

Elegant Earless Lizard

Holbrookia elegans Bocourt, 1874

Author: Ralph W. Axtell

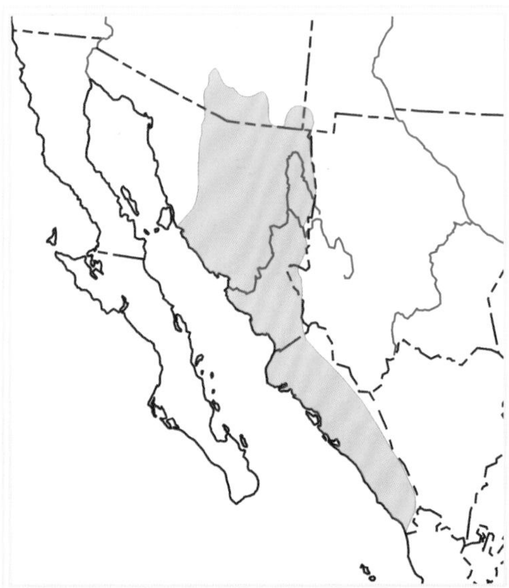

See page 559 for map color codes. Mexican subspecies not shown. There are different interpretations of taxonomy, nomenclature, and range for this species complex.

Description: This is a small, slim lizard, with males reaching about 74 mm SVL and females slightly shorter. The tail is longer than the SVL in adult males, but often slightly shorter in females. The head is chunky, with the upper lip flaring because these scales are overlapping and strongly keeled. The dorsal head scales encircling the supraoculars are similar in size to the adjacent scales on and around the supraoculars, and the ear opening is hidden by scales. There are no black spots or cross-bands beneath the tail. The ground color is gray-tan to reddish tan. **Sexual Variation:** Adult males have 2 rows of darker brown blotches on each side of the midline. These are margined behind with white lines or spots. Much of the trunk is covered with small light spots, and the tail has a single row of 8–10 fine-pointed chevrons that extend to near the tip (diagnostic for *H. elegans*). On the sides of the trunk opposite each elbow are 2 robust black bars surrounded by a vivid bluish areola several scales (3–4) in width. Adult females usually lack the pale

Juvenile H. elegans, *Kartchner Caverns State Park, AZ.*

Gravid female H. elegans, *Sycamore Pajarito Mountains, Santa Cruz Co., AZ. Compare blotches and breeding colors to* H. maculata *on p. 157.*

speckling of males, and their blotches are usually more distinct. The lateral bars are gray in females, never black (diagnostic), and gravid individuals (and some males) have a distinct, circular, reddish-orange spot on the throat (diagnostic). Gravid females (and occasional males) have bicolored areas on the sides of the trunk: reddish in front of the dark bars, and yellowish behind (diagnostic). **Juveniles:** Juveniles are similar to females, but without any gravid coloration.

Similar Species: Differentiating it from the Elegant Earless Lizard, the Common Earless Lizard has the following features: The circumorbitals are granular, not of similar size to the adjacent supraoculars. The tail is shorter than the SVL in both adult males and females. The tail chevrons are fewer (5 or 6 instead of 8–10), and usually disappear on the anterior half rather than extending to the tip. Both sexes have smaller lateral black bars with much thinner blue areolas (usually only one scale wide in males) or none at all (in females). Gravid females have an irregular orange-yellow throat patch (not a discrete red-orange spot), with a single color (pinkish to vermilion) both before and after the dark lateral bars (not reddish before and yellow behind). Both the Greater Earless and the Zebra-tailed lizards have distinctive black crossbands beneath their tails.

Habitats: This species is most commonly found in mesquite grasslands and open, grassy oak and juniper woodlands with bare patches intermingled with trees. During the mating season, males frequently use isolated rocks or rock outcrops for perching sites. Later in the year gravid females may use similar sites to bask.

Natural History: This species is an egg-laying insectivore. As far as I know, no one has studied reproductive behavior in this lizard, but probably from 6 to 10 eggs are laid after the summer monsoon rains begin (from late June to late August or early September). Emergence from brumation (in deeper rodent burrows) usually takes place in mid-April. Smaller flying and ground-dwelling insects and arthropods are taken by adults. Juveniles eat ants and other small insects. Occasionally I've seen adults jump into the air and grab an insect in flight. Individuals get moisture from their food and from dew. Salts are excreted by special glands in the nose, and if not worn off, may accumulate around the nostrils. This sun-loving lizard is active at about 33–42°C. When it is cloudy or cool they don't emerge from their dens. Often they employ "shimmy burial" to quickly sink into a friable substrate, whether to escape predators or for a temporary den during summer months.

Range: Elegant Earless Lizards occur from coastal southern Sinaloa, Mexico, northward through much of central and eastern Sonora to south central Arizona and then eastward along the Arizona border to extreme southwestern New Mexico. Mexican populations follow larger river valleys in Sonora eastward into the western uplands of Chihuahua.

Viewing Tips: This lizard is too small for distant viewing, but if one can get close enough to catch one or view one by using binoculars it can be a treat. Brightly colored males perch on conspicuous rocks in the spring along roadways and trails. Individuals are common at Kartchner Caverns State Park (AZ), in the foothills of the northern Santa Rita Mountains (AZ), and in Guadalupe Canyon (NM). Most individuals will allow you to get within 1–2 m of them before they move, but once they move they tend to be difficult to follow. View-

Ventral view of male H. elegans, *Santa Rita Mountains, AZ. Note the blue coloration on ventrolateral blotches.*

Male H. elegans, *Pajarito Mountains, Santa Cruz Co., AZ.*

ing of males is best in April and May, and of females after the rains start in July and August. Hatchlings and juveniles are rarely seen in the wild.

Taxonomy: The Elegant Earless Lizard has been confused in the literature for many years and remains confused to this day (see Taxonomy and Nomenclature section). The name *Holbrookia elegans* for Arizona populations first appeared in 1964. In the older literature and more recently, this lizard has been confused with both *H. approximans* and *H. maculata.* The taxon "*pulchra,*" first proposed as a distinct species from the Huachuca Mountains of south-central Arizona, should be subsumed into this species. In the 2003 edition of *Western Reptiles and Amphibians,* a male *H. elegans* (Plate 28) is labeled as *H. maculata.*

Subspecies and Variation: *Holbrookia e. elegans* is an all-Mexican form that occurs from coastal southern Sinaloa northward to northern Sinaloa, where it intergrades extensively with *H. e. thermophila. Holbrookia e. thermophila* occurs from northern Sinaloa through much of eastern and northern Sonora and western Chihuahua, and northward to southern Arizona. Some herpetologists continue to inappropriately use the name *H. m. approximans* for Arizona populations. An interesting color variant known from several areas in Arizona and Sonora is pale brownish above and completely devoid of any dorsal markings, although the lateral bars are still present in both sexes (grayish in females). Subspecies are not shown in the range map.

Common Lesser Earless Lizard

Holbrookia maculata Girard, 1851

Authors: Erica Bree Rosenblum, Doug Burkett, and Russell Blaine

Description: The Common Lesser Earless Lizard is a small, slightly dorsoventrally flattened lizard that reaches about 60 mm SVL and 100 mm TL. This species has no external ear openings. Dorsal scales are smooth and granular (slightly keeled in several populations). The tail is relatively wide and dorsoventrally flattened at the base, becoming more rounded toward the tip. There are 2 dark lateral bars on each side of the body, slightly forward of mid-body (these are reduced in several populations). This species has labial scales that are angled and overlap one another. Overall color of the species varies depending on location and predominant soil color, ranging from tan to dark brown or even nearly white. Darker dorsal blotches are found in 2 rows down the back. **Sexual Variation:** Males have more pronounced lateral black bars than females (narrowly edged with blue) as well as a more speckled dorsum. During the breeding season, females may obtain dramatic pink to red coloration on the sides of the trunk, more pronounced gular blotch coloration, and yellow tinges on the head. **Juveniles:** Apart from their small size, juveniles are similar to adults, but lack secondary sexual and breeding characters.

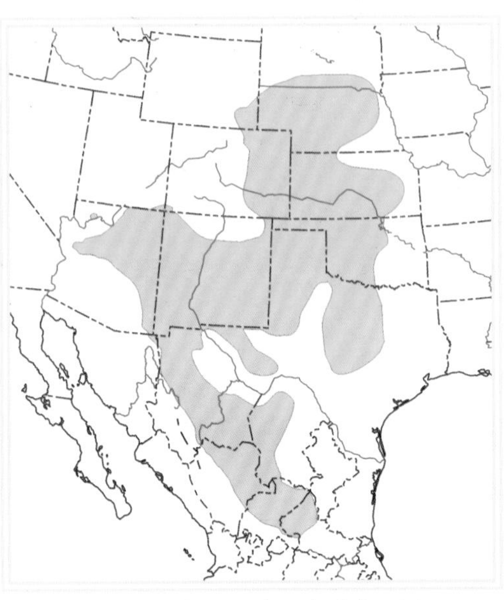

See page 559 for map color codes. Subspecies' ranges not differentiated. There are different interpretations of taxonomy, nomenclature, and range for this species complex.

Juvenile H. maculata, *showing the difference between the White Sands, NM, pattern, and the nearby Jornada, NM, pattern.*

Male H. maculata, *Mescalero Sands, Chaves Co., NM.*

Similar Species: The Elegant Earless Lizard does not have granular intraorbitals, has sharply pointed dorsal tail chevrons, and has a tail longer than SVL; males have lateral black bars more broadly edged with blue, and breeding females have a reddish orange throat patch. The Greater Earless Lizard is larger (up to 190 mm TL) and has subcaudal black crossbands. The Zebra-tailed Lizard is also larger (up to 200 mm TL) and has subcaudal black crossbands, but has ear openings. The Common Side-blotched Lizard is similar in size but has ear openings and the diagnostic side-blotch.

Habitats: This species is associated with a variety of vegetative communities, from homogeneous Alkali Sacaton flats to mixed grass-shrub communities. They prefer habitats with sandy soils for burrowing and are generally found on flats or rolling grasslands at elevations ranging from 500 to 2,200 m. This species has experienced severe habitat loss due to cattle grazing. Populations are spotty, but may be quite abundant.

Natural History: This species eats a variety of insects and spiders, and occasionally other small lizards. *Holbrookia maculata* is most active from mid-spring through early fall, and breeding generally occurs from May to July. During this time, stereotypical territorial and courtship displays can be observed. Females display low-intensity breeding coloration when reproductively receptive and high-intensity breeding coloration when gravid. Females generally lay clutches of 4–6 eggs. Home range size among dif-

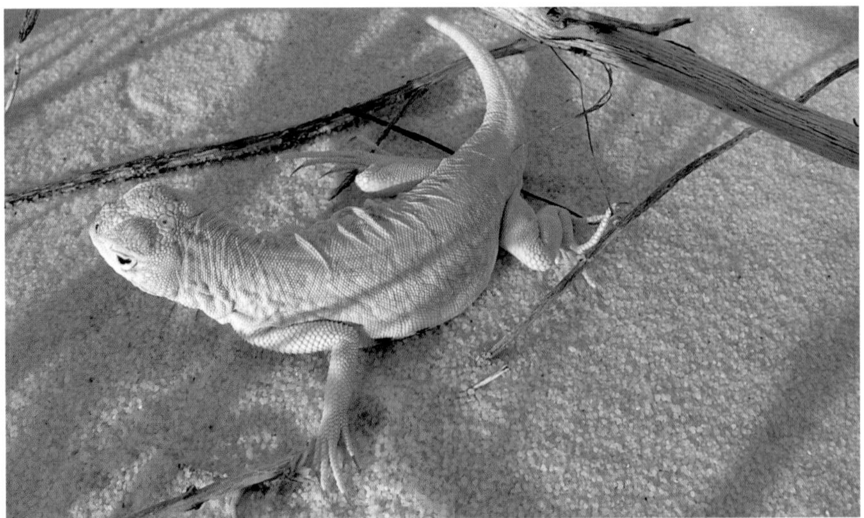

Male H. maculata ruthveni. *The Bleached Earless Lizard is a subspecies or color phase matching the gypsum sand dunes, White Sands National Monument, Otero Co., NM.*

ferent populations of *H. maculata* has been consistently measured at between 3,000 and 4,500 m^2, and individuals can overlap by as much as 60%. Overlapping home ranges may be a result of low individual site fidelity and may increase the probability of mating opportunities. Field-based experiments with *H. m. ruthveni* have shown that males of this species can discriminate among females with different breeding color intensities. Field experiments also suggest mate discrimination among members in different populations: males from the White Sands population will preferentially display to White Sands females when experimentally presented with a choice among mates. The White Sands formation is geologically young (approximately 6,000 years old). So it is particularly noteworthy for studies of speciation that White Sands populations of *H. maculata* have rapidly adapted to this environment and may have a mechanism for choosing like-colored mates.

Range: This species occurs across the central and southwestern U.S. from western Nebraska south to northern Durango, Mexico, and southeastern Kansas west to about Prescott, Arizona.

Viewing Tips: This species is well background-matched, so patience is required for viewing. Individuals can be spotted in areas where prairie dog and kangaroo rat burrows are prevalent. Early morning tends to be a good time for viewing, when individuals are warming on sunny hillocks. When startled, this species will run short distances, then remain motionless—approaching slowly at this point can afford close-up views.

One of the easiest places to view this species is at White Sands National Monument (NM), where the light-colored form is abundant. The more typical darker form can be found along Highway 80 from Douglas, Arizona, to the New Mexico border.

Taxonomy: *Holbrookia maculata* was originally described from 2 specimens collected in Adams County, Nebraska. Since the original description, numerous subspecies have been recognized. Recent morphological and genetic data suggest as many as 6 independent lineages are currently grouped as *H. maculata.* The taxonomy of this genus is confusing, and future taxonomic revisions are likely.

Subspecies and Variation: There is considerable disagreement on the taxonomic placement and nomenclature of species and subspecies of *Holbrookia*. The standard used in this book includes 6 subspecies: Speckled Earless Lizard (*H. m. approximans*), Bunker's Earless Lizard (*H. m. bunkeri*), Great Plains Earless Lizard (*H. m. maculata*), Prairie Earless Lizard (*H. m. perspicua*), Huachuca Earless Lizard (*H. m. pulchra*), and Bleached Earless Lizard (*H. m. ruthveni*). The specific epithets *bunkeri*, *maculata*, and *perspicua* are generally agreed upon as being valid names in most uses for *H. maculata*, but *approximans*, *pulchra*, and *ruthveni* are more controversial. See the Taxonomy and Nomenclature section for more details. To avoid confusion, there are no subspecific designations shown in the map.

Holbrookia maculata shows considerable morphological variation. Populations across the Colorado Plateau are smaller, with more dorsoventral flattening and shorter tails. Populations from the Cabeza de Vaca Basin in southern New Mexico and extreme western Texas are larger than other populations, with pronounced ventral lateral bars and highly developed dorsal tail chevrons. Populations from the Peloncillo and Pendregosa mountains have relatively longer tails and a high prevalence of ventral tail striping (unique to this species). Populations of *H. maculata* from areas south of the Río Conchos, Mexico, are larger, lack prominent ventral lateral bars, and exhibit slight dorsoventral flattening. Individuals from White Sands National Monument may be nearly white.

Gravid female H. maculata, *Mescalero Sands, Chaves Co., NM.*

Banded Rock Lizard

Petrosaurus mearnsi (Stejneger, 1894)

Author: Eric A. Dugan

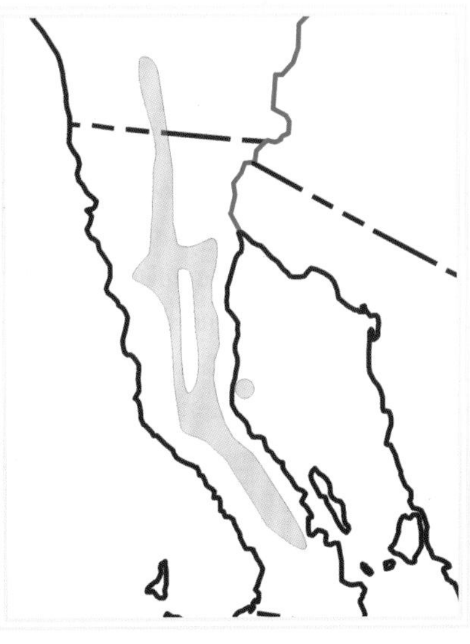

See page 559 for map color codes.

Description: A relatively small lizard, with a flat triangular head, a dorsoventrally compressed body, and a banded tail that is longer than the body. Adult size ranges from 75 to 85 mm SVL. Scales on the limbs and tail are keeled, and body scales are small and granular. Head scales are enlarged and flat. Coloration is gray-brown on the dorsum and blue to tan on the ventral surface. A distinct narrow black neck band (not bordered in white) and banded tail aid in field identification of the species. Pink-white spots are found on the throat. Five weak to moderately distinct bands are located between the forelimbs and the base of the tail. **Sexual Variation:** Males tend to have a vibrant and distinctly colored throat compared to females. During the breeding season, gravid females develop orange coloration on the head above the eyes and on the throat. **Juveniles:** Juveniles resemble the adults in coloration and morphology.

Adult P. mearnsi, *Anza-Borrego Desert State Park, CA.*

Similar Species: Adult *P. mearnsi* are relatively easily identified. However, juveniles may be confused with adult Baja California Brush Lizards, a smaller yet similar species found in the same habitats as *P. mearnsi*. Baja California Brush Lizards lack the black neck band and banded tail of *P. mearnsi*.

Adult P. mearnsi, *San Diego Co., CA. Lizards of this genus are aptly called rock lizards.*

Habitats: This species is restricted to the Baja California Peninsular Ranges. Almost exclusively a rock-dwelling species, it is confined to habitats with abundant rock. Common inhabitants of deep canyons with steep rocky faces, Banded Rock Lizards are frequently observed along washes, riparian areas, and desert palm oases, where large boulders and vertical rock faces provide fissures and cracks for refuge. Individuals have been observed from sea level to 2,000 m. Areas devoid of rocks are avoided, as locomotion in these areas in difficult.

Natural History: The entire rock lizard group is renowned for its climbing ability. This lizard spends the majority of its time climbing or basking on large boulders and rock faces. Primarily an insectivore, the Banded Rock Lizard will prey upon anything it can overpower, including bees, flies, caterpillars, beetles, and spiders. However, this species has also been observed feeding upon leaves, flowers, and juvenile Common Side-blotched Lizards.

They are generally active from March through October, but a period of inactivity or brumation has been noted from late fall to early spring. However, individuals from southern populations may become surface-active on warm fall and winter days. During brumation, rock cracks and fissures are used for refugia. Throughout the active season, individuals emerge during morning hours to thermoregulate and begin feeding. Breeding occurs during the spring months, with egg-laying commencing in the summer. Clutches ranging from 2 to 6 eggs are laid between June and August. Neonates begin to appear as early as August after a 60-day incubation period. Neonates begin to forage as soon as they hatch, eating a similar diet to that of adults. Sexual maturity is likely reached after 2 years.

This can be an extremely wary species, rendering a close approach difficult at times. When alarmed they simply relocate to the other side of a rock, trying to avoid capture and predation. Males will defend a small territory from other males, displaying a wide variety of behaviors including head bobbing, biting, and chasing during territorial defenses. Home range sizes were estimated at 0.008 ha for males and 0.004 ha for females. The home range of a single adult male may overlap with the home range of numerous females, if ample resources are available. Predators include snakes, mammals, and birds. Given their extreme mobility in rocky habitats, individuals are most likely to be preyed upon at night while sleeping.

Range: Banded Rock Lizards occur throughout the arid portions of the Peninsular Ranges in Baja California, Mexico, and southern California. Numerous populations have been confirmed as far north as the San Gorgonio Pass, near the town of Cabazon. They range as far south as Bahía de Los Ángeles, Baja California. It is likely that they occur farther south, given the uniform nature of the habitat. A single insular population has been recorded from Isla Muerto, Baja California.

Adult P. mearnsi, *San Diego Co., CA.*

Viewing Tips: This species is best viewed by walking slowly among large boulders and rocks. Individuals are often observed moving or sunning on the sides of large boulders. The use of a spotting scope or binoculars will result in the best viewing opportunities. Small groups

Juvenile P. mearnsi, *San Diego Co., CA.*

of rock lizards are often observed sunning at the edge of a rock fissure during the morning. After they warm up, individuals will disperse and begin feeding. Habitats that contain surface water are ideal for observing rock lizards. In these situations, several adults may be observed foraging for insects near the water's edge. Patience is at a premium if you intend to capture one, as they have the uncanny ability to stay just out of reach. Palm Canyon in the Anza-Borrego Desert State Park is a great place to view (and not touch) this species.

Taxonomy: Although this species was described as a species of *Uta*, it was later placed in the genus *Streptosaurus*, but now its placement in the genus *Petrosaurus* is well accepted.

Subspecies and Variation: There are no subspecies currently recognized. Dorsal ground coloration varies across the range of this species. Populations inhabiting lightly colored granite rocks usually have bluish ground coloration. Populations that occupy dark volcanic rocks have dark brown ground coloration. In the dark populations, white spots on the dorsum result in a more spotted than banded appearance. Color pattern appears to vary in a manner allowing the species to be highly cryptic in any given environment. The population occurring on Isla Muerto in the Sea of Cortez lacks the turquoise caudal scales found on peninsular populations. They also have a more boldly patterned gular region.

Blainville's Horned Lizard

Phrynosoma blainvillii Gray, 1839

Author: Tracey K. Brown

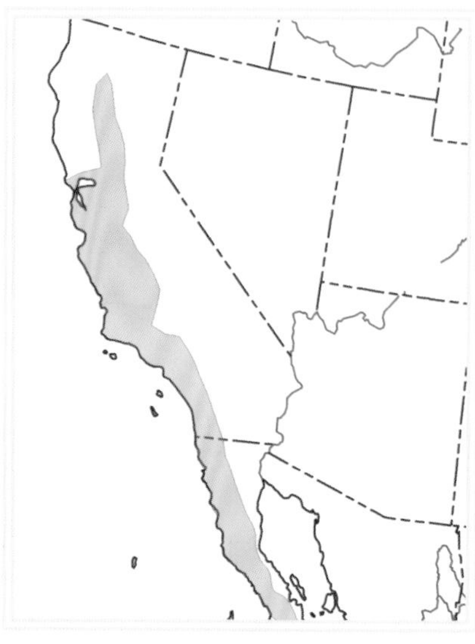

See page 559 for map color codes.

Description: This medium-sized horned lizard may be up to 110 mm SVL and 45–55 g in mass (gravid females up to 70 g). The pair of large, bony occipital horns (~ 10 mm in adults) is separated by a small scale. The dorsum of this species is very spiny, and 2 rows of fringe scales line the lateral edge of its dorsoventrally flattened abdomen. Body color is quite variable, but often includes hues of browns, tans, or reds. There are paired transverse blotches of a darker color, often edged in white, along the back, and a large dark blotch also occurs under each of the 2 largest occipital horns. Venters are smooth and pale, often with small dark dots or blotches; some individuals have a strong yellow hue. **Sexual Variation:** There are few differences between the sexes, although the largest individuals are almost always female, and males have 2 enlarged post-anal scales, evident even in hatchlings. **Juveniles:** Hatchlings (~ 25–30 mm SVL) resemble small adults in color, but have proportionally larger heads and small occipital horns.

Female P. blainvillii, *Lakeside, CA.*

Similar Species: Blainville's Horned Lizard is easily distinguished from other horned lizard species in or near its range by its double row of lateral fringe scales (vs. single row in Desert Horned Lizard) or the lack of a dorsal stripe (vs. Flat-tailed Horned Lizard).

Habitats: The defining characteristics of Blainville's Horned Lizard

Male P. blainvillii, *Lakeside, CA. Until recently, this species was called the Coast Horned Lizard,* P. coronatum, *so most of the literature refers to those names.*

habitat are widely spaced shrubby vegetation, a supply of native ants (typically harvester ants), and soils loose enough for the lizards to bury themselves. Although commonly associated with coastal sage scrub, this species inhabits a surprising array of other habitats. Dense chaparral stands, conifer, hardwood and mixed woodlands, and coastal dunes are all potential locations for this species. They occur from sea level to about 2,500 m elevation.

Natural History: The activity season for this species begins when males emerge from brumation in late March, followed by females about one month later. During late spring males tend to travel farther and more frequently, presumably in search of females. Daily activity begins when individuals first reveal their heads, and later bodies, to raise body temperatures. Following a short basking period, individuals often travel to a few harvester ant mounds for foraging and then resume basking. They retreat deep into shrubs midday on hot days, and often have a short afternoon period of activity before burying themselves for the night. Native ants comprise the majority of prey items for this species, although other insects are taken opportunistically.

Adult P. blainvillii, *McCain Valley, San Diego Co., CA.*

Although not territorial, individuals tend to remain in a given area (~ 1.0–2.5 ha) throughout the year, and male and female activity ranges can overlap. Courtship involves ritualized head bobs, tail movements, and chasing. Males will actually grab a female's occipital horns with his mouth and flip her over before mating belly-to-belly. Males typically begin summer aestivation by the end of July and may not be encountered until the next year. In early summer females lay a single clutch of 6–20 eggs in a burrow they dig themselves over several days. Females actively forage throughout summer to regain mass before beginning brumation in mid-September. Hatchlings emerge in late July or August and actively forage into November to fuel their growth; they reach reproductive size after about 20 months. No individuals are typically seen from mid-November until mid-March. Whether burying themselves for aestivation or brumation, individuals bury themselves only about 5–10 cm under soil and leaf litter. Despite their horns and thorny bodies, there are many predators of this species, including most carnivorous mammals, birds of prey, Greater Roadrunners, shrikes, and large-bodied snakes.

Range: This westernmost horned lizard species is found from north-central California south into northern Baja California. It can be found along the western Sierra Nevada foothills from Butte County south to Kern County, and along the coastal plains and inland valleys from San Mateo and Contra Costa counties south into Baja California. In southern California, the range of this species includes nearly all of San Diego, as well as western portions of San Bernardino and Riverside counties.

Viewing Tips: Blainville's Horned Lizards are notoriously difficult to find, owing to their cryptic coloration, scalation, and behavior. They may be observed on dirt roads early in the day, as they seem to use available roads for travel and finding mates. Individual *P. blainvillii* from southern California populations seem to avoid perching on rocks, while some individuals in other populations actively use rocks as perches. Successful searching for *P. blainvillii* often comes from logging many hours in appropriate habitat, during mid-morning hours of the late spring and early summer periods. Search in appropriate habitat within the Angeles and Cleveland national forests (CA), Henry W. Coe State Park (CA), and Mission Trails Regional Park in San Diego (CA).

Taxonomy: The taxonomy of horned lizards along coastal California and Baja California has been revised repeatedly. At one time, all of these lizards were called Coast Horned Lizards and placed in the *P. coronatum* species, with 4 or 5 recognized subspecies. Two of these subspecies, *P. c. frontale* and *P.c. blainvillii*, were found in northern and southern California, respectively (splitting just north of Los Angeles by the Transverse Ranges), and readers may still come across these names. Recently, both California subspecies and a northern Baja California subspecies were synonomized into *P. blainvillii* and are now called Blainville's Horned Lizards.

Remarks: This species is among the 11 (of 17) horned lizard species that can squirt blood from a sinus located behind each eye as an anti-predator defense. California populations are in severe decline because of habitat destruction from human development and the introduced Argentine Ant (displaces native ants), which Blainville's Horned Lizards will not readily eat. Owing to this decline, this species cannot be internationally traded (CITES), is a California Species of Special Concern, and is included in many southern California multiple species conservation planning programs.

Juvenile P. blainvillii, *Sweetwater, CA.*

Texas Horned Lizard

Phrynosoma cornutum (Harlan, 1825)

Author: Wendy L. Hodges

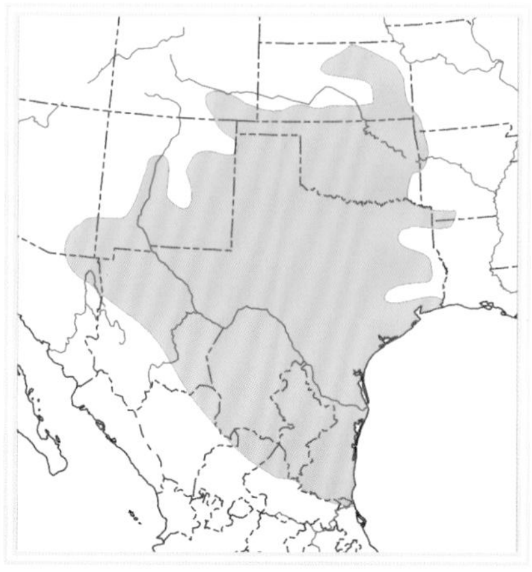

See page 559 for map color codes.

Description: Texas Horned Lizards are medium-sized, reaching 90–130 mm SVL. Tail length is about half as long as SVL. They are wide-bodied, dorsoventrally flattened, covered with keeled and granular scales, and have 2 rows of abdominal fringe scales. Background color varies from dark red to light tan. Yellow and white highlights border dark spots or chevron patterns around pyramidal scales on the back, and they have a pale middorsal stripe. Dark lines radiate from the eye to the upper lip and over the head. Their most distinctive features are their horns, which are bony extensions of the cranium. Two central occipital horns are longer than 3 pairs of temporal horns that are adjacent to them. A short horn between the occipitals is often present. They have horns above the eye and along the margin of the lower jaw. **Sexual Variation:** Adult females are larger than males. Males in breeding condition have prominent femoral pores and wider tail base. Males do not have enlarged post-anal scales. **Juveniles:** Young hatchlings have a larger head in proportion to their body size, although their horns are poorly developed and their bodies appear less spiny. They tend to be drab in color and show less pattern than adults.

Adult P. cornutum, *Willcox, Cochise Co., AZ.*

Similar Species: This species may be confused with other phrynosomatids. They differ from spiny lizards (*Sceloporus*) by their cranial horns and wide body shape. They contrast from other sympatric horned lizards (*P. modestum*, *P. hernandesi*, and *P. solare*) by a single pair of long occipital horns, 2 rows

Adult P. cornutum, *Sierra Co., NM. This species has disappeared from much of its range.*

of abdominal fringe scales, pyramidal dorsal scales with 4 distinct keels, and a single row of enlarged gular scales.

Habitats: Texas Horned Lizards live in the Chihuahuan Desert and southern Great Plains in a variety of habitats including arid and semi-desert grasslands, chaparral, and thorn scrub. Habitat components include cacti, yuccas, mesquites, acacias, grasses, oaks, and junipers. They are predominantly ground-dwelling on sandy or rocky substrates, but seek refuge in subterranean burrows and vegetation. They occur at elevations from 0 to about 1,830 m.

Natural History: Texas Horned Lizards produce clutches of 13–50 eggs, averaging 25. Body size largely determines clutch size—bigger females produce bigger clutches. Mating occurs in the spring to late summer; eggs are laid and hatch from midsummer to early fall. Hatchlings are small, 19–21 mm SVL. Seasonal activity varies based on geographic location. Southern populations are active February to late October, while northern populations are active from May through September. Early and late in the active season, lizards are out during midday but switch to a bimodal daily pattern during the hottest months.

Two-thirds of their diet consists of ants, primarily harvester ants, which are large ants that live in large colonies with foraging trails radiating out from a central hole or cone. This species can detoxify ant venom, which is lethal to small mammals and other reptiles. Texas Horned Lizards can eat other toxic insects such as blister beetles and velvet ants, but the remaining third of their diet consists of insects such as beetles and grasshoppers. They obtain water metabolically, by licking dew off vegetation or the substrate, and by harvesting rainwater. Predators include reptiles (rattlesnakes, whipsnakes, Long-nosed Leopard Lizards), mammals (Coyotes, foxes, grasshopper mice), and birds (shrikes, hawks, Greater Roadrunners). Predation among hatchlings is very high, while adults are protected by their horns and spines. Texas Horned Lizards employ many defenses ranging from passive camouflage (lying perfectly still and flat) to inflating their bodies with air and assuming an attack or shielding position. The most impressive behavior is blood squirting. The latter is usually restricted to canid predators but also happens in 4–5% of human encounters.

Texas Horned Lizards occupy a home range that includes other horned lizards, ant colonies, and appropriate vegetation. Home range size varies by sex and depends on available resources. During mating season, males expand their home range in search of females. Males are aggressive toward each other at this time, especially in the presence of females, but they are not territorial. During copulation, males grasp females by their occipital horns.

Juvenile P. cornutum, *Mescalero Sands, Chaves Co., NM. Note how the proportions usually differ in juvenile lizards, and horned lizards tend to have smaller horns as juveniles.*

Adult P. cornutum, *western TX.*

Range: *Phrynosoma cornutum* occurs in the midwestern and southern U.S. and northern Mexico. It ranges from central Kansas, extreme southwestern Missouri, and the southeastern corner of Colorado southward and westward through most of Oklahoma and Texas (including coastal barrier islands), the southeastern portion of New Mexico, and the southeastern corner of Arizona to the Mexican states of Sonora, Chihuahua, Durango, Coahuila, Nuevo León, Tamaulipas, San Luis Potosí, and Zacatecas.

Viewing Tips: Texas Horned Lizards can be difficult to spot, as they rely on camouflage for protection. They are easier to see in open habitats because they run a short distance when approached on foot. They bask in the morning on rocks, small berms, or clumps of grass. During the heat of the day, they can be spotted at the base of plants or in small shrubs. Occasionally they are found under rocks. Texas Horned Lizards are found on many public lands throughout the range, including Chaparral Wildlife Management Area (TX), Caprock Canyon State Park (TX), Cimarron National Grasslands (KS-CO-OK), and White Sands National Monument (NM).

Subspecies and Variation: No subspecies are recognized. Texas Horned Lizard colors and patterns vary between individuals and populations and closely match substrate and vegetation. Some lizards show vibrant highlights on their dorsal surfaces, while others lack bright colors.

Remarks: Texas Horned Lizards have been collected by humans since Europeans settled the western U.S. Settlers moved populations into east Texas, Louisiana, and as far as Florida and the Carolinas. In the 1950s and 60s, so many horned lizards were collected that Texas passed laws banning their exportation. Today they are protected in most states, and though over-collection has ended, populations continue to decline from a combination of factors: loss of habitat, chemicals used to kill insects, and invasion of nonnative species like red imported fire ants. If you encounter a horned lizard, please do not remove it from its habitat.

Pygmy Short-horned Lizard

Phrynosoma douglasii (Bell, 1829)

Authors: Megan E. Lahti and Daniel D. Beck

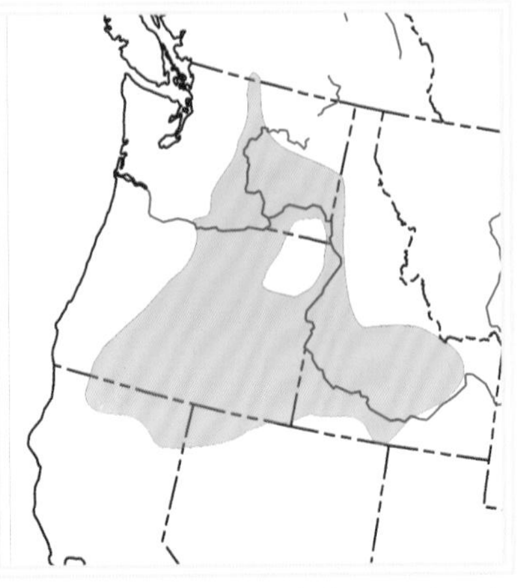

See page 559 for map color codes.

Description: The Pygmy Short-horned Lizard is easily recognized by its round body, relatively short limbs and tail, and small occipital horns that appear more like nubbins. They have one row of lateral fringes and enlarged scales that project from their dorsal surface. The Pygmy Short-horned Lizard is cryptically colored. Dorsal coloration is primarily brown and gray with patchy or spotty regions accented with yellow, white, orange, black, and sometimes red. Adults reach no more than 62 mm SVL; however, most adults are 40–50 mm SVL and weigh about 6.5 g. **Sexual Variation:** Males are smaller than females and can be distinguished from females by the presence of enlarged post-anal scales, pronounced femoral pores, and a rounded bulge extending from the base of the tail, where the hemipenes are housed. **Juveniles:** Neonates average 22 mm SVL, weigh 0.8 g, and typically lack the brighter coloration seen in adults.

Juvenile P. douglasii.

Similar Species: The Pygmy Short-horned Lizard is similar to other horned lizards, but is only sympatric with the Desert Horned Lizard in the southeastern portion of its range. It can be distinguished from the Desert Horned Lizard by its extremely reduced horns and smaller body. The Pygmy Short-horned Lizard is easily distinguishable from other lizards by its rounded body form, relatively short limbs and tail, presence of occipital horns, and cryptic coloration.

Adult P. douglasii, *Kittitas Co., WA. Until fairly recently* P. hernandesi *was included within* P. douglasii, *but the ranges of the two species are different.*

Habitats: The Pygmy Short-horned Lizard is the only horned lizard currently found exclusively in the U.S. It occurs in the Pacific Northwest (east of the Cascade Crest) and primarily inhabits shrub-steppe but also occurs in openings within high-elevation pine forests and piñon/juniper woodlands. Common vegetation associated with shrub-steppe habitat includes Big Sage, buckwheats, Stiff Sage, and Bluebunch Wheatgrass. Although much shrub-steppe habitat has been converted to agriculture, lizards can still be found in farm fields, particularly in patches of exposed basalt rocks and native vegetation. They occur at elevations ranging from 300 to 2,200 m.

Natural History: The Pygmy Short-horned Lizard is the smallest horned lizard. Unlike many other horned lizard species, the Pygmy Short-horned Lizard's distribution is not limited to the vicinity of harvester ant mounds. Although its diet consists primarily of ants, individuals consume many non-ant insects and arthropods including grasshoppers, beetles, spiders, and true bugs.

Populations vary greatly in density, ranging from less than 2 up to 15 lizards/ha. Although adults are non-territorial, they are usually moderately spaced across the terrain. They tend to occupy localized home ranges throughout their activity season and show a clumped movement pattern within those home ranges. Males appear to have larger home ranges during spring, which may serve to increase their chances of encountering females. Neonates remain within close proximity to their birthing sites throughout the activity season and during overwintering.

Adults and yearlings emerge from overwintering in early May and are most frequently observed in June when breeding activity peaks. This species is viviparous, as are many high-elevation and high-latitude species, and females typically give birth to 3–15 neonates from July to September. Mating is suspected to occur up to 2 times during years with sufficient rainfall.

These lizards are most active during the afternoon in spring and fall, while in summer they are most active during early morning and early evening. During summer, neonates are active throughout the day. They begin to brumate in September and by mid-October most are in brumation. Neonates are commonly encountered near their mothers, are active longer throughout the day, and enter brumation later than adults. When threatened, these lizards employ a variety of anti-predatory behaviors including pausing, burial into substrate, hissing, inflating the body, jumping, and gaping. Blood-squirting has not been reported in the Pygmy Short-horned Lizard.

Range: The Pygmy Short-horned Lizard occurs east of the Cascade Mountains throughout Washington and Oregon and into the southern half of Idaho. Its southern range extends into northeastern California and northwestern Nevada. Historically it was reported in south-central British Columbia, Canada; however, it is presumably extirpated there, since no records have been validated since the early 1900s.

Viewing Tips: Look for this species on the ground at the periphery of vegetation or open patches such as roads on warm days, especially in the morning. They are most easily observed by walking throughout the terrain, as they are very cryptic and do not typically move until you are within 1–2 m. They are fairly easy to catch by hand, since they do not sprint long distances. Noteworthy places to look for these lizards include Quilomene Wilderness Area (WA), Hart Mountain National Antelope Refuge (OR), Lava Beds NM (CA), and Craters of the Moon National Monument (ID).

Adult P. douglasii, *Siskiyou Co., CA.*

Taxonomy: Prior to 1997, the Pygmy Short-horned Lizard was considered a subspecies of *P. douglasii,* along

Adult P. douglasii, *Grant Co., WA.*

with 2 other currently recognized species: the Greater Short-horned Lizard (*P. hernandesi*) and the Rock Horned Lizard (*P. ditmarsi*). These 3 species and the Mexican-Plateau Horned Lizard (*P. orbiculare*) belong to the short-horned lizard clade. This clade is distinguished by body-size reduction, horn-length reduction, and an absence of blood-squirting.

Subspecies and Variation: Currently no subspecies are recognized. Local variation in pattern and coloration has been observed that corresponds with terrain coloration. Those encountered in sandy, brown soils typically lack the orange, white, and yellow coloration and instead have an overall browner and more muted coloration. In contrast, lizards that occupy more ferrous or rocky soils with cryptobiotic crust, mosses, and lichens have brighter colors and vivid color patterns. Also, lizards occupying lava fields, such as Craters of the Moon National Monument (ID), often have near-black dorsal coloration.

Remarks: Since its reclassification, minimal research has been conducted on the Pygmy Short-horned Lizard. Much research on this species needs to be done, since basic life history information is not known. Habitat alteration and weed infestations are considered the primary threats behind population declines. Fortunately, this lizard appears more resiliant to habitat alterations than other horned lizard species, likely due to its more generalized feeding habits.

Goode's Horned Lizard

Phrynosoma goodei Stejneger, 1893

Author: Daniel G. Mulcahy

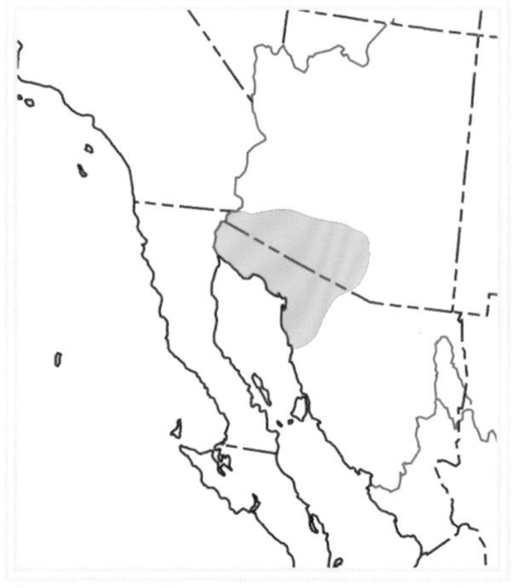

See page 559 for map color codes.

Description: Goode's Horned Lizards are flattened dorsoventrally, with adults reaching 65–90 mm SVL, and the tail is more than twice the length of the head. Two rows of lateral abdominal fringe scales are present, with the ventral row much smaller and diminishing posteriorly. There are 3 enlarged temporal horns, the second slightly larger than the first, with the third nearly the same size as the occipital horns. There are 2 occipital horns oriented upward, outward, and posteriorly. The ear opening is completely covered by scales, the last 3 chin shields are enlarged, and there are 7–10 femoral pores. Dorsal color pattern is variable and usually matches the native background. There are typically 2 rows of dorsal spots, sometimes forming wave-like patterns, and no prominent dorsal stripe, but sometimes a faint, pale stripe is present. The ventral surface has sparse, faint flecking, generally more concentrated on the chin and chest, and no umbilical scar in adults. **Sexual Variation:** Females lack enlarged post-anal scales, femoral pores are smaller than in males, and the base of the tail is not broad, as in males. **Juveniles:** Juveniles are similar to adults, but may show an umbilical scar on the ventral surface.

Adult P. goodei, *Sonora, Mexico.*

Similar Species: Goode's Horned Lizard is similar in appearance to the Desert Horned Lizard and shows some characteristics of the Flat-tailed Horned Lizard.

Adult P. goodei, *Mohawk Valley, Yuma Co., AZ. Until recently, this species was considered the Desert Horned Lizard (in part),* P. platyrhinos. *Another common name of* P. goodei *is Sonoran Horned Lizard.*

In fact, *P. goodei* is known to hybridize with *P. mcallii* in the Yuma Desert. Goode's Horned Lizards can be easily distinguished from the Flat-tailed Horned Lizard by the lack of a dark dorsal stripe. Also, *P. mcallii* has 2 complete rows of lateral fringes, an immaculate ventral surface, and an umbilical scar in adults. Hybrid individuals may show a mix of these characteristics (e.g., presence of a dorsal stripe and flecking on the venter). It is more difficult to distinguish *P. goodei* from *P. platyrhinos.* Desert Horned Lizards have only one row of lateral fringes, a wave-like dorsal pattern (as opposed to spots), occipital horns that are directed posteriorly, ventral surface with prominent flecking, and an ear opening usually not covered by scales, although some as far north as Nevada and Utah have concealed ear openings.

Habitats: Goode's Horned Lizards are typically associated with sandy areas and dunes, but are also found on pebbly bajadas, the edges of dry lake beds, and desert pavement, including volcanic substrate. They are found from near sea level to about 915 m.

Natural History: Very little is known about the natural history of *P. goodei*; most aspects are generalizations from other horned lizards, particularly from *P. platyrhinos.* Ants make up about 90% of the diet, whereas other insects are occasionally taken. Adult *P. goodei* may be found typically from February to September, with breeding taking place in March and females producing one to 2 clutches per year, averaging 2–10 eggs per clutch, with later clutches being smaller. Hatchlings, 20–30 mm SVL, emerge July-August, and may be active to early November. Predators include a variety of carnivores ranging from hawks, shrikes, Greater Roadrunners, and other birds, to Coyotes, Kit Foxes, Long-nosed Leopard Lizards, snakes, and even large spiders. Goode's Horned Lizards are not known to squirt blood from the eyes. They dig horizontal, D-shaped burrows, for retreat during the heat of the day and at night. Adults usually brumate toward the end of September, but may also aestivate during the hot dry months (June–July).

Range: Goode's Horned Lizards are found south of the Gila River in southwestern Arizona, as far east as Avra Valley west of Tucson, west to the Yuma Desert east of the Colorado River, and along the coastal areas of northwestern Sonora, Mexico, to about Bahía Puerto Lobos. Their presence in California has not been detected; however, anecdotal evidence suggests this species may occur in Baja California Norte near Puertecitos.

Viewing Tips: Goode's Horned Lizards can be "tracked" on sand dunes in the early morning and late afternoon hours, when temperatures are below ~ 32°C. Their tracks are characterized by the footprints being slightly farther apart than in most other lizards and by lack of a prominent tail-drag, but with subtle arcs between the footprints, made by the sides of their bodies. Follow tracks in the directions of movement, away from the pushed-up edges of sand. Another way to find these lizards is to slowly drive roads and look for them basking, especially on berms at the edges of dirt roads. Areas where this species can commonly be found in Arizona include the western slope of the Gila Mountains, the Mohawk Dunes, the Tule Desert near Pinta Playa sand dunes, BLM lands north of the Barry M. Goldwater Range, and along Highway 85 south of Ajo into the northern portion of Organ Pipe Cactus National Monument and Avra Valley Road (near Tucson).

Generally, arthropods are prey for horned lizards, but a Giant Hairy Scorpion can easily handle this young P. goodei.

Adult P. goodei, *southwestern AZ.*

Taxonomy: The Goode's Horned Lizard was described as a distinct species in the late 1800s, but in the early 20th century it was placed as a subspecies of *P. platyrhinos.* Recent genetics work has shown that *P. goodei* is distinct. Based on morphology, researchers have allied *P. platyrhinos* (including *goodei*) with the Round-tailed Horned Lizard (*P. modestum*), but mitochondrial genetics allied *P. platyrhinos* (and *goodei*) with *P. mcallii.* More recent work shows nuclear genetic data agrees with the morphology.

Subspecies and Variation: There are no subspecies of the Goode's Horned Lizard and very little is known about geographic variation other than color patterns generally matching the substrate.

Remarks: Where Goode's Horned Lizard and the Flat-tailed Horned Lizard hybridize in the Yuma Desert, there is a gradient of pebbles from the western slope of the Gila Mountains to sand east of the Colorado River. The 2 species co-occur, and hybrid individuals have been found where these soil types merge. Based on molecular data and the morphological intermediacy of *P. goodei,* between *P. platyrhinos* and *P. mcallii,* it was hypothesized that the species *P. goodei* may be of a "hybrid origin"—that is, resulting from hybridization between *P. platyrhinos* and *P. mcallii.*

Greater Short-horned Lizard

Phrynosoma hernandesi Girard, 1858

Author: Wendy L. Hodges

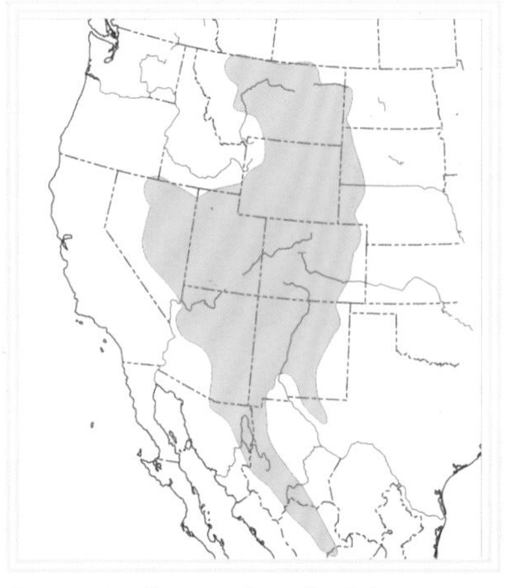

See page 559 for map color codes. Subspecies not differentiated.

Description: Greater Short-horned Lizards are small to medium-sized, reaching 50–112 mm SVL. The tail is less than half the length of the body. Their most distinctive feature is the head, which is wider than long and heart-shaped. The back of the head is enlarged or flared out and tipped with small horns. Two central occipital horns are very short, widely separated by a deep notch, and often do not extend as far back as 3 (occasionally 4) pairs of temporal horns. Greater Short-horned Lizards are wide and dorsoventrally flattened, covered with rows of keeled and granular scales and one row of abdominal fringe scales. Background color and dorsal patterns vary extensively throughout this species' range, generally matching the background soils. Paired dorsal spots or blotches along the midline are often present and outlined by lighter colors. **Sexual Variation:** This species shows pronounced sexual size dimorphism, especially in northern populations, where adult males are significantly

Juvenile P. hernandesi, *Cochise Co., AZ. The hatchlings lack the lateral fringe scales of the adult.*

Adult P. hernandesi, *Cochise Co., AZ. This taxon was recently split out from* P. douglasii, *so that should be considered when consulting older literature. The range of these 2 species is different.*

smaller than females. Males have 2 large post-anal scales and an enlarged tail base. Femoral pores in males are more prominent, especially in fully mature adults. **Juveniles:** Young Greater Short-horned Lizards tend to be dull in coloration relative to adults, though on close inspection they show intricate background patterns. Their heads appear larger relative to their body size, and their cranial horns are not developed.

Similar Species: Greater Short-horned Lizards may be confused with other horned lizards in areas of sympatry (*P. cornutum, P. modestum, P. platyrhinos,* and *P. solare*) but can be distinguished by the cranial horns. This species has the shortest occipital horns that are widely separated rather than elongated and sharp.

Habitats: Greater Short-horned Lizards live in a variety of habitats, including short-grass communities of the Great Plains, sagebrush and greasewood communities of the Great Basin, semi-desert and plains grasslands of the Mexican Highlands, and the arid Colorado Plateau. They also occur in montane environments, including coniferous and evergreen forests. The species generally lives at high altitudes and may be found between 600 and 3,200 m.

Natural History: *Phrynosoma hernandesi* are viviparous and give birth to an average litter size of 16 neonates. Shortly after birth, young disperse: they do not have maternal care. Neonates range in size from 25 to 32 mm SVL. Because they live in colder climates at high altitudes and latitudes, Greater Short-horned Lizards have very short growing seasons, and females are not sexually mature until the season after their second brumation. Males are sexually mature at a younger age than females. Females delay sexual maturity, giving them more time to grow before investing in reproduction, which allows them to reach a larger adult body size than males.

Greater Short-horned Lizards are active April to September, with some early- and late-season activity in favorable years during March or October. They can be active at colder temperatures than most lizards—when air temperatures are as low as 1.5°C—and manage relatively high body temperatures ranging from 25 to 41°C. This species' diet consists primarily of ants, with beetles contributing a substantial portion. Large invertebrate prey, like grasshoppers and crickets, are eaten opportunistically only by larger lizards. Because large lizards have large heads, they can eat a broader range of sizes of prey than small lizards, which are restricted to small prey. Females typically eat a broader diet than males because females are larger. This species is capable of squirting blood defensively at canid predators such as Coyotes. Additional predators include grasshopper mice, rattlesnakes, Glossy Snakes, Northern Goshawks, American Kestrels, and other birds of prey, which elicit defensive behaviors excluding blood squirting.

Range: *Phrynosoma hernandesi* is a wide-ranging species and occurs from southern Alberta and Saskatchewan, Canada, through the western U.S. states of Montana, Wyoming, Utah, Colorado, Arizona, New Mexico, and Texas, and into northeastern Sonora, Chihuahua, and Durango, Mexico. In the U.S., the range also extends to the western edges of North and South Dakota and Nebraska and may occur in the southeastern corner of Idaho.

Female P. hernandesi, *Santa Cruz Co., AZ. In its montane setting, it matches the native background.*

Viewing Tips: Greater Short-horned Lizards are easier to see in open habitats because they will run a short distance when approached on foot. Hiking trails are good places to see them as they run to seek refuge in nearby rocks or grass. On hot days they are found in the dappled shade of forests or moving between grass clumps in open areas. In early morning, they will bask on east-facing hillsides and perched on top of rocks with their

Male P. hernandesi, *in a semi-desert grassland of the Apachean Ecoregion, Santa Cruz Co., AZ.*

backs to the sun. These lizards can be seen in most national parks and forests in the western U.S. including Guadalupe Mountains National Park (TX), Gila National Forest (NM), Tonto National Forest (AZ), and Ouray National Wildlife Refuge (UT).

Taxonomy: This species has been a member of the "Short-horned Lizard" taxon, *Phrynosoma douglasii*, throughout most of its history, with up to 6 subspecies recognized. The arrangement and definition of species and subspecies have changed as information about its geographic range, morphology, and molecular diversity has accumulated. The single "Short-horned Lizard" taxon was split into 2 species, *P. hernandesi* and *P. douglasii*.

Subspecies and Variation: Two subspecies are currently recognized, *P. h. hernandesi* (Hernandez's Short-horned Lizard) and *P. h. brachycercum* (Smith's Short-horned Lizard). They are separated primarily by location; *P. h. brachycercum* has an entirely Mexican distribution and occurs in Chihuahua and Durango, Mexico, while *P. h. hernandesi* includes the remaining distribution in Mexico, U.S., and Canada. *Phrynosoma h. brachycercum* has a shorter tail than *P. h. hernandesi*. Greater Short-horned Lizard populations vary in coloration and pattern: some show little pattern and single background colors of brown or grey, while other populations show intricate background patterns of small dots and mosaics of bright colors including orange, yellow, white, red, blue, and green.

Flat-tailed Horned Lizard

Phrynosoma mcallii (Hallowell, 1852)

Authors: James C. Rorabaugh, Kevin V. Young

See page 559 for map color codes.

Description: The Flat-tailed Horned Lizard has a squat, roundish body and prominent cranial horns. Distinguishing markings include a dark, middorsal stripe, 2 dark round spots on each side of the vertebral line, and a venter that is uniformly white to cream colored with the exception of a prominent umbilical scar. Maximum SVL is 87 mm and tail length is about 38% of total length. **Sexual Variation:** Males have enlarged post-anal scales. **Juveniles:** They resemble small adults, but the head is proportionally larger, the horns proportionally smaller, and the tail relatively short. Juveniles measure 30–64 mm SVL.

Similar Species: The only other horned lizards known to occur with the Flat-tailed Horned Lizard are the Goode's Horned Lizard and Desert Horned Lizard, which are best distinguished from the Flat-tailed by shorter occipital horns and absence of a dark, middorsal stripe.

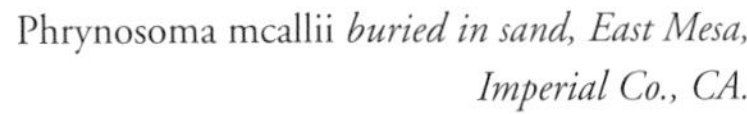

Phrynosoma mcallii *buried in sand, East Mesa, Imperial Co., CA.*

Habitats: This lizard thrives in some of the hottest and most barren examples of the Sonoran Desert. It attains its greatest abundance below about 230 m in broad, sandy valleys, sparsely vegetated with Creosote Bush and White Bursage. Substrates are typically fine sands, often silica, but in large unstable dunes the species is not abundant and may be absent. On the upper edges of its range, where this species is often sym-

Adult P. mcallii, *Gran Desierto, Sonora, Mexico. This species lives on or near stabilized sand dunes.*

patric with the Goode's and Desert Horned Lizards, soils are typically coarser and vegetation communities can be richer, with occasional trees and Ocotillos. The Flat-tailed Horned Lizard can also be found in badland habitats in California and Sonora.

Natural History: Among horned lizards, Flat-tails have the most ant-specialized diet. An individual may consume hundreds of harvester ants per day, yet it will readily eat other prey that is abundant and easy to capture (such as small beetles or caterpillars). Flat-tailed Horned Lizards typically deposit a single scat each morning. The scat is cylindrical, fragile, and composed of ant body parts, and can be useful in determining horned lizard presence. Mating typically occurs in May and June. Females have been observed to travel far from their home range to dig a deep (80–100 cm) burrow, lay eggs, and then return. Typically 4–6 hatchlings per clutch emerge from July through October. When resources are abundant, 2 clutches may be laid. If ants are in good supply, hatchlings can attain adult size by the following spring, but in general, breeding is delayed until the second year. Home range can be large and unstable, but is smaller and more stable when lizard density is high. Flat-tails are active all day in spring and fall, but during the summer, most of the day is spent in a 20–30-cm-deep burrow that the lizard digs. It emerges in the early evening and typically spends the night fully exposed on the surface, perhaps helping it begin activity earlier in the morning. This species does not squirt blood from its eyes. It is generally docile when handled, although it can use its horns forcefully on occasion.

Range: In California, the Flat-tail's range extends from the Coachella Valley southeast to the Imperial and Borrego valleys, where it occurs west into Anza-Borrego Desert State Park and east to Glamis and Ogilby. In Baja California it occurs on the eastern edges of Laguna Salada and Andrade Mesa between Mexicali and Algodones. In Arizona, the species is found in the Lower Colorado subdivision of the Sonoran Desert near Yuma, from Yuma south and east to the bajadas of the Gila and Butler mountains. The range extends south into the valleys of the Gran Desierto of Sonora from San Luis Río Colorado south and east to Bahía San Jorge or beyond. The species has disappeared from most of the Coachella Valley and other developed areas, such as the croplands of the Imperial, Yuma, and Mexicali valleys.

Viewing Tips: The Flat-tailed Horned Lizard is very cryptic and tends to freeze or shuffle under the sand when approached. Even where it occurs in relative abundance, inexperienced observers are unlikely to find more than one per day while searching on foot. Those trained to recognize the sign of this lizard, particularly its tracks, can significantly improve detection rates. Searching along the crest of mud hills in badlands can be effective in the early morning, and searching along columns of ants may also be helpful. Searching on paved or unpaved roads through their habitat can also be an effective way to find them. The species is most likely to be encountered from April through September when air temperatures are 25–37°C, but adults may be active as

Male P. mcallii, *near Yuma, AZ. This species is of conservation concern due to habitat destruction and development.*

Juvenile P. mcallii, *near Salton Sea, CA.*

early as mid-February and as late as mid-November, and juveniles can be found active during warm winter days. Good places to view these lizards include East Mesa, West Mesa, and the Yuha Desert in Imperial County, California.

Taxonomy: The Flat-tailed is closely related to the Goode's and Desert Horned Lizards. Apparent hybrids of *P. mcallii* with *P. goodei* and *P. platyrhinos* have been found southeast of Yuma, Arizona, and near Ocotillo, California, respectively.

Subspecies and Variation: There are no subspecies, and color variations among populations are subtle. In badlands, individuals tend to be brownish gray instead of orange-hued, with a less prominent vertebral stripe. Very rarely, the dark middorsal stripe and spots may be absent in lizards from the Coachella Valley.

Remarks: About 43–50% of this species' habitat in the U.S. has been lost to urban and agricultural development, and some remaining habitats have been degraded by off-highway vehicles and other human activities. Habitat loss is less in Mexico, but substantial losses have occurred locally, particularly in the Mexicali valley. The lizard is listed as threatened on Mexico's list of species at risk and is protected by the states of Arizona and California. Ten state and federal agencies in California and Arizona cooperate through a conservation agreement to protect the species and its habitat in the U.S. If you find this species in the wild, photograph it and count yourself lucky, but do not collect it.

Round-tailed Horned Lizard

Phrynosoma modestum Girard, 1852

Author: Wendy L. Hodges

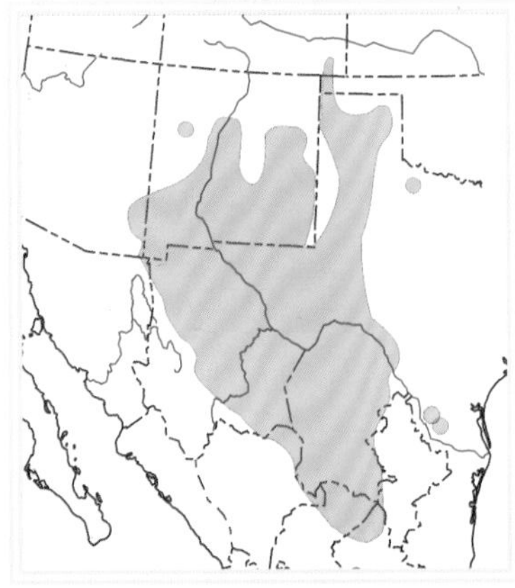

See page 559 for map color codes.

Description: This is a small, delicate lizard, reaching about 50–70 mm SVL. The tail is slender and round in cross-section (hence the common name), with a series of dark bars breaking up the background color; it is about half the length of the body. Dorsal coloration is variable, usually matching the substrate. No dorsal stripe is present, but dark blotches can be present on the neck and along the side of the body where the abdomen and hind legs meet. This species has a round body shape when viewed from above, but it is flattened dorsoventrally. Two occipital horns are the same length as adjacent temporal horns. An additional series of very short horns extends from the longer temporal horns to just below the eye. Other cranial spines or horns are small and poorly developed. This species lacks abdominal fringe scales, and the dorsal scales are not developed into spines. Dorsal scales may be enlarged and flattened or keeled and arranged as rosettes irregularly scattered. The majority of scales are granular. **Sexual Variation:** Males have enlarged post-anal scales. **Juveniles:** The head appears large for the body size of small hatchlings, but the tips of the horns are usually not well developed until the end of the first year. Color patterns are often muted, and the dark patches on the neck and torso are small.

Juvenile P. modestum, *Durango, Mexico.*

Similar Species: To the casual observer, a Round-tailed Horned Lizard may superficially look like an earless lizard (e.g., *Cophosaurus*), but on further inspection it is easily dif-

Adult P. modestum, *with a gray ground color, Culberson Co., TX.*

ferentiated by the cranial horns. The species is readily distinguished from sympatric *Phrynosoma* (*P. cornutum*, *P. solare*, *P. hernandesi*, and *P. solare*) by the lack of abdominal fringe scales and the arrangement of the posterior cranial horns that essentially form a straight line behind the head. The lack of dorsal patterning and presence of a round, striped tail are species identifiers.

Habitats: Round-tailed Horned Lizards live in the Chihuahuan Desert and southern Great Plains. They may be found in a variety of arid and semiarid grasslands and shrublands. Components of their habitat include cacti, yuccas, acacias, Creosote Bush, and grasses. They are ground-dwelling on predominantly rocky or gravelly substrates in bajadas and on arroyo slopes. They occur at elevations from about 180 to 2,225 m.

Natural History: Round-tailed Horned Lizards are egg layers and produce 6–19 eggs (12–13 on average). Mating occurs early after emergence from brumation. Egg deposition occurs between May and July with young hatching from July to October, coinciding with summer monsoon rains. Males and females are reproductively active at small body size, around 40 mm SVL. They may reach this size from hatching to first brumation and can be reproductive in less than one year. Brumation occurs from late October to the following March or April and active seasons vary with geographic location. They are active during the day from morning through early evening. They begin basking and then seek shade in midday when surface temperatures exceed 40°C. They seek refuge in burrows or climb under and into shrubs, where they can continue foraging.

Round-tailed Horned Lizards are ant eaters and 67–88% of their diet consists of ants. They can eat large harvester ants, but may prefer smaller species like honey pot ants (*Myrmecocystus*) or big-headed ants (*Pheidole*). Additional arthropods make up the remaining diet, with termites, true bugs, and insect larvae more commonly consumed than other taxa. Round-tailed Horned Lizards have many predators including collared lizards, Loggerhead Shrikes, Greater Roadrunners, and grasshopper mice. Their smaller body size and relatively short horns offer less protection than that of other horned lizards. The primary means of defense is camouflage. Color patterns mimic substrate conditions, and individuals show extreme changes in pattern intensity and hue. Dark neck and posterior-lateral body blotches provide shading patterns, and in concert with the ability to hunch their backs, they can mimic stones with amazing precision. These animals, when perfectly still, seem to disappear in front of your eyes. Trials with canids and humans suggest they are unable to squirt blood like some other *Phrynosoma*.

Range: *Phrynosoma modestum* occurs from extreme southeastern Colorado and western Oklahoma through west Texas and into New Mexico and southeastern Arizona. The species range extends south into the Mexican states of Chihuahua, Coahuila, Zacatecas, and San Luis Potosí.

Adult P. modestum, *orangish individual from orangish soils, Marijilda Canyon, Graham Co., AZ.*

Juvenile P. modestum, *Tamaulipas, Mexico.*

Viewing Tips: Round-tailed Horned Lizards are among the most difficult lizards to observe. They are masters of crypticity. When in their range and appropriate habitat (rocky substrates), look for them within a small area, approximately one square meter, around your feet as you walk. They will only scurry a few inches away from your steps at the last moment. They may be seen by driving very slowly along small paved roads. Look for them on top of vegetation clumps in late morning during their active season or on the internal branches of small shrubs in the middle of the day. You may see this species at Seminole Canyon State Park (TX), Big Bend National Park (TX), Lower Swift Trail and Marijilda Canyon, Pinaleño Mountains (AZ), and White Sands National Monument (NM).

Subspecies and Variation: No subspecies are recognized. Individuals and populations vary in dorsal background color, which closely correlates with substrate color. Colors may be white, pale to dark gray, pink, tan, yellow, or hues of blue. Individuals may also have a light peppering of black flecks irregularly scattered throughout the dorsal surface. Ventral surfaces are immaculate white to pale yellow, with some spotting near the vent. Dark blotches on the neck and posterior-lateral body vary in size and shape.

Remarks: This species is understudied, and our understanding of it would benefit from efforts to understand its biology. Though some states regulate the number of individuals that can be collected, the species receives little protection. It can occur in abundance in local populations that can be extirpated by intense commercial collecting. Searches for populations in western Oklahoma suggest the species may be extirpated from the state.

Desert Horned Lizard

Phrynosoma platyrhinos Girard, 1852

Author: Tracey K. Brown

Description: This is one of the smaller, less spiny species of horned lizards. Adults typically weigh 20–25 g and are about 80–85 mm SVL (max 95 mm). The Latin species name recognizes its noticeably blunt snout, making the head seem small for its body size. A single row of lateral fringe scales line the side of its abdomen, and the longest 2 occipital horns do not come in contact with each other at the base. This dorsoventrally flattened species is extremely variable in color, hue, and pattern—traits that often strongly match the soils of its location. Tan, pink, brown, white, and orange are all possible dorsal hues and accents for this species, and dramatic variation within a population is possible. Two large dark blotches occur on the dorsum under the occipital horns. Two or 3 matched pairs of wavy, transverse color blotches typically run down the back; the tail may appear banded. Their venters are pale and minimally

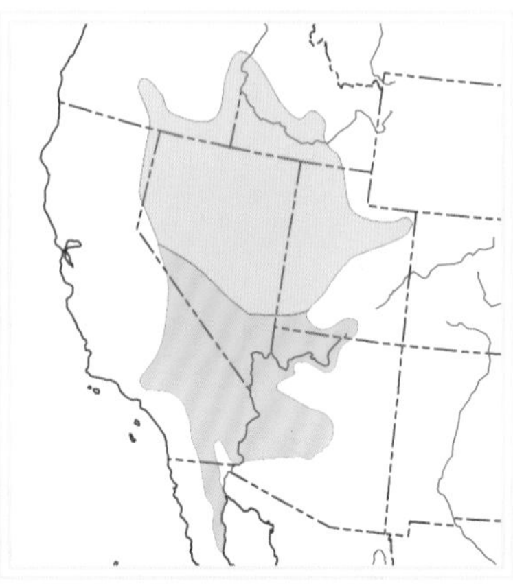

See page 559 for map color codes.

Juvenile P. platyrhinos calidiarum, *Esmeralda Co., NV.*

Adult P. platyrhinos calidiarum, *San Bernardino Co., CA.*

marked, although some spotting is seen on the tail and underside of the legs. **Sexual Variation:** Although similarly colored, males can be distinguished from females by their wider tails and possession of a pair of enlarged post-anal scales. The largest individuals in a population are typically females, especially in the northern part of the species' range. **Juveniles:** Young Desert Horned Lizards resemble adults, although proportionally their heads are larger and occipital horns are shorter.

Similar Species: The range of Desert Horned Lizards grossly overlaps with 6 other horned lizard species; habitat preferences separate many of these species from actual contact. The single row of lateral fringe scales found on Desert Horned Lizards differs from the double row found in Flat-tail and Blainville's Horned Lizards. The 2 large, non-touching occipital horns of Desert Horned Lizards differ from the 4 large, touching occipital horns of Regal Horned Lizards and the nearly absent horns of the Greater and Pygmy Short-horned lizards. Goode's Horned Lizards are very similar, but look for a scale-covered ear opening, a small second row of lateral fringe scales, and occipital horns that point more upward and outward than on Desert Horned Lizards.

Habitat: Desert Horned Lizards inhabit areas characterized by sparse, shrubby vegetation and sandy or loose soils within the Great Basin, Mojave, and Sonoran deserts.

They can be found from below sea level (in desert sinks) to nearly 2,000 m elevation in flatlands, alluvial fans, washes, along dune edges, and even atop volcanic outcrops. Dominant plants in areas used by this species include saltbushes, sagebrushes, Greasewood, and Creosote Bush.

Natural History: Several extensive studies on *P. platyrhinos* were done 30–40 years ago, and much is known about its life history. Large-bodied harvester ants make up the bulk of this species' diet, although other prey items are regularly taken, and they are even known to eat vegetative material. The remarkable ability of this species to endure drought years by curtailing above-ground activity, growth, and reproduction no doubt adds to its long life span (over 7 years in the field). The activity season for this species begins in late March, and adults begin brumation in September in self-dug burrows, found to be up to 500 cm deep in the Mojave Desert. Morning emergence becomes increasingly earlier as the activity season progresses, and daily activity becomes bimodal during summer. Lizards will retreat to shrubs or even rodent burrows during the hottest part of the day and will bury themselves a few centimeters deep in loose soil at the base of a shrub after sunset. Courtship during the late spring and early summer can be elaborate, and females may mate with more than one male. Eggs are laid in a single clutch during June, July, or August, and clutch size averages 8 eggs (maximum of 16). There is evidence that females from southern populations may lay more than one clutch during years with abundant food resources. Hatchlings (~ 25 to 30 mm SVL) emerge after a 45–50 day incubation period. Juveniles do not reach breeding size until their second spring after hatching.

Range: The Desert Horned Lizard's distribution largely overlaps the Great Basin, Mojave, and Sonoran deserts. Found throughout the arid areas of Nevada, the species ranges north into southwestern Idaho and southeastern Oregon, east into western Utah and Arizona, west into the desert portions of eastern California, and south past the U.S. border into northern Baja California and extreme northwestern Mexico.

Viewing Tips: Because this species seems to use road berms and rocks as basking platforms, mid-morning cruising along dirt roads in early summer often results in sightings. If you approach them slowly they will often slowly hunker down; otherwise, they will run a short distance and go into or behind rocks or bushes. Careful searching around the area may reveal these lizards (be careful to not step on them). Good places to view this species include Anza-Borrego Desert State Park (CA), Joshua Tree National Park (CA), and Great Basin National Park (NV).

Subadult P. platyrhinos calidiarum, *at Gila River, in Phoenix, AZ.*

Taxonomy: The Desert Horned Lizard was first described in 1852, and 2 subspecies were recognized about 40 years later. One subspecies was later elevated to the species level, and is now called Goode's (or Sonoran) Horned Lizard. Various other studies have also closely allied Desert Horned Lizards with both Round-tailed Horned Lizards and Flat-tailed Horned Lizards; it is thought Goode's Horned Lizards may have resulted from hybridization between the Desert and Flat-tailed Horned Lizard species.

Subspecies and Variation: The Northern Desert Horned Lizard, *P. p. platyrhinos*, is found mainly in the Great Basin, and the Southern Desert Horned Lizard, *P.p. calidiarum*, inhabits the Mojave and Sonoran deserts; these 2 subspecies are distinguished largely by location.

Remarks: Habitat destruction by off-road vehicles and collection by people for pets are still conservation issues for this species. Collecting one from the wild usually results in its eventual death, as they are incredibly hard to keep healthy in captivity. This species is not known to squirt blood from its eyes.

Regal Horned Lizard

Phrynosoma solare Gray, 1845

Author: Craig S. Ivanyi

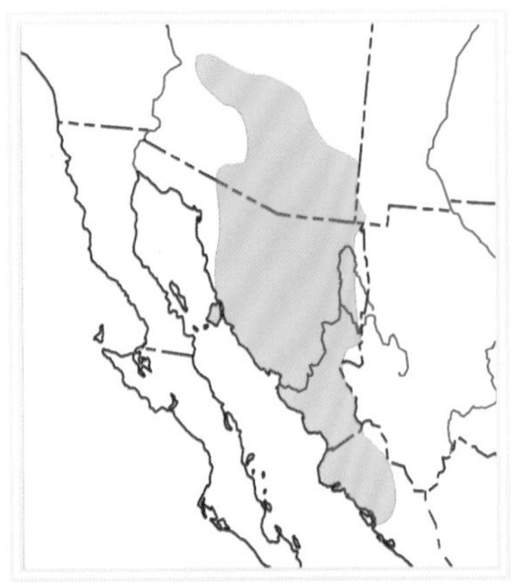

See page 559 for map color codes.

Description: This is a relatively large species of horned lizard, with adults ranging from 75 to over 115 mm SVL. It has 4 large cranial horns ringing the posterior margin of the head, where the bases of the horns are in contact with one another. Dorsally this lizard has matte-finished, strongly keeled scales, several of which are raised, giving it a slightly thorny appearance. Pattern and color range from tan to light brown or rust with brown or black blotches. Laterally, a single row of fringe scales marks the boundary between the uneven, rough dorsal surface and the smooth, shinier ventral scales, which are white to cream with scattered black spots. It may have a distinct or faint middorsal stripe, and the dorsolateral surface has darker shading. **Sexual Variation:** Males are similar in appearance but generally smaller than females, but the base of the tail is visibly distended (especially during the breeding season), due to the presence of large, inverted hemipenes. Males also have enlarged post-anal scales. Older females may lack portions of the horns on the back of the head due to males biting them off during copulation. **Juveniles:** The head (relative to body) is proportionately larger, the horns are not as well developed (much shorter), and dorsal scales are smoother.

Adult P. solare, *Vekol Valley, Maricopa Co., AZ.*

Similar Species: This lizard should not be confused with any others in North America. This is the only Horned Lizard in the U.S. with the 4 large cranial horns in contact with one another at the posterior margin of the head.

Adult P. solare, *Saguaro National Park (Rincon Mountains section), Pima Co., AZ.*

Habitats: The Regal Horned Lizard is primarily a lizard of rocky and gravelly flats and valleys in a variety of arid and semiarid habitats—including Arizona Upland desert scrub, Lower Colorado desert scrub, Chihuahuan desert scrub, semi-desert grassland, and Sea of Cortez coastal scrub. Some specimens occur up into oak and juniper woodlands. This species occurs from sea level to over 1,400 m in elevation.

Natural History: This animal may be active from sunup until after sundown from March to October, when temperatures are around 21–35 °C, avoiding midday heat in desert areas. The Regal Horned Lizard shows a strong preference for harvester ants, which may make up to 90% of its diet. Regal Horned Lizards usually capture their prey with their sticky tongues rather than by grabbing it with their jaws (a more typical way for lizards to capture prey). Harvester ants can sting and have toxic venom, but apparently this has little effect on the lizard, for a variety of reasons. The lizard coats the ants with mucus as they are consumed, and research has shown that the blood of at least some ant-eating horned lizards has the ability to detoxify the venom of harvester ants. Even so, when confronted with a large swarm of ants the lizard usually makes a hasty retreat. Predators can include other lizards, snakes (though more than one snake has died trying to eat such thorny prey), birds of prey, and carnivorous mammals.

Breeding occurs in the spring and summer, with complex courtship behaviors taking place before copulation. Generally, in July or August, the female will burrow in loose soil and generally only lay one (sometimes 2) clutches of up to 33 eggs in this underground chamber. Incubation lasts from 5 to 9 weeks.

Range: The Regal Horned Lizard is found almost exclusively in the Sonoran Desert region from south-central and southeastern Arizona through most of Sonora and northern Sinaloa, Mexico, and on Isla Tiburón in the Sea of Cortez. It also barely enters New Mexico and may occur in Chihuahua, Mexico.

Viewing Tips: The Regal Horned Lizard is extremely well camouflaged and very difficult to see when not moving. Often it is easier if you locate harvester ant colonies, by looking for characteristic clearings and then widening your field of search to a large circle around the ant nest. During the warm (but not hot) times of the day, when ants and lizards are both active, you are much more likely to find a Regal Horned Lizard feeding on ants close to the ant nest. As temperature rises, look for these animals around the base of shrubby vegetation, but be careful where you place your feet; when it's chilly or too hot, this species will burrow in loose soil. Sometimes the head, tail, or even dorsal surface of the abdomen will still be visible. In addition, try driving slowly on roads in the morning or very late afternoon, as it is not uncommon to encounter one on the road. Good locations to look for this species include Saguaro National Park (eastern and western portions adjacent to Tucson, AZ) and lower Swift Trail in the Pinaleño Mountains (AZ).

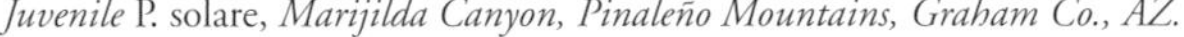

Juvenile P. solare, *Marijilda Canyon, Pinaleño Mountains, Graham Co., AZ.*

Adult P. solare, *Pima Co., AZ.*

Taxonomy: At one time, this species was considered to be most closely related to the Texas and Flat-tailed Horned Lizards. Recent evidence suggests that it is actually more closely aligned with the Flat-tailed and Blainville's Horned Lizards.

Subspecies and Variation: No subspecies or pattern classes are recognized.

Remarks: The Regal Horned Lizard has a variety of defensive tactics, many of which are only used with specific predators. For instance, when confronted by a fast-moving coachwhip, this species stays put and presents the largest part of its body to convince the snake that it's too large to swallow. However, it's likely to flee from an approaching rattlesnake—which suggests that it knows it can outrun the rattler, but *not* the coachwhip! This species can squirt blood from its eyes, an adaptation primarily to ward off canid predators.

Cute as it is, don't be tempted to take one home, as the Regal Horned Lizard does *not* make a good pet. If you want a better chance of having one in your yard, consider curtailing the use of pesticides (which kill off their prey) and prevent dogs and cats from having access to them.

Dunes Sagebrush Lizard

Sceloporus arenicolus Degenhardt and Jones, 1972

Author: Lee A. Fitzgerald and Charles W. Painter

See page 559 for map color codes.

Description: The Dunes Sagebrush Lizard is a relatively small *Sceloporus*, with males reaching 65 mm SVL and females only slightly smaller. The dorsal scales are keeled and pointed; scales on the rear of the thigh are granular. There are 41–52 scales around the mid-body; the supraoculars are separated from superciliaries and the median head scales by one or more rows of small scales; femoral pores number 9–16 on each leg, with 8 or more scales separating the most medial pores. The ear opening is partially covered by 6 or 7 scales. The dorsum is light golden brown or yellowish, with a faint gray-brown band extending from ear opening to tail. The venter is white or cream-colored. **Sexual Variation:** Mature males have widely separated blue patches on the venter; the chin coloration is reduced or absent. Breeding females have yellowish to orange lateral coloration from the throat to the base of the tail. **Juveniles:** Hatchlings and juveniles are similar in dorsal coloration to adults, with white venter.

Similar Species: The Prairie Lizard in the Mescalero Sands is difficult to distinguish unless in the hand. The 2 species differ in number of scales separating the medial ends of the femoral pores; the Prairie Lizard generally has 7 or fewer scales, whereas the Dunes Sagebrush Lizard has 8 or more. Some individuals of the Side-blotched Lizard may exhibit coloration similar to the Dunes Sagebrush Lizard, but have a blotch on the flank behind the front limbs.

Female S. arenicolus, *Winkler Co., TX.*

Male S. arenicolus, *Mescalero Sands, NM. Shown here on leaves of Shinnery Oak, a critical component of the sand dunes it inhabits.*

Habitats: Dunes Sagebrush Lizards are habitat specialists and occur only in sand-dune complexes dominated by Shinnery Oak. Shinnery Oak dunes support dense stands of Shinnery Oak and scattered Sand Sage as co-dominant plant species. The Shinnery Oak sand-dune landscape is created by a dynamic interaction between sand dunes and these stunted trees growing within them to create a unique configuration of dune topography and open sandy depressions called sand-dune blowouts. Dunes Sagebrush Lizards have an extremely strong affinity for sand-dune blowouts and do not occur within thickets of Shinnery Oak. Elevation ranges from about 775 to 1,400 m.

Natural History: Dunes Sagebrush Lizards are most active from mid-April through October. They feed on various invertebrates such as spiders, ants, beetles, grasshoppers, and crickets. Activity peaks during May and June, then declines as summer temperatures increase. Habitat selection studies showed they avoid microhabitats that are too hot, such as south-facing slopes in small blowouts. They disproportionately prefer large, deep blowouts and apparently do not occur across large areas where the composition of sand is relatively fine. Dunes Sagebrush Lizards are well adapted to living in loose sand. They readily dive into the sand as an escape behavior and often sleep buried under sand. Individuals that were radio-tagged routinely moved several meters underneath the sand.

Mating occurs from May to early July. Males are territorial and compete for females; they often have bite marks and scars from fighting. Females likewise show bite marks and scars from mating attempts by males, but are not territorial and have overlapping home ranges. After mating, females develop the yellowish-orange coloration. Females may reproduce once or twice in a season, laying clutches of 3–6 eggs in mid-June, and again in late July or early August. Based on radio-tracking studies, females move out of their immediate home range to nest and construct nests about 18 cm deep in the loose sand, at the interface between moist and dry sand. Hatchlings appear in late July and live in sand-dune blowouts, behaving similarly to adults. Some, but not all, females may reach sexual maturity the following spring; the smallest mature female documented was 49 mm SVL. Dunes Sagebrush Lizards usually live 3–4 years.

Dunes Sagebrush Lizard probably diverged from its Common Sagebrush Lizard ancestors during formation of Shinnery Oak sand-dune landscapes in the late Pleistocene. Recent genetics research revealed differences among populations, with limited gene flow between these groups. It appears the northern populations are youngest; thus expansion may have occurred from south to north, giving rise to the present distribution.

Range: *Sceloporus arenicolus* is endemic to Shinnery Oak sand dunes, referred to as the Mescalero Sands in southeastern New Mexico and the Monahans Sandhills in adjacent Texas. In New Mexico, the species exists as fragmented populations within an area of about 2,313 km^2 in parts of Chaves, Eddy, Lea, and Roosevelt counties. In Texas the distribution is patchy; Dunes Sagebrush Lizards have been found there in parts of Andrews, Crane, Gaines, Ward, and Winkler counties.

Viewing Tips: This species can be observed by walking through sand-dune blowouts in Shinnery Oak sand-dune complexes and looking ahead for lizards running upslope into the Shinnery Oak. They are more readily found in large, deep sand-dune blowouts. Specific localities include the BLM Caprock Wildlife Area, 61 km east of Roswell (NM) and the Monahans Sandhills State Park (TX).

Ventral patches of a male S. arenicolus, *Mescalero Sands, NM.*

Subadult S. arenicolus, *Chaves Co., NM.*

Taxonomy: This species was originally described as *Sceloporus graciosus arenicolus* in 1972. Reports of *S. g. graciosus* from New Mexico and Texas were determined in 1960 to be *S. arenicolus*. Based on modern phylogenetic analyses of *Sceloporus* lizards using genetic and morphological information, and its isolated distribution, the Dunes Sagebrush Lizard is now considered a valid species.

Subspecies and Variation: No subspecies of *S. arenicolus* are currently recognized.

Remarks: The Dunes Sagebrush Lizard is currently listed as endangered by the New Mexico Department of Game and Fish. The species is threatened by landscape fragmentation and Shinnery Oak removal. Experts believe these disturbances degrade areas of suitable habitat by disrupting the interaction between Shinnery Oak and moving sand, which forms and maintains open sand-dune blowouts. Dunes Sagebrush Lizards disappeared from areas where Shinnery Oak was removed by herbicides, and areas with high densities of oil wells and caliche roads were shown to have fewer Dunes Sagebrush Lizards than undisturbed areas.

Twin-spotted Spiny Lizard

Sceloporus bimaculosus Phelan and Brattstrom, 1955

Author: Robert G. Webb

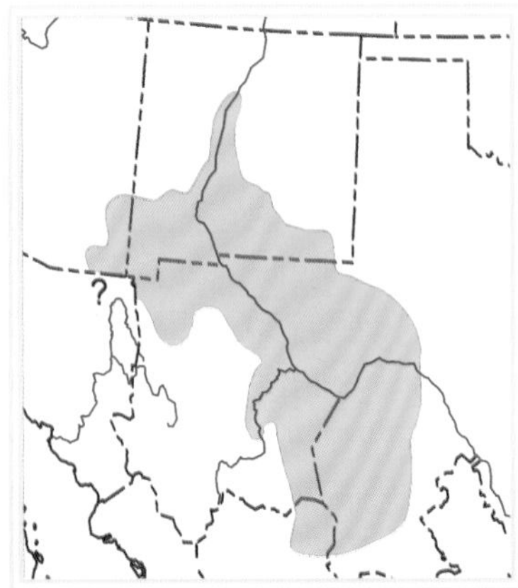

See page 559 for map color codes. May occur in Sonora. There are different interpretations of taxonomy, nomenclature, and range for this species complex.

Description: These are relatively large, rather stocky, spotted, and generally yellowish to grayish-brown lizards. Adult males attain a larger size (at least 121 mm SVL) than females (103 mm SVL). The tail is at least 130% of the SVL. The dorsal body scales are large, strongly keeled and spinose; the belly scales are smaller and less pointed. The 5–7 scales extending backward over the ear opening are large and pointed. The head has a dark line extending posteriorly from under the eye. The spotted body has distinct paravertebral rows of rather large dark brown blotches (may be staggered or confluent across the back) that may fade posteriorly and on the tail. Pale areas just below these blotches may be aligned to suggest indistinct dorsolateral stripes. The lower side of the body may be orangish and have a row of smaller, brown blotches and other markings, some arranged as vertical bars. A black, vertically oriented, wedge-shaped mark occurs on each side of the neck in both sexes. The limbs are dark-streaked in adults. Dorsal scales average about 32 (range 30–34) and femoral pores per hind leg about 13 (range 11–15). **Sexual Variation:** In males, the black wedge-shaped marks are broadened ventrally and may be continuous across the throat; dorsally these marks are narrowed and may partly fuse with blackish dorsal blotches to form a broken collar. Adult males have larger femoral pores than females and have dark blue throats and large black groin patches bordering blue belly patches, which may meet midventrally. In

Male S. bimaculosus, *Brewster Co., TX.*

Male S. bimaculosus, *Potrillo, Doña Ana Co., NM. Until recently, this taxon was generally considered a subspecies of* S. magister, *and some authorities still consider it so.*

females, the black wedge-shaped mark is unmodified, not extending dorsally or ventrally. Dark-streaked limbs are not as prominent as in males. **Juveniles:** Juveniles have dorsal patterns not unlike that of adults, except dark streaking on the limbs is absent. Ventral surfaces are whitish and immaculate.

Similar Species: These lizards may occur in the same general area inhabited by other large spiny lizards, including Clark's and Crevice Spiny Lizards. The range of the Desert Spiny Lizard abuts that of the Twin-spotted Spiny Lizard in southeastern Arizona and that of the Texas Spiny Lizard in west Texas. The divided supraoculars; broad, black, white-bordered collar; and contrasting black and white tail bands distinguish Crevice Spiny Lizards from these 4 species. Twin-spotted Spiny Lizards differ from Clark's in having distinct paravertebral rows of dark brown blotches on the back, and black-streaked limbs (instead of narrow dark crossbands on the forearms), while adult females lacking both blue throats and blue, black-bordered, ventrolateral patches on the belly. Twin-spotted Spiny Lizards differ from Texas Spiny Lizards in having the 2 posteriormost enlarged supraoculars in contact with the medial head scales. Aside from genetic data, Desert Spiny Lizards differ from Twin-spotted Spiny Lizards in that adult males have a black or deep-purple middorsal stripe (about 4.5–5 scales wide) bordered by light stripes.

Juvenile S. bimaculosus, *Columbus, NM. The twin spots are sometimes easiest to discern in juveniles.*

Habitats: This species is largely terrestrial and confined to the desert scrub landscape in parts of the Chihuahuan Desert. These lizards may occur on semi-isolated patches of large rocks and boulders, on lava flows, or in relatively thick, shrubby vegetated areas, either in dry canyons and arroyos or along rivers and streams; known Texas localities indicate a concentration along drainage basins. Often they are associated with low, dense mesquite bushes and associated mammal burrows (which are used for escape) and commonly with woodrat nests. Twin-spotted Spiny Lizards have arboreal tendencies, climbing at least Saltcedar and mesquite trees, as well as upright wooden structures (abandoned ruins, sheds, etc.), and basking atop fence posts. Elevations range from about 427 m (TX) to 1,980 m (NM).

Range: Twin-spotted Spiny Lizards occur in southeastern Arizona (as far as the Whetstone Mountains), southern New Mexico (northward along the Rio Grande drainage), west Texas, and south into northern and eastern Chihuahua, western Coahuila (and probably extreme northeastern Sonora), and northeastern Durango (north of Nazas River).

Natural History: These lizards bask and feed after emergence from winter brumation. The activity season may extend from late March into November. Body temperatures of active lizards average about 33–35°C. Food is primarily insects (ants most frequent), but also spiders and some plant material. Ingestion of hatchling lizards (same and other species) is also reported. The species exhibits territoriality and habitat fidelity. Both sexes probably are sexually mature near 80 mm SVL at an age of about 21–23 months, with some females reproductive in the season after the first brumation. Females lay eggs and some may have more than one annual clutch of eggs. Reproductive activity (mating through egg-laying) extends from early spring into late summer. Egg clutches may number 2–19, averaging about 6–7, with the larger (older) females averaging about 9 eggs/clutch. In ideal incubation environments, eggs hatch in about 2 months. Hatchlings (about 30–40 mm SVL) may appear from late May into September. Snakes (Coachwhip), Long-nosed Leopard Lizards, Eastern Collared Lizards, and hawks are known predators.

Viewing Tips: Some searching throughout the habitat may be necessary to find these lizards, as their occurrence is often patchy and unpredictable. Binoculars are useful in observing these lizards on sun-exposed surfaces among rock piles (but such perches are quickly abandoned when approached). These lizards may be seen on rock-boulder shoulder areas along roadways. They are also expected in and around ground debris and structures sourced from abandoned man-made construction sites. Good viewing areas in southern New Mexico are the black basaltic bouldered roadsides along the Santa Teresa-Columbus paved highway (County Road A003) and the rims of the volcanic Hunt's Hole and Aden Crater.

Taxonomy: For many years this species was considered a subspecies of the widespread Desert Spiny Lizard, adjacent westward. Recent studies that include genetic information recommend recognition as a distinct species. A colleague has relayed his perception of a large hiatus in genetic samples between Desert and Twin-spotted Spiny Lizard populations.

Female S. bimaculosus, *Columbus, NM.*

Subspecies and Variation: No marked consistent geographic variation has been described in this species. A hybrid specimen with parentage involving the Texas Spiny Lizard is reported from Langtry, Val Verde County, Texas.

Clark's Spiny Lizard

Sceloporus clarkii Baird and Girard, 1852

Authors: Cecil R. Schwalbe and Philip C. Rosen

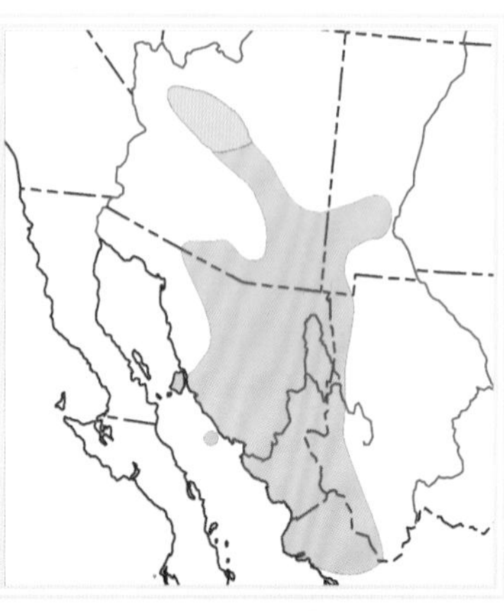

See page 559 for map color codes.

Description: This is a large, stout, sexually dimorphic lizard, with males reaching 144 mm SVL, females 120 mm SVL. The tail is usually uniformly colored (with faint tail rings in some adults) and is 1.33 to 1.5 times SVL. Scales are heavily keeled, pointed, and overlapping. Dorsal ground color is gray or brown, often with a bluish or greenish cast, with distinct blue-green scales sometimes occurring on the back and sides, especially in adult males. Black wedges on each shoulder give an impression of an incomplete collar. Dark bars on each forelimb are diagnostic for this species. The ear openings are covered by 3 backwards-projecting scales, sometimes 4. Lower labial scales are usually separated from the mental scale (see Figure 3) by small scales. **Sexual Variation:** Adult males have blue or green throat and belly patches, often outlined in black, and 2 enlarged post-anal scales. Females often have dark mottling on the throat, but seldom have blue markings on throat or venter. Adult females often retain vestiges of juvenile banding. **Juveniles:** Immature lizards have 5–7 narrow, wavy, dark bands on the back, with similar bands on the dorsal surfaces of the limbs and tail. Juveniles also have the diagnostic banded forearm.

Female S. c. clarkii, *Organ Pipe Cactus National Monument, AZ.*

Similar Species: Desert Spiny Lizards lack dark bars on the forelimbs, have 5–7 scales covering the ear openings, and the lower-labial scales (see Figure 3) touch the mental scale. Yarrow's and Crevice Spiny Lizards both have complete collars, and Crevice Spiny Lizards also have conspicuously banded tails.

Male S. c. clarkii, *Scotia Canyon, Huachuca Mountains, AZ. The turquoise coloration on some scales is commonly seen in adult males.*

Habitats: This lizard is widespread and abundant in oak and pine/oak woodlands between 1,275 and 1,848 m elevation in southeastern and central Arizona and southwestern New Mexico. It occurs as low as 713 m in riparian woodland communities of broadleaf deciduous trees, including mesquites, cottonwoods, willows, ashes, Arizona Sycamore, Arizona Walnut, Netleaf Hackberry, or urban plantings, and is widespread, though less abundant, in Arizona Upland Sonoran desert scrub on productive rock slopes as low as 510 m elevation. Highly arboreal, this species also uses boulders and outcrops regularly and is only occasionally seen on the ground.

Natural History: This is a wary lizard that often shuttles to the far side of a tree trunk or branch or seeks refuge in a hole in the trunk or higher in the tree when a potential predator approaches. Lizards living on rocks hide in crevices or under boulders when pursued. They are active from March or April into October, with activity beginning earlier at lower elevations. Body temperatures of about 34°C are preferred and are actively selected by thermoregulatory behavior in the field, with the lizards usually being at about 32–37°C. Coachwhips and whipsnakes are known to eat Clark's Spiny Lizards, as are the Rock Rattlesnake and the Gray Hawk. The diet consists of a variety of invertebrates, along with occasional leaves, buds, and flowers. In one study, Clark's Spiny Lizards had consumed a variety of invertebrates, especially caterpillars. Seventy percent of the lizards

Ventral patches of a male S. c. clarkii, *Chiricahua Mountains, Cochise Co., AZ.*

had beetles in their diet, 52% had ants and wasps, 48% had hemipterans, 30% had butterflies and moths, 22% had spiders, and 22% had grasshoppers making up a significant portion of the diet. Clark's Spiny Lizards readily eat small Ornate Tree-lizards in captivity and likely in the wild, where they often occupy the same tree.

Yolk production begins between March and mid-May in central Arizona, with egg-laying occurring in June; most females probably produce a single large clutch of 7–28 eggs each year, with averages of 14 and 20 reported in different studies. Clutch weight may make up more than 1/4 of female body weight prior to laying. Hatchling mortality is high, about 90%. One study indicated between-year survivorship for male and female lizards as only 28% and 50%. Reported population densities in an Arizona riparian area varied from 6 to 46 lizards/ha over 6 years.

Range: This species extends from the Mogollon Rim of west-central Arizona and the Mogollon Plateau of southwestern New Mexico southward along the Sierra Madre Occidental to northern Jalisco, Mexico. In New Mexico it is restricted to the southwest corner, with isolated populations in the Alamo Hueco and Little Hatchet mountains. Its northern and western boundaries in Arizona extend to the margin of the Arizona Upland desert scrub near Valentine and in the Growler Mountains. It ranges south in Sonora, Mexico, to the coast near Bahía Kino and on Tiburón and San Pedro Nolasco islands in the Sea of Cortez.

Viewing Tips: Visit almost any Coronado or Prescott national forest lands (AZ) between 1,275 and 1,850 m elevation during April through September and watch for silhouettes of these lizards on tree trunks, often facing head-down. Be alert for their movements as they shift to hide behind the tree trunk! If there are 2 (or more) observers along, the old squirrel-hunting tactic of having one observer stand still while the other circles a tree often works for many arboreal lizards. This species is abundant at many localities in Arizona, including Sabino Canyon, Saguaro National Park (especially in the Rincon Mountains District), and in Chiricahua National Monument and Coronado National Memorial.

Taxonomy: Recent studies of the evolutionary relationships within the genus *Sceloporus* suggested that the Clark's Spiny Lizard's closest relative occurs on the Pacific slopes of southern Mexico, providing further evidence of the tropical affinities of many of our southwestern reptiles and amphibians.

Subspecies and Variation: Two subspecies are recognized. The Plateau Spiny Lizard (*Sceloporus c. vallaris*) occurs north of Payson, Arizona, and differs from the Sonoran Spiny Lizard (*S. c. clarkii*) by its retention of the juvenile banding pattern in adults. A third subspecies, no longer recognized, described lizards in the southern portion of the range. A range-wide analysis of the geographic variation in the species is needed to verify the status and distribution of the forms of this lizard.

Remarks: When it is necessary to capture this species for research or education, telescoping noosing poles up to 5 m long are often used.

Juvenile S. c. clarkii *on a palm tree, San Carlos, Sonora, Mexico. The diagnostic bands on the forearm are easily seen, even in juveniles.*

Prairie Lizard

Sceloporus consobrinus Baird and Girard, 1853

Authors: Megan E. Lahti and Adam D. Leaché

See page 559 for map color codes. Range in Mexico not well known, so not shown.

Description: The Prairie Lizard has spiny, keeled dorsal scales and an incomplete gular fold. The Prairie Lizard is relatively small, reaching about 59 mm SVL in males and about 68 mm SVL in females. Dorsal background color is typically brown or gray, usually accompanied by distinctive light longitudinal stripes. In some populations, the stripes are less distinct and are accompanied by crossbars or chevrons. The blue belly and throat patches are either absent or faint in some populations. **Sexual Variation:** The blue belly patches are narrow and separated widely. Unlike females, males have a swollen tail base and enlarged post-anal scales, and they are typically smaller than females. The blue coloration on the throat and belly is reduced or absent in females. **Juveniles:** Juveniles are similar to adults, although their body proportions are different in that they have relatively larger heads. The blue coloration on the throat and belly is often absent, and the dorsal pattern may be less distinctive or absent.

Similar Species: Prairie Lizards are similar in appearance and color pattern to other small brown *Sceloporus* in the region, particularly those species belonging to the *undulatus* complex (*S. tristichus* and *S. cowlesi*). However, other species in the *undulatus* complex are generally larger and have more blue pigmentation on the throat and belly, sometimes bordered by black. *Sceloporus arenicolus* may be confused with the Prairie Lizard where they co-occur; however, *S. arenicolus* is slightly larger, is restricted to

Pale phase S. consobrinus, *Mescalero Sands, Chaves Co., NM.*

Male S. consobrinus, *Corona, Lincoln Co., NM. The* Sceloporus undulatus *complex was recently split into three southwestern species, which do not coincide well with formerly named subspecies.*

sand dunes/Shinnery Oak complexes, and has more than 12 scales between the medial ends of the femoral pores series.

Habitats: Prairie Lizards are predominantly terrestrial and occupy a wide range of habitats, including prairies, stabilized sand dunes, rocky outcrops, and grasslands. They range in elevation from approximately 0 to 3,000 m. In these habitats, adults are typically found basking on low-lying debris, rocks, or logs that are close to the ground. During temperature extremes, these lizards often retreat to upright vegetation such as yucca plants for refugia from the heat. This behavior also allows them to remain active longer throughout the day than other strictly terrestrial lizards.

Natural History: Prairie Lizards reproduce during early April to early May, and females can lay 1–3 clutches per year. Females lay on average 5.5 eggs per clutch and lay more clutches during years of extended warm temperatures. Neonates first begin hatching in midsummer and can continue into early October, just weeks prior to the onset of brumation. Prairie Lizards generally brumate from late October to March; however, they will occasionally emerge from brumation during periods of warmth during winter.

The Prairie Lizard is primarily insectivorous but also consumes other arthropods. Common prey items include a diversity of ants, beetles, grasshoppers, flies, spiders, termites, and centipedes. Similarly, these lizards also have a diversity of predators

Ventral patches of male S. consobrinus, *Rock Springs, Edwards Co., TX.*

because they occur throughout many habitats. Common predators include snakes, hawks, and larger carnivorous lizards. Badgers, skunks, and other scavengers are known to excavate and consume egg clutches. When startled, the lizards often dart behind an object, circle around it, and peer out to monitor the situation with their sharp eyesight. This behavior is often repeated using other surrounding objects, as the lizard moves so as to maintain a safe distance from the situation.

Prairie Lizards are known to be territorial, and males employ a series of head bobs and push-up displays to warn off intruders. Males display their blue coloration to further warn off intruders, particularly during mating season when competition to mate with females is greatest. Females and juveniles are not territorial, and females are allowed to roam freely throughout male territories.

Range: The Prairie Lizard occurs throughout the central U.S., from the grasslands in eastern New Mexico and eastern Colorado to the Mississippi River, where they occur in forested areas, have arboreal tendencies, and more closely resemble the Eastern Lizard (*S. undulatus*). Their northern range extends into South Dakota and tapers eastward into southwest Illinois, while their southern range extends into San Luis Potosí and Zacatecas, Mexico, and continues northeast to Louisiana.

Viewing Tips: Although Prairie Lizards are not as abundant and easy to find as other members of the *S. undulatus* complex, they are often among the most common lizards encountered where they occur. Look for this species basking on fallen debris, rocks, or clumps of vegetation during morning hours when temperatures are increasing and in the late afternoon when temperatures begin to cool. These lizards are wary, so be sure to make a slow approach if you want a closer look. An interesting spot to look for this species is the Mescalero Sands in southeastern New Mexico, where they can be found on the outskirts of the dunes along with *S. arenicolus* and a number of other reptile species.

Taxonomy: Genetic research has shown that the Prairie Lizard encompasses populations that were previously regarded as the subspecies *consobrinus*, *erythrocheilus*, *garmani*, *hyacinthinus*, *tedbrowni*, *tristichus*, and *undulatus* of the wide-ranging Eastern Fence Lizard (*S. undulatus*). Some of the population boundaries between the Prairie Lizard and adjacent members of the *undulatus* complex remain uncertain.

Subspecies and Variation: This species shows substantial levels of variation in color and color pattern, particularly considering the broad scope of the species distribution throughout the central U.S. Currently, no subspecies of the Prairie Lizard are recognized. Populations at the Mescalero Sands in southeastern New Mexico have a less distinctive dorsal pattern, which is thought to be an adaptation for living on the sand dunes. In Colorado, the Prairie Lizard is suspected of hybridizing with the Plateau Lizard (*S. tristichus*), but this has not been confirmed with genetic data.

Remarks: As with other members of the *Sceloporus undulatus* complex, the population boundaries of this species are currently defined by genetic data. These genetic boundaries do not always agree with traditional concepts of taxonomy based on morphological or ecological variation.

Juvenile S. consobrinus, *Weld Co., CO.*

Southwestern Fence Lizard

Sceloporus cowlesi Lowe and Norris, 1956

Authors: Randall D. Babb and Adam D. Leaché

Description: This is a small, stout lizard of 75 mm SVL with strongly keeled, pointed, overlapping scales. The tail, if unbroken, is about as long as the body. Regenerated tails are shorter and sport a different scale pattern and often different coloration. Scales on the sides of the body are arranged in diagonal rows. The head has average proportions for a typical lizard, with a short snout and a few pointed scales projecting posteriorly from the anterior of the ear opening. Overall coloration or ground color is tan, brown, beige, black, or white. This lizard often appears dark gray or nearly black on cold days or early mornings before warming up. Pattern is somewhat variable, but the dorsum is typically slate gray, bordered on either side by the ground color and a dorsolateral light stripe, which may be broken, running from the base of the head onto the anterior portions of the tail. Ventral surfaces are white or cream with paired dark-edged blue patches on the belly and ventral sides of the throat.

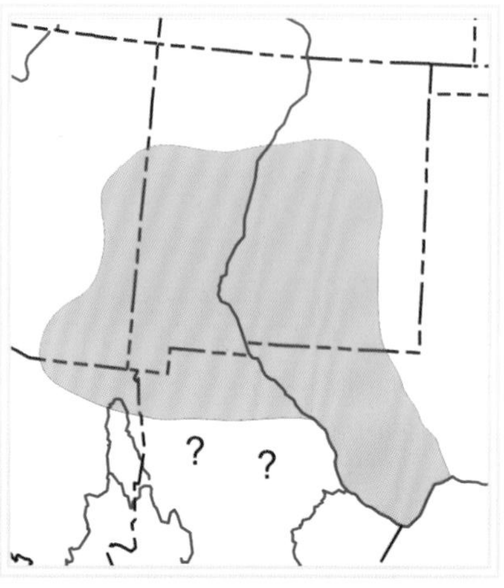

See page 559 for map color codes. Range in Mexico not well known.

Sexual Variation: Males have enlarged post-anal scales, a broad tail base in sexually mature specimens, and a vivid blue belly and throat patches. Females are marked similarly to males, except that the belly patches are faint or absent. Females often have a chubby appearance through much of the warm months due to developing eggs. **Juveniles:** Hatchlings and juveniles have similar color patterns, except they generally lack the blue ventral coloration of males and have a disproportionately large head when compared to adults.

Adult S. cowlesi, *Big Bend National Park, Brewster Co., TX.*

Adult S. cowlesi, *Cochise Co., AZ. Formerly considered within* S. undulatus *taxon.*

Similar Species: The Southwestern Fence Lizard resembles many of the other smaller members of the genus and young of the larger species of the genus. The distribution of this lizard overlaps or abuts that of several similar-sized small spiny lizards, including 2 others of the Eastern Fence Lizard complex. It is essentially identical to the Plateau Lizard and can only be distinguished with certainty by distribution (if away from potential areas of contact) or genetic analysis (in areas where it comes in contact with similar species). The Striped Plateau Lizard lacks the paired blue belly patches and is slightly smaller (70 mm SVL). The Common Sagebrush Lizard differs from the Southwestern Fence Lizard in that it lacks the paired blue throat blotches. Slevin's Bunchgrass Lizard has parallel scalation on the torso (as opposed to diagonal scale rows of other species), is a little smaller with a longer body, and often has distinctive markings.

Habitats: The Southwestern Fence Lizard inhabits the Apachean, Chihuahuan, and eastern half of the Mogollon Rim ecoregions. Within these ecoregions it frequents semi-desert and other grasslands, chaparral, woodlands, and montane conifer forests.

Natural History: This is a diurnal lizard that prefers areas that offer suitable structure for escape from predators and for basking. It is frequently seen basking atop rocks, logs, debris piles, tree trunks, fence posts, or nearly anything it can climb. The same lizard may be encountered day after day as it sits atop its favorite perch. Males defend small territories against other males. Territorial and mating displays consist of head bobs, push-ups, and display of ventral coloration, as is seen in many lizard species. Confrontations between males may result in violent but typically short-lived battles ending with the victor pursuing the defeated combatant. These lizards can be very abundant when habitat conditions are optimal, and in these situations it is not unusual to see a lizard on nearly every rock or log in the area. These small lizards are voracious predators, darting from their resting places to grab ants, grasshoppers, flies, spiders, and a variety of other small invertebrates. Smaller lizards are also occasionally eaten. Southwestern Fence Lizards lay up to 10 eggs during spring and summer months, and adults and young are important prey items for a variety of other wildlife species.

Range: This species is found from southeastern and east-central Arizona eastward through much of New Mexico to southwestern Texas's Trans-Pecos region and adjacent north-central Mexico. The boundaries of its range are imprecisely known due to its strong similarities to other fence lizards. Genetic work done to date has not defined the precise edges of its distribution.

Viewing Tips: Watch for this lizard basking atop rocks, logs, fence posts, or other structures, particularly in the morning. This lizard species is likely to be seen on almost any outing in appropriate habitats during the warm months. This species can often be approached quite closely if the observer moves cautiously. Disturbed animals will typically dart out of sight to the back side of the object they are sitting on. Animals can

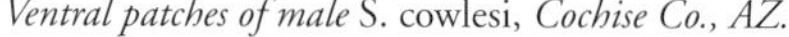

Ventral patches of male S. cowlesi, *Cochise Co., AZ.*

Juvenile S. cowlesi, *Willcox Playa, Cochise Co., AZ.*

usually be easily noosed for closer examination but should be released at the exact spot from which they were captured (note: most states require permits to capture reptiles). Southwestern Fence Lizards are widespread and abundant and can be found on a number of public lands, including the Apache-Sitgreaves National Forest (AZ), in the Gila, Cibola, and Lincoln national forests (NM) and Fort Davis National Historic Site and Guadalupe Mountains National Park (TX).

Taxonomy: Genetic research has shown that the Southwestern Fence Lizard encompasses populations that were previously regarded as the subspecies *consobrinus*, *cowlesi*, and *tristichus* of the wide-ranging Eastern Fence Lizard (*Sceloporus undulatus*). Some of the population boundaries between the Southwestern Fence Lizard and adjacent members of the *undulatus* complex remain unclear. These diverse lizards are part of a multispecies complex, and it is difficult to provide a taxonomy that captures all of the relevant morphological and genetic variation among populations.

Subspecies and Variation: There are no recognized subspecies of the Southwestern Fence Lizard. The dorsal coloration of these lizards is highly variable, and they exhibit a high degree of substrate matching that is presumably a camouflage mechanism. Lizards from White Sands National Monument have immaculate white dorsal surfaces that match the surrounding gypsum sand dunes, and lizards with black dorsal coloration are found on the nearby lava flows at Valley of Fire State Park.

Common Sagebrush Lizard

Sceloporus graciosus Baird and Girard, 1852

Author: Mason J. Ryan

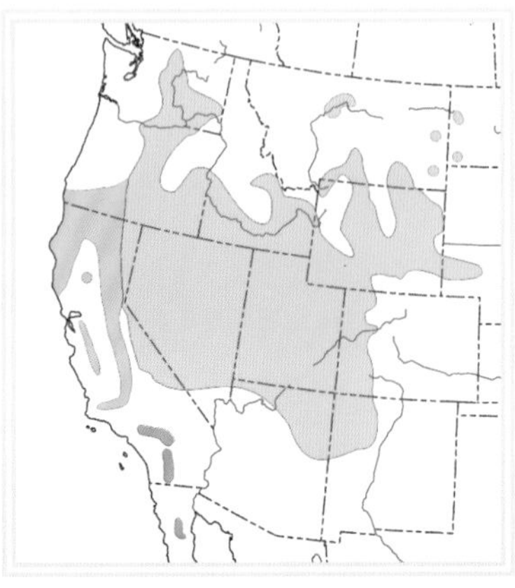

See page 559 for map color codes.

Description: This is a small lizard reaching up to 55 mm SVL and 89 mm TL. It is grayish brown with small, weakly keeled and pointed scales. The scales on the backs of the thigh are mostly granular. The pattern on the back is variable, but usually has black blotches or irregularly spaced crossbars. There is often a dark bar on the anterior portion of the shoulder and sometimes a small rusty patch posterior to the axilla. A broad gray-brown stripe begins behind the head scales and extends to the base of the tail. A lateral or dorsolateral light stripe is usually present. The ventral surface may range from white to a light cream color. **Sexual Variation:** Adult males have a blue throat patch or blue mottling on the throat. The sides of the belly are dark blue and separated by a white mid-ventral stripe. Occasionally the chest and ventral surface of the legs and underside of the tail may possess blue coloring. Adult males also possess enlarged post-anal scales and a swollen tail base. Males in some areas possess bright orange breeding coloration. Adult females have a nearly uniform white to cream ventral surface, but some may possess slight blue mottling on the throat. **Juveniles:** Juveniles are similar to females in overall coloration, but may have faint blue mottling on the throat and stomach.

Juvenile S. g. graciosus, *Grant Co., WA.*

Similar Species: The Common Sagebrush Lizard most closely resembles the slightly larger Western Fence Lizard and Plateau Fence Lizard, but they can be distinguished by scalation and coloration. Common Sagebrush Lizards have smaller and more numerous scales than the other 2 species. Common Sage-

Female S. g. vandenburgianus, *Kern Co., CA. This taxon is often considered a distinct species,* S. vandenburgianus.

brush Lizards also have a black shoulder bar that is lacking in those species. Male Plateau Fence Lizards have paired blue blotches on the sides of the throat. The Common Side-blotched Lizard is superficially similar but can be distinguished by its bluish-black spot behind the forelimbs and its lack of the more strongly keeled dorsal scales.

Habitats: The Common Sagebrush Lizard is found over much of the western U.S. in several ecoregions, including the Great Basin and Great Basin Desert, Colorado Plateau, and western montane environments. As the name implies, Common Sagebrush Lizards can be found in sagebrush-dominated habitats, but they also inhabit a variety of other vegetation communities, including chaparral, piñon/juniper woodland, pine/fir forest, canyon bottoms, open riparian areas, and other relatively open areas. They are found between 150 and 3,200 m in elevation. The Common Sagebrush Lizard is mainly a ground-dwelling species found in areas of cover that can be used for refuge, such as boulder fields, rock crevices, small mammal burrows, and debris piles.

Natural History: Common Sagebrush Lizards are diurnal and usually abundant where they occur. They are most active at temperatures between 21.7 and 36.8°C, and the preferred body temperature is 30.9°C. They are agile animals that can climb well and may leap to capture prey. Their prey consists of small arthropods including ants, flies, aphids, beetles, and spiders. When frightened they quickly run for cover under leaf

Female S. graciosus gracilis, *Tulare Co., CA. Sagebrush lizards are not as spiny as similar* Sceloporus.

litter, debris piles, in holes, or under logs or rocks. They bask on logs, stumps, and rocks to thermoregulate, and in the warmer part of the day seek refuge in the shade of bushes, rocks, and woodpiles.

In Utah, the home range of Common Sagebrush Lizards ranges from 400 to 600 m^2, and males are known to exhibit fighting behavior, which includes biting and wrestling. Males defend territories before and after the breeding season. Their displays include puffing out their throats with belly lowered to the ground and tail sticking straight out. The fighting and displaying is primarily directed at rival conspecific males that enter their territories, especially during the breeding season.

Female lizards lay 1–2 clutches per year, and clutch size is 1–10 eggs. These are laid in June through August, and hatch in 45–75 days. Eggs are laid in loose soil a few centimeters below the surface. Nests are usually located near the bases of shrubs. Hatchlings can reach sexual maturity in about 12–24 months depending on latitude and elevation.

Annual survival rates in populations studied from southern Utah and west-central California ranged from 60% in adults and approximately 30% in juveniles and eggs. The main predators of Common Sagebrush Lizards are numerous snake species, larger lizards, and a variety of predatory bird species.

Range: Common Sagebrush Lizards have a broad distribution, ranging from Washington, Idaho, Montana, and North Dakota south to northern Baja California, northern

Arizona, and northwestern New Mexico. They are found as far east as western Nebraska.

Viewing Tips: This species is easily observed in a variety of localities and habitats throughout its range. Where these lizards occur, they are usually very common. When approached, Common Sagebrush Lizards scurry to cover objects, so it is best to observe them through binoculars. Some public places to observe this species include Great Basin National Park, the many low-lying national parks and monuments of the Four Corners area of the Colorado Plateau, and many of the national forests in coastal California.

Taxonomy: Some authors have treated *Sceloporus vandenburgianus* as a distinct species. The closely related *Sceloporus arenicolus* was considered a subspecies of *S. graciosus* in recent literature, but is now generally considered to be a distinct species.

Subspecies and Variation: Three subspecies are generally recognized. They can usually be separated by scale and coloration patterns, but it is easiest just linking the locality with the subspecies. The Western Sagebrush Lizard (*S. g. gracilis*) has 50–68 (average 61) scales between the interparietal and rear of the thigh, indistinct dorsolateral striping, and white separating the blue patches on the throat and venter. The Northern Sagebrush Lizard (*S. g. graciosus*) has the same scale count of 42–53 (average 48) and distinct dorsolateral striping. The Southern Sagebrush Lizard (*S. g. vandenburgianus*) has 48–66 (average 55) scale count and more blue and less white in the throat and ventral patches, and often the ventral surface of the thigh and tail.

Male S. graciosus gracilis, *Tulare Co., CA.*

Yarrow's Spiny Lizard

Sceloporus jarrovii Cope, 1875

Author: Cecil R. Schwalbe

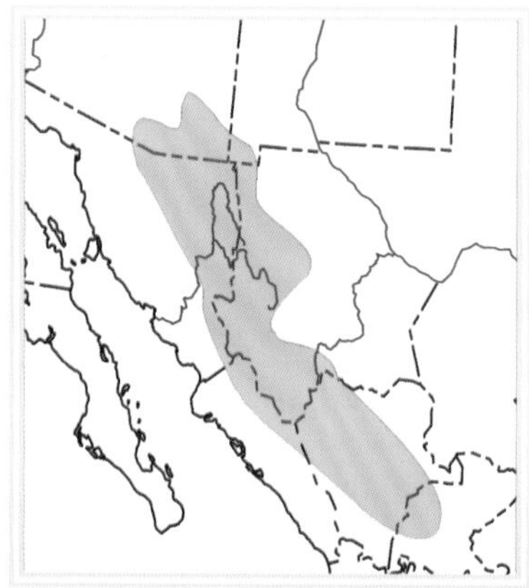

See page 559 for map color codes.

Description: This is a medium-sized, sexually dimorphic lizard, with males reaching 105 mm SVL, females 97. The tail is about 1 to 1.5 times SVL, with indistinct narrow bands and a black tip. Dorsal scales are weakly keeled, pointed, and slightly overlapping, more so on the tail, which appears more spinose than the body. **Sexual Variation:** Adult males have a characteristic lace-stocking pattern on the back, an effect created by a light spot in the center of each black scale that can appear white, pink, copper, blue, or green. They have a broad black collar with a thin, white, posterior border. White stripes are usually found through the eye, along the upper lip, and on both sides of the head and neck. There are blue throat and belly patches and 2 enlarged post-anal scales. Adult females are usually brown spotted with gray on the back and are less brightly colored than males. They have a less conspicuous collar than males. Blue throat and belly patches are subdued or absent. **Juveniles:** Juveniles are similar to females. All ages and sexes can be almost coal black when first emerging into the sun on cold mornings, especially at high elevations.

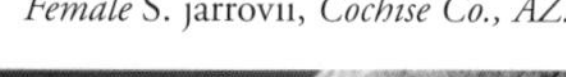

Female S. jarrovii, *Cochise Co., AZ.*

Similar Species: Crevice Spiny Lizards also have a distinctive black collar but are larger than Yarrow's, appear more spinose, and have a conspicuously banded tail. Clark's Spiny Lizards are larger, more spinose, and have an incomplete black collar. Juvenile Yarrow's Spiny Lizards are not striped, which distinguishes them from the smaller *Sceloporus* species with which they co-occur.

Male S. jarrovii, Chiricahua Mountains, AZ. Note the fishnet stocking pattern.

Eastern Collared Lizards have smooth, non-overlapping scales and a double black collar.

Habitats: This species thrives at mid to high elevations (1,370–3,550 m). In Arizona and New Mexico, they occur on rocky substrates in Mexican evergreen oak woodlands, up through pine-oak woodlands, Ponderosa Pine forests, and Douglas-fir forests, into subalpine conifer forests of Engelmann Spruce, Subalpine Fir, Douglas-fir, and Quaking Aspen. They use talus slopes, rocky outcrops, and steep cliffs extensively. They are found occasionally on trees and buildings. They avoid thick forest and north-facing slopes.

Natural History: Yarrow's Spiny Lizard activity is affected by body size, elevation, season, and weather. The variation in ambient temperature with elevation has profound effects on the physiology and behavior of this species, with lizard activity limited by high temperatures at some low-elevation sites and by low temperatures at high elevations. Both sexes establish territories in spring, with rocks with abundant crevices one of the defended resources. Males increase territory size during the breeding season and shift boundaries to increase overlap with females. Lizards abandon summer territories and move to winter aggregation sites, usually steep, south-facing rocky cliffs with deep crevices, where as many as 63 individual lizards have been observed emerging from a single crevice, in an area less than a meter wide. In one study, during 3 winters at 2,542–2,560 m elevation, lizards emerged to bask on every sunny day on site visits during December through February, if crevice temperatures exceeded 7.5°C. In Arizona, this species has been observed active every month.

These lizards are live bearers. Males sexually mature at SVLs as short as 46 mm SVL, females at 50–55 mm SVL. Breeding occurs in the fall, with live birth in late spring or early summer, later at higher elevations. Females can store sperm. Litter sizes vary from 2 to 14 and correlate with female body size. Over a 4-year period, density estimates of 2 populations varied from 32–71 lizards/ha at a low-elevation site (1,675 m) to 148-229 lizards/ha at a high-elevation site (2,542 m).

These sit-and-wait predators consume a wide variety of insects and other arthropods. Quite aggressive in pursuing prey, they occasionally leap off a cliff face to capture food, falling 10 m or so. They return to their original perch within a few minutes, apparently unharmed. All lizard-eating snakes and lizards in the area likely eat this abundant lizard. All 4 montane rattlesnakes (Rock, Ridge-nosed, Twin-spotted, and Northern Black-tailed) eat them, as do Sonoran Mountain Kingsnakes and Sonoran Whipsnakes. Ten or more predatory birds and several mid-sized mammal predators, such as White-nosed Coatis, Ringtails, and skunks, likely consume them as well.

Range: This species ranges from southern Arizona and extreme southwest New Mexico south along the Sierra Madre Occidental through parts of Sonora, Chihuahua, and Durango to central Zacatecas, Mexico. In Arizona it occurs in the Baboquivari, Chiricahua, Dos Cabezas, Dragoon, Huachuca, Galiuro, Pinaleño (Graham), Quinlan, Santa Catalina (introduced), Santa Rita, Santa Teresa, Whetstone, and Winchester mountains; in New Mexico, the Peloncillo, Pyramid, San Luis, Animas, Big Hatchet, and Alamo Hueco mountains.

Viewing Tips: At Barfoot Park and Cave Creek in the Chiricahua Mountains, you can observe high- and low-elevation populations, respectively. Madera Canyon in the Santa Ritas and the crest trails in the Huachucas provide great hikes with lots of lizards. Visit the picnic area and road cut at Kitt Peak in the Baboquivaris to see these lizards any month of the year.

Taxonomy: Yarrow's Spiny Lizard was previously recognized as one of 7 subspecies of the Mountain Spiny Lizard, *S. jarrovii* (as *S. j. jarrovii*). A phylogenetic study of those populations recognized at least 5 species formerly referred to *S. jarrovii*, and *S. jarrovii* now is applied to those populations formerly referred to as *S. j. jarrovii* and *S. lineolateralis*.

Juvenile S. jarrovii, *Chiricahua Mountains, AZ. These high-elevation lizards are an important food source for montane rattlesnakes within their ranges.*

Subspecies and Variation: No subspecies are currently recognized.

Remarks: In the early 1980s an estimated 5,000–10,000 Yarrow's Spiny Lizards were illegally collected in southern Arizona, smuggled into Mexico, then brought back into the United States under a commercial import permit to be sold on the pet market. Collectors were paid a dollar a lizard, which were then marketed for $10–$15 apiece. Authorities were unable to gather enough evidence to prosecute the ringleader, but he finally got out of the business. Apparently no populations were collected to extinction, but some Arizona herpetologists thought that the size of the largest adults declined in several populations.

Desert Spiny Lizard

Sceloporus magister Hallowell, 1854

Authors: Lawrence L. C. Jones and Cecil R. Schwalbe

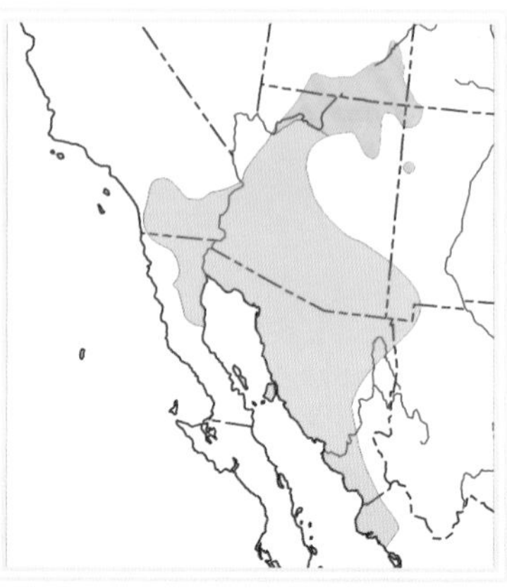

See page 559 for map color codes. May occur in Chihuahua. There are different interpretations of taxonomy, nomenclature, and range for this species complex.

Description: This is a large, robust spiny lizard, reaching about 140 mm SVL. Tail is slightly longer than SVL and limbs are relatively thick. The dorsum is covered with large, keeled overlapping scales. Coloration is variable, but usually consists of a light-brown ground color, with various dorsal markings, depending on age, sex, and locality. Adults have dark wedge-shaped markings on the neck above the shoulders. Thin, dark lines extend posteriorly from the rear of the eye and mouth. **Sexual Variation:** Adult males are larger, generally more colorful, and more distinctively marked than females. Males have conspicuous bluish patches on the sides of the venter, edged with black, as well as blue throat markings, enlarged post-anal scales, and a swollen tail base. **Juveniles:** Juveniles have smaller scales with dark and/or light spots or blotches on the dorsum. They lack the dark nuchal wedges and secondary sexual coloration of adults.

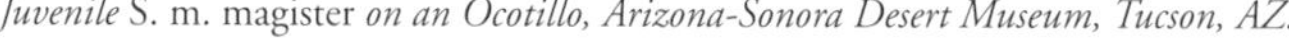

Juvenile S. m. magister *on an Ocotillo, Arizona-Sonora Desert Museum, Tucson, AZ.*

Male S. m. magister, *showing why this taxon is called Purple-backed Spiny Lizard. Mohawk Dunes, AZ.*

Similar Species: The Desert Spiny Lizard is most similar to other members of the Desert Spiny Lizard complex: the Yellow-backed and Twin-spotted Spiny Lizards. The former tends to be yellow to tan above, without markings or with less distinctive markings than the Desert Spiny Lizard. The Twin-spotted Spiny Lizard has paired spots or blotches down the dorsum. Other sympatric large *Sceloporus* may be confused with adult *S. magister*. Clark's Spiny Lizard has diagnostic dark bars on the forearm. The Granite Spiny Lizard lacks the distinctive dark wedges on the neck, as do smaller species of *Sceloporus*.

Habitats: The Desert Spiny Lizard rarely ventures above the desert or semi-desert valleys. It is associated with the Sonoran Desert (*Sceloporus m. magister*) and Colorado Plateau (*S. m. cephaloflavus*). Characteristic upland plant associations include Creosote Bush, Velvet Mesquite, Burro Bush, Greasewood, yuccas, cacti, sagebrushes, saltbushes, junipers, and grasses. They may also be found in riparian areas, where they are associated with Arrow Weed, Tamarisk, Fremont Cottonwood, palms, and willows. This species is usually found in areas with large structures, including boulders, trees, logs, shrubs, woodrat nests, and natural and artificial debris piles; it may also be common in suburban areas. It is found from sea level to about 1,520 m.

Natural History: Because the Desert Spiny Lizard has generally been regarded as a single species that encompassed the 2 other members of the species complex recognized here, the literature on life and natural history often refers to more than one of these

Female S. m. magister, *Tucson, Pima Co., AZ.*

taxa, but most of the literature is skewed to the western hot deserts (Sonoran and lower Mojave), so should be representative of *S. m. magister*. Definitive studies of *S. m. cephaloflavus* are lacking, and that subspecies occurs in a somewhat different environment (arid semi-desert with cold winters).

Desert Spiny Lizards are generally active in the morning and afternoon during the active season (March through October), but may be active at dusk or night, especially after summer rains. They brumate during the winter. Preferred body temperature is about 35°C, but they can be active at temperatures more than 10°C lower. They bask on structures to reach their preferred temperature, which they maintain fairly precisely by shuttling in and out of shade. Adults usually reach sexual maturity at 2–3 years of age. Females lay 3–19 eggs from May to August, and hatchlings are usually seen from August to October; they are about 31–33 mm SVL at hatching. Females may lay more than one clutch per year.

Males are highly territorial, exhibiting their ventral colors during push-up displays at rival males, and encounters may involve biting. Desert Spiny Lizards are generally sit-and-wait predators, but may also actively forage. They are generalist feeders, but studies show that ants, beetles, and true bugs are their primary prey. They occasionally eat small vertebrates, including lizards and bird nestlings.

Range: As currently recognized, this species occurs in the Sonoran Desert of Arizona, southern California, Sonora, and northern Baja California and the Colorado Plateau in southeastern Utah, and adjacent Arizona and Colorado, plus extreme northwestern New Mexico.

Viewing Tips: This species is common and widespread in the Sonoran Desert and Colorado Plateau. They are conspicuous while basking on structures. This species is fairly wary, so it is best to observe them at a distance through binoculars, and then approach them slowly. Good places to view the southern subspecies include Saguaro National Park (AZ), Organ Pipe Cactus National Monument (AZ), the lower Colorado River (AZ/CA), and the Salton Sea (CA). The northern subspecies can be seen at the lower elevations of several national parks and monuments in the Four Corners area. On overcast mornings following summer rains one can see incredible numbers of Desert Spiny Lizards foraging on the ground; some herpetologists call this the "maggie [from *magister*] moment."

Taxonomy: The members of the *Sceloporus magister* complex are widespread in the arid lands of the American Southwest. There is currently no consensus on how to relegate the complex to species and/or subspecies. There have been several named subspecies that basically conform to certain geographically oriented color patterns, but there is considerable variation and the zones of intergradation or hybridization are large. Three species from the U.S. in the *Sceloporus magister* complex are recognized in this book, but there is considerable justification for not splitting the 2 currently recognized subspecies of *S. magister* into separate species.

Subspecies and Variation: There are 2 subspecies, *S. m. magister* (Purple-backed Spiny Lizard) and *S. m. cephaloflavus* (Orange-headed Spiny Lizard). The latter has long been recognized as the form occurring on the Colorado Plateau. It is characterized by having 5 to 6 distinct dark bands or chevrons and a yellow to orange head and/or forebody background color. Adult male Purple-backed Spiny Lizards have a blue, purple, or black dorsal patch on the anterior dorsal surface.

Ventral patches of a male S. m. magister, *Mohawk Dunes, AZ.*

Remarks: The literature shows how important it is to document precise locality information in research, as taxonomy is subject to change. Recent evidence suggests subsumation of *S. m. cephaloflavus* into *S. uniformis.*

Canyon Lizard

Sceloporus merriami Stejneger, 1904

Author: Lee A. Fitzgerald

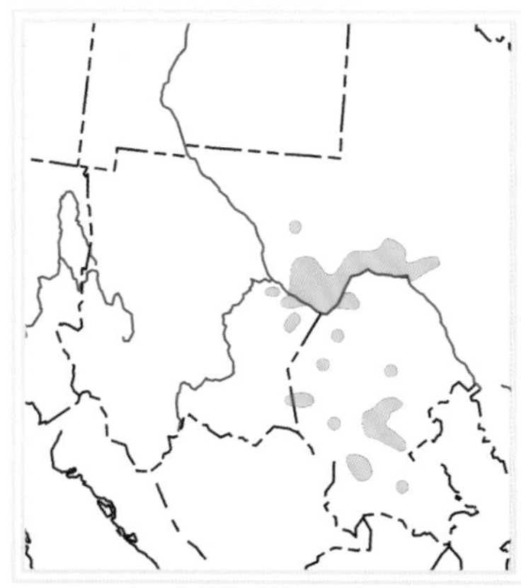

See page 559 for map color codes. Subspecies' ranges not differentiated.

Description: The Canyon Lizard is a small light to dark brown *Sceloporus*, 45–62 mm SVL. The tail is about 1.5 times the SVL. A Canyon Lizard has 4 rows of dark spots on the back, a black bar on the shoulder, and a partially developed gular fold, which is visible in front of the shoulders. There are numerous pale blue and white flecks on the body and tail. This species has small keeled scales on the dorsum; scales on the sides are granular; post-femoral pockets are lacking. **Sexual Variation:** Females are similar to males in dorsal coloration. Males have 2 large blue belly patches margined with black, which may touch or be separated by a white midventral stripe; a noticeable dewlap; blue and black lines on the throat; and may have transverse bars under the tail. Females have much less developed ventral markings. **Juveniles:** The juveniles of this species are similar to adults, and the same characteristics serve to identify them.

Male S. m. longipunctatus, *Big Bend Ranch State Park, Presidio Co., TX.*

Male S. m. annulatus, *Big Bend National Park, Brewster Co., TX.*

Similar Species: Other *Sceloporus* that occur together with Canyon Lizards have large keeled scales on the sides of the body. Ornate Tree Lizards and Common Side-blotched Lizards have a complete gular fold and distinctive markings.

Habitats: Canyon Lizards are aptly named, as they occur in rocky canyons and live on rocks, boulders, and canyon walls.

Natural History: Canyon Lizards are sit-and-wait foragers that prey on a variety of small arthropods such as spiders, ants, beetles, grasshoppers, and crickets. Breeding occurs from spring to late summer, and females lay about 4 eggs on average. Some females may lay 2 clutches in a single season. Clutch size varies with location, elevation, and the size and age of females. Males are socially dominant between 50 and 55 mm SVL, depending on elevation. Some females breed the first spring after they hatch; the minimum size of breeding females was 42 mm SVL. Long-term studies by ecologist Arthur E. Dunham revealed that Canyon Lizards living at high, medium, and low elevations have very different life histories and population dynamics, largely because of differences in availability of food resources and activity periods of the lizards. At high elevations, there is more rainfall, more arthropod prey, and cooler temperatures. Canyon Lizards at higher elevations can remain active throughout the day compared to lower elevations, where they are inactive during midday. Interestingly, lizards at both low and high elevations have relatively slow growth rates compared to mid-elevation sites, but for different reasons. Reduced activity at low elevations constrains activity and foraging, whereas at high elevations slow growth is probably due to higher energy expenditures associated with more activity, and inefficient food processing because of lower temperatures in refugia. At high elevations the activity season is less, which results in smaller yearlings compared to lower elevation sites. Population densities of these lizards can surpass 100 individuals per ha, but vary greatly according to location and year. One experiment in which either Canyon Lizards or Ornate Tree-lizards were removed from study plots showed the 2 species competed, but only when food resources were limited by drought. During dry years when Canyon Lizards were removed, foraging rate, growth, body mass, survival, and population density of Ornate Tree-lizards all increased; however, removal of Ornate Tree-lizards had little effect on population density of Canyon Lizards. This remains an elegant and compelling demonstration of ecological competition.

Range: In the U.S., Canyon Lizards are found in Texas from Edwards County west through the Big Bend region. In Mexico, they are known from Coahuila, Chihuahua, and northern Durango.

Viewing Tips: Canyon Lizards are easy to find in rocky canyons and arroyos in the Big Bend region. They can be found at many accessible localities throughout Big Bend National Park and Big Bend Ranch State Park. Canyon Lizards are not particularly wary and can be readily observed and photographed *in situ*.

Male S. m. merriami *doing a push-up display. Sanderson, Terrell Co., TX.*

Venter of male S. m. merriami, *Sanderson, Terrell Co., TX.*

Taxonomy: The Canyon Lizard has been recognized as a valid taxon since it was described in 1904. The species was named for the American naturalist C. Hart Merriam, who originated the U.S. Biological Survey that later became the U.S. Fish and Wildlife Service. Taxonomic work on Canyon Lizards has focused on describing subspecies and understanding relationships among them.

Subspecies and Variation: Seven subspecies of Canyon Lizards are described, 3 of which occur in the United States: *S. m. annulatus*, Big Bend Canyon Lizard, with 52 scales from back of head to tail, a dark dorsal pattern, transverse bars of equal breadth, and prominent tail rings dorsally and ventrally; *S. m. longipunctatus*, Presidio Canyon Lizard, with paravertebral spots shaped like a transverse comma and poorly defined tail rings; and *S. m. merriami*, Merriam's Canyon Lizard, with 58 or more dorsal scales, and small paravertebral dark spots. The remaining 4 subspecies occur in Coahuila, Durango, and Chihuahua, Mexico: *S. m. ballingeri, S. m. williamsi; S. m. sanojae,* and *S. m. australis.*

Remarks: Canyon Lizards are not protected by the Texas Parks and Wildlife Department or the U.S. Fish and Wildlife Service. However, much of their range is within Big Bend National Park and Big Bend Ranch State Park, where they are protected.

Western Fence Lizard

Sceloporus occidentalis Baird and Girard, 1852

Author: Robert E. Espinoza

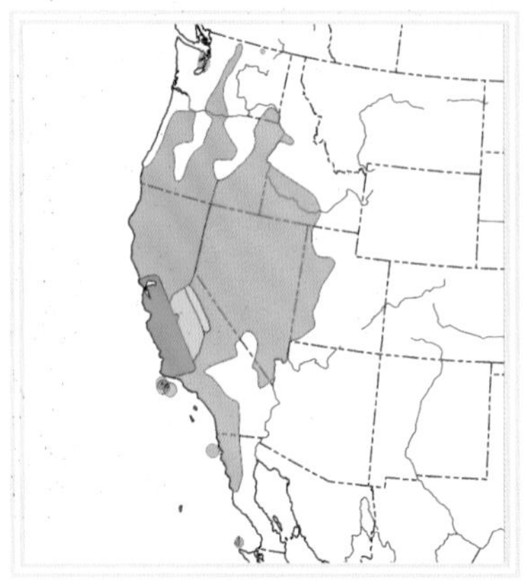

See page 559 for map color codes.

Description: These are medium-sized lizards (70–94 mm SVL) with tails about 1.5 times the length of the body. Their scales are keeled and pointed, giving their bodies a spiny appearance. The dorsal background color varies from grayish brown to dark brown to black. The back usually has brown to black bars or blotches that may form parallel rows on either side of the midline, but these markings are not visible on dark individuals. In some populations individuals are striped rather than barred or banded. The posterior surfaces of the limbs are usually orange-yellow. **Sexual Variation:** Adult males average 10% larger than females and have throat and belly patches in varying shades of vibrant blue. The belly patches are outlined in black and usually separated medially by gray (rarely black) scales. Individuals that are lighter dorsally may also have scattered blue to turquoise-green scales. The tail base is swollen, the femoral pores are prominent (exuding waxy secretions in the breeding season), and there are 2 enlarged postanal scales. Markings on the backs of females are more distinct than on males, but females lack blue scales dorsally. Throat and belly patches are smaller and less vibrant than in males. **Juveniles:** Juveniles are similar to females, but ventral coloration is faint or absent.

Juvenile S. occidentalis bocourtii, *Elkhorn Slough, Monterey Co., CA.*

Similar Species: Aside from the Common Side-blotched Lizard, which has a single black or dark blue blotch behind each forelimb and a complete gular fold, Western Fence Lizards are unlikely to be confused with lizards in their range except other spiny lizards. In contrast to

Adult S. occidentalis bocourtii, *Elkhorn Slough, Monterey Co., CA.*

other spiny lizards, Western Fence Lizards have pointed, moderately sized, overlapping (not granular) scales; a single throat patch (occasionally partly to completely divided) that is not flecked with other colors; yellow on their posterior limbs; and, if present, the gular fold is incomplete.

Habitats: This species can be found in a variety of natural habitats including coastal sage scrub, grassland, chaparral, sagebrush, oak and conifer woodlands, and in open forests at higher elevations. It is common in disturbed habitats in both rural and urban areas, but absent from extreme deserts. Although regularly encountered foraging on or near the ground, the preferred microhabitat is elevated perches (typically 0.5–4 m above ground) such as boulders, tree trunks and stumps, woodpiles, brick and stucco walls, and of course, fence posts. This species occurs from sea level to above 3,300 m.

Natural History: Commonly known as "blue bellies" for the vibrant ventral patches of males, Western Fence Lizards are among the most familiar reptiles in the Southwest. These lizards are usually observed basking on elevated perches on sunny days. From these vantage points, males perform push-up displays and use lateral body compressions to flash the bright colors of their ventral region. These displays serve to defend localized territories (7.5-m radius) from encroaching males and to attract females. Occasionally, competing males will engage in physical combat. The home-range size in a population studied in Nevada was 0.2–0.7 ha for males and 0.04–0.2 ha for females.

Mating occurs from spring to early summer and 1–3 clutches of 3–17 eggs are deposited. Eggs hatch after about 60 days in late summer or early fall. Western Fence Lizards primarily eat insects and other small arthropods, although cannibalism has been reported. They are parasitized by mites, ticks, and a variety of internal worms. Their propensity to bask on elevated perches and their conspicuous behavior makes them vulnerable to a variety of diurnal predators including small mammals, birds, snakes, and other lizards.

Range: This widespread lizard occurs from northern Washington and southwestern Idaho south to southern California (including 3 of the Channel Islands), Nevada, and western Utah. It also occurs in northwestern Baja California and on 2 islands off the Mexican coast.

Viewing Tips: Their ability to thrive in association with humans (e.g., ranches, urban parks, and backyards, etc.), high density, and conspicuous behaviors make these lizards easy to find and observe. The best time to view them is from spring to early summer (March through early June) when males are performing territorial and courtship displays, but they remain active throughout the year in milder climates (e.g., coastal southern California), particularly on sunny days. When startled, they typically race for the nearest elevated perch and remain out of sight briefly. However, individuals from areas with high human traffic (e.g., hiking paths in city parks like those surrounding

Female S. o. occidentalis, *Mendocino Co., CA.*

Ventral view of a male S. o. longipes, *Escondido, San Diego Co., CA.*

the San Diego Zoo/Balboa Park, CA) may allow a viewer to approach to within arm's length or closer.

Taxonomy: Until recently, 5 to 6 subspecies were recognized (see below). A taxonomic revision of the species based on genetic and morphological data is currently under way. In most cases, the current taxonomy does not reflect the species boundaries delineated by this research: several subspecies warrant full-species recognition, but others apparently interbreed at their contact zones, and thus represent clinal variation. Additionally, several new genetically distinct populations have been discovered that also warrant species recognition.

Subspecies and Variation: The subspecies include the Island Fence Lizard (*S. o. becki*) (sometimes considered a full species), San Joaquin Fence Lizard (*S. o. biseriatus*), Coast Range Fence Lizard (*S. o. bocourtii*), Great Basin Fence Lizard (*S. o. longipes*), Northwestern Fence Lizard (*S. o. occidentalis*), and Sierra Fence Lizard (*S. o. taylori*).

Remarks: This abundant species is one of the most well-studied lizards in the Southwest. Recent studies revealed that Western Fence Lizards might lower the incidence of Lyme disease. A disease-causing bacterium (*Borrelia burgdorferi*) inhabits the guts of at least 2 species of western ticks (*Ixodes* and *Dermacentor*). This bacterium is transferred to humans after a tick bites and attaches to its victim for 1–2 days; however, when these ticks feed first on Fence Lizard blood, which contains a special protein, the disease-causing spirochetes are eliminated. The protein is so effective that in areas where Western Fence Lizards occur, only 5% of ticks carry the disease, whereas the infection prevalence may reach 50% in other areas.

Texas Spiny Lizard

Sceloporus olivaceus Smith, 1934

Author: James R. Dixon

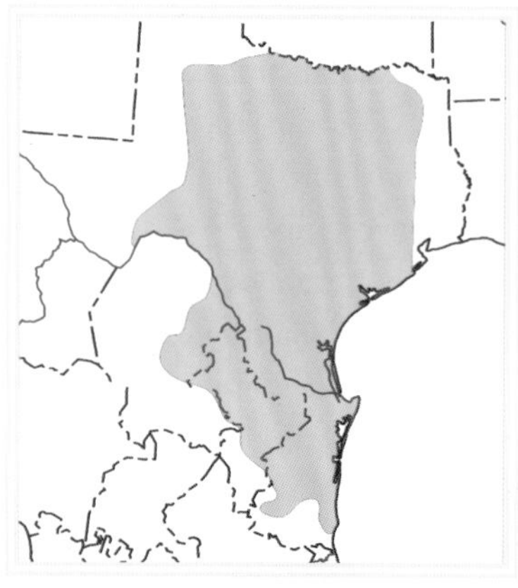

See page 559 for map color codes.

Description: This is a large species of spiny lizard. The body is somewhat dorsoventrally compressed. The largest male measured 98 mm SVL, while the largest female was 124 mm SVL. In adults, the tail is approximately 1.6 times the SVL. The body scales are large, keeled, in parallel rows, and not strongly mucronate. Those scales around the middle of the body vary from 28 to 41, and those from the rear of the head to the base of the tail vary from 28 to 35. Neither of the latter 2 characteristics shows sexual variation. Male and female lizards show indications of femoral pores, but female pores do not pierce the scale, while male femoral pores do, and vary from 11 to 33. Head scales are smooth. The supraoculars are large, 5–6 in number, and are sepa-

Female S. olivaceus, *Wise Co., TX. Females, unlike males, have distinct crossbars on the dorsum.*

Male S. olivaceus, *Burnet Co., TX. Males have the dorsolateral light lines, as do females.*

rated from the median head scales and the supercilliaries by a single row of small scales. **Sexual Variation:** There is strong sexual dimorphism between the sexes. Males have 2 enlarged ventrolateral post-anal scales, whereas the females have none. The ground color of males may be gray to pale brown. The dorsum has 2 broad pale gray to yellowish gray dorsolateral lines from the shoulder to the base of the tail. These pale stripes are bordered interiorly by dark brown to almost black borders. Males have narrow ventrolateral blue belly patches without dark edges. Their heads are normally brown but may vary to pale brown. The venter is gray to dusky, with a median, thin black line from the chin to the middle of the belly and occasionally to the tail. The dorsum of females also has pale dorsolateral lines. However, they have 5–7 undulating brown to blackish brown crossbars from the rear of the head and onto the tail that frequently interrupt dorsolateral pale lines. **Juveniles:** Juveniles are similar to adult females in coloration until they become young adults. They have relatively larger heads and shorter tails (only 1.2 times the SVL).

Similar Species: Young and juveniles of fence lizards are difficult to distinguish from Texas Spiny Lizards. Crevice Spiny Lizards have a similar body shape but a different color pattern, while the Twin-spotted Spiny Lizard's body is not dorsoventrally compressed and has a different color pattern.

Habitats: The Texas Spiny Lizard is primarily a forest species. Both young and adults of this species use medium to large tree trunks for perches. They are relatively common in Texas on the trunks of Live Oak, Post Oak, Water Oak, cedars, hackberries, elms, and large shrubs. They are limited by grass prairies, but follow riparian forests along streams into grasslands and deserts. When suitable trees and shrubs are not available in desert areas, they occasionally use boulders along washes. Occasionally they are found on wooden poles, fence posts, and other man-made structures.

Natural History: This lizard is an ambush predator. It usually sits on a tree trunk or other object whereby it can scan the ground and grass for moving objects. Its position is normally tail up and curled toward its back, and the head down. The stance is approximately 1–2 m above the ground. The lizard dashes to the ground, grabs the prey, and immediately returns to its original tree to consume the prey. Prey items are normally crickets, grasshoppers, ants, flies, true bugs, butterflies, and caterpillars. In periods of drought, vertebrate prey may be taken. In turn, the lizard and/or its eggs may be eaten by patch-nosed snakes, Coachwhips, crows, Greater Roadrunners, Blue Jays, and mockingbirds. The lizards live about 4 years, with males maturing in one year and females in 2. The average size of sexual maturity in males is 65 mm SVL, but 80 mm for females. Males are territorial, combat other males, and occasionally lose their tails while fighting. Normally there is only one adult male per tree during the breeding season. Mature females may lay 4 clutches per year, with 19–30 eggs per clutch. Of this number of eggs, only 2–5% of the young reach maturity.

Juvenile S. olivaceus, *Edwards Co., TX.*

Female S. olivaceus, *Guadalupe Co., TX.*

Range: The distribution of this lizard is extreme southern Oklahoma south through east central Texas to the Gulf Coast, southward to southern Tamaulipas, Mexico, west into central Coahuila, Mexico, then north into the edge of the Big Bend region of Texas, ending just below the caprock of northwest Texas.

Viewing Tips: The use of a pair of binoculars would allow anyone to observe this lizard. If you walk slowly toward the lizard at rest, it generally will remain in place until you are approximately 5 steps away. A closer approach may make the lizard flee up the tree. It is generally active during the warm months from about 8:00 to 11:30 a.m. and from 4:00 to 6:00 p.m. While driving at 45 miles per hour, you can easily see it in its ambush position along a wooded roadway. Within its Texas range, walking around a roadside park with trees at the proper time of day will normally reveal one or more lizards in their ambush position.

Taxonomy: The taxonomy of this species has been relatively stable since the 1940s.

Subspecies and Variation: A thesis concerning the morphology and genetics of the Texas Spiny Lizard within its total range was completed in 1984. The work essentially says that variation is greatly reduced, and all of the 13 geographic samples (a total of 963 individuals) showed congruence in all of the characteristic states without major derivation.

Granite Spiny Lizard

Sceloporus orcutti Stejneger, 1893

Author: Eric A. Dugan

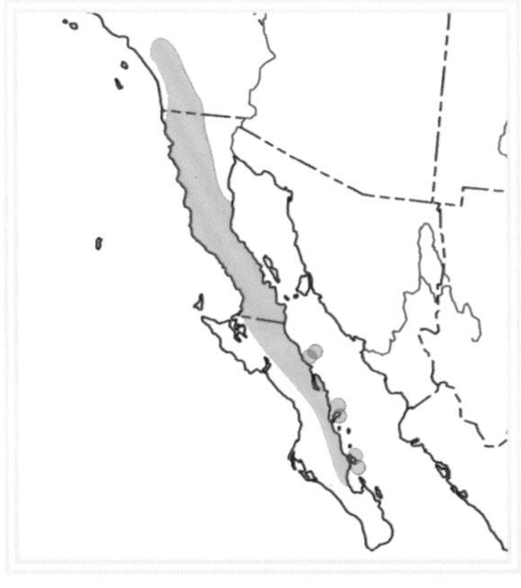

See page 559 for map color codes.

Description: The Granite Spiny Lizard is medium-sized, reaching an adult SVL of 115 mm. The body is robust and covered with moderately keeled dorsal scales. The triangle-shaped head is covered with plate-like scales. Slightly longer than the length of the body, the tail is covered with strongly keeled scales. In general, this is a dark-colored lizard. Ground coloration ranges from a light rusty brown to a nearly melanistic form. A dark wedge-shaped mark is present on each side of the neck. Crossbands on both the body and tail are distinct in females and juveniles, but may be faint in melanistic individuals. **Sexual Variation:** Males exhibit significant geographic variation in coloration. Males have blue or blue-green coloration on the throat and ventral surfaces and possess enlarged post-anal scales. A pale purple middorsal stripe runs the length of the dorsum. Females lack the blue and green coloration of the males and the crossbands are more distinct. Females also lack the purple coloration on the dorsum. The blue-green coloration on the neck and ventral surface is less conspicuous to absent in females. **Juveniles:** Juveniles display a distinctly rust-colored head and vivid crossbands and neck markings.

Venter of male S. orcutti, *Lake Perris, Riverside Co., CA.*

Similar Species: The Desert Spiny Lizard is another large-bodied Spiny Lizard, and the likeliest to be confused with the Granite Spiny Lizard. The two species often occupy habitats that are nearby, yet distinct. Desert Spiny Lizards have strongly

Female S. orcutti, *San Diego Wild Animal Park, CA.*

keeled dorsal scales that are more pointed than those of *S. orcutti* and have more conspicuous dark neck markings. Granite Spiny Lizards may also be confused with the Western Fence Lizard. However, the noticeably larger adult size, distinct black shoulder bars, and distinct forearm bands of the Granite Spiny Lizard are diagnostic.

Habitats: Granite Spiny Lizards occur in a wide range of habitats including rocky desert, chaparral, oak woodland, semi-desert grassland, and coastal sand dunes. It is a rock-dwelling species primarily associated with mid-elevation habitats containing granite rock outcroppings, as reflected in its common name. Populations occur from sea level to 2,100 m elevation.

Natural History: The active season ranges from February to November. Granite Spiny Lizards begin to emerge from brumation in late January. This is one of the few species of lizard documented to brumate communally. Adults have been noted to use the same rock crack in consecutive years. Interestingly, this species has been documented to migrate to hibernacula outside of the spring and summer home range, returning to their respective home ranges the following spring. Adults typically emerge in the morning hours to bask, after which they begin to forage for insects. As with other spiny lizards, *S. orcutti* are aggressive insectivores. Prey items include flies, grasshoppers, beetles, bees, and moths. Vegetation has also been noted in their diet, as has cannibalism. Cracks, fissures, and granite exfoliations are used as overwintering and thermoregulation sites as well as refugia from predators. Once in a crack, the large keeled scales help wedge the lizard into the crack, thus preventing removal by predators. A hierarchal order has been reported between different age classes, with adult lizards having access to the deepest sections of rock cracks and fissures. Subadults and juveniles were observed to occupy marginal refugia at the edge of the cracks, where temperatures fluctuated drastically. Large numbers of Granite Spiny Lizards are often observed using the same crack. Some consider this to be one of the more social species in the spiny lizard group.

Mating occurs from March to April. From May to July, up to 15 eggs are deposited in small holes, mammal burrows, or under surface cover such as logs and rocks. Eggs hatch in approximately 60 days. Hatchlings are independent upon emerging from the egg and don't reach sexual maturity until the second or third years. Predators include mammals, birds, and snakes. A large majority of the individuals that fall prey to predators are taken at night while they sleep. Adults have been removed from the stomachs of Red Diamond Rattlesnakes. Juveniles may also fall prey to carnivorous species of lizards such as leopard lizards and collared lizards.

Range: This species ranges from southern San Bernardino County southward into the Baja California peninsula. Individuals have been recorded from as far south as the area northwest of La Paz, Baja California, Mexico. Seven insular populations are located on the islands of Carmen, Coronados, San Francisco, San Ildefonso, San Jose, San Marcos, and Tortuga off the coast of the Baja peninsula.

Viewing Tips: *Sceloporus orcutti* are commonly observed basking on rocks in the early morning and late afternoon on warm days. Look for these often-conspicuous lizards in

Juvenile S. orcutti, *Anza-Borrego Desert State Park, San Diego Co., CA.*

Male S. orcutti, *Toro Canyon, CA. Among the more spectacularly colored lizards in the American Southwest, they are very unapproachable and may appear black in the distance.*

granite boulder fields, at mid to low elevations. Adults can be observed emerging from large rock fissures to thermoregulate. Known as an alert and nervous species, individuals can be difficult to approach. Within proper habitat, this will often be the most conspicuous lizard species, of which numerous individuals can be observed at the same time. Sitting quietly among large granite boulders will allow the lizards to emerge, at which time they can be easily observed with binoculars. This species is readily observed among boulders in the Anza-Borrego Desert State Park (CA).

Taxonomy: *Sceloporus orcutti* is most closely related to the Baja endemics *S. licki* and *S. hunsakeri*. *Sceloporus orcutti* attain a larger adult size than both *S. licki* and *S. hunsakeri*, and vary slightly in scalation.

Subspecies and Variation: Currently no recognized subspecies. As with many lizard species that have large distributions, color pattern variation can be significant between populations. Several insular trends in coloration have been noted by some authors.

Remarks: Granite Spiny Lizards are well studied. Several published studies detailing their biology can be looked up by those interested in information not detailed herein.

Crevice Spiny Lizard

Sceloporus poinsettii Baird and Girard, 1852

Author: Robert G. Webb

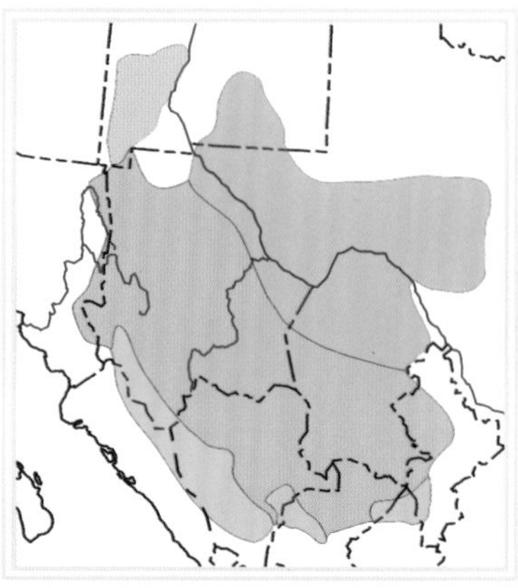

See page 559 for map color codes.

Description: Crevice Spiny Lizards are relatively large, with males attaining a larger maximal size (137 mm SVL) than females (128 mm SVL). Characteristic pattern features include a broad, black uninterrupted collar with white borders (may be lengthened and curved posteriorly), a small pale bluish spot just above the shoulder within the black collar, a whitish crossband or series of spots on the rear of the head between the ear openings, and a tail with contrasting black (widest) and white bands. Dorsal body scales may have black edges aligned to form longitudinal black lines. The basic dorsal body pattern is usually 3–4 crossbands, but patterns vary rangewide and may be sexually dimorphic. Supraoculars are divided, usually subequal in size, but the medial row may be noticeably enlarged. The posterior frontal-frontoparietal area is often fragmented into irregularly arranged small scales. Rangewide, dorsal scales (vertebral rows mostly smooth in large adults) vary from 25 to 43, and femoral pores 7–16 (per leg) with extremes of 7–7 and 14–16. **Sexual Variation:** Adults of both sexes have blue throats and ventrolateral dark-bordered blue belly patches, but the colors are brightest and most extensive in males. **Juveniles:** Juveniles have crossbanded backs and dark bluish barred throat patterns, usually with pale midventral streaks.

Adult S. p. axtelli, *Brewster Co., TX.*

Similar Species: In the U.S., Crevice Spiny Lizards may occur in the same general area with other large spiny lizards including Twin-Spotted, Clark's, Texas, and Yarrow's Spiny Lizards, all of which can be distinguished

Adult male S. p. poinsettii, *southwest NM.*

from Crevice Spiny Lizards in having large undivided supraoculars, and in lacking the contrasting black and white banded tail. Juveniles of Crevice and Yarrow's Spiny Lizards are often confused; the throat pattern of Crevice Spiny Lizards usually includes a pale, medial, longitudinal streak (persists in larger lizards), which is lacking in Yarrow's Spiny Lizard.

Habitats: Crevice Spiny Lizards occur in parts of the Chihuahuan Desert, semi-desert grasslands, and in pine/oak forested mountainous terrain. They may occasionally climb trees, but are characteristic of rocky landscapes, including lava flows, especially large rocks and boulders associated with outcrops of either low dry hills or mountainous highlands. Rangewide elevations range from 231 m (Texas) to near 2,743 m (Durango, Mexico).

Range: Crevice Spiny Lizards occur in southwestern New Mexico (but are absent in the Peloncillo Mountains) and southeastern New Mexico (distributional gap across southern New Mexico) and central and west Texas, extending south into northern Mexico through Coahuila, Chihuahua, and Durango, including the eastern highland parts of Sonora and Sinaloa, into northern Zacatecas and San Luis Potosí, and eastern Nuevo León.

Natural History: After emergence from brumation, lizards bask on sun-exposed rock perches and feed in spring and summer. These lizards are mostly insectivorous with ants, beetles, and grasshoppers common in the diet. Spiders and a centipede have also been reported as food items. Plant material is also consumed, especially among larger lizards. The reproductive period (mating through ovulation) occurs in fall months, with slowed winter embryonic development increasing through spring. Young (29–35 mm SVL) are born alive in late May–June, and females produce only one litter each season. Females mature in about 15–17 months and males after at least 12 months. Sexual maturity in both sexes is reported to be near 75 mm SVL in New Mexico, but near 85–90 mm SVL in females and about 95 mm in males in Texas. Litter size varies from 6 to 23 (average 10.4) with numbers of young increasing with size of females. Known predators include snakes, hawks, and, in one instance, a Bobcat.

Viewing Tips: Binoculars are useful in observing these lizards (readily identified by their broad black collars and black and white banded tails) basking on distant rocks on warm sunny days during morning and afternoon hours in spring and summer. Startled lizards retreat into rocky crevices and may inflate the body as an antipredator device. Viewing areas may include rocky roadcuts, rocks and boulders along highways, small bridges over culverts, or any campground or rest area having nearby appropriate large rocks and boulders associated with mountainous or hilly terrain. Good rocky viewing sites are in Hueco Mountains State Park (TX) and the Animas Mountains foothills along Highway 81, about 4 miles north of Antelope Wells (NM).

Male S. p. poinsettii *Hidalgo Co., NM.*

Female S. p. axtelli, *Reeve's Co., TX.*

Taxonomy: Crevice Spiny Lizards have been continually recognized as a valid taxon. Although originally proposed as a distinct species in 1852 and so stabilized since the late 1930s, these lizards were often recognized in intervening years as a subspecies of the Mexican species *S. torquatus*.

Subspecies and Variation: Two subspecies occur in the U.S.: New Mexico Crevice Spiny Lizard, *S. p. poinsettii*, in southwestern New Mexico, and the Texas Crevice Spiny Lizard, *S. p. axtelli* in eastern New Mexico and Texas (including northeastern Chihuahua and northern Coahuila). New Mexico Crevice Spiny Lizards have a black, white-spotted top of head, pale body crossbands with black-edged scales, and no sexual pattern dimorphism. Lower sides of the body may be orangish. Texas Crevice Spiny Lizards have a black cruciform blotch on rear of the head, and exhibit sexual dimorphism (but not absolute) with males having body crossbands reduced except for black vertebral blotches (separated by white spots), and females with complete crossbands (vertebral areas may be darkened). Three other subspecies and intergradient specimens occur in Mexico, including the Largescale Crevice Spiny Lizard, *S. p. macrolepis*; the Clouded Crevice Spiny Lizard, *S. p. amydrus*; and the Smallscale Crevice Spiny Lizard, *S. p. polylepis*.

Slevin's Bunchgrass Lizard

Sceloporus slevini Smith, 1937

Author: Charles W. Painter

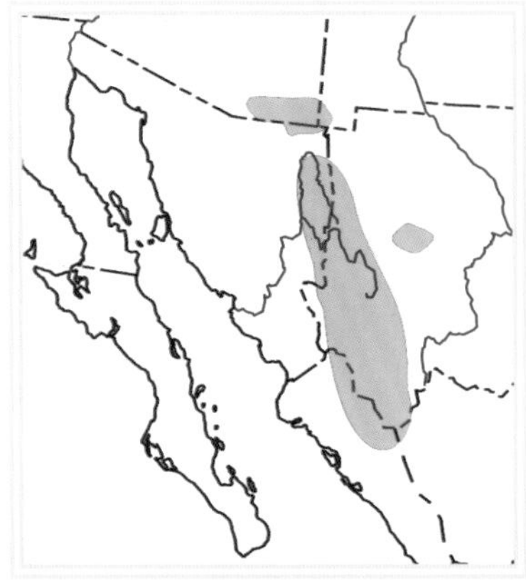

See page 559 for map color codes.

Description: Slevin's Bunchgrass Lizard is a small species of *Sceloporus*, with a maximum SVL of 68 mm. The dorsal scales are keeled and mucronate, and overlap only slightly; lateral scales may be smooth or keeled. Lateral scale rows are arranged parallel to the longitudinal dorsal scale rows. There are only 2 post-rostral scales (see Figure 3). There are 12–18 femoral pores on each side. The limbs are relatively small compared to those of other *Sceloporus*. There is no gular fold. The ground color of most individuals is light brown. There are 2 distinct light lines, one scale row wide and separated from each other by 7–8 scale rows extending from the parietal region posteriorly onto the tail. There are paired rows of 10–13 crescent-shaped, brown markings on the dorsum. A longitudinal light line extends from the lips through the ear opening onto the front of the hind leg. A small number of individuals in each population may be unicolored. **Sexual Variation:** Females are slightly larger than males, averaging 50–56 mm SVL. Mature females from southwestern New Mexico averaged 51.9 (41–68) mm SVL, while mature males averaged 47.9 (35–59) mm SVL. The sexually dichromatic coloration of breeding males is spectacular, with a bright salmon-colored streak 3–5 scales wide bordering dorsally a somewhat wider, bright pale blue streak on each side of the abdomen.

Adult S. slevini, *Huachuca Mountains, AZ. This is the plain phase, infrequently encountered.*

Female S. slevini, *Huachuca Mountains, AZ. Unlike most other lizards, the female is more showy than the male (except for the ventral colors!).*

Similar Species: Size, coloration, lack of a gular fold, and the lateral scale rows arranged parallel to the longitudinal dorsal scale rows should distinguish *S. slevini* from all other *Sceloporus* in North America. *Sceloporus virgatus* and *S. cowlesi* have blue patches on the throat and broad longitudinal light dorsal lines. These species both lack granular scales on the posterior surface of the thigh and the longitudinal series of dorsal chevron markings.

Habitats: Although typically ascribed to montane habitats, Slevin's Bunchgrass Lizard is also known to occur in intermountain valleys and along riparian areas. Montane habitats feature various vegetation types, including woodlands or forests dominated by pines. Regardless of the habitat type this species may inhabit, the essential feature appears to be clumps of thick grass. Grasses in valley grasslands might include sacatons, grammas, panic grasses, and Tobosa, while in montane areas bromes and muhlys are important. These grasses serve this secretive and wary lizard in various ways, including as refuge or thermoregulation sites. Elevation in Arizona ranges from 1,300 m (Sonoita Plains) to near 2,683 m (Barfoot Park, Chiricahua Mountains). The species is restricted to elevations between 1,561 and 1,611 m in New Mexico.

Natural History: Slevin's Bunchgrass Lizards remain active throughout the year, even during the coldest months. They actively thermoregulate and maintain body temperatures significantly higher than the surrounding ambient. Body temperature of 851 individuals from southeastern Arizona averaged 32.6°C. Males generally have higher body temperatures than females. Females reach sexual maturity at 41 mm SVL during their first spring at approximately 8–9 months of age. Mating in southeastern Arizona takes place in April at the higher elevations and perhaps somewhat earlier in the lower and warmer, intermountain valleys (e.g., the Sonoita Plains). In the montane areas ovulation occurs from late May through mid-June, oviposition begins in late June–early July, and hatchlings appear in September. In the Animas Valley in southwest New Mexico hatchlings as small as 20 mm SVL and 0.02 g have been observed as early as August 5. Considerable embryonic development occurs in the eggs prior to oviposition. Only one clutch of eggs is produced each year per female, with the size of the clutch significantly correlated with female SVL. In southeastern Arizona the average number of eggs in 153 clutches was 8.5. True bugs, ants, beetles, and grasshoppers comprise most of the food items identified in food habit studies of the species in southeastern Arizona and central Mexico.

Range: In the U.S., *S. slevini* ranges into the mountain islands and high-elevation grasslands of southeastern Arizona and southwestern New Mexico, where it is common especially on east- and south-facing slopes having a vegetative cover of dense grasses. In southeastern Arizona the species occurs in the Santa Rita, Dragoon, Huachuca, and Chiricahua mountains and in the Empire, San Rafael, and Sulfur Springs valleys. In southwestern New Mexico it occurs in southwestern Hidalgo County in the southern end of the Animas Valley in the vicinity of Cloverdale. This intermountain valley lies between the Animas and Peloncillo mountains, although despite extensive searches *S. slevini* does not appear to occupy these mountain ranges.

Viewing Tips: These small, secretive lizards scurry between bunchgrasses in sunlit areas. Their coloration renders them cryptic and difficult to observe. This species may

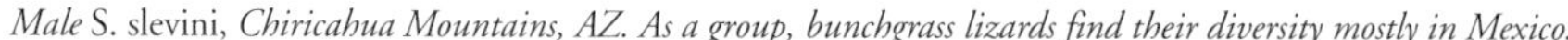

Male S. slevini, *Chiricahua Mountains, AZ. As a group, bunchgrass lizards find their diversity mostly in Mexico.*

Ventral coloration of S. slevini, *Chiricahua Mountains, AZ. The ventral color of males is quite distinctive.*

be observed in the Chiricahua Mountains in southeastern Arizona. Specific localities include the grassy meadows around Rustler Park and Barfoot Park at approximately 2,591 m elevation. Localities of occurrence near Cloverdale in the southern end of the Animas Valley of southwest Hidalgo County, New Mexico, are on private land and therefore unavailable for observation without landowner permission.

Taxonomy: *Sceloporus slevini* was originally described as a subspecies of *S. scalaris,* although recent investigations suggest the taxa should be elevated to full species, based on geographic isolation and meristic characteristics.

Subspecies and Variation: No subspecies of *S. slevini* are currently recognized. Some individuals from southeastern Arizona lack a dorsal pattern. These unicolored individuals, with a gray, yellowish, or dark brown dorsal ground color, appear in both sexes and may constitute 14–20% of the population. Such unicolored individuals have not been reported from New Mexico.

Remarks: Microhabitat condition, especially at high altitudes, is important in the conservation of this species because of its importance for cover and thermoregulation during winter months. Studies have suggested that the species' apparent restriction to montane meadows may be a historic artifact associated with chronic and ubiquitous grazing of lower-elevation perennial grasslands. Populations of Slevin's Bunchgrass Lizard seem to have declined significantly in sites in the Chiricahua Mountains where the species reached densities of 100–200 per ha. Severe overgrazing by livestock was implicated in this decline.

Plateau Fence Lizard

Sceloporus tristichus Cope in Yarrow, 1875

Authors: Trevor B. Persons and Adam D. Leaché

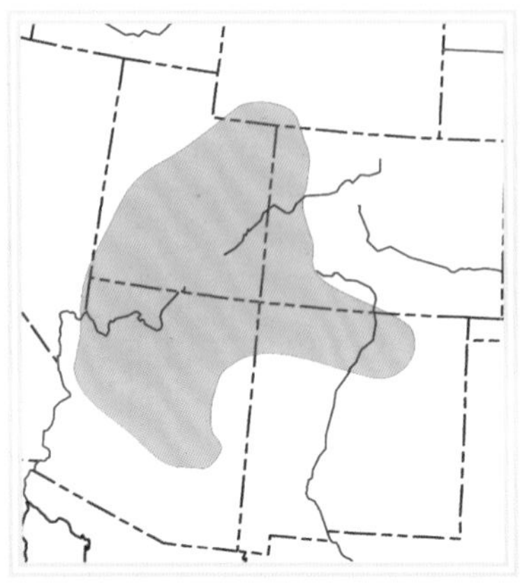

See page 559 for map color codes.

Description: The Plateau Fence Lizard has pointed, keeled, overlapping dorsal scales and an incomplete gular fold. Plateau Fence Lizards reach a maximum SVL of around 90 mm, although 70–80 mm is more usual. Tail length is about 1.5 times the SVL. Ground color is brown or gray, often matching local rock or soil color, with a dorsal pattern of stripes, crossbars, or chevrons. **Sexual Variation:** Adult males have bright blue patches on each side of the throat and belly, which are edged with black in some populations, and the base of the tail is noticeably swollen from the inverted hemipenes. Males of all ages have enlarged post-anal scales. Females lack enlarged post-anal scales, and the blue patches on the throat and belly are much reduced. When gravid, the skin directly above the eyes may become orange or red. **Juveniles:** Plateau Fence Lizards are about 25 mm SVL upon hatching and look like adults, except that the ventral blue patches are faint or absent, especially in females.

Female S. tristichus, *Yavapai Co., AZ.*

Male S. tristichus, *Yavapai Co., AZ. This taxon was formerly within* S. undulatus.

Similar Species: Small Plateau Fence Lizards are readily distinguished from Common Side-blotched Lizards and Ornate Tree Lizards, 2 frequent neighbors, by having pointed scales and lacking a complete gular fold. The distribution of the Plateau Fence Lizard overlaps or approaches that of 9 other spiny lizards: species in the Desert Spiny Lizard complex (*S. magister*, *S. uniformis*, and *S. bimaculosus*) are larger and show black wedge-shaped markings on the sides of the neck. The Clark's Spiny Lizard is larger and has dark crossbars on the wrists and forearms. The Yarrow's Spiny Lizard has a dark, iridescent mesh-like dorsal pattern and a prominent black collar. The Common Sagebrush Lizard is smaller, less spiny, and has small, granular scales on the rear of the thighs. In male Common Sagebrush Lizards the throat is uniformly blue, rather than forming 2 distinct patches. Adult Western Fence Lizards from the narrow zone of overlap in the Pine Valley Mountains of southwestern Utah usually lack lateral striping and have blue flecking on the back, and adult males have yellow or orange on the underside of the limbs and a single large blue throat patch. The Southwestern Fence Lizard and the Prairie Lizard are difficult to distinguish in the field where their ranges meet.

Habitats: Plateau Fence Lizards occur in almost every habitat within their range, including Great Basin desert scrub, chaparral, semi-desert grassland, Plains and Great

Basin grassland, piñon/juniper woodland, Ponderosa Pine forest, and even into mixed conifer forest. Elevations range from about 900 to 2,750 m. In all habitats, Plateau Fence Lizards are most commonly found in rocky areas (outcroppings, lava fields, etc.), but they also climb on trees, buildings, fences, and other structures.

Natural History: Plateau Fence Lizards are among the first lizard species to emerge from brumation in the spring, often appearing in March. Adults are active into October, and juveniles can sometimes be seen on warm days in November. They are more likely than other species to be abroad on cooler days, and individuals may be active from early morning to sunset. Body temperatures of active Plateau Fence Lizards are usually between 29 and 37°C. Adult males defend territories against other Plateau Fence Lizards (and sometimes humans) with a series of push-up displays whereby they expose their bright blue ventral coloration to chase away conspecific intruders. Densities of studied populations range from 14 to 35 individuals (excluding hatchlings) per ha. Plateau Fence Lizards eat a wide variety of insects and other arthropods, and sometimes small lizards. They are sit-and-wait predators, perching on rocks or tree trunks until suddenly dashing off to catch an unsuspecting prey item. Plateau Fence Lizards mate in spring, and females lay 1–3 clutches of 5–12 (usually 7–8) eggs in May, June, or July, and hatchlings emerge about 2 months later. Most lizards do not reach maturity until almost 2 years of age, and few individuals live longer than 4 years. Females are about 60 mm SVL when reproductively mature.

Juvenile S. tristichus, *Yavapai Co., AZ.*

Ventral patches of male S. tristichus, *Canyon Pintado, CO.*

Range: The Plateau Fence Lizard occurs throughout most of the Colorado Plateau region, including central and northern Arizona, northwestern New Mexico, southern and eastern Utah, western Colorado, and extreme southern Wyoming. The Plateau Fence Lizard and the Southwestern Fence Lizard meet in a narrow hybrid zone south of Holbrook, Arizona, and similar contact zones probably exist elsewhere in eastern and southeastern Arizona and northern New Mexico. The distribution of these 2 species in and near these contact zones needs further study.

Viewing Tips: Plateau Fence Lizards are common in almost all habitats within their range, and are easily observed almost anywhere. In recent surveys of National Park Service lands across the Colorado Plateau, the only areas without Plateau Fence Lizards were high-elevation Bryce Canyon National Park and Cedar Breaks National Monument in Utah. In addition to national parks such as Arches, Grand Canyon, or Mesa Verde, these lizards are common throughout national forests within their range. Plateau Fence Lizards are often seen basking on rocks, fences, or other structures. They can usually be approached to within a few feet, where an observer can experience the full wrath of a territorial push-up display at close range.

Taxonomy: Genetic research has shown that the Plateau Fence Lizard more or less encompasses populations that were previously regarded as the subspecies *elongatus*, *erythrocheilus,* and *tristichus* of the wide-ranging Eastern Fence Lizard (*Sceloporus undulatus*). These diverse lizards are part of a multi-species complex, and it is difficult to provide a taxonomy that captures all of the relevant variation among populations.

Subspecies and Variation: No subspecies are currently recognized. Lizards from the southern portion of the range (formerly classified as *S. undulatus tristichus*) have dorsal stripes and are difficult to distinguish from the Southwestern Fence Lizard. Northern lizards (formerly *S. u. elongatus*) are somewhat larger and generally have faint dorsal stripes (if any) and prominent crossbars. In older adults these crossbars may be faint or absent, resulting in an overall plain appearance.

Yellow-backed Spiny Lizard

Sceloporus uniformis Phelan and Brattstrom, 1955

Author: Paulette M. Conrad

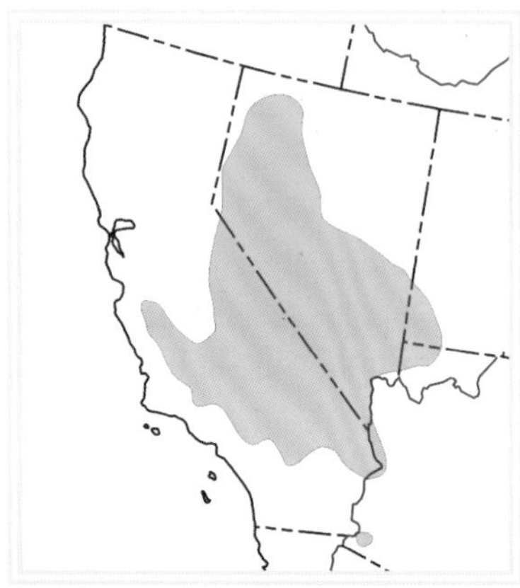

See page 559 for map color codes. There are different interpretations of taxonomy, nomenclature, and range for this species complex.

Description: Yellow-backed Spiny Lizards are stout, strong-looking lizards that are yellowish-brown with a black wedge-shaped mark on the shoulders. They have keeled dorsal scales, creating a spiny appearance, and have 4 to 8 pointed ear scales. Males can reach 140 mm SVL, while females reach 112 mm SVL. Tail lengths are slightly longer than the SVL for each individual. This species has a rather dull coloration compared to other large spiny lizards and lacks distinctive dorsal markings. **Sexual Variation:** Adult males have blue lateral abdominal patches edged in black, as well as a central blue throat patch. Males have a light yellow or tan uniform dorsum grading into darker brown on the sides. Adult males also have larger post-anal scales. Females are generally smaller than males and have faint or absent blue throat patches and generally lack color on the venter. The head of the female may be orange or reddish when breeding, and the post-anal scales are smaller. **Juveniles:** Juveniles are smaller than adults of this species and have faint or absent blue abdominal or throat patches. The post-anal scales are smaller in juvenile males until they reach sexual maturity.

Adult S. uniformis, *Lovell Canyon, NV. This dark individual has not warmed up to show its normal, active color pattern.*

Adult male S. uniformis. *This taxon was formerly within* S. magister.

Similar Species: Desert Spiny Lizards are somewhat larger, and adult males will have a black, deep purple, or red middorsal longitudinal stripe bordered by light stripes (*S. m. magister*) or an orange head with contrasting dorsal crossbands (*S. m. cephaloflavus*). Yellow-backed Spiny Lizards also look similar to Western Fence Lizards. The Western Fence Lizard is smaller, lacks the dark wedge on its shoulders, and its spiny scales protrude less than the Yellow-backed Spiny Lizard's. Other morphologically similar species such as the Twin-spotted Spiny Lizard, Clark's Spiny Lizard, and Granite Spiny Lizard do not overlap the distribution of the Yellow-backed Spiny Lizard.

Habitats: This species is found only in the southwestern portion of North America, typically in association with yuccas and Joshua Trees. However, in the Central Valley of California individuals inhabit rock outcrops and rodent holes in the banks of dry streambeds, while in the Great Basin they are found in eroded landscapes and not found in the flats around shrubs. The species occurs from near sea level to around 1,520 m.

Natural History: Individuals of this species emerge from brumation around April, when temperatures begin to rise, and will be most active when ambient temperatures are above 22°C but below 33°C. This species has a complex social organization and is probably territorial, as it achieves densities of 6–50 per ha. These spiny lizards communicate with other individuals of their species by bobbing their heads, doing push-ups, and mouth gaping. This communication is used to identify territories and attract

Male S. uniformis, *Churchill Co., NV. As with most other large* Sceloporus, *the dark wedge on the neck is much broader ventrally in males than in females.*

mates. One or more clutches of 4–19 eggs per adult female will be laid from May to August each year. This species presumably lays eggs in nests constructed in friable, sandy, well-drained soil. Yellow-backed Spiny Lizards occasionally eat flowers, buds, leaves, and berries, but mostly rely on insects, spiders, and other smaller lizards for food. Their predators are primarily birds and snakes, but the young are probably taken by predatory lizards such as Leopard and Collared Lizards. Yellow-backed Spiny Lizards use good vision to detect these predators and will sometimes inflate their bodies to look larger so the predator will avoid them. If a predator gets too close, the lizard will attempt to elude it by moving quickly to seek shelter in crevices, under debris, or in rodent burrows. If a predator catches its tail, Yellow-Backed Spiny Lizards have the ability to autotomize the tail from the rest of the body to escape capture. They will also bite when captured as a last defense mechanism.

Range: The Yellow-backed Spiny Lizard occurs primarily in the Mojave and Great Basin deserts of California, Nevada, Utah, and northwestern Arizona. It also occurs in California's Central Valley.

Viewing Tips: This species is diurnal and most active in the spring and summer, April through August. However, they are commonly observed outside of this time frame if the weather is right. They are quick to retreat to cover, so it is best to use binoculars to view this species before attempting to get closer. You can also find Yellow-backed Spiny Lizards basking on paved roads early in the morning. Good places to view these lizards include Red Rock Canyon National Conservation Area (NV), Lake Mead National

Park (NV, AZ, CA), Joshua Tree National Park (CA), Death Valley National Park (CA), Inyo National Forest (NV), and Walker Lake (NV).

Taxonomy: Two former subspecies of the Desert Spiny Lizard, *S. magister uniformis* (in part) and *S. m. transversus*, were recently combined and elevated to the species level and currently make up the *S. uniformis*, or Yellow-backed Spiny Lizard, species. The former *S. m. uniformis* from the Lower Colorado subdivision of the Sonoran Desert was synonymized with *S. m. magister*. This taxonomic change was based on differences among color patterns, habitats, and DNA sequences. While this recent genetic work has assisted in elevating the Yellow-backed Spiny Lizard to a species level, large areas within the former distribution of the Desert Spiny Lizard (*S. magister*) complex were not sampled (northwest Arizona, southeast Utah, and southeast Arizona/southwest New Mexico), raising questions about contact zones and current ranges.

Subspecies and Variation: There are currently no subspecies of the Yellow-backed Spiny Lizard. However, males from populations near Walker Lake, Nevada; east Mineral or Esmeralda counties, Nevada; or Kern County, California, tend to have 6 to 7 dark dorsal crossbands extending onto the sides. Individuals from the rest of this species' distribution have a uniform dorsum with no distinct pattern.

Remarks: The specific epithet *uniformis* comes from the Latin words *uni* meaning "one" and *formis* meaning "shape," which refer to the patternless dorsum of the Yellow-backed Spiny Lizard. Recent evidence suggests subsumation of *S. m. cephaloflavus* into *S. uniformis*.

Female S. uniformis, *Stoddard Ridge, San Bernardino Co., CA.*

Striped Plateau Lizard

Sceloporus virgatus Smith, 1938

Author: Lawrence L. C. Jones

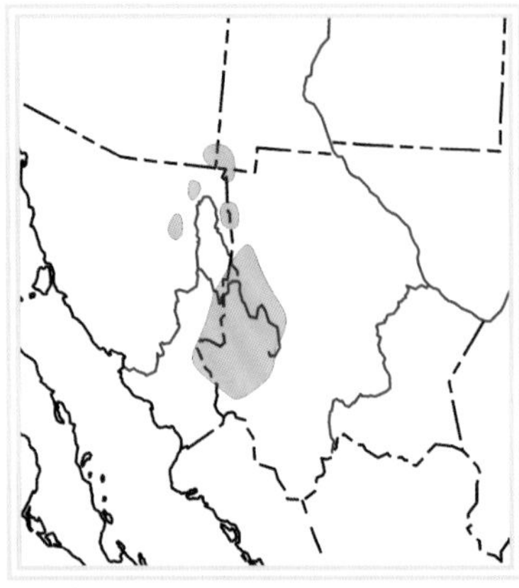

See page 559 for map color codes.

Description: This is a small brown lizard, reaching about 61 mm SVL in males and 71 mm SVL in females. It has 2 distinct, cream-colored, dorsolateral stripes, extending from the rear of the head onto the tail. Between the dorsolateral stripes are 2 parallel rows of dark brown and white spots. There is a broad brownish to gray middorsal stripe between the spots. There are 2 lateral stripes, which are separated from the dorsolateral stripes by dark brown stripes. The venter of the torso and tail is patternless and cream-colored. **Sexual Variation:** Sexual dimorphism is fairly subtle in this species. Unlike other members of the genus, males lack the familiar "blue-belly" pattern, but males do have blue throat patches that are more distinctive than those found in females. The dorsal spots of males are more obscure than those of females, and may even be absent. Males tend to be more intensely striped than females. Males also have swollen tail bases and enlarged post-anal scales. The throat patches of females are pale blue when not in breeding condition and turn progressively more orange with hormonal changes associated with the reproductive cycle. **Juveniles:** Juveniles are similar to adults, but have a relatively larger head, poorly developed dorsal spotting, and no throat patches.

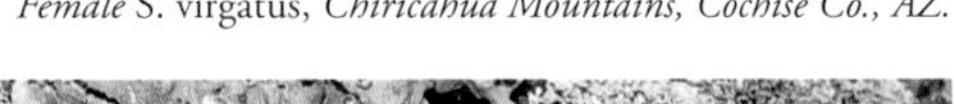

Female S. virgatus, *Chiricahua Mountains, Cochise Co., AZ.*

Male S. virgatus, *Chiricahua Mountains, Cochise Co., AZ.*

Similar Species: Striped Plateau Lizards are similar to other small brown *Sceloporus* in the *undulatus* complex (*tristichus, cowlesi,* and *consobrinus,* in our region) that have longitudinal stripes, but can be separated by the lack of a blue belly in males. *Sceloporus virgatus* has a smaller maximum adult size than species in the *undulatus* complex, and has posteriorly notched femoral-pore scales. Slevin's Bunchgrass Lizard has parallel rows of scales.

Habitats: This is a montane species, found from about 1,490 to 3,080 m above sea level, but is normally observed between 1,600 and 1,900 m. It is most frequently observed in Madrean oak and pine-oak woodlands, but also inhabits forests of Apache and Ponderosa Pine, and sometimes mixed conifers. These lizards are most frequently found in canyons and along drainages, but are also found in upland situations. Adults are generally associated with rocks, including boulders, especially near the edges of perennial or ephemeral streams, or rockslides, but are sometimes observed on logs and trees. Juveniles do not tend to climb.

Natural History: Males and females are born at a 1:1 ratio. Males reach sexual maturity at a minimum of about 43 mm SVL and females at about 47 mm SVL, but there is variation depending upon food availability and time of hatching. Males are reproductive in their second year, and females become reproductive in 10–22 months after hatching (first or second year after hatching). Females lay a single clutch per year, averaging 9.5 eggs. Oviposition is triggered by the onset of summer rains. Eggs are laid in sunny areas. Hatchlings measure about 21 or 22 mm SVL and usually appear on the surface during late August and September. The female's reproductive cycle can be tracked by color changes in the throat patches. During non-reproductive periods, they are blue, then become increasingly more orange, starting when eggs are well developed, peaking after ovulation and fading after oviposition.

Both males and females are territorial. Females have well-defined home ranges, while males tend to venture outside of home ranges during breeding forays. Densities have been recorded as high as 130 individuals/ha. Territorial displays may be observed, but females rarely fight. Striped Plateau Lizards may be active through much of the year, but activity peaks in the summer months; juveniles are more likely to be seen on the surface during winter months, when warm conditions prevail. Field-recorded body temperatures of active adults are usually about 33°C. This species is closely tied with monsoonal moisture; rainy years translate to increased reproductive output, feeding, and growth. This species eats small arthropods and presumably is preyed upon by a variety of larger bird, mammal, and reptilian predators that share its habitat.

Range: *Sceloporus virgatus* is a Madrean montane endemic, found only in some of the mountains of the Apachean ecoregion. In the U.S., they are only known from the Chiricahua, Peloncillo, and Animas mountains of Arizona and New Mexico. They range into the Sierra Madre Occidental of Sonora and Chihuahua, but the southern limits are poorly known.

Viewing Tips: The Striped Plateau Lizard is easily observed in the Coronado National Forest in the Chiricahua Mountains of southeastern Arizona. Look for it in pine/oak

S. virgatus, *Chiricahua Mountains, AZ. Color pattern differences between the sexes are subtle, but the swollen tail base indicates a male.*

Juvenile S. virgatus, *Chiricahua Mountains, Cochise Co., AZ.*

woodlands along any of the major roads at the proper elevations. It is most easily observed in areas with boulders, especially along drainages. They are usually seen basking on rocks, especially during the summer months. As lizards go, this species is easily approachable. Juveniles may be observed during the late summer and early fall.

Taxonomy: This species was originally described as a subspecies of *S. undulatus,* but has been regarded as a full species by herpetologists for many years.

Subspecies and Variation: No subspecies are recognized. Unlike the *S. undulatus* complex, this species shows relatively little intraspecific variation. Variation is usually limited to the intensity of stripes and degree of spotting. The stripes are sometimes broken.

Remarks: The natural history of this species is well researched, due in part to the fact that the lizards are abundant, easy to capture, and found in the vicinity of the American Museum of Natural History's Southwestern Research Station in the Chiricahua Mountains. They share habitat with 3 other montane *Sceloporus,* including *S. clarkii, S. jarrovii,* and *S. slevini,* as well as *Urosaurus ornatus* and some ground-dwelling species. The mechanisms allowing for sympatry of so many lizards has been the focus of several studies. *Sceloporus cowlesi* is a superficially similar species found in the adjacent valleys. It is not known to overlap the range of *S. virgatus,* but they occur within 2 km of each other.

Coachella Fringe-toed Lizard

Uma inornata Cope, 1895

Authors: Cameron W. Barrows and Mark Fisher

See page 559 for map color codes.

Description: Coachella Fringe-toed Lizards are medium-sized dorsoventrally flattened lizards (70–122 mm SVL) that are superbly adapted to windblown sand habitats. These adaptations include an elongated fringe of scales along the trailing edge of each toe, enlarged scales that partially cover their ear openings, a countersunk jaw, a shovel-shaped nose, and slit-shaped nasal openings. Their dorsal pattern consists of small ocelli that overlay a background hue that closely matches that of the local sand. The ocelli are fused into broken diagonal lines over the shoulders. The throat is marked with thin black chevrons that become faded or absent at mid-throat; there are black bars on the underside of the tail. Fewer than 5% of these lizards have ventrolateral clusters of small black spots, sometimes present only on one side, located where the prominent ventrolateral blotches on other fringe-toed lizards would be. The eyelids have an orange color that is present in all ages and sexes. **Sexual Variation:** Males average 99 mm SVL (range 80–122 mm) and differ from females primarily in their larger size and enlarged

Male U. inornata, *Coachella Valley, CA. Ventral color patterns are good for differentiating some species of* Uma.

Adult male U. inornata *near Palm Springs, CA, showing scars on the shoulder from territorial battles.*

post-anal scales. Sexually active males develop a very pale pink to orange wash along their flanks. Females average 79 mm SVL (range 70–99 mm). When gravid they develop vivid orange color laterally along their flanks, faces, and anterior portions of their tails. This bright color is obvious only when viewed at "lizard level" and may be a "not available" signal to otherwise amorous males. Females observed in copulation lacked this additional orange color. **Juveniles:** Juveniles resemble adults.

Similar Species: This is the only fringe-toed lizard found in California's Coachella Valley. Sympatric lizards within the Coachella Valley that could be confused with Coachella Fringe-toed Lizards include Desert Iguanas and Zebra-tailed Lizards. Adult iguanas are considerably larger and are rounder in cross section than the distinctly dorsoventrally flattened fringe-toed lizards. Desert Iguanas have relatively longer tails and lack a well-formed pattern of ocelli. Zebra-tailed lizards are slimmer with thinner legs and a tail that they often flick back and forth in a cat-like fashion; males have 2 distinct ventrolateral bars. The Colorado Desert Fringe-toed Lizard differs in having prominent black ventrolateral blotches, and adult males have a permanent orange ventrolateral band. The Mohave Fringe-toed Lizard differs in that the ocelli do not fuse into lines over the shoulder, a ventrolateral blotch is present, and the throat chevrons are complete and widest at midthroat.

Habitats: This species is restricted to the windblown sands in the northwestern corner of the Sonoran Desert's Colorado Desert subdivision, at elevations ranging from below sea level up to 400 m. On expansive, sparsely vegetated dunes these may be the only lizards encountered. They prefer loosely compacted sand with moderate to sparse vegetation and can be especially common on sand-dune avalanche faces. Typical shrub associations include Creosote Bush, Indigo Bush, Honey Mesquite, and Four-winged Saltbush.

Natural History: Sparsely vegetated, actively moving sand presents a challenge for most organisms, yet for fringe-toed lizards this is home. Their physical and behavioral adaptations are so attuned to this habitat that they are rarely found on any other substrate. Fringe-toed lizards will dive headfirst into loose sand and bury a few centimeters below the sand surface to avoid predators or temperature extremes. They often lie below the sand with just their eyes above the surface, superbly camouflaged yet ready to dash out to grab a meal or escape a predator. They tend to be most active April through October, in mornings after sand surface temperatures reach 35°C and before they exceed 45°C. Males can often be seen surveying their surroundings from atop dune crests. Midday temperatures can be lethal, forcing the lizards to relocate and burrow into the sand below a shrub or get greater temperature relief by burrowing in the sand or in a rodent burrow. Both locations carry risks, as the Sidewinder, a fringe-toed lizard predator, often seeks the same daytime refuges. Fringe-toed lizards do not maintain a territory, but within their home range adult males will display at other males to claim access to a receptive female. Displaying males circle each other, expanding their rib cages and tilting toward each other to assess who is larger. Female Coachella Fringe-toed lizards dig burrows to lay a clutch of 2–3 eggs and, depending on available food resources, can lay 0–3 clutches from May to September; hatchlings usually emerge August through October. Coachella Fringe-toed Lizards feed on various arthropods and, when available, flowers and leaves of dune plants. Harvester ants can be a key prey item in dry years, but in wetter years, plants, true bugs, grasshoppers, and beetles all become important components of their diet.

Juvenile U. inornata, *Riverside Co., CA.*

Range: This species is confined entirely within southern California's Coachella Valley. It once ranged over roughly 32,000 ha but, due primarily to development, now occurs on scattered locations totaling less than 1,300 ha.

Gravid female U. inornata, *Coachella Valley, CA.*

Viewing Tips: This species was listed as a threatened (federal) and endangered species (California state) in 1980, and as a result access to the Coachella Fringe-toed Lizard's protected habitat is restricted. Occasional tours are provided into protected preserves to see this species as well as other sand-dune endemics. For a less structured viewing, they can sometimes be seen through binoculars on dune hummocks from the parking lot of the Palm Springs train station, located just west of Indian Avenue and south of Interstate 10.

Taxonomy: Taxonomists have previously considered the Coachella Fringe-toed Lizard a subspecies of the Colorado Desert Fringe-toed Lizard, referring to it as *U. notata inornata.*

Subspecies and Variation: No subspecies are recognized.

Remarks: A multiple-species, multiple-agency Habitat Conservation Plan (with federal, state, and county funding) was created in 1986 to ensure protection of the Coachella Fringe-toed Lizards' remaining habitat. Habitat has been lost to suburban and agricultural development and by blocking wind and sand movement, which eventually stabilizes down-wind habitat and renders it unsuitable for fringe-toed lizards. Intense off-road vehicle activity has degraded habitat locally by eliminating vegetation critical for thermal relief and food.

Colorado Desert Fringe-toed Lizard

Uma notata Baird, 1859 "1858"

Author: James C. Rorabaugh

See page 559 for map color codes.

Description: This lizard is flattened white or buff-colored with dark spots or ocelli. Adults have a permanent bright orange or orange/pink ventrolateral patch that intensifies during the breeding season from May through September. The pattern of ocelli form interrupted black stripes over the shoulder. Adaptations for sand dune life include fringes on the toes, enlarged scales over the ears, valves over the nostrils, eyelids that exclude sand, a countersunk jaw, flattened head and snout, and smooth, granular scales on the body. **Sexual Variation:** Adult males range from about 80 to 121 mm SVL and have 2 enlarged post-anal scales; adult females are smaller at 70–94 mm SVL. **Juveniles:** The orange or orange/pink ventrolateral patch is absent or faint.

Adult U. notata, *Algodones Dunes, Imperial Co., CA.*

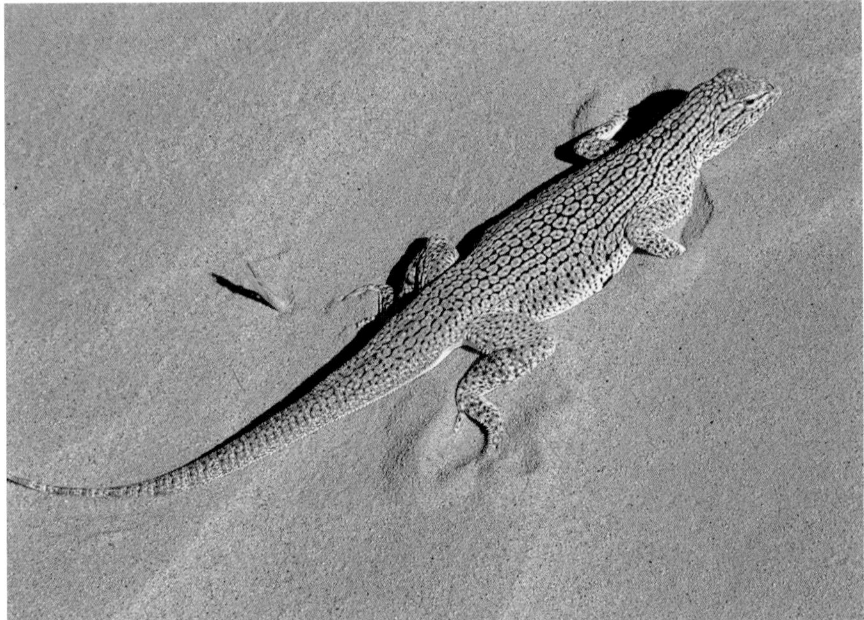

Male U. notata, *Ocotillo Wells, CA.*

Similar Species: The Colorado Desert Fringe-toed Lizard is distinguished from all other fringed-toed lizards by the permanent orange or orange/pink ventrolateral patch in adults; such coloration in other species occurs only during the breeding season. Other features distinct from other fringe-toed lizards include a prominent black ventrolateral blotch (absent or just a cluster of black dots in Coachella Fringe-toed Lizards) and an absence of black blotches in the pre-femoral pocket on the upper surface of the thigh (as present in Mohave Fringe-toed Lizards).

Habitats: Fine, uncompacted, and windblown sand is the key habitat feature. This can take the form of large dune systems, such as the Algodones Dunes in California, smaller barchan dunes that move with the winds, and/or sandy plains, or broad, sandy washes, such as Pinto Wash west of Calexico. Substrates found over much of the range of this species and the Yuman Fringe-toed Lizard are buff-colored silica sands that were deposited throughout the region over millions of years by the Colorado River. These sandy habitats, which occur at elevations of about –74 to 180 m, are sparsely vegetated with many plant species of the Lower Colorado River subdivision of Sonoran Desert scrub, including a number of species endemic to dunes. Colorado Desert Fringe-toed Lizards can occupy barren, shifting dunes, but they are seldom found far from vegetated areas, which are important for forage and escape cover.

Natural History: The unique challenges of living in sand dunes have shaped the morphology and natural history of the Colorado Desert Fringe-toed Lizard. This species is most active from February into November, but juveniles are often active on warm days in winter. Colorado Desert Fringe-toed Lizards are known for diving a few centimeters into the sand to avoid predators and extreme surface temperatures; however, adults spend the winter buried as deep as 30 cm. A clutch of 1–5 (mostly 2) eggs is laid from May to August. Two clutches may be produced in favorable years, but breeding is delayed following dry winters. Hatchlings appear from early July to mid-September. Diet includes insects, especially those that live on or near the sand surface or on annual plants, such as ants, beetles, moths, grasshoppers, sand roaches, spiders, and caterpillars. However, the flowers, buds, leaves, and seeds of some plants are eaten as well, and juvenile lizards are sometimes taken. Predators are many and include, among others, Sidewinders, Glossy Snakes, Coachwhips, Loggerhead Shrikes, Greater Roadrunners, Common Ravens, Badgers, and Coyotes.

Range: The Colorado Desert Fringe-toed Lizard ranges over portions of southeastern California and northeastern Baja California. On the western side of the Salton Sea, this species is found from Clark Dry Lake, northeast of Borrego Springs, and just south of Salton City south to around Superstition Mountain, West Mesa, and Pinto Wash. East of the Salton Sea, the species occurs throughout the Algodones Dunes and in windblown, sandy flats in East Mesa west of the Coachella Canal. The Colorado Desert Fringe-toed Lizard has apparently disappeared from the limited dunes surrounding Bat Cave Butte, just east to Highway 111 in Riverside County, in extreme southern California. In Baja California, the species occurs in the dunes and sandy flats on the edge of Laguna Salada, the western base of the Sierras los Cucapás, northern end of the Sierra las Pintas, at the southern end of the Algodones Dunes, and likely on the eastern edge of the Sierra Juarez.

Adult U. notata, *Algodones Dunes, Imperial Co., CA.*

Viewing Tips: This species is easily observed on the edges of the Algodones Dunes, in windblown sand around Superstition Mountain, and in other dunes of

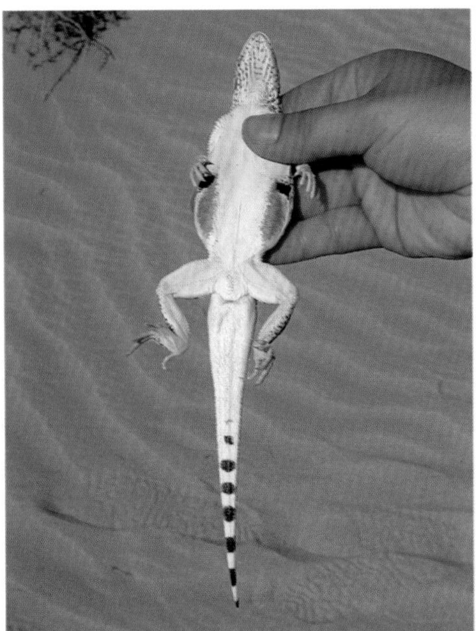

Ventral coloration of male U. notata, *Ocotillo Wells, CA. Both sexes have similar ventral markings.*

Imperial County, California, when surface temperatures range from about 32 to 47°C. These temperatures may occur midday in March or April, but as the season progresses surface temperatures suitable for lizard activity occur only in the morning and near dusk. The Colorado Desert Fringe-toed Lizard is typically the most abundant lizard species where it occurs and is virtually the only lizard to inhabit the interior of large dune systems. They are often seen running at high speed across the dunes, only to disappear abruptly into the sand. Their tracks consist of 2 rows of alternating dots or impressions in the sand, which may lead to where the lizard dove into the sand. It elevates the tail off the sand while running, but a tail drag between the impressions of the feet is evident when the lizard is moving more slowly.

Taxonomy: Until recently, the Colorado Desert and Yuman Fringe-toed Lizards were considered subspecies of *U. notata*. However, molecular genetic analyses indicate they are separate species.

Subspecies and Variation: No subspecies are recognized; however, dorsal coloration varies among populations, probably as a local adaptation to substrate color.

Remarks: Colorado Desert Fringe-toed Lizards are rarely found far from windblown sand, which tends to occur in discrete, isolated patches. As a result, many populations are isolated. *Uma* species likely evolved from a more widespread, less dune-adapted ancestor that may have become a dune specialist in response to competition from similar species, such as the Zebra-tailed Lizards and earless lizards. Populations, particularly small populations, are susceptible to the impact of off-highway vehicles. The Colorado Desert Fringe-toed Lizard is listed as *amenazada* (threatened) on Mexico's list of species at risk.

Yuman Fringe-toed Lizard

Uma rufopunctata Cope, 1895

Authors: Dale S. Turner and James C. Rorabaugh

See page 559 for map color codes.

Description: This is a medium-sized lizard with a flattened body and countersunk lower jaw. Adult males range from 80 to 98 mm SVL, while adult females are somewhat smaller at 66–80 mm SVL. A dorsal pattern of ocelli forms broken longitudinal lines over the shoulder. There is a black, ventrolateral blotch on each side. While the smooth scales of black, brown, and orange on cream form distinct patterns when viewed closely, they blend together when viewed from a distance into a color that precisely matches the surface of the lizard's native sand dunes. They have a fringe of enlarged scales on toes of the hind feet. **Sexual Variation:** Males have enlarged postanal scales. **Juveniles:** Hatchlings measure 35–40 mm SVL, but are otherwise similar to adults.

Juvenile U. rufopunctata, *Mohawk Dunes, Yuma Co., AZ.*

Adult U. rufopunctata, *Dateland, Yuma Co., AZ.*

Similar Species: No other species of fringe-toed lizard occurs within the range of the Yuman Fringe-toed Lizard. The similar Zebra-tailed Lizard can be found in sandy flats and dune edges, but has a boldly striped, black-and-white tail that it frequently waves over its back when threatened.

Habitats: The Yuman Fringe-toed Lizard is closely associated with windblown sand deposits in the Lower Colorado River subdivision of the Sonoran Desert. These include the bare sand of active dunes, dunes that have been partially stabilized by vegetation, and the vegetated sand sheets that surround some dune fields. Perennial plants are typically in low density and low species diversity, with the most common being White Bursage and Big Galleta Grass.

Natural History: This species is superbly adapted to living in windblown, sandy habitats. It often occurs in sand that is too loose or friable for construction of open burrows. The Yuman Fringe-toed Lizard is adept at diving into the sand head-first, accompanied by rapid sideways movements of the head and kicks or thrusts with the hind legs to bury itself within a few centimeters of the surface. Midday in summer, when surface temperatures frequently exceed 65°C, Yuman Fringe-toed Lizards burrow into the sand beneath large shrubs (especially White Bursage), into the floor of mammal burrows (if present), or in other shaded or protected sites that provide better thermal cover. This species is most active when surface temperatures are 35–47°C.

Thus they are active only morning and evening during the hot summer months and only at midday during spring and fall. The highest activity levels occur in April and May, during the peak breeding season. The parietal eye is particularly well developed in the Yuman Fringe-toed Lizard. With both lens and retina, it helps the lizard monitor solar radiation and regulate activity periods.

Yuman Fringe-toed Lizards are relatively abundant in good habitats. They reproduce in the spring following winters with adequate rainfall, but reproduction may be timed to the summer rains after a dry winter. Two clutches may be produced in wet years. Clutch size ranges from 1 to 3 (average 1.85). The diet of the Yuman Fringe-toed Lizard includes a variety of arthropods as well as plants. Common prey includes ants, beetles, spiders, and roaches, along with seeds and flowers of legumes. As lizards mature, plants make up a greater proportion of their diet.

Range: The Yuman Fringe-toed Lizard is restricted to southwestern Arizona and northwestern Sonora. In Arizona, its range includes the sandy valleys and dunes near Yuma, east to Dateland, and south through the northwestern San Cristobal and Mohawk valleys (including the Mohawk Dunes) to Pinta Sands on Cabeza Prieta National Wildlife Refuge. The largest populations in Arizona occur in the Yuma and Mohawk dunes, and Pinta Sands, all of which appear to be disjunct. In Sonora, the species occurs in the extensive sand fields and dunes of the Gran Desierto from near San Luis Río Colorado to east of the Sierra Pinacate and southeast along the coastal plain to Punta Tepoca.

Viewing Tips: Yuman Fringe-toed Lizards can be challenging to see well because they are nearly invisible when motionless and very fast when running. They are wary and have good eyesight, and will often dash for cover when an approaching person is still more than 20 m distant. Lizard-watchers should focus well out in front of themselves, and visually follow the path of a running lizard. By keeping their eyes fixed on where the lizard disappeared, they can often pick up the distinctive trail in the sand and follow their fresh tracks to the animal's hiding place. Temperatures are critical, with the best time to observe this species being in April and May during morning times when temperatures are 35–47°C.

Permits are needed to visit most occupied areas in the U.S., either from the Marine Corps in Yuma or Fish and Wildlife Service in Ajo. A few small populations can be visited without permits north and west of the Barry M. Goldwater Range. Much of the Gran Desierto is accessible without permits, although the lack of roads and road maintenance, remoteness, and extreme temperatures bring significant risks to the unprepared traveler.

Taxonomy: This was recently elevated to full species status, having been formerly a subspecies of *U. notata*. The Mohawk Dunes population has a genetic signature that is distinct from other populations and may lead to future taxonomic recognition.

Subspecies and Variation: There are no recognized subspecies, but some variation in overall color occurs among local populations, matching the variation in local sand color.

Remarks: This lizard and its habitat are susceptible to the impacts of off-highway vehicles, but much of the habitat and the three largest populations in Arizona are protected by public access closures (Yuma Dunes) or limited vehicle use (Mohawk Dunes and Pinta Sands). In Sonora, large portions of the Gran Desierto are protected by Biosphere designations. An additional threat is invasion by non-native annual plants, such as Sahara Mustard, which can fuel destructive fires or cause other ecological changes. The lizard is listed as *amenazada* (threatened) on Mexico's list of species at risk, and a hunting license is needed to collect or possess them in Arizona.

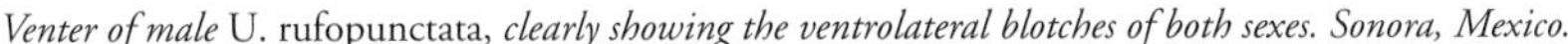

Venter of male U. rufopunctata, *clearly showing the ventrolateral blotches of both sexes. Sonora, Mexico.*

Mohave Fringe-toed Lizard

Uma scoparia Cope, 1894

Author: Robert E. Espinoza

See page 559 for map color codes.

Description: This medium-sized lizard (maximum 114 mm SVL) is dorsoventrally compressed, with distinct red-centered ocelli irregularly spotting the tan or faint yellow background of the dorsal surface. The body scales are small and granular, giving them a velvety appearance. The tail is approximately the length of the body. The snout forms a sharp wedge and the lower jaw is countersunk. The throat has 1–3 dark crescent-shaped markings. The scales of the eyelids, anterior border of the ear opening, and toes form elongate fringes, which are particularly long on the third and fourth toes. The legs are short and stout. The ventral side is white, except for the throat markings, dark bars on the distal region of the tail, and a prominent ventrolateral spot behind each forelimb. During the breeding season both sexes develop a yellowish-green wash ven-

Adult U. scoparia, *San Bernardino Co., CA.*

Adult U. scoparia, *Bouse Dunes, La Paz Co., AZ.*

trally, which fades to pink laterally. **Sexual Variation:** Adult males tend to be larger (averaging 97 mm SVL) than females. The base of the tail has hemipenal bulges, and the femoral pores are distinct, particularly in the breeding season. Males also have two enlarged post-anal scales. Females average 83 mm SVL and lack most male sexual characteristics. Post-anal scales, when present, are smaller than in males. **Juveniles:** Juveniles are similar to adult females.

Similar Species: Because of their distinctive characteristics—countersunk jaw, fringed eyelids and toes, and dorsal ocelli—Mohave Fringe-toed Lizards can only be confused with other species of fringe-toed lizards (Coachella, Colorado Desert, Yuman), none of which have an overlapping range. Unlike these other species, Mohave Fringe-toed Lizards have throat markings that form crescents, ventrolateral spots behind their forelimbs, dorsal ocelli that are scattered (not arranged into rows), and usually five internasals.

Habitats: This species occurs exclusively on fine wind-blown sand associated with Creosote Bush scrub in the Mojave and northern Colorado deserts. This habitat occurs on dune complexes, margins of dry lakebeds and washes, and in isolated pockets along hillsides. This species has been recorded from below sea level to approximately 900 m.

Natural History: Mohave Fringe-toed Lizards are active from March to October and brumate in the intervening months. These heat-loving reptiles are rarely active until sand temperatures approach 38°C, which is close to their "preferred" body temperature (37.3°C) when active, although body temperatures as high as 44°C are tolerated. They are most commonly encountered at midday in spring, but activity shifts to morning and late afternoon in summer and early fall. Unlike most lizards, adults of this species are principally herbivorous, eating grasses, leaves, flowers, and dried seeds. Juveniles eat primarily arthropods (ants, beetles, and scorpions), but a small proportion of their diet also includes plants. Cannibalism has been reported. Adults exhibit breeding coloration from April through July. Males and females are territorial, but only the former aggressively defend their territories. Home ranges for adult males (0.10 ha) are three times the size of those for adult females, and female home ranges overlap the territories of several males. Male displays include dewlap extensions, lateral orientation and compression of the body, and push-ups. Courtship displays include head bobbing and rapid, alternate, up-and-down waving of the front legs and feet. Females deposit 2–5 eggs in sandy hummocks from May through July and can produce more than one clutch per season in wet years, but may suppress reproduction in dry years. Hatchlings appear in early fall (September) and reach sexual maturity in their third year. Predators include American Badgers, Coyotes, hawks, shrikes, Greater Roadrunners, Burrowing Owls, Long-nosed Leopard Lizards, and snakes.

Range: The historical range of the Mohave Fringe-toed Lizard included wind-blown sand habitats in the following southern California counties: southern Inyo, San Bernardino, northeastern Los Angeles, and eastern Riverside. The species is also known from La Paz County, Arizona. Recent studies, however, indicate that this species has been extirpated from several historical localities, and other populations have severely declined.

Viewing Tips: These swift lizards usually dart across a dune to a shrub or rodent burrow. On occasion they dive headfirst and disappear into the sand, usually under a bush. Searching for them in pairs (or more) is helpful, and with practice (and a little luck), one can observe and follow the line traversed, or track their prints in the sand and find the characteristic impression left after they bury. Alternatively, moving very slowly will often permit an approach to within a few meters. Mohave Fringe-toed Lizards are most commonly encountered from late spring (May) through early fall (into October), with adults more likely to be found earlier in the activity season and juveniles later. They require high body temperatures for activity (as described earlier). Indeed, they are among a small number of lizards that are active on very hot days, but

Juvenile U. scoparia, *Bouse Dunes, La Paz Co., AZ.*

when sand temperatures exceed 49°C, even these thermophiles seek cover. Perhaps the most accessible and reliable place to observe Mohave Fringe-toed Lizards in large numbers is Kelso Dunes, which lie within the Mojave National Preserve (CA).

Taxonomy: There are two major genetic groups associated with either the Amargosa or Mojave River drainage systems. These probably split in the mid-Pleistocene.

Subspecies and Variation: No subspecies are recognized.

Remarks: These lizards are well-suited for life on wind-blown sand. The toe fringes improve locomotory performance (traction, speed, and reduced sinking). In fact, they often achieve bipedal locomotion when fleeing. The eyelids are fringed and overlap. Projecting fringes cover the ear opening. The nostrils are valved, and the keeled jaw scales and countersunk lower jaw allow rapid penetration and prevent sand from entering the mouth when dune diving. When burying, the hind limbs provide propulsion, the forelimbs are pressed close to the body, and the torso shimmies, ratcheting the body into the sand with the aid of enlarged imbricate scales on the shoulders and upper arms. The California Department of Fish and Game has designated this as a Species of Special Concern.

Long-tailed Brush Lizard

Urosaurus graciosus Hallowell, 1854

Author: Charles S. Rau

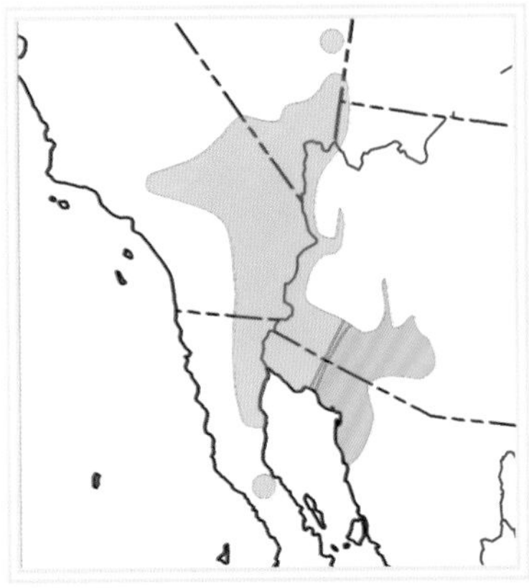

See page 559 for map color codes.

Description: A small, slender lizard with short limbs and a very long tail. Adults range in size from 41 to 52 mm SVL. The tail is slender and long, twice the SVL or longer. Dorsal coloration can be a light gray to a light brown or tan, but is highly variable. There are light gray to blackish crossbars from near the mid-dorsal line to the sides of the body. The underside is pale. The throat can be a light yellow, orange, or red in color. There is an undivided broad band of enlarged dorsal scales, 5–7 scale rows in width, running down the length of the back. The frontal scale is usually divided. **Sexual Variation:** Males have a pale blue to green elongated patch on either side of the belly, often speckled with white; this is lacking in females. Adult males also have enlarged post-anal scales. **Juveniles:** Juveniles of both sexes are similar to adult females but have proportionately larger heads.

Adult U. g. shannoni, *Maricopa Mountains, Maricopa Co., AZ.*

Male U. g. shannoni, *Gila Bend, Maricopa Co., AZ.*

Similar Species: The Long-tailed Brush Lizard is similar to other members of the brush and tree lizard genus, *Urosaurus*. The single dorsal row of enlarged scales and the long, slender tail distinguishes this species from the Ornate Tree Lizard and the Baja California Brush Lizard, as well as the Common Side-blotched Lizard. The Cataviña Brush Lizard (*U. lahtelai*) from Baja California, Mexico, is very similar in appearance to *U. graciosus*. In Baja California, their ranges come to within 16 km of each other and are not known to overlap.

Habitats: This lizard is found in Lower Colorado River desert scrub and Mojave desert scrub. It inhabits desert washes and drainages and flat areas with loose sand and gravel. The Long-tailed Brush Lizard is frequently found on the branches of shrubs and trees such as Creosote Bush, Desert Willow, palo verdes, Smoke Tree, salt bushes, Galleta Grass, mesquites, and Catclaw Acacia. In some areas, they can be found on larger trees, including Fan Palms and introduced Tamarisk. It is found from near sea level to about 1,070 m.

Natural History: This species is usually found on the branches and exposed roots of shrubs and trees where it may lie motionless with its body and tail held flat along the branch (often pointing downward to facilitate escape). This is a territorial species. Generally, only one individual or a pair will inhabit a small shrub or a few small shrubs, whereas several individuals may occupy larger trees. Young and juveniles are usually found in smaller shrubs than adults. This species has a characteristic "push-up" display that is most prominent between males defending their individual territories, but males can also direct their displays towards females or sometimes at other species of lizards. Females also exhibit these displays, but to a lesser degree. This is a heat-tolerant species, with preferred body temperatures above 36°C. During the hottest part of the day it may seek shelter in the sand or in the burrows of other animals. During the hotter months, it may spend nights in the branches of shrubs and bushes. This species breeds in April or May. One or two clutches of 2–10 eggs are deposited in soft sand or loose gravel from May through August. Juveniles usually appear in August and September after about a 60-day gestation period. Primarily this lizard eats a variety of small arthropods, including beetles, ants, bees, leaf hoppers, termites, and spiders, but also consumes small flowers and leaves. Predators are poorly known, but probably include lizard-eating snakes, Long-nosed Leopard Lizards and Collared Lizards, and some mammals and birds such as shrikes, roadrunners, and ravens.

Range: This lizard ranges from northwestern Sonora and northeastern Baja California, Mexico, to desert areas of southern California, and from southern Nevada along the Colorado River into southwest and central Arizona. The northern part of their range in Arizona is near Wickenburg and the Hassayampa River drainage. It has been found a little east of Casa Grande in south-central Arizona.

Viewing Tips: Look for these cryptic lizards on branches of various desert shrubs and trees, where they may be found lying lengthwise and motionless along branches. Occasionally, they may be spotted on the ground, running toward a bush or tree. Areas of sparse vegetation over loose sand and gravel in or near dry desert washes are good places to find them. Search for these lizards in the early morning on the sunny sides of bare lower branches and exposed roots of Creosote Bushes and other shrubs. These lizards become wary when approached closely and will slide around to the other side of a branch, or down the branch. During the hottest periods of the summer these lizards may be seen sleeping on the outer tips of branches at night. This is a good way to spot many individuals, and their pale venters reveal them at night. Some good public lands to see Long-tailed Brush Lizards include Anza-Borrego Desert State Park (CA), Joshua Tree National Park (CA), Valley of Fire State Park (NV), and Kofa National Wildlife Refuge (AZ).

Taxonomy: This species has been considered taxonomically distinct for many years, but subspecies have not always been recognized.

Juvenile U. g. shannoni *on a Creosote Bush branch, Sierra Estrella, Maricopa Co., AZ. These animals are very cryptic on branches, so close inspection is in order, or flash-lighting bushes at night may reveal their pale undersides.*

Subspecies and Variation: There are two subspecies, the Western Long-tailed Brush-lizard (*U. g. graciosus*) and the Arizona Long-tailed Brush Lizard (*U. g. shannoni*). The latter occurs in southwestern Arizona and has a bolder pattern, while the former is primarily southern Californian and has a duller pattern. Long-tailed Brush Lizards are noted for their dramatic color-change abilities. Individuals can change from dark to light phase within 2 or 3 minutes, which is among the fastest for any Southwestern lizards. This color change is also temperature-dependant, with lighter color becoming evident with higher temperatures.

Remarks: These lizards are fast runners, but spend most of their time in bushes, shrubs and trees. They can move very quickly and are very nimble among the roots and branches, and the extra-long tail may be used for balance.

Baja California Brush Lizard

Urosaurus nigricaudus (Cope, 1864)

Author: Robert E. Lovich

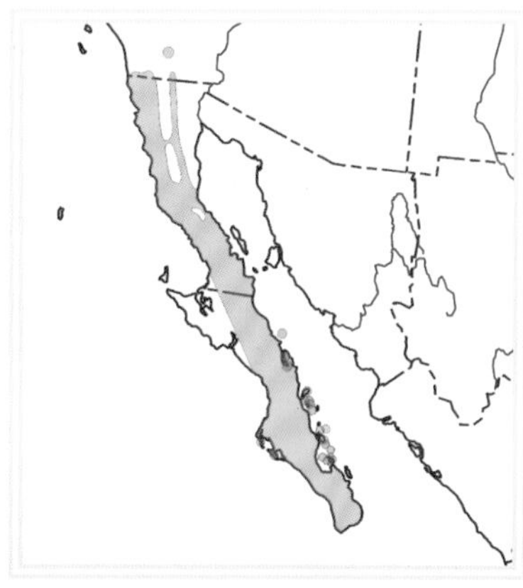

See page 559 for map color codes.

Description: The Baja California Brush Lizard is a relatively small lizard, with adults averaging 38–51 mm SVL. The eyes are small relative to the SVL and have movable eyelids. Enlarged keeled scales run down the length of the back but give way to smaller, more granular scales at the sides. The coloration is gray with paired black blotches running the length of the body, and these blotches are usually bordered by pale blue and white spots or bars. The tail is conspicuously black. The ventral side is grayish. **Sexual Variation:** Males have blue or blue-green metallic patches and an orange or yellow throat patch; these colors are most vivid during breeding season. Females are similar in appearance to males but with reduced dark blotches, and blue spotting is almost absent. Sometimes a yellowish-orange throat patch is also present in females. Females lack the ventral patches. **Juveniles:** Juveniles are nearly identical in appearance to adult females in coloration and shape.

Similar Species: Baja California Brush Lizards are generally similar in appearance to the Long-tailed Brush Lizard and Ornate Tree Lizard. From a distance, they all appear to be relatively small, slender, nondescript brown lizards. Upon closer inspection the observer will find that the black tail, coloration and pattern differences, and overall scalation differentiates them easily from these 2 lizard species in the same genus. They also look like proportionately smaller spiny

Male U. nigricaudus, *Anza-Borrego Desert State Park, CA.*

Male U. nigricaudus, *Anza-Borrego Desert State Park, CA.*

lizards, although they lack strongly keeled scales. This species may also be confused with the Common Side-blotched Lizard, which is slightly smaller and has large dark spots behind forearms.

Habitats: These lizards frequent rocky hillsides and canyon bottoms, from coastal to montane areas, and are seldom found on level terrain. Vegetation includes chaparral, oak and sycamore woodland, or willow. They seem to be especially abundant near streams or oases. Since these lizards prefer rocky canyon areas, they are frequently found in association with other rock-dwelling lizards like spiny lizards, collared lizards, Banded Rock Lizards, and night lizards. They are agile climbers and move quickly on vertical surfaces such as rocks, trees, buildings, and embankments. Cracks, crevices, and burrows are the areas most often used by this lizard for shelter. Elevational range is from just above sea level to as high as 2,120 m.

Natural History: These lizards are diurnal and are fairly conspicuous when active on light-colored surfaces, since their conspicuously dark tails stand out on light backgrounds. They can be seen basking in the open and exposed to sunlight during warm months. Otherwise, they seek retreats in the form of rock cracks, tree hollows, or burrows in the soil. Most seasonal activity occurs in the spring when mating takes place, then continues at a reduced level through the summer and fall. They are egg-layers, and hatchlings can be found in mid-summer. They are reported to eat insects, including termites, ants, moth and butterfly larvae, beetles, bees, and other arthropods.

Male U. nigricaudus, *Anza-Borrego Desert State Park, CA.*

Their varied diet indicates a relatively opportunistic feeding strategy. They will readily lose their tails as a predation-avoidance mechanism and will also do so if handled roughly or handled by the tail itself.

Range: Baja California Brush Lizards occur from extreme southwestern California, southward to the Cape Region of Baja California. In the U.S. they can be found along the desert canyons in San Diego County and in some of the coastal canyons of extreme southern San Diego County.

Viewing Tips: These lizards can easily be enjoyed during daytime hours by slowly walking and observing movements on streamside and hillside rocky outcrops. They will flee for cover when approached; thus binoculars or a spotting scope can be used to treat the viewer to their natural movements from a distance, after they have been located with the naked eye. During spring and summer when these lizards have breeding coloration, they stand out with their dark tails and blue throats against the rocks, and can be easily picked out by the casual observer. Good places to view this species include Anza-Borrego Desert State Park (CA), where it may be seen near California Fan Palm oases, as along the Borrego Palm Canyon trail.

Taxonomy: Generally accepted as a valid species, this lizard was stabilized taxonomically only in the late 1990s or so. It was first described in the early 20th century as a distinct species; problems in resolving its correct taxonomy since that time resulted in *U. nigricaudus* and *U. microscutatus* as representing 2 distinct species, the former found only in Baja California. In fact, *U. microscutatus* was the name of all members of this species occurring in the U.S. in the recent past. This is no longer the case, and our current understanding indicates that *U. microscutatus* and *U. nigricaudus* together constitute the single species *U. nigricaudus.*

Subspecies and Variation: There are currently no subspecies within this species, although historically it was at one time considered a subspecies itself! Also, there is little or no variation recognized within its range in the U.S. One variable characteristic within the species is throat coloration; in males it is blue, but in its southern range in Baja California, Mexico, this coloration changes to orange or gray.

Remarks: This species almost observes the international border between Mexico and the United States as the northern edge of its natural range, since it occurs only as far north as Borrego Palm Canyon in Anza-Borrego Desert State Park. Most of its range is within Baja California, Mexico, where is found along the entire length of the Baja California peninsula.

Male U. nigricaudus, *Dulzura, San Diego Co., CA.*

Ornate Tree Lizard

Urosaurus ornatus (Baird and Girard, 1852)

Author: Robert Haase

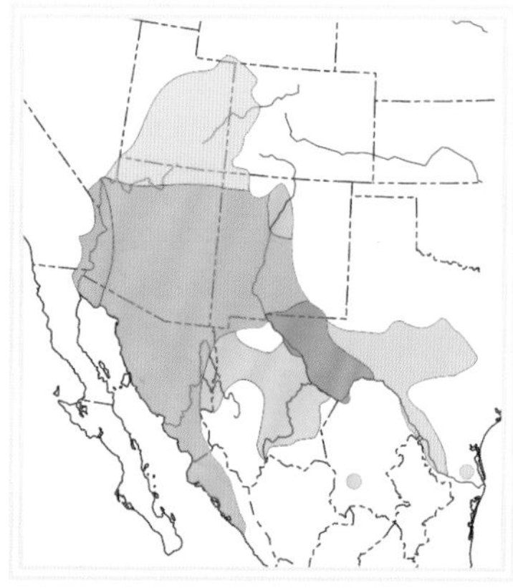

See page 559 for map color codes.

Description: The Ornate Tree Lizard is a small, slim-bodied species up to 56 mm SVL with a slender tail less than twice the body length, 2 rows of enlarged middorsal scales separated by small granular scales, 2 longitudinal folds along the body sides, and a prominent throat fold. One or more scales on the head are enlarged; tail and legs have noticeable keeled scales. Dorsal coloration is gray, brown, or tan, marked by contrasting dark brown or black irregular blotches, crossbars, or striations, often edged in lighter gray. Some populations have light stripes extending from the side of the head down each body side. The tail base is a rusty red-brown. Ornate Tree Lizards can appear very dark when first emerging, during periods of cool ambient temperatures, or during courtship or territorial displays. **Sexual Variation:** Adult males have 2 metallic blue or blue-green

Juvenile U. o. schottii, *Tucson, Pima Co., AZ*

Adult U. o. schottii, *Marijilda Canyon, Graham Co., AZ.*

ventral patches; a blue, blue-green, yellow, or orange throat; and paired enlarged post-anal scales. Adult females have faint or no belly patches; a white, pale yellow, or yellow-green throat; and lack enlarged post-anal scales. **Juveniles:** Juveniles are similar to females in color pattern, but have somewhat different body proportions, including a relatively larger head.

Similar Species: Other southwestern lizards comparable in body shape and color pattern to the Ornate Tree Lizard are the Baja California Brush Lizard, Long-tailed Brush Lizard, and Common Side-blotched Lizard. Baja California Brush Lizards are similar in size and color pattern, but occur only in extreme southwestern California and in Baja California, Mexico, and do not overlap ranges with the Ornate Tree Lizard. Long-tailed Brush Lizards are distinguished by a longer tail (greater than twice the body length), a broad band of enlarged middorsal scales unbroken by smaller scales, and light tan dorsal coloration with faint or no blotches. Common Side-blotched Lizards have a blue-black blotch behind each forelimb, a stouter body lacking obvious enlarged dorsal scales or longitudinal body folds, and a relatively shorter tail. Male Common Side-blotched Lizards have light blue and yellow dorsal flecking; females have brown or black-brown irregular dorsal blotches or crossbars; and both sexes lack ventral color patches.

Habitats: Ornate Tree Lizards inhabit arid or semiarid habitats including rocky slopes, canyons, cliffs, wooded grasslands, and ephemeral riparian woodlands from near sea level to above 2,440 m elevation. Habitats are typified by mesquites, alders, and cottonwoods; also oak, pine, and juniper woodlands. They prefer trees, fallen branches, or rocks for basking and foraging, as well as areas around human habitation where rocks, stumps, or other surface objects are present. They are common residents of urban lots and backyards. Ornate Tree Lizards are often sympatric with Common Side-blotched Lizards where the geographic ranges are shared.

Natural History: Ornate Tree Lizards feed on invertebrates, taking a varied diet of insects and other small arthropods. They are in turn prey for various small carnivorous mammals, raptorial birds, larger lizards, and snakes. In parts of its range, the Ornate Tree Lizard can be active on warm days year-round and be observed even during cool winter months. Virtually any sunny day with ambient temperatures above 15°C can bring them out to bask. In parts of their range prone to subfreezing temperatures, they brumate from late fall through winter, sometimes aggregating in sizeable numbers in prime refuges. They may also aestivate during drought or very hot conditions to minimize water loss and retain fat reserves. Both sexes are territorial. Female mate selection is influenced by male displays, or a female may simply occupy a suitable territory and mate with a male occupying an overlapping territory. Females are oviparous, capable of producing multiple clutches of 2–16 eggs from spring into summer, depending on available resources. Hatchlings can appear from May to September.

Male U. o. schottii, *Cochise Co., AZ.*

Range: They occur in extreme southeastern California, southern Nevada, southern Utah, western Colorado, throughout Arizona and New Mexico, and into western and central Texas; also northern Mexico.

Viewing Tips: Ornate Tree Lizards are one of the most conspicuous and easily observed southwestern species. Any area that has scattered trees and numerous rocks is a likely location to observe them. They are most active (and easily viewed) during morning or afternoon hours and are excellent climbers that are well camouflaged on the bark of trees or fallen branches. Locate individuals by

Ventral coloration of male U. o. schottii, *Hidalgo Co., NM.*

spotting them basking in the open on rocks, or by scanning trunks and branches for movements. Typical behaviors are short dashes while watching the offending interloper, or bobbing the body up and down, doing push-ups. When approached, Ornate Tree Lizards will often climb higher or traverse the surface they are on, keeping to the side away from the perceived threat. Urban individuals become accustomed to humans and will often tolerate being approached closely; in wild settings they can be more wary. They will often sleep aloft during summer and can be located by examining terminal branches on shrubby trees such as mesquites with hand-held lights. Good public viewing areas include Bandelier National Monument (NM), Big Bend National Park (TX), Capitol Reef National Park (UT), Colorado National Monument (CO), Gila National Forest (NM), Natural Bridges National Monument (UT), Organ Pipe National Monument (AZ), and Saguaro National Park (AZ).

Taxonomy: *Urosaurus ornatus* has been recognized as a species for a long time, but subspecific designations have been shuffled around or contested.

Subspecies and Variation: Six subspecies of *U. ornatus* are currently recognized: the Smooth Tree Lizard, *U. o. levis*; Texas Tree Lizard, *U. o. ornatus*; Big Bend Tree Lizard, *U. o. schmidti*; Schott's Tree Lizard, *U. o. schotti*; Colorado River Tree Lizard, *U. o. symmetricus*; and the Northern Tree Lizard, *U. o. wrighti*.

Remarks: These small lizards are often very approachable, especially in urban settings, and thus are an ideal species to introduce to children, students, or novice wildlife enthusiasts. They are interesting to observe jumping after flying insects and engaging in territorial or courtship displays.

Common Side-blotched Lizard

Uta stansburiana Baird and Girard, 1852

Author: Thomas C. Brennan

Description: This is a small lizard with an average build. Males reach a maximum SVL of 64 mm and females reach 58 mm. The dorsal scales are small and weakly keeled, the caudals are large and keeled, and a gular fold is present. Coloration is shades of orange-brown or gray-brown, with a large blue-black blotch on each side of the body just behind the forelimb. Dorsal markings usually include a pale dorsolateral stripe on each side of the body, extending from snout to tail. Stripes can be partial, broken, or complete, with straight or barbed edges. Two longitudinal rows of dark blotches often mark the mid-dorsum. Some populations are patternless. The venter is plain and pale, and the throat is blue, yellow, or orange. Alternating gray and cream or yellow-orange bars often radiate from the throat to the sides of the face. **Sexual Variation:** Males have 2 enlarged post-anal scales, dorsal markings that are faded or obscured by small light spots, and turquoise-blue speckles on the tail, body, and hind limbs. Females usually have a distinct dorsal pattern. **Juveniles:** Young are similar in pattern to females.

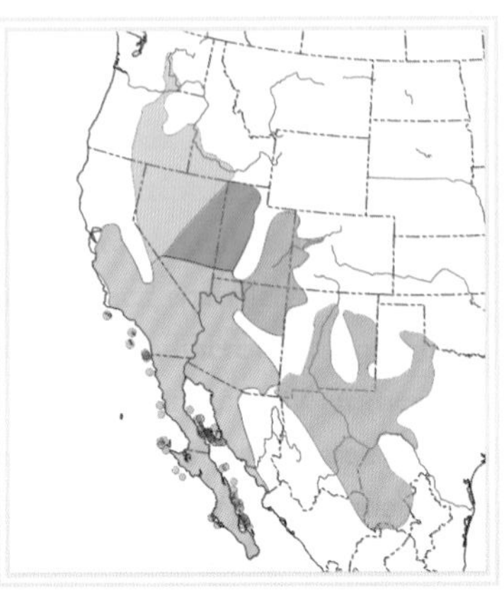

See page 559 for map color codes.

Similar Species: Spiny lizards lack side-blotches and have spiny scales. Tree and brush lizards lack side blotches. Earless lizards lack external ears and have paired side-blotches.

Female U. stansburiana, *Sierra Estrella, Maricopa Co., AZ.*

Habitats: The Central Valley of California, Great Basin, Mojave, Sonoran, and Chihuahuan ecoregions are home to this lizard. It occurs in desert scrub, semi-desert grassland, coastal scrub, chaparral, and woodlands at elevations ranging from sea level to 2,700 m in the south and

Male U. s. elegans, *Kern Plateau, Tulare Co., CA. Males have more vibrant coloration.*

1,900 m in the north. It can be found in a variety of terrains including dunes, flatlands, bedrock, boulders, and rocky slopes. In some northern localities it inhabits cliff faces. Vegetation in suitable habitat can include Creosote Bush, yuccas, bunchgrasses, low shrubs, mesquites, palo verdes, Ironwood, and junipers.

Natural History: This lizard is active from February to November and, at lower elevations, on warm winter days. Diurnal, it emerges after sunrise and exposes its back to the sun to warm up. In summer it is most active in the morning and late afternoon, avoiding the midday heat.

Crypsis is the primary defense against predation. Predators include the Long-nosed Leopard Lizard, Tiger Whiptail, Coachwhip, whipsnakes, rattlesnakes, patch-nosed snakes, nightsnakes, kingsnakes, tarantulas, and various birds and mammals. The tail can be lost and regenerated. This opportunistic insectivore sits and waits for prey to wander within close proximity. It eats grasshoppers, beetles, ants, termites, leaf-hoppers, insect larvae, scorpions, spiders, and juvenile conspecifics. Prey is seized and beaten on the ground with a vigorous back and forth motion before being ingested.

Studies in California revealed 3 territorial strategies, each associated with a different throat color. Orange-throated males usurp and defend high-quality territory. Blue-throated males defend small territories but do not usurp. Yellow-throated males sneak copulations and are not territorial. Territories are defended via displays that include elevating and laterally compressing the body, arching the back, nodding, push-ups, extending the dewlap, and fighting. Territoriality ceases in winter, when lizards often share group hibernacula. Although this species is polygynous, males defending small territories often guard a single female. Courtship and mating begin in late winter. During courtship the male performs territorial-like displays, approaches the female, relaxes his posture, licks her, and then performs push-ups and nods. Prior to copulation he grasps her neck or shoulder in his jaws, lifts her, performs push-ups, drags her, and pulls her from side to side. One to 7 clutches of 1–8 eggs each are laid from March through August. Females can store sperm for up to 3 months to fertilize ensuing clutches. Eggs incubate in an underground nest for 60–80 days, and hatchlings begin to emerge in June. Adult size can be reached in as little as 3 months, but lizards do not reproduce until the following spring. Longevity can exceed 4 years, but the average life span is less than one year.

Range: This lizard ranges across much of the western United States and northern Mexico from Washington to Zacatecas. In this region it occurs in southern and central California, Nevada, Utah, western Colorado, Arizona, New Mexico, and west Texas.

Viewing Tips: Nearly every public land in arid or semiarid areas within the range provides opportunities to observe this common lizard. On warm days within suitable habitat it is a regular feature of the trailside scenery. Keep an eye out for lizards basking on low rocks or scurrying under bushes.

Juvenile U. stansburiana. *Who says lizards aren't cute?*

Male U. s. uniformis, *Chaco Canyon, McKinley Co., NM.*

Taxonomy: Evidence gathered from populations in Mexico suggests that *U. s. stejnegeri* might be a distinct species.

Subspecies and Variation: This species was described in 1852 based on specimens from the Great Salt Lake Valley, Utah. Five subspecies are recognized. The Western Side-blotched Lizard (*U. s. elegans*) occurs in western and southern Arizona, southern California, and southern Nevada. Males are often heavily speckled with blue on the tail and posterior body. An average of 91.3 dorsals (counting along the mid-dorsum from the interparietal to a point above the hind limbs) and more than 8 interfemorals distinguish it from *U. s. stejnegeri*. The Nevada Side-blotched Lizard (*U. s. nevadensis*) occurs in northwestern Nevada. It is distinguished by a reduced and relatively uniform dorsal pattern, usually consisting of scattered light and dark dots. The Northern Side-blotched Lizard (*U. s. stansburiana*) occurs in western Utah and northeastern Nevada. It is distinguished from adjacent subspecies by its relatively distinct dorsal pattern. The Eastern Side-blotched Lizard (*U. s. stejnegeri*) occurs in extreme southeastern Arizona, New Mexico, and west Texas. Males are often profusely speckled with blue on the tail and posterior body. It averages 85.1 dorsals and fewer than 8 interfemorals. The Plateau Side-blotched Lizard (*U. s. uniformis*) occurs in eastern Utah, western Colorado, northeastern Arizona, and northwestern New Mexico. It lacks dorsal markings or has a uniform pattern of dark and light dots. Uniformly small body scales further distinguish it from other subspecies, which have body scales that grade from largest middorsally to smallest laterally.

FAMILY EUBLEPHARIDAE: Eyelidded Geckos

Author: Aaron M. Bauer

This is a small family of lizards (about 26 species) with a disjunct distribution in North and Central America, east and west Africa, middle Asia, India, southeast Asia, Borneo, and the Ryukyu Islands. There are 6 genera, only one of which, *Coleonyx*, with 7 species, occurs in the New World, from southern California to west Texas and as far south as Costa Rica and possibly Panama, but with distributional gaps in between. Four species occur in the American Southwest: *Coleonyx brevis* in south and southwest Texas, south-central New Mexico, and adjacent parts of northern Mexico; *C. reticulatus* in the Big Bend area of Texas; *C. switaki* in inland southern California and the northern half of Baja California; and *C. variegatus* (with many subspecies) from east-central California, east to extreme southwestern Utah and south through the whole of Baja California and western Sonora.

Eublepharids form a distinct group within the geckos and their relatives. Like most geckos, they are relatively small, with soft, granular skin, large heads, and prominent eyes with vertical pupils. Unlike all other geckos, however, they possess true eyelids and can blink and close their eyes. They also differ from the Gekkonidae in this book in lacking adhesive toe pads. Eublepharids have long, thin legs and short, slender toes, with small but well-developed claws. The tail is used as a fat storage organ, and healthy eyelidded geckos usually have thick, cylindrical tails. Color patterns vary considerably across the species, but those in the area covered by this book have either banded or spotted dorsal patterns in pastel colors or earth tones.

The status of the eyelidded geckos as a family separate from the Gekkonidae remains controversial, but phylogenetic studies verify that eublepharids have a long history independent of other geckos, probably diverging from their relatives in the early to mid-Cretaceous. The members of the genus *Coleonyx* are each other's closest relatives and are only distantly allied to the Old World genera. *Coleonyx switaki* was originally described as the sole representative of a new genus, *Anarbylus*, but it is now accepted that it too belongs in *Coleonyx*.

Eublepharids occur from relatively moist tropical habitats to temperate deserts. In the American Southwest they range across many vegetation types, and from sandy flats at low elevations to piñon/juniper woodlands to 1,524 m. Most are associated with areas that provide some rocky cover, although they may also inhabit dunes or dry forests. Several *Coleonyx* occur in the warm, wet forests of Central America, but those covered in this book prefer dry areas—although they typically choose retreat sites with a more humid microclimate.

All eublepharids are nocturnal, emerging from daytime retreats in burrows or crevices or under rocks, vegetation, or surface debris to forage at night for arthropod prey, including spiders, scorpions, and insects, on the ground. In comparison to other geckos, they forage more widely, alternating periods of movement and search with bouts of immobility. A combination of visual and chemosensory cues is probably used to locate the prey. Eyelidded geckos are most often encountered by humans at night, when they are seen thermoregulating on warm paved road surfaces, and they may be noted by attentive drivers traveling at slow speeds. They also may be located when cover items they are sheltering under are dislodged, or they can be found by walking with a flashlight or headlamp on mild-to-warm spring and summer nights, particularly following rains (although intentional disruption of the habitat should be avoided, as should direct exposure to bright lights, which may disturb or disorient eyelidded geckos).

Coleonyx elegans *(Yucatan Banded Gecko), Mountain Pine Ridge Forest Reserve, Belize.*

Because they are active at night when temperatures are cooler, eublepharids are restricted in their activity to warmer periods of the year. Winter nights in their range in the American Southwest are too cold to allow activity, and they may spend 4–5 months of the year hibernating in retreat sites. After spring emergence, eyelidded geckos breed and typically lay clutches of 2 leathery-shelled eggs at a time, usually from late spring to late summer, depending on the species and locale. Females, which are usually slightly larger than males, may lay up to 3 clutches per year.

Eublepharids use a stereotypic defensive posture when threatened. They rise up on their thin legs and arch their backs, often slowly waving their tails or curving them over their backs like scorpions. A similar tail waving may be seen in *Coleonyx* as they stalk their prey. They also vocalize, squeaking when distressed or handled and they readily autotomize the tail, usually at the base, when attacked by predators such as snakes or small mammals, or handled roughly by humans.

Texas Banded Gecko

Coleonyx brevis Stejneger, 1893

Author: James R. Dixon

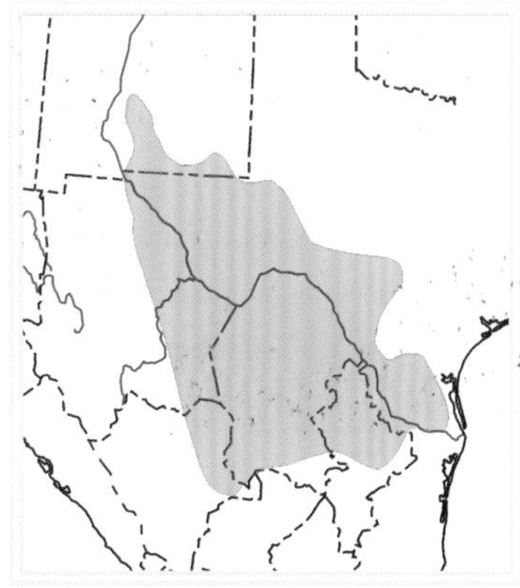

See page 559 for map color codes.

Description: The Texas Banded Gecko is a small lizard with a maximum SVL of 63 mm. The tail is covered with rows of imbricate scales and represents 90–100% of its TL. The skin is thin, granular, and without tubercles. Granular scales around the middle of the body vary from 102 to 142. The eyes have functional eyelids. The toes are straight, unexpanded at the tips, and the claw lies between 2 lateral, shell-shaped scales, capped above with a long, thin pointed scale.

The dorsal ground color is cream to sulphur yellow. There are usually 4 distinct reddish-brown cross-bands on the body between the shoulder and the hind limb, and about 7–11 on the tail. These bands are chestnut colored, fading laterally, and not present on the belly. The ground color interspaces are

Adult C. brevis, *Brewster Co., TX.*

Female C. brevis, *Terrell Co., TX.*

narrow, less than half the width of the dark bands. The pale nape area area is crescent in shape and extends forward toward the labials. A narrow chestnut line behind the head is the anterior border of the pale nape band, and the same band is bordered posteriorly by the first dark band on the body. As the lizard grows, the chestnut bands break up into small dark spots, and small dark spots also appear in the pale interspaces. The dark crossbands may be absent or appear as obscure dusky areas. **Sexual Variation:** Males have 3–6 pre-anal pores, 1–5 scales between the pre-anal pore series, and cloacal spurs with a flat distal end; these features are lacking in females. **Juveniles:** The pattern and basic colors of juveniles are bolder than observed in adults. The juveniles retain the banded pattern until they become young adults.

Similar Species: The only other species similar to the Texas Banded Gecko is the Western Banded Gecko. It lacks the enlarged tubercles on the dorsum and contains reddish-brown cross-bands, but differs in having a cloacal spur that is pointed, and generally retains the juvenile pattern as an adult.

Habitats: This species is a typical inhabitant of the Chihuahuan Desert, where it is common in the Creosote Bush association. It also occurs in cedar/live oak plant formation, Tamaulipan brush plains, and the flat, arid bolson basins from 30 to 1,570 m. However, it is usually associated with canyons, rocky hills, and desert pavement, utilizing small stones and boulders as daytime retreats. Elsewhere it may be found in cracks in the earth when rock cover is not available.

Female C. brevis, *Black Gap Wildlife Management Area, Brewster Co., TX.*

Natural History: Texas Banded Geckos feed upon grasshoppers, moths, termites, spiders, ants, solpugids, crickets, cockroaches, cicadas, lycaeid bugs, blister beetles, and larvae of various insects. The geckos walk slowly with one foot in front of the other until prey is observed. An attack is generally a series of short runs at the prey, grabbing it in the mouth and vigorously shaking it, and occasionally banging the prey against the substrate. Males reach sexual maturity in one year at 45 mm SVL, and females mature usually in one year at 48 mm SVL. Egg clutches always contain 2 soft leathery eggs, and usually 2 clutches are laid each reproductive season. The eggs usually hatch in late May and early to mid-July. Hatching size is 24 to 26 mm SVL. Females that hatch in May will likely be reproductive the following summer, while those that hatch in July will probably breed in their second year of life. Because of the small clutch size, this gecko is considered a long-lived species.

Texas Banded Geckos regulate their body temperature beneath stones by pressing their backs against the bottom of the rock retreat. They cool themselves in the same fashion, by lowering their bodies into the cooler substrate below. Territoriality is displayed by tail-wagging, side stances, and back-arching, but biting and combat seldom occur between individuals. The defense posture (toward snakes, for example) is identical. When the predator is within 4 cm of the gecko, the gecko flees. Many of the Texas Banded Geckos have regenerated or missing tails. It is suspected that tails are lost because waving the tail at a potential predator directs the predator's attention to the tail. As a predator bites the tail, it is autotomized, and the lizard escapes.

Range: The species occurs from south central New Mexico southeast to the eastern extent of the Chihuahuan Desert in Texas, southeast along the Rio Grande to the end of the brush zone of southern Texas, south into the Mexican state of Nuevo León, then westward to eastern Durango, Mexico, and finally north to New Mexico.

Viewing Tips: This lizard is nocturnal. Any viewing should be done with black light, gas lantern, a night scope, or a flashlight. The lizard is terrestrial and walks slowly across the desert floor, with its tail arched up and waving slowly back and forth. Upon first sight, it looks like a large scorpion. It crosses paved roads at night.

Taxonomy: Texas Banded Geckos were once thought to represent a subspecies of the Western Banded Gecko. Both geckos occupy desert environments, but the Western Banded Gecko occurs in the Sonoran and Mojave deserts and does not share its habitat with the Texas Banded Gecko.

Subspecies and Variation: A 1975 thesis on the ecology and systematics of the Texas Banded Gecko suggests that there may be evidence to describe 3 new subspecies. According to the analyses of 7 characteristics, west Texas samples are very distinct from samples representing the Edwards Plateau of Texas. In addition, the eastern Durango, Mexico, samples are very distinct from the southern Coahuila, Mexico, samples. The author supposed that the grasslands that lie between these 2 areas are barriers to their dispersal, and likewise, the shift from Chihuahuan Desert plant formation to wetter live oak/juniper plant formation of the Edwards Plateau may be the major cause of the character shifts between those samples.

Reticulate Banded Gecko

Coleonyx reticulatus Davis and Dixon, 1958

Author: James R. Dixon

See page 559 for map color codes.

Description: This gecko has an elongate rounded body, and eyelids are present. It is relatively large, with no sexual dimorphism in size, reaching an SVL of 94 mm. The tail is 48–51% of the TL. The toes are straight, each claw is partially enclosed within 2 lateral shell-shaped scales, and the fourth toe contains 23–31 lamellae. The skin is thin, covered with granular scales, and, in addition, the body contains 13–16 rows of enlarged tubercles. The tubercular rows begin occasionally on the nape, usually at the shoulder, and infrequently at mid-body. The tubercular rows normally end above the vent, but occasionally 2–3 transverse rows pass beyond the base of the tail. In addition, there are 18–20 pre-anal pores, with no granular rows of scales between the pores. The ground color is pink-buff with a profusion of small dorsal and lateral auburn spots scattered throughout the head, body, and tail. **Sexual Variation:** Males have bony cloacal spurs that are visible under the skin; these are lacking in females. **Juveniles:** The young and occasionally adults have diffuse auburn bands. The bands become broken as the animal grows and eventually form spots. The spots often coalesce and form a reticulated pattern.

Adult C. reticulatus, *Presidio Co., TX.*

Similar Species: The Texas Banded Gecko, Switak's Banded Gecko, and Western Banded Gecko are the only other U.S. geckos with eyelids and straight toes, but of these, only the Texas Banded Gecko occurs sympatrically with the Reticulate Banded Gecko. These species all differ from the

Female C. reticulatus, *Black Gap Wildlife Management Area, Brewster Co., TX. A permit is needed from the state of Texas to even photograph this rare species in the wildlife management area.*

Reticulate Banded Gecko by lacking enlarged tubercles, having a much smaller body size as adults, and possessing 5–6 distinct dark bands on the body and 6–11 bands on the tail.

Habitats: This species is largely restricted to large boulders and rock cliff faces with cracks and deep crevices in the Chihuahuan Desert. Although it may be found away from cliffs and boulders after dark, it is generally moving about in search of food. It is a good climber and may move vertically in search of food or horizontally on the desert floor at elevations between about 520 and 1,070 m.

Natural History: The Reticulate Banded Gecko is an egg-layer, depositing 2 leathery soft-shelled eggs at a time. The only data for egg laying and sexual activity is from captive individuals. There are 2 clutches per season of 2 eggs each. Historically, Reticulate Banded Geckos are related to tropical forest species in southern Mexico. They are nocturnal, active following rains, and are found at lower temperatures than the sympatric Texas Banded Gecko. In one study, cloacal temperatures varied from 24 to 32°C during the hours of 11:30 p.m. to 1:10 a.m. during a rain in the month of August. These geckos climb readily in vertical cracks, shrubs, and boulders. The tail is long, thin, and probably less useful for fat storage than in other banded geckos, because the tail is somewhat prehensile and used for balancing. Although the tail may be autotomized during predation, it occurs more frequently in Texas Banded Geckos. Known food items are tenebrionid beetles, grasshoppers, and spiders. Adult geckos stalk their prey, walking slowly toward it, one foot in front of the other, until they are close. They arch their backs and lunge toward the prey. On the other hand, when approached within 7 cm by a predator, such as a snake, they flee rapidly. They are known to bite when handled and show aggression toward others of the same species.

Range: This species occurs in the Chihuahuan-Zacatecan biotic province in Mexico and only the Chihuahuan biotic province in Texas. It is known from 7 miles east of León Guzmán, Durango, and from just north of Cuatro Cienegas, Coahuila, Mexico, as well as from several localities in Brewster and Presidio counties, Texas.

Viewing Tips: Although these nocturnal geckos may be active from April through September, they are not easy to observe. On rainy nights they are normally out of their crevices and on pavement at road cuts through the hills in Presidio and Brewster counties. The rainstorms are usually scattered, and one would have to be tuned in to local radar stations to be able to move from one storm to another in search of a specimen. The color of this species makes an individual difficult to observe, even under the

Female C. reticulatus, *Lajitas, Presidio Co., TX.*

Female C. reticulatus, *Presidio Co., TX.*

brightest light. Any time you are in Texas looking for this gecko, you must obey the game department laws, especially at night. You cannot "road hunt" for specimens without a valid Texas Parks and Wildlife hunting license or a scientific collecting permit. You are allowed to walk the road cuts, but first you must park your vehicle.

Taxonomy: Since the original description of this species in 1958, the name has been stable.

Subspecies and Variation: Because of the rarity of this species there are too few specimens to determine variation within the samples. No subspecies are described.

Remarks: There has been no effort by Mexican herpetologists to locate other populations of this species. Texas has been searched thoroughly for additional populations, but to no avail. There is ample habitat to search for additional populations between the Big Bend area of Texas and Cuatro Cienegas, Coahuila, and between the Mexican states of Coahuila and Durango.

Switak's Banded Gecko

Coleonyx switaki (Murphy, 1974)

Author: Eric A. Dugan

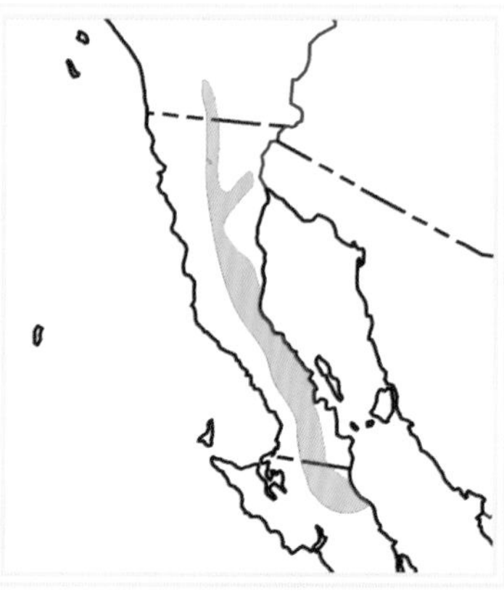

See page 559 for map color codes.

Description: This is a small, delicate lizard that attains an adult size of 60–85 mm SVL. This species has movable eyelids and no gular fold. The head is triangular and distinctly wider than the neck. Both the front and hind limbs are thin and moderate in length. Lamellae are present on the ventral surfaces of the feet and toes. Small tubercles are interspersed among granular scales throughout the body. Ground color is highly variable, ranging from yellow or beige to reddish brown. Ground color matches the coloration of the surrounding substrate. The dorsal surface has numerous spots that form weak to distinct body bands. The dorsal surface can be either banded or spotted. Unregenerated tails are often distinctly black-and-white-banded. Regenerated tails are always spotted and slightly off color compared to the original tail. **Sexual Variation:** Males can be identified by prominent spurs on each side of the base of the tail. Sexually mature males develop bright yel-

Juvenile C. switaki.

Adult C. switaki, *Anza-Borrego Desert State Park, San Diego Co., CA.*

low coloration during the breeding season. **Juveniles:** Neonates hatch with a bright yellow-orange ground coloration and a vibrantly colored black and white banded tail. These characteristics begin to fade as juveniles approach a year of age.

Similar Species: The Western Banded Gecko is sympatric throughout the range of *C. switaki*. Western Banded Geckos are smaller, lack body tubercles, and are much more commonly observed. Juvenile *C. switaki* have a distinctly black and white banded tail and are bright yellow, distinguishing them further from similarly sized Western Banded Gecko. The most reliable method to distinguish the 2 species is by noting the presence or absence of small body tubercles. The only other species of gecko found in the same habitat as *C. switaki* is the Peninsular Leaf-toed Gecko. These small geckos differ by having expanded toe pads.

Habitats: Switak's Banded Geckos are restricted to the arid eastern slope of the Baja California Peninsular Ranges. There they inhabit a variety of habitats, the majority of which are rocky. Observations of this species have been made in granite boulder fields, lava flows, sandstone arroyos, and areas dominated by small rocks. Vegetation is usually limited to small, sparsely distributed shrubs and bushes, as areas with dense vegetation are usually not occupied by this species. They occur from sea level to 600 m in elevation.

Natural History: Switak's Banded Geckos are egg-laying insectivores that are nocturnal, secretive, and rarely observed. Individuals typically emerge from brumation in the

Juvenile C. switaki.

early spring. Hibernaculum includes mammal burrows and surface objects such as rocks. Adults have been observed under rocks as early as January. As they are derived from tropical ancestors, dry and hot desert conditions appear to limit surface activity. Surface activity increases during May and June during warm nights when humidity levels are elevated.

This species preys on small invertebrates such as crickets, scorpions, spiders, moths, and beetles. Captive adults have eaten neonate Western Banded Geckos; however, it is unlikely that small vertebrate prey species are taken with any regularity in the wild. This species has the unusual behavior of elevating the tail while waving it back and forth during predatory strikes. Daytime retreats include mammal holes, cavities under rocks, and rock fissures. Individuals leave their daytime retreats on warm evenings to forage. Mating begins as early as May and continues through July. Up to 2 eggs are laid from June to July. Females may deposit up to 3 clutches from a single mating. Hatchlings begin to appear in early August.

Range: This gecko inhabits the arid desert slopes on the east side of the Baja California Peninsular Ranges. More specifically, *C. switaki* is distributed from Santa Rosalia, Baja California, in the south to the vicinity of Borrego Springs in northern San Diego County, California. An isolated population exists in the Coyote Mountains of Imperial County. The apparent absence of this species in the Vallecitos Mountains of Imperial County, California, is puzzling. Populations have been documented to both the south and north; however, species-specific surveys within suitable habitat have yielded no observations. This species has yet to be observed south of the vicinity of Santa Rosalia, Baja California. This too comes as somewhat of a surprise, given that contiguous habitat stretches farther south. It has been hypothesized that the change in vegetation density limits a more southerly distribution. Additional work documenting the full geographic range of this species is needed.

Viewing Tips: This species is notoriously difficult to find. Walking through proper habitat during the evening hours is a good way to find them. Individuals can be

Juvenile C. switaki, *showing the vibrant coloration of juveniles.*

observed as they forage among rocks and canyons. Driving at night while looking for geckos as they cross roads has also proven to be a successful method of observation.

Taxonomy: Originally described as *Anarbylus switaki* in 1974, this species' taxonomic relationship to other eublepharid geckos was unclear. Subsequent investigation has resulted in Switak's Banded Gecko being placed in the genus *Coleonyx*. *Coleonyx switaki* is the sister species of the insular Isla San Marcos Banded Gecko (*C. gypsicolis*).

Subspecies and Variation: There are currently no recognized subspecies.

Remarks: Given the secretive nature of this species, it wasn't discovered until the early 1970s and went undiscovered in California until the early 1980s. This is quite remarkable, as southern California deserts were among the most well-explored regions of the southwestern United States during that time. It is sometimes called the Magic Gecko because of its secretive nature, or the Barefoot Gecko.

Coleonyx switaki is protected by the State of California and cannot be legally collected. However, this species is highly sought after by private collectors and is collected illegally every year from the Anza-Borrego Desert State Park. The author has recorded as many as 7 collectors in the park on a single night. It is unlikely that this collecting pressure has affected local populations.

Western Banded Gecko

Coleonyx variegatus Baird, 1859 "1858"

Author: Robert E. Espinoza

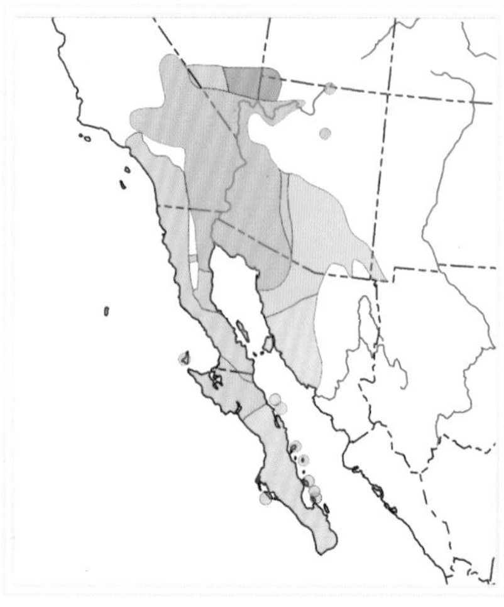

See page 559 for map color codes.

Description: Western Banded Geckos are small to mid-sized lizards with slender toes that lack enlarged pads, velvety skin with uniformly granular scales, functional eyelids, vertical pupils, and a fat tail that is constricted at the base and tapers toward the tip. Adults can reach 75 mm SVL and 150 mm TL. The dorsal background color typically matches the substrate of the local environment, varying from light cream or gray to pale yellow to pink. As the name *variegatus* implies, the dorsal pattern is highly variable—even within a population. The body and tail may have distinct bands or spots and irregular blotches that may form mottled bars of tan, reddish-brown, or dark brown. The bands or bars, typically numbering 5 on the body and up to 10 on the tail, are usually more lightly colored in the center and do not extend to the ventral surface. Tail bands tend to be more distinct toward the tip. The head, flanks, and limbs have small dark flecks, spots, or irregular markings of similar color. The neck is often marked with a crescent-shaped ring. The belly is immaculate cream and semitransparent. **Sexual Variation:** Males are similar to females in coloration and markings, but males have a slightly smaller maximum size (68 vs. 75 mm SVL), conspicuous pre-anal pores, a pair of hemipenal bulges, and spurs at the base of the tail. In adult females, pairs of developing eggs may be seen through the belly in the breeding season. **Juveniles:** The nuchal crescent is well defined and the banding pattern is more prominent in juveniles, but this pattern fragments into

Juvenile C. v. abbotti, *showing the banding pattern, Escondido, CA.*

Adult C. v. bogerti, *Stanfield, Pinal Co., AZ.*

irregular blotches or spots with maturity (except in western California populations, which tend to retain the juvenile pattern).

Similar Species: Because of their uniformly minute scales, thick tails, slender toes, vertical pupils, and movable eyelids, Western Banded Geckos can be confused with only other banded geckos (*Coleonyx* spp.). Switak's and Reticulate Banded Geckos are larger and have interspersed tubercles on the body, and Texas Banded Geckos are smaller and have 4–6 pre-anal pores in an interrupted series (vs. 6–10 in an uninterrupted V-shaped series in Western Banded Geckos).

Habitats: These terrestrial geckos are most common in the deserts of the Southwest U.S., but also reach near-coastal chaparral habitat in southern California. They can be found in a diversity of habitats including chaparral, desert scrublands, foothill and desert washes, volcanic mesas, sandstone, and sand dunes. They occur from below sea level in desert sinks to about 1,500 m.

Natural History: Western Banded Geckos are nocturnal, oviparous, and eat small arthropods (primarily insects and spiders). When foraging, Banded Geckos curl the tail over the body and sway the appendage in undulating waves. Banded Geckos have relatively low body-temperature preferences and high rates of evaporative water loss. They compensate for these physiological handicaps by sheltering in rodent burrows and under boulders and rubbish piles by day, and by restricting activity to the cooler and relatively more humid nighttime. Mating occurs in spring, and as many as 3 clutches of eggs are deposited in pairs in early to mid-summer and hatch in mid- to late summer. The scent of one predator, the Spotted Leaf-nosed Snake, is avoided by adult Western Banded Geckos.

Range: The distribution of Western Banded Geckos follows the Mojave and Sonoran deserts of the southwestern U.S. and adjacent northern Mexico (Baja California and western Sonora). In the U.S., this includes parts of eastern central and southern California, southern Nevada, southern and western Arizona, and extreme southwestern New Mexico and Utah.

Viewing Tips: Because they are nocturnal, Western Banded Geckos are encountered by day only by searching under cover, a practice that is generally discouraged. But at night, particularly in spring, this species is among the most frequently encountered desert reptiles in the Southwest. Peak activity occurs in spring (March through early June) from 8:00 to 11:00 p.m. and at temperatures of 27–29°C. During these times they are commonly found resting or foraging on paved roads. The best way to find them is to drive slowly (less than 40 km/hour) along asphalt roads in the appropriate habitat starting about dusk. Because of their light color, their bodies will contrast with dark pavement. Note that the foraging posture of Banded Geckos—tail waving and

Male C. variegatus, *Owl's Head Buttes, Pinal Co., AZ.*

arched over their back—may cause one to be mistaken for a scorpion at a distance. Good places to observe this species include Anza-Borrego Desert State Park and Joshua Tree National Park (CA); Ironwood Forest National Monument, Organ Pipe Cactus National Monument, and Saguaro National Park (AZ); and Valley of Fire State Park (NV).

Coleonyx v. abbotti *are sometimes found in small groups. This is not a breeding pair.*

Taxonomy: Seven subspecies have been recognized (see below). Research currently under way suggests that some of these warrant recognition as full species, whereas others are mere pattern classes with overlapping characteristics resulting from intergradation. The geographic distribution of some of the taxa in the pending revision is not consistent with the currently recognized subspecies.

Subspecies and Variation: There have been as many as 7 subspecies recognized, 4 of which occur in the Southwest: San Diego Banded Gecko (*C. v. abbotti*), Tucson Banded Gecko (*C. v. bogerti*), Utah Banded Gecko (*C. v. utahensis*), and Desert Banded Gecko (*C. v. variegatus*). The remaining subspecies occur in Mexico.

Remarks: Banded Geckos detach their tails readily upon capture and are commonly found with a regenerated portion, which is spotted and typically lacks the banding of the original, yet is no less able to store fat. When handled, they may emit a defensive squeak, which sounds like the whine of a tiny motor. By day, these lizards may aggregate, usually in pairs, but as many as 8 individuals have been found in a single subterranean retreat. Recent research has shown that aggregating lowers their rate of evaporative water loss by increasing the humidity of the retreat cavity. Western Banded Geckos eat their shed skin by pulling off large patches and swallowing them whole. In Mexico, Banded Geckos are erroneously considered to be venomous and to have poisonous skin.

FAMILY GEKKONIDAE: Geckos

Author: James R. Dixon

This family includes some of the oldest lizards; some fossils are more than 50 million years old (Miocene Epoch). Geckos are thought to have risen in Southeast Asia and radiated out from that primitive beginning. Currently, members of this family occur around the world between the 50th parallels north and south. They are very successful colonizers and occupy a wide variety of habitats (except water) from sea level to 3,960 m elevation. Geckos are very diverse, and the family contains about 100 genera and 1,200 species. Only one native member of the Gekkonidae occurs in the southwestern U.S.: the Peninsular Leaf-toed Gecko. This species is found mainly in the Borrego Desert area of southern California, and southward into Baja California, Mexico. The non-native Mediterranean House Gecko is a familiar resident in many areas of the American Southwest, especially in urban areas.

Most gecko species are nocturnal, but some are crepuscular and diurnal. Members of this family may vocalize, emitting a series of chirps, squeaks, tics, tocks, and barks. Some members are small, less than 30 mm SVL, while a few geckos reach 350 mm TL. Geckos come in various shapes. Most have bodies that are somewhat compressed dorsoventrally. Their bodies may be short or long, and the tails in various shapes, including leaf-like, turnip-shaped, fat and short, long with leaf-like appendages on its tip, or just long and thin. The tips of the toes may be straight, bent, pointed, fan-shaped, leaf-shaped, etc. All species have

Phyllodactylus tuberculosus, *Sonora, Mexico.*

adhesive toe pads. The pupil of the eye lacks an eyelid (present in the Family Eublepharidae). The pupil shape is also highly varied, from a vertical slit to round, with or without lobes, depending upon the amount of available light. The body scales are generally granular, but may be cycloid, imbricate, or a combination of granular scales intermixed with large tubercles. The head may be short or long, deep or flattened, and may even have spines across the back. The color patterns are varied and extremely numerous. The amount of light present often changes the pattern from almost black to uniform pale cream.

Most geckos can swim, and some species can leap from a tree and glide to another or to the ground, utilizing skin flaps along the sides of the body and tail. Those species that are the best colonizers are all-female species that lay one or 2 hard-shelled egg(s). The eggs can be laid beneath bark of a tree, in a crevice, beneath palm fronds on or off the tree, and any number of other places. Most gecko eggs are easily transported via driftwood or floating debris of all kinds. In modern times, transport may be via cardboard boxes, crates, boats, ships, planes, cars, and other means. In the case of all-female species, the absence of males eliminates the search for a mate, and reproduction occurs on a regular basis. Some species maintain communal nests, where eggs may number in the hundreds.

Habitats range from the deserts to rain forests. Daytime or nocturnal retreats include burrows in the ground; crevices or holes in small shrubs, rock cliffs, boulders, leaf litter, caves, canopy of large trees, or tree trunks; and man-made structures.

The diet of geckos usually consists of insects and spiders, but large geckos also eat smaller ones. In turn, geckos are preyed upon by other lizards, snakes, birds, bats, monkeys, and other mammals. Our local member of the Gekkonidae, the Peninsular Leaf-toed Gecko, consumes a variety of insects, ants, and spiders. Some geckos show passive resistance to competing species, while others are more territorial. In one study, 2 species of different genera occupied the same walls of a building. The original inhabitant was forced out by the later arrival simply taking over the best feeding sites. No aggression was noted over several observation periods. Undoubtedly, competition for food, space, and shelter is common in successful colonizers.

Because the Peninsular Leaf-toed Gecko is nocturnal and occurs on boulders, cliff walls, and deep rock crevices, an observer must use some sort of illumination to peer within or upon these structures. At the same time, careful observance of the ground around these structures is a must. But use caution—rattlesnakes often use the same habitat in search of food and may coil at the base of rocks or walls in wait of prey. The color pattern of these geckos is cryptic and blends well onto the rock surface, so one must look for movement across the surface in order to locate a Peninsular Leaf-toed Gecko.

Peninsular Leaf-toed Gecko

Phyllodactylus nocticolus Dixon, 1964

Author: James R. Dixon

See page 559 for map color codes.

Description: This lizard is moderately small, with males and females reaching 62 mm SVL. The tail is fragile and often regenerated. The tail is approximately 54% of the TL. The terminal ventral tips of the toes have 2 leaf-like lamellae, usually white or gray, which are their most distinctive feature. The skin is thin and covered with both granular and enlarged tubercular scales. The belly and the ventral part of the tail have enlarged scales. The number of scales in a row across the snout at the level of the third labial is usually fewer than the interorbital scales in a row between the middle of the orbits. There are usually 5 tan to dark-brown transverse bands on a ground color of gray, tan, or pinkish tan, to pale brown, between the axilla and groin, and occasionally on the tail. The dorsal bands may become obscure, break up into spots, become reticulated, or form lines. The head may be a uniform gray or have dark reticulations, spots, or lines. A brown to black line is usually present from slightly in front of the eye to the temporal region, and occasionally to the ear or arm insertion. Occasionally there is a gray to pale pink mid-dorsal stripe from the rear of the head to the pelvic region. The dorsal surfaces of the limbs, including the digits, may be uniform gray, with obscure dark spots or reticulations. The tubercles may be white-tipped. The dorsal part of the tail may be uniform gray to spotty, reticulated, or banded with darker color. The venter is pale yellow, cream, or dusky, generally without darker spots. **Sexual Variation:** There are usually no differences in color between the sexes. Males have post-anal bony spurs beneath the skin, but not externally visible as in eublepharid geckos. **Juveniles:** The pattern in young and juveniles is similar to that of adults but bolder in color and outline.

Similar Species: There are no other lizards in the U.S. with leaf-like toe pads, dorsal tubercles, and fragile skin. However, other species of leaf-toed geckos are common from Mexico to Chile.

Adult P. nocticolus *on granite, Anza-Borrego Desert State Park, CA. This rock-dwelling, nocturnal species is similar to species found in the Cape Region of Baja California, Mexico (compare to* P. unctus, *page 505).*

Habitats: This lizard is generally found on large granite boulders along the desert slope of the Baja California Peninsular Ranges, and the slopes of the Borrego Desert Mountains at elevations between sea level and 1,000 m. They occur beneath exfoliating sheets and deep within crevices of boulders. In areas south of California this lizard is found beneath bark of dead trees and cacti, and occasionally in bird nests. They occasionally are seen scampering across a rocky beach zone at night. It may occur around human habitation, such as abandoned stone or concrete buildings, towers, wells, and caves.

Natural History: Peninsular Leaf-toed Geckos are nocturnal and crepuscular. They typically live in rock crevices or under bark during the day and begin their activity at dusk. Occasionally with a flashlight you may see them moving about during the day, deep within crevices. Their movements may occur because they are startled by the sudden illumination. After dark, the geckos forage over and around boulders, looking for insect prey. They are also known to eat invertebrates, including amphipods and isopods. They may use buildings, dead trees and shrubs, and rocky beaches in the same manner. When disturbed while foraging among beach rocks, one gecko leaped into the water and swam a few cm away from the beach; others immediately sought cover under the nearest object. Although they are not known to defend territories, both sexes have been observed chasing one another within the crevices, with males more often chasing other males. Males apparently mark their territories with fecal pellets. This was observed in captive individuals. The seasonal activity patterns are unusual. Whereas most lizards seek a harbor for winter temperatures, this gecko has been found active in southern California during February to December at temperatures approaching 10°C. Adult females normally lay 2 hard-shelled eggs at a time. The number of clutches varies by seasonal temperatures, but in the tropics the females lay eggs throughout the year. Nothing has been published on growth rates between hatchling and adult.

Range: Peninsular Leaf-toed Geckos occur from the south side of San Gorgonio Pass near Cabazon, California, to the Cape Region of Baja California Sur, including many of the islands of the Sea of Cortez. Two other species occupy the Cape Region.

Viewing Tips: Because of their small size, nocturnal habits, and habitat, the only safe way to observe this species is with the aid of artificial light. This lizard has excellent hearing, and any movements by the observer must be kept to a minimum. In most cases, the observer would have to be within 2 m of the crevice (or the lizard, if it is out of the crevice) to observe its activity. A black light or infrared source may be a better observation tool than a normal flashlight. The best sites for observation are the large

Juvenile P. nocticolus *with regenerating tail, Anza-Borrego Desert State Park, San Diego Co., CA.*

Adult P. nocticolus. *Note the expanded toe tips for clinging to boulders, and large eyes with vertical pupils for night vision. San Diego Co., CA.*

boulders of Anza-Borrego Desert State Park, especially in the vicinity of Yaqui Wells, Yaqui Pass, Scissors Crossing, and Sentenac Canyon.

Taxonomy: This species was once thought to be a subspecies of *P. tuberculosus,* during the mid-19th century to the early 20th century. During the late 19th century it occasionally became *P. xanti.* During the 1960s the Peninsular Leaf-toed Gecko became a subspecies of *P. xanti.* With a re-examination of its morphology and the use of the new techniques of genetic research, the subspecies *nocticolus* was elevated to species level.

Subspecies and Variation: There are no subspecies of *P. nocticolus,* depending upon whom the reader accepts as the final author of its taxonomy. One researcher proposed that all described subspecies of *P. xanti* become subspecies of *P. nocticolus,* and that *P. xanti* become a monotypic species. More recently, the reverse of this taxonomy has been proposed for a second time. Currently, all of the named subspecies of *P. nocticolus* are island forms in the Sea of Cortez and on one Pacific coast island.

FAMILY TEIIDAE: Whiptails and Their Allies

Authors: Trevor B. Persons and John W. Wright

Teiidae is a New World lizard family closely related to its sister family Gymnopthalmidae. About 130 species in 10 genera range from the northern U.S. to central Argentina, including islands throughout the Caribbean. Most are small or medium-sized, but the South American tegu lizards reach almost 500 mm SVL. Most teiids occupy open areas, mostly in a variety of arid habitats, but some South American species use clearings in tropical forests, and members of 2 genera are largely aquatic. Most are streamlined, actively foraging terrestrial species with high preferred body temperatures.

Only members of the genus *Aspidoscelis* (formerly *Cnemidophorus*) reach the U.S., and these are the whiptails. About 60 species of whiptails are currently recognized throughout the Americas. Of the 22 species occurring in the American Southwest, the only one not occurring in the area covered by this guide is the Laredo Striped Whiptail (*A. laredoensis*) of the southern Rio Grande Valley of Texas. Whiptails range in habitat from Creosote Bush scrub to Ponderosa Pine forest, and from below sea level (as in Death Valley) to over 2,400 m elevation. Almost every acre of natural habitat in our area has a resident whiptail, and frequently 2 or more species occur together.

Whiptails are small to medium-sized lizards, with adults in the American Southwest ranging from about 50 mm (Little Striped Whiptail) to 140 mm (Giant Spotted Whiptail) SVL. Their dorsal surfaces are covered with small scales (dorsal granules), and they have 8 lengthwise rows of large, square ventral scales. The number of dorsal granules in a row across the back, which requires a hand lens and a stationary lizard to count, differs significantly between some species. The long whip-like tail, which is usually over twice the body length and is covered with keeled scales, breaks

A putative hybrid between Aspidoscelis tigris *(bisexual) and* A. sonorae *(unisexual/all-female). Hybridization is the source for all-female, parthenogenetic species.*

Aspidoscelis burti stictogramma. *This impressive lizard is the largest whiptail in the United States.*

easily. Whiptails have pointed snouts and large, symmetrical head scales. The frontoparietal scale is divided in all our species except the Orange-throated Whiptail. A row of small scales bordering the supraocular scales above the eyes, called the supraocular semicircle, varies in how far forward it penetrates between the adjacent larger scales and is useful in discriminating between some species. The scales directly in front of the gular fold (mesoptychials) and on the back of the foreleg (postantebrachials) are often abruptly enlarged relative to neighboring scales—also important characteristics in identifying some species. The dorsal patterns of most species are striped or striped and spotted, but a few are reticulated. In most striped and spotted species, juveniles and young adults are boldly striped and faintly spotted, but as they age the stripes become fainter and the spots become more prominent. Old individuals of some species (e.g., Chihuahuan Spotted Whiptail, Giant Spotted Whiptail, Sonoran Spotted Whiptail) may lose their stripes altogether. Appreciating this age-related variation in color pattern is often the key to sorting out what otherwise may seem to be an impossibly complicated array of different-looking whiptails at a given site.

Whiptails are diurnal, terrestrial, widely foraging lizards active during the warmest times of the day and year. As such, they have shorter active seasons than many other lizards they share their habitats with. Whiptails are constantly on the move in search of food, which they usually find by rooting among leaf litter under shrubs. Prey consists almost entirely of insects, spiders, and other arthropods. Termites are especially favored when available and often make up a large portion of the diet.

An intriguing aspect of whiptail biology is their reproductive mode. About a third of all whiptail species consist only of females. These unisexual species reproduce by parthenogenesis, whereby a female lays unfertilized eggs that hatch into more females, all genetically identical to their mother. All unisexual species arose through hybridization between 2 bisexual species or (in the case of triploids) through backcross hybridization between a diploid unisexual and a bisexual species. Parthenogenesis is rare in vertebrates, but common in whiptails. Nine of the covered species are all-female, and additional unisexual species are undescribed. Parthenogenetic reproduction has a theoretical advantage in that population size increases twice as much each generation compared with a sexually reproducing species in which half its members (the males) do not produce offspring. This has likely helped many unisexual species to rapidly colonize large areas. Unisexual whiptails often occupy transitional or disturbed habitats, and in this respect resemble botanical weeds, an observation that gave rise to the so-called "weed hypothesis" to explain their origin and distribution. The wide variety of rapidly shifting habitats in the Southwest during and after the Pleistocene provided opportunities for hybridization between bisexual species on the one hand and available habitat for the new unisexual species on the other. Pseudocopulation, in

Aspidoscelis t. tigris, *Harney Co., OR.*

Aspidoscelis tigris *copulating. This is a bisexual species, but some all-female species have been known to "pseudo-copulate," even though no genetic material can be exchanged.*

which 2 females engage in stereotypical courtship and mating behaviors (mounting, biting, body twisting, etc.) identical to those in bisexual species, has been observed in many parthenogenetic whiptails. Pseudocopulation has been studied extensively in captive lizards, although rarely observed in the wild; it is unknown how important this behavior is for free-ranging whiptails.

The identification and systematics of whiptail lizards have frustrated herpetologists for decades, even before the discovery of parthenogenesis in the group. Recently, the generic name for North American whiptails was changed from *Cnemidophorus* to *Aspidoscelis*. However, more recent analyses have not supported the partitioning of *Cnemidophorus*, and it has been proposed that *Aspidoscelis* be reduced to a subgenus of *Cnemidophorus*. Regardless, most herpetologists will probably always call them "cnemies" (pronounced "nem-eez"). Much controversy in whiptail taxonomy has focused on how to treat the parthenogenetic species. Most workers now regard any lineage derived from an independent hybridization event to constitute a species. For example, the Gila Spotted and Sonoran Spotted Whiptails originated by hybridizations between the same combination of parental species (possibly sharing the same diploid parthenogenetic intermediary), but involving different individual lizards. Thus these species, while similar, are morphologically and ecologically distinct.

Arizona Striped Whiptail

Aspidoscelis arizonae (Van Denburgh, 1896)

Author: Brian K. Sullivan

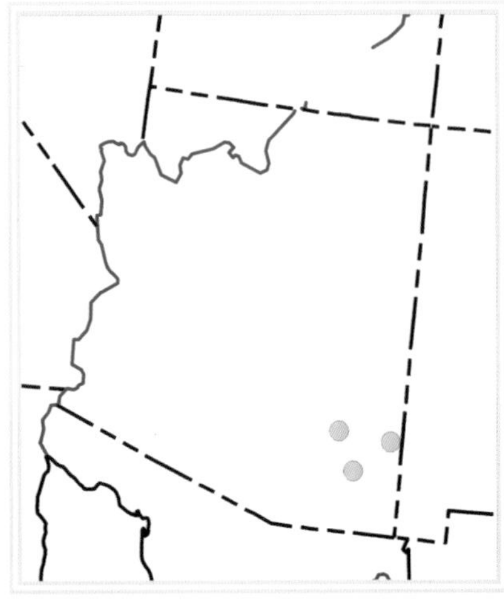

See page 559 for map color codes.

Description: This is a small (SVL to 75 mm), unspotted brown whiptail with 7 yellow stripes, and blue wash on the sides and especially on the face. Ground color appears to vary with the dominant soil coloration: near Bonita (AZ), on red sandy substratum, the dorsal color is rust tinged. Near the Willcox Playa, in white sand dunes, the ground color is pale. The seventh, middorsal stripe may be weaker (though rarely incomplete) than the dorsolateral stripes. The tail is about twice the SVL, and hindlimbs are somewhat larger than forelimbs. There are usually 9–11 scales between the paravertebral stripes in the space that includes the seventh, middorsal stripe. Usually a total of 28–30 femoral pores are present. Postantebrachial scales (see Figure 4) are not enlarged, relative to other scales on the forearms. **Sexual Variation:** Adult males have larger femoral pores and more blue coloration than females. **Juveniles:** Juveniles are similar to females.

Similar Species: These colorful lizards, especially females, are easily confused with a sympatric all-female species, the Desert Grassland Whiptail (an all-female descendant of the Arizona Striped Whiptail), but the Arizona Striped Whiptail has a seventh, middorsal stripe and distinct sky-blue coloration; aqua or green-blue coloration is the rule for other

Female A. arizonae, *Willcox Playa, Cochise Co., AZ.*

Male A. arizonae, *Willcox Playa, Cochise Co., AZ.*

striped, unspotted whiptails in southern Arizona. In the hand, Arizona Striped Whiptails can be identified on the basis of unenlarged postantebrachial scales, unenlarged scales on the gular fold, around 28 femoral pores, and 9–11 scales between the paravertebral stripes. Hybrids between Desert Grassland and Arizona Striped Whiptails have been documented at a number of sites where these 2 occur sympatrically (e.g., southeast, southwest, and immediately north of Willcox, Cochise County, Arizona). Hybrid individuals are typically intermediate to the 2 parental forms in morphology and coloration, thus difficult to identify with certainty in the absence of genetic and cellular (e.g., hybrids possess larger, tetraploid blood cells) analysis.

Habitats: This species is primarily a whiptail of grasslands, especially sandy and alkali areas (Willcox Playa) in the Sulphur Springs Valley of southeastern Arizona. Bunch grasses are typically present, but some shrubs, especially mesquite, may also be present. Rarely, individuals are found in Creosote Bush shrubland (e.g., Whitlock Valley). Although grazing is thought to be detrimental, Arizona Striped Whiptails generally occur with cattle throughout their range, and may take refuge under cow dung and even forage for termites in the droppings colonized by these insects. They co-occur most commonly with Desert Grassland Whiptails, and infrequently with Tiger Whiptails. They have been observed at elevations between 1,000 and 1,500 m.

Natural History: These are diurnal lizards with relatively restricted activity periods; they emerge generally late in the morning and retire in the early afternoon. Relative to most other sympatric lizards, these whiptails are primarily active in May, with a second peak of activity during July, but adults are rarely seen from September to April. Wind and cloud cover discourages activity. They are active lizards, pausing regularly to probe or dig in soil, primarily for termites and ants, and other insects. They are almost constantly on the move, actively tongue flicking the substratum as they move. Relative to some congeners (e.g., the Tiger Whiptail), they can be approached relatively closely (i.e., within 3–5 m), especially while they are basking in the morning. They will take refuge in grass clumps or under shrubs and cow dung when pursued, or even retreat into rodent or other burrows. Long-nosed Leopard Lizards are often observed in habitats with Arizona Striped Whiptails and, along with whipsnakes, presumably represent important predators on these lizards. Mating occurs in late spring, and females lay one or 2 clutches of 1–3 eggs in summer. Young of the year (about 100 mm TL) are generally seen in late August and often are the only individuals active in late summer and early fall.

Range: Restricted to the vicinity of Willcox (AZ) and at least 2 areas of southern Graham County (near Bonita and the Whitlock Valley), Arizona.

Viewing Tips: Activity peaks in the late spring, generally following the emergence of most other lizards. They are also active during the summer monsoon, but activity is

Male A. arizonae, *Willcox Playa, Cochise Co., AZ. Adult males are more intensely blue than females.*

Female A. arizonae, *Willcox Playa, Cochise Co., AZ.*

greatly reduced when the monsoon ends. Search for these lizards on warm mornings with little wind, before it is hot. They often take refuge in the shade of shrubs or in holes if hard pressed, so remain 4–6 m away to avoid stimulating a complete retreat on the part of the individual under view. Public lands, including Cochise Lakes, immediately south of Willcox, AZ, offer opportunities for viewing these lizards.

Taxonomy: Some consider the Arizona Striped Whiptail a subspecies of the Little Striped Whiptail, while others consider it a full species, based on divergence in genes and morphology, and its allopatric distribution. Recent analysis of sequence divergence (in mitochondrial DNA) indicates 2–3% difference between the Arizona Striped Whiptail and its sister taxon, the Pai Striped Whiptail of central and northern Arizona. Together these 2 lizards most likely represent the evolutionary sisters of the remaining, more easterly populations of Little Striped Whiptails of New Mexico.

Subspecies and Variation: No subspecies are recognized.

Remarks: Arizona Striped Whiptails may be in jeopardy due to habitat alterations associated with overgrazing (i.e., conversion of grassland to shrubland), but recent fieldwork was unable to document any significant shift in historic distribution over the past 100 years; rather, it appears that this lizard has occupied a relatively restricted range near Willcox for some time. It has been suggested that the unisexual Desert Grassland Whiptail may be replacing the Arizona Striped Whiptail in habitats degraded by overgrazing and undergoing conversion to shrubland.

Canyon Spotted Whiptail

Aspidoscelis burti (Taylor, 1938)

Author: Philip C. Rosen

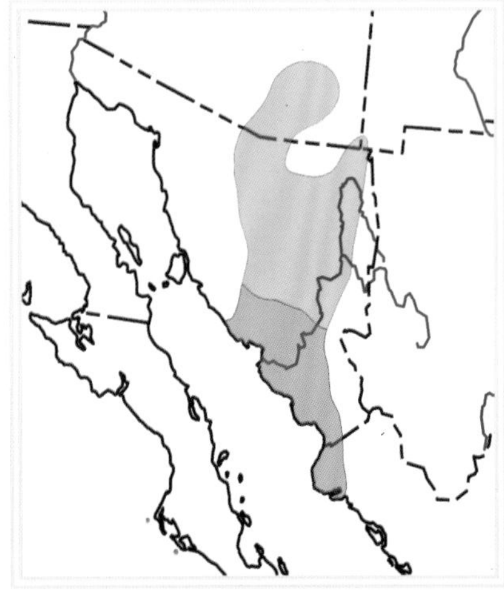

See page 559 for map color codes.

NOTE: *Aspidoscelis burti* in the U.S. is represented only by the Giant Spotted Whiptail, *A. b. stictogramma.* This subspecies differs markedly from Mexican subspecies, so the following refers to it only.

Description: The Giant Spotted Whiptail subspecies of Canyon Spotted Whiptail is the largest whiptail in the U.S., reaching 140 mm SVL and 468 mm TL. It has long legs, and the tail, brown in the adult, is typically over twice the body length. Large, old individuals are distinctive, unstriped, heavily spotted, and often washed on the dorsum and sides with reddish, blue, and yellow. There are marked ontogenetic changes in coloration, with the 6 light stripes of the juveniles breaking up into rows of spots and heavy yellow spotting often developing on the legs, as adult size is approached at about 90 mm SVL. **Sexual Variation:** Males are similar to females but average slightly larger, with slightly larger heads and

Adult A. b. stictogramma, *Sabino Canyon, Santa Catalina Mountains, AZ. Small adults still retain stripes.*

Large adult male A. b. stictogramma, *Santa Catalina Mountains, AZ. Large adults have lost the stripes and are covered in large spots.*

femoral pores. **Juveniles:** Hatchlings and small juveniles are unspotted, with an orange-red tail, and retain an orange-brown "glow" on the tail base and hind legs as they grow and develop numerous sharp-edged spots.

Similar Species: Although large adult Giant Spotted Whiptails are huge and more heavily spotted than other whiptails, younger individuals can only be distinguished with careful attention to detail. The only certain way to identify them is to count the granular scales around mid-body. The Giant Spotted Whiptail has 90 or more, while other species except the Tiger Whiptail have fewer than 89, but whiptails are hard to catch, and coloration must be used to identify species. The tails of juvenile Tiger, Desert Grassland, and Arizona Striped Whiptails are blue, and darken with age. The adult Tiger Whiptail has distinctive black pigment on the throat and shoulders. Gila Spotted and Sonoran Spotted Whiptails are striped with spots developing in older adults. However, they do not acquire the heavy, sharp-edged spotting and large size of the Giant Spotted Whiptail, and they have bluish-green or brownish tails as juveniles. The Red-backed Whiptail, which geographically abuts the range of the Giant Spotted Whiptail, occupies rock slopes in desert scrub, and is spotted with a slaty-grayish to bluish tail as a hatchling.

Juvenile A. b. stictogramma, *Sycamore Canyon, AZ. Juveniles are striped and lack spots. At this stage, they are easily differentiated from congeners by the orange tail.*

Habitats: This whiptail has a restricted niche in the U.S., primarily in thorn scrub environments in mountain canyons in semi-desert grassland, the Arizona Upland portion of the Sonoran Desert, and lower Madrean oak woodland. It also occurs along perennial streams, cienegas, and surrounding thorn scrub in arid valleys. Thorn scrub plants in its preferred thickets include Velvet Mesquite, Desert Hackberry, Catclaw Acacia, Coursettia, Catclaw Mimosa, and many others. Riparian woodland is also used, as are thickets in surrounding environments. The elevational range is about 722–1,463 m, but mostly 822–1,219 m.

Natural History: This lizard is particularly wary and quick to flee into impenetrable cover. It employs rock slopes and arroyo embankments as well as densely vegetated bottomlands. Its large body mass enables it to retain heat gained in the sun as it forages deep into the shade, with body temperatures usually in the range of 37–42°C. Its spots serve as camouflage in dappled sunlight, and individuals may appear greenish as they vanish into dense herbaceous foliage. The diet probably includes arthropods as well as small juvenile lizards. Individuals search widely and actively for food within areas about 150 m in diameter. They probe with their pointed snouts and dig in organic litter under desert trees to find arthropods, and are alert to the movement of key predators, notably Sonoran Whipsnakes and Greater Roadrunners. Activity begins as hot weather commences in late April to mid-May and continues into mid-September or October. Mating occurs in May–July with females producing one or more clutches of 3–9 eggs from early June through July. Hatchlings appear in mid-summer.

Range: The Canyon Spotted Whiptail is a subtropical thorn scrub species that enters the U.S. in southeastern Arizona and extreme southwestern New Mexico in the Baboquivari, Pajarito, Peloncillo, and Perilla mountains. It occurs mainly in numerous canyons in the Santa Catalinas, Rincons, Santa Ritas, and Whetstones, and extends north into the Galiuro, Pinaleño, and Santa Teresa mountains. It persists near existing or former mid-valley streams at Arivaca, Empire Ranch, Nogales, Tucson, and a few tanks in Altar Valley, and it may occur locally on the San Pedro River. In Sonora, Mexico, it occurs more widely on the landscape.

Viewing Tips: To see this big, striking whiptail, go to Sabino Canyon or Catalina State Park (near Tucson, AZ) or Muleshoe Ranch (Galiuro Mountains, AZ) in mid-to-late morning when it is hot and sunny, and look for the lizards in canyon-bottom thickets, especially near perennial water. Watch 10–35 m ahead, and listen for the rustling of these wary lizards. On most warm days, lizards remain active through the heat of the day, although you may need to search them out in the shade.

Taxonomy: The species was described in 1938 from near Guaymas, Sonora, but the population there, which is *A. b. burti*, is very different from the Giant Spotted Whiptail and closely related whiptails in Sonora, which were previously confused with other striped, spotted species, and not accurately understood scientifically until the 1950s. The Red-backed Whiptail was considered a subspecies of *A. burti* until recently.

Subspecies and Variations: *Aspidoscelis b. stictogramma* is the only subspecies of this species in the U.S. In central and southern Sonora there are transitions between this and other large, spotted taxa and the smaller, striped *A. b. burti*.

Remarks: The Canyon Spotted Whiptail or a related taxon is one of the parental species that has hybridized with grassland whiptails in the *A. inornata* complex, producing unisexual parthenogenetic species. These unisexuals are favored by human-caused habitat disruption and are probably important competitors with their parental species, which may partially explain the restricted niche of the Giant Spotted Whiptail. Desiccation of valley streams and frequent damage to dense riparian vegetation appear to have significantly diminished its distribution in valley environments.

Gray Checkered Whiptail (unisexual)

Aspidoscelis dixoni (Scudday, 1973)

Author: Charles W. Painter

See page 559 for map color codes.

Description: This is a rather large, boldly marked whiptail, with individuals reaching at least 108 mm SVL. Average size of 402 individuals from southwest Hidalgo County, New Mexico, was 81 mm SVL and 15.5 g. The dorsal scales are small and granular; there are 94–112 scales around mid-body. The well-defined striped pattern of hatchlings changes as individuals age, often producing a finely vermiculated dorsal pattern of small squarish blotches that obscure the original lined pattern. Larger individuals often have a conspicuous orange-brown coloration on the posterior half of the body, which may extend well onto the tail. Ventrally, the throat is light tan with a slight touch of orange and without dark spots. The chest is paler than the throat, with a few small black dots. The belly is cream or white and lacks any black markings. **Juveniles:** Juveniles have 10–14 cream or yellow longitudinal dorsal stripes on a black or dark brown background.

Similar Species: The finely vermiculated dorsal pattern of small squarish blotches and the conspicuous orange-brown coloration on the posterior half of the body in mature adults may help observers distinguish the Gray Checkered Whiptail. However, the species is easily confused with numerous sympatric whiptails (up to 7 species) throughout its range in New Mexico and Texas. Until the casual observer becomes familiar with the subtle differences of these closely related species, only detailed examination of meristic characteristics of certain scales will help separate these species.

Habitats: In New Mexico, the Gray Checkered Whiptail occurs in desert scrub regions of Creosote Bush flats with little undergrowth and sandy to gravely soils. It is not found in sandy arroyo bottoms or adjacent grasslands. These grasslands likely serve as barriers to dispersal and result in a range of only a few square kilometers. Elevation in New Mexico is 1,303–1,426 m. Dominant plants in the New Mexico range include Creosote Bush, Tarbush, mesquites, Allthorn, Little Leaf Sumac, Mormon teas, vari-

Female A. dixoni, *Chinati Mountains, Presidio Co., TX.*

ous cacti, grasses, and annuals. In west Texas, general habitat includes rocky soils in desert shrublands and degraded grasslands on alluvial benches, canyon bottoms, and the lower slopes of the Chinati Mountains; elevation ranges between 908 and 1,460 m. Characteristic vegetation at these sites includes Creosote Bush, acacias, mesquites, Ocotillo, and various cacti and grasses.

Natural History: Individuals mature at approximately 67 mm SVL, with reproduction from May through July. Average clutch size is 3 (TX) to 4 (NM). The eggs are creamy in color, elliptical, and approximately 10 x 18 mm. An adult captured in New Mexico on June 4 laid 5 eggs on June 5; 4 of the eggs hatched during the third week in September. Hatchlings are 32–36 mm SVL; of 402 individuals collected at Antelope Pass, the smallest was 34 mm SVL collected on August 5. Gray Checkered Whiptails can live at least 6 years in the wild. A mature adult, at least 2 years of age when first captured at 85 mm SVL, was marked at Antelope Pass and recaptured 1,473 days later at 101 mm SVL.

In one study, the stomach content of 22 individuals from New Mexico included termites in 82% of the lizards, ants in 41%, beetles in 32%, and spiders in 23%. Other items included beetle larvae, desert cockroaches, solpugids, robber flies, and plant debris. The species is a deliberate forager and a generalized, opportunistic insectivore.

Female A. dixoni, *Antelope Pass, Peloncillo Mountains, Hidalgo Co., NM.*

Range: The Gray Checkered Whiptail occurs in 2 extremely limited areas separated by approximately 500 km: Antelope Pass in the Peloncillo Mountains, southwest New Mexico, and Chinati Mountains in Presidio County, west Texas.

Viewing Tips: Because of their diurnal habits and active foraging strategy, Gray Checkered Whiptails may be easily observed in Hidalgo County in southwest New Mexico if population density does not continue to decline. Specific localities include Antelope Pass in the Peloncillo Mountains approximately 10.5 km west of Animas. Individuals are most often observed in Creosote Bush flats during May through late July, although in New Mexico active individuals have been observed between April 5 and October 13. Activity is generally confined between 9:00 a.m. and 12 noon. The species may also be observed on the alluvial fans on the southwestern slopes of the Chinati Mountains in Presidio County, northwest of Presidio (TX). When startled, Gray Checkered Whiptails may rapidly flee from an observer for a distance of several meters before they stop. Binoculars greatly aid in identification of this species.

Taxonomy: This is a diploid unisexual whiptail belonging to the *A. tesselata* species group. When the Gray Checkered Whiptail was first recognized as a distinct clone it was described as pattern class F of *A. tesselata*. It was later designated a full species, with pattern classes A and B recognized. Parental species are male *A. scalaris* and female *A. marmorata*.

Subspecies and Variation: No subspecies of *A. dixoni* are recognized. Comparative genetic data indicate that although populations of *A. dixoni* from New Mexico and Texas are similar, the population in New Mexico is distinctive and represents a unique clone. This form is referred to as *A. dixoni* pattern class C.

Remarks: The unique New Mexico form of the Gray Checkered Whiptail appears to be declining in its extremely limited range of only a few square kilometers at Antelope Pass. Recent research suggests this decline may be a result of negative interactions with the Sonoran Tiger Whiptail (*A. tigris punctilinealis*), including competition and hybridization. Three sterile female hybrids between *A. dixoni* pattern class C and *A. tigris punctilinealis* have recently been reported from Antelope Pass in the Peloncillos. The Gray Checkered Whiptail is sympatric with at least 18 species of lizards and 22 species of snakes at Antelope Pass in the Peloncillo Mountains just west of Animas, Hidalgo County, New Mexico, an area of approximately 8.8 km^2. The scientific name of this species honors Dr. James R. Dixon—gentleman, mentor, and student extraordinaire of southwestern herpetofauna.

Desert scrub habitat of A. dixoni, *Peloncillo Mountains, Hidalgo Co., NM. This area has at least 18 species of sympatric lizards, including other whiptails.*

Chihuahuan Spotted Whiptail (unisexual)

Aspidoscelis exsanguis (Lowe, 1956)

Author: Randall D. Babb

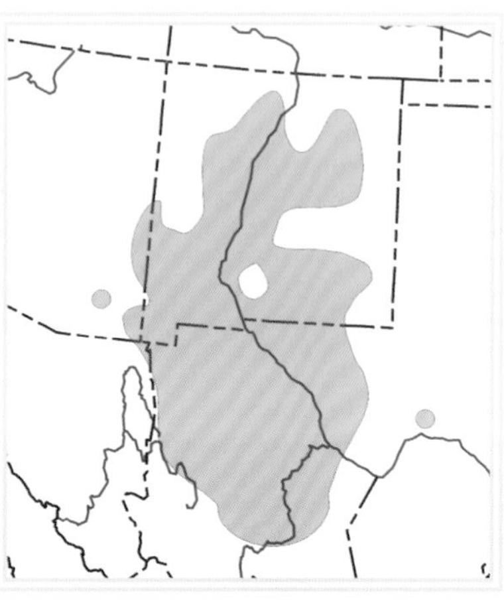

See page 559 for map color codes.

Description: A slender, all-female species covered with small granular scales dorsally, reaching about 100 mm SVL. Its tail is blue or greenish to gray and is long and slender and, when complete, much longer than the body. The head is narrow with a long snout and covered with large plate-like scales. A series of enlarged scales is also found on the anterior and posterior surfaces of the front limbs and the anterior surfaces of the hind limbs. The dorsal coloration is brown or rust with 6 (sometimes 7) thin diffused light stripes that run from the head to the base of the tail. Light spots are scattered across the back in both stripes and dark fields and are somewhat brighter on the rump. Light spots are also found on the hind legs. The venter is white, grayish, or bluish, unmarked and covered with larger rectangular scales arranged in rows. There are typically 3 enlarged preanal scales. The throat may also be bluish or white, with enlarged scales along the edge of the gular fold. **Juveniles:** Juveniles have blue or green tails with more distinct stripes dorsally and usually have light spotting.

Female A. exsanguis, *Eddy Co., NM.*

Similar Species: The spotted and striped parthenogenetic species of whiptails all look very similar. The Gila Spotted Whiptail is typically darker-colored dorsally, not as profusely spotted, and has 6 (rarely 7) distinct light stripes, which tend to be more brightly colored on the anterior portions of the body. Its tail is greenish or bluish, and it typically has 2 enlarged pre-

Female A. exsanguis, *Sierra Vieja Mountains, Presidio Co., TX.*

anal scales. The Sonoran Spotted Whiptail is slightly smaller (to about 89 mm SVL), tends to be darker dorsally, and is less heavily spotted, with 6 well-delineated light stripes; the tail often has an orange tint, and this species typically has 3 pre-anal scales.

Habitats: This species inhabits the Chihuahuan ecoregion, where it frequents rocky slopes, canyons, canyon bottoms, and riparian corridors in desert scrub, semi-desert grasslands, woodlands, and lower montane coniferous forests. It is commonly encountered in canyon bottoms in oak and pine-oak woodlands.

Natural History: Chihuahuan Spotted Whiptails are one of the most conspicuous lizard species in the habitats they occupy. Their characteristic nervous, jerky movements while foraging and long slender body make them easily recognizable. Chihuahuan Spotted Whiptails are diurnal, wide-ranging foragers that cover a lot of ground while hunting for a variety of prey. Activity is often punctuated by brief stops to cool off or bask, depending on the temperature. It is not unusual to see them scratching through leaf litter or digging beneath rocks or other surface objects in search of a meal. Prey items are chiefly invertebrates, including insects such as grasshoppers, grubs, termites, beetles, and other arthropods like spiders and scorpions. Chihuahuan Spotted Whiptails are active for only a few hours each day and maintain their body temperatures within narrow ranges near 38°C while doing so. This is one of several species of parthenogenetic whiptails of the Southwest that sometimes exhibit

Juvenile A. exsanguis, *Grant Co., NM. Note the faint light spots on the dark fields, which help distinguish this lizard from other juvenile whiptails.*

pseudocopulatory postures that mimic mating among sexually reproducing species. Depending on the stage of egg development within the lizard's body, it will assume either a male or female role. Research has shown that this behavior actually stimulates the female to lay more eggs than if this "ritual" were not employed. Chihuahuan Whiptails lay up to 6 eggs from June through August.

Range: Chihuahuan Spotted Whiptails are distributed from extreme southeastern Arizona (Greenlee and Cochise counties) eastward through most of the southern two-thirds of New Mexico to southwestern Texas (Tran-Pecos region) and most of adjacent Sonora and Chihuahua, Mexico. There is a disjunct population in northwestern Cochise County, Arizona.

Viewing Tips: Watch for this lizard foraging among the underbrush in canyons and in riparian corridors on benches and areas adjacent to the channel. These lizards are most likely to be seen before the heat of summer days makes temperatures too hot for activity. Look for Chihuahuan Spotted Whiptails starting about mid-morning on hot days. Close approach to these nervous lizards will be difficult, so close-focusing binoculars will be helpful in identifying and watching this animal. In Arizona, look for it along the Gila River and its tributaries, including the Blue River Wilderness in Greenlee County; Chiricahua National Monument; and the Coronado National Forest in the Chiricahua

Mountains of Cochise County. In New Mexico, look for this species on the Gila, Cibola, and Lincoln national forests; Carlsbad Caverns National Park; and Bosque del Apache, San Andres, and Bitter Lake national wildlife refuges. In Texas, Fort Davis National Historic Site and Guadalupe Mountains National Park are good places to view this species.

Taxonomy: The Gila Spotted Whiptail, Sonoran Spotted Whiptail, and Chihuahuan Spotted Whiptail were at one time all considered a single species. The Chihuahuan Spotted Whiptail has a 2-staged origin resulting from hybridization among 3 different species of whiptails and an intermediate ancestor. Genetic work done in 2002 shows the Chihuahua Spotted Whiptail likely originated through hybridization between the Texas Spotted Whiptail and an intermediate ancestor that in turn originated from hybridization between the Canyon Spotted Whiptail and the Little Striped Whiptail.

Subspecies and Variation: No subspecies are recognized.

Remarks: Chihuahuan Spotted Whiptails are important lizards ecologically. They are efficient predators and consume large numbers of prey due to high energy demands. Many birds, mammals, and other reptiles in turn prey upon these lizards.

Female A. exsanguis, *Chiricahua Mountains, Cochise Co., AZ. The faint stripes on the neck distinguish this species from* A. sonorae *and* A. flagellicauda, *which have bolder stripes and also occur in the Chiricahuas.*

Gila Spotted Whiptail (unisexual)

Aspidoscelis flagellicauda (Lowe and Wright, 1964)

Authors: Lawrence L. C. Jones, Trevor B. Persons, and John W. Wright

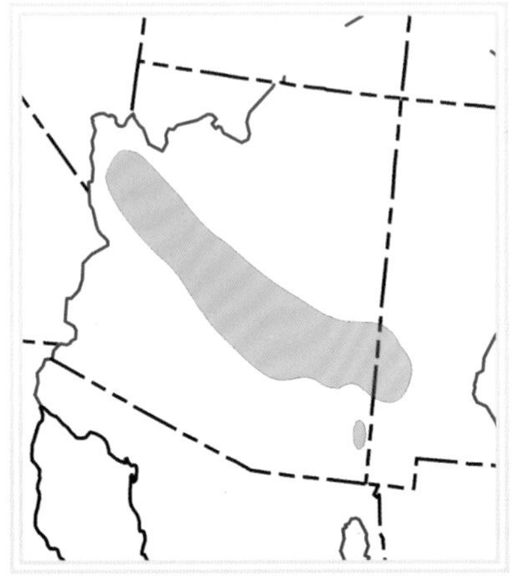

See page 559 for map color codes.

Description: This is a moderately large all-female whiptail, with some adults reaching almost 100 mm SVL, although 80–90 mm is typical adult size. The tail is about twice the SVL and becomes progressively more olive-green toward the end. This is a striped and spotted species of whiptail. There are 6 distinct longitudinal dorsal light stripes, with the paravertebral stripes often quite close together. There are relatively few light spots in the dark fields, but spots may extend onto (and be lighter than) the light stripes. Spotting is most pronounced in older adults. In adults, the upper thigh and foreleg are often a uniform tan color, although in some individuals they may be indistinctly mottled. The venter is unmarked and cream-colored. In adults, the nuchal and head region is heavily suffused with a gold or chartreuse color. There are usually only 2 enlarged pre-anal scales, and the mesoptychial and postantebrachial scales are abruptly enlarged. **Juveniles:** Juveniles are similar but have few spots, and the contrast between the light stripes and dark fields is more pronounced. Also, the upper hind-limb surfaces are usually indistinctly mottled.

Subadult A. flagellicauda *with fused paravertebral stripes, Montezuma Well, Yavapai Co., AZ.*

Similar Species: The striped and spotted whiptails are among the most difficult lizards to differentiate. The Chihuahuan Spotted (*A. exsanguis*) and Sonoran Spotted (*A. sonorae*) whiptails look very similar to *A. flagellicauda*, and there is overlap in many scale counts. *Aspidoscelis exsanguis* is the most distinctive of

Female A. flagellicauda, *Montezuma Well, Yavapai Co., AZ.*

the 3 species. Unlike the other 2, hatchling *A. exsanguis* have discrete red or white spots in the dark fields between the lowest lateral stripes, and distinct white spots or dashes along the midline. Adult *A. exsanguis* are heavily spotted and indistinctly striped, and unlike the other 2 species their paravertebral light stripes are wavy, and both the front and rear limbs are distinctly mottled. In both *A. flagellicauda* and *A. sonorae*, hatchlings have only faint, diffuse yellowish spots in the upper lateral dark fields, with spotting becoming more pronounced and spreading to the lower dark fields as they mature. Compared with *A. sonorae*, *A. flagellicauda* is less heavily spotted at a given age, and the paravertebral light stripes are usually noticeably closer together, even sometimes touching. The Gila Spotted Whiptail is the only one of these 3 species that usually has 2, rather than 3, enlarged pre-anal scales. The distributions of these 3 similar species overlap only partially in southeastern Arizona and southwestern New Mexico. In the Canyon Spotted Whiptail, whose range overlaps that of the Gila Spotted Whiptail in a few areas, juveniles and young adults are also striped and spotted, but they usually have orange hind legs and tail.

Habitats: This species is found primarily in Madrean evergreen woodlands of oak and pine, piñon/juniper woodlands, and interior chaparral, but it may extend lower into semi-desert grasslands, especially along riparian corridors. It occurs primarily between 1,220 and 1,980 m. It is occasionally found in the lower edge of coniferous forests. This is the characteristic whiptail in chaparral and woodland habitats throughout much of the Mogollon Rim region (AZ and NM) and west to the Cerbat Mountains (AZ).

Natural History: This species is active from about April through October, although most adult activity occurs between May and August. This species is a widely foraging, opportunistic insectivore that maintains a high body temperature (about 40°C) when active. Although diet has not been extensively studied, Gila Spotted Whiptails probably eat a variety of adult and larval insects and other arthropods. This is an all-female species, so females lay unfertilized eggs that hatch into genetically identical females. Gila Spotted Whiptails usually lay a single clutch of 2–6 eggs in June or July, and hatchlings appear about 2 months later. Pseudocopulation has been observed rarely in captivity or in the wild for this species, and it is unknown if this behavior is important.

Range: The Gila Spotted Whiptail occurs throughout much of the Mogollon Rim ecoregion, ranging from the headwaters of the Gila River drainage in southwestern New Mexico northwestward through Arizona to the Cerbat Mountains west of the Grand Canyon. Populations have also been found farther south in the Santa Catalina, Chiricahua, Galiuro, and Pinaleño mountains.

Viewing Tips: Gila Spotted Whiptails are common and easily observed throughout most of their range. In the Mogollon Rim country of central Arizona, where neither *A. exsanguis* nor *A. sonorae* occur, they can be observed on such public lands as Mon-

Juvenile A. flagellicauda, *Galiuro Mountains, Graham Co., AZ. Hatchlings lack light spots in the dark fields, but in this young animal the light spots are just starting to become visible.*

Female A. flagellicauda, *Yavapai Co., AZ. The bold neck stripes help distnguish it from* A. exsanguis, *but not* A. sonorae.

tezuma Castle National Monument (Montezuma Well unit), Tonto National Monument, and many areas in Prescott and Tonto national forests. They can also be observed in the Pinaleño Mountains, at many locations along the Swift Trail (AZ Route 366). For more challenging whiptail-watching, one can look for this species in the Santa Catalina, Chirichahua, or Galiuro mountains in Arizona, or near the Gila or San Francisco rivers in New Mexico, where Chihuahuan Spotted and/or Sonoran Spotted Whiptails may also be found.

Taxonomy: The hybrid parentage of the Gila Spotted Whiptail is similar to that of the Sonoran Spotted Whiptail, but because the two species arose through separate hybridization events they are considered distinct species.

Subspecies and Variation: As with other unisexual whiptails, subspecies are not recognized. The color pattern of the Gila Spotted Whiptail is relatively uniform throughout its range, suggesting it may consist of a single, hybrid-derived lineage.

Remarks: The Gila Spotted Whiptail is a triploid species that arose by hybridization between the Canyon Spotted Whiptail (or the closely related Western Mexico Whiptail, *A. costata*) and a diploid parthenogenetic species, which in turn originated by hybridization between the Canyon Spotted or Western Mexican Whiptail and a member of the Little Striped Whiptail complex.

Common Spotted Whiptail

Aspidoscelis gularis (Baird and Girard, 1852)

Authors: Daniel J. Leavitt and Allison F. Leavitt

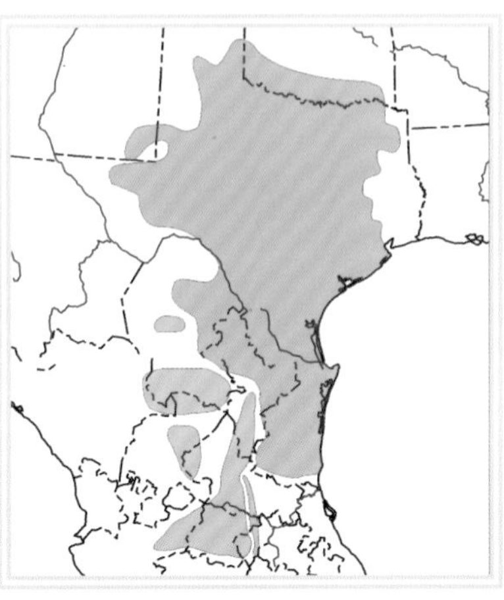

See page 559 for map color codes. There are different interpretations of taxonomy, nomenclature, and range for this species complex.

Description: This is a medium-sized, striped and spotted whiptail, reaching a maximum of 105 mm SVL. It has rectangular belly scales, and the long slender tail is up to 2 times longer than the SVL. The brownish-green body is adorned with 7–8 longitudinal yellowish-white stripes containing many similarly colored spots within the margins. With this species both the postantebrachial and the mesoptychial scales are enlarged. This species is sexually dimorphic: males are larger than females, and there are differences in ventral coloration. **Sexual Variation:** Adult males have distinguishing marks on the venter. The gular region is often orange, red, or pink; abdominal ventral coloration can be blue or light blue, occasionally with black patches. Adult females do not have any bright coloration on the venter, which appears white or cream colored. **Juveniles:** Juveniles tend to have reddish rumps that fade with age. Dorsal spots are either absent or indistinct.

Similar Species: The Common Spotted Whiptail is similar to the Chihuahuan Spotted Whiptail, but can be distinguished by its dorsal stripes and chest color. Common Spotted Whiptails have 7 or 8 dorsal stripes with dark ventral coloration, and Chihuahuan Spotted Whiptails have 6 dorsal stripes with lighter ventral color. They may be differentiated from the Plateau Spotted Whiptail by their spots, which are located within the fields of

Aspidoscelis gularis, *Austin, Travis Co., TX.*

Male A. gularis, *Devil's River, Val Verde Co., TX.*

dark coloration in the Common Spotted Whiptail, whereas they merge with the dorsal stripes in the Plateau Spotted Whiptail. Six-lined Racerunners may appear somewhat similar, though they lack spots and are generally smaller than Common Spotted Whiptails.

Habitats: In the U.S., Common Spotted Whiptails are found on the southern plains, portions of the Chihuahuan Desert, Post Oak savanna, and cross timbers regions. This species can be found in prairies, grasslands, desert scrub, mesa tops, rocky hillsides, dense thickets, and canyon bottoms. Altitudinal ranges are from under 900 m to over 1,400 m. They are often found near watercourses and occur in both disturbed and undisturbed landscapes.

Natural History: Common Spotted Whiptails are highly active insectivores. Emergence from brumation occurs in late spring and is dependent upon temperature. Most often, these diurnal lizards prey upon termites, grasshoppers, crickets, beetles, and spiders. Research has shown no apparent difference in food preferences between age or sex classes. Much of their daily energy is invested in rooting and probing the soil litter in search of food. Common Spotted Whiptails are most active when morning air temperatures reach 35 to 40°C. Research has shown these lizards to be most active in the morning; activity is then curtailed by midday. Female egg development may begin in mid-April. Males reach their peak reproductive output from May through early June.

Females can lay 1–8 (usually 2–3) eggs in July. Yearling females (~ 65 mm SVL) can be reproductive. Eggs are laid in a separate chamber within the adult female's burrow, which can be as deep as 30 cm. Nests often occur in abandoned rodent burrows, though they have also been found in road embankments. Hatchlings begin to emerge in the late summer and early fall when they become common. Hatchlings measure 25 to 40 mm SVL and their tails are pinkish or reddish. While numerous animals prey upon Common Spotted Whiptails, the most common predators include Greater Roadrunners, Cactus Wrens, and many species of snakes and medium-sized mammals. In suburban areas this lizard's presence is challenged by predation pressure from both domestic and feral cats.

Range: In the U.S., Common Spotted Whiptails occur in southern Oklahoma, extreme southeastern New Mexico, and much of Texas. Within Mexico, they can be found in northern Coahuila, Nuevo León, and Tamaulipas.

Viewing Tips: Because of their manner and abundance, these lizards are easy to find in proper habitat. They scare easily and often retreat in a straight line before stopping to reassess the danger from the cover of vegetation. Binoculars are handy, since approaching within 5 m may not be easy. The best time of year to view Common Spotted Whiptails is during the late spring and summer (April through August), when insects

Underside of a male A. gularis, *one of the few whiptails with colorful venter, Devil's River, Val Verde Co., TX.*

Juvenile A. gularis, *Marfa, Presidio Co., TX. Juveniles have a red rump, similar to the related* A. scalaris.

are most abundant and the animals are surface-active for much of the day. The most opportune time to find these lizards is early in the morning when they are beginning to warm up for the day. Typically, these lizards will begin to forage after the ground temperature reaches 30 to 35 °C. Good places to observe Common Spotted Whiptails include Amistad National Recreation Area (TX), Carlsbad Caverns National Park (NM), Fort Davis National Historic Site (TX), and many Texas state parks located on the Edwards Plateau, including Pedernales State Park.

Taxonomy: With the exception of the change to the genus from *Cnemidophorus*, there have been few changes to the taxonomy of this lizard. For some time the Plateau Spotted Whiptail (*A. scalaris septemvittata*) was considered a subspecies of the Common Spotted Whiptail.

Subspecies and Variation: Over the years, there have been as many as 7 subspecies recognized for the Common Spotted Whiptail (*A. gularis*). Within the range of this book, the Texas Spotted Whiptail, *A. g. gularis*, is the only subspecies currently recognized.

Remarks: Common Spotted Whiptails are known to squeak when disturbed. Their purpose for this high-pitched monosyllabic vocalization is not well understood.

Little White Whiptail

Aspidoscelis gypsi (Wright and Lowe, 1993)

Authors: Erica Bree Rosenblum and Doug Burkett

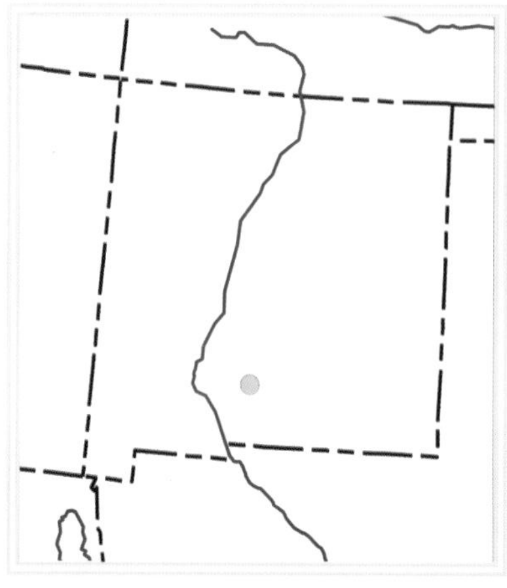

See page 559 for map color codes.

Description: The Little White Whiptail is a relatively small whiptail with an average SVL of approximately 65 mm and an extremely long tail (much longer than the head and body). This whiptail lizard is most obviously characterized by its pale dorsal color and faint pattern, which provides excellent camouflage on the gypsum dunes of White Sands (NM). The dorsal field may be fairly uniform in color or may have 6–8 relatively dim longitudinal stripes running from the back of the neck to the base of the tail. The head and tail are light blue. The limbs and side body also typically exhibit a pale blue hue. **Sexual Variation:** In males, the blue head and tail coloration is more pronounced than in females, and the hemipenal bulge is relatively easy to discern when the lizard is in the hand.

Adult A. gypsi, *White Sands National Monument, NM.*

Adult A. gypsi, *White Sands National Monument, NM.*

Juveniles: Juveniles are rarely seen in the field; however, they are smaller than adults with little ontogenetic change as they mature.

Similar Species: There are no other species of whiptail lizards found on the white gypsum dunes of south central New Mexico. *Aspidoscelis gypsi* is very closely related to *A. inornata* (see Taxonomy section below) and can be distinguished most obviously by its pale coloration and restricted distribution. *Aspidoscelis gypsi* shares the diagnostic scale morphology of *A. inornata*, having only slightly enlarged postantebrachial and mesoptychial scales.

Habitats: *Aspidoscelis gypsi* is found in sandy white gypsum habitat. This landscape consists of barren dunes separated by low inter-dune areas dominated by Rabbitbrush, yuccas, Mormon teas, Sand Verbena, and a variety of grasses. Little White Whiptails are observed in the vegetated inter-dune areas much more frequently than on the barren dunes themselves. White Sands National Monument is at an elevation of approximately 1,200 m.

Natural History: This species eats a variety of invertebrates, with insect larvae generally comprising a large proportion of the diet. These lizards are fast runners and are capable of quick bursts of speed for short distances. Little White Whiptails are active foragers, favoring persistent movement in search for prey. As with most other diurnal, actively foraging lizards, this species is quite heat-tolerant and is most often seen during warm ambient temperatures (30 to 35°C) with ground temperatures soaring well above 38°C. During non-active periods (ambient temperatures over 38°C and nighttime) they make use of their narrow burrows, which they typically excavate themselves. Little White Whiptails have many predators, including avians, reptiles, and mammals. Specific predators on the gypsum dunes include the Greater Roadrunner, American Kestrel, Coachwhip, Massasauga, and Kit Fox. Tail autotomy is sometimes used as an escape strategy, and they will use any available hole or vegetative cover when fleeing predators. Females lay an average of 2 eggs per clutch, primarily between mid-June and early August.

Range: *Aspidoscelis gypsi* is geographically restricted to the white sands of the gypsum dune fields of the Tularosa Basin in south-central New Mexico. The entire habitat of this species lies within White Sands National Monument and White Sands Missile Range. This is the largest gypsum dune field in the world, covering approximately 71,280 ha. Although the range of this species is quite restricted, populations at White Sands National Monument are abundant.

Viewing Tips: This species is most typically observed foraging in the inter-dune areas of White Sands National Monument. Lizards are abundant even in the sparsely vegetated heart of the dune system. The lizards will typically flush from a short distance (2–20 m). Walk slowly through low-lying vegetated areas between the dunes and watch for *A. gypsi* darting between clumps of vegetation. These lizards are most easily seen once surface temperatures are quite high, in the late morning and early afternoon throughout the spring, summer, and fall.

Taxonomy: *Aspidoscelis gypsi* was formerly known as *Cnemidophorus inornatus* and was reassigned to the genus *Aspidoscelis* in 2002. The species was described in 1993 as a subspecies of *C. inornatus* (Little Striped Whiptail, now *A. inornata*) but was considered a full species in 1997. *Aspidoscelis gypsi* is certainly distinct in coloration from other populations of *A. inornata*; however, whether *A. gypsi* should be considered a full species or a form of *A. inornata* is still debated. *Aspidoscelis gypsi* is not distinguishable from *A. inornata* based on available genetic data. This means that there has been recent or ongoing gene flow between populations inhabiting the gypsum dune habitat at White Sands and those in the surrounding Chihuahuan Desert soils. Another difficulty of delineating *A. gypsi* as a full species is that populations of *A. inornata* are continuously distributed throughout the Tularosa Basin of New Mexico. This means that the lighter *A. gypsi* is found within meters of the darker *A. inornata*. The likelihood of ongoing contact between these forms is therefore high.

Gravid females of A. gypsi *(top) and* A. inornata *(bottom), from nearby localities.* Aspidoscelis gypsi *more closely matches its gypsum dunes background, and some authorities regard it as a light color phase of* A. inornata.

Subspecies and Variation: There are no subspecies of *A. gypsi*.

Remarks: The light coloration of *A. gypsi* appears to have a genetic basis and is not merely induced by environmental conditions. The color of *Aspidoscelis gypsi* varies somewhat with temperature (darker at colder temperatures), as is common in lizards. However, even at its darkest, *A. gypsi* is still significantly lighter in color than *A. inornata*. Further, there is evidence that variation in one particular gene, the melanocortin-1 receptor gene, may lead to the light coloration of *A. gypsi*. Interestingly, this is the same gene responsible for color variation in some populations of pocket mice in deserts of the Southwest.

Orange-throated Whiptail

Aspidoscelis hyperythra (Cope, 1863)

Author: Jeffrey M. Lemm

Description: This is a relatively small whiptail, with adult males reaching 72 mm SVL. The tail is long and slender, and is approximately twice as long as the body. The snout is pointed and the head is yellow-brown to olive-gray with a single, fused frontoparietal scale. Males are usually larger than females and there are slight differences in coloration. **Sexual Variation:** Adult males are gray, reddish-brown, dark brown, or black, with 5 to 6 pale yellow, tan, or white stripes down the dorsum. The middle stripe is often forked at both ends. The ventral surfaces of the body and tail may be completely orange, but this coloring is usually restricted to the throat and chest. The venter of females is usually cream or white. Males also have larger femoral pores than females. Some older females may exhibit some orange coloration on the throat. **Juveniles:** Juveniles are similar to adults; however, the striping is more vivid. The venter is cream or white, and the tail and hind limbs are cobalt blue.

See page 559 for map color codes.
Subspecies not differentiated.

Similar Species: The only other whiptail within the American range of the Orange-throated Whiptail is the Tiger Whiptail, which is much larger than the Orange-throated Whiptail and has a broken dorsal striped pattern, as well as a divided frontoparietal scale. Juvenile Tiger Whiptails also have more distinct stripes than the adults and a blue or green tail, are larger than Orange-throated Whiptail juveniles, and have an average of 8 dorsal stripes.

Juvenile A. hyperythra, *Escondido, San Diego Co., CA.*

Male A. hyperythra, *showing the characteristic orange throat. Escondido, San Diego Co., CA.*

Habitats: This species is confined to coastal southern California and much of Baja California. Orange-throated Whiptails are associated with coastal sage scrub, chaparral, thorn scrub, and many other habitats in Baja California, including some offshore islands. The species is most commonly found in areas with patches of thick vegetation surrounded by open areas with loose soil and rocks. In southern California, Buckwheat, Black Sage, White Sage, and Chamise are usually present where Orange-throated Whiptails are found. The elevational range of the species is from near sea level to about 1,040 m. In southern California, Orange-throated Whiptails are usually found only in pristine areas and are exceedingly rare or absent in marginal habitats and developed areas.

Natural History: Orange-throated Whiptails are wary, fast-moving lizards. They are most active from early spring until late summer. Daily activity occurs within a narrow range of substrate temperatures, and high midday temperatures are often avoided. Orange-throated Whiptails usually become active when substrate temperatures reach 27–29°C and will remain active through much of the day, thermoregulating between shade and sunshine. In midsummer, midday heat is often avoided, and the lizards remain in the shade of bushes or retreat underground. Most of the winter is spent underground in the northern part of the range, although they may become active on warm winter days. Yearlings often remain active until December. Dietary specialists, they feed primarily on termites; however, in the summer months, when termites are difficult to find, they often feed on other insects such as beetles, cockroaches, grasshoppers, silverfish, and spiders. Orange-throated Whiptails are not territorial. Home ranges of numerous males and females overlap, and average home ranges measure 0.03 ha for males and 0.06 ha for females.

The reproductive season of the Orange-throated Whiptail varies slightly with latitude. In southern California the breeding season lasts from May through July, whereas in southern Baja California the season may not commence until July. Two to 3 eggs are laid per clutch, and hatchlings usually emerge around August or September. Hatchlings measure roughly 30 mm SVL and weigh 0.50 g. They grow quickly and often reach sexual maturity within a year; however, most probably do not reproduce until their second year. Females may have multiple clutches when conditions are optimal. Orange-throated Whiptails may live up to 6 years or more. They are often host to pterygosomatid mites. Predators include other lizards, snakes, birds, and mammals.

Range: In the United States, Orange-throated Whiptails occur from Orange and San Bernardino counties in southern California on the western side of the Peninsular Ranges to the U.S.–Mexico border in San Diego County. In Baja California they

Male A. hyperythra, *San Diego Wild Animal Park, San Diego Co., CA.*

Adult A. hyperythra. *The male (left) has the orange ventral coloration, most pronounced on the throat, while the female (right) has a cream-colored venter.*

occur throughout the cismontane northwestern portion of the peninsula (excluding the high elevations). The southern range extends from around San Ignacio in the west, southeast in an arc down near San Evaristo in the east.

Viewing Tips: Orange-throated Whiptails may be difficult to find in many regions of California. They are most easily viewed in the late morning in spring and summer in pristine coastal sage and chaparral habitats in reserve areas and open-space parks. They do not stay on open ground long and when approached often dart to the nearest cover. Collection or possession is illegal without proper permits, so the animals should never be handled.

Taxonomy: Until recently, whiptails from North America were assigned to the genus *Cnemidophorus*; however, with recent genetic and morphological research the North American whiptails were placed back into the resurrected genus *Aspidoscelis*.

Subspecies and Variation: Over time, 3 subspecies of *hyperythra* have been recognized by various authors: *A. h. beldingi* in the north, *A. h. schmidti* in central Baja California, and *A. h. hyperythra* in southern Baja California Sur. Some authors believe *schmidti* to be an intergrade between the other 2 subspecies, and others believe only one taxon should be recognized (*A. hyperythra*). The most current taxonomy suggests *A. h. beldingi* occurs from southern California south into Baja California near San Ignacio and southeastward to near San Evaristo, and *A. h. hyperythra* occurs in the Cape Region.

Remarks: The Orange-throated Whiptail has a relatively small range compared to other lizards in the United States. The species is tied closely to endangered ecosystems such as coastal sage scrub in southern California, but where it occurs it is often the most common lizard found.

Little Striped Whiptail

Aspidoscelis inornata (Baird, 1859 "1858")

Authors: Trevor B. Persons and John W. Wright

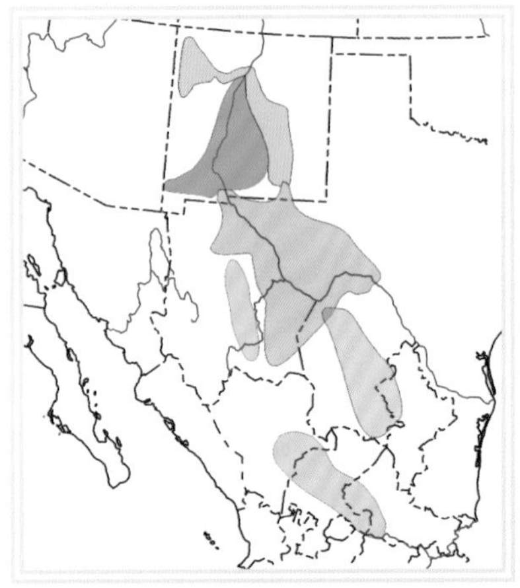

See page 559 for map color codes.

Description: This is a small whiptail, reaching a maximum size of about 70 mm SVL, with most adults only about 50–65 mm. The tail is about twice the SVL, and is bright blue. Throughout much of its range the dorsal pattern consists of 7 light stripes on a brown or dark gray background, although some populations lack the seventh (middorsal) stripe. The dark fields between the light stripes are unspotted, and the upper surfaces of the hind limbs are frequently unpatterned. The whitish ventral surfaces are suffused with blue, as are the upper surfaces of the limbs. The postantebrachial and mesoptychial scales are not enlarged. **Sexual Variation:** The bellies, throats, and undersides of the limbs of males are a brilliant sky blue, and the base of the tails usually appears somewhat swollen from the inverted hemipenes. In females the ventral blue coloration is reduced. **Juveniles:** Juveniles are similar to adults, and hatchlings emerge at about 30–35 mm SVL.

Female A. i. heptagramma, *Marfa, Presidio Co., TX.*

Male A. i. heptagramma, *Pecos Co., TX.*

Similar Species: Rely on range to distinguish between this species and 3 very similar members of the *A. inornata* complex: Arizona Striped, Pai Striped, and Little White whiptails, all considered to be conspecific by many (see Taxonomy, below). The Little White Whiptail is also distinguished by its bleached coloration and faded pattern. The larger Plateau Striped Whiptail usually has 4 or more enlarged pre-anal scales (vs. 2–3 in the Little Striped Whiptail) and lacks an extensive series of small interlabial scales between the chin shields and lower labials (usually 2–5, vs. 10 or more in the Little Striped Whiptail). The Desert Grassland Whiptail has only 6 light stripes, the ventral surfaces are white or only very faintly blue, the tail of adults is greenish-blue, and the postantebrachial and mesoptychial scales are abruptly enlarged.

Habitats: Little Striped Whiptails occur in a variety of grassland habitats, especially where various shrubs such as yuccas, Mormon teas, mesquites, Creosote Bush, and Snakeweed are present. They also occur in open juniper savannas and piñon/juniper woodlands. They are usually found in areas with markedly sandy soils, but they occupy gravelly or rocky areas in Trans-Pecos Texas. Little Striped Whiptails, along with Common Lesser Earless Lizards, are often abundant residents of prairie dog towns. Although most common at low to mid-elevations (*ca.* 900–1,600 m), they occur up to almost 2,300 m in parts of New Mexico.

Natural History: Little Striped Whiptails emerge in April and are among the first lizards to cease activity for the year, usually by mid-September. Like other whiptails, this is a widely foraging species that maintains a high body temperature (38-40°C) when active. They may be abroad both morning and afternoon, depending on temperature and availability of shade. They are opportunistic insectivores, eating whatever small insects, insect larvae, and other arthropods they find as they poke through leaf litter under shrubs. Termites are especially favored and are usually available. Individual home ranges overlap, but males may defend temporary foraging territories, and they often chase away both female and other male conspecifics. Little Striped Whiptails lay 1–2 clutches of 1–3 eggs each in June or July, and hatchlings appear about 45 days later. In northern areas (e.g., Albuquerque) they do not breed until they are almost 2 years of age. However, studies in Texas indicate that many individuals there are reproductively mature in their second year, as is the closely related Arizona Striped Whiptail in southeastern Arizona.

Range: The Little Striped Whiptail ranges throughout much of southern and central New Mexico, Trans-Pecos Texas, and into north-central Mexico. Populations in northwestern New Mexico (San Juan River watershed) are isolated from the bulk of the species range.

Viewing Tips: Throughout much of their range, Little Striped Whiptails are common and easily observed. They move almost constantly, and although they invariably flee from an observer they usually resume their normal behavior quickly. The best time for watching them while not moving is soon after they emerge in the morning, when one can find them basking in the open. They can be readily found at Petroglyph National Monument and at the Gran Quivira unit of Salinas Pueblo Missions National Monument in New Mexico, and at Big Bend National Park in Texas. Shrubby, sandy roadsides in grasslands are good places to find this whiptail.

Taxonomy: Until recently the Little Striped Whiptail included populations in Arizona that are currently regarded as the species Arizona Striped Whiptail and Pai Striped Whiptail, as well as the Little White Whiptail inhabiting White Sands in New Mexico. Although subspecies are not universally in vogue, they best describe the relationship among the various forms in the Little Striped Whiptail complex. Although the large-bodied, woodland populations of Pai Striped Whiptail in central Arizona and near Grand Canyon may be distinct, the small-bodied, grassland populations elsewhere in northeastern Arizona are likely more closely related to Little Striped Whiptails in northwestern New Mexico. The Arizona Striped Whiptail is similarly one end of a

Adult A. i. junipera, *Doña Ana Co., NM.*

relict cline between it and populations of Little Striped Whiptail in southern New Mexico. The Little White Whiptail is likely a population of Little Striped Whiptail that is subject to extreme natural selection for light coloration (for predator avoidance) within the white gypsum sands it inhabits.

Subspecies and Variation: Currently, 3 subspecies are recognized in the U.S. portion of the range. The Trans-Pecos Striped Whiptail (*A. i. heptagramma*) occurs from extreme southern New Mexico through Trans-Pecos Texas and eastern Chihuahua, Mexico; the Woodland Striped Whiptail (*A. i. junipera*) occurs in eastern and northwestern New Mexico; and the Plains Striped Whiptail (*A. i. llanuras*) occurs in the Rio Grande Valley and nearby areas in central and southern New Mexico. Four other subspecies, including an unpatterned (i.e., inornate) form, occur in Mexico. Both *heptagramma* and *junipera* usually have 7 complete stripes, while *llanuras* generally lacks the seventh (middorsal) stripe.

Marbled Whiptail

Aspidoscelis marmorata (Baird and Girard, 1852)

Author: James R. Dixon

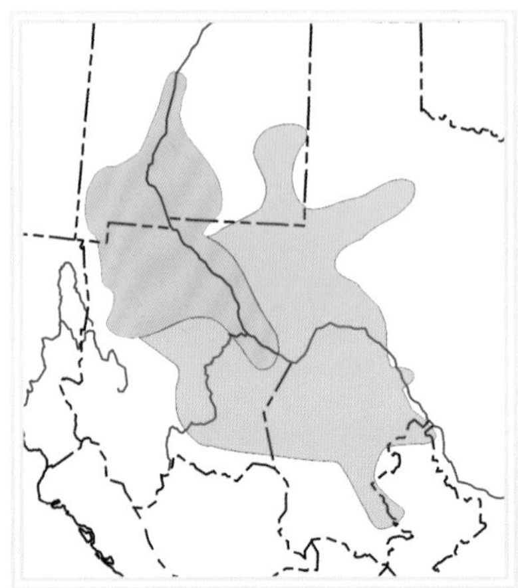

See page 559 for map color codes.

Description: The Marbled Whiptail reaches about 107 mm SVL. The body is elongate and torpedo shaped. The limbs are relatively long and muscular. The tail is extremely long and whip-like, representing 69 to 72% of the TL of the lizard. The dorsal and lateral skin of the body and limbs is granular, the belly is covered with large rectangular scales, and the tail scales are imbricate, somewhat square, and in regular rows. The head is somewhat pointed and relatively long. The dorsal and lateral surfaces of the head have large shields. The color pattern consists of a ground color of gray brown to brown, with bold pale spaces surrounded or partly surrounded by dark brown to black markings that tend to form reticulations over the dorsum and sides of the body. It is common for the pale spaces to become predominant in larger adults. Throat and ventral pattern of young female adults is predominantly white and occasionally has faint black spots. The latter spot-

Male A. m. reticuloriens, *Mescalero Sands, Chaves Co., NM.*

Female A. m. marmorata, *Doña Ana Co., NM.*

ting is bold and the throat black spotting is more distinct in adult males. **Sexual Variation:** The dark throat and ventral pattern of adult males is more distinct. Adult males tend to be larger than females, with the larger males reaching 107 mm SVL and females 97 SVL. **Juveniles:** The juvenile dorsal pattern has about 6 distinct narrow pale stripes on a brownish gray to brown ground color. These stripes are usually broken into a series of pale dashes that tend to become reticulated posteriorly. As juveniles mature, the reticulations become more pronounced on the posterior part of the body and move anteriorly.

Similar Species: The Tiger Whiptail and Gray Checkered Whiptail are the only 2 whiptail species that approach the size and color pattern of the Marbled Whiptail. Both of the former have slightly different patterns and color, and occupy different habitats than those of the Marbled Whiptail.

Habitats: The Chihuahuan Desert areas of New Mexico and Texas that range in elevation from 900 to 1,575 m and contain Creosote Bush, Desert Willow, mesquites, Fourwing Saltbush, Russian Thistle, Desert Salt Grass, and various cacti are prime areas for Marbled Whiptails. The lizards apparently like desert pavement, wide sandy washes, and undulating bajadas with some gravel and adobe soils.

Natural History: Foraging activity of Marbled Whiptails is rapid and jerky. As a consequence, this species covers almost twice the foraging range of other species of whiptails in the vicinity. The prey of this species consists of beetles, grasshoppers, ants, insect larvae, butterflies, moths, and termites. Termites appear to be the staple item in their diet and are common throughout the deserts where the lizard lives. This lizard is in turn preyed upon by Greater Roadrunners, Harris's Hawks, Long-nosed Snakes, Coachwhips, and Long-nosed Leopard Lizards.

Male Marbled Whiptails mature at 70 mm SVL and females at 60 mm. They first emerge from brumation in March or April. Breeding has been observed during July, and the first appearance of young occurs in July. There is apparently a single clutch of eggs each summer, and the number of eggs per clutch varies from 1 to 5, with an average of 2.6 eggs. The life span of Marbled Whiptails is 3–4 years, with one known individual surviving until the age of 8 years.

One author suggested that each species of whiptail occupies a particular plant community, but overlaps other plant communities when environmental conditions are favorable. This is especially true where topography allows several plant associations to occur in close proximity to one another. In this case, as many as 5 species of whiptails may occur together. Marbled Whiptails apparently prefer flat desert pavement where visibility is excellent. However, they are also found on bajadas, in dry sandy creek beds, and occasionally in desert grasslands that contain adequate visibility between clumps of grass. Home range in this lizard is basically its foraging territory, about 267 m^2. Competition between Marbled Whiptails and other species of whiptails is mostly avoided by their choice of habitat and their behavior while feeding.

Range: Marbled Whiptails are generally confined to the Chihuahuan Desert. They usually occur below 1,520 m in elevation in the southern half of New Mexico, far western Texas, most of the states of Chihuahua and Coahuila, and extreme western Nuevo León, Mexico. One isolated population is found just north of Laredo, Texas, along the Rio Grande.

Viewing Tips: A good watch, a pair of 10 x 50 binoculars, a wide-brim hat, walking boots, light-colored clothes, and a canteen are important while observing the Marbled Whiptail. From about 8:00 to 11:00 a.m. are good observation times. The desert is gen-

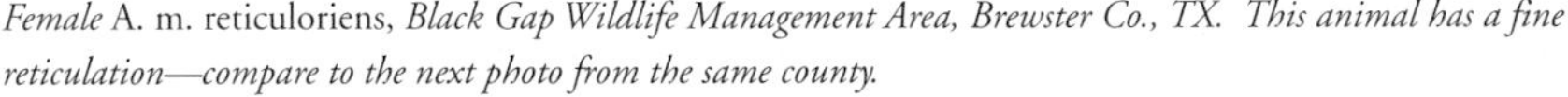
Female A. m. reticuloriens, *Black Gap Wildlife Management Area, Brewster Co., TX. This animal has a fine reticulation—compare to the next photo from the same county.*

Male A. m. reticuloriens, *Brewster Co., TX. This taxon has been within* A. tigris *in much of the literature.*

erally too hot for observations for the rest of the day. Find a nice, somewhat flat, desert area, with Creosote Bush and some grass, and you will likely encounter the Marbled Whiptail. It can be seen in many public areas of the Chihuahuan Desert, including Big Bend National Park (TX) and several state parks in southern New Mexico.

Taxonomy: For many years in the desert Southwest, this whiptail lizard was considered a subspecies of the Tiger Whiptail. It has now been accepted as a full species based upon hybridization events in a very narrow zone of contact at the eastern edge of the Peloncillo Mountains in extreme western New Mexico.

Subspecies and Variation: Four subspecies are recognized. The nominate subspecies (Western Marbled Whiptail, *A. m. marmorata*) occurs primarily in the United States. One subspecies (Eastern Marbled Whiptail, *A. m. reticuloriens*), is found in both Mexico and the U.S., and 2 subspecies are confined to Mexico. The subspecies are separated primarily by each having its own unique color pattern and some differences in scale characters.

Remarks: Both the Marbled and Tiger Whiptails are extremely common lizards in the desert areas of the Southwest. The ecology and behavior of both species have been studied in great detail over the past 35 years.

New Mexico Whiptail (unisexual)

Aspidoscelis neomexicana (Lowe and Zweifel, 1952)

Author: Randy D. Jennings

Description: This is a medium-sized, slender, unisexual lizard, with individuals reaching about 82 mm SVL. The slender tail is longer than the body. This whiptail has a narrow, pointed snout and a somewhat tubular body. The front limbs are relatively small, with well-developed digits and claws, while the back limbs are relatively larger with more elongated digits. Adults have a dark brown or almost black background coloration. Usually there are 7 longitudinal, cream-colored to yellowish stripes on the back and sides. This species exhibits a unique middorsal stripe that is well developed, wavy, and possesses a "Y" at its anterior terminus. This whiptail possesses spots that are present in the dark fields of the back and sides, but typically very faint or absent from those adjacent to the wavy middorsal line. The long, slender tail is brownish to grayish at the base, while the more distal part of the tail is gray-green to bluish-green. The venter is white but may possess a faint bluish wash throughout. Postantebrachial and mesoptychial scales are not enlarged. **Juveniles:** Juveniles are similar to adults, but dark fields are generally darker, stripes are better defined with more intense color, and the tail is blue. Spots are less conspicuous in hatchlings and juveniles. In neonates the tail is bright blue.

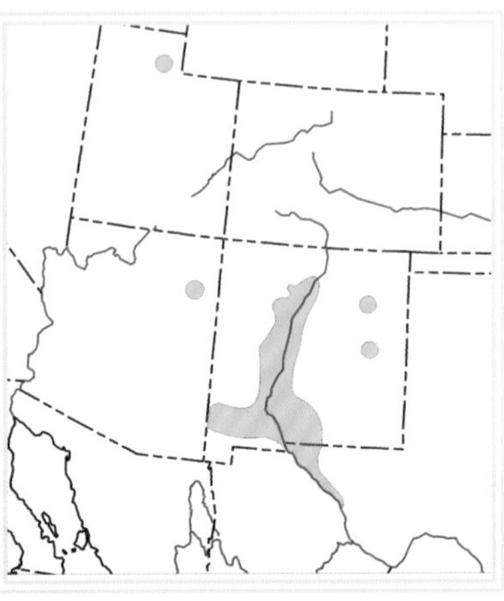

See page 559 for map color codes. May occur in Chihuahua along the Rio Grande.

Female A. neomexicana, *Petrified Forest National Park, Apache Co., AZ, where it is likely a non-native species.*

Similar Species: The New Mexico Whiptail is most likely to be confused with other striped and spotted whiptails, including Chihuahuan Spotted Whiptail, Gila

Female A. neomexicana, *Petroglyph National Monument, Bernalillo Co., NM. Note the characteristic wavy vertebral stripe.*

Spotted Whiptail, and Sonoran Spotted Whiptail. It can be distinguished from these other species by the distinctive wavy middorsal line, gray-green colored tail, and by the further anterior extent of supraorbital scales.

Habitats: This species is common in disturbed (flood, fire, road cuts, overgrazing, and urbanization) habitats associated with interior basin grasslands and shrublands and up to piñon/juniper woodlands along and adjacent to the Rio Grande corridor within the Chihuahuan Desert. It is often associated with saltbushes, dropseed grasses, mesquites, and Creosote Bush. It occurs at elevations ranging from about 1,000 to 1,900 m.

Natural History: New Mexico Whiptails are egg-laying insectivores. They are active foragers, searching among organic detritus and litter for insects. One study of their food habits identified moths, butterflies, beetles, grasshoppers, ants, and a variety of insect larvae as prey items; termites were also important components of the diet. New Mexico Whiptails overwinter in burrows that they excavate themselves. Burrows are about 30 cm below the surface, with entrances that are plugged with dirt. These lizards may become active as early as April and remain active as late as October. Activity periods vary with elevation and ambient temperatures. These whiptails exhibit early-morning and late-afternoon bouts of activity. One study showed that New Mexico Whiptails became active as soil temperatures reached 26 to 30°C and retreated into shelters as temperatures approached 50°C. All-female New Mexico Whiptails have home ranges that overlap. Eggs are laid from June through July, about 2 eggs per clutch, and some females lay a second clutch within the reproductive season. Hatchlings typically are observed during late July and early August. Documented predators include the Long-nosed Leopard Lizard.

Range: As the name suggests (*neomexicanus* refers to New Mexico), the range of this species is found largely within New Mexico. New Mexico Whiptails are found along the Rio Grande Valley from west Texas near Candelaria, Presidio County, and north to the vicinity of Española, Sandoval County, New Mexico. They also have been found to the east in the Tularosa Basin and to the west in the vicinity of Lordsburg, Hidalgo County, New Mexico. Populations near Conchas Lake, San Miguel County, New Mexico, and in the Petrified Forest, Apache County, Arizona, are reportedly introduced.

Viewing Tips: Because New Mexico Whiptails are typically associated with sandy soils in disturbed areas, this species is not hard to find along roadways, around urban areas, and along rivers and washes experiencing periodic flash flows. Look for them around the bases of woody shrubs in relatively open, sandy habitats. However, because they are wary and so similar in appearance to many other whiptails, it is best to observe through binoculars. It is also best to observe them early in the day before they warm up and are more quick to flee. When active, body temperatures range between 39 and 40°C. Whiptails, especially parthenogenetic species, quickly grow accustomed to the presence of people when not approached too closely. With binoculars it is easy to watch whiptails forage, dig nests, and interact with other lizards. New Mexico Whip-

Female A. neomexicana, *Petroglyph National Monument, Bernalillo Co., NM.*

Juvenile A. neomexicana, *Petroglyph National Monument, Bernalillo Co., NM. Except for the bright blue tail, the juvenile blends perfectly with grasses.*

tails are common along the Rio Grande Valley and are commonly observed in the rest area north of Socorro along Interstate 25.

Taxonomy: The New Mexico Whiptail is a diploid parthenogenetic species that originated through a single hybridization event between 2 bisexual parental whiptails. The parental species were *A. marmorata* (female) and *A. inornata* (male). Because there has been little genetic variation detected among populations of *A. neomexicanus*, most assume that this species may have arisen from a single ancestral female and that the species is relatively young. Confusion was generated around the taxonomic status of this species with the discovery of a whiptail formerly referred to as *Cnemidophorus perplexus*. This confusion was alleviated after the lizard was realized to be a hybrid between *A. neomexicanus* and *A. inornata*.

Subspecies and Variation: No subspecies of this whiptail have been identified.

Remarks: It is not uncommon to find New Mexico Whiptails syntopically with a variety of other whiptails species, both unisexual and bisexual. Because of this, whiptails have been the foci of many studies involving competition among species and the relative successes of parthenogenetic and bisexual species. Much work has gone into unraveling the complexities of the hybrid origins of *A. neomexicanus* and other parthenogenetic species.

Colorado Checkered Whiptail (unisexual)

Aspidoscelis neotesselata (Walker, Cordes and Taylor, 1997)

Author: Lauren J. Livo

See page 559 for map color codes.

Description: Colorado Checkered Whiptails are long, slender lizards that reach a maximum SVL of about 107 mm. The tail is more than twice the SVL. Dorsal scales are granular, while the belly scales are larger and rectangular. The snout is somewhat pointed. The head grades into the body, resulting in the lack of a distinct neck dorsally; a gular fold with enlarged scales is conspicuous on the ventral side. Several pattern classes exist, all composed of 6 longitudinal primary stripes, which are relatively straight and colored gray, cream, or yellowish, against a dark background that contains additional bars or spots. A middorsal stripe may be relatively straight in the neck region or reduced to spots. **Juveniles:** Juveniles have a pattern of 6 gray, cream, or yellowish stripes on a black background, with smaller light bars or spots compared to adults.

Similar Species: Colorado Checkered Whiptails are very similar to Common Checkered Whiptails and are sympatric with this species in portions of Otero County (CO). Colorado Checkered Whiptails tend to have better-organized dark fields, more extension of the stripes onto the base of the tail, and an unbroken, irregular streak on the rear of one or both thighs. Common Checkered Whiptails have less-organized dark fields, reduced appearance of stripes on the tail base, and a spotted or reticulated pattern on the rear of the thigh.

Juvenile A. neotesselata, *Otero Co., CO.*

Female A. neotesselata, *Otero Co., CO. This triploid species is endemic to Colorado.*

Habitats: The Colorado Checkered Whiptail occupies canyon, arroyo, and foothill habitats. Sites supporting populations of this whiptail are often disturbed by humans, including at a campground site in a state park, overgrazed areas, and a wasteland area along the Arkansas River. Colorado Checkered Whiptails have been reported at elevations between 1,230 and 2,105 m.

Natural History: Beginning in April, Colorado Checkered Whiptails are active on most warm or hot days. Although they may begin surface activity before 7:00 a.m., most daily activity peaks between 10:00 a.m. and 1:00 p.m. After emerging from an overnight retreat, a lizard normally spends some time basking, often repeatedly selecting the same favored spot. Colorado Checkered Whiptails actively forage for small invertebrates. While searching for prey they may flick their tongues over the substrate and paw into it. Lizards that obtain large food items often remain inactive on the following day. These lizards first reproduce when they have reached a minimum SVL of about 68–71 mm. Beginning in June or July, a female selects an open, sunny site to dig the burrow in which she will deposit 1–5 eggs. The larger (and older) lizards in a population tend to lay their eggs earlier in the season than small lizards. A female digs and enters an underground nest, where she stays for a day or more. Beginning in late August, after an incubation period of 60–74 days, the first hatchlings appear. Because there is both a prolonged period of egg deposition and considerable temperature variability within nests, hatchlings appear over a span of several weeks, with later clutches hatching out into October. Beginning in August for large adults, Colorado Checkered Whiptails select overwintering sites on southeast-facing slopes and dig down into the substrate half a meter or more, where they can remain above freezing. Predators include snakes such as Coachwhips.

Range: Colorado Checkered Whiptails occur only in southeastern Colorado. All records to date have been from localities in the Arkansas River drainage and its tributaries, including the Purgatoire, Huerfano, St. Charles, and Apishapa rivers.

Viewing Tips: Colorado Checkered Whiptails are fast and wary, and always seem to be on the move. You can observe Colorado Checkered Whiptails skittering nervously from one shrub to another on warm or hot days beginning in mid-April. The best viewing is usually in May, when days are sufficiently warm for activity by these lizards but grasses and weeds have not reached their full height. By October, usually only hatchlings remain active. Public areas where it is possible to observe the Colorado Checkered Whiptail include Lake Pueblo State Park (Juniper Breaks Campground) west of Pueblo (CO). In the Comanche National Grassland south of La Junta (CO), hiking trails into Vogel Canyon provide an opportunity to observe not only the Colorado Checkered Whiptail but also its parental species, the Common Checkered Whiptail and Six-lined Racerunner, which are all sympatric in this area.

Juvenile A. neotesselata, *Otero Co., CO. Like other hybrid, all-female species, this juvenile is a clone of its mother.*

Female A. neotesselata, *Las Animas Co., CO.*

Taxonomy: Before 1997, most references to the Colorado Checkered Whiptail included it as pattern (and ploidy) variants of *Cnemidophorus tesselatus* (now *Aspidoscelis tesselata*). In 1997, it was described as a separate species, *Cnemidophorus neotesselatus.*

Subspecies and Variation: No subspecies of the Colorado Checkered Whiptail are recognized. However, 3 well-defined pattern types (A, B, and C) have been described. These pattern types differ in details of the stripes, spots or blotches, coloration, and scale counts.

Remarks: Mating between a female Western Marbled Whiptail (*A. marmorata marmorata*) and a male Big Bend Spotted Whiptail (*A. scalaris septemvittata*) resulted in the production of the Common Checkered Whiptail (*A. tesselata*), an all-female species with a total of 46 chromosomes. In this diploid (2n) species, 23 chromosomes were derived from the female ancestor and 23 from the male ancestor. Subsequently, a mating of a female Common Checkered Whiptail (after all, there are no males in this species!) with a male Six-lined Racerunner yielded yet another parthenogenetic species: the Colorado Checkered Whiptail. This is an all-female species, but instead of having the diploid (2n) number of chromosomes, it has an extra set and so is triploid (3n), with 69 chromosomes. The "extra" 23 chromosomes in these lizards come from the Six-lined Racerunner. This extra genome may also provide Colorado Checkered Whiptails with an increased flexibility to exploit habitats that were unsuitable for the species from which it derived.

Pai Striped Whiptail

Aspidoscelis pai (Wright and Lowe, 1993)

Author: Brian K. Sullivan

See page 559 for map color codes.

Description: This is a small (SVL typically less than 75 mm, large individuals to 85 mm SVL), unspotted, brown-bodied whiptail, typically with 6 yellow stripes, and with blue to violet wash along the sides, limbs, and face. A seventh, middorsal stripe is rarely present (or partially so). The tail is roughly twice the SVL, and hindlimbs are larger than forelimbs. There are usually 9–11 scales between the paravertebral stripes, 28–30 femoral pores, and unenlarged postantebrachials and mesoptychials. **Sexual Variation:** Adult females have less blue and violet coloration than males, and femoral pores on the underside of the hindlimbs are less well developed. **Juveniles:** Juveniles are similar to females.

Similar Species: The sympatric, all-female Plateau Striped Whiptail is larger, lacks the blue and violet coloration, has enlarged postantebrachial scales, fewer scales between the paravertebral stripes (usually 6), and more femoral pores (usually more than 32). One hybrid between these 2 whiptails has been reported from north of Flagstaff,

Male A. pai, *Alpine Ranches, Coconino Co., AZ.*

Adult A. pai, *formerly within* A. inornata, *Mazatzal Mountains, AZ.*

Coconino County, Arizona. Other striped, unspotted whiptails in central and northern Arizona possess aqua or green-blue wash on the tail and lateral surfaces, rather than the deep blue to violet blue of the Pai Striped Whiptail.

Habitats: This whiptail is found in a variety of non-desert habitats. It typically occurs in open grassland, which is usually heavily grazed, but is also found in forest, woodland, and chaparral associations (Music and Mazatzal mountains, and southeast of the Grand Canyon). In the Mazatzal Mountains it occurs in relatively dense chaparral, heavily grown with manzanita, Scrub Oak, and other shrubs. In northern Arizona south of the Grand Canyon, it occurs in piñon/juniper woodland mixed with sagebrush flats, where it is usually associated with sandy soil in sunny, open areas. It has been found from just above 1,400 to almost 2,200 m in elevation.

Natural History: An active whiptail is usually encountered moving in open areas between shrubs or grass clumps. It moves almost constantly, tongue-flicking the soil and probing for insect prey with its snout and forelimbs. It takes refuge in grass clumps, shrubs, or mammal burrows when pursued. Activity appears to peak in late May and early June, and during the summer monsoon (July and August); it is rarely encountered from September through April. North and east of Flagstaff it generally co-occurs with Common Lesser Earless Lizards in heavily grazed grasslands in which

Adult A. pai, *Four Peaks, Maricopa Co., AZ.*

invader shrubs are often present. Eastern Collared Lizards and Long-nosed Leopard Lizards are often associates in these habitats and presumably prey on these smaller whiptails. Mating occurs in late spring, and females lay one or 2 clutches of 1–3 eggs in summer. Hatchlings are often apparent in August and early September when adults are scarce.

Range: This species occurs primarily in northern Arizona on the southwestern edge of the Colorado Plateau, with an isolated population in the Mazatzal Mountains of central Arizona and the Music Mountains of northwestern Arizona. Its patchy distribution is perhaps best envisioned as a series of isolated populations.

Viewing Tips: The Pai Striped Whiptail is most active in May and early June, and during the summer monsoon. Search for it in open grassland during the early morning on relatively windless days, or in open areas associated with woodland or forest habitats, or in chaparral in some areas (e.g., Four Peaks, Mazatzal Mountains, Gila County, AZ). North and east of Flagstaff, Coconino County (AZ), Pai Striped Whiptails can be found in the relatively open, grazed grassland habitats along Interstate 40 and Arizona Highway 89. They are typically abundant in these habitats, but patchy in distribution, co-occurring with Common Lesser Earless Lizards, Long-nosed Leopard Lizards, and Plateau Lizards.

Taxonomy: The Pai Striped Whiptail is considered a subspecies of the Little Striped Whiptail by some, but recent genetic analysis suggests the Pai Striped and Arizona

Striped whiptails are both diagnosable and on separate evolutionary trajectories, and thus should be recognized as distinct species. In addition, size and habitat variation among Pai Striped Whiptails (i.e., between those found in woodland, forest, and chaparral associations, and those found in grassland) suggest that there is within-species variation. Analysis of populations on the eastern edge of the range, especially in relation to populations of Little Striped Whiptails in northwestern New Mexico, would also help clarify systematic relationships.

Subspecies and Variation: No subspecies are recognized, although genetic and morphometric analysis of disjunct populations (e.g., Mazatzal Mountains) are currently under way.

Remarks: Pai Striped Whiptails have a patchy distribution along the southern edge of the Colorado Plateau, and it is unclear to what degree this distribution has been shaped in part by recent anthropogenic changes in habitat conditions (e.g., reduction in grass cover and increase in shrub density due to overgrazing). Similar to the situation with the Arizona Striped Whiptail and its all-female descendant, the Desert Grassland Whiptail in southeastern Arizona, changes in the distribution of the Pai Striped Whiptail and interactions with the sympatric all-female and much more common and widespread Plateau Striped Whiptail remain to be fully understood. A hybrid between the Pai Striped Whiptail and Plateau Whiptail, found north of Flagstaff, Coconino County, Arizona, suggests that interactions between these 2 species warrant additional study.

Adult A. pai, *Wupatki National Monument, Coconino Co., AZ.*

Plateau Spotted Whiptail

Aspidoscelis scalaris (Cope, 1892)

Author: Daniel J. Leavitt

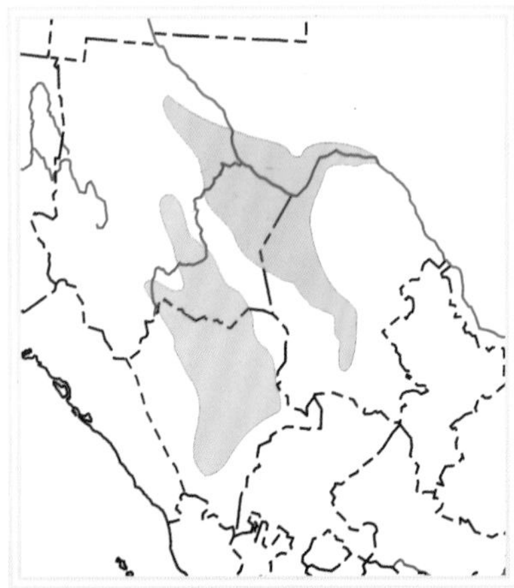

See page 559 for map color codes. There are different interpretations of taxonomy, nomenclature, and range for this species complex.

Description: Plateau Spotted Whiptails are one of North America's largest species of whiptail, with maximum lengths of up to 115 mm SVL. This is a spotted and striped whiptail with a slender tail much longer than the SVL. The white spots on this lizard are usually fused with the 7 longitudinal white lines that run along the dorsum. Rarely are the spots found within the margins. These lizards have a full rusty brown or tan dorsal posterior that begins above the hind legs, and their forearms may appear grayish-blue. The postantebrachial and mesoptychial scales are enlarged. In Mexico, many of the traits used above to distinguish this species are variable from population to population, and more than 40 pattern classes may exist. **Sexual Variation:** Males are larger than females and have white throats. Often adult females will have orange speck-

Female A. scalaris septemvittata, *Brewster Co., TX.*

Male A. scalaris septemvittata, *Presidio Co., TX. This subspecies, the Big Bend Spotted Whiptail, has had a variety of scientific names over the years.*

les or flecking on the throat. **Juveniles:** Juveniles are similar to adults, though the tail may appear green or blue.

Similar Species: Plateau Spotted Whiptails look similar to some other species of North American whiptails. Outwardly their appearance is similar to the Chihuahuan Spotted Whiptail, from which they can be distinguished by their spotting pattern. Also, the Plateau Spotted Whiptail's pale dorsal lines become obscured posteriorly instead of extending beyond the back legs, as they do with the Chihuahuan Spotted Whiptail. Regions of sympatry between these 2 taxa are restricted to the foothills in the Chinati and Davis mountains of west Texas. Plateau Spotted Whiptails can be confused with the Common Spotted Whiptail, though the 2 are only slightly sympatric. However, the spots are located within the fields of dark coloration in the Common Spotted Whiptails rather than merging with the dorsal lines in the Plateau Spotted Whiptail.

Habitats: Typical habitat for Plateau Spotted Whiptails can be found on moderately vegetated hillsides and foothills or upper-elevation grasslands and piñon/oak/juniper associations. Plateau Spotted Whiptails are common at middle and high elevations, where there may be a slight to moderate slope. Elevations range from just over 800 m to the tallest peaks in their range. They are found on volcanic, sedimentary, and alluvial substrates within their range. In Big Bend National Park, this lizard has benefited from the expansion of shrub and brush cover in recent decades.

Male A. scalaris septemvittata, *Brewster Co., TX.*

Natural History: Plateau Spotted Whiptails are egg-laying insectivores. Emergence from brumation occurs in late spring and is temperature-dependent. These whiptails prey upon termites, grasshoppers, crickets, beetles, and spiders. Research has shown no apparent difference in prey capture between age or sex classes. Much of their day is spent scouring the land, rooting and probing the soil litter for their prey. These lizards have strong olfactory senses that they depend upon for finding food. Plateau Spotted Whiptails are most active when morning air temperatures are 35 to 40°C.

Female egg development does not occur until mid-April. Males reach their peak reproductive output in May through early June. Females lay 1–5 (usually 2–3) eggs in July. It is assumed that egg chambers are found about 30 cm below the ground surface, as with the Common Spotted Whiptail. Hatchlings are prolific during the late summer and fall after emergence. Hatchlings measure 25–40 mm SVL and are not as wary as adults. Being somewhat prolific and active for long periods of the day, these lizards are often eaten by predators. Of these, the most obvious predators are Greater Roadrunners, Cactus Wrens, and Eastern Collared Lizards, along with many species of snakes and medium-sized mammals. Where they overlap territory with Marbled Whiptails there is competition, which often results in Marbled Whiptails chasing Plateau Spotted Whiptails away from their territory.

Range: This species is confined to the northern Chihuahuan Desert. Plateau Spotted Whiptails are found in the United States in the Big Bend region of Texas. In Mexico, they are found in the states of Chihuahua, Coahuila, Durango, and Zacatecas.

Viewing Tips: For a trained whiptail watcher or an enthusiast, Plateau Spotted Whiptails are easy to locate. Simply pulling off the road in proper habitat may produce one or 2 within a short walk. They are wary, though, and you are most likely to spot one after you have spooked it a short distance from your feet. Have your binoculars ready—they usually do not scurry very far. They often flee to the closest patch of vegetation, from which they can reassess the danger. The best time of year to view these whiptails is during the late spring and summer months (April through August). These whiptails can be found at mid-morning foraging beneath and around shrubby vegetation. Good places to observe Plateau Spotted Whiptails in Texas include the Chisos Mountains of Big Bend National Park, the Deadhorse Mountains of Black Gap Wildlife Management Area, and Big Bend Ranch State Park. In Mexico, look for them at the Peguis Canyon overlook south of Ojinaga, Chihuahua.

Taxonomy: This species was referred to as *Cnemidophorus sacki* and more recently *C. septemvittata.* For some time it was included as a subspecies of *Aspidoscelis gularis.* A zone of hybridization was found in Terrell County, Texas, where the 2 taxa hybridized. The genotypes observed from this location were determined to be no less variable between these 2 taxa than they are for individual species in the sexlineatus group; thus, it is suggested that each should be considered an individual species.

Subspecies and Variation: Within the range of this book, the only subspecies that occurs is the Big Bend Spotted Whiptail, *A. scalaris septemvittata.*

Remarks: This lizard is one of the parental contributors to a couple of parthenogenetic whiptails. It is suggested that Gray Checkered Whiptail and the Common Checkered Whiptail were both the results of a hybrid crossing of *A. scalaris* with *A. marmorata.*

Six-lined Racerunner

Aspidoscelis sexlineata (Linnaeus, 1766)

Author: Matthew A. Kwiatkowski

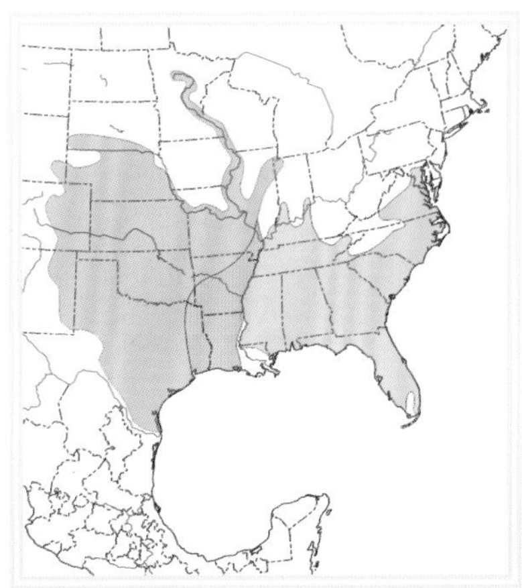

See page 559 for map color codes. Range of A. sexlineata stephensae *not differentiated.*

Description: This is a smaller species of whiptail with maximum SVL of 86 mm and 267 mm TL. Typical SVL varies from 55 to 75 mm. The head and body color is green anteriorly, which is the most distinctive feature when viewed from a distance; the Six-lined Racerunner is the only whiptail with this green color. The green dorsal color fades to brown posteriorly. Contrary to its name, 7 light dorsal stripes are typically present in the western subspecies, although the vertebral stripe may fade to light brown or split into 2 anteriorly. No spots are present on the body, and the mesoptychial scales are conspicuously enlarged. **Sexual Variation:** Adult males have green on the dorsal surface, which may be brighter than on females, with the dorsal stripes often "washed out" by green anteriorly. Males may also have a blue throat and belly. Male tail length was found to be relatively longer than in females in one study. Females are slightly larger than males in some populations. **Juveniles:** In juveniles, the dorsal stripes are often more distinct

Male A. s. viridis, *Mescalero Sands, Chaves Co., NM.*

Male A. s. viridis, *Laclede, Linn Co., MO. The subspecific epithet* viridis *means "green" in Latin, so it is easy to tell where it got its name.*

than in adults, and the tail is bright blue. Juvenile males do not develop the green dorsal color until adulthood.

Similar Species: The Little Striped Whiptail looks very similar, with 6–8 light dorsal stripes; however, it lacks greenish color, and the mesoptychial scales are only slightly enlarged, if at all. The Plateau Striped Whiptail also has 6–7 stripes but is slightly larger, has enlarged scales on the posterior side of the forelimbs, and may have dorsal spots, although spots are uncommon in this species. The Common Spotted Whiptail has 7–8 dorsal stripes, but has spots between the stripes, has enlarged postantebrachial scales, and is larger than *A. sexlineata*.

Habitats: These lizards are typically associated with sandy or loamy soils but can occupy a wide variety of habitats, including open grasslands, shrublands, river banks, and floodplains, and can extend into piñon/juniper woodlands. They are most commonly found in lowlands and hills, but may be found at elevations up to around 2,100 m.

Natural History: Six-lined Racerunners are a bisexual species. Individuals emerge from brumation in April and reach peak activity in June. Although there is little evidence that males defend territories *per se*, males will chase off rivals when encountered. Females become sexually mature in their second year at around 68 mm SVL. Eggs are laid May–August, and clutches are typically 1–6 eggs. Two clutches may be laid, which is common in the eastern subspecies. Eggs have an incubation period of 46–63 days and hatch June–September. They are active foragers, searching in the open or digging for subterranean prey. The long tail acts as a counterbalance during sprints when capturing prey or escaping predators. Diet consists of various arthropods, with spiders and grasshoppers making up a considerable portion of prey consumed. Other prey may include termites, leafhoppers, beetles, ants, moths, and butterflies. Home ranges can vary dramatically among populations, from approximately 0.1–1.3 ha, with female home ranges slightly larger than those of males. Densities can be highly variable among populations both spatially and temporally, ranging from 15 to almost 70 lizards per ha. Adults are active through July, but as summer temperatures rise, their activity becomes bimodal, peaking in the morning and afternoon. Adult activity wanes in August, but juvenile activity peaks during that time, and they are more likely to be encountered than adults.

Range: They are found along the Atlantic coast from Maryland to Florida; westward through Virginia, Tenessee, Kentucky, and Missouri;, then extending north along the Mississippi and Illinois river valleys through Illinois into Indiana, Wisconsin, and Minnesota. They occur from southern South Dakota and southeast Wyoming southward through eastern Colorado and New Mexico to south Texas. The eastern sub-

Juvenile A. s. viridis, *Adams Co., CO. As with several species of whiptails, juveniles have bright blue tails.*

species is primarily east of the Mississippi River, with an intergrade zone between the 2 subspecies found west of the Mississippi River from southwest Illinois through southeast Missouri, most of Arkansas and Louisiana, and into eastern Texas.

Viewing Tips: Six-lined Racerunners are best viewed during sunny weather with temperatures between 36 and 42°C. Look for lizards foraging out in the open or thermoregulating in the shade of a plant. They may spend the night under logs, rocks, or trash, although many use burrows at night. Six-lined Racerunners are quite fast and readily flee when approached. If they run, try to keep sight of them until they stop and you can approach again slowly. Potential viewing sites can be found throughout much of eastern New Mexico, including Mescalero Sands east of Roswell and Oasis State Park southwest of Clovis.

Taxonomy: Members of the genus *Aspidoscelis* found in the U.S. were in the genus *Cnemidophorus* until recently, which could cause some confusion when reading older texts. Hybridization events between Six-lined Racerunners and both Common Spotted Whiptails and Common Checkered Whiptails have resulted in unisexual whiptail species complexes. Hybridization between Six-lined Racerunners and New Mexico Whiptails has also been described.

Subspecies and Variation: Two subspecies occur in the U.S., with *Aspidoscelis sexlineata viridis*—the Prairie Racerunner—the western subspecies found within the range of this book. The eastern subspecies, *A. s. sexlineata*, is found primarily east of the Mississippi River and has 6 dorsal stripes rather than 7 or 8. Dorsal background color is not as distinctly green in the western subspecies and instead ranges from greenish-brown to black. Note: while most texts recognize 2 subspecies in the U.S., a third subspecies, *A. s. stephensi*, has been described by a study in 1992 as occurring in south Texas.

Remarks: Because of the extensive range of this species, Six-lined Racerunners are relatively well studied compared to other whiptails. Yet there is still much that can be learned about this species, given that it can be found in such dramatically different environments, ranging from the mesic Southeast to the arid Southwest. Generally, populations are healthy, although there is some concern that certain northern populations are declining due to habitat loss from human development.

Sonoran Spotted Whiptail (unisexual)

Aspidoscelis sonorae (Lowe and Wright, 1964)

Authors: Michael J. Sredl, Trevor B. Persons, and John W. Wright

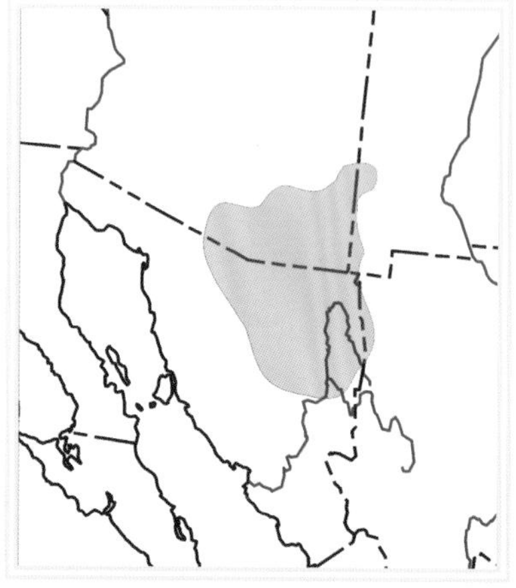

See page 559 for map color codes.

Description: The Sonoran Spotted Whiptail is a moderately large all-female whiptail, with adults reaching a maximum SVL of 91 mm; the tail is approximately twice the length of the SVL. It is a striped and spotted whiptail, with a dark brown to black dorsal ground color and 6 distinct longitudinal dorsal light stripes that remain distinct on the neck, even in older lizards. Light spots are present in the dark fields between stripes on young adults, becoming more intense and overlapping the light stripes on older individuals. The upper thigh and foreleg of adults are indistinctly mottled. The tail is orange-tan, often grading to olive toward the tip. The ventral surface of the body is unmarked and cream-

Female A. sonorae, *Kartchner Caverns State Park, Whetstone Mountains, Cochise Co., AZ.*

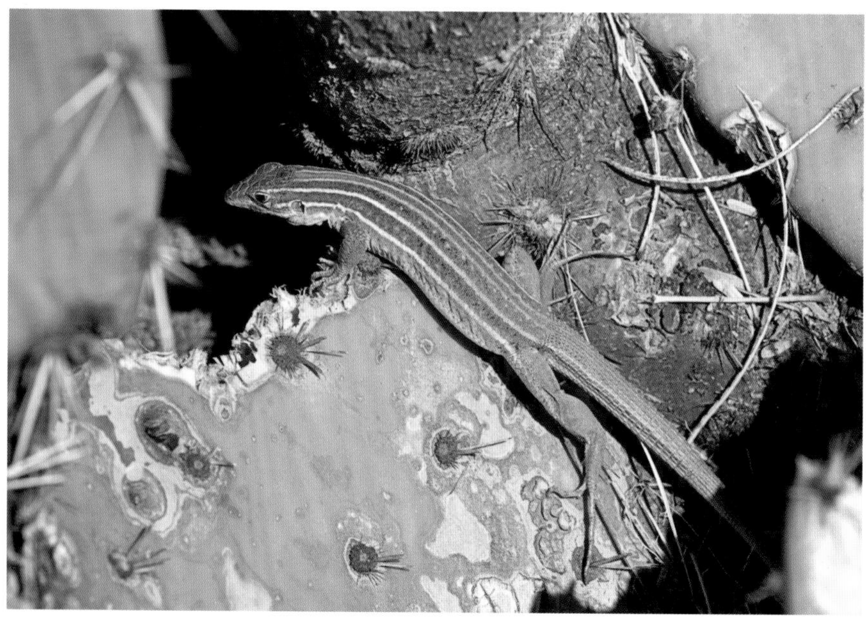

white. The mesophtychial and post-antebrachial scales are enlarged. **Juveniles:** Juveniles are similar to adults, but spotting is reduced or absent (in hatchlings), and the contrast between the longitudinal stripes and dark fields is more pronounced. Also, the upper hind limb surfaces have a bold vermiculate pattern.

Female A. sonorae, *Santa Rita Mountains, Pima Co., AZ.*

Similar Species: Other striped and spotted whiptails, the Gila Spotted and Chihuahuan Spotted whiptails, are found within the range of the Sonoran Spotted Whiptail. They look very similar to one another and there is overlap in many scale counts. Of these species, the Chihuahuan Spotted Whiptail is the easiest to distinguish. Adult Chihuahuan Spotted Whiptails are heavily spotted and indistinctly striped, and, unlike the other 2 species, the longitudinal light stripes are wavy, and both the front and rear limbs are distinctly mottled. Longitudinal stripes of the Sonoran Spotted and Gila Spotted whiptails are distinct on the head and neck. Hatchlings of both Gila Spotted and Sonoran Spotted whiptails have only faint, diffuse yellowish spots in the upper lateral dark fields, with spotting becoming more pronounced and spreading to the lower dark fields as lizards age. Compared with Gila Spotted Whiptails, Sonoran Spotted Whiptails are more heavily spotted at a given age, and the paravertebral light stripes are usually noticeably farther apart. The Sonoran Spotted and Chihuahuan Spotted whiptails usually have 3 or more enlarged pre-anal scales, while Gila Spotted Whiptails usually have 2. Unlike the other 2, hatchling Chihuahuan Spotted Whiptails have discrete red or white spots in the lowest dark fields and distinct white spots or dashes along the midline.

Habitats: This species is found primarily in oak woodlands and oak grassland, but it ranges into pine/oak woodlands at higher elevations and desert scrub and semi-desert grassland at lower elevations. It seems to be especially abundant along riparian corridors. In Mexico, it also inhabits thorn scrub. Elevation ranges from 610 to 2,130 m in the U.S., but occurs down to around 215 m in Sonora, Mexico.

Natural History: Sonoran Spotted Whiptails can be active from April through October, although most adult activity occurs between May and September. During the activity season, these lizards can maintain a high body temperature (about 40°C) when active. On sunny days, lizards are active in the morning and afternoon. Activity is inhibited by hot weather, and lizards become inactive on the surface when soil temperatures exceed 50°C. Activity is also depressed on cloudy days. This species is an actively foraging insectivore. Diet consists mainly of insects and other arthropods, with termites making up the greatest percentage by frequency of any prey item. It is an all-female, parthenogenetic species. Females lay 2 or 3 unfertilized clutches of eggs from June through August. Average clutch size is nearly 4 (clutches range from 1 to 7 eggs). Eggs hatch into more females, all genetically identical to their mother. Hatchlings begin appearing by the end of July.

Range: The range of the Sonoran Spotted Whiptail extends from the Río Sonora and Río Yaqui basins of northern Sonora, Mexico, northward and westward to the Santa Catalina and Baboquivari mountains in Arizona and eastward to the Peloncillo and Animas mountains and the Gila River basin in extreme southwestern New Mexico.

Viewing Tips: Look for adults when they are most active, between May and August. Hatchlings remain active into October. Listen for foraging lizards, which can often be

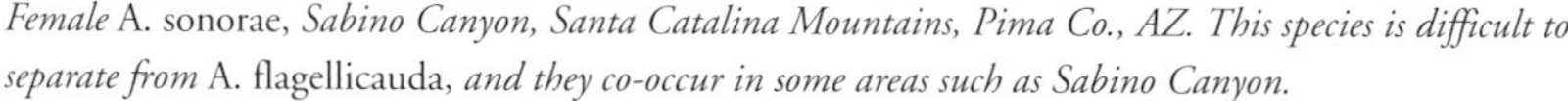

Female A. sonorae, *Sabino Canyon, Santa Catalina Mountains, Pima Co., AZ. This species is difficult to separate from* A. flagellicauda, *and they co-occur in some areas such as Sabino Canyon.*

heard rustling in leaf litter. Places to find Sonoran Spotted Whiptails in Arizona include many areas of the Coronado National Forest, including Sabino Canyon (Santa Catalina Mountains), Madera Canyon (Santa Rita Mountains), Cochise Stronghold (Dragoon Mountains), Carr Canyon (Huachuca Mountains), and Parker Canyon Lake (Canelo Hills). Search the areas where the grasslands and oak woodlands converge, and along riparian areas. In New Mexico, look along the Gila River up to the town of Redrock or Guadalupe Canyon (Peloncillo Mountains) near the Arizona–New Mexico border. In some of these areas they are sympatric with other striped and spotted whiptails.

Juvenile A. sonorae, *Arizona-Sonora Desert Museum, AZ. Juveniles lack spots and do not have blue tails.*

Taxonomy: The Sonoran Spotted Whiptail is a triploid, parthenogenetic species of hybrid origin. Genetic work has identified the probable paternal and maternal parent species of an intermediate lineage (presumably parthenogenetic and extinct) as either the Canyon Spotted Whiptail (*A. burti*) or Western Mexico Whiptail (*A. costata*) and Little Striped Whiptail (*A. inornata* complex). This diploid, intermediate species then hybridized with either the Canyon Spotted Whiptail or Western Mexico Whiptail to produce the triploid Sonoran Spotted Whiptail.

Subspecies and Variation: As with other unisexual whiptails, subspecies are not recognized. Additional color pattern classes of Sonoran Spotted Whiptails, which may represent undescribed species, have been identified from populations in Arizona and New Mexico.

Remarks: The distributions of the similar-looking Gila Spotted, Chihuahuan Spotted, and Sonoran Spotted whiptails overlap in only a few areas of southeastern Arizona and southwestern New Mexico. The hybrid parentage of the Sonoran Spotted Whiptail is similar to that of the Gila Spotted Whiptail, but because they arose through separate hybridization events they are considered distinct species.

Common Checkered Whiptail (unisexual)

Aspidoscelis tesselata (Say, 1823)

Author: Randy D. Jennings

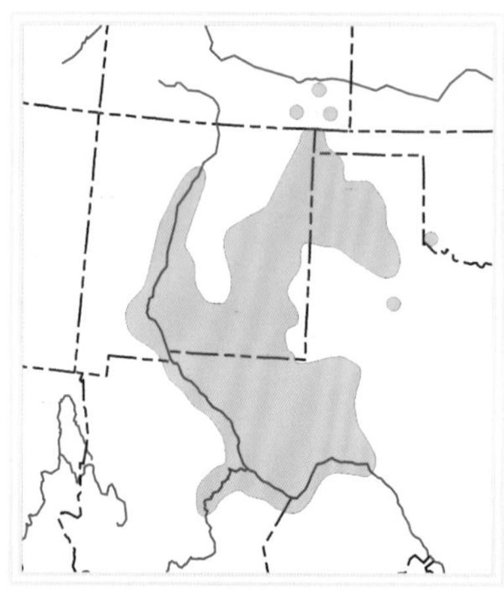

See page 559 for map color codes.

Description: This is a large whiptail, with individuals reaching about 106 mm SVL. The tail is long and slender, and much longer than the body. It has a narrow, pointed snout and a somewhat tubular body. The forelimbs are relatively small, with well-developed digits and claws, while the back legs are relatively larger, with more elongated digits. Its long hindlimbs make rapid locomotion possible. This species is parthenogenetic and consists of only females. Adult females have a dark brown or almost black to reddish-brown background coloration. There are 6 to 8 longitudinal cream-colored, gray, tan, or brown stripes on the back and sides that may be interrupted or indistinct due to coalescence with spotting and barring. This whiptail possesses dorsal spots or bars that often connect adjacent lines, giving it a distinctly checkered appearance. The dorsal thigh is dark and covered with large yellowish to tan or gray spots that often coalesce. The tail is yellowish tan, brown, or gray with dark markings. The venter is white with sparse black marks. Postantebrachial scales are not enlarged, but mesoptychial scales are enlarged. **Juveniles:** Juveniles differ from adults in having more conspicuous lines and spots that typically become larger and more obscure with age. Lines are initially more cream or yellow than in adults.

Juvenile A. tesselata, *Sierra Vieja, Presidio Co., TX.*

Similar Species: There are 8 species of whiptails that are likely to be found sympatrically with the Common Checkered Whiptail, but it is most likely to be confused with other large species,

Female A. tesselata, *Sierra Vieja, Presidio Co., TX.*

including the Marbled Whiptail, Gray Checkered Whiptail, and Colorado Checkered Whiptail. It can be distinguished from the Marbled Whiptail by possessing little or no black coloration on the chin, throat, chest, and tail; the better defined pattern dorsally above the shoulders; enlarged postantebrachials; and the absence of males. It can be distinguished from Gray Checkered Whiptails by the boldness of its pattern and by having fewer longitudinal lines (Gray Checkered Whiptails have 10–14 stripes). Additionally, Gray Checkered Whiptails are found only in Hidalgo County, New Mexico, and Presidio County, Texas. They can be distinguished from Colorado Checkered Whiptails by having smoother, straighter lines on the anterior part of the body, especially above the shoulders and middorsal and lowermost lateral stripes.

Habitats: This species is found in a broad variety of desert and grassland habitats, including yucca grasslands, mesquite/Creosote Bush grasslands, and semi-desert and Plains grasslands. It is often associated with rocky or gravel soils, but is also found in sandy areas. This whiptail also may be found in piñon/juniper woodlands and riparian corridors running through the above-mentioned habitats. They occur at elevations ranging from about 250 to 2,000 m.

Natural History: Common Checkered Whiptails are egg-laying insectivores. Studies of the food habits of this species indicate that termites are an important component of the diet. Other food items include beetles, grasshoppers, moths, and butterflies.

Observations of this lizard's foraging suggest that it is quite tenacious at seeking and digging its prey out of leaf litter and soil.

These lizards may become active as early as April and remain active as late as October. Activity periods vary with elevation, ambient temperatures, and age class of the lizards. Juveniles are active earlier in the spring and later in the fall than adults. These whiptails exhibit early morning (8:30–10:30 a.m.) and late afternoon (5:00–7:00 p.m.) bouts of activity. Again, the actual timing of these bouts varies across different environmental situations.

Individual females have overlapping home ranges, ranging from 0.06 to 0.10 ha. While home ranges and individual burrows are not rigorously defended from other females, agonistic encounters between females occur. Population sizes range from 2 to 100 individuals/ha, varying across years and habitats. Pseudocopulatory behavior has been observed in captivity among females.

Females carry eggs from May to July. They average 3–4 eggs/clutch (range 1–8 eggs/clutch) depending on location. Clutch size has been reported to increase with increasing body size. Hatchlings typically are observed during late July through September. Common Checkered Whiptails may live up to 4 or more years of age. Documented predators include birds and snakes, such as the Coachwhip.

Range: Common Checkered Whiptails are found throughout Trans-Pecos Texas and adjacent portions of Chihuahua and Coahuila, Mexico. They range north into New Mexico along the Rio Grande and Pecos River valleys to San Ildefonso and Santa Rosa, respectively. This species extends its distribution into northeastern New Mexico, southeastern Colorado, and the panhandles of Oklahoma and north Texas.

Female A. tesselata, *Indio Mountain, Hudspeth Co., TX.*

Viewing Tips: Because Common Checkered Whiptails are especially approachable, observation at close range is not uncommon. This is a relatively large species and therefore relatively easy to find and identify within their range. Look for them around the edges of woody shrubs in relatively open habitats. With binoculars it is easy

Female A. tesselata, *Culberson Co., TX.*

to watch whiptails forage, dig nests, and interact with other lizards. *Aspidocelis tesselata* is a common lizard along the Rio Grande on mesas with Creosote Bush, like those found in Elephant Butte Lake State Park (NM).

Taxonomy: The Common Checkered Whiptail is a diploid parthenogenetic species that originated through a hybridization event between *A. marmorata marmorata* and *A. scalaris.* This species has a complicated taxonomic history. Originally 6 morphological variants were identified. Two variants were later confirmed to be a different triploid species and named the Colorado Checkered Whiptail, *A. neotesselata.* One diploid variant was named the Gray Checkered Whiptail, *A. dixoni.* The remaining diploid lizards constitute *A. tesselata.*

Subspecies and Variation: No subspecies of this whiptail have been identified.

Remarks: It is not uncommon to find Common Checkered Whiptails syntopically with a variety of other whiptails species, both unisexual and bisexual. Because of this, whiptails have been the foci of many studies involving the relative successes of parthenogenetic and bisexual species. Sympatry with other whiptail species makes further hybridization between females of this species, as with all parthenogenetic species, and a male of a bisexual species possible.

Tiger Whiptail

Aspidoscelis tigris (Baird and Girard, 1852)

Author: Brian K. Sullivan

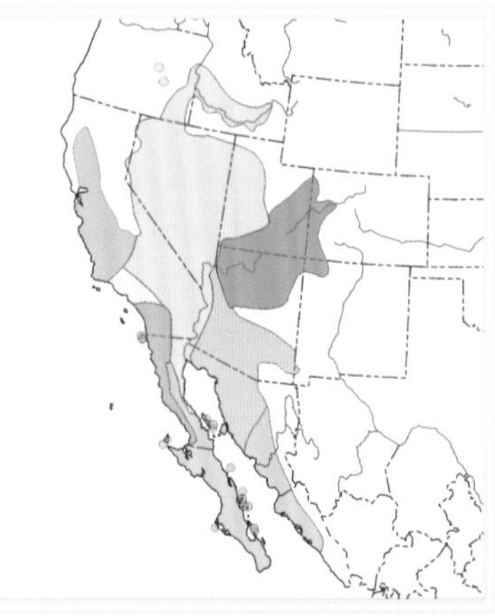

See page 559 for map color codes.

Description: This is a large, sometimes heavy-bodied whiptail reaching 120 mm SVL, though adults are more typically between 75 and 95 mm SVL. This tail can be between 2 and 3 times the length of the body, and often darkly colored (black). Generally some evidence of striping is present dorsally, but this often fades with age and can be broken by various patterns of bars and spots, which in turn may coalesce into larger spots and crossbars between the stripes. Ventrally there is usually some degree of black spotting, especially on throat and chest. Postantebrachials and mesoptychial scales are not enlarged. **Sexual Variation:** Males can be considerably more robust than females; the jowls and forelimbs are

Juvenile A. t. punctilinealis, *Sierra Estrella, Maricopa Co., AZ.*

Adult A. t. stejnegeri, *Escondido, San Diego Co., CA.*

often much larger than in a similarly sized female. Coloration of adult females is similar to that of males but generally less darkly pigmented ventrally, and they possess smaller femoral pores. **Juveniles:** Juveniles are similar to females but generally well striped (though they can be heavily spotted or marked with crossbands and bars like adults), developing the adult color pattern as they grow. Their tails are often bright blue.

Similar Species: Most other whiptails of the Southwest are striped, or striped and spotted (with stripes still very distinct), and all lack the dark ventral pigmentation seen in Tiger Whiptails. Over most of its range, no other sympatric whiptail is as large, has such extensive mottling, and has ventral spotting of at least some degree.

Habitats: The Tiger Whiptail frequents a variety of habitats including desert, grassland, chaparral, woodland, and even forest-edge habitats. It is especially fond of riparian corridors with sandy soil. It occurs even in relatively barren sand dune regions (e.g., Yuma in Arizona and Death Valley in California) and heavily grazed, open grassland in some areas (northwestern Arizona, near Kingman, Mohave County). In northern California (e.g., San Francisco Bay region) it can be found in relatively dense chaparral, while in south-central California (e.g., east of Bakersfield, Kern County), it occurs in oak woodland with extensive grassland habitats.

Natural History: These lizards are seemingly always on the move, tongue-flicking and scratching at the substratum regularly as they move through the environment, pausing frequently to uncover and consume insects that they apparently detect by chemical and perhaps auditory means. They also prey on small lizards. They are often the most apparent reptile species in desert habitats. They are perhaps the least approachable of whiptails: when pursued, they generally run 10 to 20 m and take refuge on the opposite side of a shrub or rock, or in a burrow. Roadrunners, whipsnakes, collared lizards, and leopard lizards are predators of this common whiptail.

Mating occurs in spring, and females may produce 1–3 clutches of 1–4 (rarely more) eggs. Fewer clutches are produced in more northerly populations.

Range: Tiger Whiptails are found from Oregon and Idaho south through California, Nevada, Utah, Arizona, and extreme western Colorado and New Mexico to Mexico. They occur from near sea level to over 2,000 m.

Viewing Tips: Tiger Whiptails are most active in the morning during spring and summer. They emerge later in the spring and retire earlier in the fall than most sympatric, non-whiptail lizards. They are often the most commonly encountered lizard in a number of habitats in the Southwest. They are especially abundant in washes associated with Creosote Bush flats and other associations of the Mojave Desert (Death Valley and Joshua Tree national parks in California) and Sonoran Desert (Sonoran Desert and Agua Fria national monuments in Arizona). Approach them slowly and persistently; they will generally emerge from shrubs or burrows where they have taken refuge and continue foraging. Binoculars really help with this species.

Taxonomy: Tiger Whiptails are a well-delineated taxon, although there continues to be some discussion over the recognition of a former subspecies, the Marbled Whiptail, as a full species. Most have concluded that the Marbled Whiptail should be recognized as distinct from the Tiger Whiptail, as treated here. Relationships among the various subspecies are under evaluation, and there is some suggestion of variation correlated with elevational or latitudinal range (i.e., northern populations from higher elevations in Arizona and Utah may be distinct).

Subspecies and Variation: Currently 5 subspecies are recognized. The Great Basin Whiptail, *A. t. tigris*, occurs in southeastern Oregon, southern Idaho, Nevada, western Utah, southeastern California, and western Arizona; it typically has 4 dorsal stripes and ventral spotting, but can vary from only a few flecks to heavily spotted, especially in northern populations. The California Whiptail, *A. t. munda*, occurs in northern

Adult A. t. stejnegeri, *Escondido, San Diego Co., CA.*

and central California. This form typically possesses 8 bright yellow dorsal stripes and reduced ventral spotting, usually restricted to the throat; again, higher-elevation populations (e.g., Walker Pass) are more heavily spotted. The similarly patterned Coastal Whiptail, *A. t. stejnegeri*, of extreme southwestern California, possesses less-well-defined lateral stripes than the California Whiptail. The Sonoran Tiger Whiptail, *A. t. punctilinealis*, of southern Arizona has a darkly pigmented throat and chest that are uniformly black in large males, and light spots are usually present dorsally among the 4 stripes. The Plateau Tiger Whiptail, *A. t. septentrionalis*, of northeastern Arizona, southeastern Utah, and western Colorado, generally lacks ventral pigment (some have flecks on the throat, some considerable spotting), and the stripes and especially the hindquarters are often yellow-orange, producing a striking appearance that matches the red sandy substrate where they occur. These subspecies are based on variation in color pattern, but there is considerable variation, especially in the dorsal pattern of stripes. Large individuals in almost all populations can manifest a uniform color pattern in which stripes are obscure; the posterior dorsal surfaces can be uniformly colored in most large (greater than 95 mm SVL) individuals.

Remarks: Tiger Whiptails are not as generalized in their activity patterns as might be surmised by their widespread occurrence and abundance. In Arizona they typically are not active before April, and adults are often inactive after August, unless rainfall occurs.

Desert Grassland Whiptail (unisexual)

Aspidoscelis uniparens (Wright and Lowe, 1965)

Author: Randy D. Jennings

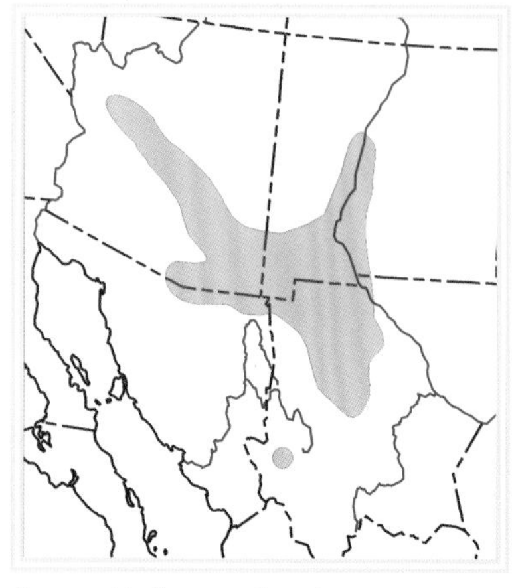

See page 559 for map color codes.

Description: This is a medium-sized, slender lizard, with individuals reaching about 86 mm SVL. The tail is long and slender and longer than the body. This species has a narrow, pointed snout and a somewhat tubular body. The front limbs are relatively small, with well-developed digits and claws, while the back limbs are relatively larger, with more elongated digits. Adult females have a dark brown or almost black to reddish-brown background coloration. Usually there are 6 longitudinal, cream-colored to yellowish stripes on the back and sides. Occasionally, there is a partial seventh middorsal stripe or the suggestion of a stripe, but usually only on the anterior quarter of the back. This whiptail possesses no dorsal light spots. The tail is brownish to grayish at the base, while the more distal part

Female A. uniparens, *Hidalgo Co., NM.*

Female A. uniparens, *San Bernardino Valley, Cochise Co., AZ.*

of the tail is olive or bluish-green to olive turquoise. The ventral surface of the face and chin, chest, and anterior aspects of forelimbs may possess a faint bluish wash, but otherwise is white. Postantebrachial scales are enlarged; there are 3 rounded pre-anal scales. **Juveniles:** Juveniles are similar to adults, but dark fields are generally darker, stripes are more clearly defined with more intense color, and the tail is bluer. In recent hatchlings the tail is intense blue.

Similar Species: The Desert Grassland Whiptail is most likely to be confused with other whiptails lacking dorsal spots. Within their range, these include the Arizona Striped Whiptail, Little Striped Whiptail, Pai Striped Whiptail, and Plateau Striped Whiptail. The Little Striped and Pai Striped whiptails and Arizona Striped Whiptails generally have tails and bodies with more blue coloration. Arizona Striped Whiptails and Little Striped Whiptails generally have 7 dorsal stripes. Plateau Striped Whiptails have more than 3 pre-anal scales that are angular, and a longer, more prominent seventh middorsal stripe.

Habitats: This species is common in grassland, semi-desert grassland, and desert grassland habitats of the Chihuahuan and Sonoran deserts. It is often associated with habitats possessing mesquites and yuccas. It is common along lower-elevation riparian corridors of the Gila, Rio Grande, and San Francisco drainages. This whiptail also may be found in woodland habitats (interior chaparral, piñon/juniper woodlands, and oak woodlands) adjacent to riparian corridors. It occurs at elevations ranging from about 1,000 to 1,500 m.

Natural History: Desert Grassland Whiptails are egg-laying insectivores. The few studies of food habits suggest that termites constitute an important component of the diet. These lizards may become active as early as March and remain active as late as October. Activity periods vary with elevation and ambient temperatures. These whiptails exhibit early morning (8:30–10:30 a.m.) and late afternoon (5:00–7:00 p.m.) bouts of activity.

Desert Grassland Whiptails are active foragers, searching among organic detritus and litter for insects. Individual females have home ranges that overlap. While ranges are not rigorously defended from other females, agonistic encounters between females occur. Population sizes, which can be 80 individuals/ha or higher, vary across habitats. Pseudocopulatory behavior has been observed among females, but the frequency and significance of such behaviors in nature are not well understood.

Eggs are laid in late spring to mid-summer. They average 2.7–3.6 eggs/clutch (range 1–4 eggs/clutch), depending on location. Clutch size has been reported to increase with increasing body size. Hatchlings typically are observed during the late summer and fall. In one location, Desert Grassland Whiptails exhibited high degrees of turnover from year to year, indicating high rates of adult and juvenile mortality. Documented predators include birds such as Greater Roadrunners, Burrowing Owls, and Loggerhead Shrikes, and other lizards like Long-nosed Leopard Lizards.

Range: Desert Grassland Whiptails range north and west from central Chihuahua, Mexico, along the Rio Grande Valley to around Bernardo, Socorro County, New Mexico, and northwest along the lower elevations along and adjacent to the Mogollon Rim to the Hualapai Mountains, southeast of Kingman, Mohave County, Arizona.

Viewing Tips: Because Desert Grassland Whiptails are typically associated with grasslands and exhibit such high population densities where they occur, this species is easy to find. Look for them around the bases of woody shrubs in relatively open sandy habitats or in grassland to woodland ecotones. However, because they are wary and so similar in appearance to many other whiptails, it is best to observe them through binoculars. It is also best to observe them early in the day before they warm up; when body temperatures approach 41°C, lizards can move extremely quickly. With binoculars it is easy to watch them forage, dig nests, and interact with other lizards. *Aspidoscelis uniparens* is a common whiptail within the Gila River valley of southwestern New Mexico. Public lands administered by the BLM and Gila National Forest allow

Juvenile A. uniparens, *Kartchner Caverns State Park, Cochise Co., AZ. The blue tail helps distinguish it from sympatric juvenile whiptails.*

access to many sites with large populations. This species is also known from Kartchner Caverns State Park, Whetstone Mountains, and Marijilda Canyon in the Pinaleño Mountains, Coronado National Forest (all in AZ).

Taxonomy: The Desert Grassland Whiptail is a triploid parthenogenetic species that originated through more than one hybridization event. The first hybridization was between *A. burti* or *A. costata* and *A. inornata,* creating an extinct, ancestral parthenogenetic whiptail. A female of that ancestral form then hybridized with a male of *A. inornata* to create the triploid *A. uniparens.* Because considerable genetic variation is detected among populations of *A. uniparens*, some speculate that this species may represent multiple hybrid origins of a similar nature. Additionally, some researchers suggest that the extinct ancestor described above may have been a common ancestor shared by the Chihuahuan Spotted Whiptail, Gila Spotted Whiptail, Sonoran Spotted Whiptail, and Plateau Striped Whiptail.

Subspecies and Variation: No subspecies of this whiptail have been identified.

Remarks: It is not uncommon to find Desert Grassland Whiptails syntopically with a variety of other whiptail species, both unisexual and bisexual. Because of this, whiptails have been the foci of many studies involving competition among species, and the relative successes of parthenogenetic and bisexual species.

Plateau Striped Whiptail (unisexual)

Aspidoscelis velox (Springer, 1928)

Authors: Trevor B. Persons and John W. Wright

Description: This is a medium-sized whiptail species, with large adults reaching about 90 mm SVL, although 70–80 mm is more usual. The long blue-green tail is slightly over twice the SVL. The dorsal ground color is dark brown, with 6–7 light stripes. In many populations the dark fields between the stripes have no spotting, but in others there are faint light spots, especially within the lowermost dark field. The belly, throat, and undersides of the limbs are white, often with a light bluish cast. There are usually 4 or more irregular, angular pre-anal scales, and the postantebrachial and mesoptychial scales are abruptly enlarged. **Juveniles:** Juveniles look similar to adults, except that the tail is brighter blue. Hatchlings emerge at about 30–40 mm SVL.

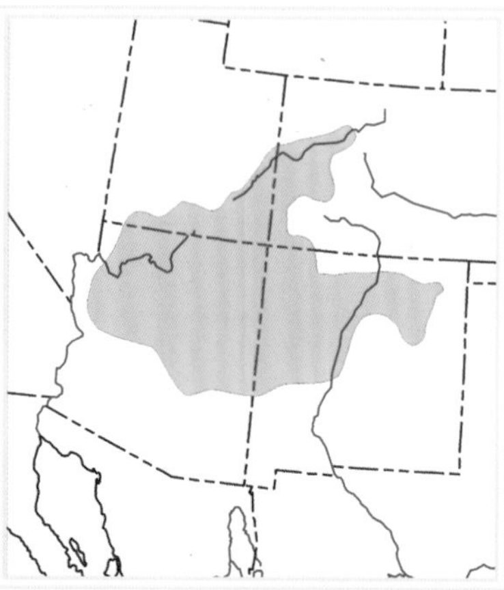

See page 559 for map color codes.

Female A. velox, *Budville, Cibola Co., NM.*

Female A. velox. *Some authorities consider* A. innotata *distinct from this taxon.*

Similar Species: Within its range, the Little Striped, Pai Striped, and Desert Grassland whiptails are most likely to be confused with this species. Although the Little Striped and Pai Striped whiptails are variable in body size and number of dorsal light stripes, both are more extensively blue than the Plateau Striped Whiptail. The Desert Grassland Whiptail is superficially similar, but the tail is more olive-green. Also, it rarely has much of a middorsal stripe, and where their ranges overlap, the Plateau Striped Whiptail is represented by a 7-striped, spotted form. In the hand, the Plateau Striped Whiptail can be separated from all these species by the lack of an extensive row of small interlabial scales between the chin shields and lower labials (usually 2–5, vs. 10 or more in the other species), in addition to usually having 4 or more angular pre-anal scales.

Habitats: Habitats occupied include Great Basin desert scrub (marginally), grassland, chaparral, piñon/juniper woodland, and Ponderosa Pine forest. Above the Mogollon Rim these lizards occur from about 1,400 to 2,440 m elevation, but may be found as low as 1,200 m in chaparral and riparian habitats farther south. They prefer open, sunny areas with scattered shrubs and loose soil, and can be locally abundant in disturbed patches (dry washes, roadsides, vacant lots) within a given habitat.

Natural History: Plateau Striped Whiptails emerge from brumation in April, although activity is limited until May. Most adults cease activity for the year by late August or early September, but juveniles (especially hatchlings) may be active through October. This species is a widely foraging, opportunistic insectivore that maintains a high body temperature of about 38°C when active, which for an individual lizard may be only an hour or two each day. In open grasslands with little shade, they largely cease daily activity by late morning, but can be found throughout the day in more shaded habitats. They are often seen darting from bush to bush, where they use their pointed snouts to rummage through leaf litter in search of food. Prey consists of adult and larval insects and other arthropods, and termites are especially favored when available. Plateau Striped Whiptails are not territorial, and home ranges overlap.

This whiptail usually lays 3–5 eggs in June, and hatchlings appear about 2 months later. Individuals do not reproduce until they are almost 2 years old, and multiple clutches have not been reported, although this would be expected in the more productive habitats in the southern portion of the range. Pseudocopulation has been reported for this species in captivity, but it is unknown how common or important this behavior is in the wild.

Range: As the name implies, this species is primarily distributed on and near the Colorado Plateau in northern Arizona and New Mexico, southern Utah, and west-central to southwestern Colorado. The distribution is spotty along the southern edge of the range, where it occurs as far south as the Pinal Mountains near Globe, Arizona. It is also uncommon and spottily distributed over much of its range in Utah. An introduced population occurs at Cove Palisades State Park in Oregon.

Viewing Tips: Throughout much of their range, Plateau Striped Whiptails are abundant and easily observed. The best time for watching them is when they are still, soon after they emerge in the morning. With binoculars, one can see color pattern details from a few meters. At this time they often bask in the open with their feet raised in the air and their belly pressed to the sun-warmed ground. They can be found at many national parks and monuments in the region, including Wupatki and Petrified Forest in Arizona; Aztec Ruins, Bandelier, and El Malpais in New Mexico; Colorado and Mesa Verde in Colorado; and Natural Bridges and Zion in Utah.

Taxonomy: The Plateau Striped Whiptail is actually a complex of species of separate hybrid origin. *Aspidoscelis innotata*, a 7-striped, spotted form described from Kanab, Utah, was later placed in synonomy with *A. velox.* We consider it a valid

Female A. velox, *Wupatki National Monument, Coconino Co., AZ.*

name applicable to one of a number of species in the complex. Other species in the complex await description.

Subspecies and Variation: Subspecies are not recognized. Marked variation in color pattern within *A. velox* stems from the fact that multiple species comprise the complex. *Aspidoscelis velox* proper generally has 6 light stripes, or if a seventh (middorsal) stripe is present, it is faint or broken, and no spots are present within the dark fields between the light stripes. Populations referable to *Aspidoscelis innotata* (which may contain several species) usually have a complete, somewhat wavy middorsal stripe and faint light spots in the dark fields. Lizards resembling *A. innotata* occupy much of the western, southern, and eastern portions of the mapped range of this book.

Remarks: The triploid Plateau Striped Whiptail arose by hybridization between a member of the Little Striped Whiptail complex and a diploid parthenoform, which in turn originated by hybridization between the Giant Spotted Whiptail or its Mexican relative, the Barranca Whiptail (*A. costata barrancorum*), and a Little Striped Whiptail. Some populations referable to *A. innotata* are diploid and may represent the diploid intermediary in the origin of both *A. velox* and *A. exsanguis.*

Red-backed Whiptail

Aspidoscelis xanthonota (Duellman and Lowe 1953)

Author: Philip C. Rosen

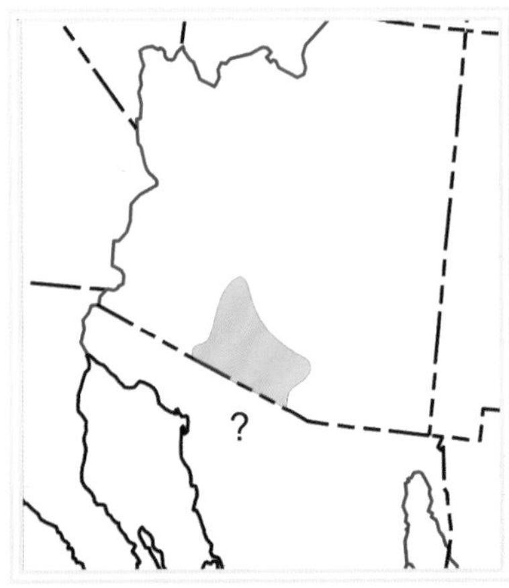

See page 559 for map color codes.

Description: This is a large whiptail, reaching 114 mm SVL and 382 mm TL. Its head is angular, with a pointed snout; its body is slender, with long hind legs and tail. Arguably, its colors mark it as our most beautiful whiptail. There are major ontogenetic changes in coloration. The light stripes of the juveniles break up into rows of spots as the lizard ages, and adults develop bright coloration covering the dorsum, ranging from profuse yellowish spotting on a dark brown background to rusty orange with inconspicuous spots. Older individuals can be heavily spotted like the Canyon Spotted Whiptail. Adults also develop slaty blue to sky-blue lateral color. **Sexual Variation:** Males are similar to females but average slightly larger. **Juveniles:** Hatchlings and small juveniles are striped and finely spotted, with a slaty-gray to slaty-blue tail. The spots often occur in 2 rows between each pair of light stripes. As the young lizard grows, the stripes fade or break up into spots.

Similar Species: The Red-backed Whiptail never has black pigment on the throat and shoulders and is thus distinguished from the sympatric Tiger Whiptail. It can be distinguished from the Sonoran Spotted Whiptail by its more numerous spots, bright dorsal and lateral coloration, and gray-blue, rather than brown, tail in juveniles.

Habitats: This whiptail occupies a restricted niche in the Arizona Upland subdivision of the Sonoran Desert. It occurs primarily on the higher desert mountains within its range, especially those that rise to 1,219 m elevation or higher. It is mostly restricted to productive, botanically diverse desert montane communities, including canyons with palo verde, mixed cactus, and diverse subtropical shrubs, and relictual mountaintop communities with unusual shrubs (such as Crucifixion Thorn and Allthorn), yuccas, agaves, prickly pears, and grasses. It occurs only on rocky slopes and adjoining canyon bottoms. The elevational range is about 396–1,402 m, but most occurrences are from the highest elevations down to 732 m.

Adult A. xanthonota, *red-backed coloration, Sierra Estrella, Maricopa Co., AZ.*

Natural History: The Red-backed Whiptail occurs in hot, remote, often inaccessible islands of montane desert scrub and desert grassland. Little is known about its diet or reproduction, though both probably follow the whiptail pattern of eating mostly arthropods and producing multiple small clutches of eggs. They forage actively and alertly on the ground and among rocks on warm to hot days, stopping to bask and retreat into soil burrows. Mating has been observed in June. Actively foraging lizards followed with radio-transmitters had body temperatures of 36–43°C. They were most active on warm to hot mornings, but surface activity sometimes continued during hot mid-afternoons. They used areas covering well over a hectare. The active season extends at least from April to October, although early and late in the season mostly hatchlings or small juveniles are seen. Although Red-backed Whiptails may permit humans to approach fairly close, they are extremely attuned to the presence of snakes. Nonetheless, one of the lizards we radio-tracked was eaten by a Sonoran Whipsnake. Other abundant predators include Gray Foxes, American Kestrels, and Red-tailed Hawks.

Range: The Red-backed Whiptail is a subtropical desert species known only in south-central Arizona, although it presumably extends south in Sonora for a substantial distance. It is restricted to the Arizona Upland, occurring as isolated populations on the

Juvenile A. xanthonota, *Sierra Estrella, Maricopa Co., AZ. Juveniles are quite different in appearance from adults.*

major mountain masses from the Ajo Mountains and Puerto Blanco Mountains at Organ Pipe Cactus National Monument to the Sierra Estrella, Table Top Mountain, and southeast nearly to the Baboquivari Mountains. Much of the range is within the Tohono O'odham Nation. Small outlying populations are known in the Quitobaquito Hills, Agua Dulce Mountains, and Growler Range at the arid edge of the Arizona Upland.

Viewing Tips: To see the Red-backed Whiptails, hike Alamo Canyon or the Bull Pasture trail at Organ Pipe Cactus National Monument in mid-morning on sunny days during May–September. More challenging, but perhaps equally rewarding, may be hiking the trail up the south face of Table Top Mountain in Sonoran Desert National Monument. The lizards are on slopes and in the canyon bottom, especially where rich, diverse vegetation occurs.

Taxonomy: The Red-backed Whiptail is closely related to, and was until recently considered a subspecies of, the Canyon Spotted Whiptail.

Subspecies and Variations: There are no currently recognized subspecies, but lizards from some of the ranges are distinctively marked. For example, adults from the region of Organ Pipe Cactus National Monument tend to have weak spotting and distinctive rusty-orange to yellow-orange backs, whereas those from the Sand Tank Mountains often bear heavy cream-yellow spotting on the dorsum.

Remarks: The Red-backed Whiptail is a bisexual species. It and the Giant Spotted Whiptail (*A. burti stictogramma*) replace one another geographically. In the southeastern portion of its known range, the Red-backed Whiptail narrowly overlaps the unisexual Sonoran Spotted Whiptail. In contrast, over its entire range, the Red-backed Whiptail is sympatric with the presumably competing Tiger Whiptail, which is the only whiptail in the desert valleys and on most of the lower, more arid hills and mountains. These 2 whiptails overlap extensively only on lower slopes and canyons. Because the Red-backed Whiptail is isolated in relatively mesic montane desert environments and is surrounded by this robust, more arid-adapted competitor, it is a relatively uncommon species. It may therefore also be sensitive to global climate change, which recent models predict will produce increased heat and drought in the American Southwest, favoring the Tiger Whiptail.

Adult A. xanthonota, *with a yellow-spotted color pattern, Sierra Estrella, Maricopa Co., AZ.*

FAMILY XANTUSIIDAE: Night Lizards

Author: Robert L. Bezy

Night Lizards of the family Xantusiidae are perhaps the least known and most misunderstood of the lizards found in the American Southwest. From their English name, they often are presumed to be nocturnal and to be related to geckos, neither of which is accurate. The moniker "Night Lizard" is used for all xantusiids and appears to be based on the presence of vertically elliptical pupils. But these are found only in members of the genus *Xantusia* occurring in the Southwest and northern Mexico, whereas round pupils are present in tropical night lizards (*Lepidophyma* found in Mexico and Central America) and the Cuban Night lizard (*Cricosaura typica*). The elliptical pupils of *Xantusia* are most likely an adaptation for vision in the dark crevices in which they live and do not indicate that these lizards are necessarily nocturnal. Although night lizards were once thought to be most closely related to geckos (which are largely nocturnal), current evidence indicates that they are more closely related to skinks (which are diurnal).

Night lizards (*Xantusia*) can be distinguished easily from all other lizards in the Southwest except geckos by the presence of eyes that have vertically elliptical pupils and that lack movable eyelids but are covered by a clear scale, or brille. From geckos, they can be distinguished by the presence of large plates on the dorsal surface of the head and rectangular ventral scales arranged in transverse and longitudinal rows.

Eight species of night lizards of the genus *Xantusia* are found in the Southwest, and 6 additional species are restricted to northwestern Mexico. Most are small with a maximum SVL of 50 to 70 mm, but the Island Night Lizard reaches 117 mm SVL and may represent an example of insular gigantism. Animals found on islands often are either significantly larger or significantly smaller than their mainland relatives. The Cuban Night Lizard, with a maximum SVL of 38 mm, is the smallest xantusiid and may represent an example of insular dwarfism.

Night lizards are highly sedentary and reclusive habitat specialists, spending much of their lives under the same cover. The Island Night Lizard is active in the day, utilizing a system of trails beneath the cover of Boxwood. The Granite Night Lizard appears to be active within its rock crevices in late afternoon and evening, but a certain percentage of the population ventures out onto the boulder surface at night, if conditions are favorable. Nocturnal activity has been extensively observed in the Sandstone Night Lizard. Time of activity may be temperature-dependent in some species of Night Lizards. Under laboratory conditions with controlled day length and temperature they have been found to be diurnal.

Xantusia wigginsi, *San Diego Co., CA.*

In the Southwest, 5 species live exclusively—or almost exclusively—in rock crevices: Granite Night Lizard, Sandstone Night Lizard, Bezy's Night Lizard, Arizona Night Lizard, and Sierra Night Lizard. These have adaptations for this habitat that include a flatter head and body, longer limbs and toes, and (except for the Sierra Night Lizard) a more boldly spotted color pattern. The 5 species differ in the degree to which these adaptations are present and are listed above in order of decreasing adaptation for the rock-crevice habitat. Evidence from DNA sequences indicates that each of 5 species has independently evolved adaptations for the rock-crevice habitat, with the exception of the Sandstone Night Lizard, which appears to have originated from populations of the Granite Night Lizard, a unique example of evolution from one rock-crevice habitat (granite) to another (sandstone).

The second microhabitat type for which 4 species of night lizards are specialized consists of decaying yuccas and agaves. All 4 are small and have relatively short limbs, permitting movement within the labyrinths inside yucca logs and agave cores. Two of the 4 yucca specialists, the Desert Night Lizard and Wiggins' Night Lizard, occur in the Southwest. The close association of the Desert Night Lizards with the fallen branches of the Joshua Tree, a giant tree-like yucca found in the Mojave Desert, was discovered by John Van Denburgh in 1895. Before this discovery the species was thought to be one of the rarest lizards in the Southwest. This habitat association has been used as a classic textbook example of a close association of a vertebrate with a particular microhabitat, and it might come as a surprise to some that there are extensive stands of Joshua Trees that lack Desert Night Lizards, and that these lizards also occur in a variety of cover, including other species of yuccas, agaves, sotols, and even pine logs.

The eighth southwestern species, the Island Night Lizard, contrasts strongly with the other members of the genus. It is larger and less specialized to the narrow confines of rock crevices and yucca branches. It occurs in a variety of microhabitats including prickly pear patches, cracks in the soil and rock outcrops, and under rocks and driftwood.

Xantusia henshawi, *San Diego Co., CA.*

There are many correlates of the habitat specialization and sedentary lifestyle of these reclusive lizards. Most of the species have very limited geographic ranges and are known from very few localities. Nearly all populations are geographically isolated and are genetically distinct. The only case of 2 species found at the same locality in the Southwest is the occurrence in southern California of the Granite Night Lizards in rock crevices of boulders surrounded by yuccas harboring the Desert Night Lizard. The Desert Night Lizard is the only widely distributed species, occurring across the Mojave Desert and the western portion of the Sonoran Desert.

Other lifestyle attributes of these reclusive lizards include low preferred body temperatures and low metabolic rates. Diet consists primarily of insects and other arthropods that are found within the microhabitat. The only exception is the Island Night Lizard, which is extensively herbivorous, perhaps a correlate of its large size, as most herbivorous lizards are large. Cannibalism has been documented in one species. In captivity the Sandstone Night Lizard has been observed to open eggs and eat the yolk of the Peninsular Leaf-toed Gecko. Home ranges are small and overlapping in the few species that have been studied. Yet, intraspecific aggression has been observed in the Desert Night Lizard under laboratory conditions. These lizards are viviparous, and a well-developed placenta has been documented in one species. One or 2 (most *Xantusia*) to 9 (Island Night Lizard) young are born, but in dry years reproduction may not occur. They often live more than 10 years. In spite of their low reproductive potential, night lizards achieve high population densities, presumably a result of low predation rates in their protected habitats, low metabolic rates, high longevity, and overlapping home ranges.

Both the family and the genus *Xantusia* are named for Janos Xantus, who collected the type specimens of Desert Night Lizards at Fort Tejon, California, in 1857.

Night Lizards are extremely difficult to observe in the wild without disturbing their habitat, the reason so little is known about their behavior and ecology. Consider it a challenge to observe one without turning some form of cover. Look for them at sunlit edges of rock crevices or of decaying yuccas and agaves when temperatures are not too hot. You may have the opportunity to make observations that have not been recorded previously for these poorly understood, reclusive lizards.

Arizona Night Lizard

Xantusia arizonae Klauber, 1931

Author: Robert L. Bezy

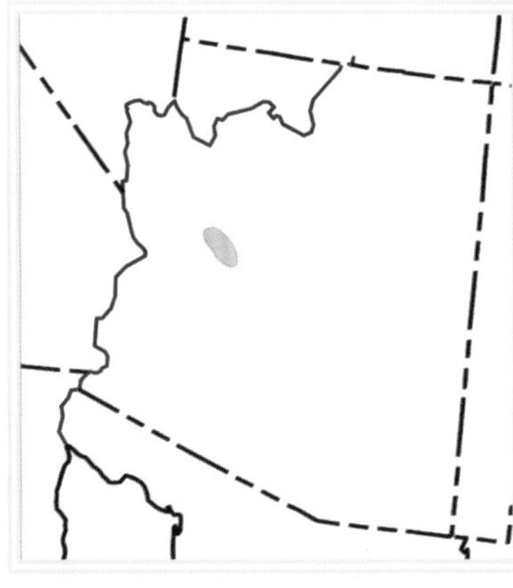

See page 559 for map color codes.

Description: This is a small lizard reaching a maximum of 60 mm SVL (84 mm tail length, 144 TL), lacking movable eyelids, and having vertically elliptical pupils (covered by a clear scale), large plates on the dorsal surface of the head, and 12 longitudinal rows of flat rectangular ventral scales. The color pattern usually is composed of medium-sized dark spots (encompassing 4 or more granular scales) on a tan to yellow-tan background. In many Arizona Night Lizards the dark spots tend to align into longitudinal rows, but some individuals have small scattered dorsal spots covering 1–2 scales. The body is moderately flat and the limbs and toes relatively long. Femoral pores are inconspicuous or absent in females. **Sexual Variation:** Males are smaller than females (55 vs. 60 mm maximum SVL) with broader heads and femoral pores with comb-shaped secretions. The femoral pores are inconspicuous or absent in females. **Juveniles:** Young Arizona Night Lizards are darker with less-conspicuous spots.

Adult X. arizonae, *Weaver Mountains, Yavapai Co., AZ.*

Adult X. arizonae, *Weaver Mountains, Yavapai Co., AZ.*

Similar Species: It most closely resembles Bezy's Night Lizard, from which it differs in having dorsal spots that tend to be aligned in horizontal rows and in lacking a dark U-shape along the posterior dorsal head plates. The geographic ranges of the 2 species do not overlap: Arizona Night Lizard is found only west of the Verde River; Bezy's Night Lizard is restricted to east of the river. The Sierra Night Lizard is smaller (51 vs. 60 mm maximum SVL), has a reticulated dorsal pattern and a conspicuous broad post-orbital stripe, and the females have well-developed femoral pores. The Arizona Night Lizard differs from the Desert Night Lizard in being larger (60 vs. 50 mm maximum SVL), more boldly spotted (spots encompassing 1–3 vs. 4 or more scales), and having a more flattened body form, longer limbs and toes, and femoral pores that are inconspicuous in females. The Granite Night Lizard and Sandstone Night Lizard are more boldly spotted and are larger (70 vs. 60 mm maximum SVL), and have a more flattened body form and 14 rather than 12 longitudinal rows of ventrals. The Arizona Night Lizard differs from the Island Night Lizard in being smaller (51 vs. 117 mm maximum SVL) and having 12 rather than 16 longitudinal rows of ventral scales. Arizona Night Lizards can be distinguished from juvenile lizards of other families by the absence of movable eyelids and the presence of vertically elliptical pupils, large scales on the dorsal surface of the head, and longitudinal row of rectangular scales on the venter.

Habitats: This species lives in crevices of granite boulders, usually on hilltops with interior chaparral dominated by manzanita, shrub oak, silk tassel, and mountain mahogany, with scattered Emory Oaks and One-seed Junipers. At some localities Arizona Night Lizards extend down to the upper edge of the Arizona Upland Sonoran Desert and have been found occasionally in packrat nests and under Banana Yuccas. The elevational range is from 1,005 to 1,465 m.

Natural History: The Arizona Night Lizard gives birth to one (43%) or 2 (57%) young in late August or early September. The diet consists of ants (30%), flies (22%), true bugs (11%), and beetles (11%), plus a wide variety of other arthropods. Bark Scorpions are abundant in the rock crevices these lizards inhabit. In their microhabitat they are protected from most predators, but Lyre Snakes are present and could represent potential predators. It is unknown whether this species is active on the boulder surfaces as are the Granite Night Lizard and Sandstone Night Lizards. Based on information available for other rock-crevice night lizards, it is likely that some Arizona Night Lizards may live for over 10 years. Night lizards have relatively low preferred body temperatures, and the rock crevices protect these lizards from the temperature and humidity extremes of the external environment. It is likely that the lizards use different parts of the crevice at different times of the day and year, perhaps occupying deeper crevices during the winter and mid-summer. A male, a female, and one or 2 young may be present in different crevices on the same boulder. They are probably territorial and may engage in intraspecific aggression. The boulders often are isolated by the stands of chaparral, and dispersal of the young may require movement across long distances. Cannibalism, which is known in the Desert Night Lizards, could be an important factor for lizards on isolated boulders.

Range: This species is endemic to Arizona west of the Verde River in the Weaver, Date Creek, and McCloud mountains.

Viewing Tips: Arizona Night Lizards are difficult to view in nature. They nearly always remain hidden within cracks and under slabs of rock. Look for these lizards at

Adult X arizonae, *Yarnell, Yavapai Co., AZ. View this species in its rocky lair by peering into crevices with a mirror or flashlight.*

Adult X. arizonae *with regenerated tail, Yarnell, Yavapai Co., AZ.*

the edge of crevices in granite boulders. Use a flashlight or mirror to peer into crevices to see this species. Under no circumstance should the rock crevices be broken or otherwise disturbed, as this destroys the microenvironment on which they depend. These lizards are found on private, state, and Bureau of Land Management lands. Make sure to comply with access regulations when looking for this species.

Taxonomy: The Arizona Night Lizard is most closely related to a species of night lizard found in Mexico. At some localities in northwest Arizona, lizards have been found that are intermediate between the Arizona Night Lizard and the Desert Night Lizard in color pattern, scalation, and body size and shape. DNA evidence indicates that these intermediate lizards are not hybrids but represent populations of Desert Night Lizards that have independently evolved adaptations to rock crevices.

Subspecies and Variation: There are no subspecies currently recognized. Arizona Night Lizards with a finely spotted color pattern resembling that of the Desert Night Lizard occur at some localities.

Remarks: Observations of activity and natural history of undisturbed lizards are needed. It is against federal and state regulations to use a prying device to uncover these and other lizards.

Bezy's Night Lizard

Xantusia bezyi Papenfuss, Macey, and Schulte, 2001

Author: Robert L. Bezy

See page 559 for map color codes.

Description: This is a small lizard reaching a maximum of 60 mm SVL (76 mm tail L, 136 mm TL), lacking movable eyelids, and having vertically elliptical pupils (covered by a clear scale), large plates on the dorsal surface of the head, and 12 longitudinal rows of flat rectangular ventral scales. The color pattern is usually composed of large dark spots (encompassing 4 or more granular scales) on a tan to yellow-tan background. There is often a dark U-shaped marking along the back and sides of the large posterior head scales. The head and body are moderately flat and the limbs and toes are relatively long. **Sexual Variation:** Males are smaller than females (54 vs. 60 mm maximum SVL), and have broader head femoral pores with comb-shaped secretions, whereas femoral pores are inconspicuous or absent in females. **Juveniles:** Juveniles are darker with less conspicuous spots.

Adult X. bezyi, *Four Peaks, Maricopa Co., AZ. Note the distinctive dark brown "U" bordering the large head scales.*

Similar Species: It is most similar to the Arizona Night Lizard, from which it differs in having dorsal dark spots that are larger (often encompassing 7 or more scales) and usually not aligned into longitudinal rows, and in having a conspicuous dark brown "U" bordering the back and sides of the large posterior dorsal head scales. The Desert Night Lizard is smaller (50 vs. 60 mm maximum SVL) and has a less boldly spotted color pattern (spots encompassing 1–3 scales rather than 4 or more scales), a less flattened body form, shorter limbs and toes, and females with conspicuous femoral pores. Bezy's Night Lizard differs from the Granite Night Lizard and Sandstone Night Lizard in being smaller (60 vs. 70 mm. maximum SVL) and less boldly spotted, and having shorter limbs and toes, a less flat body form, and 12 (vs. 14) longitudinal rows of ventral scales. The Sierra Night Lizard differs from Bezy's Night Lizard in having a reticulated dorsal pattern and females with well-developed femoral pores. The Island Night Lizard is larger and has 16 longitudinal rows of ventral scales. Bezy's Night Lizards can be distinguished from juvenile lizards of other families by the absence of movable eyelids and the presence of vertically elliptical pupils, large scales on the dorsal surface of the head, and longitudinal rows of rectangular scales on the venter.

Habitats: Bezy's Night Lizards live in crevices in granite boulders in Arizona Upland Sonoran Desert and interior chaparral. The species has also been found in decaying Sotols and may occur in decaying yuccas, agaves, and Saguaros. The elevational range extends from 760 m to 1,770 m.

Natural History: Nothing has been published on this species beyond systematics, distribution, and habitat. Based on the limited natural history information available for other species of Night Lizards that inhabit rock crevices, it may be conjectured that Bezy's Night Lizard likely mates during May and gives birth to one or 2 live young in September. The lizards probably spend most of their lives in the same rock crevice. Two or more lizards may live on the same boulder, but usually not in the same crevice. They may be territorial and may engage in intraspecific aggression. They may approach the edges of the crevice to sun, but whether they are ever active on the boulder surfaces needs to be studied. The crevices afford a microhabitat that is buffered from the temperature and moisture extremes of the Sonoran Desert and chaparral. They likely use different parts of the crevice in different seasons and different times of the day. They may inhabit the deeper recesses of the crevices during extremely hot or cold weather conditions. Activity may take place within the crevice in late afternoon and early evening. Within the crevices they are protected from most predators and may live for 10 or more years. Their diet likely consists primarily of ants and other arthropods that occur within the crevices. Crevice-dwelling snakes are potential predators.

Range: This is an Arizona endemic found east of the Verde River from the Mazatzal Mountains and Superstition Mountains east to the northwest base of the Pinal Mountains and south across the Gila River to the Galiuro Mountains.

Viewing Tips: This species is difficult to view in nature. They nearly always remain hidden within cracks and under slabs of rock. They may also be seen in dead Sotols. Look for these lizards at the edge of crevices in granite boulders. Use a flashlight or mirror to peer into crevices to see this species. Under no circumstance should the rock crevices be broken or otherwise disturbed, as this destroys the micro-environment on which they depend. These lizards are found primarily in national forests, on a national monument, and on BLM land. Make sure to comply with all access regulations when looking for this species. It is against federal and state regulations to use a prying device to uncover these and other lizards.

Taxonomy: Bezy's Night Lizard and the Arizona Night Lizard are similar rock-crevice specialists and were originally considered to be members of the same species. Recent DNA evidence indicates that they are genetically very different and that the adaptations to the rock-crevice habitat evolved independently in the 2 species.

Subspecies and Variation: There is considerable variation in color pattern within populations and across the limited range of the species, but no subspecies have been described. At certain localities some Bezy's Night Lizards have dark reticulations, and at others they have a slightly red hue.

Remarks: Field observations of activity and behavior are needed.

Adult X. bezyi, *Mazatzal Mountains, AZ.*

Sandstone Night Lizard

Xantusia gracilis Grismer and Galvan, 1986

Author: Robert E. Lovich

See page 559 for map color codes.

Description: The Sandstone Night Lizard is a relatively small lizard, with adults averaging 60–71 mm SVL. It is somewhat dorsoventrally flattened, with splayed limbs reminiscent of its sister species, the Granite Night Lizard. The eyes are large, with vertically elliptical pupils and no movable eyelids. The tail is generally longer than SVL. Back, sides, and limbs are covered with granular scales. The head has large plate-like scales, and the venter has wide scales that run from one side to the other. The body pattern is composed of round spots across the dorsal surface and a nearly immaculate ventral surface. Dark dorsal spots are set against a lighter coloration of white to gray or tan. **Sexual Variation:** Males possess enlarged femoral pores, which are lacking in females. **Juveniles:** Juveniles are similar in appearance to adults.

Similar Species: The Sandstone Night Lizard is most closely related to the Granite Night Lizard and resembles that species in general. Granite Night Lizards are slightly larger, darker and "flatter," with their limbs splayed out more than is evident in Sandstone Night Lizards. Also, Granite Night Lizards do not co-occur within the limited distribution of the Sandstone Night Lizard.

Habitats: Sandstone Night Lizards are found in the low desert subdivision of the Sonoran Desert. They are only known from a unique rock formation called the Truckhaven Rocks in Anza-Borego Desert State Park (CA). This formation is composed of sandstone, and they have not been found outside of this formation. Cracks, crevices, and burrows in rocks are the areas most often used by this lizard for shelter, although it can be found active outside cover at night. Plants are sparsely distributed where this species occurs, but scattered Creosote Bush, Ocotillo, and other typical Sonoran Desert vegetation can be found in the narrow range this species inhabits. Elevational range is known from about 150 m to just over 400 m.

Natural History: Sandstone Night Lizards are most active at night. Most of their seasonal activity occurs in the spring when mating takes place, then continues at a reduced level through the summer and fall. They are live-bearing and generally have no more than 1–3 offspring per year. Sandstone Night Lizards are more terrestrial than their exclusively rock-dwelling sister species, the Granite Night Lizard, which rarely leaves the surfaces of boulders it inhabits. Their overall body shape is smaller and thinner than the Granite Night Lizards', which presumably helps in thermoregulation, since they live in the Sonoran Desert, where temperatures commonly exceed 49°C in the summer. They will also use rodent and other burrows as shelter, besides cracks and crevices of sandstone. Behavioral observations have shown this species to be comfortable moving around on loose dirt away from sandstone rock, and even digging as if foraging in the dirt for concealed prey. During monsoonal rain events and flooding, they have been found to be surface-active when quite literally flushed from their retreats. As a result, they have been observed "swimming" through shallow pools in a side-to-side motion in order to cross the water to dry land. Longevity, diet, and home range size are not precisely known for this species and require further research. They are thought to be similar to the Granite Night Lizard in being long-lived, having a

Adult X. gracilis, *Truckhaven Rocks, Anza-Borrego Desert State Park, CA.*

Adult X. gracilis, *Truckhaven Rocks, Anza-Borrego Desert State Park, CA.*

slow metabolism, and taking several years to reach sexual maturity. Their diet is also poorly known. They will readily lose their tails as a predation-avoidance mechanism, and will also do so if handled roughly or handled by the tail itself. It is unknown what species chiefly prey upon these lizards, although bats, numerous species of snakes, other lizards, Coyotes, owls, and ravens all occur in the Truckhaven Rocks and are potential predators. Predation is offset by their coloration, which closely resembles the light-colored sandstone they inhabit. No other species of night lizards are known to occur in the Truckhaven Rocks.

Range: Sandstone Night Lizards occur only in the Truckhaven Rocks of Anza-Borrego Desert State Park. Their range is restricted to, and they are endemic to, the unique sandstone rock formation in this area of northeastern San Diego County, California.

Viewing Tips: Bring your lanterns! Sandstone Night Lizards are highly secretive and will attempt to flee when approached. They are best encountered by walking at night with a lantern (thus illuminating a larger area than with a flashlight) in desert arroyos, and looking for active individuals. Only viewing from a distance is permitted, however, since capture, handling, or any disturbance of the habitats of this lizard require permits from both the California Department of Fish and Game and Anza-Borrego Desert State Park. The Sandstone Night Lizard is listed as a California Species of Special Concern.

Taxonomy: Sandstone Night Lizards were first described as a subspecies of the Granite Night Lizard and referred to as *X. henshawi gracilis*. They have since been elevated to full species and are now referred to as *X. gracilis*.

Subspecies and Variation: There are no subspecies within this species, and variation is seen in the number and types of speckles on the dorsal surface. While general color pattern remains consistent as dark or black dots on a gray background, the number and size of black dots may vary among individuals, as will the shade of background coloration.

Remarks: This species has been known to prey upon eggs of other lizard species in captivity! Also, it is fortunate that this lizard's entire range occurs within a state park. As a result, impacts to it and its habitat are against the law, although off-road vehicles, careless habitat destruction from curious hikers and campers, and collecting pressure all threaten this incredibly cool and very rare lizard.

The author searching for X. gracilis, *using the environmentally acceptable method of night-lighting, at Truckhaven Rocks in Anza-Borrego Desert State Park, CA.*

Granite Night Lizard

Xantusia henshawi Stejneger, 1893

Author: Robert E. Lovich

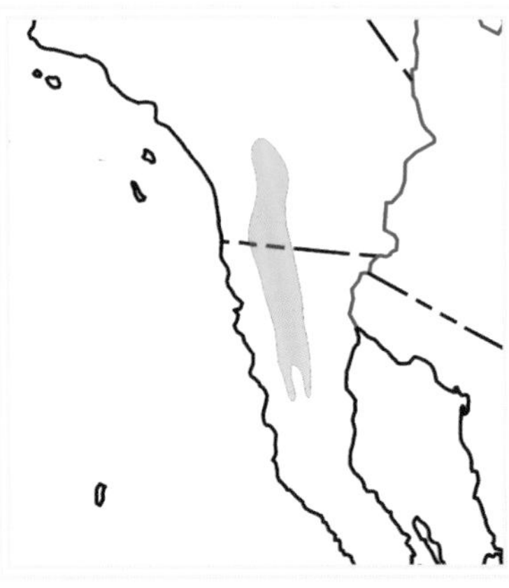

See page 559 for map color codes.

Description: The Granite Night Lizard is a dorsoventrally flattened small lizard, with adults reaching 70 mm SVL. Tail length is usually slightly longer than SVL. Limbs are widely splayed, with long, narrow toes. The eyes are large, with a vertically elliptical pupil and no movable eyelids. Back, sides, and limbs are covered with granular scales. The ventral scales are smooth, and rows of overlapping scales as wide as the vent run the length of the ventral side. The body pattern is composed of round spots across the dorsal surface and a light ventral surface peppered with dark small spots. Dark dorsal spots are set against a lighter coloration of white to gray or tan. They have a diel color-phase change, and their pattern is dark in the daytime, with light-colored spots, and light at night, with dark spotting. **Sexual Variation:** Males possess enlarged femoral pores. **Juveniles:** Juveniles are similar in appearance to adults.

Similar Species: Granite Night Lizards are similar in appearance and most closely related in the U.S. to the Sandstone Night Lizard. Sandstone Night Lizards are slightly thinner, less dorsoventrally flattened, much lighter in coloration, and generally more round and less prostrate in appearance, with their limbs not as widely splayed as in Granite Night Lizards. Granite Night Lizards do not overlap in range with the Sandstone Night Lizard.

Adult X. henshawi. *At night the blotches are smaller than in the day.*

Habitats: The Granite Night Lizard is found exclusively in association with cracks and crevices in exfoliating granitic and volcanic rock. These lizards

Adult X. henshawi, *San Jacinto Mountains, Riverside Co., CA.*

are built for rocks and are habitat specialists. They can be found from about 200 to 2,500 m in elevation. They are rarely seen far from the boulders and rocky habitats they inhabit, although a number of different vegetative associations may be found within their range. They can be found in association with coastal sage scrub, chaparral, oak and sycamore woodland, and desert intergrade vegetation along the east side of the Peninsular Ranges.

Natural History: Granite Night Lizards are most active at night but may be active in the day, moving along the fringes of rock cracks. These lizards rarely stray far from the rocks they inhabit. Most of their seasonal activity occurs in the spring when mating takes place, then continues at a reduced level through the summer and fall. They are live-bearing and have one to 2 offspring per brood. These lizards are found in close association with rocky and boulder habitats, where they can be seen along cracks and crevices created by the natural weathering of these surfaces. Their overall body shape is wide and flat, with widely splayed limbs that help them navigate the surfaces of rocks and get into the narrow retreats that they use. They are rarely found in association with riparian habitats, but rather are found on hillsides and ridge tops. They are known to prey on ants, insects, spiders, ticks, scorpions, and centipedes. They will

Adult X. henshawi, *on the prowl at night on a granite boulder. Riverside Co., CA.*

readily lose their tails if being preyed upon or roughly handled. It is unknown what species chiefly prey upon these lizards, but their habitats are prohibitive to access by most predators, and instances of predation are likely confined to the evening when these lizards are surface-active. Nocturnal predators such as bats, some snakes, Coyotes, and owls may prey upon Granite Night Lizards. Fires are also a common feature in the habitats where this species is found, yet they survive them well as a result of the protection that their rock habitats afford.

Range: Granite Night Lizards are endemic to the northern Peninsular Ranges in California and Baja California. They occur on both desert and coastal slopes of the Peninsular Ranges and occur from Banning, California, in the north to Arroyo Encantada, Mexico, in the south.

Viewing Tips: They are sometimes found just inside the cracks and crevices of rocky outcrops and boulders in the daytime, but are more commonly encountered at night when active on the surface of the same rocky habitats. Otherwise they will attempt to flee when approached. Another tip for daytime viewing is to look along sunlit edges of rocky cracks and crevices, since they will expose their bodies to the sun's rays to gain heat during the daytime, while at the same time staying far enough within the rocks to avoid predation. Only viewing from a distance is allowed without a permit. Capture, handling, or any disturbance of the habitats of this lizard requires a Scientific Collecting Permit from the California Department of Fish and Game.

Taxonomy: The Granite Night Lizard was first described in 1893. Since its original description there have been several taxonomic changes, most related to subspecies of this lizard. Historically it has shared both *X. h. bolsonae* and *X. h. gracilis* as subspecies. This is no longer the case, as both are recognized as full species now, and there are no subspecies within *X. henshawi*.

Subspecies and Variation: There are no subspecies of the Granite Night Lizard currently, but some variation exists in the species. A clinal variation of scale differences has been noted, and color variation exists in the form of dorsal spotting size and number, and background color shading. Further research is needed to determine whether variation seen in this species reflects any taxonomic differences.

Remarks: The Granite Night Lizard is a habitat specialist and has never been found to move more than 200 m from a boulder outcrop. It is also believed that earthquake fault zones have resulted in high genetic variation for this species. Creation of the boulder flakes and crevices it inhabits can take thousands of years, and damage or destruction of such habitat is strictly illegal. The Granite Night Lizard is listed as a California Species of Special Concern, and collecting is prohibited.

Juvenile X. henshawi, *San Jacinto Mountains, Riverside Co., CA.*

Island Night Lizard

Xantusia riversiana Cope, 1883

Authors: Gary M. Fellers and Charles A. Drost

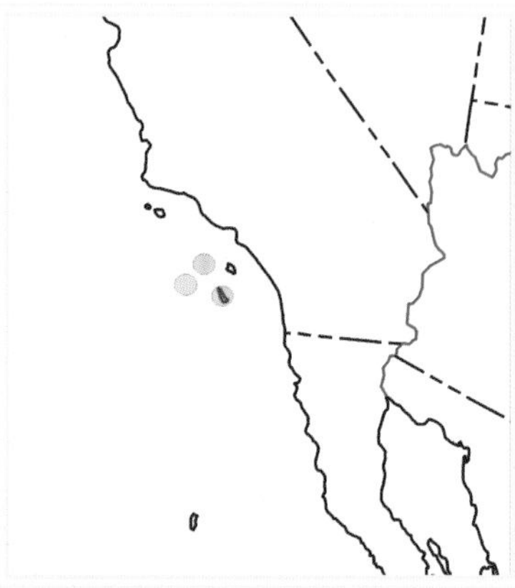

See page 559 for map color codes.

Description: The Island Night Lizard is medium sized, ranging from 70 to 117 mm SVL. The eyes are fairly large, with a vertically elliptical pupil and no movable eyelids. Dorsal scales are smooth and granular, while the caudal scales are faintly keeled. Ventral scales are large and plate-like, as are the head scales. Dorsal color pattern varies widely, ranging from a uniformly unmarked to finely mottled, boldly mottled, reticulated, and striped, with many intermediates. Dorsal color ranges from light gray (infrequent) to olive-brown (most common) to dark brown or black. **Sexual Variation:** There is no sexual dimorphism. **Juveniles:** Size at birth is about 31 mm SVL. Juveniles usually have more subtle dorsal patterns, except for striped juveniles, which are as boldly marked as striped adults.

Juvenile X. riversiana, *Santa Barbara Island, CA.*

Adult X. riversiana, *mottled individual, San Nicolas Island, CA.*

Similar Species: Island Night Lizards are quite distinctive and are not likely to be confused with other species. The only other similar-sized lizard within the range of the Island Night Lizard is the Southern Alligator Lizard, which has keeled scales, a lateral skin fold, and a different color pattern.

Habitats: Island Night Lizards occur only on the California Channel Islands. This lizard is most common in areas of Boxthorn, prickly pear cacti, and fissured rock. Boxthorn is a low-growing shrub with branches armed with sharp, thorn-like tips. In mature prickly pear stands, dead cactus pads fall to the ground and provide abundant cover for both lizards and their invertebrate prey. Cracks and crevices in and around rock outcrops and boulders provide cover similar to that afforded by Boxthorn and prickly pear. Elevationally, this lizard ranges from sea level to nearly 610 m on San Clemente Island.

Natural History: In spite of their common name, Island Night Lizards are active during the day, with little activity during cool conditions and none at night. Seasonal activity peaks in the spring when mating occurs and continues at a lower level through the summer and fall. Island Night Lizards have a low reproductive rate; roughly half of adult females bear young in a given year, and females may not have their first young until 5 years of age. Island Night Lizards breed in April, and 2–9 fully developed young are born in September. Juveniles can be active through the winter, while adults are active primarily during the spring and summer. Island Night Lizards are notably sedentary and have very small home ranges, averaging only 17 m^2. This species is slow-growing and long-lived, with some individuals reaching 12 or more years of age. Island Night Lizards feed on a wide variety of invertebrates but also eat plant material as adults. Common prey includes ground-dwelling spiders, beetles, moth larvae, ants, and many other invertebrates. Plant foods include saltbush fruits and flowers, Boxthorn fruits and leaves, and fruits of Mediterranean Iceplant and other species.

Island Night Lizards living in Boxthorn on Santa Barbara Island occur at higher densities than any other terrestrial lizard, 1,700–3,200 lizards/ha. The high densities are probably due to several factors. These lizards have an unusually low metabolic rate and can survive on half the caloric intake of other similar-sized lizards. With their varied diet, Island Night Lizards can obtain sufficient food from a wide range of both plant and animal foods. Their sedentary nature, combined with small, overlapping home ranges, permits more individuals to live in a small area. Island Night Lizards are preyed on by Island Foxes, feral House Cats (on San Clemente and San Nicolas islands), and predatory birds, primarily Barn Owls, American Kestrels, and, on San Clemente Island, Loggerhead Shrikes. During their long lives, Island Night Lizards accumulate many injuries including tail breaks, scale injuries (missing or damaged scales), cuts and scrapes, missing toes, eye injuries, and embedded cactus spines. All large lizards have some injuries, while about one-third of smaller lizards do. The most common injuries apparently result from fighting with other Island Night Lizards.

Range: Island Night Lizards occur on only 3 of the Channel Islands off southern California. They are found on San Clemente, San Nicolas, and Santa Barbara islands, as well as one small islet (Sutil Island) 1.3 km offshore from Santa Barbara Island.

Viewing Tips: Island Night Lizards are almost strictly diurnal, but they are quite secretive and sedentary. The authors have seen only a few free-ranging individuals during more than 25 years of research on this lizard. Since this species is federally listed, searching under ground cover or otherwise disturbing this lizard is illegal.

Taxonomy: In 1957 Island Night Lizards were placed in a new monotypic genus (*Klauberina*), named for Lawrence M. Klauber; this taxonomic classification was based on differences in scalation and skeletal features. They were subsequently returned to

Adult X. riversiana, *striped individual, San Nicolas Island, CA.*

the genus *Xantusia* on the basis of chromosomal, morphological, and biogeographical similarities with mainland species of night lizards.

Subspecies and Variation: The uniform, unmarked color pattern is present only on San Clemente and San Nicolas islands. Olive is a fairly common color on Santa Barbara Island, but absent on San Clemente; reddish-brown individuals are present on San Clemente and San Nicolas Islands, but absent on Santa Barbara Island.

Island Night Lizards on San Clemente and Santa Barbara Islands have been described as *X. r. reticulata*, while those on San Nicolas Island are sometimes referred to as *X. r. riversiana*. Though there are some minor inter-island differences in color, pattern, morphology, and reproductive rates, the subspecific names are not widely accepted among herpetologists.

Remarks: The Island Night Lizard is the most distinctive, strongly differentiated vertebrate species on the California Channel Islands. Genetic and biogeographic analyses suggest they have been isolated on the islands for perhaps one million years or more. Divergence from mainland fossil forms (*Paleoxantusia*) dates to Miocene time or earlier.

Sierra Night Lizard

Xantusia sierrae Bezy, 1967

Author: Robert L. Bezy

See page 559 for map color codes.

Description: This is a small lizard reaching a maximum of 51 mm SVL (76 mm tail L, 127 mm TL), lacking movable eyelids, and having vertically elliptical pupils (covered by a clear scale), large plates on the dorsal surface of the head, and 12 longitudinal rows of flat rectangular ventral scales. Femoral pores are well developed in both sexes. The color pattern is reticulated, consisting of an interconnected network of dark brown markings on a gray-tan background. Extending from behind the eye to above the ear opening is a conspicuous broad, yellow-tan stripe bordered above and below by dark brown. The head and body are slightly flat. **Sexual Variation:** Males are smaller than females (54 vs. 60 mm maximum SVL), have broader heads, and femoral pores with comb-shaped secretions. **Juveniles:** The young are darker, with less conspicuous markings.

Similar Species: It is most similar to the Desert Night Lizard, from which it differs in having a reticulated dorsal color pattern, a conspicuous broad post-orbital stripe, and a slightly flattened body form. Arizona Night Lizard and Bezy's Night Lizard are larger (60 vs. 50 mm maximum SVL), with boldly spotted color patterns, and the females lack conspicuous femoral pores. The Sierra Night Lizard differs from the Granite Night Lizard and Sandstone Night Lizard in being smaller (51 vs. 70 mm maximum SVL), having a color pattern that is reticulated rather than boldly spotted, a conspicuous broad post-orbital stripe, a less flattened body form, shorter limbs and toes, well-developed femoral pores in females, and 12 rather than 14 longitudinal rows of ventral scales. The Island Night Lizard is larger (117 mm) and has 16 rather than 12 longitudinal rows of ventral scales. Sierra Night Lizards can be distinguished from juvenile lizards of other families by the absence of movable eyelids and the presence of vertically elliptical pupils, large scales on the dorsal surface of the head, and longitudinal rows of rectangular scales on the venter.

Adult X. sierrae, *Kern Co., CA.*

Habitats: The Sierra Night Lizard lives in crevices of granite boulders in California Prairie with a few scattered Blue Oaks, Mexican Elderberries, and California Buckeyes. It is also found in Digger Pine logs in Blue Oak/Digger Pine woodland above the grassland. The elevational range is from 485 to 610 m.

Natural History: This is a species that is found in both rock crevices and decaying logs. No information has been published on life history or behavior. Based on field studies of the Desert Night Lizard and the Granite Night Lizard, some guesses can be made about the ecology of the Sierra Night Lizard. One or 2 young are probably born in September. The lizards likely are active only under cover, but field studies are needed to determine if they can be observed outside of the crevices on the surfaces of the boulders day or night. In the protection of the granite crevices they probably have few predators and may live for about a decade. Their diet likely includes ants and other arthropods that occur within the crevices. Two or 3 lizards may live on a single boulder, but usually not in the same crevice. They can be expected to have a low preferred body temperature and low metabolic rate. The boulders on which they live are separated by large expanses of grassland, and dispersal requires long-distance movements though inhospitable terrain.

Range: The species is known only at a few localities along the eastern edge of the San Joaquin Valley and the western foothills of the Greenhorn Mountains in south-central California. The distribution does not appear to overlap that of the Desert Night Lizard, which occurs a few miles to the south in the Kern River Canyon and on the eastern slope of the Greenhorn Mountains. The upper slopes of the Greenhorn Mountains have wet forests that appear to lack night lizards.

Viewing Tips: It is a difficult species to observe. Look for the lizards along the edges of crevices in granite boulders. Use a flashlight or mirror to peer into crevices to see this species. Under no circumstance should the rock crevices be broken or otherwise disturbed, as this destroys the micro-environment on which they depend. These lizards are found primarily on privately owned land. It is against federal and state regulations to use a prying device to uncover these and other lizards.

Taxonomy: The Sierra Night Lizard presents a taxonomic and evolutionary enigma that occurs repeatedly in the Xantusiidae. The Sierra Night Lizard has the body form, proportions, and scalation of a weakly adapted rock-crevice specialist. Its reticulated color pattern is unique and unlike that of other rock-crevice night lizards. Its occur-

Habitat of X. sierrae, *Kern Co., CA. This species occurs almost entirely on private land in sensitive habitat, so it is best to concentrate on viewing other lizard species.*

Adult X. sierrae *with broken tail, Kern Co., CA.*

rence in massive boulders scattered in the grasslands of the eastern Central Valley of California is unique as well. The distinctive color pattern and scalation, the grassland boulder habitat, and the presence of unique DNA sequences suggest that the Sierra Night Lizard qualifies as an independent evolutionary species. However, recognizing the Sierra Night Lizard as a separate evolutionary species renders the Desert Night Lizard an unnatural (non-exclusive) species, as DNA evidence indicates that some populations of the Desert Night Lizard are more closely related to the Sierra Night Lizard than they are to other Desert Night Lizards. Whether interbreeding between the Desert Night Lizard and the Sierra Night Lizard occurs in the area of the Kern River Canyon merits additional study, which may help resolve this puzzle.

Subspecies and Variation: There appear to be no differences in DNA sequences or in external features between Sierra Night Lizards found in crevices of boulders in the grassland and those found under logs in the adjacent pine-oak forest.

Remarks: Observations on activity and natural history of undisturbed lizards are needed. It is against federal and state regulations to use a prying device to uncover these and other lizards. This is a California Species of Special Concern.

Desert Night Lizard

Xantusia vigilis Baird, 1859 "1858"

Author: Robert L. Bezy

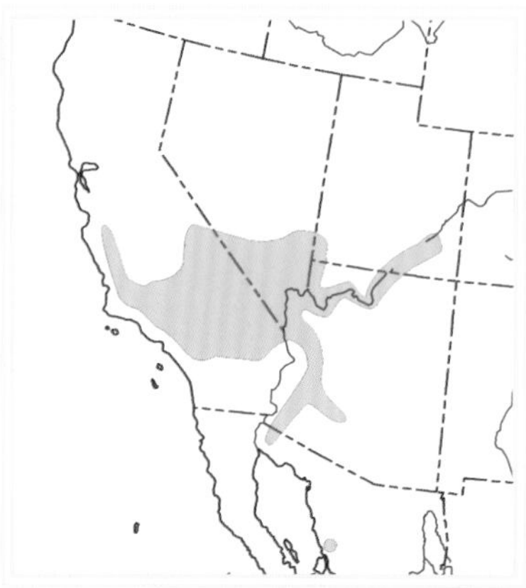

See page 559 for map color codes. Recent research suggests additional cryptic species in Mexico.

Description: This is a small lizard, reaching a maximum of 50 mm SVL (60 mm tail L, 110 mm TL), lacking movable eyelids and having vertically elliptical pupils, relatively short limbs, large plates on the dorsal surface of the head, and 12 longitudinal rows of rectangular ventral scales. Femoral pores are well developed in both sexes. The dorsal color pattern usually consists of small dark brown spots (encompassing 1–2 granular scales) on a tan background. Some individuals have a patternless, uniformly tan coloration. Dark-edged dorsolateral light stripes may be present on the side of the neck, sometimes extending the full length of the body and onto the tail. **Sexual Variation:** Males are smaller than females (44 vs. 50 mm maximum SVL) and have broader heads and femoral pores with conspicuous comb-shaped secretions. **Juveniles:** They usually have a dark brown color pattern but are otherwise similar to adults.

Similar Species: It is most similar to Wiggins' Night Lizard, from which it can be distinguished only by DNA and by geographic distribution. Desert Night Lizards range south in California to the southern edge of the Mojave Desert; Wiggins' Night Lizards are found to the south in the Sonoran Desert of California and Baja California. The Sierra Night Lizard has a reticulated color pattern and a conspicuous post-orbital stripe. The Desert Night Lizard differs from Bezy's

Juvenile X. vigilis, *Sierra Estrella, Maricopa Co., AZ.*

Adult X. vigilis, *Kern Co., CA. This tiny lizard is usually found under succulents.*

Night Lizard and Arizona Night Lizard in being smaller (50 vs. 70 maximum SVL) and having a color pattern that is less boldly spotted, shorter limbs and toes, a less flattened body form, and conspicuous femoral pores in females. Granite Night Lizards and Sandstone Night Lizards have more boldly spotted color patterns, more flattened body forms, 14 rather then 12 longitudinal rows of ventrals, and inconspicuous femoral pores in females. The Desert Night Lizard differs from the Island Night Lizard in being smaller (50 vs. 117 mm maximum SVL) and having 12 rather than 16 longitudinal rows of ventral scales. Desert Night Lizards can be distinguished from juvenile lizards of other families by the absence of movable eyelids and the presence of vertically elliptical pupils, large scales on the dorsal surface of the head, and longitudinal rows of rectangular scales on the venter.

Habitats: This species is found primarily in the Mojave and Sonoran deserts, but ranges up into the adjacent chaparral and lower pine woodland habitats. It lives in and under decaying yuccas (such as Joshua Trees and Mohave, Whipple, and Banana yuccas), agaves, Bigelow's Nolinas, Saguaros, prickly pears, and pine logs. They may also be found in rock crevices and woodrat nests, under boards, and other similar situations. The elevational range is from 335 to 2,835 m.

Natural History: This species is viviparous. One to 3 (mode: 2; mean: 1.87) young are born in September or early October, although in exceptionally dry years no reproduction takes place. The newborns average 23 mm SVL. Females produce their first litter at 3 years of age and may survive for 9 years or more. These are reclusive, sedentary lizards that usually remain under the same cover for much of their life, although in some areas they may aggregate during the winter. They have overlapping home ranges but exhibit interspecific aggression. Diet consists of ants, beetles, termites, and other arthropods that can be obtained under their cover. An instance of cannibalism has been noted. Most Desert Night Lizards lose their tails at least once in their lifetime (perhaps from fighting with other members of the species), and this loss may retard growth. In their microhabitat they have few predators and achieve population densities of at least 47 lizards per hectare. Night Snakes occur in the same yuccas and agaves as Desert Night Lizards and often are considered to be potential predators. Other potential predators include Coyotes and Kit Foxes. It is unknown whether they are eaten by woodrats in whose nests they occur.

Range: They are found in the Mohave Desert in southern California, southern Nevada, northwestern Arizona, and southwestern Utah. Isolated populations occur in California along the Inner Coast Ranges from Mount Pinos to Pinnacles National Monument, and in the Owens Valley and eastern flank of the Sierra Nevada north to the White Mountains; in southeastern Utah near the Henry Mountains and Escalante

Adult X. vigilis, *San Bernardino Co., CA.*

Adult X. vigilis, *Harquahala Mountains, La Paz Co., AZ.*

Canyon; in Arizona in the Grand Canyon and in Sonoran Desert ranges from the Kofa Mountains east to the Sierra Estrella and north to the Hualapai Mountains.

Viewing Tips: These lizards are rarely observed outside of yuccas, agaves, and other cover. Their time of activity is unknown but likely depends on season. Look for them along the edges of fallen branches of Joshua Trees and Mohave Yuccas. They may be seen briefly by turning a fallen yucca log in the Mohave Desert, but care should be taken not to damage the habitat, injure the lizards, or cause tail breakage. This species occurs in several public lands that are protected from disturbance, such as Joshua Tree National Park; never disturb cover objects in these protected landscapes. Instead, search for them on BLM or Forest Service lands within their range, where looking under cover objects is approved by the land manager (i.e., check ahead).

Taxonomy: Studies of mitochondrial DNA indicate the presence of significant genetic differences between many of the populations currently assigned to the species.

Subspecies and Variation: No subspecies are currently recognized. Desert Night Lizards in southeastern Utah are more reddish than those in the Mohave Desert.

Remarks: These tiny lizards are abundant in the litter under Joshua Trees in the Mohave Desert, but observing them undisturbed presents a challenge.

Wiggins' Night Lizard

Xantusia wigginsi Savage, 1952

Author: Robert L. Bezy

See page 559 for map color codes. Recent research suggests additional cryptic species in Mexico.

Description: This is the Southwest's smallest lizard, reaching a maximum of 44 mm SVL (53 mm tail length, 97 mm TL). It lacks movable eyelids and has vertically elliptical pupils, relatively short limbs, large plates on the dorsal surface of the head, and 12 longitudinal rows of rectangular ventral scales. Both sexes have well-developed femoral pores. The dorsal color pattern is highly variable and 3 morphs exist: spotted, with small dark brown spots (encompassing 1–4 granular scales) on a tan background; striped, with a pale dorsolateral stripe bordered above and below by a narrower dark stripe, extending from the posterior edge of the head plates onto the tail; and patternless, tan without dark marking. **Sexual Variation:** Males are smaller than females (37 vs. 44 mm maximum SVL) and have broader heads and femoral pores with comb-shaped secretions. **Juveniles:** Juveniles are darker and lack a conspicuous color pattern.

Juvenile X. wigginsi, *Jacumba, San Diego Co., CA. Adults are very small, so juveniles are diminutive.*

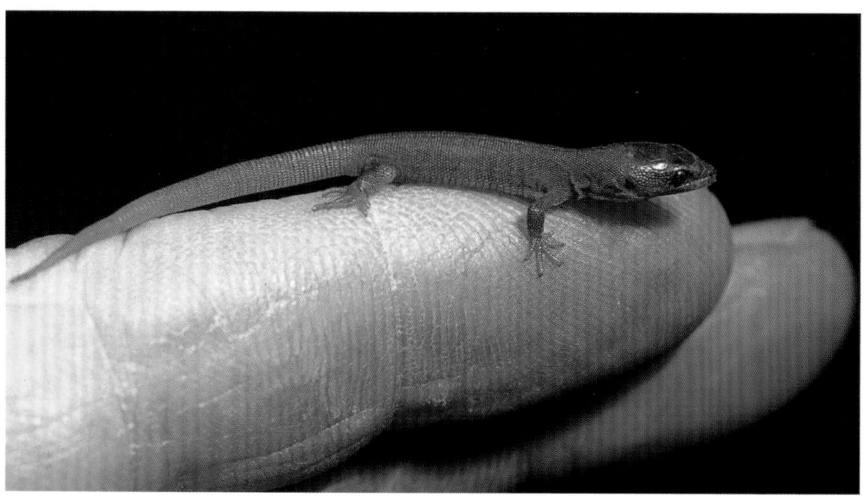

Adult X. wigginsi, *San Diego Co., CA.*

Similar Species: It differs from the Desert Night Lizard in nuclear and mitochondrial DNA, but no distinguishing external features of color pattern or scalation have been identified. The 2 species differ in their geographic ranges, with Wiggins' Night Lizard occurring primarily in the Sonoran Desert in Baja California and southern California north to Yucca Valley, where it comes into contact with the Desert Night Lizard of the Mohave Desert. The Sierra Night Lizard is larger (51 vs. 44 maximum SVL) and has a reticulated color pattern, a conspicuous broad post-orbital stripe, and a slightly flattened body form. Wiggins' Night Lizard differs from Bezy's Night Lizard and the Arizona Night Lizard in being smaller (44 vs. 70 mm maximum SVL), and having a less boldly spotted color pattern, a less flattened body form, shorter limbs and toes, and conspicuous femoral pores in females. The Granite Night Lizard and Sandstone Night Lizard have more boldly spotted color patterns, more flattened body forms, longer limbs and toes, 14 rather then 12 longitudinal rows of ventrals, and inconspicuous femoral pores in females. Wiggins' Night Lizard differs from the Island Night Lizard in being smaller (50 vs. 117 mm) and having 12 (vs. 16) longitudinal rows of ventral scales. Wiggins' Night Lizards can be distinguished from juvenile lizards of other families by the absence of movable eyelids and the presence of vertically elliptical pupils, large scales on the dorsal surface of the head, and longitudinal rows of rectangular scales on the venter.

Habitats: Wiggins' Night Lizards are found under decaying agaves, Mohave Yuccas, Joshua Trees, and datilillos (Baja California tree yuccas). They are often found under dead agaves around the edges of live agave colonies, into which they take refuge if uncovered. In Baja California members of the species also have been recorded under decaying barrel cacti and Boojum Trees. They are sometimes found under trash. Wiggins' Night Lizards occur predominantly in the Sonoran Desert extending into piñon/juniper woodland and into the southern edge of the Mohave Desert. The elevational range is from sea level to 1,370 m.

Natural History: Virtually nothing has been reported on the ecology, life history, and behavior of this species. Populations of Wiggins' Night Lizards in the Sonoran Desert appear to be less dense than populations of the Desert Night Lizard in the Mohave Desert. From a study of the ecology of the Desert Night Lizard it is presumed that Wiggins' Night Lizards are viviparous and that one or 2 young are born in September or early October in southern California; reproduction may occur earlier in Baja California Sur. Their home ranges are likely small and overlapping, restricted to the confines of a dead yucca or agave. Territorial aggression may take place and perhaps result in tail loss. Diet likely consists of ants, beetles, termites, and other arthropods that can be obtained under their cover. They likely live for 10 years or more. Potential predators include Coyotes, Gray Foxes, Ringtails, and nightsnakes.

Range: It extends from Baja California Sur north into southern California to the San Jacinto Mountains, San Gorgonio Pass, and the southernmost Mohave Desert in Homestead Valley. In Baja California Sur it is notably absent from the Vizcaino Peninsula.

Adult X. wigginsi, *San Diego Co., CA.*

Viewing Tips: No observations have been recorded of activity of Wiggins' Night Lizards outside their cover. Look for them along the edges of decaying yucca logs and agaves, day or night when temperatures are not too hot.

Taxonomy: Nuclear and mitochondrial DNA evidence indi-

Adult X. wigginsi, *San Diego Co., CA.*

cates Wiggins' Night Lizard includes 3 highly distinctive lineages (*X. wigginsi* ranging from the Vizcaino Desert in Baja California Sur north to the Anza Borrego region of southern California; the San Jacinto lineage, found in the region of the San Gorgonio Pass; and the Yucca Valley lineage in the southernmost Mohave Desert). Genetic markers indicate that little or no interbreeding occurs among these 3 lineages or between the Wiggins' Night Lizard and the Desert Night Lizard in the southern Mohave Desert. Additional studies are needed to determine if there are any differences in scalation, color pattern, and body shape among these 3 lineages that appear to be genetically isolated and likely represent separate species.

Subspecies and Variation: Considerable differences in DNA exist across the range of the species.

Remarks: Observations of activity and natural history of undisturbed lizards are needed. Identification of distinctive features of color pattern and scalation would be helpful.

FAMILY SCINCIDAE: Skinks

Author: Jonathan Q. Richmond

Members of the Scincidae, commonly referred to as skinks, are found worldwide and reach their highest diversity (~ 250 species) in Australia. The number of species in the U.S. is uncertain, but likely exceeds the 20 or so that are currently recognized. Skinks in the American Southwest are members of the genus *Plestiodon* (formerly *Eumeces*). Historically, the systematics of *Plestiodon* have been complicated by a high degree of geographic and individual variation, and a general lack of fixed character differences for distinguishing taxa. Current genetic work is revealing higher levels of diversity than previously expected, and many forms traditionally recognized as single species are almost certainly composed of more.

Skinks are characterized by smooth, overlapping cycloid scales that are relatively equal in size all over the body. Their shiny appearance and hard exterior of the body are a result of osteoderms, which are bony plates that lie just beneath the scales. Body forms are extremely variable, ranging from some having robust limbs and stout bodies to fully limbless forms with snake-like bodies. Limb reduction has evolved many times independently, with substantial variation between major clades; a number of species

Adult Plestiodon callicephalus, *Pajarito Mountains, Santa Cruz Co., AZ.*

Striped adult female Plestiodon "gilberti," *Argus Range, Inyo Co., CA.*

are completely limbless, while others have limb vestiges, weak limbs, or reduced numbers of digits. Size range is large, from less than 50 mm SVL in some North American species to greater than 32 cm SVL in *Macroscincus coctei* of the Cape Verde Islands. Most skinks are egg-layers, but some species give birth to live young. Females are also known to tend the eggs and young.

Color patterns change markedly as individuals grow older; juveniles typically have conspicuous longitudinal stripes overlaying a dark ground color on the flanks and the dorsum. This pattern becomes faded or disappears in the adults, and the number of stripes can be used to distinguish certain species. Larger species tend to have the greatest change in color pattern as individuals age. Nuptial coloration is common in the breeding season (usually mid-March through May); males often have reddish-orange coloration on the head and on the underside of the tail during the spring and early summer. Nuptial colors are far less pronounced in females. As with many other lizards, the tails break off easily when predators latch onto them; juveniles have brightly colored tails (typically blue, but in some areas pinkish-red) that are far more conspicuous than the body during high-speed chases, so predators are often left with a writhing tail rather than the more substantial morsel that is the skink itself.

Habitat diversity is substantial, with terrestrial and fossorial species predominating. However, some species are adept at climbing in trees, while others are more or less aquatic. Skinks will typically seek shelter under rocks, debris, and decaying logs. In many ways their preferred habitats are more similar to those of salamanders than to those of typical lizards; they are often found near springs, swamps, or in humid underground burrows. Insects are the chief food, but larger skinks can manage small rodents or nesting birds. Foraging is generally done during the day.

Mountain Skink

Plestiodon callicephalus Bocourt, 1879

Authors: Don E. Swann, Matthew D. Caron, and Taylor Edwards

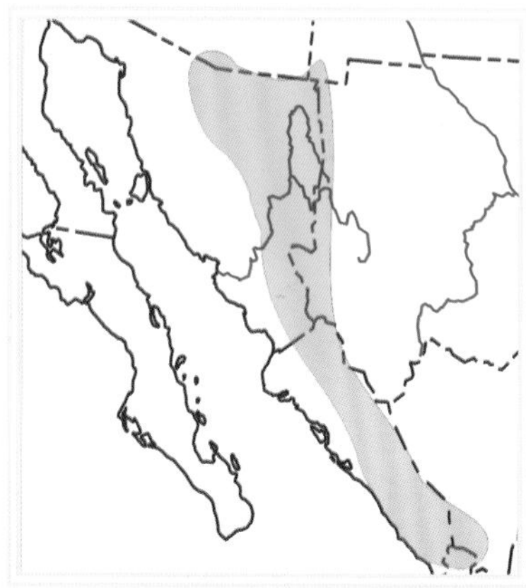

See page 559 for map color codes.

Description: This medium-sized skink reaches a maximum length of 76 mm SVL. Its legs are small, and the tail is approximately twice as long as the body. The color of this species is shiny copper, golden brown, or olive-brown, which makes individuals cryptic in oak leaf litter. Adults retain the blue tail color of juveniles, although the color is much less vivid as they age. A pale, narrow stripe on the 4th scale row extends on each side of the animal from the eye to the trunk, but more distinctive is the dark lateral band that runs beneath it to the hind limbs. The scales of this species are shiny, smooth, and cycloid. **Sexual Variation:** Adult males have bright red lips. **Juveniles:** Juveniles are dark brown with bright blue tails. Some juveniles and young adults also have a light-colored Y-shaped line on top of the head, although in large adults this pattern may be faded or completely absent.

Juvenile P. callicephalus, *Cochise Co., AZ.*

Similar Species: The Great Plains Skink is larger, lacks stripes, and has a dark, net-like scale pattern along its body. Juvenile Great Plains Skinks are black with bright blue tails. The Many-lined Skink ranges north of this species and has a light stripe running the length of its upper back.

Habitat: In the U.S., the Mountain Skink typically inhabits wooded riparian areas and oak woodlands in or near

Adult P. callicephalus, *Pajarito Mountains, Santa Cruz Co., AZ. Adults retain the brilliant blue tail.*

mountains, up to an elevation of approximately 1,980 m. Usually, the species occurs in moderately mesic areas. In typical habitat in the "sky island" mountain ranges of southeastern Arizona and southwestern New Mexico, the ground cover includes large boulders or loose rocky soils, with logs and dry leaf litter often present. Dense stands of grass may sometimes be present as well. Associated tree species include Arizona Sycamore, Arizona Walnut, Velvet Mesquite, Silver-leaf Oak, Mexican Blue Oak, junipers, and Piñon Pine. In parts of Mexico, the species ranges down to sea level.

Natural History: Little is known about the diet of this insectivorous species, but prey such as beetles, flies, and spiders have been recorded. Captive Mountain Skinks easily handle insects such as large crickets. They are active from May through September, and they are diurnal until mid-afternoon. In general, little or no crepuscular or nocturnal activity is observed in this species. Mountain Skinks are secretive lizards, seldom venturing far from cover and avoiding open, dry areas. They are alert and fast-moving animals; when observed or disturbed they quickly retreat and disappear in leaf litter or boulder piles.

Only anecdotal information is available on reproduction in this species. Female Mountain Skinks lay clutches of 3–6 eggs and are known to guard these eggs. Somewhat surprisingly, some individuals have been observed guarding hatchlings as well. There is one report of a Mountain Skink from Arizona giving birth to live young.

Hatchlings have been found as early as July 23 in New Mexico, suggesting that reproduction is timed with the summer monsoon rains. Hatchlings have an SVL of 20–25 mm. Little is known about predation on this species, but Mountain Skinks are probably taken by lizard-eating snakes that occur in their range, such as the Arizona Mountain Kingsnake, as well as diurnal mammals such as White-nosed Coatis.

Range: This species reaches the northern limits of its range in the sky islands of southeastern Arizona and extreme southwestern New Mexico. Mountain Skinks are known in the U.S. only from the Pajarito, Baboquivari, Huachuca, Santa Rita, and Peloncillo mountain ranges. In Mexico the range includes the Sierra Madre Occidental of Sonora, Chihuahua, and Sinaloa, and extends south to Nayarit and Jalisco.

Viewing Tips: Mountain Skinks are probably one of the most difficult lizards in the Southwest to find and view. They are extremely wary, very habitat specific, cryptic, and uncommon, even in optimal habitat. The best time to spot them is on summer mornings in wooded canyons in the few sky island mountain ranges where they occur in the Coronado National Forest. One viewing tip is to listen for them as they forage or flee; Mountain Skinks' very rapid movements in dry leaves create a sound that is different from that of other lizards. Finding the best habitat for Mountain Skinks and waiting quietly for them to appear may also be an effective strategy. Prime areas for viewing this species are also great for seeing many other interesting animals, including Yarrow's Spiny Lizards, Rock Rattlesnakes, and Arizona Mountain Kingsnakes.

Taxonomy: A few taxonomists still consider the Mountain Skink to be a subspecies of the Four-lined Skink. However, most experts consider the Mountain Skink to be a separate species, because it is geographically isolated from the Four-lined Skink and morphologically distinct. This species was recently placed in the genus *Eumeces*, a name that was replaced by an earlier published name, *Plestiodon*.

Subspecies and Variation: There are no recognized subspecies.

Remarks: The scientific name of the Mountain Skink, *callicelphalus,* is a Greek word meaning "beautiful head." The name is believed to refer to the Y- or lyre-shaped light line on the head of this species. Little is known about the Mountain Skink, leaving gaps in our understanding of its natural history, but this beautiful and distinctive species is one of the more elusive treasures of southwestern herpetofauna.

Gilbert's Skink

Plestiodon "gilberti" Van Denburgh, 1896

Author: Jeffrey M. Lemm

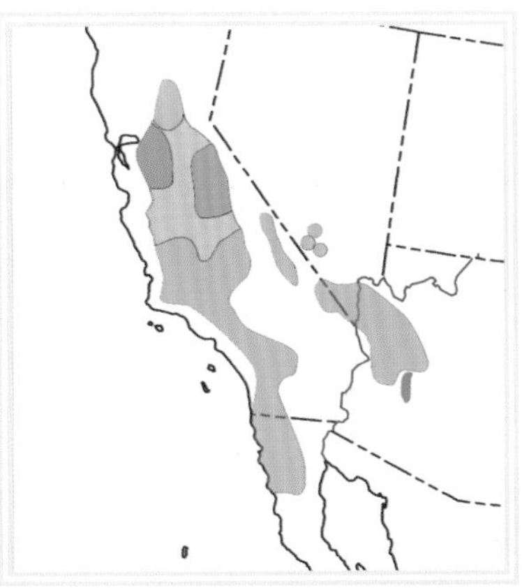

See page 559 for map color codes.

Description: This is one of California's largest skinks, with adult males reaching 117 mm SVL. The tail is as long as or slightly longer than the body and may become brick-red or orange in both sexes with age, depending on locality. It has short limbs, smooth scales, and a heavy body. The adult is brown, gray, olive, or green, and may have dark spotting, which may form intricate patterns. Light and dark striping is more or less distinct in adults of some populations and varies with age and locality. **Sexual Variation:** Adult males tend to lose striping sooner than females and have large heads, often orange or red, which the females lack. Female head coloration is not usually as bright as the males'. **Juveniles:** Young have a pair of whitish stripes on each side, which enclose a broad black or dark brown stripe that disappears at the base of the tail. The tail is blue in the northern and eastern parts of the range and salmon or pink in the south.

Male P. "gilberti" gilberti, *Greenhorn Mountains, Kern Co., CA. The intense orange markings indicate that this is a male.*

Similar Species: The Gilbert's Skink is most commonly confused with the Western Skink, in which the lateral stripe is uniformly brown. This stripe is absent or variegated in the Gilbert's Skink. In Western Skinks the blue or gray tail persists in adults. In juvenile Gilbert's Skinks the dark lateral stripe usually stops at the base of the tail, whereas in juvenile Western Skinks, the stripe extends well out onto the tail.

Habitats: The Gilbert's Skink is found in a wide variety of habitats. It is most common in open areas within grasslands, salt flats, various desert communities, chaparral, coastal sage scrub, piñon/juniper woodlands, and pine forests. It extends into the desert along riparian corridors. Heavy brush and densely forested areas are generally avoided. Gilbert's Skink occurs from sea level to an elevation of about 2,200 m.

Natural History: Gilbert's Skinks are fairly common and active from early spring to early fall. They overwinter underground but may be active in the southern parts of the range on warm winter days. They emerge in the spring, when daily activities are mostly restricted to late morning and afternoon. Minimum activity temperature is 21.5°C. They are seldom seen in the open, foraging through leaf litter and dense vegetation, occasionally digging through loose soil. The diet is primarily made up of ground-dwelling insects, although cannibalism has been reported. Adept at burrowing, they often construct their own shelters by burrowing under surface objects such as rocks or rotting logs. Gilbert's Skinks are not believed to be territorial, and home range size has been estimated at 0.4 ha.

The reproductive season for this species varies geographically and from year to year, depending on local conditions. Little is known about the timing of reproduction, but mating probably occurs in the late spring and summer. Clutches are laid in the summer from June to August, and clutch size varies from 3 to 9 eggs. Females construct nest chambers in loose, moist soil several centimeters deep, especially under flat stones. It is thought that females stay with the eggs and guard them from predators. In southern California, hatchlings are often observed in August, but fresh hatchlings have been found as early as May. They weigh and measure 0.5 g and 30–35 mm SVL, respectively, at hatching. Gilbert's Skinks grow quickly and reproduce by their second year of age. They can live for up to 6 years or more. Gilbert's Skinks are often host to external parasites such as pterygosomatid mites and are preyed upon by other lizards (including adults of their own species), snakes, birds, and mammals.

Range: Gilbert's Skinks occur mainly in California. They are found in the northern San Joaquin Valley, in the foothills of the Sierra Nevada from Butte County southward, and along the coastal regions of the Coast Ranges from the San Francisco Bay to the Mexican border and into northern Baja California. They are also found in the mountains of southern California and at scattered montane localities in the eastern desert from Mono County to San Bernardino County. Isolated populations also occur in western Arizona and southern Nevada.

Juvenile P. "gilberti" rubricaudatus, Argus Range, Inyo Co., CA. Other "subspecies" tend to have a blue tail as juveniles.

Viewing Tips: Gilbert's Skinks are nearly impossible to view in the open. Most open ground sightings occur on warm, overcast days; however, Gilbert's Skinks generally flee to cover when encountered. The easiest way to see them is by looking under rocks and logs in the early morning, before the skinks are active. In many regions, they can be found throughout the year in this manner. However, all cover objects should always be replaced to their original positions to reduce the disturbance to the fragile microenvironment; never look under objects on public lands where it is prohibited.

Taxonomy: The genus *Plestiodon* was found to take priority over the genus *Eumeces*, which appears in nearly all literature for this species. Recent research has shown that "*gilberti*" has 3 lineages that probably merit species recognition. *Plestiodon "gilberti"* is shown in quotations to indicate that it refers to a group of species until those animals are described.

Subspecies and Variation: Gilbert's Skink is represented by 5 subspecies: The Arizona Skink (*P. g. arizonensis*), in which the young have a pinkish coloration on the underside of the tail and adults tend to retain the juvenile striping; the Variegated Skink (*P. g. cancellosus*), in which the young have a pink tail and older adults develop a network of dark bars or lattice markings on the back; the Greater Brown Skink (*P. g. gilberti*), in which the young have a blue tail; the Northern Brown Skink (*P. g. placerensis*), in which the young have a blue tail; and the Western Red-tailed Skink (*P. g. rubricaudatus*), in which the young have a pink tail, except in the Panamint and other desert mountains where the tail is blue.

Remarks: For such a common species, very little is known about the Gilbert's Skink.

Many-lined Skink

Plestiodon multivirgatus (Hallowell, 1857)

Author: Lauren J. Livo

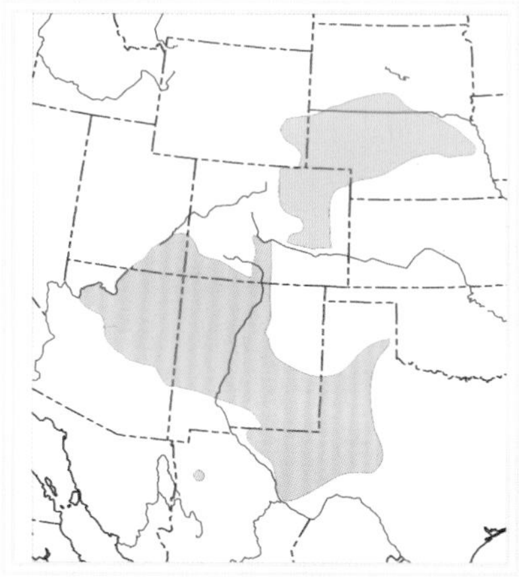

See page 559 for map color codes.

Description: Many-lined Skinks have a maximum SVL of 76 mm. The tail is 1.5 to 2 times longer than the body, but most adults have a broken and regenerated tail that is shorter than the original. These slender, relatively cylindrical lizards have tiny limbs and smooth, shiny cycloid scales that overlap tightly and have rounded rear edges. The color pattern varies geographically and even within a single brood. Most individuals in the northeastern part of the range have alternating light and dark stripes running the length of the body. These stripes become less distinct on the tail. In the southwestern portion of the range, the pattern is highly variable, with striped individuals (often with a darker background color and distinct white dorsolateral stripes), other individuals lacking a pattern, and intermediate individuals. **Sexual Variation:** Males have orange or reddish labial scales during the breeding season. Males have a smaller average body size (42–68 mm SVL) compared to females (49–70 mm SVL). **Juveniles:** Young Many-lined Skinks have very dark bodies with a variable number of light stripes and a bright blue tail.

Juvenile P. m. multivirgatus, *Weld Co., CO.*

Similar Species: This long-bodied species should be confused only with other skinks, all of which possess the smooth, shiny cycloid scales. Mountain Skinks (which are not sympatric) and Four-lined Skinks have tails that are shorter in proportion to the body and a Y- or lyre-shaped mark on

Adult P. m. multivirgatus, *Weld Co., CO. Typical pattern for this subspecies.*

the head and neck (especially in younger adults) compared to the Many-lined Skink. In addition, the position of a white or light stripe on the back varies among species. Counting from the mid-dorsum, striped individuals of the Many-lined Skink have a white stripe restricted to scale row 3.

Habitats: In the northeastern portion of its range, Many-lined Skinks occupy high shortgrass plains and sandhills, including in urban and suburban areas. To the southwest, this species occurs in a wide variety of habitats, including grasslands, open coniferous forests, oak thickets, sandy greasewood habitats, along montane streams, and rocky areas such as talus slopes and canyons. Many-lined Skinks have been reported from a low elevation of about 450 m in Nebraska to at least 2,590 m in Colorado.

Natural History: In the south, this skink may be active from February through October. An activity season beginning in April is typical for more northerly populations. After mating in the spring or early summer, a female Many-lined Skink will dig a burrow in a protected underground location and produce 3–5 eggs (range 3–9 eggs) per clutch. The timing of egg deposition varies, with some clutches produced as early as May or as late as August. Consequently, the time when hatchlings appear varies across the range of the species, from mid-June in southern populations to August or later in the north. The Many-lined Skink female broods her eggs and remains with her offspring for several days after hatching. Hatchlings begin life with a bright blue tail, which presumably acts to divert visual predators such as birds from attacking the body. As the skink grows, the blue color fades. At a suburban grasslands conservation center in Aurora, Colorado, juvenile Many-lined Skinks were observed around prairie dog burrows. Many-lined Skinks brumate underground, sometimes with other reptile species. Excavation of a partially buried boulder in Santa Fe, New Mexico, revealed Many-lined Skinks brumating with Smooth Greensnakes and Terrestrial Gartersnakes in a rodent burrow system. These skinks eat a variety of small invertebrates. Specimens from Nebraska contained spiders, grasshoppers, beetle larvae, and unidentified insects. An American Kestrel was observed preying on a Many-lined Skink, and Many-lined Skinks may also be impaled by shrikes.

Male P. m. epipleurotus, *Linclon Co., NM. Unstriped adult male; note the orange labial scales of the breeding males.*

Range: The Many-lined Skink ranges from central Arizona through New Mexico and west Texas, northwest to southeastern Utah, through Colorado, southeastern Wyoming, and most of Nebraska, to extreme southern South Dakota.

Viewing Tips: When encountered in the open, a Many-lined Skink tends to slither quickly into shrubbery or other cover. This skink is much more frequently found under objects, including rocks, downed branches, boards, and even cowpies (return such objects to their original positions to maintain habitat). When captured—even when held carefully—the wriggling of the skink as it tries to escape may result in detachment of the tail. When held, this skink may try to bite, although its small size makes the bite a mere pinch. Because of its secretive habits, the Many-lined Skink may be infrequently encountered, including at sites that support large numbers. Public lands for which there are records of this skink include the Cherry Creek Reservoir State Park and the Great Sand Dunes National Park and Preserve, both in Colorado. Do not turn over cover objects in these protected areas, unless you have special permits.

Taxonomy: This skink has had a confusing taxonomic history, due in part to the variability of its color pattern. Some biologists argue that the northern and southern subspecies represent distinct species, but more research is needed to clarify this issue. Most previous literature uses the genus *Eumeces* in reference to this skink, but the genus name *Plestiodon* was recently applied to many North American skinks, resulting in a revision of the scientific name for this species.

Subspecies and Variation: Two subspecies are recognized: the Northern Many-lined Skink (*P. m. multivirgatus*) in the northeastern part of the range, and the Variable Skink (*P. m. epipleurotus*) in the southwestern part of the range. In the northeastern subspecies (*P. m. multivirgatus*), which typically has alternating dark and light stripes, the dark markings on scale rows 1 and 2 (counting from the mid-dorsum) do not form a zigzag pattern. On striped individuals in the southwestern subspecies (*P. m. epipleurotus*), these dark markings frequently form a zig-zag pattern. Some researchers consider west Texas populations to be intergrades between these 2 subspecies. No intergrades have been reported from central Colorado, where the nearest records of these 2 subspecies are separated by a distance of at least 60 km.

Female P. m. epipleurotus, *striped phase, Encino, Torrance Co., NM. Note the differences in striping between this subspecies and the other pictured on p 453.*

Great Plains Skink

Plestiodon obsoletus (Baird and Girard, 1852)

Authors: Matthew D. Caron and Don E. Swann

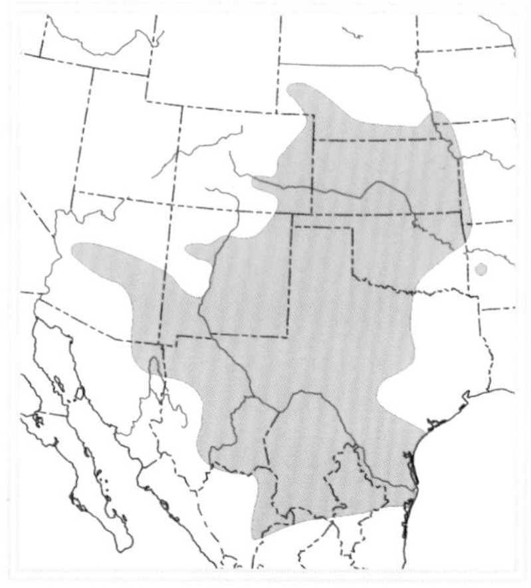

See page 559 for map color codes.

Description: The Great Plains Skink is a large skink, with males reaching a maximum SVL of 142 mm. The limbs are short, the body stout, and the thick tail, if unbroken, is approximately 1.5 times the SVL. Adults are shiny and vary in color from grayish-brown to tan or olive-brown. The tail and limbs are yellow to pale orange, and the lower sides often have orange spots. The most important feature in identifying this species is a net-like pattern of dark lines over the entire body, created by the cumulative effect of dark crescents on the rear of each dorsal scale. Great Plains Skinks have cycloid scales that are smooth and shiny. **Sexual Variation:** Adult males are slightly larger than adult females, but are otherwise similar. Adult males also have enlarged, more muscular heads during breeding season. **Juveniles:** Juveniles are a shiny jet black, with bright blue tails and white spots on the labial scales.

Similar species: Skinks are not likely to be confused with species in other families, except possibly alligator lizards, which have a lateral fold, and whiptails, which have granular body scales. Four other species of skinks are found within the range of the Great Plains Skink. The Many-lined, Mountain, and Four-lined skinks are smaller than the Great Plains Skink, usually darker in coloration, and have body stripes (sometimes absent in the Many-lined Skink). Gilbert's Skink is only slightly

Juvenile P. obsoletus, *Cochise Co., AZ.*

Adult P. obsoletus, *San Bernardino Valley, Cochise Co., AZ.*

smaller, but it lacks the net-like pattern and has no dorsal markings, and juveniles are striped.

Habitat: In the central and eastern part of its range, this species primarily occurs in open prairie. In the Southwest it is somewhat of a habitat generalist wherever moist conditions exist. Individuals can be found in areas ranging from low valleys to rocky canyons and up into the mountains. Vegetative communities inhabited include Creosote Bush desert, desert grassland, riparian corridors, piñon/juniper woodland, and pine/oak woodlands. Great Plains Skinks are especially fond of rocky outcrops near riparian corridors that are characterized by sandy to gravelly soils and loose ground cover, including leaf litter and logs. In arid parts of southern Arizona, they are almost always found where wet soils and springs or seeps occur nearby. Over its entire range, the Great Plains Skink occurs from sea level to 2,650 m in elevation.

Natural History: A secretive species, the Great Plains Skink is chiefly fossorial and spends most of its time under rocks and logs or in rodent burrows. It is active at a preferred temperature range of between 31 and 34°C, and is most often encountered above ground in shaded areas, on cool mornings or overcast days, after rainstorms, and just before and after dark. The species is primarily diurnal but is sometimes seen at night. Its diet consists of insects (including grasshoppers, roaches, caterpillars, ants, and beetles), spiders, snails, and other lizards. Little is known about predation on this species, but it is presumably eaten by a variety of snakes, birds, and mammals. As with many other lizards, the tail of the Great Plains Skink is easily detached but will grow back in time, although it will be shorter.

Female Great Plains Skinks reach sexual maturity at about 3 years of age. Females may produce a single clutch of eggs annually, although mature females may not breed every year. Females guard their clutches, which are laid in underground nests during spring or summer. Clutches vary from 7 to 24 eggs, with larger, older females producing larger clutches. Hatchlings have an SVL of 33–43 mm and usually appear in July. Males become sexually mature following the third brumation and develop muscular enlargements on either side of the head during the breeding season.

Range: The Great Plains Skink is a wide-ranging species in the Southwest. It is found throughout the southern central Great Plains, from southern Nebraska, southwestern Iowa, and western Missouri, and south through Kansas and central and west Texas. It also occurs throughout the Chihuahuan Desert into the northern Sonoran Desert, ranging west to the Mogollon Plateau of central Arizona. In Mexico, the species occurs from northwestern Sinaloa southeast to central Durango, Nuevo León, and northern Tamaulipas.

Viewing Tips: Great Plains Skinks are among the most secretive of lizards, rarely seen for longer than a flash. They are sometimes found under rocks and logs and in rodent

Juvenile P. obsoletus, *Sierra Anchas, AZ. Juveniles are so different in appearance from adults that they were initially described as a different species.*

Male P. obsoletus.

burrows, but are more often heard than seen as they scurry in bursts through leaf litter. The best tip for viewing this species in the Southwest is to spend a lot of time in mesic habitats, especially during optimal temperature conditions, which often occur in early morning and late afternoon. Look for them along stream corridors where trees and other vegetation provide shade and cover, but use your ears as well as your eyes to detect this cryptic, elusive lizard.

Taxonomy: In part due to the abrupt color-pattern change between younger and older Great Plains Skinks, adults and juveniles were once described as separate species in separate genera. However, the relationship between adults and juveniles was known by 1935, and this species has remained a distinct taxon since. Most literature refers to it in the genus *Eumeces*, a name that was subsequently replaced by an earlier published name, *Plestiodon*.

Subspecies: No subspecies are currently recognized, nor have any been described.

Remarks: The juveniles' bright blue tails and shiny black bodies also make them very distinctive. When they are older, Great Plains Skinks are somewhat aggressive and will bite when handled; in large individuals this bite can be painful, and it is reported that individuals will sometimes retain this trait in captivity. In captivity, skinks readily take crickets and may live up to 8 years or more.

Western Skink

Plestiodon skiltonianus (Baird and Girard, 1852)

Author: Mason J. Ryan

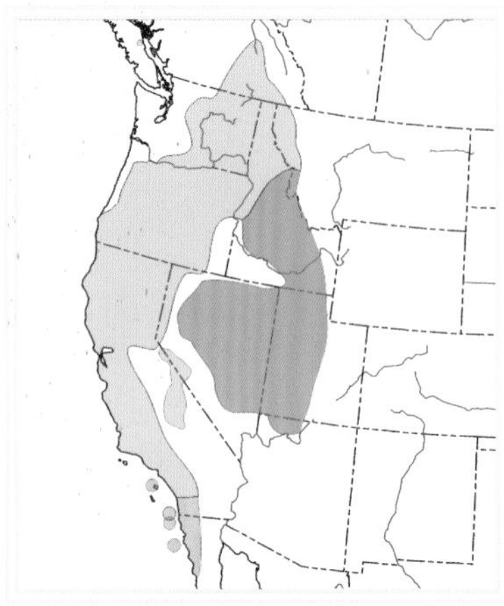

See page 559 for map color codes.

Description: This is a small to medium-sized slim lizard reaching up to 75 mm in SVL. The tail may be up to twice the length of the body. All of the body scales are cycloid, giving the lizard a glossy appearance. The scale rows across the middle of the body range from 24 to 28, but are usually 26. Their limbs are relatively small in relation to their elongate body. Adults of both sexes are similarly colored, with a wide dorsal stripe that is dark brown to reddish brown, bordered by 2 light tan dorsolateral stripes that extend from the snout to the base of the tail. These dorsolateral stripes are about 2 to 3 scales wide. A second, narrower pair of ventrolateral stripes extends from the rear of the mouth to the tail. The tail of adults may be suffused or speckled with blue and brown on a gray ground color. The ventral surface of the throat, chest, hind legs, and tail may be cream to gold, with the belly having a bluish tint. **Sexual Variation:** During the breeding season males develop an orange, yellow, or red coloration on the lower jaw, head, and snout. Otherwise, there is no sexual dimorphism. **Juveniles:** Juvenile Western Skinks have a bright blue tail (usually) that starkly contrasts with the dorsum. As these lizards age the colors fade, including the tail, to the adult coloration.

Similar Species: Gilbert's Skink may closely resemble the Western Skink at some localities, but they can be differentiated by their dorsal patterns and tail color. Adult Western Skinks have more contrasting dorsolateral stripes that extend to the tail, while adult Gilbert's Skinks may be monocolored or at least lack strongly contrasting dorsolateral stripes. The tail of juvenile Western Skinks is bright

Adult P. s. interparietalis, *San Jacinto Mountains, CA.*

Male P. s. skiltonianus, *Greenhorn Mountains, Kern Co., CA, showing the blue tail typical of juveniles (and some populations of adults) and orange labial scales.*

blue in contrast to a pink to salmon-colored tail of southern populations of Gilbert's Skinks. However, juveniles of northern populations of Gilbert's Skinks also have blue tails or blue and red-tinged tails, but the dark stripes extend farther out onto the tail in Western Skinks than in Gilbert's Skinks. Many-lined Skinks are similar to Western Skinks, but have more, narrower stripes.

Habitats: The Western Skink is found in a wide range of habitats west of the Rocky Mountains. It occurs in treeless meadows, grasslands, riparian areas, chaparral, piñon/juniper, juniper/sage woodland, and open pine/oak forests from sea level to 2,400 m above sea level. Because the Western Skink occurs over such a wide geographic area, the habitat used varies geographically. In arid regions east of the Coast Ranges and Sierras, this species is restricted to the more mesic microhabitats. West of the California Coast Ranges and Sierras this species is commonly distributed in coastal sage scrub, woodlands, treeless meadows, wooded streams, and rivers.

Natural History: Western Skinks are secretive and are seldom found on the surface of the ground. They are typically found hidden under rocks, woody debris, leaves, or thick vegetation. The diet includes moths, beetles, crickets, grasshoppers, leafhoppers, and other invertebrates.

Western Skinks have a loose social system wherein males and females live separately, but males may live near a female. Western Skinks are adept burrowers, using their snouts while keeping their limbs to the sides of their bodies, wriggling into soft, friable soils, creating tunnels that may be up to 380 mm long. These tunnels are important to the breeding strategy of this species.

Females lay one clutch of 2–5 eggs per year during May or June. Eggs are laid in a pear-shaped excavation under embedded rocks in loose, friable soil. Females may remain in the nest, guarding the eggs until they hatch, which occurs between July and late August, when juveniles can be found. The females may stay with the hatchlings for a few days in the nest until all of the hatchlings disperse. Female nest-guarding behavior varies from flight to fight. Females that flee from the nest eventually return to tend the remaining eggs and repair any damage that may have occurred. Hatchlings emerge from the eggs at about 24–26 mm SVL and apparently grow rapidly in their first 3 months, reaching sexual maturity at about age 2.

Juvenile P. s. interparietalis, *San Jacinto Mountains, CA.*

When disturbed they are surprisingly quick, scurrying away in dense grass or other cover. Western Skinks move in an undulating manner. To further deter or avoid predators, Western Skinks easily autotomize their tails when caught. The tail may wriggle for several minutes, allowing the skink to escape danger.

Range: The Western Skink ranges from about San Quintín, northwestern Baja California, north to British Columbia, and ranges east from coastal mountains to central Idaho and Utah. It is found throughout much of the Great Basin and just entering northern Arizona. It is apparently absent from the San Joaquin Valley, the central Sierra Nevada, and the lowland deserts of California.

Viewing Tips: The Western Skink can be found under rocks, coarse woody debris, forest clearings and edges, and rocky hillsides. The best way to observe a Western Skink is to search through woodpiles, lift up rocks, or look under debris piles. It is important to remember to place rocks and logs back where you found them, even if you did not find any animal underneath. Good public lands to observe these lizards include Cleveland National Forest (CA), Great Basin National Park (NV), and many other public lands of the West.

Taxonomy: Until recently, this species was generally referred to in the genus *Eumeces*. Current research suggests the currently named subspecies are not aligned genetically. Gilbert's and Western Skinks need taxonomic revision.

Subspecies and Variation: Three subspecies are currently recognized: Coronado Skink (*P. s. interparietalis*), Skilton's Skink (*P. s. skiltonianus*), and Great Basin Skink (*P. s. utahensis*). The subspecies are similar, but one population of putative *P. s. utahensis* has red-tailed juveniles.

Four-lined Skink

Plestiodon tetragrammus (Baird, 1859 "1858")

Author: Lee A. Fitzgerald

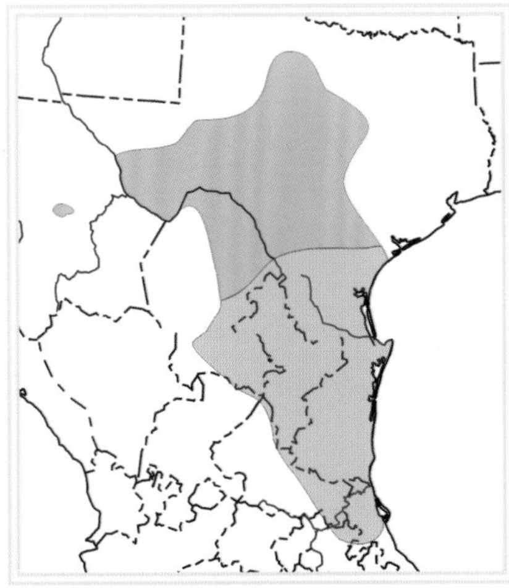

See page 559 for map color codes.

Description: The Four-lined Skink is a medium-sized skink, with adults about 50–60 mm SVL; the maximum size reported was 76 mm. Hatchlings are 25–26 mm SVL. These are smooth and shiny lizards, similar in body form to all other North American skinks. The Four-lined Skink is characterized by 4 light stripes on the sides that terminate in the groin; however, there is substantial individual variation, and the subspecies (described below) differ in the pattern of stripes. A broad black band runs between the stripes along the flanks. The dorsum is dark gray or gray-brown, tending to be lighter with age. As in all North American skinks, the scales are small and smooth. In this species scales are arranged in 26 or 28 rows around the body, 53–59 scales from the interparietal to the base of the tail, with 7 upper labials. **Sexual Variation:** This species is not sexually

Male P. t. brevilineatus, *showing bright orange lips of males, Val Verde Co., TX.*

dimorphic, except that males may have brilliant orange coloration on the upper and lower lips and along the lateral part of the throat. **Juveniles:** Young have bright blue tails, are black, and may have orange lines on the head and neck. A pair of lines is present on the head in juveniles, but disappears in juveniles and adults.

Similar Species: Great Plains Skinks are larger and do not have distinct stripes. Little Brown Skinks are small, slender, and brown. Southern Prairie Skinks (*P. septentrionalis obtusirostris*) are sympatric with Four-lined Skinks in south-central Texas, outside the range of this book. Southern Prairie Skinks have middorsal stripes and a dark lateral stripe that is not more than 2 scales wide.

Habitats: These skinks occupy many habitats, including grasslands, thorn scrub, pine-oak woodlands, and forests along creeks and rivers from sea level up to 2,300 m elevation. They tend to be found in relatively moist, sheltered microhabitats with leaf litter and debris. They can be found under almost any sort of cover, including the base of clump grass or under bark, debris, or rocks.

Natural History: Four-lined Skinks are diurnal, active foragers that prey on a variety of small arthropods such as spiders, ants, beetles, grasshoppers, and crickets. These are secretive skinks that bask early in the morning near refugia, but largely remain hidden in burrows and shady spots. Breeding occurs from spring to late summer, and females lay from 3 to 12 eggs. Hatchlings are 25–26 mm SVL and appear from mid-July through August. As is common in other scincids, embryos undergo some development inside the female before shell deposition and egg laying. Females have been observed guarding their eggs, which are laid in a depression in the female's refuge. Females breed only once in a season and may not reproduce every year.

Juvenile P. t. brevilineatus, *Kimble Co., TX.*

Range: Four-lined Skinks are found from north-central Texas throughout the Trans-Pecos and south Texas, and in Mexico through Tamaulipas to northern Veracruz and eastern San Luis Potosí. Disjunct populations are known from Cuatro Cienegas, Coahuila, and Sierra del Nido, Chihuahua.

Female P. t. brevilineatus, *Crocket Co., TX.*

Viewing Tips: These secretive lizards are most easily observed by turning rocks, logs, and debris, then carefully replacing the cover objects. They may sometimes be observed basking outside refugia in morning hours. Within this region, Big Bend National Park may be the only public land where these animals may be observed; they have not been recorded in Big Bend Ranch State Park, but probably occur there. Note that it is illegal to look under surface objects in national parks, so try to find them when they are outside their refugia or when they are surface-active after summer rains. At Big Bend National Park, they are best known from the Chisos Mountains.

Taxonomy: The Four-lined Skink has been recognized as a species since its original description in 1859. The epithets for the species and subspecies, *tetragrammus* and *brevilineatus*, refer to the characteristics of possessing 4 lines or short lines. Taxonomic issues have pertained to whether disjunct geographic populations of Four-lined Skinks may be valid species or subspecies. The Mountain Skink was considered a subspecies until fairly recently. Based on broad consensus among herpetologists, it is treated as a valid species in this volume. Four-lined Skinks belong to a natural group of related North American and eastern Asian skinks, along with the Florida Sand Skink (*P. reynoldsi*), which recently was designated to the genus *Plestiodon*. According to a recent analysis relying on genetic data, *Plestiodon* is the sister group to all remaining skinks, including 2 other groups of "*Eumeces*" in North Africa and southwest Asia, and Mexico and Central America, respectively.

Subspecies and Variation: Two subspecies of the Four-lined Skink are currently recognized: the Short-lined Skink (*P. t. brevilineatus*) and the Long-lined Skink (*P. t. tetragrammus*). In the former, the light stripes end at the tail, whereas in the nominal subspecies stripes continue to the base of the hindlimbs. The 2 subspecies come into contact and populations intergrade in southern Texas and Coahuila, Mexico. The Short-lined Skink occurs outside the range of this book, in central and southwest Texas, northern Coahuila and northern Nuevo León, and the Sierra del Nido, Chihuahua.

Little Brown Skink

Scincella lateralis (Say in James, 1823)

Author: Matthew A. Kwiatkowski

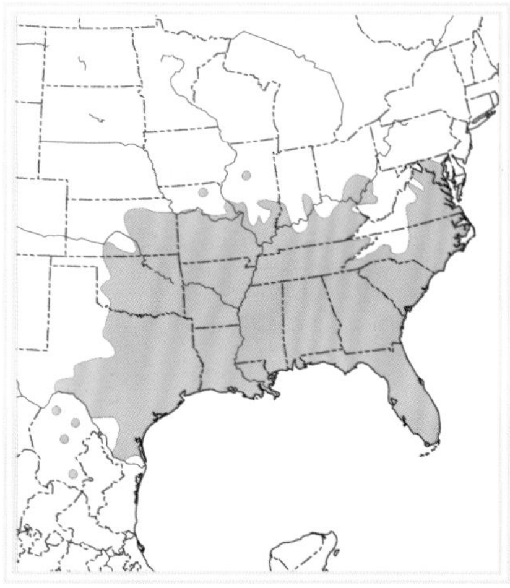

See page 559 for map color codes.

Description: This is a small skink with a maximum SVL of 57 mm and TL ranging from 75 to 146 mm. Little Brown Skinks are slender, with small limbs and relatively long tails that can be over twice the length of the body. Individuals have smooth scales and may have a shiny appearance. Dorsal coloration is typically darker than lateral coloration, ranging from tan or gold to dark brown. Dorsolateral stripes divide the dorsal and lateral colors, extending from the snout, through the eye, to the tail. These stripes are typically darker than even the dorsal coloration. However, coloration can vary considerably among populations, with some individuals appearing uniformly dark. The ventral surface is light and has few to no markings. The lower eyelid has a transparent membrane that may allow the lizard to see when the eye is closed. **Sexual Variation:** Males and females are not sexually dimorphic. **Juveniles:** The young look similar to adults and are approximately 44 mm at hatching.

Similar Species: Few species can be confused with Little Brown Skinks. Only other skinks will have smooth scales that have a shiny appearance. Two skinks overlap with the western range of Little Brown Skinks: the Great Plains Skink and the Four-lined Skink. Both of these species are larger than Ground Skinks, with heavier bodies and shorter tails relative to their body lengths. Juvenile Great Plains Skinks and Four-lined Skinks are similar to Little Brown Skinks in size, and young Four-lined Skinks can be boldly striped, but their jet-black bodies and blue-purple tails make them easily distinguishable from Little Brown Skinks. East of the range in our book, this species is sympatric with a number of other skink species, but none are as diminutive or have the same color pattern.

Adult S. lateralis, *College Station, Brazos Co., TX.*

Habitats: Little Brown Skinks are found primarily in moist or humid woodland leaf litter (especially oak), although a variety of other habitats may also be used. Occasionally they can be found in more open grassy hammocks. They are chiefly terrestrial and rarely climb on rocks or vegetation. They are typically encountered skittering through leaf litter and soil. Ground Skinks are apparently tolerant of human disturbance and are often found in gardens and neighborhood parks.

Natural History: The Little Brown Skink is a diurnal, active forager. Its long body and small limbs give it a snake-like appearance as it moves quickly through forest leaf litter. It feeds on a variety of small invertebrates, including small beetles, flies, and spiders. Behavioral studies suggest that Little Brown Skinks are quite aggressive toward each other when competing for food. They are prey for a wide diversity of predators including various snakes, other lizards, Domestic Cats, Eastern Bluebirds, and Nine-banded Armadillos. I have witnessed a large wolf spider preying on a moderately sized Little Brown Skink. Individuals may enter water to escape predators. Breeding occurs between January and August, and they may lay as many as 5 clutches in one year. However, in western populations, breeding is likely limited to spring and early summer months. Clutch sizes range from 1 to 7 eggs. Females in some eastern populations nest communally, with 66 eggs deposited at one site. Unlike some other skinks, female Little Brown Skinks do not tend to the nest after depositing eggs. Very little is known about population demographics in the West. In the East, population density can vary considerably, with typical estimates between 30 and 60 individuals/ha (although a

Adult S. lateralis, *Guadalupe Co., TX.*

Florida estimate was as high as 560/ha). Population densities in the West are likely considerably lower than in the East. Male home ranges are typically larger than those of females, with one study finding home range averages of 52 m^2 and 14 m^2 for males and females, respectively.

Range: Little Brown Skinks are found throughout the southeastern U.S. Their northern range extends from southern New Jersey westward through southern Ohio, Indiana, Illinois, and most of Missouri. Their western range extends from eastern Kansas south through most of Oklahoma and across central Texas. The westernmost part of their range is in south-central Texas, in Crockett and Val Verde counties. Specimens are also known from 2 localities in Coahuila, Mexico.

Viewing Tips: Little Brown Skinks are mainly associated with oak woodland leaf litter. Although this species is fairly secretive, they are commonly seen flitting among leaves and may be caught by quickly, yet gently, grabbing a handful of leaf litter. In the West, they can be found along canyon bottoms and on slopes above waterways. Places to look include areas along the Pecos River and its tributaries, such as Independence Creek. Public land in the western range of this species is sparse, so look along waterways where they are crossed by roads, or else seek permission of land owners before searching.

Taxonomy: Little Brown Skinks represent the only species in the genus *Scincella* found in North America. Species diversity in this genus is highest in Asia, and phylogenetic studies suggest that ancestors of *Scincella lateralis* migrated across Beringia (the Pleistocene land bridge that is now the Bering Strait) from Asia to North America. Recent genetic study suggests that Little Brown Skinks are more closely related to New World members of another genus, *Sphenomorphus*, than to Asian *Scincella*. Because these 2 New World species appear to be more closely related to Asian *Scincella* rather than Asian *Sphenomorphus*, it has been recommended that neotropical skinks in the genus *Sphenomorphus* be reassigned to the genus *Scincella*.

Subspecies and Variation: Most variation found in Ground Skinks is related to the darkness of the dorsum, ranging from a dark chocolate brown to a golden color.

Remarks: While Little Brown Skink ecology in the eastern part of the species' range is relatively well studied, little is known about western populations. These populations experience a xeric environment that is very different from the humid, moist forests that most populations experience. Hence, any study or observations of this species in the western part of its range would be quite informative.

Adult S. lateralis, *Neuces Canyon, Edwards Co., TX.*

FAMILY ANGUIDAE:
Alligator and Legless Lizards

Author: Daniel D. Beck

Anguidae is an ancient and widespread lizard family that originated in Laurasia, the supercontinent in the Triassic, over 100 million years ago. Today 4 subfamilies (15 genera; just over 100 species) are distributed in tropical and temperate regions in Europe, Asia, southeast Asia, the Caribbean, South America, Central America, and North America.

Anguids are members of Scleroglossa (meaning "hard tongue"), a major branch of the lizard/snake evolutionary tree that uses the jaws, rather than the tongue, to draw food into the mouth, freeing the tongue to be used as a powerful chemosensory organ. The slightly forked tongues of anguid lizards are important chemical detectors used in searching for food, refuges, and mates. Anguid lizards (along with the Helodermatidae and 3 other lizard families outside our range of coverage) are also members of the Anguimorpha, a lizard group (including the Old World monitor lizards) herpetologists believe to be most closely allied to the snakes. In fact, anguimorph lizards share a more recent common ancestor with snakes than they do with many other lizards, such as the familiar iguanas, chuckwallas, and horned lizards.

Our region of coverage harbors 2 Anguidae subfamilies: alligator lizards (Gerhonontinae) and legless lizards (Anniellinae). Anniellines comprise but one genus, *Anniella*, with 2 species: the California Legless Lizard and the Baja California Legless Lizard. These snakelike lizards spend much of their lives underground in sand or loose soil, where they seem to "swim" through the soil. Legless lizards have several traits that aid in burrowing, including smooth, cycloid scales, a countersunk lower jaw, and a shovel-shaped snout. They have small eyes with movable lids, but no external ear openings. Adults are about the diameter of a pencil, with a body length up to 17.8 cm. Legless lizards are viviparous, giving birth to 1–4 young in late summer or early autumn. The species within our range of coverage, the California Legless Lizard (*A. pulchra*), lives in loose soil along beaches, chaparral, pine-oak woodlands, and canyons from central to southern California. In some habitats in southern California, they may be common in litter under juniper trees, where they likely feed on termites.

Alligator lizards (Gerhonontinae) have short limbs and slim bodies covered with large scales that only barely overlap one another. Adults range in body length from 70 mm (*Elgaria coerulea*) to 178 mm (*E. multicarinata*) up to 500 mm TL (*Gerrhonotus infernalis*). The squarish dorsal and ventral scales are underlain with osteoderms, which provide a stiff, protective coat of body armor. An alligator lizard in hand can be readily identified by the distinctive fold on the sides of its body. This ventrolateral fold provides a line of elasticity between back and belly that allows the armored bodies of alligator lizards to expand for breathing, and for food, eggs, or developing young.

If you travel along southern California's Ventura Highway, it is unlikely that you'll see "alligator lizards in the air" (alligator lizards were thus referred to in the 1970s song lyrics for "Ventura Highway," by the band America), but if you follow that road off the beaten path you might find these beautiful, fierce lizards shuffling about in open forest, woodland, and chaparral habitats, or hiding under rocks, logs, boards, trash, and other surface cover. Alligator lizards have impressed humans long before pop music took notice of them. The famous lizard motif of Mimbres pottery shows a lizard likely inspired by that ancient culture's contact with both alligator lizards and Gila Monsters in their native southwestern New Mexico.

Alligator lizards generally occur in moist microenvironments in foothills and mountains, but also frequent arid lowland canyons and springs. The species included in this guide are found from southern British Columbia south through Washington, Oregon, California, southeastern Arizona, southwestern New Mexico, and (for *Gerrhonotus*) in a band from central Texas to the Big Bend area. Alligator lizards may be active by day or night, depending on temperature and season. Their cryptic, copper patterns, laced with various ground hues, blend well with their forest, chaparral, grassland, and desert habitats. Seldom conspicuous, alligator lizards are often encountered scurrying over rocks and through leaf litter, grasses, and forest openings where they often seek cover among woody debris, rocks, or vegetation. They commonly occur in

Baja California Legless Lizard, Anniella geronimensis.

urban areas in southern California, providing the casual lizard observer an opportunity to watch these lizards in their own backyard. When handled, alligator lizards may bite as tenaciously as a Gila Monster (although they are *not* venomous), and may squirm vigorously in attempts to smear feces on their captors. Their long, fragile tail may break off easily, and it seldom grows back to its original length. Good swimmers, some species may flee to water to escape a predator.

Males have wider, more triangular heads than females, a trait that may be related to male-to-male combat. In some populations of the Northern Alligator Lizard, females grow to be larger than males. Most alligator lizards lay eggs, but the Northern Alligator Lizard (along with the California Legless Lizard) is a live-bearer. Alligator lizards are ferocious, widely roaming predators of arthropods, centipedes, spiders, lizards, and small mammals. Some species may even climb into trees and feed on bird eggs and young.

Alligator lizards and the California Legless Lizard select a broad range of body temperatures during activity (between approximately 24 and 33°C), and their thermal preference tends to be lower than many other southwestern lizards. This affords them the option to be active during warm rainy periods and at cooler nighttime temperatures during the summer. The highest temperatures tolerated by alligator lizards (around 39°C) are within the range of body temperature that most heliothermic lizards would find optimal.

Interestingly, alligator lizards have become a model creature for physiologists and engineers investigating the functioning of tiny hair cells within the inner ear. This research has led directly to a better understanding of the mechanism of hearing, and to the development of hearing aids. Alligator lizards provide yet another reminder of the value of biodiversity. Without them not only would we be deprived of the beauty and wonder that has inspired art and song, but we would know less about the workings of our inner ears. Ironic for an iconic pop-song lizard?

Elgaria panamintina, *Inyo Co., CA.*

California Legless Lizard

Anniella pulchra Gray, 1852

Author: Gary M. Fellers

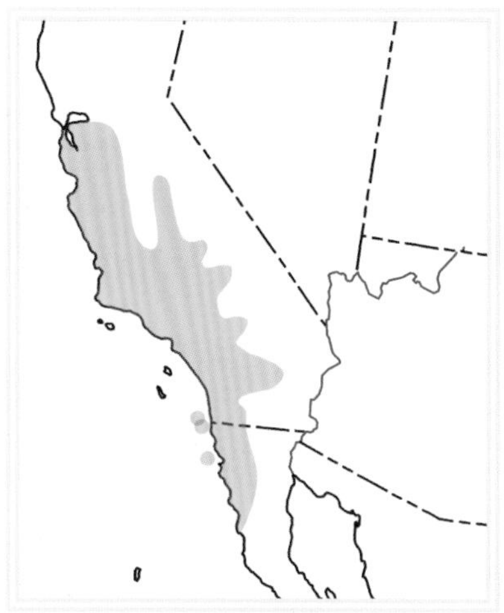

See page 559 for map color codes.

Description: This is a small, slender lizard that reaches 90–180 mm SVL. There are vestigial pectoral and pelvic girdles internally, but no visible fore or hind limbs. Legless lizards lack external ear openings. The eyes are small and deep set, but they have lower eyelids that can be seen in good light. When the mouth is closed, the lower jaw is covered by the rostral and labial scales. This countersunk arrangement helps keep sand or debris from entering the mouth while burrowing. Body scales are small and have a shiny, highly polished look. Body color varies geographically. Throughout most of the range, the body is silver, beige, or gray, with a dark middorsal stripe and several less-well-defined lateral stripes. In some coastal areas, the body is black or dark brown. Ventral color ranges from pale to bright yellow. When a lizard is about to shed, the skin becomes light blue-green and will remain that color for several days. **Sexual Variation:** The sexes are not distinguishable externally. **Juveniles:** Juvenile California Legless Lizards are born with a distinct dorsal stripe, silvery upper parts, dark lateral stripe, and flesh-colored venter, through which the internal organs can be seen. In areas where adults are dark, juveniles acquire the dark coloration as they mature.

Adult A. pulchra, *Monterey Co., CA. The dark phase from Monterey Bay is sometimes considered a distinct subspecies,* A. p. nigra.

Similar Species: There are no other legless lizards in the southwestern U.S. California Legless Lizards are most likely to be confused with a snake, but snakes do not have eyelids. There are no snakes within the range of this lizard with a similar color pattern.

Habitats: California Legless Lizards are fossorial and need substrates that are porous and loosely packed. They are usually found in sand or sandy-loam soils, sometimes with gravel, stones, or boulders mixed with finer soils. There is often a layer of leaf litter. This combination of habitat requirements is found in sand dunes, chaparral, pine and oak woodlands, and riparian areas with cottonwood and sycamore. Lizards are typically within 25 cm of the surface, but they have been reported up to 1.5 m underground. Densities of 2,200 lizards per hectare have been reported near Moss Landing. Elevationally, the lizard occurs from sea level to 1,800 m in the Sierra Nevada foothills.

Natural History: California Legless Lizards are viviparous and give birth to 1–4 live young between September and November. The young are 45–75 mm SVL at birth. Lizards mature in 2–3 years, with males becoming sexually mature at a smaller size than females: 90 vs. 120 mm SVL. Legless lizards are normally subterranean and are known to bask in warm sand during the day. They are active primarily in the morning and evening. California Legless Lizards do not avoid moderate levels of light, but activity is strongly influenced by temperature. Preferred temperatures range from 20 to 25°C; higher temperatures are preferred when there is more soil moisture. Below 13°C, lizards become inactive, though they can tolerate temperatures down to at least 3°C. Temperatures above 34°C are lethal. California Legless Lizards primarily use their senses of smell and touch. Hearing has shifted from detecting air-borne sounds to detecting vibrations through the substrate. These vibrations are conducted to sensory organs through bones in the head. California Legless Lizards feed predominantly on beetles, larval moths, spiders, and termites. Legless lizards have an unusually low metabolic rate that is not strongly influenced by ambient temperature. California Legless Lizards readily lose their tails, though they can be regenerated. The percentage of lizards with regenerating tails in a population is often 60–70%.

Range: California Legless Lizards range from the edge of the San Joaquin River at Antioch, California, south to the northern portions of Baja California, Mexico, in the vicinity of Colonia Guerrero. The lizard occupies the Coast Range south of San Francisco, the Transverse and Peninsular Ranges farther south, and the southwestern part of the Sierra Nevada. California Legless Lizards are found on the floor of the San Joaquin Valley and in parts of the Mojave Desert, but increasing agricultural and mining activities have greatly reduced or eliminated populations in many of these areas.

Viewing Tips: This lizard is not normally seen on the surface of the ground, though it has been found on roads and road shoulders on occasion. California Legless Lizards can be found at the State Vehicular Recreation Areas at Hunter Valley (Los Angeles

Adult A. pulchra, *silvery color phase, shown here with Mediterranean Ice Plant, which is a non-native decorative plant that threatens coastal habitats.*

and Ventura counties) and Hollister Hills (San Benito County). This lizard can also be found along tributaries to the Salinas River in Los Padres National Forest.

Taxonomy: Two subspecies of California Legless Lizards have been described. Black Legless Lizards (*Anniella p. nigra*) are found in the vicinity of Monterey Bay, and lizards throughout the rest of the range are referred to as Silvery Legless Lizards (*Anniella p. pulchra*). These subspecies are not supported by recent genetic work (see below).

Subspecies and Variation: Lizards in the vicinity of Monterey Bay (Seaside, Fort Ord, Spanish Bay) are jet black or dark brown. Lizards in the vicinity of Morro Bay and south to the Santa Maria River mouth are nearly as dark, but have never been included in the *nigra* subspecies. Recent genetic work shows that the Monterey and Morro Bay populations evolved independently, though neither population is sufficiently unique to be recognized as a distinct taxon.

Remarks: California Legless Lizards move by body undulation. There are no scutes to aid in gripping the substrate. If there is a solid object available, the lizard will push against it; the point of contact then shifts along the body as the lizard travels forward. On smooth sand, lateral movements of the body generate small ridges that are then used as traction points. When burrowing in sand, a 200-mm-long lizard can disappear in 6 seconds. Observations of captive lizards indicate that the eyes are closed when the lizards move in dry, unconsolidated soils, but in open burrows in damp sand, they are open.

Northern Alligator Lizard

Elgaria coerulea (Wiegmann, 1828)

Author: Daniel D. Beck

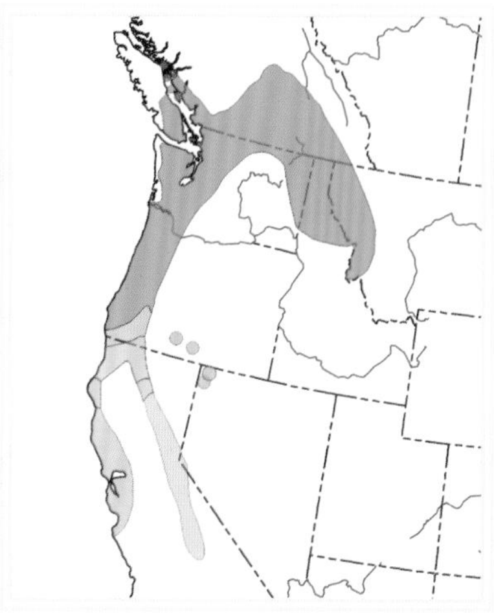

See page 559 for map color codes.

Description: The Northern Alligator Lizard ranges in body size from 70 to 136 mm SVL, although individuals over 120 mm are rare. It has large, squarish scales, a slender body with short limbs, and a distinctive band of small granular scales (the lateral fold) along the sides of its body. The long, easily broken tail regenerates to only a portion of its original size. The color is brown, rust, gray, olive, or blue above, with dark blotches or irregular crossbands edged with white spots. Northern Alligator Lizards occasionally have no pattern, faint dark markings, or a broad stripe on the back. Belly scales are usually dark along the lateral edges, giving the appearance of faint dark lines running between ventral scale rows. The eyes are dark around the pupils and the head is often darkly mottled. **Sexual Variation:** Males have a broader, more triangular head than females. **Juveniles:** Young usually have few dark markings and can have a brownish or copper stripe on the back.

Juvenile E. c. shastensis *(or intergrade), Crescent City, Del Norte Co., CA.*

Adult E. c. palmeri, *Butte Co., CA.*

Similar Species: The distinct lateral folds on the sides of the trunk distinguish alligator lizards from other superficially similar lizards, like skinks (genus *Plestiodon*) and spiny lizards (genus *Sceloporus*). The Northern Alligator Lizard differs from the Southern Alligator Lizard, with which it shares nearly half its range, by being smaller, having brown eyes (rather than yellow), and dark lines along the lateral edges of its ventral scales.

Habitats: *Elgaria coerulea* prefers moister, cooler microhabitats than the Southern Alligator Lizard, but still frequents sunny, open environments chiefly in forests, forest clearings, and woodlands, and also sagebrush habitats, grassland, chaparral, coastal dunes, and marshes. In the northern part of its range, it shows great site fidelity and little movement between summer microhabitats and winter brumation sites. Some form of cover is very important for these fairly secretive lizards, which are often found hiding under rocks, logs, bark, boards, driftwood, trash, or other surface objects. They are found from sea level in coastal habitats up to 3,200 m in montane coniferous forests.

Natural History: The Northern Alligator Lizard is a ferocious little predator that moves with a snake-like undulating motion and feeds on insects and other small invertebrates including slugs, ticks, spiders, centipedes, millipedes, snails, and worms. Because they are active at cooler temperatures than many other lizards, Northern Alligator Lizards may swim in cool streams and forage on rainy nights. Northern Alligator

Male E. c. shastensis, *Lockerman Canyon, Plumas Co., CA.*

Lizards do not lay eggs. The young are born live, having been carried within the female until they are fully developed. By retaining the embryos in this way, female Northern Alligator Lizards are better able to regulate temperature during gestation and thereby enhance the likelihood of successfully producing a brood in the cooler, thermally constrained environments inhabited by this species. Mating, which may last several hours, occurs from April to June and usually involves the male biting and holding the head or neck of the female or grasping her with his prehensile tail. Females produce one litter per year of 3–8 offspring, depending on locality. Young are born between July and early September, after a gestation period of about 3 months. Females become sexually mature by 32–44 months in northern California. In northern populations, females older than 3 years may be larger than males, a possible result of natural selection for larger body size. The skin is shed, unlike for most lizards, in a single piece. They are commonly parasitized by ticks, which may attach to the neck or lateral fold.

Range: *Elgaria coerulea* ranges from southern British Columbia south through the Cascade Mountains and Coast Ranges to northern Monterey County, California, east into northern Idaho and northwestern Montana, and south through the Sierra Nevada Mountains to Kern County, California. Isolated populations are found in southeastern Oregon, northwestern Nevada, and northeastern California.

Viewing Tips: The best way to find Northern Alligator Lizards is to watch (and listen in dry understory litter) for their snake-like, undulating motion as they move through openings and rocky areas in forests, woodlands, and other suitable habitats described above. Individuals may often be found by carefully turning (and replacing) cover objects, such as bark, logs, stones, and boards, especially after spring and summer rains. Forest and woodland habitats at moderate elevations in the Sierra Nevada and

Cascade Mountains, as well as coastal dune and scrub habitats of northern California and Oregon, all provide fruitful opportunities for finding *E. coerulea.*

Taxonomy: This species was formerly placed in the genus *Gerrhonotus,* as *Gerrhonotus coeruleus.*

Subspecies and Variation: Four subspecies are recognized. The Northwestern Alligator Lizard (*E. c. principis*) is the smallest and most widespread. It usually has a broad stripe of tan, olive, golden brown, or grayish down the back, with or without spots. Its dorsal scales are in 14 rows, and weakly keeled. Temporal scales are also weakly keeled. The Shasta Alligator Lizard (*E. c. shastensis*) is the most variable of the 4 subspecies. It has 16 rows of dorsal scales, smooth temporal scales, and a variety of color morphs. The young are crossbanded. The Sierra Alligator Lizard (*E. c. palmeri*) has dorsal scales in 16 rows and keeled temporal scales. Its markings may be absent or confined to the sides, or extend across the back. The San Francisco Alligator Lizard (*E. c. coerulea*) resembles the Northwestern Alligator Lizard except that it has heavily keeled scales on its back and sides and dark blotches, or irregular crossbands, on its back. Intergrades occur in areas of contact between subspecies.

Remarks: When captured, these lizards will not hesitate to bite and hang on. When they eat they occasionally grasp their prey and spin the body along the long axis. Such behavior—along with their relatively large heads, powerful jaws, elongated bodies, and large bony scales—most likely give these fierce lizards their common name. Some individuals of *E. c. shastensis* have no faint dark lines on the abdomen, making them a little more difficult to distinguish from *E. multicarinata.*

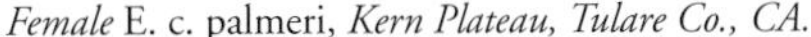

Female E. c. palmeri, *Kern Plateau, Tulare Co., CA.*

Madrean Alligator Lizard

Elgaria kingii Gray, 1838

Author: Thomas C. Brennan

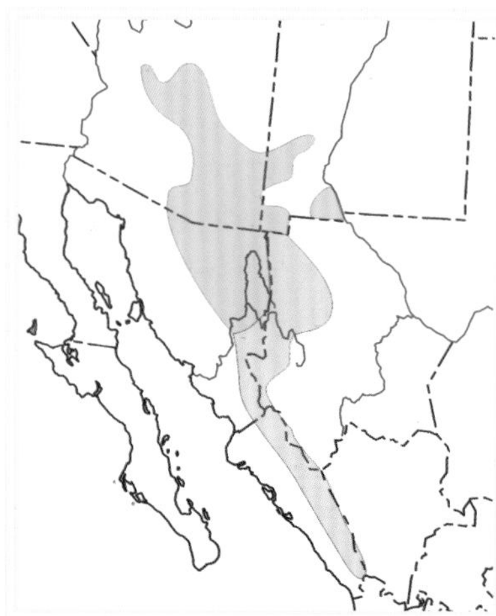

See page 559 for map color codes.

Description: This is a slender lizard with an extremely elongated body, diminutive limbs, and a long tail. It reaches a maximum SVL of 140 mm. The unregenerated tail is more than twice the length of the body. The head is somewhat flattened, and the dorsal and ventral surfaces are armored with large, rectangular, bone-reinforced scales. Most of its scales are smooth and shiny, but the 6–8 middorsal rows are mildly keeled. The ventral scales are larger and more plate-like than the dorsal scales. A lateral fold covered by small granular scales extends along each lower side of the body from behind the ear to the groin. This fold presumably allows the body to expand for breathing, ingesting large meals, and oogenesis. Base coloration is olive-gray, gray-brown, beige, or tan. There are usually 9 or 10 (range 8–15) dark reddish-brown or olive-brown bands on the body, and more than 20 on the tail. Regenerated portions of the tail lack bands. Each side of the face is usually marked with 3–5 distinct, black-edged white spots. The lateral fold is dull gray and is often overlaid with small black and white markings. The underside is cream or pale gray with dark gray or black spots that are often arranged in longitudinal rows. **Sexual Variation:** Males are more heavy-bodied than females, have a broad temporal region, and are boldly patterned, usually with a crisp dark line running along the posterior margin of each dorsal band. Females are slender and have an overall less distinct pattern. **Juveniles:** Young Madrean Alligator Lizards are boldly patterned with crisp black or dark brown bands, dark limbs, dark lateral surfaces, and plain olive-tan coloration on the top of the head.

Similar Species: Skinks (*Plestiodon*) lack a lateral fold and have smooth middorsal scales.

Habitats: This species occurs in montane conifer forests, woodlands, riparian corridors, grasslands, semi-desert grasslands, and desert scrub communities within the

Adult E. kingii, *Black River, Apache Co., AZ.*

Mogollon Rim, Apachean, and Chihuahuan ecoregions. It inhabits a variety of terrain types, including steep rocky canyons, talus, open forest, grassy flatlands, and low valleys, at elevations ranging from approximately 1,150 m to 2,675 m. Conspicuous plants in suitable habitat can include junipers, oaks, Ponderosa Pine, Arizona Sycamore, willows, grasses, and, in some localities, Creosote Bush. It is most frequently encountered in moist areas with abundant surface cover such as pine needles, leaf litter, dead Sotol and yuccas, rock piles, and fallen wood.

Natural History: This secretive terrestrial lizard emerges from brumation in April and remains active through November. Although it is primarily diurnal, it often prowls well into the evening during the warm summer months. As it forages and explores its environment, it flicks its tongue in and out to pick up chemical information. Its unusual method of locomotion involves bending from side-to-side in a way that sends a traveling "wave" down the long and slender body from head to pelvic girdle. This traveling wave may contribute propulsive force and increase stride length. When moving through surface debris it often folds its legs against the body and crawls in a serpentine fashion.

Known predators include the Ring-necked Snake and Striped Whipsnake. It is likely in the diet of raptors and a variety of mammals as well. When pursued it quickly slithers under and through surface cover and can be quite difficult to focus on and capture. The long tail is easily lost but will regenerate. In response to being seized by a Striped Whipsnake this lizard was observed to bite and hold the base of its own tail. In this looped posture the lizard would be difficult for a snake to swallow. If the snake were to "walk" its mouth around the loop in an effort to swallow the lizard, the snake would likely end up ingesting only a shed lizard-tail. The Madrean Alligator Lizard feeds on insects including crickets, grasshoppers, caterpillars, and moths. It also preys on scorpions and likely takes a variety of other invertebrates.

Mating takes place in late summer and early autumn. Females apparently store sperm and delay embryonic development until the following spring. Eggs in the oviduct are present in April and May, and oviposition occurs in June and July. Clutch sizes of 9, 12, and 15 eggs have been recorded, and evidence suggests that parents stay with the eggs to guard them. Emerging hatchlings have been observed in August in New Mexico. Lifespan in captivity exceeds 15 years.

Range: The Madrean Alligator Lizard ranges from central Arizona and western New Mexico, south along the Sierra Madre Occidental to Jalisco, Mexico. In our area it occurs throughout the Mogollon Rim country of central Arizona and western New Mexico, and the sky islands and valleys of southeastern Arizona and southwestern New Mexico.

Viewing Tips: A considerable effort is often required to find this relatively secretive lizard. Walk through suitable habitat during the day or evening searching under (and replacing) surface cover such as fallen logs, woodpiles, and dead plants. It is often heard

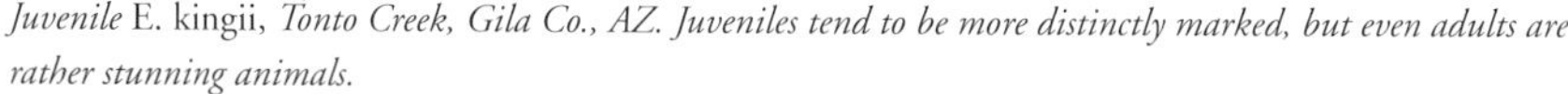

Juvenile E. kingii, *Tonto Creek, Gila Co., AZ. Juveniles tend to be more distinctly marked, but even adults are rather stunning animals.*

Adult E. kingii, *Dragoon Mountains, Cochise Co., AZ. The light and dark labial markings are clearly seen in this photograph.*

before it is seen, so listen for rustling in the leaf litter. Good places to search for this lizard include Chiricahua National Monument (AZ), Tonto Natural Bridge State Park (AZ), and Gila Cliff Dwellings National Monument (NM).

Taxonomy: In much of the older literature this lizard is referred to as *Gerrhonotus kingii.*

Subspecies and Variation: The species description is based on a specimen from the Huachuca Mountains, Arizona. Three subspecies have been recognized (*E. k. ferrea, E. k. kingii,* and *E. k. nobilis*). Only the Arizona Alligator Lizard (*E. k. nobilis*) occurs in our area. A nearly patternless female was collected in Grant County, New Mexico. The specimen was plain olive-gray with the typical black and white markings on the labials and sporadic black flecking on the lateral surfaces.

Southern Alligator Lizard

Elgaria multicarinata (Blainville, 1835)

Author: Daniel D. Beck

See page 559 for map color codes.

Description: The Southern Alligator Lizard ranges in body size from 73 to 178 mm SVL. It has large, square scales, a slender body with short limbs, and a distinctive lateral fold along the sides of its body. The long, semi-prehensile tail can reach twice the length of the body and, if broken, will regenerate to only a portion of its original size. Dorsal and limb scales are strongly keeled. Well-defined, regular dark crossbands usually occur on the back and tail. The sides have black or dusky wavy bars, which are usually spotted white. Background coloration is mostly brown, gray, reddish, or yellowish dorsally. Ventral scales have light lines along their lateral edges, which may give the appearance of a dark lengthwise stripe or dashed line running down the middle of ventral scale rows, but sometimes the venter is unmarked. The eyes are pale yellow, and the head is either unmarked or spotted with black. **Sexual**

Adult E. m. webbii, *Tulare Co., CA.*

Adult E. m. multicarinata, *Point Mugu State Park, Santa Monica Mountains, Ventura Co., CA.*

Variation: Males have a broader, more triangular head than females. **Juveniles:** They lack the dark dorsal crossbars and often have a wide dorsal stripe of tan, reddish, beige, or gray extending onto the tail, with barred sides as in adults.

Similar Species: The distinct lateral folds on the sides of the trunk distinguish alligator lizards from other superficially similar lizards, such as skinks (genus *Plestiodon*) and spiny lizards (genus *Sceloporus*). The Southern Alligator Lizard differs from the Northern Alligator Lizard, with which it shares nearly half its range, by being larger, having yellow eyes (rather than brown), and light lines along the lateral edges of its ventral scales.

Habitats: Southern Alligator Lizards frequent a diversity of habitats including grassland, chaparral, oak woodland, and open pine forest. In drier regions, they most often occur along streams or in other moist, vegetated areas. Microhabitats include logs, thickets, rocks, and old woodpiles and trash heaps around houses. They sometimes climb into bushes and trees. Egg-laying sites include burrows or stable talus. They are found from sea level to 1,524 m.

Natural History: Southern Alligator Lizards have variable body temperatures during activity (with an average only around 21°C), which may allow them to be active earlier and later in the day than most lizards. Activity generally decreases during the hottest periods of summer, although Southern Alligator Lizards are occasionally encountered abroad on warm summer nights. In cooler areas, activity shuts down during the winter, but elsewhere individuals may be active all winter long. Compared to other lizards, *E. multicarinata* also have very low metabolic rates, and consequently use energy slowly. They feed on slugs, insects, centipedes, scorpions, spiders (including Black Widows), lizards, and small mammals. A ferocious predator, *E. multicarinata* may climb into shrubs and trees in search of prey and may even feed on eggs and young of birds. Some individuals appear to rely predominantly on ambush foraging, whereas others may spend more time searching for prey. Southern Alligator Lizards lay 1–3 clutches of eggs (5–20 eggs per clutch) from May to July. Eggs hatch in late summer and early fall after an incubation period of about 55 days. Males occasionally fight with one another, possibly for access to females and breeding opportunities. The larger, more triangular head of males may be related to these male-to-male agonistic behaviors. When broken, the long tail of *E. multicarinata* will writhe on the ground, distracting a potential predator long enough for the lizard to escape. Southern Alligator Lizards are also good swimmers and may sometimes escape a threat by diving into the water and swimming away. Significant predators include snakes (racers, rattlesnakes, garter-snakes), birds (Loggerhead Shrikes, Red-tailed Hawks), and Domestic Cats.

Range: *Elgaria multicarinata* ranges from south-central Washington westward into Oregon and California mostly west of the Cascade and Sierra Nevada mountains, southward through much of California (including some of the Channel Islands), into

Juvenile E. m. webbii, *La Mesa, San Diego Co., CA. This individual does not show a distinct dorsal stripe, as many juveniles do.*

northwestern Baja California. It has been introduced into Las Vegas, where it is apparently common on some casino properties.

Male E. m. multicarinata, *Bass Lake, Madera Co., CA. This photograph shows why the group is called "alligator lizards."*

Viewing Tips: Southern Alligator Lizards are most common in oak woodland, chaparral, and open forest habitats, where the best way to see them on the surface is to watch (and listen) for their snake-like, undulating shuffle as they travel through the dry understory or across roads. Southern Alligator Lizards are generally secretive, tending to hide under brush or cover—so look for them also under potential hiding places: rocks, logs, boards, trash, or other surface cover (and always restore the hiding place to its original condition). These lizards are also common denizens of suburban yards and garages, especially in southern California. Peaks in activity occur in the spring and after summer rains.

Taxonomy: This species was formerly placed in the genus *Gerrhonotus*, as *G. multicarinatus.*

Subspecies and Variation: Three subspecies are recognized. The Oregon Alligator Lizard (*E. m. scincicauda*) has moderately keeled dorsal scales and smooth temporal scales (or only upper temporals weakly keeled). The head is usually unmarked, and the lateral fold is cinnamon-colored. The California Alligator Lizard (*E. m. multicarinata*) has red blotches on its back and a mottled head. Its scales are weakly keeled. The San Diego Alligator Lizard (*E. m. webbii*) is larger, with more prominently keeled dorsal and temporal scales than the other 2 subspecies. Intergrades occur in areas of contact between subspecies.

Remarks: When captured, these lizards will not hesitate to bite and hang on. They may also twist their bodies and attempt to smear feces on their captor. A relatively large head, powerful jaws, and large bony scales on an elongated body most likely give these fierce lizards their common name. A record in the 1970s of "alligator lizards in the air" along southern California's Ventura Highway has not been substantiated.

Panamint Alligator Lizard

Elgaria panamintina (Stebbins, 1958)

Authors: Clark R. Mahrdt and Kent R. Beaman

See page 559 for map color codes.

Description: The Panamint Alligator Lizard has a maximum SVL of 150 mm and a tail nearly twice the body length. The limbs are small compared to the body size. The scales on the tail are weakly keeled; head scales are smooth. This species possesses 14 smooth or weakly keeled dorsal scale rows. There are 7–8 complete, well-defined light to dark-brown crossbands on the body. The ventral surface is whitish with gray spots at the center or margin of scales which appear as irregular, scattered blotches. The iris is pale yellow. **Sexual Variation:** There is no obvious sexual dimorphism, although adult males have larger, broader, more triangular heads than adult females. **Juveniles:** Hatchlings and subadults have prominent dark brown to blackish

Juvenile E. panamintina, *White Mountains, Inyo Co., CA.*

Female E. panamintina, *Inyo Mountains, Inyo Co., CA.*

crossbands separated by light gray or pale ground color. Ventral blotching on the throat and chest is reduced.

Similar Species: This species may be confused with the Madrean Alligator Lizard because of a similar color pattern, orange or pink iris, and 8–11 crossbands, but that species occurs nearly 500 km to the southeast in Arizona. The Southern Alligator Lizard, occurring less than 10 km from the nearest Panamint Alligator Lizard population, is larger (max. SVL 178 mm) with strongly keeled dorsal scale rows, and 9–13 crossbands.

Habitats: This species occurs most frequently in isolated canyons with riparian and permanent spring habitats in desert mountain ranges of the western Great Basin and northern Mohave Desert. Dominant plant species include Red Willow, Arroyo Willow, Virgin's Bower, Wild Grape, Scarlet Monkey Flower, and Southern Maidenhair Fern. These habitats have a thick layer of plant debris where lizards may seek refuge. Individuals also occur in riparian habitat on boulder and talus slopes dominated by xeric plant species such as Creosote Bush, Wormwood, Shad Scale, California Buckwheat, Acton's Encelia, Beavertail Cactus, and barrel cacti. Individuals have been observed in dry washes and on rocky slopes in Creosote Bush scrub, desert scrub, and lower piñon/juniper woodland plant communities. The altitudinal range of the species extends from 760 to 2,290 m.

Natural History: Very little is known about the ecology and natural history of this secretive species; no data exist on population density and status. This species is not frequently encountered in the open and spends much of its time under rocks and dense vegetation. Individuals have been observed basking in late afternoon. Although primarily diurnal, this species is sometimes active at night. Activity occurs from late March through mid-October, peaking in June. Air temperatures when lizards are active range from 15 to 24°C. The diet is chiefly composed of insects, spiders, and other arthropods. A study on reproduction based on 6 males and 2 females suggests breeding occurs in spring (April–May), followed by egg deposition in September. One female was reported to contain 4 developed eggs. Juvenile lizards appear during April–June. Potential reptilian predators include Coachwhip, Striped Whipsnake, Western Patch-nosed Snake, California Kingsnake, and Long-nosed Snake.

Range: The Panamint Alligator Lizard is endemic to California. It is known from approximately 24 isolated localities in Mono and Inyo counties. In Inyo County, it occurs in the Argus Range (Homewood Canyon, Margaret Ann Spring, Mountain Springs Canyon), Coso Range, Panamint Range (Brewery Spring, Limekiln Spring, Pleasant Canyon, Surprise Canyon, Wildrose Canyon), Nelson Range (Grapevine Canyon), Inyo Mountains (Daisy Canyon, French Spring, Lime Hill, Long John Canyon), and the White Mountains (Black Canyon, Marble Canyon, Silver Creek Canyon, Tollhouse Spring, Westgard Pass). Individuals have been reported from the middle fork of Hanaupah Canyon on the east side of the Panamint Mountains in Death Valley National Park. In Mono County, it occurs in the White Mountains (Coldwater Creek, Cottonwood Canyon, near Hammil Valley). It is expected to occur in the Benton and Queen Valleys of Mono County and in adjacent mountain ranges of western Nevada.

Viewing Tips: Because of its secretive habits and presumed rarity, this species is seldom encountered in the field. It may occasionally be found under rocks in damp canyon bottoms and along streams or basking in open areas—for example, Limekiln Spring, Brewery Spring, Batchelder Spring, Daisy Canyon, and Grapevine Canyon. However, carefully turning objects and replacing them is generally discouraged for this species, due to conservation concerns. Throughout most of its range, access to preferred habitat is difficult and requires considerable hiking.

Taxonomy: The species description in 1958 was based on 2 adult specimens, 3 juveniles, and 3 shed skins collected in October 1954 from Surprise Canyon on the west side of the Panamint Mountains, Inyo County, California. There is no evidence sug-

Male E. panamintina, *Inyo Mountains, Inyo Co., CA.*

gesting that the species is sympatric with other members of the genus. Its closest relative is the Madrean Alligator Lizard.

Subspecies and Variations: There are no subspecies currently recognized, and variation within this species is minimal.

Remarks: There are only 25 museum specimens and an additional 14 reputable sight records of this species. Although there are no baseline data suggesting a current decline in population numbers, habitat loss or alteration due to expanded mining operations, off-highway vehicle activity, grazing, and introduction of non-native invasive plant species (e.g., Tamarisk) could have serious adverse effects on the riparian habitat where this species occurs. Long-term illegal collecting using pitfall traps and coverboards may also substantially reduce population numbers. Several localities where suitable habitats exist are on private, BLM, and national forest lands. It is critical that conservation efforts be directed at protecting habitats through restricted land use and enforcement.

Texas Alligator Lizard

Gerrhonotus infernalis Baird, 1859 "1858"

Authors: Harry W. Greene, Philip M. Ralidis, and Edward W. Acuña

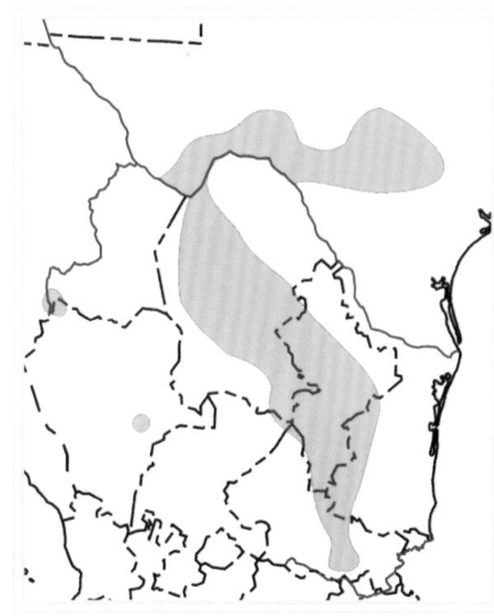

See page 559 for map color codes.

Description: This is a relatively large, somewhat slender and flattened lizard, reaching 180–200 mm SVL, with rather short legs and short, sharp claws. The snout is elongate and somewhat triangular. The intact tail tapers gradually and can be almost twice as long as the body, so that large adults might reach 500 mm TL. All scales are small, and except for those on the head, more or less rectangular; a tiny bone underlies each scale, which gives the skin a slightly armored feel, and dorsal scales are keeled. A flexible lateral fold of granular scales, from the neck to just above the vent, allows expansion for eggs, stomach contents, and defensive body inflation. Adult ground color ranges from light tan to dark brown, sometimes with a reddish cast. Seven to 10 irregular, narrow, black- and white-flecked bands cross the body, and this pattern continues at least to the anterior portion of the tail. Large, old individuals may be nearly uniform tan, with cross-bands reduced to small white flecks. **Sexual Variation:** Large males have broader heads than females of comparable body size. **Juveniles:** Hatchlings are strikingly marked, with copper-colored heads and black-and-cream banded bodies, so that they resemble centipedes or millipedes, but after a few weeks of growth they more closely resemble adults.

Female G. infernalis, *Neuces Canyon, Edwards Co., TX.*

Similar Species: The combination of obvious legs and a lateral fold (also found in the related but limbless glass lizards, *Ophisaurus*) readily distin-

Male G. infernalis, *Neuces Canyon, Real Co., TX.*

guishes adults of this species from all other Texas lizards. Small Texas Alligator Lizards look and move somewhat like skinks, but the latter are shinier, lack lateral folds, and never have cross-banded color patterns.

Habitats: This species is most commonly found in moist, shady, wooded ravines and slopes, often near limestone rock outcrops; elevation records range from about 180 m in Austin to 2,300 m in the Chisos Mountains. It also occurs in bunchgrass meadows and rarely in near-desert conditions, among Sotol, yuccas, and small oaks.

Natural History: Texas Alligator Lizards move slowly and methodically, often one foot at a time, and frequently extend the dark, slightly forked tongue as they investigate their surroundings. If pursued they can move fastest by lateral undulation, with limbs folded. They eat grasshoppers, crickets, beetles, spiders, scorpions, other invertebrates, and perhaps small vertebrates. Arthropods are carefully stalked, often while the lizard twitches its tail tip, and are seized with a rapid forward strike. Prey is immobilized by repeated biting and often swallowed headfirst.

Texas Alligator Lizards can be active during every month, but they are much less likely to be seen during unusually cold or hot and dry weather. They bask at the openings of rock fissures on sunny winter days, but in warmer weather prefer shade and dappled exposure rather than bright sunlight. During the fall mating season, males follow and court females for hours, and at least in captivity they fight each other. Females lay at least one clutch of 5–31 eggs between February and June, under rocks and in crevices, and remain with their clutches throughout the 32–62-day incubation period. Captives readily attack a human finger or a snake intruding into the nest, occasionally leave to feed and defecate, and abandon their neonates after hatching. Females may produce a second clutch within a single season.

Our recent field studies disclose that these lizards are often arboreal, especially in the spring, mating and feeding in vine tangles and foliage up to 3 m above the ground. Their color pattern is exceedingly cryptic under those conditions, especially when they lie immobile on horizontal branches. The tail is strongly prehensile. Texas Alligator Lizards also forage in leaf litter and spend inactive periods under rocks and logs, as well as in limestone fissures. At least in drier parts of the range and during hot weather they may be active after dark. When discovered they freeze or slip into the nearest refuge, and if handled roughly or otherwise threatened, they face an adversary with open mouth, inflate the body, writhe, defecate, bite, and autotomize their tails. Known predators include Ringtails and Striped Whipsnakes. The skin is shed intact and reversed, as in snakes.

Range: Texas Alligator Lizards occur in northeastern Mexico, as well as at a few disjunct localities in the Chihuahuan Desert and throughout much of the Edwards Plateau in Texas; there is an isolated population along bluffs of the Colorado River in LaGrange, and several doubtful records for north-central Texas.

Juvenile G. infernalis, *Neuces Canyon, Edwards Co., TX.*

Male G. infernalis, *Neuces Canyon, Real Co., TX.*

Viewing Tips: These lizards are alert, slow-moving, cautious, and sometimes difficult to locate. In Big Bend National Park they are occasionally encountered along trails in the Chisos Mountains, especially under cool, cloudy conditions after summer rains. On the Edwards Plateau they are most frequently found in canyons of the Balcones Escarpment, as for example at Lost Maples Natural Area, by carefully searching limestone outcrops and in nearby vine tangles and trees during the fall mating season.

Taxonomy: Although originally described as a distinct species, Texas Alligator Lizards were long treated as a subspecies of *G. liocephalus*, whose range extended to southern Mexico. The most recent studies of the genus recognize 5 species, of which *G. infernalis* is a northern relict of this essentially tropical group.

Subspecies and Variation: No subspecies are recognized, and there is little variation among U.S. populations. Animals from the Edwards Plateau evidently have more completely banded tails than do those from the Chisos Mountains.

Remarks: Texas Alligator Lizards are sharp-eyed and responsive, well worth watching. They actively defend themselves if forcibly restrained, and the bite of a large individual produces painful scratches that bleed readily; they particularly resent being grasped by the neck, but can usually be handled gently without difficulty, even when first caught.

FAMILY HELODERMATIDAE:
Gila Monsters and Beaded Lizards

Author: Daniel D. Beck

The Helodermatidae is a famous lizard family with only 2 species: the Gila Monster (*Heloderma suspectum*) and the Beaded Lizard (*H. horridum*). It has a rich and diverse evolutionary history that dates back 98 million years across Europe, Asia, and North America to a time well before many dinosaurs had appeared. The fossil record shows that the remaining species of helodermatid lizards are descendants of a more diverse lineage, called the Monstersauria, which included at least 6 other genera inhabiting subtropical desert, forest, and savanna habitats. The genus *Heloderma* has existed since at least the early Miocene (about 23 million years ago). Today, helodermatid lizards, or monstersaurs, are found in desert, grassland, and tropical dry forest habitats of the American Southwest, western Mexico, and southeastern Guatemala. The American Southwest harbors only the Gila Monster, but the Beaded Lizard occurs in Sonora and Chihuahua, within a day's drive of the international border.

The name *Heloderma* is derived from Greek for "studded skin," in reference to the distinctively textured skin consisting of osteoderms on the dorsal surfaces of these lizards. Their lumbering gait, thick forked tongues, robust skull architecture, and venom glands in the lower jaw give helodermatids a cumbersome appearance that some consider "monster-like." The body markings can be bright and colorful, or faded and cryptic. Juveniles have banded patterns that usually break up with age into a variety of adult markings consisting of spots (in *H. horridum*), blotches, or chain-like crossbands of black, yellow, or orangish on a background of pink, orange, yellow, slate gray, or black. The limbs are relatively short and strong; the clawed feet are reminiscent of tiny human hands. Fat reserves are stored in the tail, which may be plump in well-fed individuals, or quite thin in wild-caught lizards. Individuals range in size from barely 150 mm TL (hatchling Gila Monster) to up to 1 m for a large Beaded Lizard, which can weigh over 2 kg.

Like members of the family Anguidae, monstersaurs are members of the Anguimorpha, a lizard group (including the Old World monitor lizards) herpetologists believe to be most closely allied to the snakes. Monstersaurs are also members of the Scleroglossa ("hard tongue"), a major branch of the lizard/snake evolutionary tree that uses the jaws, rather than the tongue, to draw food into the mouth, freeing the tongue to be used as a powerful chemosensory organ. The forked tongues of monstersaurs (Beaded Lizards have pink tongues, whereas Gila Monsters have black tongues) are important chemical detectors used in searching for food, refuges, and mates. During the breeding season, monstersaurs perform spectacular male-to-male combat rituals, similar to those of monitor lizards (*Varanus*) and snakes. The entwining postures of these fights (reminiscent of the way males of some snake species twist their bodies together during combat) provide a telling reminder of the evolutionary ties between monstersaurs and snakes.

Beaded Lizards inhabit primarily tropical dry forest and thorn scrub, occurring less frequently in lower pine-oak woodland, whereas the Gila Monster is a desert dweller that also inhabits semi-desert grassland and woodland communities along mountain foothills.

Monstersaurs are the only lizards with a well-developed venom delivery system. The venom apparatus consists of multi-lobed glands that empty through ducts at the base of grooved, venom-conducting teeth. In contrast to snakes, the venom glands of monstersaurs are housed in the lower jaw, rather than the upper jaw. Unlike other lizards that can rapidly skitter out of harm's way, monstersaurs are not sprinters. Top speed for a Gila Monster is around 1.9 km/hr, barely walking speed for a human. The threat of a painful, venomous bite is, therefore, very important for monstersaurs in defending themselves against potential predators such as Coyotes, foxes, hawks, and cats.

A bite from a Gila Monster or Beaded Lizard causes excruciating pain, swelling, and, in more severe bites, a rapid drop in blood pressure, profuse sweating, and vomiting. Gila Monsters pose little threat to human health and safety, however. Bites to people are rare and almost always result from careless handling. Despite numerous exaggerated accounts before 1950, there has not been a human death reported from a Gila Monster bite since 1930. No first aid measures are recommended aside from carefully cleaning the wound and seeking immediate medical attention.

Adult H. horridum, *Alamos, Sonora, Mexico. Both species of Helodermatidae occur near Alamos.*

In addition to compounds that cause pain, several important biologically active peptides occur in the venom of helodermatid lizards. Most of

Adult male Heloderma suspectum suspectum, *Cochise Co., AZ.*

these peptides are similar to a mammalian hormone known as vasoactive intestinal peptide (VIP), which relaxes smooth muscle and mediates the flow of water and electrolytes across intestinal membranes. One of the peptides, known as helospectin, binds to VIP receptors in human tissues of the gut, the brain, the lungs, and even the genitalia, where VIP may play a role in regulating secretions and local blood flow. Another monstersaur peptide known as helodermin binds to receptors on breast-cancer cells and inhibits the growth of lung-cancer cells. The best-known lizard peptide is Exendin-4, which occurs naturally only in Gila Monster venom. It mimics a mammalian hormone known as glucagon-like peptide, which mediates insulin release and glucose uptake from the blood after a meal, and also suppresses appetite. Exendin 4 has been developed into a leading new drug called Byetta, which is helping thousands of people suffering from type 2 diabetes. Why Gila Monsters possess such peptides remains a mystery, but they provide another excellent example of the value of biodiversity.

Both Gila Monsters and Beaded Lizards receive full legal protection from collecting, transport, or killing throughout their ranges. Their greatest threat is from habitat loss due to development of their dry forest and desert habitats, and from poaching. The Guatemalan Beaded Lizard (*H .h. charlesbogerti*) is critically endangered.

Gila Monster

Heloderma suspectum Cope, 1869

Author: Daniel D. Beck

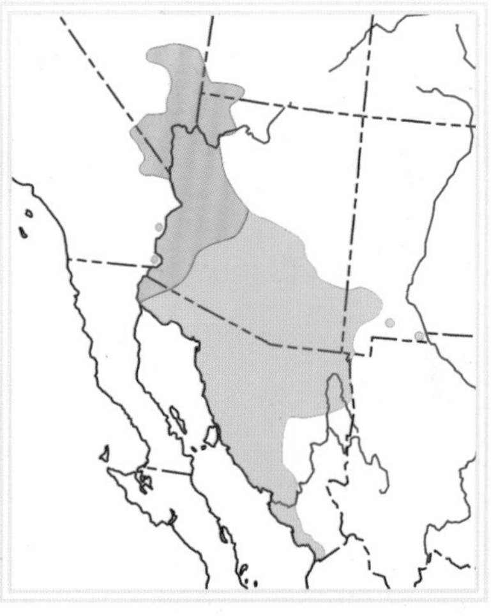

See page 559 for map color codes.

Description: This is a large, stout, venomous lizard with distinctive, bead-like osteoderms on the dorsal surfaces of its head, limbs, body, and tail. The legs are short; the trunk is relatively long; the thick, forked tongue is black; and the feet are reminiscent of tiny, clawed human hands. The thick, short tail, used to store fat, does not regenerate if broken. The black snout is bluntly rounded. Adults reach up to 360 mm SVL and 570 mm TL and weigh 450–900 g. Adult patterns vary from chainlike double crossbands on a yellowish to salmon-pink background to a reticulated pattern of black blotches on a rose, orange, or yellow background. **Sexual Variation:** Adult male Gila Monsters have slightly wider heads and shorter trunks than females. **Juveniles:** Juveniles have 4–5 distinct black saddlelike crossbands on a pale background.

Adult H. s. cinctum. *Legal captive specimens like this one include educational animals, often those confiscated from poachers and given to zoos and universities for care and educational purposes.*

Adult H. s. suspectum, *Phoenix, AZ.*

Similar Species: Adult Gila Monsters are distinctive and seldom confused with other species. The only other large, bulky lizard in our region is the Common Chuckwalla, but it has a much longer tail, a small head, long 4th toes on its hind feet, and smoother scales. Juvenile Gila Monsters are sometimes mistaken for Western Banded Geckos, but the largest adult Western Banded Gecko (under 80 mm TL) is never more than half as long as the smallest Gila Monster (hatchings average 165 mm TL).

Habitats: Gila Monsters occur in desert scrub habitats, semi-desert grassland, and (more rarely) woodland communities along mountain foothills. They frequent canyons or adjacent rocky slopes and more rarely open valleys from near sea level (in coastal Sonora) up to about 1,550 m. Presence is strongly influenced by availability of suitable microenvironments (boulders, rocky crevices, burrows, packrat middens, etc.) used as shelters, where Gila Monsters spend most of their time. Individuals are very faithful to familiar habitats and shelters; lizards translocated to unfamiliar habitats show greatly increased mortality.

Natural History: Gila Monsters are widely searching foragers of the contents of vertebrate nests, primarily reptile and bird eggs, and juvenile mammals. Among the most common food items are juvenile cottontail rabbits and rodents, lizard eggs, and quail eggs. In nature, adult Gila Monsters have been observed eating meals weighing up to a third of their body mass, a quantity sufficient to fulfill a third of their annual maintenance energy requirements. Although they spend most of their time hidden within shelters, Gila Monsters may travel distances in excess of one km/day in search of food and mates. Gila Monsters may be diurnal or nocturnal; the specific timing of activity varies among individuals, seasons, and geographic locations.

Gila Monsters have very low metabolic rates but fairly high rates of evaporative water loss, especially for a desert lizard. Water can be stored in the urinary bladder and later absorbed, helping to delay the onset of dehydration during hot, dry periods. During activity, their preferred body temperature is around 30°C, and they do not tolerate body temperatures in excess of 37°C. When stressed at higher temperatures, Gila Monsters can evaporate significant quantities of water from the cloaca.

Sperm maturation, courtship, and mating occur in late April through early June. Eggs are laid in July and August, which coincides with the onset of summer rains in the southwestern deserts. Hatchlings do not emerge until at least April of the following year. During the spring mating season, male Gila Monsters fight for access to females through spectacular ritualized wrestling matches. Combatants face and circle each other, and then one lizard straddles the other. Combatants entwine their bodies in efforts to gain or maintain the superior position, often pointing their snouts to the sky. Each bout ends when pressure exerted by twisting causes the lizards to separate, but bouts can be repeated many times over. In nature, male Gila Monsters have been observed fighting for 3 hours continuously, and over 10 hours off and on during a single day.

Range: Gila Monsters are found in the eastern Mojave Desert (southern Nevada, southwestern Utah, southeastern California, and western Arizona) in habitats receiving at least 25% of their annual precipitation as summer rain; throughout much of the Sonoran Desert in Arizona and Sonora, Mexico (but not Baja California); and at the northeastern edge of the Chihuahuan Desert in southwestern New Mexico and southeastern Arizona.

Juvenile H. s. suspectum, *Organ Pipe Cactus National Monument, AZ. Juveniles have a more distinctly banded pattern than adults.*

Viewing Tips: Gila Monsters are secretive and fairly rarely seen in nature. Most people encounter them during May when they show the greatest diurnal surface activity. As summer progresses and the nights warm up, Gila Monsters may also be encountered nocturnally along roadways crisscrossing suitable habitat. Good places to observe Gila Monsters include Saguaro National Park and the foothills of the Catalina Mountains (AZ), Snow Canyon State Park (UT), Valley of Fire State Park (NV), and other public lands harboring healthy desert scrub or semi-desert grassland habitats.

Taxonomy: Compared to their sister species, *H. horridum*, Gila Monsters show fairly low genetic diversity, even between the 2 subspecies discussed below. Interestingly, New Mexico and Utah populations appear to be the most genetically similar.

Subspecies and Variation: Two subspecies are recognized. The Banded Gila Monster (*H. s. cinctum*) occurs in southwestern Utah, extreme southeastern Nevada and California, and western Arizona. Adults usually retain the juvenile dorsal pattern of chain-like double crossbands on a yellowish or salmon pink background. The Reticulate Gila Monster (*H. s. suspectum*) occurs in southern Arizona, southwestern New Mexico, and Sonora. In most individuals of this subspecies (New Mexico populations being an exception), the dorsal bands of juveniles break up to become a reticulated pattern of black blotches on a rose, orange, or yellow background.

Remarks: Nobody has died from a Gila Monster bite in over 75 years. Nearly all bites to people result from careless handling. Nevertheless, anyone bitten should go immediately to a hospital. With the development of Byetta, a promising new diabetes drug derived from Gila Monster venom (see Helodermatidae family account), these lizards seem poised to become new icons of the value of biodiversity.

Adult H. s. suspectum, *Maricopa Co., AZ.*

LIZARDS OF BAJA CALIFORNIA (NORTE) AND BAJA CALIFORNIA SUR, MÉXICO

Authors: Robert E. Lovich and L. Lee Grismer

Male Petrosaurus thalassinus, *Baja California Sur, México.*

The Baja California peninsula and associated islands in the Pacific Ocean and Sea of Cortez (also called Mar de Cortés or Gulf of California) have long captured the interest of naturalists and herpetologists. This second-longest peninsula in the world spans almost 10 degrees latitude, extends approximately 1,300 km in length, and is only 230 km across at its widest point. It has elevational extremes that range from desert regions below sea level to mountainous peaks exceeding 2,600 m in elevation. Rainfall averages from less than 5 cm in some places to over 763 cm in others; some desert regions may receive no rain in certain years! Forming the backbone of the peninsula are the Peninsular Ranges, a complex of mountain ranges running almost unbroken from within the state of California to the cape of Baja California. A complex tectonic origin of interactions between the Pacific and North American Plates caused Baja to break away from mainland México and resulted in the latest land configurations, formed within the last 7 million years. During the resulting geologic history, numerous islands have formed between the peninsula and the mainland, providing over 3,300 km of coastal habitats, with islands in the Pacific Ocean also. Highway 1, which runs the length of the peninsula, was not completed until 1973, and before its construction very few people, biologists or otherwise, made the inhospitable trip to the remote lands and islands associated with Baja California. As a result, Baja California—which is actually split into the Mexican states of Baja California Norte and Baja California Sur—was notably understudied until the past few decades.

Travel in Baja California and the Sea of Cortez is much less arduous in this modern age. A road trip to the tip of the peninsula used to be a rugged and grueling 2- to 6-week journey over worn and narrow, unpaved roads, but can now be accomplished in 2 to 3 days. The convenience of a maintained and paved highway for the length of the peninsula, as well as numerous other highways that connect with it, has opened up Baja California's interior and gulf waters to a wide variety of vacationers, ranging from sport fishermen and sun worshipers to hikers and off-roaders. There is still, however, a wild, intangible, alluring element about Baja California—something that teases to the surface an innate sense of adventure, heightened by an invitation to danger and the unknown.

Habitats in Baja California vary by latitude, longitude, and elevation. The major ecoregions have distinctive vegetation communities including coastal scrublands, desert scrub, montane woodlands and forests, and subtropical thorn scrub. Each of these communities has a distinctive assemblage of lizards. Coastal shrublands, which have a mild climate, are found along Baja's northwest Pacific coast. They are characterized by coastal scrub plant communities. Inland from there, elevations rise from chaparral to oak woodland and coniferous forests. The northeast part of the peninsula contains low Sonoran Desert habitats, some below sea level. South of these 2 habitat types, the central deserts of Baja California are composed of a varied Sonoran Desert terrain, interrupted in the center of the peninsula by the Vizcaino fog desert, one of only 3 fog deserts in the world—a place with arid plant communities that may be

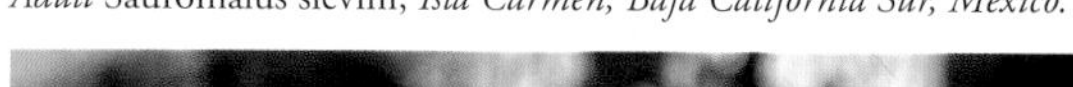
Adult Sauromalus slevini, *Isla Carmen, Baja California Sur, México.*

shrouded by fog. Farther south, the eastern central coast is called the central gulf coast, and the inland and western deserts are called the Magdalena Plains. Arid subtropical habitats can be found ranging along the mountainous areas from Loreto southward to the Cape Region, and finally the montane habitat of the Sierra La Laguna in the southern portion of the peninsula has oak woodlands comprising numerous endemic species at the upper elevations.

Adult Phyllodactylus unctus, *one of two species of the genus in the region of Cabo San Lucas, Baja California Sur, México.*

Lizard aficionados are rewarded richly for travels to Baja California and associated islands. Baja California is home to 79 species of lizards from 10 families, and 23 genera. The most speciose family is the Phrynosomatidae, with 30 species, and the least speciose is the Bipedidae, with only a single species represented (*Bipes biporus*). Baja California has only 18 fewer lizard species than are found in the entire southwestern United States (79 vs. 97), and lizard seekers are rarely far from a number of lizards to enjoy and observe! Thirty-two of Baja's species are shared with the southwestern United States; many of these are wide-ranging Sonoran Desert or Pacific Coast species. Forty-two total species are found *only* in Baja California, 25 of which are insular endemic species that have evolved on the islands of the Sea of Cortez and Pacific Ocean. They represent an extraordinary number highlighting the complex natural processes of the region, and the diversity of habitats available in which these species evolved. Equally impressive are the 17 peninsular endemic species.

It is important to consider that all of the above numbers as they relate to lizards are subject to change, as new species from Baja California continue to be described. Within the last several years, a new alligator lizard was described for Baja California. Recent studies also determined that the former "Coast Horned Lizard" was actually composed of 4 distinct species! New species of side-blotched and spiny lizards have also been added in recent years. Further studies will

The odd little Five-toed Worm Lizard is subterranean in loose soils.

Male Sceloporus hunsackeri, *of the cape region.*

no doubt result in changes to the number of species listed for Baja California, both as discoveries of previously unrecognized species take place and changes in taxonomy result in additions or subtractions of species recognized.

Four species of lizards are non-native, 3 of which are geckos restricted generally to urbanized areas where they can be found around artificial lighting at night, preying on the insects attracted to those lights. The other, *Sauromalus varius,* is actually native to Baja California, but also was introduced to Isla Roco Lobos from the Sonoran Gulf Island of Isla San Esteban, where it is endemic. The introduced population on Isla Roca Lobos is reproducing and viable.

Lizard activity patterns are dictated for the most part by seasonal weather patterns on the peninsula. As ectotherms, lizards are predictably active during warmer times of year in spring and summer, but excessive heat can also reduce activity in some species. Northern Baja California receives most of its rainfall from winter storms coming out of the north, but as one moves south, tropical storms originating in the southern Pacific Ocean provide the bulk of the rainfall during the mid- to late-summer monsoon season. Likewise lizard activity is affected by these climatic events, with cold winter storms in the north causing reduced levels of activity, and lizards of northern Baja California becoming active during spring and summer when temperatures are elevated. The southern half of the peninsula stays relatively warm throughout the year, and some species may be active during all months, with summer monsoonal events causing pulses of activity. Looking for lizards following rain events can be especially productive and rewarding!

The Baja California peninsula has much to offer those interested in lizards, regardless of your background or experience. Its varied habitats have an equally varied lizard fauna that can be enjoyed, and the potential for exploration is high, given the remoteness of much of the peninsula. There are 4 major ecoregions that have distinctive biotic communities and characteristic lizard fauna. They are described here in very simple form, considering the complex number of habitats found across the length and breadth of the peninsula and its islands. Some species range widely across ecoregions and are considered to be a fifth ubiquitous lizard group. Some additional species cannot be considered characteristic of these ecoregions, as they are narrow endemics from islands and other regions of the peninsula.

Northwestern Coastal Assemblage

Members of this group are cismontane species whose distributions are in the coastal scrub, chaparral, and lower-elevation forested habitats of northwestern Baja California, and which are adapted to the less arid conditions of the region north and west of El Rosario. This group includes *Sceloporus occidentalis, S. orcutti, Xantusia henshawi, Gambelia copeii, Phrynosoma blainvillii, Plestiodon "gilberti," P. skiltonianus, Anniella pulchra, A. geronimensis, Aspidosceles labialis, Elgaria cedrosensis,* and *E. multicarinata.*

Sonoran Desert Assemblage

Species in this group occupy Sonoran Desert habitats of Baja California in the Lower Colorado River Valley, but with a larger distribution outside of Baja California for the most part. This group includes *Gambelia wislizenii, Phrynosoma mcallii, P. platyrhinos, P. cerroense, P. wigginsi, Sceloporus magister, Dipsosaurus dorsalis, Callisaurus draconoides, Xantusia wigginsi, Ctenosaura hemilopha, Sceloporus zosteromus, Uma notata,* and *Urosaurus graciosus.* It also includes saxicolous species such as *Crotaphytus grismeri, C. vestigium, Sauromalus ater, Petrosaurus* spp., *Urosaurus lahtelai, U. nigricaudus, Coleonyx switaki,* and *Phyllodactylus nocticolus.* Rock-dwelling species are generally restricted to arid, rocky habitats of the Peninsular Ranges and occupy a range of vegetative communities. One species, *Urosaurus ornatus,* is confined entirely to the Lower Colorado River Valley region.

Montane Assemblage

Northern montane species of Baja California are restricted to the coniferous forests of the Sierra de Júarez and Sierra de San Pedro Mártir mountains in the north. This "group" includes one species, *Sceloporus graciosus.*

Subtropical Assemblage

This group is composed of endemic species restricted to the arid tropical habitats and Sierra la Laguna in the Cape of Baja California. This group includes *Petrosaurus thalassinus, Phrynosoma coronatum, Sceloporus hunsakeri, S. licki, Elgaria paucicarinata,* and *Phyllodactylus unctus.* Several species in this group are endemic and occur exclusively in the Cape Region's arid tropical habitats and in the Sierra la Laguna. This group includes *Plestiodon lagunensis, Elgaria velazquezi,* and *Bipes biporus.* None of these last 3 species is endemic to the Cape Region; *E. velazquezi* doesn't even reach the Cape Region.

Ubiquitous Group

This group ranges across much of the peninsula, and includes *Uta stansburiana, Coleonyx variegatus, Aspidoscelis hyperythra,* and *A. tigris.*

LIZARDS OF SONORA, MÉXICO

Authors: James C. Rorabaugh and Erik F. Enderson

Of the Mexican states, Sonora is second only to Chihuahua in size, with a mainland territory encompassing 185,430 km^2. Sonora is topographically diverse, characterized by plains and low (mostly less than 1,000 m) ranges in the west to dramatic mountains and river valleys in the east. Fourteen islands in the Mar de Cortés (Gulf of California) are also part of the state of Sonora. Elevations range from sea level to 2,625 m at the top of the Sierra de los Ajos in the northeast. The continental divide is in the Sierra Madre Occidental near the Chihuahuan border, and as a result, most of Sonora's rivers drain to the gulf. Rainfall generally increases from north to south and west to east, and is bimodal—with winter and summer rainy seasons—the latter of which becomes increasingly dominant to the south and east. Sonoran desert scrub and Sinaloan thorn scrub biotic communities dominate the western plains and lower mountains. Oak and conifer forests blanket the tops of the eastern mountains, with grasslands or Sinaloan thorn scrub typically occurring in the intervening valleys. Tropical deciduous forest is found in the foothills of the southeast, which gradually gives way to Sinaloan thorn scrub in the north and west, and montane woodlands to the east. Sonora's diverse and often extreme climate and topography foster its biodiversity.

Subadult Ctenosaura macrolopha, *emerging from a sewer pipe in Alamos, Sonora, México.*

Occurring statewide and present in every biotic community—often in great abundance—lizards are one of Sonora's most conspicuous terrestrial vertebrate life forms. Sixty-four species in 21 genera and 11 families are currently known from Sonora. Of these, 32 are regionally endemic to the Sonoran Desert, and 8 live nowhere else in the world. Eight horned lizards are known from the state—a regional diversity unmatched on Earth. The world's 2 venomous lizards (*Heloderma horridum* and *H. suspectum*) occur in and are possibly sympatric in Sonora. Ten different spiny lizards, 9 whiptails, 6 geckos, and 4 iguanas punctuate Sonora's wondrous lizard diversity.

Each major biotic community contains, to varying degrees, distinct herpetofaunal assemblages and transition zones. Five lizard assemblages may be recognized on the basis of regional distribution: the Sonoran Desert assemblage (35 species), montane assemblage (13 species), tropical/subtropical assemblage (8 species), Chihuahuan Desert assemblage (3 species), and grassland assemblage (3 species). Two species, *Sceloporus clarkii* and *Urosaurus ornatus,* are generalists found across the various biomes, with the exception of the extremely arid valleys of the Gran Desierto in northwestern Sonora.

Sonoran Desert Assemblage

Lizard diversity in Sonora reaches its peak in the Sonoran Desert. Forty species live in this region, and of these, 35 are Sonoran Desert specialists, while the remaining 5 are considered peripheral species. The high diversity of this region is traced to its tropical origin and the historical southward expansion of the North American temperate zone, creating deep interdigitation of tropical and temperate herpetofauna.

Northwestern Sonora is a study in stark beauty and contrast. The Río Colorado valley, along the border with Baja California, is a dramatic greenbelt through an otherwise arid and barren desert. In the remnant riparian forests along the river, but also in adjacent agricultural and rural lands, are found arboreal *Sceloporus magister* and *Urosaurus ornatus*, along with the ground-dwelling *Aspidoscelis tigris* and *Callisaurus draconoides*—often in great abundance. The introduced *Hemidactylus turcicus* has been found on buildings at El Golfo de Santa Clara and was reported from San Luis Río Colorado. Perhaps Sonora's most ecologically distinct area exists to the east in the Lower Colorado River subdivision of the Sonoran Desert, where high lizard diversity exists despite the area's extreme aridity (annual precipitation of 55 mm at San Luis Río Colorado) and heat (daytime highs frequently exceed 43°C in summer). This area, known as the Gran Desierto, is characterized by vast, sandy plains where Creosote Bush, White Bursage, and Galleta Grass interdigitate with dunes and scattered dry mountain ranges. The Gran Desierto has the largest sand dune complex in the western hemisphere, and the 3,300 km^2 Pinacate lava field, as well as granitic ranges such as the Sierra del Rosario, increase topographic and habitat diversity. The highly specialized, sand-dwelling *Uma rufopunctata* may be the only lizard encountered on the larger dunes, but *Phrynosoma mcallii, Callisaurus draconoides, Dipsosaurus dorsalis, Uta stansburiana, Urosaurus graciosus, Coleonyx variegatus, Aspidoscelis tigris,* and *Gambelia wislizenii* can also be found here on low dunes, dune edges, and adjacent sandy flats and plains. On the bajadas of the region's mountains, where dunes mingle with coarser alluvium and outcrops, *Phrynosoma goodei, P. solare,* and *Sceloporus magister* make their appearance. *Heloderma suspectum* occurs on the slopes of the Sierra Pinacate, and observations suggest they venture into the lava fields. In the mountains of the Gran Desierto, *Sauromalus ater* is indeed a common sight, but *Crotaphytus nebrius* is also occasionally encountered.

Thirty-three km south of the Sierra Pinacate, the desert meets the Sea of Cortez at the resort community of Puerto Peñasco (Rocky Point). At about 130 km southeast of Puerto Peñasco, the lower Colorado River valley subdivision yields to the rugged, mountainous, and increasingly arborescent central gulf coast subdivision near Punta Lobos, where the similarity to Baja California's Vizcaíno subdivision of Sonoran desert scrub is unmistakable. The central gulf coast subdivision becomes increasingly tropical from north to south and eventually grades into Sinaloan thorn scrub in the city of Guaymas. The stem-succulent elephant trees and limberbushes along with massive columnar cacti and palm-lined tropical canyons help define the region. Although the area is largely unexplored herpetologically, lizards are well represented and include the endemic *Crotaphytus dickersonae,* the males of which are a spectacular blue. The geckos *Coleonyx variegatus* and *Phyllodactylus homolepidurus* are sympatric here, as are the iguanas *Dipsosaurus dorsalis* and *Ctenosaura macrolopha.* Introduced *Hemidactylus turcicus* occur on beachside resorts at Bahía Kino, but *Hemidactylus frenatus* is known from Guaymas and likely also occurs at Empalme. Included in the central gulf coast subdivision are the islands San Pedro Mártir, San Pedro Nolasco, and San Esteban—each containing endemic lizards.

East of the central gulf coast subdivision is the Plains of Sonora subdivision. This generally flat and open region is best described as a desert-to-tropical transition that grades south and east into Sinaloan thorn scrub and north into the Lower Colorado River Valley and Arizona Upland subdivisions. Ironwood, mesquites, and palo verdes, common in the Sonoran Desert areas of Arizona and southeastern California, are found here among frost-sensitive Elephant Trees, Organpipe Cactus, Tree Ocotillos, and bright blue-flowered Guayacan, among others. Historically, this community generally lacked an understory, and that is still the case where the introduced Buffelgrass does not occur. However, this introduced African grass has invaded much of the Plains of Sonora, where it is planted for livestock forage. Buffelgrass has brought fire to this and other arid plant communities in Sonora; fire destroys many of the native trees, shrubs, and cacti and dra-

Gravid female Crotaphytus dickersonae, *Sonora, México. Compare to the cobalt-blue male on p. 99.*

matically alters lizard habitats. Lizard diversity here is relatively low among Sonoran Desert scrub subdivisions; however, one tropical denizen can be observed with some frequency by those willing to look to the treetops. The often-arboreal *Ctenosaura macrolopha* maximizes the sun's rays by thermoregulating above the tree canopy. In the southern portions of the Plains of Sonora, it is not at all uncommon to observe these iguanas perched atop one of Sonora's most distinctive plants—the Lollipop Tree or Palo Jito. These impressive lizards reach their northern distributional limits near Benjamin Hill west of Highway 15. Others commonly observed in the region include *Phrynosoma solare, Sceloporus magister, Aspidoscelis tigris, Coleonyx variegatus,* and *Uta stansburiana.*

North of the Plains of Sonora and extending well into southern Arizona is the Saguaro-palo verde-dominated Arizona Upland subdivision. The eastern and wetter examples of this woodland-like community can be particularly luxuriant, contradicting common perceptions about deserts. This subdivision is the Sonoran Desert's most speciose lizard realm, due in part to habitat diversity in the form of lush, tree-lined arroyo bottoms contrasting with intervening upland shrublands, as well as a diversity of substrates from silty or sandy valley bottoms that give way to gravelly bajadas and then to rocky montane slopes. However, perhaps even more important, the Arizona Upland is often at the confluence of biotic communities, borrowing from western, xeric desert scrub herpetofauna, but also from eastern and southern Sinaloan thorn scrub and grassland faunas. At least 21 species are known to occur in the Arizona

Upland subdivision in Sonora. Commonly observed species include *Aspidoscelis burti, A. tigris, Callisaurus draconoides, Coleonyx variegatus, Crotaphytus nebrius, Holbrookia elegans, Phrynosoma solare, Sauromalus ater, Sceloporus magister, Urosaurus ornatus,* and *Uta stansburiana.*

Tropical/Subtropical Assemblage

The tropical/subtropical assemblage includes species characteristic of Sinaloan thorn scrub and tropical deciduous forest (TDF). About 28 lizard species occur in these communities. Sonora's TDF is the northernmost extension of a drought-deciduous tropical forest type that extends south along the Pacific coast to northwestern Costa Rica. In Sonora, TDF occurs in the foothills of the southeast where enough rainfall occurs to support a woodland, but also at moderate elevations where freezing temperatures occur only rarely. This forest undergoes a dramatic transition twice a year. In most years, from about November through June, TDF is nearly leafless and predominantly colored gray, except for the columnar cacti, species of trees with green, photosynthetic bark, and occasional palms and flowering trees. With the onset of the summer rains in June or early July, TDF almost explodes into a lush, vibrant green landscape with all the looks and sounds of a tropical forest. Nearly all of the trees have tropical origins, as do the many vines and epiphytic bromeliads and orchids. To the west and north, TDF grades into Sinaloan thorn scrub, which, like TDF, is also distinctly drought-deciduous. This is a transition community between TDF and Sonoran desert scrub in which the columnar cacti generally exceed the stature of trees (the opposite is true in TDF). Occurring in this tropical landscape with Boa Constrictors, Jaguars, Ocelots, and Military Macaws are an assemblage of lizard species with southern origins. Anoloid lizards (Family Polychrotidae), represented by about 391 often confusing but mostly tropical semiarboreal or arboreal lizards, reach their northernmost distribution in western México in *Anolis nebulosus,* which occurs in TDF and thorn scrub in southeastern and south-central Sonora.

Adult Beaded Lizard, Heloderma horridum, *a considerably larger member of the genus than the Gila Monster,* H. suspectum.

Adult Anolis nebulosus, *Sonora, México. Anoles comprise a large group that is mostly distributed in the more southerly tropics.*

Sceloporus albiventris, similar to the *Sceloporus clarkii* in appearance and habitats in southeastern Sonora, is found on rocks or tree trunks in the foothills north to about Highway 16. *Sceloporus nelsoni,* a small, dark, or occasionally orange spiny lizard, is commonly encountered on rocks or cliffs in shaded arroyos near streams in TDF. Looking in rock crevices in those same arroyos will often reveal *Phyllodactylus tuberculosus,* which can also be found on the walls of buildings and houses in rural areas at night. *Heloderma horridum,* which grows to an astounding and hefty 0.9 m, is at times surprisingly common. Other species of the tropical/subtropical assemblage include *Urosaurus bicarinatus, Coleonyx fasciatus,* and *Aspidoscelis costata.*

Montane Assemblage

Upslope and to the north of TDF and thorn scrub, occasional freezing temperatures limit the distribution of tropical trees, which are gradually replaced by frost-tolerant oaks and conifers. These trees occur in montane woodlands of the Sierra Madre Occidental along Sonora's eastern border, but also in isolated mountain ranges in the northeast known as "sky islands" because of their distinctive montane floras and faunas that are isolated from other such assemblages by largely xeric valleys. On the lower slopes, several species of oaks are often intermingled with junipers and mesquites. Moving upslope, one finds oak woodlands, then pine/oak woodlands, and on the highest peaks (mostly above 2,135 m), mixed conifer forests. Examples of the latter can be found near Yecora and in the Sierras de los Ajos, San José, San Luis, and El Tigre. About 21 lizard species inhabit these montane woodlands in Sonora. Characteristic lizards of the montane assemblage include the secretive *Elgaria kingii* and *Plestiodon callicephalus,* typically found under logs and rocks or in leaf litter on the forest floor, and the more conspicuous *Sceloporus jarrovii, S. lemosespinali, S. poinsettii,* and *S. virgatus,* which can be observed on rocks or in trees. *Aspidoscelis sonorae,* an active and highly visible species, is the most common montane woodland whiptail. Some species, such as *Sceloporus slevini* and *Phrynosoma hernandesi,* occur in the mountains, but also bridge the gap between sky islands in intervening grassland or shrubland valleys. *Phrynosoma orbiculare* reaches its northernmost limits in the higher, wooded sierra around Yecora. Also in the southeastern mountains and ranging downslope into TDF is the rarely encountered *Plestiodon parviauriculatus.* Similar to *P. callicephalus, P. parviariculatus* can be distinguished by the presence of a single postmental scale (see Figure 3; *P. callicephalus* usually has 2) and the absence of a light Y-shaped head marking. *Phrynosoma ditmarsi,* endemic to Sonora, is known from only 4 discrete areas of northeastern Sonora. After the first collections in 1890–1897, the species was not seen again until 1970.

Grassland Assemblage

Semi-desert grassland, which occurs at approximately 1,100–1,700 m elevation, is the dominant grassland community in Sonora. Transitional in character, it grades into or adjoins Sonoran desert scrub or Sinaloan thorn scrub to the west, and Chihuahuan desert scrub, plains grassland, and montane woodlands in northeastern Sonora. Grasslands, particularly semi-desert grasslands, have been degraded by decades of overgrazing and perhaps other factors that have resulted in invasions by desert shrubs and cacti. These communities are now often similar floristically to adjoining desert scrub and thorn scrub, but may lack some of the lizards characteristic of those communities. In the northeast, good examples of plains grassland still exist at elevations of 1,200–2,300 m in the upper Río San Pedro Valley, just west of the Sierra San Luis, and northeast of Bacerac. Roughly 21 lizard species can be found in Sonora's grasslands. Representative members of the grassland assemblage include *Aspidoscelis uniparens, Plestiodon obsoletus,* and *Sceloporus cowlesi.* Other species entering the grasslands, often along riparian or other woodland or shrubland stringers, include, among others, *Aspidoscelis sonorae, Elgaria kingii, Holbrookia elegans, Phrynosoma hernandesi, P. cornutum,* and *Sceloporis slevini.*

Chihuahuan Desert Assemblage

In the valleys of the northeast, Chihuahuan desert scrub occurs at elevations of about 900–1,430 m. This biome, which reaches its western limits in northeastern Sonora and southeastern Arizona, is characterized by relatively cool, dry winters and a distinct summer rainy season. It is dominated by Creosote Bush and other shrubs, and where livestock grazing is well managed, a diversity of warm-season grasses. Several yuccas, sotols, and their relatives may visually dominate. About 13 species of lizards are known from the Chihuahuan Desert in Sonora. Three species are considered characteristic of the Chihuahuan Desert assemblage, including *Aspidoscelis exsanguis, Phrynosoma cornutum,* and *P. modestum. Aspidoscelis inornata* and *Sceloporus bimaculosus* are not currently known from Sonora, but may occur in this community in the extreme northeast.

LIZARDS OF CHIHUAHUA, MÉXICO

Author: Julio A. Lemos-Espinal

Chihuahua is the largest state in the Mexican Republic; its 245,612 km^2 represent 12.6% of the total territory of the nation. Its extensive surface is physiographically complex, and affects the distribution of the lizard fauna in equally complex ways. Almost all of the western part of the state is occupied by the Sierra Madre Occidental, along the crest of which the Continental Divide passes. The highest altitude in the state is on Cerro Mohinora in the extreme southwestern part, at 3,300 m. Other major elevations are Sierra de Gasachic at 3,060 m, and Cerro Güirichique at 2,740 m. The altitude of the Sierra Madre diminishes to the north, terminating where the Sierra de San Luis extends northward nearly to the borders of Arizona and New Mexico, and reaches an altitude of ~ 2,100 m.

The extreme southwestern Pacific slopes of the Sierra Madre are characterized by deep canyons that drop down to about 250 m in the Barranca del Septentrión/Cañón de Chínipas. The Sierra Madre varies in width from about 130 to 160 km in the south (west of Hidalgo de Parral) to about 65 to 80 km in the north (west of Casas Grandes).

Over half of the state of Chihuahua, east of the Sierra Madre, is represented by high plains at about 1,200–1,700 m. However, from these plains arise a large number of small to medium-sized, isolated sierras, some of which reach altitudes of over

Adult Plestiodon brevirostris, *Durango, México.*

Male Sceloporus edbelli, *Durango, México.*

2,000 m. Some are high enough to support coniferous forests, constituting continental "islands" surrounded by a "sea" of semiarid plains, where population differentiation is enhanced by isolation.

In the extreme northeast, deep canyons, analogous to those on the Pacific side of the Sierra Madre, cut into the edge of the high plains, and support their own distinct lizard assemblage. Among those canyons is the great Cañón de Santa Elena, in the Zona de Protección de Flora y Fauna Silvestre Cañón de Santa Elena, an extension of the Big Bend National Park of the United States. It has elevations less than 800 m.

This complex topography has fundamental effects on the distribution of types of vegetation and human activities. In the Sierra Madre, as well as in the highest parts of the ranges throughout the rest of the state, dense coniferous forests occur, dominated by Chihuahua Pine, Apache Pine, Mexican White Pine, Durango Pine, and White Oak, among others. This type of vegetation represents 29.42% of the surface area of the state.

The deep barrancas of the west and southwest support tropical deciduous forests that have been relatively little disturbed, due to the low density of human occupation. Notable plants are Mauto, Tree Morning Glory, Guacimo, and Fragrant Bursera. This type of vegetation covers 2.38% of the surface area of the state.

East of the Sierra Madre the terrain is dominated by xerophytic shrubs such as Creosote Bush, American Tarwort, mesquites, Texas Sotol, and Ocotillo, among other species.

The principal grasslands are in the central and northeastern parts of the state. Some of the dominant species are Blue Grama, Hairy Grama, Three-awn, Sacaton, and Spear Grass. These parts make up 23.89% of the surface area of the state, and all that is suitable for grazing is grazed. Cultivated parts of the state account for 7.38% of its area.

Chihuahua is inhabited by a total of 51 native and one introduced species of lizards. These 52 species represent 10 families and 20 genera, of which *Sceloporus* is the most speciose with 12 species, followed by *Aspidoscelis* with 9, and *Plestiodon* with 7. The distribution and behavior of these lizard taxa have been greatly influenced by the varied ecologies arising from the diverse physical properties of the state. The major barrier to a more or less uniform distribution is the Sierra Madre Occidental, which prevents most eastern species from reaching western slopes, and vice versa, as well as supporting an extensive intrinsic biota. The lowland species that occur on both sides of the Sierra Madre (e.g., *Urosaurus ornatus, Uta stansburiana*) do not cross the divide but extended southward on both sides from the north.

Adaptations of the Chihuahua lizard fauna to variables of the environment have given rise to 4 distinct assemblages, each sharing more or less common environmental preferences. (1) Tropical/subtropical assemblage: species confined to the deep canyons with tropical deciduous forests that occur also in extreme southeastern Sonora and northeastern Sinaloa. (2) Montane assemblage: species occurring in the Sierra Madre and Sierra de San Luis. Many are limited to high elevations of the various sierras that arise from the adjacent high plains east of the Sierra Madre, such as the Sierra del Nido, Sierra del Pajarito, and Sierra Azul. (3) Chihuahuan Desert assemblage: species adapted to the arid/semiarid environment of the Chihuahuan Desert east of the Sierra Madre and its associated sierras. (4) Generalist assemblage: species that occur in more than one of the major habitats of the state, and are not uniquely characteristic of any one of them.

Tropical/Subtropical Assemblage

Eight species are included in this assemblage: *Anolis nebulosus, Aspidoscelis costata, Ctenosaura macrolopha, Heloderma horridum, Phyllodactylus tuberculosus, Sceloporus albiventris, S. nelsoni,* and *Urosaurus bicarinatus.* None of these occur in the U.S.

Except for *P. tuberculosus,* all these species are relatively abundant in the southwestern part of the state. Of them, *A. costata, C. macrolopha,* and *S. nelsoni* are the most common species, followed by *A. nebulosus, S. horridus, U. bicarinatus,* and *H. horridum.* Surprisingly, *H. horridum* is locally common near Chínipas (municipality of Chínipas) and Tubares (municipality of Urique). At Sierra de Chínipas and Palmarejo we have observed this lizard species reaching elevations of up to 1,000 m in a mixture of oak and tropical deciduous forest. However, its greatest abundance is observed in the surroundings of the tropical deciduous forest associated with the Río Chínipas. Due to the secretive and nocturnal habits of *P. tuberculosus* this species has been less frequently observed than the other 7. However, a careful examination of rock crevices and refuges on human buildings, such as behind hanging frames, corners of windows, under light lamps, etc., will reveal the presence of this species.

The density of human populations is quite low in these tropical zones, and as a result anthropogenic alteration is also quite low, which aids in conservation. Near Chínipas *H. horridum* has been especially persecuted, and in a large part of the distribution of *C. macrolopha* people tend to consume it occasionally.

Montane Assemblage

Fifteen species are limited to this area and constitute the montane assemblage: **Barisia ciliaris, *B. levicollis, Elgaria kingii, *Gerrhonotus taylori, Phrynosoma hernandesi, *P. orbiculare, Sceloporus jarrovii, *S. lemosespinali, S. slevini, S. virgatus, *Plestiodon brevirostris, P. callicephalus, *P. multilineatus, *P. parviauriculatus, Aspidoscelis sonorae.* Eight (each indicated by an asterisk*) are limited to México.

Three of these 15 species are considered rare in the state: *Barisia ciliaris,* which has been recorded only in one locality (Mesa de Agostadero, village of Cerro Blanco, municipality of Balleza); *Plestiodon parviariculatus,* limited to 3 localities in the western part of the state; and *Aspidoscelis sonorae,* limited to the extreme northwestern part of the state in the municipality of Janos. Although some other species can be considered rare they are locally abundant, such as *Barisia levicollis,* which is very abundant in the mountain grasslands at the top of Sierra del Nido (municipalities of Chihuahua and Namiquipa), and the skinks, which in general are locally abundant. Although lizards of the genus *Phrynosoma* are seldom encountered in mountainous habitats, they occur widely there. *Phrynosoma hernandesi* is found along all of the Sierra de San Luis and Sierra Madre Occidental, including Sierra del Nido, whereas *P. orbiculare* is limited in the state to the southern half of the Sierra Madre Occidental (including Sierra del Nido). The 4 lizards of the genus *Sceloporus* (*S. jarrovii, S. lemosespinali, S. slevini,* and *S. virgatus*) that occur in montane habitats are abundant and widespread in all localities of the Sierra del Nido and Sierra Madre Occidental.

Juvenile Phrynosoma orbiculare, *Durango, México.*

Chihuahuan Desert Assemblage

Although the Chihuahuan Desert is characterized by a definite climatic continuity, it nevertheless has considerable habitat diversity. Extensive grasslands occur in the central and northwestern parts of the state; sand dunes, both live and stabilized, occur to the north (Bolsón Cabeza de Vaca, Samalayuca system) and to the south (Bolsón de Mapimí); extensive swales or *barreales* in extreme northern and central parts; ecotones of mixed xerophytic and wooded areas around isolated sierras in the middle of the desert; and riparian vegetation along the Conchos, Bravo, and Santa María rivers.

Twenty-two species are exclusive to the Chihuahuan Desert, within the boundaries of the state: *Coleonyx brevis, Hemidactylus turcicus, Cophosaurus texanus, Crotaphytus collaris, Gambelia wislizenii, Holbrookia maculata, Phrynosoma cornutum, P. modestum, Sceloporus cowlesi, *S. edbelli, S. bimaculosus, S. merriami, *Uma paraphygas, Uta stansburiana, Plestiodon multivirgatus, P. obsoletus, Aspidoscelis gularis, A. inornata, A. marmorata, A. scalaris, A. tesselata,* and *A. uniparens.* Two (each indicated by an asterisk*) are limited to México.

Unfortunately, considerable anthropogenic environmental degradation has occurred in the Chihuahuan Desert. Stock ranches, especially of cattle, have drastically affected the face of the land, where in the mid-19th century the extensive grasslands were relatively free of bushes. Rivers traversing the region were bordered by dense gallery forests, and frequently overflowed into large barreales that retained a relatively high level of humidity for the region. At present, cattle-ranching has resulted in domination of much of the former prairie grassland by shrubby vegetation. The barreales now retain water scarcely beyond the rainy season itself. Several large species of vertebrates have been extirpated from most or all of the state.

In addition, intensive agricultural practices have destroyed the native vegetation of thousands of hectares. Overuse of subterranean aquifers and reservoirs for irrigation and the needs of burgeoning cities like Ciudad Chihuahua, Juárez, and Cuauhtémoc have seriously affected the flow of rivers such as the Bravo, Conchos, Florido, San Pedro, and others, and hastened the desertification of the Chihuahuan Desert.

The lizard fauna of the area have also suffered from increasing human activity; one of the 22 lizard species, *Plestiodon multivirgatus,* has almost been extirpated. This species has been recorded only at Ojo de Galeana (7.2 km southeast of Galeana, municipality of Galeana). The springs that maintained the mesic habitat are no longer present, and this lizard species has not been recorded recently. The other skink that inhabits the Chihuahuan Desert (*Plestiodon obsoletus*) has been recorded only from a few localities, although this could be the result of the secretive habits of this species. Most of the other species are at least locally abundant. Some of them (*Coleonyx brevis, Sceloporus merriami, Uma paraphygas, Aspidoscelis marmorata, A. gularis,* and *A. tesse-*

Adult Uma paraphygas, *Chihuahua, México.*

lata) are limited to the eastern part of the state. *Uma paraphygas* is confined to the sand dunes system of the Bolsón de Mapimí. *Holbrookia maculata* is limited to sandy areas in the northern and northeastern parts of the state. Some others (*Cophosaurus texanus, Crotaphytus collaris, Gambelia wislizenii, Phrynosoma cornutum, P. modestum, Sceloporus cowlesi, S. edbelli, S. bimaculosus, Uta stansburiana, Aspidoscelis inornata* and *A. scalaris*) are widespread in most of the state's Chihuahuan Desert. Only *A. uniparens* is limited to the arid/semiarid western part of the state. Finally, one of the 22 lizard species of the Chihuahuan Desert assemblage, *Hemidactylus turcicus*, is an introduced species recorded only at one locality at eastern Chihuahua (La Perla, municipality of Camargo). This species no doubt arrived in the state through traffic from the east (state of Coahuila), where it has been widely recorded.

Generalist Assemblage

Seven species whose range in Chihuahua involves more than one of the 3 major habitats of the state constitute a generalist assemblage: *Holbrookia approximans, H. elegans, Sceloporus clarkii, S. poinsettii, Urosaurus ornatus, Plestiodon tetragrammus*, and *Aspidoscelis exsanguis*. Of these only *Holbrookia approximans* is limited to México.

The lizard species using the most diverse habitats is *S. clarkii*; it can be found in a variety of conditions that range from tropical deciduous forest in the lowlands of the

Barrancas del Cobre to the semiarid valley of the Pradera de Janos at the northwestern end of the state. *Urosaurus ornatus* occurs in almost the entire state except for the lowlands of the Barrancas del Cobre. This species is one of the most conspicuous in rocky mountains of the Chihuahuan Desert and in the pine-oak forest of the Sierra Madre Occidental. The presence of this species on both sides of the Sierra Madre Occidental implies that it extended southward on both sides from the north. *Holbrookia elegans* shows its greatest abundance in the lowlands of the southwestern part of the state. However, it has also been recorded from the pine/oak forest between the towns of Moris and Ocampo, and it is a common inhabitant of the pine forest of Yécora, Sonora, and the Sonora Desert. *Sceloporus poinsettii* also occupies a large part of the state. This is one of the most abundant and conspicuous lizard species found among boulders and in crevices in the rocky areas of the Chihuahuan Desert and the Sierra Madre Occidental.

Holbrookia approximans is widespread in most of the Chihuahua Desert in the state, but it is also present in oak forests of the foothills of the Sierra Madre Occidental, Sierra de San Luis, and Sierra del Nido. In the Sierra de San Luis this species extends up the Arroyos del Oso and La Madera to dense piñon, juniper, pine, and oak forests, where it occurs at an unusually high density. *Aspidoscelis exsanguis* prefers more or less mesic areas in open, grassy woodlands with piñon, juniper, pine, and oak forest at elevations as great as 2,424 m in the numerous sierras of central Chihuahua (Sierra del Nido, Sierra del Pajarito) and northwestern Chihuahua (Sierra de San Luis and the northern tip of the Sierra Madre Occidental west of Casas Grandes). However, it is also abundant under semiarid conditions in central-north Chihuahua. Finally, *Plestiodon tetragrammus* has been recorded at only 4 localities in the state, all represented by semiarid conditions and pine-oak forests in central Chihuahua.

CHECKLIST BY STATE (U.S. AND MEXICO)

SCIENTIFIC NAME/ BROWN TYPE = NON-NATIVE SPECIES	ENGLISH STANDARD NAME	SPANISH STANDARD NAME/ MEXICAN VERNACULAR
Family Anguidae		
Anniella geronimensis	Baja California Legless Lizard	Lagartija Sin Patas/ Culebra
Anniella pulchra	California Legless Lizard	Lagartija Ápoda/Culebra
Barisia ciliaris	Northern Mexico Alligator Lizard	Escorpión de Montaña/ Escorpión
Barisia levicollis	Chihuahuan Alligator Lizard	Escorpión de Chihuahua/ Escorpión
Elgaria cedrosensis	Isla Cedros Alligator Lizard	Lagarto de Isla Cedros/ Ajolote
Elgaria coerulea	Northern Alligator Lizard	NA/NA
Elgaria kingii	Madrean Alligator Lizard	Lagartija Lagarto de Montaña/ Escorpión del Bosque, Lagartija, Lagarto de Montaña
Elgaria multicarinata	Southern Alligator Lizard	Lagarto Meridional/Ajolote
Elgaria nana	Isla Coronado Alligator Lizard	Lagarto de Isla Coronado/ Ajolote
Elgaria panamintina	Panamint Alligator Lizard	NA/NA
Elgaria paucicarinata	San Lucan Alligator Lizard	Lagarto de Cuatro Patitas/ Ajolote
Elgaria velazquezi	Central Baja California Alligator Lizard	Lagarto de Baja California/ Ajolote
Gerrhonotus infernalis	Texas Alligator Lizard	Cantil de Tierra/Escorpión
Family Bipedidae		
Bipes biporus	Five-toed Worm Lizard	Dos Manos de Cinco Dedos/ Ajolote

U.S. STATES:							MEXICAN STATES:				FOOTNOTES (see page 543 for key)
AZ	CA	CO	NM	NV	TX	UT	BC	BCS	CH	SO	
											non-native in NV
											6.
											1.

SCIENTIFIC NAME/ BROWN TYPE = NON-NATIVE SPECIES	ENGLISH STANDARD NAME	SPANISH STANDARD NAME/ MEXICAN VERNACULAR
Family Chamealeonidae		
Chamaeleo jacksonii	Jackson's Chameleon	NA/NA
Family Crotaphytidae		
Crotaphytus bicinctores	Great Basin Collared Lizard	NA/NA
Crotaphytus collaris	Eastern Collared Lizard	Cachorón de Collar/Lagartija Cabezona, Lagartija de Collar, Cachorón
Crotaphytus dickersonae	Sonoran Collared Lizard	Cachorón Azul de Collar/ Lagartija de Collar, Cachorón, Hast Coof
Crotaphytus grismeri	Sierra Los Cucupás Collared Lizard	Cachorón de Sierra de los Cucapas/Escorpión
Crotaphytus insularis	Isla Ángel de la Guarda Collared Lizard	Cachorón de Collar Isla Ángel de la Guarda/Escorpión
Crotaphytus nebrius	Sonoran Collared Lizard	Cachorón de Sonora/Lagartija de Collar, Cachorón, Hast Coof
Crotaphytus vestigium	Baja California Collared Lizard	Cachorón de Baja California/ Escorpión
Gambelia copeii	Cope's Leopard Lizard	Cachorón Leopardo de Baja California/Cachora
Gambelia sila	Blunt-nosed Leopard Lizard	NA/NA
Gambelia wislizenii	Long-nosed Leopard Lizard	Lagartija Mata Caballo/Lagartija Mata Caballo, Cachorón, Hantpizal
Family Eublepharidae		
Coleonyx brevis	Texas Banded Gecko	Salamanquesa del Desierto/ Salamanquesa de Colores
Coleonyx fasciatus	Black Banded Gecko	Geco de Bandas Negras/Geco de Manchas Negras, Salamanquesa
Coleonyx gypsicolus	Isla San Marcos Banded Gecko	Salamanquesa de Isla San Marcos/Salamanquesa

U.S. STATES:							MEXICAN STATES:				FOOTNOTES (see page 543 for key)
AZ	CA	CO	NM	NV	TX	UT	BC	BCS	CH	SO	
											2, 6.
											2.
											2, 6.

SCIENTIFIC NAME/ BROWN TYPE = NON-NATIVE SPECIES	ENGLISH STANDARD NAME	SPANISH STANDARD NAME/ MEXICAN VERNACULAR
(Family Eublepharidae, continued)		
Coleonyx reticulatus	Reticulate Banded Gecko	Geco Reticulado/NA
Coleonyx switaki	Switak's Banded Gecko	Geco Descalzo/Salamanquesa
Coleonyx variegatus	Western Banded Gecko	Geco de Bandas Occidental/ Salamanquesa de Franjas, Cozixol
Family Gekkonidae		
Gehyra mutilata	Mutilating Gecko	Salamanquesa que Mutila/ Salamanquesa
Hemidactylus frenatus	Common House Gecko	Besucona/Salamanquesa, Besucona
Hemidactylus turcicus	Mediterranean House Gecko	Geco del Mediterráneo/ Salamanquesa, Geco Pinto
Phyllodactylus bugastrolepis	Isla Santa Catalina Leaf-toed Gecko	Salamanquesa de la Isla Santa Catalina/Salamanquesa
Phyllodactylus homolepidurus	Sonoran Leaf-toed Gecko	Salamanquesa de Sonora/ Salamanquesa de Sonora
Phyllodactylus nocticolus	Peninsular Leaf-toed Gecko	Salamanquesa Insular/ Salamanquesa
Phyllodactylus partidus	Isla Partida Norte Leaf-toed Gecko	Salamanquesa de Isla Partida Norte/Salamanquesa
Phyllodactylus tuberculosus	Yellow-bellied Gecko	Geco Panza Amarilla/ Salamanquesa, Geco Tuberculoso
Phyllodactylus unctus	San Lucan Leaf-toed Gecko	Salamanquesa, Salamanquesa de San Lucas/Salamanquesa
Tarentola mauritanica	Moorish Gecko	NA/NA
Family Helodermatidae		
Heloderma horridum	Beaded Lizard	Escorpión/Escorpión, Escorpión Grande, Goowli
Heloderma suspectum	Gila Monster	Monstruo del Gila /Escorpión, Escorpión Pequeño, Escorpión Pintado, Paaza

U.S. STATES:							MEXICAN STATES:				FOOTNOTES (see page 543 for key)
AZ	CA	CO	NM	NV	TX	UT	BC	BCS	CH	SO	
											2, 6.
											6.
											2.

SCIENTIFIC NAME/ BROWN TYPE = NON-NATIVE SPECIES	ENGLISH STANDARD NAME	SPANISH STANDARD NAME/ MEXICAN VERNACULAR
Family Iguanidae		
Ctenosaura conspicuosa	Isla San Esteban Spiny-tailed Iguana	Iguana de Isla San Esteban/ Iguana
Ctenosaura hemilopha	Cape Spiny-tailed Iguana	Iguana del Cabo/Iguana de Palmo
Ctenosaura macrolopha	Sonoran Spiny-tailed Iguana	Iguana de Sonora/Iguana, Iguana de Tierra Firme, Heepni
Ctenosaura nolascensis	Isla San Pedro Nolasco Spiny-tailed Iguana	Iguana de Isla San Pedro Nolasco/ Iguana
Dipsosaurus catalinensis	Isla Santa Catalina Desert Iguana	Cachorón de Isla Santa Catalina/ Cachora; Cachorón
Dipsosaurus dorsalis	Desert Iguana	Cachorón Güero/Porohui, Iguana, Coof Coopol, Cachora, Cachorón Güero
Sauromalus ater	Common Chuckwalla	Cachorón de Roca/Iguana, Coof Coopol
Sauromalus hispidus	Spiny Chuckwalla	Iguana Espinosa de Pared/ Iguana
Sauromalus klauberi	Spotted Chuckwalla	Iguana de Pared Manchada/ Iguana
Sauromalus slevini	Isla Monserrate Chuckwalla	Iguana de Pared de Isla Monserrate/Iguana
Sauromalus varius	Piebald Chuckwalla	Iguana de Pared de Piebald/ Iguana
Family Phrynosomatidae		
Callisaurus draconoides	Zebra-tailed Lizard	Cachora Arenera/Cachora, Perrita, Ctamñfi, Cachorita Blanca, Cachimba
Cophosaurus texanus	Greater Earless Lizard	Lagartijón Sordo/Perilla de Roca, Perrita de Roca, Lagartijon Sordo, Cachora
Holbrookia approximans	Blue-bellied Earless Lizard	Lagartija Sorda Manchada/ Perrilla de Arena, Perrita

U.S. STATES:							MEXICAN STATES:				FOOTNOTES (see page 543 for key)
AZ	CA	CO	NM	NV	TX	UT	BC	BCS	CH	SO	
											2, 6.
											2.
											2; non-native in AZ
											2, 6.
											2, 6.
											6; non-native in SO
											6.
											2, 6.
											6.; non-native in BC
											3.

SCIENTIFIC NAME/ BROWN TYPE = NON-NATIVE SPECIES	ENGLISH STANDARD NAME	SPANISH STANDARD NAME/ MEXICAN VERNACULAR
(Family Phrynosomatidae, continued)		
Holbrookia elegans	Elegant Earless Lizard	Lagartija Sorda Elegante/Lagartija Sorda Mexicana, Cachorrita, Perilla, Perrita, Lagartija Blanca
Holbrookia maculata	Common Lesser Earless Lizard	Lagartija Sorda Pequeña/Perrilla de los Arenales, Perrita de los Arenales, Cachorrita
Petrosaurus mearnsi	Banded Rock Lizard	Lagarto de Roca Rayada/ Lagartija de la Piedra
Petrosaurus repens	Short-nosed Rock Lizard	Lagarto de Roca de Hocico Corto/ Lagartija de la Piedra
Petrosaurus slevini	Slevin's Banded Rock Lizard	Lagarto de Roca Bandeado/ Lagartija de la Piedra
Petrosaurus thalassinus	San Lucan Rock Lizard	Lagarto de Roca de San Lucas/ Cocodrilo, Lagartija Azul
Phrynosoma blainvillii	Blainville's Horned Lizard	Camaleón de Blainville/ Camaleón
Phrynosoma cerroense	Isla Cedros Horned Lizard	Camaleón de Isla Cedros/ Camaleón
Phrynosoma cornutum	Texas Horned Lizard	Camaleón Común/ Camaleón, Camaleón Tejano
Phrynosoma coronatum	Coast Horned Lizard	Camaleón del Litoral/ Camaleón
Phrynosoma ditmarsi	Rock Horned Lizard	Camaleón de Roca/ Camaleón de Piedra
Phrynosoma douglasii	Pygmy Short-horned Lizard	NA/NA
Phrynosoma goodei	Goode's Horned Lizard	Camaleón de Sonora/ Camaleón de Sonora
Phrynosoma hernandesi	Greater Short-horned Lizard	Camaleón Cuernitos de Hernández/Camaleón, Camaleón de Cola Plana, Camaleón del Gran Desierto
Phrynosoma mcallii	Flat-tailed Horned Lizard	Camaleón de Cola Plana/ Camaleón
Phrynosoma modestum	Round-tailed Horned Lizard	Camaleón/Camaleón

U.S. STATES:							MEXICAN STATES:				FOOTNOTES (see page 543 for key)
AZ	CA	CO	NM	NV	TX	UT	BC	BCS	CH	SO	
											3.
											3.
											2, 6.
											2.
											2.
											2.
											2.

SCIENTIFIC NAME/ BROWN TYPE = NON-NATIVE SPECIES	ENGLISH STANDARD NAME	SPANISH STANDARD NAME/ MEXICAN VERNACULAR
(Family Phrynosomatidae, continued)		
Phrynosoma orbiculare	Mountain Horned Lizard	Camaleón de Montaña/Camaleón, Camaleón de Montaña, Sapo Cornudo
Phrynosoma platyrhinos	Desert Horned Lizard	Camaleón del Desierto/Camaleón
Phrynosoma solare	Regal Horned Lizard	Camaleón Real/Camaleón Real, Hant Coáaxoj
Phrynosoma wigginsi	Gulf Coast Horned Lizard	Camaleón de la Costa del Golfo/ Camaleón
Sceloporus albiventris	Western White-bellied Spiny Lizard	Espinosa de Vientre Blanco/ Torosa, Cachorón, Bejore, Bejori, Cochasza, Rochaca, Roñoso
Sceloporus angustus	Isla Santa Cruz Spiny Lizard	Espinosa de la Isla Santa Cruz/ Cachora
Sceloporus arenicolus	Dunes Sagebrush Lizard	NA/NA
Sceloporus bimaculosus	Twin-spotted Spiny Lizard	Cachora/Roñoso, Lagartija Rasposa
Sceloporus clarkii	Clark's Spiny Lizard	Bejori de Clark/Bejore, Bejori, Cochaca, Rochaca, Lagartija Espinosa de Clark, Cachora, Haasj
Sceloporus consobrinus	Prairie Lizard	Lagartija de las Cercas/NA
Sceloporus cowlesi	Southwestern Fence Lizard	Lagartija de Cowles/Lagartija de Cerca, Cachora
Sceloporus edbelli	Bell's Lizard	Espinosa de Bell/Lagartija de los Mezquites, Roñoso de los Mezquites
Sceloporus graciosus	Common Sagebrush Lizard	Meridional de las Salvias/Bejori, Lagartija
Sceloporus grandaevus	Isla Cerralvo Spiny Lizard	Espinosa de la Isla Cerralvo/ Cachora
Sceloporus hunsakeri	Hunsaker's Spiny Lizard	Espinosa de Hunsaker/ Bejori, Canarro
Sceloporus jarrovii	Yarrow's Spiny Lizard	Lagartija de Yarrow/Roñoso, Rochaca, Cachorón, Lagartija Espinosa de Yarrow

U.S. STATES:							MEXICAN STATES:				FOOTNOTES (see page 543 for key)
AZ	CA	CO	NM	NV	TX	UT	BC	BCS	CH	SO	
											2.
											2, 6.
											2.
											4.
											2.
											2, 6.

SCIENTIFIC NAME/ BROWN TYPE = NON-NATIVE SPECIES	ENGLISH STANDARD NAME	SPANISH STANDARD NAME/ MEXICAN VERNACULAR
(Family Phrynosomatidae, continued)		
Sceloporus lemosespinali	Lemos-Espinal's Spiny Lizard	Lagartija de Lemos-Espinal/ Lagartija Negra de los Árboles, Cachora
Sceloporus licki	Cape Arboreal Spiny Lizard	Bejori Arborícola del Cabo/ Bejori
Sceloporus lineatulus	Isla Santa Catalina Spiny Lizard	Bejori de Isla Santa Catalina/ Bejori
Sceloporus magister	Desert Spiny Lizard	Lagartija del Desierto/Lagartija Espinosa del Desierto, Cachorón, Haasj, Bejori
Sceloporus merriami	Canyon Lizard	Lagartija de Cañón/Lagartija de las Peñas
Sceloporus nelsoni	Nelson's Spiny Lizard	Espinosa de Nelson/Lagartija Espinosa de Nelson, Cachorrita, Bejore Chico, Bejori Chico, Lagartija de Panza Azul, Rochaquita
Sceloporus occidentalis	Western Fence Lizard	Bejora de Cerca Occidental/ Bejori
Sceloporus olivaceus	Texas Spiny Lizard	Espinosa de los Árboles/Lagartija Espinosa.
Sceloporus orcutti	Granite Spiny Lizard	Espinosa del Granito/Bejori, Canarro
Sceloporus poinsettii	Crevice Spiny Lizard	Lagartija de las Grietas/Lagartija Espinosa de Barrada, Cachorón
Sceloporus slevini	Slevin's Bunchgrass Lizard	Espinosa de Pastizal de Slevin/ Lagartija del Zacate, Lagartija de Pastizal de Slevin, Cachora
Sceloporus tristichus	Plateau Fence Lizard	NA/NA
Sceloporus uniformis	Yellow-backed Spiny Lizard	Bejora de Espalda Amarilla [Roño de Suelo]/NA
Sceloporus virgatus	Striped Plateau Lizard	Lagartija Rayada de la Meseta/ Lagartija, Lagartija de Meseta Rayada, Cachora
Sceloporus zosteromus	Baja California Spiny Lizard	Bejori/Bejori, Canarro

U.S. STATES:							MEXICAN STATES:				FOOTNOTES (see page 543 for key)
AZ	CA	CO	NM	NV	TX	UT	BC	BCS	CH	SO	
											6.
											2.
											2.
											2.
											2.

SCIENTIFIC NAME/ BROWN TYPE = NON-NATIVE SPECIES	ENGLISH STANDARD NAME	SPANISH STANDARD NAME/ MEXICAN VERNACULAR
(Family Phrynosomatidae, continued)		
Uma inornata	Coachella Fringe-toed Lizard	NA/NA
Uma notata	Colorado Desert Fringe-toed Lizard	Arenera del Desierto del Colorado/Cachora
Uma paraphygas	Chihuahuan Fringe-toed Lizard	Arenera de Chihuahua/Perrilla de los Arenales, Perrita de los Arenales
Uma rufopunctata	Yuman Fringe-toed Lizard	Arenera de Manchas Laterales/ Lagartija de Manchas Laterales, Cachora
Uma scoparia	Mohave Fringe-toed Lizard	NA/NA
Urosaurus bicarinatus	Tropical Tree Lizard	Roñito Arborícola/Roñino, Lagartija, Cachorrita, Salamanquesa, Salamanquesca
Urosaurus graciosus	Long-tailed Brush Lizard	Roñito de Matorral/Lagartija de Matorral, Cachorrita, Lagartija
Urosaurus lahtelai	Cataviña Brush Lizard	Roñito de Matorral Bajacaliforniano/Lagartija
Urosaurus nigricaudus	Baja California Brush Lizard	Roñito de Matorral Cola-negra/ Lagartija
Urosaurus ornatus	Ornate Tree Lizard	Roñito Ornado/Roñosa, Lagartija de Árbol, Cachorrita, Hehe Iti Cooscl
Uta encantadae	Enchanted Side-blotched Lizard	Mancha Lateral Encantadas/ Lagartija
Uta lowei	Dead Side-blotched Lizard	Mancha Lateral Muerta/ Lagartija
Uta nolascensis	Isla San Pedro Nolasco Lizard	Mancha Lateral de San Pedro Nolasco/Lagartija
Uta palmeri	Isla San Pedro Mártir Side-blotched Lizard	Mancha Lateral de San Pedro Mártir/Lagartija
Uta squamata	Isla Santa Catalina Side-blotched Lizard	Mancha Lateral Santa Catalina/ Lagartija Verde
Uta stansburiana	Common Side-blotched Lizard	Mancha Lateral Común/ Lagartija, Cachora Gris, Tozipla
Uta tumidarostra	Swollen-nosed Side-blotched Lizard	Mancha Lateral Narigona/ Lagartija

U.S. STATES:							MEXICAN STATES:				FOOTNOTES (see page 543 for key)
AZ	CA	CO	NM	NV	TX	UT	BC	BCS	CH	SO	
											2.
											2.
											2.
											2, 6.
											2, 6.
											2, 6.
											2, 6.
											2, 6.
											2.
											2, 6.

SCIENTIFIC NAME/ BROWN TYPE = NON-NATIVE SPECIES	ENGLISH STANDARD NAME	SPANISH STANDARD NAME/ MEXICAN VERNACULAR
Family Polychrotidae		
Anolis nebulosus	Clouded Anole	Roño de Paño/Pañuelo, Lagartija, Cachorrita, Lagartija de Papada Rosa
Family Scincidae		
Plestiodon "gilberti"	Gilbert's Skink	Lincer de Gilbert/Ajolote Rayado
Plestiodon brevirostris	Short-nosed Skink	Alicante/Axolote, Sorcuate
Plestiodon callicephalus	Mountain Skink	Lincer de Barranco/Lagartija de Cola Azul, Lincer de Barranco, Salamanquesa, Ajolote
Plestiodon lagunensis	San Lucan Skink	Lincer de la Laguna/Ajolotito Rayado
Plestiodon multilineatus	Chihuahuan Skink	Eslaboncillo/Ajolote
Plestiodon multivirgatus	Many-lined Skink	None given/Lagartija Azul, Lagartija Brillante
Plestiodon obsoletus	Great Plains Skink	Lincer de Llanura/Lagartija Amarilla, Lincer Llanero, Salamanquesa
Plestiodon parviauriculatus	Northern Pygmy Skink	Lincer Pigmeo Norteño/ Salamanquesa, Ajolote, Axolote
Plestiodon skiltonianus	Western Skink	Lincer Occidental/Ajolote Rayado
Plestiodon tetragrammus	Four-lined Skink	Lincer de Cuatro Líneas/Lagartija Azul
Scincella lateralis	Little Brown Skink	Escincela de Tierra/Lagartija
Family Teiidae		
Aspidoscelis arizonae	Arizona Striped Whiptail	NA/NA
Aspidoscelis bacata	Isla San Pedro Nolasco Whiptail	Huico de Isla San Pedro Nolasco
Aspidoscelis burti	Canyon Spotted Whiptail	Huico Manchado de Cañón/Güico Güico, Huico, Ctoixa
Aspidoscelis cana	Isla Salsipuedes Whiptail	Huico de la Isla Salsipuedes/ Güico

U.S. STATES:							MEXICAN STATES:				FOOTNOTES (see page 543 for key)
AZ	CA	CO	NM	NV	TX	UT	BC	BCS	CH	SO	
											2.
											2, 4.
											2.
											2.
											2, 6.
											6.

SCIENTIFIC NAME/ BROWN TYPE = NON-NATIVE SPECIES	ENGLISH STANDARD NAME	SPANISH STANDARD NAME/ MEXICAN VERNACULAR
(Family Teiidae, continued)		
Aspidoscelis carmenensis	Isla Carmen Whiptail	Huico de Isla Carmen/Güico
Aspidoscelis catalinensis	Isla Santa Catalina Whiptail	Huico de la Isla Santa Catalina/ Güico
Aspidoscelis celeripes	Isla San José Western Whiptail	Huico Occidental de la Isla San José/Güico
Aspidoscelis ceralbensis	Isla Cerralvo Whiptail	Huico de la Isla Cerralvo/Güico
Aspidoscelis costata	Western México Whiptail	Huico Llanero/Guico, Huico, Huico Llanero
Aspidoscelis danheimae	Isla San José Whiptail	Huico de la Isla San José/Güico
Aspidoscelis dixoni	Gray Checkered Whiptail	Huico Gris/NA
Aspidoscelis espiritensis	Isla Espíritu Santo Whiptail	Huico de Isla Espíritu Santo/Güico
Aspidoscelis estebanensis	Isla San Esteban Whiptail	Huico de Isla San Esteban/Güico
Aspidoscelis exsanguis	Chihuahuan Spotted Whiptail	Corredora de Chihuahua/Lagartijo, Huico, Huico Pinto de Chihuahua
Aspidoscelis flagellicauda	Gila Spotted Whiptail	NA/NA
Aspidoscelis franciscensis	Isla San Francisco Whiptail	Huico de Isla San Francisco/Güico
Aspidoscelis gularis	Common Spotted Whiptail	Corredora Pinta Texana/Lagartijo
Aspidoscelis gypsi	Little White Whiptail	NA/NA
Aspidoscelis hyperythra	Orange-throated Whiptail	Huico Garganta Naranja/Güico
Aspidoscelis inornata	Little Striped Whiptail	Huico Liso/Lagartijo de Cola Azul
Aspidoscelis labialis	Baja California Whiptail	Huico de Baja California/Güico
Aspidoscelis marmorata	Marbled Whiptail	Huico Marmóreo/Lagartijo
Aspidoscelis martyris	Isla San Pedro Mártir Whiptail	Huico de Isla San Pedro Mártir/ Güico
Aspidoscelis neomexicana	New Mexico Whiptail	NA/NA
Aspidoscelis neotesselata	Colorado Checkered Whiptail	NA/NA
Aspidoscelis opatae	Opata Whiptail	Huico Opata/Huico, Huico Opata
Aspidoscelis pai	Pai Striped Whiptail	NA/NA
Aspidoscelis picta	Isla Monserrate Whiptail	Huico de la Isla Monserrate/ Güico
Aspidoscelis scalaris	Plateau Spotted Whiptail	Corredora Pinta Occidental/ Lagartijo

U.S. STATES:							MEXICAN STATES:				FOOTNOTES (see page 543 for key)
AZ	CA	CO	NM	NV	TX	UT	BC	BCS	CH	SO	
											2, 6.
											6.
											2, 6.
											6.
											6.
											5.
											2, 6
											2, 6.
											2, 6.
											3.
											2.
											4, 6.
											non-native in AZ, UT
											6.
											3.

SCIENTIFIC NAME/ BROWN TYPE = NON-NATIVE SPECIES	ENGLISH STANDARD NAME	SPANISH STANDARD NAME/ MEXICAN VERNACULAR
(Family Teiidae, continued)		
Aspidoscelis sexlineata	Six-lined Racerunner	Huico de Seis Líneas/Huico
Aspidoscelis sonorae	Sonoran Spotted Whiptail	Huico Manchado de Sonora/ Lagartijo, Huico, Huico Manchado de Sonora
Aspidoscelis tesselata	Common Checkered Whiptail	Huico Teselado/Lagartijo del Río
Aspidoscelis tigris	Tiger Whiptail	Huico Tigre/Huico, Huico Occidental
Aspidoscelis uniparens	Desert Grassland Whiptail	Huico de la Pradera del Desierto/ Lagartijo, Huico de la Pradera del Desierto
Aspidoscelis velox	Plateau Striped Whiptail	NA/NA
Aspidoscelis xanthonota	Red-backed Whiptail	Huico de Dorso-rojo/NA
Family Xantusiidae		
Xantusia arizonae	Arizona Night Lizard	NA/NA
Xantusia bezyi	Bezy's Night Lizard	NA/NA
Xantusia gracilis	Sandstone Night Lizard	NA/NA
Xantusia henshawi	Granite Night Lizard	Nocturna de Granito/ Salamanquesa
Xantusia riversiana	Island Night Lizard	NA/NA
Xantusia sierrae	Sierra Night Lizard	NA/NA
Xantusia vigilis	Desert Night Lizard	Nocturna del Desierto/ Salamanquesa, Cozixoj
Xantusia wigginsi	Wiggins' Night Lizard	Nocturna de Wiggins/ Salamanquesa

REVIEWERS AND COMPILERS OF THIS CHECKLIST:

AZ: Thomas C. Brennan

BC and BCS: Robert E. Lovich and L. Lee Grismer

CA: Robert E. Espinoza

CH: Julio A. Lemos-Espinal

CO: Lauren J. Livo

NV: Paulette M. Conrad

NM: Charles W. Painter

SO: James C. Rorabaugh and Erik F. Enderson

TX: James R. Dixon

UT: Daniel G. Mulcahy

Mexico overall: Julio A. Lemos-Espinal

Entire checklist overall: Lawrence L. C. Jones and Robert E. Lovich

U.S. STATES:							MEXICAN STATES:				FOOTNOTES (see below for key)
AZ	CA	CO	NM	NV	TX	UT	BC	BCS	CH	SO	
											2.
											2, 5.
											6.
											2.

KEY TO FOOTNOTES:

1. A worm-lizard
2. Taxonomy and/or nomenclature of Liner and Casas-Andreu (2008) modified to correct typographic errors, agree with standards of de Quieroz and Reeder (2008), or meet standard nomenclatural conventions.
3. Significant differences in taxonomic and nomenclatural interpretations between de Quieroz and Reeder (2008) and Liner and Casas-Andreu (2008) cannot be resolved in this checklist.
4. Not in Liner and Casas-Andreu (2008)
5. In Liner and Casas-Andreu (2008), but not recorded in Mexico
6. Island endemic

ACKNOWLEDGMENTS

We would like to acknowledge all of the authors who contributed to this book, as well as those potential authors who were equally qualified, but could not be accommodated as contributors. We thank all of our fine photographers—they make our book look good, and we hate to think of what it would look like if we had to rely on our own photographs! We also thank the other contributors who helped with specific parts of this book, including Randy Babb (illustrations), Esther Nelson (maps), Janet Jones (editing), and Jim Rorabaugh (photograph editing). While the editors' names appear alone on the front cover, this entire book was a team effort and could not have been completed without all of the people mentioned and highlighted in this section. Also, this book would not have been possible without the financial assistance of the sponsors listed in the front of the book.

We thank the staff of Rio Nuevo Publishers for their support throughout this project: Christine Barry, Ross Humphreys, Carrie Stusse, Lisa Anderson, and Caroline Cook.

We the editors, authors, and other contributors also relied on the personal contacts covering a lifetime of experience with the people we interacted with. Thus, it is impossible to really thank all of the people who helped us to contribute to this field guide. We thank the following people: Matt Anderson, Jim Archie, Kevin Baker, Kevin Bonine, George Bradley, David Brown, R. Bruce Bury, Young Cage, Anne Casey, Chip Cochran, Charles (Jay) Cole, Joe Collins, Charles Conner, Taylor Cotton, Brian Crother, David Cundall, Kevin de Queiroz, Taylor Edwards, Daniel Esterbrooks, Linda Ford, Glenn Frederick, Darrel Frost, Ernie Garcia, Brooke Gebow, Elizabeth Goldstein, Matt Goode, Randy Gray, Paul Hamilton, Bob Hansen, Arthur Harris, Mike Hill, Peter Holm, Andy Holycross, Jerry Husack, Tina Jackson, Kent Jacobs, Josh Jones, Kris Karsten, Shawn Kuchta, Jennifer Lancaster, Dean Leavitt, Ernie Liner, Day Ligon, Matt Lovern, Charles Lowe, Mark Madrid, Roy McDiarmid, Joe Mitchell, Priya Nanjappa-Mitchell, Kirsten Nicholson, Erika Nowak, Elissa Ostergaard, Jennifer Ramirez, Tod Reeder, Roger Repp, Daren Riedle, Stephen Romaniello, Don Sias, Kary Schlick, Debbie Sebesta, Jackson Shedd, Wade Sherbrooke, Raymond Skiles, Tom Skinner, Dan Silver, Hobart Smith, Lora Smith, Nikki Smith, Jerre Ann Stallcup, Robert Stebbins, Keith Sullivan, Josh Taiz, Harry Taylor, Gail Tunberg, Don Virgovic, Bruce Weissgold, Michael White, and Joe Yarchin. And to those of you who should have been acknowledged, but were forgotten, please accept our humblest apologies—then write your name in this section!

Let's not forget the agencies and nongovernment organizations that helped support this book by allowing their employees to work on the *Lizards of the American*

Southwest or by allowing access to their lizard-bearing grounds. In-kind service acknowledgment is extended to all of the affiliations shown in the Contributors section. Plus there was additional support from all of the state game and fish agencies of Arizona, California, Colorado, Nevada, New Mexico, Texas, and Utah. Federal agency support included the Department of Defense, Fish and Wildlife Service, Forest Service, National Park Service, and Geological Survey. We also thank all state and local governments for their support.

—*Larry Jones and Rob Lovich*

CONTRIBUTORS AND PHOTOGRAPHY CREDITS

Edward W. Acuña (text)

Brad Alexander (photos), Kernville, CA: photos on pages 190, 191, 219, 246, 278, 300, 437, 472, 475, 477, 562 row 2 left

Ralph W. Axtell (text), Southern Illinois University, Edwardsville, IL

Randall D. Babb (text, photos, illustrations except for maps), Arizona Game and Fish Department, Phoenix, AZ: photos on pages 328, 375, 561 row 4; illustrations on pages 43, 45, 47, 49

Aaron M. Bauer (text), Villanova University, Villanova, PA

Cameron W. Barrows (text, photos), University of California, Riverside, Palm Desert, CA: photo on page 185

Kent R. Beaman (text), Natural History Museum of Los Angeles, Los Angeles, CA

Daniel D. Beck (text), Central Washington University, Ellensburg, WA

Robert L. Bezy (text)

Russell Blaine (text), Washington University in St. Louis, St. Louis, MO

Thomas C. Brennan (text, photos), Tempe, AZ: photos on pages 37, 42, 100, 132, 143, 144, 145, 148, 151, 153, 166, 175, 250, 251, 274, 275, 279, 282, 294, 313, 330, 331, 376, 394, 399, 407, 408, 409, 413, 414, 417, 419, 436, 447, 457, 458, 481, 482, 499, 560 row 3 left, 561 row 1 left, 562 row 1 left

Tracey K. Brown (text, photos), California State University, San Marcos, CA

Doug Burkett (text, photos), White Sands Missile Range, NM: photos on pages 8 top, 107 bottom, 127

Matthew D. Caron (text), Saguaro National Park, Tucson, AZ: photo on page 258

Paulette M. Conrad (text, photos), Nevada Department of Wildlife, Las Vegas, NV: photo on page 258

James R. Dixon (text), Department of Wildlife and Fisheries Sciences, College Station, TX

Charles A. Drost (text), US Geological Survey, Flagstaff, AZ

Eric A. Dugan (text, photos), Loma Linda University, Loma Linda, CA: photos on pages 308, 310

Taylor Edwards (text), University of Arizona, Tucson, AZ

Erik F. Enderson (text), Drylands Institute, Tucson, AZ

Robert E. Espinoza (text, photos), California State University, Northridge, CA: photos on pages 19, 46, 314, 315

Gary M. Fellers (text, photos), U.S. Geological Survey, Point Reyes, CA: photos on pages 428, 429, 431, 484, 561 row 5

Mark Fisher (text), University of California–Natural Reserve System, Palm Desert, CA

Lee A. Fitzgerald (text), Texas A&M University, College Station, TX

Stanley F. Fox (text), Oklahoma State University, Stillwater, OK

David J. Germano (text, photos), California State University, Bakersfield, CA: photos on pages 120, 121, 122, 123

Harry W. Greene (text), Cornell University, Ithaca, NY

L. Lee Grismer (text), La Sierra University, Riverside, CA

Robert Haase (text), Oceanside, CA

Terry Hibbitts (photos), Camp Wood, TX: photos on pages 187, 202, 240, 248, 263, 301, 304, 307, 340, 359, 363, 364, 365, 378, 379, 380, 392, 393, 464, 487

Toby Hibbitts (photos), Texas A&M University, College Station, TX: photos on pages 34, 86, 189, 198, 236, 238, 239, 335, 338, 362, 460, 462, 467, 506

Troy and Marla Hibbitts (photos), Camp Wood, TX: photos on pages 30, 125, 203, 204, 205, 211, 212, 220, 221, 231, 232, 233, 245, 257, 261, 295, 297, 302, 305, 306, 339, 347, 348, 349, 358, 383, 390, 391, 425, 426, 427, 439, 449, 454, 455, 461, 463, 465, 469, 476, 479, 488, 489, 491, 492, 493, 494, 495, 515, 516, 517, 560 row 1 left and row 5 right, 562 row 1 right and row 2, 563 row 2 middle and right

Wendy L. Hodges (text), University of Texas at Austin, Austin, TX

Bradford D. Hollingsworth (text), San Diego Natural History Museum, San Diego, CA

Jeffrey M. Howland (text), Bitter Lake National Wildlife Refuge, Roswell, NM

Craig S. Ivanyi (text), Arizona-Sonora Desert Museum, Tucson, AZ

Randy D. Jennings (text), Western New Mexico University, Silver City, NM

Lawrence L. C. Jones (text, photos, maps), Casa Araña, Tucson, AZ: photos on front cover, pages 1, 14, 24, 26, 27, 28, 29, 32, 35, 39, 40, 41, 48, 51, 53, 54 bottom, 55, 56, 57, 58, 59, 60, 61, 62, 63, 64, 65, 67, 68, 70, 73, 74, 75, 76, 77, 78, 80, 81, 82, 85, 104, 105, 107 top, 111, 124, 131, 137, 139, 140, 146, 147, 149, 150, 152, 155,

156, 157, 158, 167, 168, 188, 194, 195, 196, 199, 200, 206, 208, 209, 214, 217, 223, 225, 226, 230, 234, 235, 241, 243, 244, 252, 253, 262, 265, 283, 285, 290, 291, 293, 316, 332, 337, 342, 344, 351, 361, 367, 368, 369, 377, 382, 386, 387, 388, 389, 398, 401, 405, 423, 468, 473, 497, 501, 508, 512, 513, 560 row 3 middle and right, 561 row 1 middle, 562 row 1 right,

Thomas R. Jones (photos), Arizona Game and Fish Department, Phoenix, AZ: photo on page 415

Matthew A. Kwiatkowski (text), Department of Biology, Stephen F. Austin University, Nacogdoches, TX

Megan E. Lahti (text, photos), Utah State University, Logan, UT: photos on pages 162, 163, 170

Adam D. Leaché (text), University of California, Berkeley, CA

Allison F. Leavitt (text), Huntsville, TX

Daniel J. Leavitt (text), Texas A&M University, College Station, TX

Jeffrey M. Lemm (text, photos), Zoological Society of San Diego (CRES), Escondido, CA: photos on pages 237, 286, 287, 288, 289, 309, 311, 312, 354, 355, 357, 395, 397, 411, 441, 486

William Leonard (photos), Olympia, WA: photos on pages 173, 197, 324, 346, 438

Julio A. Lemos-Espinal (text, photos), Unidad de Biología, Tecnología y Prototipos, UNAM, Tlalnepantla, edo. de México: photos on pages 71, 520

Lauren J. Livo (text, photos), University of Colorado, Boulder, CO: photos on pages 69, 106, 213, 370, 371, 372, 373, 384, 452, 453

Kim Lovich (text), Zoological Society of San Diego, San Diego, CA

Robert E. Lovich (text, photos), Loma Linda University, Loma Linda, CA: photos on pages 17, 165, 242, 277, 296, 320, 356, 421, 422, 424, 505 bottom

Clark R. Mahrdt (text, photos), San Diego Natural History Museum, San Diego, CA: photos on pages 117, 118, 119

Daniel G. Mulcahy (text, photos), Brigham Young University, Provo, UT: photos on p. 31, 271, 273

Brad Moon (photos): photos on pages 9, 79, 169, 416, 444

Gary Nafis (photos): photos on pages 8 bottom, 171, 172, 266, 341, 350, 433, 434, 435, 440, 471, 504, 505 top

Larry Neel (photos): photos on pages 259, 260, 478

Esther I. Nelson (maps), Santa Fe National Forest, Las Vegas Ranger District, Las Vegas, NM

Charles W. Painter (text), New Mexico Department of Game and Fish, Santa Fe, NM

Trevor B. Persons (text, photos), USGS Southwest Biological Science Center, Flagstaff, AZ, and Norridgewock, ME: photos on pages 343, 366, 374, 402

Philip M. Ralidis (text)

William R. Radke (photos): photos on p. 33, 178, 201, 210, 218, 268, 269, 456

Charles S. Rau (text, photos): photos on pages 2, 6, 10, 44, 133, 179, 215, 216, 222, 292, 336, 446, 459, 498

Jonathan Q. Richmond (text, photos), Cornell University, Ithaca, NY: photos on pages 445, 451

James C. Rorabaugh (text, photos), US Fish and Wildlife Service, Tucson, AZ: photos on back cover and pages 22, 52, 54 top, 92, 129, 130, 134, 160, 164, 174, 176, 177, 182, 183, 184, 193, 207, 228, 247, 264, 267, 270, 272, 299, 319, 321, 322, 323, 412, 442, 443, 483, 485, 500, 502, 503, 560 row 2 left, 561 row 3, 562 row 3

Philip C. Rosen (text), University of Arizona, Tucson, AZ

Erica Bree Rosenblum (text, photos), University of Idaho, Moscow, ID: photos on pages 87, 154, 353

Mason J. Ryan (text), University of New Mexico, Albuquerque, NM

Cecil R. Schwalbe (text, photos), US Geological Survey, Southwest Biological Science Center, Sonoran Desert Research Station, University of Arizona, Tucson, AZ photos on pages 36, 102, 126, 186, 227, 229, 281

Michael J. Sredl (text), Arizona Game and Fish Department, Phoenix, AZ

Brian K. Sullivan (text, photos), Arizona State University at the West Campus, Phoenix, AZ: photos on pages 326, 327, 329

Don E. Swann (text), Saguaro National Park, Tucson, AZ

Dale S. Turner (text), The Nature Conservancy, Tucson, AZ

Robert G. Webb (text, photos), University of Texas at El Paso, El Paso, TX: photo on pages 249

William Wells (photos), Surprise, AZ: photos on pages 38, 99, 101, 103, 108, 109, 110, 112, 113, 114, 115, 135, 136, 138, 142, 159, 161, 180, 181, 254, 255, 256, 325, 345, 403, 511, 560 row 1 right and row 2 right, 560 row 5 left and middle

Steve Wilcox (photos), Lakewood, CO: photos on pages 69, 106, 213, 370, 371, 372, 373, 384, 452, 453

John W. Wright (text), Natural History Museum of Los Angeles County, Los Angeles, CA

Kevin V. Young (text), Logan, UT

REFERENCES AND OTHER RESOURCES

Web Pages

There are many Web resources available, and URLs often change, so we just list the main societies for herpetology, the primary American Southwest regional scientific organization, and 2 important herpetological Web links. However, we encourage everyone to do searches for the sponsors listed in the front of the book, as well as on the species in the book and other areas of interest. These searches can be quite productive if you want to know more about lizards or are preparing for a lizarding adventure.

Partners in Amphibian and Reptile Conservation (www.parcplace.org).

Society for the Study of Amphibians and Reptiles (www.ssarherps.org/), publisher of the scholarly journals *Journal of Herpetology* and *Herpetological Review*, and *Catalogue of American Amphibians and Reptiles.*

The Herpetologists' League (www.hljournals.org/), publisher of the scholarly journal *Herpetologica.*

American Society of Ichthyologists and Herpetologists (www.asih.org/), publisher of the scholarly journal *Copeia.*

Southwestern Association of Naturalists (www.biosurvey.ou.edu/swan/), publisher of the scholarly journal *The Southwestern Naturalist.*

Center for North American Herpetology (www.naherpetology.org/).

Literature

There are thousands of scientific and popular papers on lizards of the American Sout west, and as with Web pages above, we are limiting the resources below to a few of the multiple-species books and symposia, plus the references for our taxonomic and nomenclatural standards and some papers on Sonoran herpetology (there are no books dedicated to the topic) and global decline.

Bartlett, R. D., and P. Bartlett. 1997. Lizard care from a to z. Hauppauge, NY. Barron's Educational Series. 180 p.

Behler, J. L., and F. W. King. 1979. The audubon society field guide to north american reptiles and amphibians. New York, NY. Alfred A. Knopf. 743 p.

Bogart, C. M. and J. A. Oliver. 1945. A preliminary analysis of the herpetofauna of Sonora. Bulletin of the American Museum of Natural History 83(6): 297–426.

Brennan, T. C., and A. T. Holycross. 2006. A field guide to amphibians and reptiles of Arizona. Phoenix, AZ. Arizona Game and Fish Department, 150 p.

Brown, D.E. ed. 1994. Biotic communities: southwestern United States and northwestern New Mexico. Salt Lake City, UT. University of Utah Press. 342 p. [This and the accompanying map by D. E. Brown and C. H. Lowe are a most valuable resource for understanding habitats of the American Southwest and targeting lizards to view.]

Brown, P. R., and J. W. Wright, eds. 1994. Herpetology of the North American deserts: proceedings of a symposium. Southwestern Herpetological Society Special Publication 5. 331 p.

Conant, R., and J. T. Collins. 1998. A field guide to reptiles and amphibians, eastern and central North America. Boston, MA and New York, NY. Houghton-Mifflin Co. 616 p.

Cornett, J. W. 2006. Desert Lizards. Palm Springs, CA. Nature Trails Press. 68 p.

Crother, B. I. (ed.). 2008. Scientific and standard English names of amphibians and reptiles of North America north of Mexico, pp. 1–84. SSAR Herpetological Circular 37.

Degenhardt, W. G., C. W. Painter, and A. H. Price. 1996. Amphibians and reptiles of New Mexico. Albuquerque, NM. University of New Mexico Press. 504 p.

de Queiroz, K., and T. W. Reeder. 2008. Squamata: lizards, pp 24–45. In: Scientific and standard English names of amphibians and reptiles of North America north of Mexico, B. I. Crother, ed. Society for the Study of Amphibians and Reptiles, Herpetological Circular 37.

Dixon, James R. 2000. Amphibians and reptiles of Texas. College Station, TX. Texas A&M University Press. 425 p.

Enderson, E. F., A. Q. Mascareñas, D. S. Turner, R. L. Bezy, and P. C. Rosen. Forthcoming. A synopsis of the herpetofauna of Sonora with comments on research and conservation priorities. In Biodiversidad de Sonora, México. Universidad Nacional Autónoma de México y la comisión nacional para el conocimiento y uso de la biodiversidad. F. M. Freaner and T. R. VanDevender (eds)

Fox, S. F., K. McCoy, and T. A. Baird. 2003. Lizard social behavior. Baltimore, MD.Johns Hopkins University Press. 456 p.

Garrett, J. D., and D. G. Barker. 1987. A field guide to reptiles and amphibians of Texas. Texas Monthly Fieldguide Series. Houston, TX. Gulf Publishing Company. 225 p.

Gibbons, J. W., D. E. Scott, T.J. Ryan, K.A. Buhlmann, T.D. Tuberville, B.M. Metts, J.L. Greene, T. Mills, Y. Leiden, S. Poppy, and C.T. Winne. 2000. The global decline of reptiles, déjà vu amphibians. Bioscience 50(8).

Grismer, L. L. 2002. Amphibians and reptiles of Baja California, its Pacific Islands, and the islands in the Sea of Cortés. Berkeley, CA. University of California Press. 402 p.

Hammerson, G.A. 1999. Amphibians and reptiles in Colorado: a Colorado field guide, 2nd ed. Niwot, CO. University Press of Colorado. 510 p.

Huey R. B., Eric R. Pianka, and T. W. Schoener, eds. 1983. Lizard ecology: studies of a model organism. Cambridge, MA. Harvard University Press. 501 p.

Lemm, J. M. 2006. Field guide to amphibians and reptiles of the San Diego region (California natural history guides). Berkeley, CA. University of California Press. 344 p.

Lemos-Espinal, J. A., and H. M. Smith. 2007. Anfibios y reptiles del Estado de Chihuahua, México. Tlalnepantla, estado de México: Universidad Nacional Autónomico de México. 613 p.

Levell, J. P. A. 1997. Field guide to reptiles and the law, 2nd ed. Lanesboro, MN. Serpent's Tale. 270 p.

Liner, E. A., and G. Casas-Andreu. 2008. Nombres estándar en Español en Inglés y nombres científicos de los anfibios y reptiles de México," 2nd ed. Society for the Study of Amphibians and Reptiles Herpetological Circular 38.

McPeak, R. H. 2000. Amphibians and reptiles of Baja California. Monterey, CA. Sea Challengers. 99 p.

Milstead, W. W., ed. 1967. Lizard ecology: a symposium, University of Missouri at Kansas City, June 13–15, 1965. Columbia, MI. University of Missouri Press. 300 p.

Pianka, E. R., and L. J. Vitt. 2006. Lizards: windows to the evolution of diversity. Berkeley, CA. University of California Press. 334 p.

Rorabaugh, J. C. 2008. An introduction to the herpetofauna of mainland Sonora, México, with comments on conservation and management. Journal of the Arizona-Nevada Academy of Science 40(1):21–62.

Sanborn, S. R. 1994. The lizard-watching guide: the common lizards of southern California's Mojave and Colorado deserts. Salt Lake City, UT. Lorraine Press. 36 p.

Sherbrooke, W. C. 1981. Horned lizards, unique reptiles of western North America. Tucson, AZ. Southwest Parks and Monuments Association. 48 p.

Sherbrooke, W. C. 2003. Introduction to horned lizards of North America. Berkeley, CA. University of California Press. 191 p.

Stebbins, R. C. A. 2003. Field guide to western reptiles and amphibians, 3rd ed. Boston, MA. Houghton Mifflin. 544 p.

Smith, H. M. 1946. Handbook of lizards: lizards of the United States and of Canada. Ithaca, NY. Comstock 557 p.

Smith, H. M., and E. D. Brodie, Jr. 1982. Reptiles of North America: a guide to field identification. New York, NY. St. Martins Press. 240 p.

Vitt, L. J., and E. R. Pianka, eds. 1994. Lizard ecology: historical and experimental perspectives. Cambridge, MA. Harvard University Press. 501 p.

Wright, J.W., and L. J. Vitt, eds. 1993. Biology of whiptail lizards (genus Cnemidophorus). Norman, OK. Oklahoma Museum of Natural History. 417 p.

Zug, G. R., L. J. Vitt, and J. P. Caldwell. 2001. Herpetology: an introductory biology of amphibians and reptiles. San Diego, CA. Academic Press. 630 p.

GLOSSARY

Note: Many of the definitions given here apply specifically to their use in lizard anatomy; many of these terms may have somewhat different meanings when referring to human anatomy.

Aestivation: A period of summer dormancy to escape hot, dry conditions.

Allopatric: Referring to ranges and populations of two or more different species that do not overlap.

Anterior: Pertaining to the front (in the case of lizards, this is usually the head and forebody). *See Figure 2.*

Anthropogenic: Caused by humans.

Areola: As used in this book, coloration around blotches on sand lizards.

Arroyo: A channel formed by a stream that is often dry.

Autotomy: The ability of a lizard to shed its tail as a defense mechanism.

Axilla: Armpit, or base of forelimb. See *Figure 2.*

Bajada: A broad, sloping deposition of alluvium, frequently associated with the coalescing of alluvial fans.

Band or Bar: A color pattern. *See Figure 1.*

Barchan dune: A crescent-shaped sand dune with the convex side in the direction of the wind.

Barranca: A ravine or canyon.

Bimodal: Characterized by dual peaks, e.g., of activity. In the cases of lizards, this typically refers to two active peaks, or increases in surface activity—one in the morning and one in the afternoon. Seasonally there may be a peak in the spring and a peak during the monsoon.

Bipedal: Literally "having two feet." In the case of lizards, this commonly describes some species that have the ability to run on their hind feet only.

Blotch: A color pattern. *See Figure 1.*

Bolson: A flat, arid valley surrounded by mountains and draining into a shallow central lake.

Brumation: Essentially synonymous with hibernation and overwintering; this is the period of lowered metabolic rate during cold periods.

Caudal: Referring to the tail or tail region.

Chevron: A color pattern. *See Figure 1.*

Cienega: A series of springs forming a large wetland. This term is commonly used in the American Southwest and presumably comes from the Spanish *cien aguas,* meaning "100 waters."

Circumorbital: A type of scale. *See Figure 3.*

Cismontane: Literally "on this side of the mountain," this term refers to how animals are distributed along mountains from a reference point.

Clade: A taxonomic group of organisms classified together on the basis of similar features traced to a common ancestor.

Cline/Clinal: Gradual changes in characteristics that occur across the geographic range of a species.

Cloaca/Cloacal opening: The common urogenital opening for excretion and reproduction. This is also known as the vent. *See Figure 2.*

Cloacal spur: A small protuberance near the cloaca on male geckos.

Congener/congeneric: Belonging to the same genus.

Conspecific: Belonging to the same species.

Crepuscular: Active during the twilight hours.

Crossbar/crossband: A color pattern. *See Figure 1.*

Cruciform: In the shape of a cross.

Cryptic: Difficult to recognize and easy to hide. For lizards, this usually means that the lizard is hard to distinguish from the background; however, it also refers to morphological crypsis, wherein a species "hides" among similar-looking or indistinguishable species—that is, they cannot be readily differentiated by their appearance, and other characters are needed to determine their identification.

Cryptobiotic: Describing a state in which an animal can shut down normal metabolic functions until environmental factors allow it to resume metabolism.

Cycloid: A type of scale. *See Figure 4.*

Dark fields: The dark part of a pattern, such as the darker ground color of some striped lizards.

Density: The number of individuals per given area.

Desert pavement: A substrate type found in deserts that is composed of gravel- to cobble-sized rocks closely arranged in a thin layer on the surface and embedded in a fine substrate.

Dewlap: The underside of the throat, which is often distended to advertise ventral throat coloration as an indication of fitness. *See Figure 3.*

Dichromorphism: Having two different color forms.

Diel: Referring to an activity pattern through the course of a 24-hour day.

Dimorphic/Dimorphism: Having different forms. Usually refers to sexual dimorphism, where females and males are distinguishable, especially by size and color.

Diploid (2n): Having two pairs of chromosomes.

Distal: Relating to the opposite (far) end of a point of reference. *See* proximal; *Figure 2.*

DNA: Deoxyribonucleic acid, a nucleic acid that contains genetic information in all organisms.

Dorsal *(adj.)*/**Dorsum** *(n)*: Pertaining to the upper part of the body; the back. *See Figure 2.*

Dorsolateral: Pertaining to the area above the sides and below the dorsum. *See Figure 2.*

Dorsoventral: From dorsum to venter. This term is often used to refer to a shape in cross-section, as with horned lizards, which are very dorsoventrally flattened. *See Figure 2.*

Ecoregion: A relatively large area wherein there are similar ecological influences, such as climate, vegetation, and species composition. Essentially synonymous with "physiographic" province, but that is a more geographically based term.

Ecotone: A transition zone between two ecological communities.

Epithet: In biology, usually refers to the species part of the genus and species nomenclature of the scientific name. For example, for *Xantusia henshawi*, the Granite Night Lizard, "*henshawi*" is the specific epithet.

Evolution: Change by descent.

Femoral: Referring to the thigh, which often has pores and enlarged scales. *See Figures 2 and 4.*

Ferrous: The color of oxidized iron (rust-colored).

Fossorial: Adapted for digging and/or life underground or beneath substrate.

Friable: Readily crumbled, such as soil that does not bind together.

Fringed: A scale type. *See Figure 4.*

Frontal: A scale type. *See Figure 3.*

Frontoparietal: A type of scale. *See Figure 3.*

Fusiform: A body type. *See Figure 2.*

Genetic sequence: The precise order of DNA nucleotides (Thymine, Adenine, Cytosine, and Guanine).

Genome: The entire complement of genetic information, or the complete code of DNA that is found in an organism.

Genotype: The respective genetic makeup of an organism.

Granular or Beaded: A type of scale. *See Figure 4.*

Gravid: Possessing eggs or in late-stage pregnancy.

Ground color/background color/base color: The predominant underlying color on a lizard, on which patterns lie.

Gular fold: *See Figure 2.*

Haplotype: A group of alleles (alternate forms of a gene) that are located closely on a chromosome and are inherited as a unit during reproduction.

Head plates: Large, flat scales on the head; *see Figure 3* for illustrated head scales.

Heliothermic: Deriving energy directly from the sun, as in basking behavior.

Hemipenes: The paired reproductive organs of male lizards and snakes.

Herp/herptile: A vernacular used by herpetologists to denote amphibians and reptiles.

Herpetofauna: Generally referring to the composition of a particular set of amphibian and reptile species.

Hibernaculum/hibernacula *(pl.)*: An area where an animal will hibernate or brumate during the cold winter periods.

Hybrid: A genetic cross between two species.

—id: Ending commonly used in the biological sciences that refers to the family of an organism. For example, canids are members of the Family Canidae (dogs, wolves, foxes), tenebrionids are members of the family of beetles, Tenebrionidae, and so forth.

Imbricate: Overlapping, like the shingles on a roof.

Immaculate: Without spots or other patterns.

Inguinal: Pertaining to the area of the groin.

Interdigitation: Referring to the infolding or interlocking of different parts. The term is derived from the relationship of fingers to the hand. As an example, in reference to ecology, different habitat types are often interdigitated along and between canyons and ridges.

Interfemoral: Between the thighs.

Intergrade: A transitional form between two other forms, usually referring to subspecies or genotypes.

Internasal: A scale type. *See Figure 3.*

Interparietal: A type of scale. *See Figure 3.*

Interspecific: Between different species, as in "interspecific variation," which shows differences between different species.

Intraorbital: A type of scale. *See Figure 3.*

Intraspecific: Within the same species, as in "intraspecific variation," which shows differences within a single species.

Keeled: A scale feature. *See Figure 4.*

Labial: A type of scale. *See Figure 3.* There are upper and lower labial scales.

Lamella: In geckos, the soft transverse plates of the toe tips that allow the animal to walk on vertical surfaces. In general use, even in biology, refers to layering. *See Figure 4.*

Lateral: Pertaining to the sides. *See Figure 2.*

Laterally compressed: Narrow from side to side.

Marbling: A color pattern resembling that of marble, with blotches and lines. *See Figure 1.*

Median/Medial: Pertaining to the midsection or midline. *See Figure 2.*

Mental scale: A type of scale. *See Figure 3.*

Meristic *(adj.)*: Describing quantitative characters—i.e., those that can be counted, such as scale rows.

Mesic: Moist.

Mesoptychial: Scales between the pregular and gular folds, or in the absence of a pregular fold, immediately preceeding the gular fold. *See Figure 3.*

Microhabitat: A smaller scale of habitat. Common usage often refers to where a species often spends most of its time or seeks cover.

Mitochondrial DNA: The DNA from mitochondria, a cellular organelle.

Mode: The most frequently appearing number, which is different from the arithmetic mean (average), as in the case of a lizard that usually has two particular scale types but sometimes has one.

Monotypic: Pertaining to only one type, such as a genus with no other genera in the family or a species with no other species in the genus.

Monsoon: A climatic season when the wind changes direction. In the American Southwest, it is usually typified by the warm, rainy summer from early to mid-June through September or so. Afternoon thunderstorms and morning clearing are typically associated with the monsoon.

Morph: Literally means "form," and refers different forms of the same organism, such as different colors, different patterns, or different shapes.

Morphometry: The measurement of shape, structure, and form.

Mucronate: A type of scale. *See Figure 4.*

Nasal: A scale type. *See Figure 3.*

Neonate/Nominal: A newly born or hatched individual.

Nominate: Referring to the genus or specific epithet common to the described taxon. For example, in *Aspidoscelis tigris tigris*, this is the nominate subspecies, whereas *Aspidoscelis tigris munda* is not.

Nuchal: Referring to the back of the neck region; also a scale type. *See Figure 3.*

Nuclear DNA: DNA found in the nucleus (an organelle) of a cell.

Occipital: Referring to the head region, particularly with regard to scales. *See Figure 3.*

Ocellus (Ocelli, *pl.***):** A type of pattern. *See Figure 1.*

Ontogenetic: Describes changes associated with development. For example, a Giant Spotted Whiptail is hatched as a striped individual lacking spots. As it develops into adulthood, it starts to lose its stripes and gain spots. Small adults have this pattern. As they grow to become large, old adults, they lose their stripes and have spots only.

Oogenesis: The process of ovum (egg) formation.

Osteoderm: A bony deposit in the dermal layer of the scale of some animals (i.e., in the scale), such as Gila Monsters (and Beaded Lizards) and Alligator Lizards.

Overwinter: Essentially synonymous with brumation or hibernation, but generally refers to what the animal does during periods of inactivity in the winter, such as where it resides.

Oviparous: Egg producing; lays eggs rather than giving birth to live young.

Oviposition: The laying of eggs.

Ovoviviparous: Describes the case of young that are born from eggs, but the eggs are incubated internally.

Paravertebral: Laterally adjacent (but relatively close) to the middorsal area. *See Figure 1.*

Parietal: A type of scale. *See Figure 3.*

Parietal eye: A sensory organ on the parietal scale of lizards that detects light and shadows. *See Figure 3.*

Parthenoform: An organism that is parthenogenetic.

Parthenogenetic: Reproducing by eggs without fertilization; i.e, offspring are clones of the female parent. For lizards, this includes a large number of all-female whiptail species (genus *Aspidoscelis*) that are of hybrid origin.

Pattern Class/Type: A group of organisms that exhibit similar patterns and color. In some usages, synonymous with subspecies. In whiptails, some pattern classes are given specific letters, such as Pattern Class A (these distinctions are too specific for this book, and one needs to access original research publications for specific descriptions).

Plate: Synonymous with shield, or large, flat scales.

Ploidy: The number of complete sets of chromosomes in a cell.

Postantebrachial: A type of scale group. *See Figure 4.*

Posterior: Pertaining to the rear area of the lizard, and may or may not include the tail. *See Figure 2.*

Postmental: A type of scale group. *See Figure 3.*

Pre-femoral: In front of the thigh.

Proximal: Referring to the part closest to a reference point, such as mid-body.

Pseudocopulation: A behavior that mimics copulation between a male and female, but involves only females.

Range: The extent of an animal's geographical distribution. It also refers geographically to a group of mountains.

Relict/Relictual: A species that has survived a contraction in range, usually accompanied by a long history, along with the extinction of others close by; a group of organisms that are isolated from closely related organisms.

Reticulation: A netlike color pattern of lines. *See Figure 1.*

Rostral: A type of scale. *See Figure 3.*

Sand lizard: A group of phrynosomatid lizards belonging to the genera *Callisaurus*, *Cophosaurus*, *Holbrookia*, and *Uma*. They all possess adaptations for sand-living.

Scute: Large scales or bony plates. In reference to snakes and some lizards (e.g., legless lizards), usually refers to the enlarged scales on the venter that aid in locomotion.

Serpentine: Snake-like, as in movement or appearance.

Shield: A large, plate-like scale.

Sky island: Small isolated mountain range that is surrounded by valleys with a different habitat type than found at higher elevations, especially deserts and grasslands.

Spinose: Spiny.

Subcaudal: Below the tail.

Subequal: Not the same size.

Substrate: The surface on or within which an organism lives, e.g., soil, rock, or leaf litter.

Superciliaries: A type of scale. *See Figure 3.*

Supraoculars: A type of scale. *See Figure 3.*

Supraorbital (semicircle): A scale type. *See Figure 3.*

SVL: Snout-to-vent length. A term referring to the standard measurement from the snout to the vent of reptiles, from the tip of the snout to the external opening of the cloaca.

Sympatric: Occupying the same area or range.

Syntopic: Different species found sharing the same habitat within the geographic range of the two.

Temporal: Referring to the region of the temple on the side of the head (note that there is also an illustrated temporal scale in *Figure 3*).

Tetraploid (4n): Having four sets of chromosomes.

Thermoregulate: Behaviorally adjusting body temperature, such as moving from shade to sun.

TL: Total length. The standard unit of measure and standard abbreviation for reptiles, from the tip of the snout to the tip of the tail.

Triploid (3n): Having three sets of chromosomes.

Tubercle: A raised bump, which in the case of this book usually refers to elevated scales of gekkonids.

Unisexual: Being composed of only one sex. In the case of parthenoforms (e.g., whip-tails), it means only female.

Variegated: Usually refers to having a variety of colors and a variety of patterns.

Vent: The external opening of the cloaca. *See Figure 2.*

Venter/Ventral: Referring to the underside. *See Figure 2.*

Ventrolateral: Referring to the venter to lateral (side) area. *See Figure 2.*

Vermiculate: Describing worm-like or wavy markings. *See Figure 1.*

Vertebral: Along the dorsal mid-body, usually associated with a color pattern. *See Figure 1* for vertebral stripe.

Viviparous: Live-bearing; gives birth to live young rather than eggs.

Xeric: Dry.

GUIDE TO STANDARD ABBREVIATIONS, METRIC CONVERSIONS, AND MAP CODES

Standard Abbreviations

(also see Metric Conversions, below)

NF = National Forest

NM = National Monument (also New Mexico)

NRA = National Recreation Area

NP = National Park

SP = State Park

sp. = species, singular (spp. = species, plural)

SVL = snout-to-vent length

TL = total length

Metric Conversions

g = gram (approx. 0.035 ounce)

ha = hectare (10,000 square meters or 2.47 acres)

m = meter (approx. 39.37 inches)

mm = millimeter (approx. 0.039 inch)

km = kilometer (approx. 0.62 mile)

km^2 = square kilometers (approx. 0.3861 square miles)

Celsius-to-Fahrenheit conversion examples: –18° C = 0° F; 0° C = 32° F; 21° C = 70° F; 38° C = 100° F

Map Codes

Subspecies are color-coded alphabetically in the range maps. The first subspecies, alphabetically, is shown in blue; the second alphabetically is shown in green, etc., as shown here:

= First subspecies (alphabetically), or no subspecies recognized by our U.S. standard, or subspecies not shown (see Range text in individual species descriptions for details)

= Subspecies 2

= Subspecies 3

= Subspecies 4

= Subspecies 5

= Subspecies 6

= Intergradation zone between subspecies

= Mexican subspecies or subspecies in the eastern U.S.

THUMBNAIL GUIDE TO THE LIZARD FAMILIES AND GENERA

Crotaphytidae, Collared and Leopard Lizards. Page 98.

Crotaphytus, collared lizards
Gambelia, leopard lizards

Crotaphytus

Gambelia

Iguanidae, Iguanas and Chuckwallas. Page 128.

Dipsosaurus, desert iguanas
Sauromalus, chuckwallas

Dipsosaurus

Sauromalus

Phrynosomatidae, Phrynosomatid Lizards. Page 139.

Callisaurus, zebra-tailed lizards
Cophosaurus, greater earless lizards
Holbrookia, lesser earless lizards

Callisaurus

Cophosaurus

Holbrookia

Petrosaurus, California rock lizards
Phrynosoma, horned lizards
Sceloporus, spiny lizards

Petrosaurus

Phrynosoma

Sceloporus

Phrynosomatidae, Phrynosomatid Lizards. **(continued)**

Uma, fringe-toed lizards

Urosaurus, tree and brush lizards

Uta, side-blotched lizards

Uma

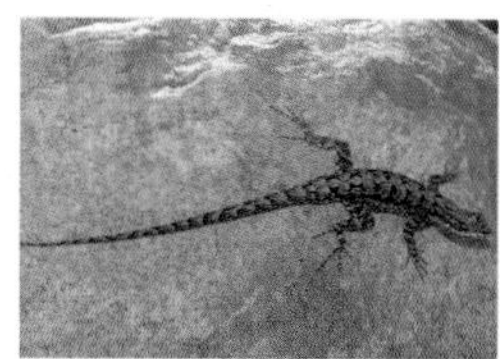

Urosaurus

Uta

Eublepharidae, Eyelidded Geckos. Page 298.

Coleonyx, banded geckos

Coleonyx

Gekkonidae, Geckos. Page 316.

Phyllodactylus, leaf-toed geckos

Phyllodactylus

Teiidae, Whiptails. Page 322.

Aspidoscelis, whiptails

Aspidoscelis

Xantusiidae, Night Lizards. Page 410.

Xantusia, night lizards.

Xantusia

Scincidae, Skinks. Page 444.

Plestiodon, toothy skinks

Scincella, ground skinks

Plestiodon

Scincella

Anguidae, Legless and Alligator Lizards. Page 470.

Anniella, North American legless lizards

Elgaria, western alligator lizards

Gerrhonotus, eastern alligator lizards

Anniella

Elgaria

Gerrhonotus

Helodermatidae, Gila Monsters and Beaded Lizards. Page 496.

Heloderma, Gila monsters and beaded lizards

Heloderma

INDEX OF SPECIES